Macroeconomics

Theory and Applications

Fourth Edition

Macroeconomics

Theory and Applications

Fourth Edition

G S Gupta

Former Professor

Indian Institute of Management, Ahmedabad

McGraw Hill Education (India) Private Limited

CHENNAI

McGraw Hill Education Offices

Chennai New York St Louis San Francisco Auckland Bogotá Caracas
Kuala Lumpur Lisbon London Madrid Mexico City Milan Montreal
San Juan Santiago Singapore Sydney Tokyo Toronto

McGraw Hill Education (India) Private Limited

Published by McGraw Hill Education (India) Private Limited,
444/1, Sri Ekambara Naicker Industrial Estate, Alapakkam, Porur, Chennai 600116, Tamil Nadu, India.

Macroeconomics: Theory and Applications, 4/e

Eighth reprint 2018
RXQLCRAERBCXX

Print Edition
ISBN (13 digits): 978-93-392-1436-4
ISBN (10 digits): 93-392-1436-6

E-book Edition
ISBN (13 digits): 978-93-392-1437-1
ISBN (10 digits): 93-392-1437-4

09 10 11 12 13 APO 22 21 20 19 18

Head—Higher Education (Publishing and Marketing): *Vibha Mahajan*
Senior Production Executive: *Atul Gupta*
General Manager—Production: *Rajender P Ghansela*
Manager—Production: *Reji Kumar*

Typeset at Script Makers, 19, A-1B, DDA Market, Paschim Vihar, Delhi 110063, and Printed and Bound in India at A.P Offset Pvt. Ltd., 25/487, Zulf-e-Bengal, Dilshad Garden, New Delhi 110095.

Visit us at: www.mheducation.co.in ; Phone (Toll free in India): **1800 103 5875**
Write to us at: info.india@mheducation.com

CIN: U22200TN1970PTC111531

To my dearest children
Indu, Jaya** and **Manish
their loving spouses
Ramakant, Raghav** and **Monika
and my wonderful grandchildren
Anu, Aditya, Ritu, Ishika, Varun, Arushi ...
for the fulfillment they have brought to my life

Preface to the Fourth Edition

Since the launching of the third edition, in 2007, not only the world has faced significant macroeconomic events but also the academicians and practitioners have developed new tools and out-of-box strategies to successfully handle the unexpected situations. In the backdrop of these a new edition of *Macroeconomics: Theory and Applications* is overdue. The events that happened include the Great Recession of 2007-09 leading even to the fall of a giant (viz. Lehman Brothers) and the Debt Crisis faced by a group of European countries (called PIIGS) from 2008 onwards; theoretical developments including Securitisation of (mortgage) Debt Bundles, Quantitative Easing and Hypothesising a causal link between public debt and GDP growth rate; and mounting of chief strategy with the formation of the Group of 20 developed, emerging and large economies (G-20) to deliberate, design and mount a coordinated attack to manage the unexpected events. In addition, my experience of teaching Macroeconomics at IIMs and other well established management schools in the country since retirement from IIMA in March 2010, and the interactions with their faculty and students, have enriched me to offer a thoroughly revised edition. Accordingly, it is my great pleasure to offer the 4th edition of this textbook.

New in this Edition

Since Macroeconomics deals with macroeconomic events not only in the country but also in the world as a whole, all the national and international latest available data have been incorporated in the text. Besides, most new global macroeconomic events have been incorporated at appropriate places in chapters/appendix. In addition, all ambiguities and misprints in the text, some even brought to the notice by the caring professionals, have been removed.

As globalisation is progressing fast and global imbalances are causing increasing troubles, Chapters 12 and 13, in particular, have been significantly strengthened by incorporating the foreign exchange (or balance of payments) market explicitly. Accordingly, twin equilibriums, viz. internal and external, have been considered, the conflict between the two has been highlighted and the appropriate alternative policies to resolve have been discussed. As a result, the IS-LM model has become IS-LM-BP model and the AD-AS model has been recast as the AD-AS-BP model. A total of seven new graphs have been added. The new theoretical/policy concepts have been added to the relevant chapters. These include:

- Wholesale vs. retail inflation in **Chapter 3**;

- Quantitative easing and the marginal standing facility tools with the Central bank of the country, and the emerging emphasis of the RBI's new Governor, Dr. Raghuram Rajan on inflation as the primary goal and interest rate as the basic tool of monetary policy in **Chapter 8**;
- Money supply vs. interest rate as the intermediate target variable and causal link between public debt and GDP growth rate in **Chapters 10 and 16** respectively;
- Effects of changes in government spending and taxation on fiscal deficit and lags in the autonomous expenditure (Keynesian) multiplier in **Chapter 11**;
- Assignment rule in **Chapters 12**, the Taylor rule for interest rate target in **Chapter 13**, the propagation effect in **Chapter 14**, pros and cons of indexation in **Chapter 15**, and demographic dividend and coupling-decoupling theory in **Chapter 16**, among others.

Old case studies (Comprehensive Case Studies) have been updated and two new, one on each of the two significant events experienced recently, have been added. These are

- The Great Recession 2007–09
- The Euro Area Crisis 2007–12.

This edition has also been pedagogically enhanced by incorporating the following:

- Learning objectives provided at the beginning of each chapter
- Key words/concepts spelled out at the end of each chapter
- Glossary as a ready reference for the students at the end of the textbook

Online Learning Centre

To facilitate classroom teaching, a wealth of resources has been provided on the companion website of the book for the faculty as well as the students. The faculty will have access to PowerPoint Presentations, Solutions Manual and a Test Bank comprising multiple choice questions, fill-in-the-blanks and true/false questions for all the chapters. The students will have access to Web-links, Objective type questions and Glossary to explore the subject and strengthen their learning. These resources can be accessed at *www.mhhe.com/guptamacro4e*

Acknowledgements

I am grateful to the students and faculty who have sustained the Textbook for last 15 years and have provided useful feedback and suggestions for revision. In particular, my thanks go to those at IIM Ahmedabad, IIM Indore, Entrepreneurship Development Institute of India – Ahmedabad, Ahmedabad University, FLAME Pune, National Insurance Academy Pune, Goa Institute of Management and Adani Institute of Infrastructure Management Ahmedabad, where I had the pleasure to offer a course on the subject since the release of its third edition in 2007. I appreciate the support provided by Dr. Anil Kumar and Mr. B. Ganapathi, Chief Librarians at IIM Ahmedabad and EDI Ahmedabad, respectively for facilitating the access to the pertinent national and international publications on macroeconomic data.

The entire work on this edition was carried out at our home in Ahmedabad. My wife, Lalita, not only rendered all the logistic and moral support; she even restrained herself from over complaining on her sacrifice of the quality time and encouraged me to bring out the BEST possible textbook. Our children and grandchildren have always been a great source of encouragement and support; their assistance in drawing some graphs and complicated tables, besides fostering a cool environment towards shouldering such a noble project is really commendable.

The publishers, McGraw Hill Education (India) Pvt. Ltd. deserve sincere thanks for pursuing me to work on this edition and for rendering the full cooperation, as always. In particular, Mr. Tapas Maji, Ms. Surabhi Khare, Ms. Shalini Negi, Ms. Hema Razdan, Mr. Manohar Lal and Mr. Atul Gupta, among others, who converted the soft copies into such a well finished product, must get a special mention.

I hope the new edition is received well both by the students and faculty of Macroeconomics, and I solicit from them continuous feedback and suggestions for improvements. Needless to say, for the errors, if any, and the imperfections that may have still remained, I alone am responsible.

G.S. Gupta
70, Green Park, Ambli, Bopal Road
Ahmedabad-380058

Publisher's Note
We value your views, comments and suggestions and hence look forward to your communication at
info.india@mheducation.com. Please feel free to report piracy issues, if any.

Preface to the First Edition

Macroeconomics deals with the measurement, fluctuations, and growth in economic aggregates like national income, employment/unemployment, and the price level. It attempts to explain the past behaviour of such variables, predicts the likely future events, and helps policy-makers to formulate the appropriate policies to stabilise the economy and to achieve other policy objectives. The present text presents, under four parts, all these through a coherent and logical approach. Part I provides an introduction to macroeconomics, explains the various macroeconomic variables in terms of the concepts and measurements, and examines the historical data of the selected countries. Part II rationalises the various macroeconomic behavioural and technological relations by appealing to the rational behaviour of individual consumers, workers, and firms. It thus provides the macroeconomic foundations to the macroeconomic functions. In Part III, these macroeconomic functions are integrated into alternative macroeconomic models to explain the fluctuations in national income, employment/unemployment and the general price level, and the role of stabilisation policies. Part IV deals with the long-run issues of economic growth, unemployment and inflation, and presents a brief account of the present state of macreconomics.

Economics draws heavily from mathematics and statistics, among other disciplines. The book uses algebra, geometry, and econometric tools to supplement the verbal explanations. A few hypothetical examples are integrated in the text and more are provided in the form of Review Questions at the end of each chapter. These should help the readers master the concepts in macroeconomics.

The book is written primarily for MBA and MA (Economics) students. However, it should be useful for advanced BA (Economics), B Com, and M Com students as well as the executives concerned with business environment. While there are several high quality texts on the subject by the USA-based economists, there is, perhaps, none that is up-to-date in theory and contains Indian data and events. When I was teaching macroeconomics at the Illinois State University, USA, I found the USA-based textbooks highly useful and fully satisfying. However, when the same books were used at the Indian Institute of Management, Ahmedabad, and the Universiti Sains Malaysia, Penang, I was only partially satisfied. The reason was, obvious—the Indian and the Malaysian students were more eager to know about the economic events and policies in their own economies, besides those of the US and other successful economies. This motivated me to write this text and I hope the Indian students would greatly benefit from this book. The highly encouraging response to my textbook on Managerial Economics (Tata McGraw-Hill) inspired me to come out with this complementary text, too.

The book has benefited immensely from my interactions with my students at the Indian Institute of Management, Ahmedabad (1970-till date), Illinois State University (1982-83, 1985-86, and 1999), Universiti Sains Malaysia (1993-94, 1997-98, and Summer 1999), and several other Indian universities and institutions where I have delivered lectures on the subject. The current batch of students in the post-graduate programme at IIMA (PGP 2000-02) have even used the pre-publication draft of this text as the background material for the course in Economic Environment and Policy—I, and have offered some useful suggestions towards its presentation. Prof Rati Ram of the Illinois State University was kind enough to supply some useful material on the subject. My academic associate at IIMA, Mr Md Munshi, helped me in terms of searching the relevant material and data from the library and collecting the feedback from students. The Indian Institute of Management, Ahmedabad, provided me the most conducive academic environment and the best of infrastructure for working on this text. I express my sincere thanks to Director Dr Jahar Saha and others for this. My high gratitude and sincere thanks are due to Ms Maya Madhavan, my Secretary at IIMA, for her prompt, very efficient, and cheerful services of putting the messy manuscript on the computer, among other things. The Personnel Officer at IIMA, Mr N V Pillai, was kind enough to promptly arrange help for the extra typing. My student Mr Shailesh Tamgadge helped in designing the cover page. The publisher, Tata McGraw-Hill, its MD, Dr N Subrahmanyam and other officers deserve all the credit for encouraging me to write this book, and for bringing it out in the present form so neatly and promptly.

An overwhelming part (80%) of this text was written during May–September 2000 when I was away from IIMA to have the pleasure of living with my children, their spouses, and my grandchildren in Dubai and Dallas. Living with them made writing easy and fulfilling. My wife Lalita rendered all kinds of assistance, including data compilation, tabulation, and proofreading.

G S Gupta

Contents

PART 1
INTRODUCTION AND MEASUREMENT

PART 2
BEHAVIOURAL AND TECHNOLOGICAL FUNCTIONS

PART 3
ECONOMIC FLUCTUATIONS AND STABILISATION POLICY: MACROECONOMIC MODELS

PART 4
ECONOMIC GROWTH AND THE STATE OF MACROECONOMICS

PART 1

INTRODUCTION AND MEASUREMENT

Ragnar Frisch divided Economics into two branches—microeconomics and macroeconomics. Though, over time, the distinction has been getting more and more blurred, it is still considered useful in defining the role of economics and in understanding and managing global and national economies as well as those of the individual firms. This part of the text elaborates upon these two branches of economics and their roles in decision-making and discusses the concepts and measurements of the various significant macroeconomic variables. Chapter 1 gives an introduction to economics, macroeconomic goals and instruments and presents latest available comparative data on significant macroeconomic variables for India and for other selected countries. Chapter 2 details national income and related concepts and looks at the methods of measurement and cross-country data. Chapter 3 dwells on other economic issues, including inflation, unemployment, poverty and income inequality. The last chapter of this part of the text, Chapter 4, deals with the other relevant macroeconomic variables like money supply, interest rate, government fiscal magnitudes foreign exchange rate and balance of payments.

Chapter 1

Introduction: An Overview

Learning Objectives

After reading the chapter you should be able to:

1. Understand what are economics, its two branches, micro and macroeconomics and what they deal with
2. Appreciate the link between micro and macroeconomics
3. Learn full gamut of macroeconomic variables, their appropriate grouping into target, indicators, intermediate and policy variables, and get a feel of their relative magnitudes across leading countries
4. Get an overview of the macroeconomic issues and learn how the macroeconomic theory and policies work to tackle such situations

Economic growth, without compromising on humanitarian concerns, is what all countries are striving for today. While some countries like the United States, Switzerland, Japan and Singapore have attained a high degree of economic prosperity, some others like Mexico, Malaysia, Thailand and China are still hovering in the high middle, and many more like India, Nigeria, Nicaragua, Bangladesh and Nepal fall in the group of middle income and/or developing countries. Also, until the onset of the great recession in 2007, while China had sustained a two-digit growth rate for about two decades, countries in East Asia and the Pacific achieved an average growth rate of around 8 per cent, over one hundred countries had attained a growth rate of only less than 4 per cent during the same period. The recession of 2007–09 affected all countries in the world, yet China continues its top position in terms of the growth rate. Inflation rate has also varied across countries and over time. While the inflation rate has usually been a one digit number in all countries during the most years, it was around zero recently in countries like Canada, New Zealand and Japan, and it crossed even 1,000 per cent per annum in Germany during 1922–23, Hungary during 1945–46, and Argentina and Brazil, among others, during some years in the 1980s and 1990s. The situation with regard to the social justice criterion (humanitarian concerns) is not very different either. We have countries like India in which about one fourth of the population still lives below the poverty line and also the countries like Singapore and Germany that are often over heated. Openness of countries has also varied considerably, and accordingly the size of exports, imports, foreign investment, and external debt take varying magnitudes across nations. Besides these factors of size and growth, fluctuations in growth rates are not small either. Japan, which was among the fastest growing economies in the 1960s, ended with a mere 1.0 per cent growth rate during the 1990s and 0.9 per cent during the first decade of the present century. Most ASEAN countries moved from the low growth rate group until 1960 to the second highest growth rate group in the 1980s and 1990s perhaps through their strategy of openness. Even India, which could achieve a mere 3.5 per cent annual average growth rate between 1950 and 1980, attained an average growth rate of around 6 per cent between 1980 and 2003, and 8 per cent during 2000–2012. Countries like Angola, Congo Democratic Republic, Georgia, and Moldova moved from a positive growth rate during the 1980s to negative growth rate during the 1990s; others like Argentina, Bolivia, Nicaragua, and Peru experienced quite the opposite trend. Currently, among the large countries, China, India, Russia, Indonesia, Nigeria and Vietnam are growing at a relatively faster rate while USA, Japan, Brazil and Mexico at a slower rate. The interesting question is: "What causes these distinct levels, their fluctuations, and growth rates?" The answer to this question is found in the study of macroeconomics theory and policy, the subject which this textbook will address.

ECONOMICS

The origin of the term 'economics' lies in the Greek words *oikon* and *nomos*, which together mean laws of households. This expounds the significance of economics to all human beings. However, to fully understand its usefulness in decision making at various levels—households, firms and government—a deeper insight into its meaning is imperative.

There are two basic definitions of economics. The first one is credited to Adam Smith (the father of economics), Karl Marx and others. According to this, **economics is a social science that deals with human behaviour pertaining to production, exchange and consumption of goods and services**. Since the goods and services constitute the tangible wealth, the definition emphasizes the material well-being. Leisure, morality, spiritual values and the like are thus ignored by economists. The second definition was inspired by the rise of the neoclassical economics and the so called 'marginal revolution' of the 1870s with which the aim of economics was re-formulated. Lionel Robbins published his book *Essay on the Nature and Significance of Economic Science* in 1932, wherein he advocated the now famous second definition of the discipline. Under this, **economics is the analysis of universal types of problems of the allocation of resources, which are scarce and versatile, among ends, which are many and varied in significance**. This makes economics the **'science of choice under scarcity'**.

All decision units, including governments, firms, workers and households are subject to the limited (scarce) and versatile resources, and unlimited needs of varying intensity. For example, though governments have unlimited powers to tax its population, it can raise and earn only limited funds, and has pressing demands for expenditures on unlimited heads. Firms have limited funds for capital and other expenditures (raised through equity and borrowings) and have plenty of alternatives to invest in and produce. Similarly, workers (students) have 24 hours/day which they must allocate between work (study) and leisure (fun); households have limited income and wealth and their consumption needs (present and future) are never satiable. Also, every country has a given amount of natural and other resources, and she desires to attain as high a standard of living for its inhabitants as possible. Thus, every decision maker is confronted with the allocation of scarce resources among unlimited ends. This involves trade-offs, to get something, you sacrifice some other thing. This is known as the **principle of scarcity or no free lunch principle**. Fortunately, all the investment opportunities and items of consumption are not equally attractive and hence, the decision maker could strike a judicial choice. Economics emphasises rationality in decision-making, though customs, traditions and emotions do influence decision-making. **Marginal (incremental) analysis**, where one compares the marginal benefit with marginal cost associated with a decision, is used for the purpose. A decision is prudent only if the marginal benefit from it is no less than its marginal cost, both measured in terms of money.

The aspect of choice making can be best explained through the **Production Possibility Curve**, illustrated in Fig. 1.1.

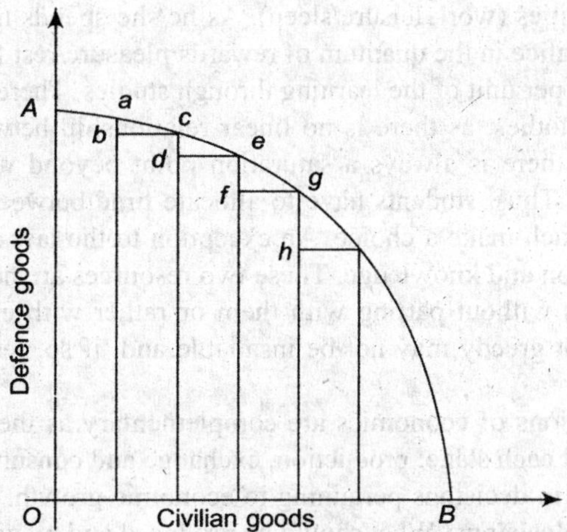

Fig. 1.1 Production Possibility Frontier

With the limited resources (land, labour, capital and entrepreneurship) a country at any given time, can at most (i.e. when resources are fully and most efficiently employed) produce only a combination of the two goods, civilian and defence, along the production possibility curve (PPC) *AB*. If it opts only for the civilian goods, the full and efficient employment of its resources could produce *OB* quantity of civilian goods. In contrast, if the country decides to concentrate on defence goods production only, it can have *OA* amount of these. A mixed basket of these two types of goods will take the country anywhere along the non-corner points of the *AB* curve. Under utilisation and/or inefficient use of the resources will lead to a production basket given by some point inside the PPC. The exact choice along the PPC will be dictated by the needs and/or the prices of the two kinds of goods. It may be noted that the curve is **concave to the origin** (bow-shaped) because while some resources are relatively well-suited for producing civilian goods, the others are well-suited for the production of defence goods. For example, some people enjoy farming the most while others trading the most, some students are good at engineering others at medicine or management or computers and some faculty prefers teaching, others research or service/administration. As the country goes for more and more units of the civilian goods, the sacrifice of defence goods goes on increasing, that is, $ab < cd < ef < gh$, and so on. This is because this process causes factors of production to move from defence to civilian goods, thereby reducing employment of resources in defence and increasing it in civilian goods. Such outcomes are achieved through forcing some resources to move to their unsuited production thereby affecting factor productivity negatively.

The above feature is called the **Principle of Increasing Opportunity Cost**. It is also called the **principle of low-hanging fruit**. Nobel laureate Milton Friedman, thus, describes economics as "there is nothing like free lunch". To get more and more units of civilian goods, one has to sacrifice an increasing quantity of defence goods. Thus, there is a trade-off. The law holds good almost universally. For example, students have 24 hours in a day. The more hours a student studies, the lesser time is left for other activities (work/leisure/sleep). As he/she spends more and more time on studies, the sacrifice in the quantum of rewards/pleasure/rest from other activities goes on increasing per unit of the learning through studies. There is an ideal quantity of time even for studies, as there is no linear relationship between the time spent and learning, and there is always a saturation point beyond which even learning becomes negative. Thus, students have to allocate time between studies and other activities, and as such make a choice. An exception to the law of scarcity could be found in information and knowledge. These two resources are not scarce as one can sell these products without parting with them or rather with enhancements. Also, people who are not greedy may not be insatiable and, if so, resources may not be scarce for them.

The two definitions of economics are complementary as the problem of choice must be resolved at each stage: production, exchange and consumption of goods and services, and even in decisions pertaining to economic growth:

(a) **Production decisions:** What should be produced and by whom? How much to produce of the chosen good at various points of time? Where to produce the chosen quantity of the chosen product and with what technique of production (i.e, how to produce)?

(b) **Exchange decisions:** What price to charge for the produced goods and to whom/where/how to sell it?

(c) **Consumption decisions:** How much to consume of each type of goods and services?

(d) **Growth decisions:** How much of a non-renewable resource (like mines and oil deposits) to use now and how much of it to leave for the future? How to grow over time, that is, growth strategies, like balanced-unbalanced growth, small scale versus medium versus large scale sector, public versus private sector, inward versus outward looking, development versus growth, civilian versus defence goods, consumption versus capital goods and so on?

Choice is inevitable due to the scarcity of resources in relation to the needs. Thus, **scarcity is the foundation of economics**. Incidentally, note that scarcity does not mean shortage rather it means 'price tag'. Anything that has a price is scarce in economics, and it is the price, in a capitalist economy, that equates demand and supply. Choice making is made difficult by the uncertainty of future events. When a firm has to decide what to produce, it only has some estimates of what it could sell and at what price, but these estimates would rarely turn out to be exact facts in the future. Similarly there is uncertainty in all the other economic decisions narrated above. Thus, **uncertainty** is the additional factor, over and above the scarcity, with which economics has to deal.

All economic decisions involve trade-offs. For example, when a household decides to spend more on consumption, less is left for its savings, given its income. Also, if a worker decides to work for a company, say, *XYZ* for 40 hours a week, she cannot work for any other company and her non-work time (leisure etc.) is reduced by 40 hours a week. Similarly, if a firm decides to employ its resources in the production of, say, two-wheelers, those resources are not available for any other use. Such trade-offs are faced by all decision makers, including the government. Further, it is not easy to decide on these trade-offs. For example, while choosing a job, students have difficulty in deciding whether they should focus on career, money, social service, family or something else. For this reason, it is said that while some choice is good, it is not necessary that more choice is better.

Human needs have multiplied over time and they are non-satiable. Once you have sufficient food at home, you want to go out and eat at luxurious hotels. If you are living in a rented house, you desire to own one, and if you own one you desire a better one. If you have a two-wheeler, you wish to own a four-wheeler, and thereafter a more expensive one. If you have all these, you would like to go for holidays and to tour around the world. There are also, of course, health, education, sports and other requirements. The list is never ending.

Scarcity is pervasive. During the periods of Adam Smith, David Ricardo, John Stuart Mills and Alfred Marshall, among others, food, clothing, shelter and transport were scarce/non-affordable goods. Even today, these products are scarce for millions of poor people around the world. The rich have material wealth, but time/leisure is a likely scarce product for them. These people often complain of being too lonely and having little time for the family and children. Human decency is perpetually in short supply everywhere. While allocating their time and material resources among various uses, people may not just look at marginal benefit and marginal cost, as mentioned above. Instead, they may compare the benefits and costs on the basis of their subjective tastes and preferences, and on the available information. To appreciate the role of subjective tastes, an example would be helpful. In 1999, the *New York Times* published an obituary of Oseola McCarthy, a woman who died at the age of 91 after spending her life as a laundress, leading a modest (e.g, small, sparsely furnished house, having black-and-white television with just one channel) life and, just four years before her death, donating US $150,000 to endow a scholarship for poor students at the University of Southern Mississippi, a school which she never attended. It seems that she derived more satisfaction from this endowment than she would have got from a lavish life style. Many such examples can be cited even from India. To mention one, Dr R.L. Sanghvi, the former Principal of the prestigious H L College of Commerce, Ahmedabad, after leading a modest life, on his retirement from the college, created an endowment at the Ahmedabad Management Association to organise an annual lecture by an eminent person on the Global Economic Environment. Adam Smith argued that every one is guided by "self interest", and the above examples are consistent with this principle. A person who hates poverty would be better off if the poverty of others (not even related to him) is alleviated.

Uncertainty has only multiplied over time. The world is becoming a global village and though information travels fast with the discovery of the internet, it is rarely accurate, on time and complete. Besides, the universe is too dynamic to warrant fair forecasts of future events. Since all decisions are based on the available data and they involve the future, uncertainty renders economics a difficult discipline.

Scotsman Thomas Carlyle once labelled economics as a '**dismal science**' and the former United States president, Harry Truman, wanted to have '**one-armed economists**' to avoid ambiguity. The term 'dismal science', may be used because the discipline was then considered difficult, boring, ambiguous and of little use, and also because it ignored the non-material aspects of life and issues such as poverty and income distribution. Nobel laureates Amartya Sen and Gary Becker, among others, have impressed upon us the anatomy of good life, which includes health, education and the availability of options. Further, some economists like Karl Marx painted a pessimistic picture about the future. Yes, economists still talk of 'on the one hand' and 'on the other hand', but this is because everything is associated with pros and cons. For example, the high interest rate, on the one hand, is welcomed by those who plan to save for the future and, on the other hand, is disliked by those who desire to invest. This may be true that economics is not that easy to learn and grasp, but some people say it is intuitive! It is difficult primarily because unlike physical sciences, economists do not have the benefit of laboratories to conduct controlled experiments and they try to explain/predict human behaviour, which is unpredictable. The tool of 'other things being equal' or ***ceteris paribus*** is used to understand the causal relationships between two variables in an otherwise complex (multivariate) relationship. The significance of economics has become obvious by the fact that currently economists are playing increasingly significant roles, both in business and the government.

Economics is also seen as money. This is because all applications of economics' principles require all benefits and costs to be expressed in terms of money. Also, economics is talked as a **science of numbers**. This is partly true because economists deal with data and use them to generate forecasts for future events. However, economics is much more than this. It also analyses data to develop theories that help predict the behaviour of decision units. How all this is done will be explained in the section on methodology. Incidentally, note that while it is easy to lie with the data, it is a lot easier to lie without it.

Microeconomics and Macroeconomics

In the 1930s, Ragnar Frisch classified economics into two branches, which are, **microeconomics** and **macroeconomics**. These terms are derived from the Greek words *micros* and *macros*, which mean small and large, respectively. Microeconomics deals with the behaviour of individuals like a household, worker, firm, industry and market, and interactions among them. In contrast, macroeconomics is concerned with the behaviour of the aggregate, the economy as a whole. Thus, while in microeconomics we study the demand, supply and price of a commodity, in macroeconomics we study the aggregate demand, aggregate supply and price of all goods and services. The latter, in turn, deals with variables such as the national income, growth rate, employment/unemployment, inflation, money supply, interest rate, wage rate, international trade, foreign exchange rate, monetary policy, fiscal policy, fiscal deficit, current account deficit, saving investment gap, and so on. Decisions pertaining to individuals are discussed in microeconomics, while those concerning the aggregate are dealt with in macroeconomics. Macroeconomics deals with national economy and its goals without worrying about the well-being of any specific group. This distinction is convenient, though it is being blurred lately. This is because economists are now looking for the micro-foundation of macroeconomics as the decisions have to mainly be taken at the individual's level. While individuals behave, nations do not.

Microeconomics and macroeconomics, though interdependent, proceed on diverse paths. What is taken as a given in one, is the prime variable to explain in the other, albeit their identical goal of **maximum material well being**. While microeconomics assumes national income and aggregate (macro) price (inflation) as given, and explains the determination of relative productions and relative prices of various goods and services, quite the opposite is true for macroeconomics. The former concentrates on the optimum allocation of resources among various goods and services and the latter aims at the full utilisation of resources, both of which help to attain the maximum material well-being for the people in the economy. The bridge between microeconomics and macroeconomics is provided by aggregation, which is explained a little later.

Micro events may produce macro consequences and *vice versa*. For example, the Organisation of Petroleum Exporting Countries' (OPEC) decision to raise the price of crude oil led to worldwide stagflation (stagnation plus inflation) during the 1970s and the 1997–98 South East Asian crisis and 2007–09 great recession have caused a fall in production, purchases and prices of houses, cars and most luxury items in corresponding countries.

Methodology in Economics

Economics deals with the efficient allocation of resources, that is, to get the most from those resources. The term 'most' thus needs definition. For this purpose, we need to understand economics' methodology with regard to

- Assumptions
- Method of enquiry
- Nature
- Economic system

The Assumption of Economics

Economics assumes that **all the behavioural agents act rationally**, as consumers they maximise utility/satisfaction/happiness, as producers they maximise profit, as government it maximises efficiency with due consideration to equity. As there is no free lunch, decision makers compare benefits and costs measured in money, associated with every decision. The benefits and costs are subjective to some extent. Recall the example of the frugal living of Oseola McCarthy and her endowment of a scholarship at the University of Mississippi. To her, the endowment was dearer than lavish living and, if so, her behaviour was very rational. While there is some necessary standard of living, obsession with luxury is not necessarily better. One needs a clear definition of what he/she wants before economics can assist one to get there. Americans are richer than most others but they also work harder, vacation lesser and retire later. They suffer from loneliness, which perhaps, they did not choose. Indians are relatively poor but they have the luxury of a lot of leisure and time for the family. Similarly, those who are familiar with the '**Prisoners Dilemma**' would realise that their decision to confess the crime was the most rational on each ones' part even though the mandated punishment was more under the chosen option than in some other option (both denying the charge). Similarly, some firms may look for maximum sales subject to some target level of profit rather than maximum profit and public sector firms may aim at maximum social gains. With regard to cost, it must be noted that for economists the relevant variable is the **opportunity cost**. The real cost of something is what you must give up in order to get it, which is almost always more than just cash. Remember, time is one of the scarcest resources, and also it is the one which cannot even be stored. Thus, if a person is getting a free ticket for a concert, should he be ready to stand in line for a couple of hours, then the concert is worth two hours of the person's time. Most parents now have fewer children than earlier, not because the food and education costs have gone up, but because the primary cost of raising a child (the cost of earnings forgone when a parent quits the job to look after the kid) has gone up considerably. Also, busy executives are often found shopping around their offices/homes, where prices are relatively high, instead of going downtown or to discount stores.

In addition, economics' principles are derived on the premise that decision makers are well informed and they are not influenced by emotions, traditions, customs, religions, etc.

Method of Enquiry

There are two methods of enquiry, namely **deductive** and **inductive**. The deductive method is employed by physical sciences like physics, chemistry and biology, where the analysis proceeds from general to particular cases. In this method, the researcher starts with a theoretical framework (hypothesis), performs certain controlled experiments and deducts results. For example, quinine is a medicine to cure malaria. In contrast, social sciences, including economics, have no controlled experiments (such as various taxes and expenditure testing) and thus employ the inductive method, which proceeds in the opposite direction. Particular phenomena are studied and generalisations are made. In this method, the researcher starts with facts (data/results), formulates and tests hypotheses, and thereby, creates laws/theories. For example, if a fan is not working, then one looks for the possible causes (reasons) and analyses them to see why the fan is not operating. Since the reasons could be many and unknown, hypothesis testing could be inconclusive. In the case of the fan, hypotheses could be:

(a) The motor is burnt out, so the fan is not working
(b) The switch is bad, so the fan is not working
(c) There is no electricity, so the fan is not working and so on.

The validity of any one or more of these hypotheses would provide a good answer to the problem. However, since the list of possible causes is rarely total, validity of any such hypothesis may not rule out the possibility of some other hypotheses. Thus, in inductive research the answer comes from empirical studies or data analysis. This is basically a **cause-effect approach** to research, which is the method used in economics. In this context, we must note a fallacy, called the **post hoc fallacy**, or "after this, therefore necessarily because of this". Mere precedence of an event does not make it a cause to an event that follows it. For example, prosperity of 1990s was followed by recession in 2001, does not conclude that all prosperities are followed by recessions. Also, the association of two events does not make the one the cause of the other. For example, if a high degree of association (positive correlation) is found between the amount of liquor drunk and the salary of a professor, this does not mean that any one of them is the cause of the other. One needs a theoretical base to attribute causation and/or statistical tests to verify the direction of causation, if any.

Nature of Economics

Concerns are expressed as to whether economics is a **science** or an **art**, and whether it is a positive or a normative discipline or both. Since all economic theories are based on causation, it is a science. However, economic policies, though basically derived from the principles of economics, cannot be devoid of art. This is so because experience and personal thoughts go a long way in setting objectives and realising the constraints, which *inter alia*, govern policies. Besides, for a discipline to qualify as a science, it must be able to predict relevant events. While economics aids in forecasting, it does not guarantee perfect accuracy. Also, a particular policy may not produce similar consequences even under similar situation. Thus, economics is both a science as well as an art, and more than that it is a social science as it studies the part of human behaviour that is concerned with the production, exchange, consumption and growth of goods and services. Incidentally, note that the institution of the Noble Prize in economics in 1969 awarded the status of a science to economics. One may thus say that which economic theory is science, its application to decision-making is an art.

Economics has both **positive** as well as **normative** roles. As a positive science, it seeks to discover and report facts (data/information) and tries to explain the facts through formulating and estimating causal relationships. For example, finding the prices of various products in various markets, combining them to compute the general price index/level, to determine the inflation rate, identifying the factors determining the inflation rate, and estimating the inflation function, is the positive aspect of economics. Also, the study of why professors get higher salaries than secretaries do, falls in the domain of positive economics. Under the normative role, economics seeks the optimum policy/decision, given the objectives and constraints facing the decision maker. Incidentally, note that economics is devoid of value judgements. Thus, for example, economics does not concern itself as to whether a firm should aim at profit maximisation or sales maximisation, subject to a given profit constraint; or whether a country should target inflation or growth, if two are in conflict; or whether a country should aim at a 5 per cent or 8 per cent economic growth rate. But economics surely helps us to formulate an optimum policy to attain a given objective, of say, a growth rate of 8 per cent, under the given scenario. Thus, under normative economics, an economist makes prescriptions for the individual consumer, firm or economy (what ought to be) on the basis of his own value judgement, not on the basis of objective scientific ground. However, the two aspects are interrelated. While all economic problems involve normative issues, thinking like an economist involves an analytical approach that usually abstracts from or at least downplays the 'value' issue. It is often said 'two economists, three opinions'. This is not a criticism of economists, rather their strength. This is so because decisions vary with objectives, and therefore, perusal of different objectives/priorities call for different recommendations. It must be noted that such differences prevail basically in normative economics and rarely in positive economics.

Economic System

Decision-making is governed by the **economic system** operating in the given economy. In a free enterprise (capitalist or market) economy, factors of production are mostly owned by the individuals, decisions are taken at the individual level and they are regulated by the market, that is, by the forces of demand and supply. Resources move out of loss-making enterprises and into the profit-making activities, and from low utility consumption to high utility ones. Such a system has been prevailing in developed economies like those of the United States of America, Canada and Great Britain. In contrast, in a totally centrally planned **(command) economy**, (also known as communism) most resources are owned/controlled by the government, all economic decisions are taken by the economic planners, and workers and firms are forced to follow them. This was the system that prevailed in the Soviet economy (USSR) until its collapse in 1989, and it exists to some extent in North Korea and Cuba. We talk of **socialism** as well, which refers to the objective of the economic system. However, most countries are operating in a mixed economy system, where some decisions are taken by the planners, the others are governed by the market forces of demand and supply. Needless to say, customs, traditions, religions, habits, emotions, etc. may exert some influence on individual decisions but the collective outcomes are expected to follow rational behaviour. The 20th century experienced an economic battle between two extreme systems, capitalism won over communism. Currently, though all countries are trying to move towards capitalism, a 'mixed economy' system still dominates. While the developed world is more capitalist, developing economies are having fairly good governmental role. To illustrate, primary and secondary education is still a monopoly of the government in the United States, and the Indian government still owns and runs many businesses. It must be emphasised that the market economy (capitalism) inspires hard work and progress by rewarding the winners and crushing the losers. For example, the discovery of the personal computer has enriched information technology based industries and crushed the electric typewriters business. In business, this is referred to as 'creative destruction'. North Korea and Cuba are the most government intensive countries, but they are not economic powerhouses. Adam Smith saw the benefits of capitalism (prosperity), Karl Marx predicted the dark side (class struggle) of it and its ultimate demise, and John Maynard Keynes (1883–1946) pleaded for a rational government policy to salvage and enrich it. Keynes is even considered the **Father of Mixed Economy**. In a mixed economy, all decisions are subject to two kinds of rules, market (demand-supply) rule and government rules.

There are evidences of both market as well as government failures, though it is hard to distinguish the two. The symptoms of the former are found in the existence of excessive income/wealth inequalities, unemployment, gluts and shortages of products, and wage differences across race, gender, region and so on, and also among workers with similar education and experience earning differential wages, besides others. These arise at least partly due to the prevalence of **imperfect competition** (monopoly, oligopoly and monopolistic competition), lack of perfect information about the market (**information barrier** and/or asymmetric information), perverse expectations (if the price is rising, people expect it to continue rising), non-private marketability of **public goods** and **externalities** and irrationality in time horizon. Public goods like national defence, lighthouse in seas, general research, general (free) broadcasts, law and order, environment, and weather service are those goods

(a) whose consumption cannot be denied to anyone (non-excludable),

(b) consumption of which by some people does not reduce the available amount to others (non-rival),

(c) that cannot usually be bought by ones' income (non-affordable on own income), and

(d) that can not be supplied by the market system.

Thus, such goods are consumed by all together and have to be provided by the government free to all (no price tag), financed through tax payer's money. Similarly, **externalities**, the so-called third party effects (like pollution suffered by the inhabitants around a textiles mill or the benefits they reap from a nearby private park), have to be checked by the government only. Further, expenditure on education, research and development etc. involves a long time horizon and thus may not be made in good amounts under the pure market system. The evidence for government failure is seen in poor enforcement of laws and orders and threat to our security/property, and inefficiency of public sector enterprises. Red tapism, corruption and discrimination in awarding government jobs, approvals, clearances, security, justice and others exist in plenty. Poor infrastructure, including illiteracy and ill-health, is a big hurdle to prosperity. Thus, the society has no perfect servant, neither the market nor the government. For the market to function smoothly, there must be a healthy legal and financial framework, where rules and regulations are well laid down and the violators are punished timely. To avoid market failure, sellers' monopolies and buyers' ignorance need to be done away with. Similarly, to check government failures, rules and regulations have to be defined unambiguously, favouritism and bribery have to be bidden goodbye and justice must be awarded quickly. There is no dichotomy between the market and the government as both are essentials, but the exact mix between the two has to be struck through trial and error. Thus, while some government is good, more is not necessarily better.

THEORY OF AGGREGATION

As microeconomics deals with individuals and macroeconomics with the aggregate; the latter is the sum of micro. For instance, microeconomics studies the demand for a good (commodity) by an individual household, and if we sum that demand over all goods and over all the households, we get the demand for all goods by all households, which is known as consumption–a major component of aggregate demand concept of macroeconomics. If the **fallacy of aggregation/composition** did not hold, what was true for an individual would be true for all. However, the fallacy exists:

- If there is fire, it is in the individual's interest to run away as fast as possible, but such a behaviour is no good for the society at large.
- If an individual's salary goes up, he is happy, but if salaries of all go up proportionately, no one may be happy (for prices may increase proportionately).
- If an individual farmer reaps a bumper crop, he is happy, but if all the farmers reap a bumper crop, all of them could be unhappy. This is known as "misery under plenty" and it arises because the farm produce may be perishable and too much production may lead to a throw away price. During the 1976–77 in India, a lot of sugar cane was burnt on the field and similarly the price of tomatoes fell to below ₹2 per kg sometime during 2006 due to over production.
- If a student gets high scores, he is happy but if all the class-mates get high marks, none of them may be happy. This is true if the grading is based on the relative performance.
- An attempt to increase savings by everyone may lead to a decrease in total savings (**paradox of thrift**, discussed later in Chapter 11).

To illustrate the fallacy of composition and thereby the principle of aggregation, consider two households' economy with the following income and consumption levels:

(Rupees)

Year	*Household - 1*		*Household - 2*		*Macro*	
	Income	*Consumption Expenditure*	*Income*	*Consumption Expenditure*	*Income*	*Consumption Expenditure*
2000	50,000	40,000	90,000	80,000	1,40,000	1,20,000
2010	1,00,000	70,000	50,000	45,000	1,50,000	1,15,000

In the above example, income and consumption move in the same direction for each household but not for the economy as a whole. This illustrates the **fallacy of composition**, which states that what is true for individuals may not be true for the aggregate or that the total may not equal the sum of the parts. However, if one goes deeper into it, it will be seen that the above apparent contradiction arises primarily due to the change in relative income of different individual households. To draw from RGD Allen (1973), consider the following consumption function example:

$$C_{jt} = a_j + b_j Y_{jt} \quad \textbf{(1.1)}$$

where C_{jt} = consumption expenditure of household j (j = 1, 2, …, n) in period t

a_j = autonomous consumption of household j
b_j = marginal propensity to consume of household j
Y_{jt} = income of household j in period t
and $a_j > 0, b_j > 0$

Function **(1.1)** is micro consumption function. The macro consumption function would be:

$$C_t = A + BY_t \quad \textbf{(1.2)}$$

where C_t = consumption expenditure of all households in period t
Y_t = income of all households (national income) in period t
A = autonomous consumption of all households
B = marginal propensity to consume in the country
and $A, B > 0$

Macro function **(1.2)** can not be derived from micro functions **(1.1)**. While

$$\Sigma C_{jt} = Ct$$
$$\Sigma a_j = A$$
$$\Sigma b_j Y_j t \neq BY_t$$

The last inequality would be equality if, and only if,

$$b_1 = b_2 = \cdots = b_n = B$$

Thus, if marginal propensity to consume (MPC) were the same for all households, macro function **(1.2)** would follow from micro function **(1.1)**. In the absence of this assumption, macro function **(1.2)** does not have the benefit of a micro foundation. However, even in the absence of uniform MPCs, if income distribution across households were constant over time, it can be shown (not shown here) that all positive micro MPCs would imply a positive macro MPC. In the hypothetical numerical example in the table above, though both micro MPCs are positive, macro MPC is negative (macro income increased by ₹10,000 but macro consumption went down by ₹5000, implying a macro MPC of – 0.5), and this is so because neither are the two MPCs same nor has the income distribution remained unaltered over time.

In the light of the above, the aggregation principle points out that the macro relations do not automatically follow from the corresponding micro relations. Thus, macro functions have to be either rationalised for themselves or how they are deduced from micro functions has to be shown, case by case. Traditionally, the two sets of functions have been hypothesised independently. But lately, efforts have been made to relate the two by way of discovering the micro foundation of macroeconomics. While microeconomics derives its principles through appealing to the rational or optimising behaviour of individuals, there can be nothing of this sort in macroeconomics (for economy does not behave), and thus, recent developments in macroeconomics are trying to look for their microeconomic foundation. In essence, the fallacy of composition is usually ignored.

MACROECONOMIC GOALS AND INSTRUMENTS

Tan Tinbergen, who shared the first Noble Prize in Economics with Ragnar Frisch, has classified macroeconomic variables into four categories:

- Target variables

- Leading indicator variables
- Intermediate variables
- Instrument variables

Target Variables

The target variables are the economy's ultimate goal variables. The three most noted ones are:

- Economic growth, which is high, inclusive and sustainable
- Inflation, which is low and stable
- Unemployment, which is low

The other economic goals include:

- Clean environment
- Globalisation with sovereignty intact/sustainable current account balance

In addition, the economy generally has intermediate target variables like, money supply, interest rate, fiscal deficit, current account deficit, etc. These variables' targets are not attempted for their own sakes but since they bear some known relationships with the ultimate target variables, they are targeted as well.

Economic Growth Since national income represents purchasing power, and therefore, command over goods and services, every economy aims at securing the highest possible level of it. Growth in national income is an obvious goal, for this alone indicates whether a relatively poor economy will catch up with a relatively rich country or whether it will further lag behind it over time. Examples of fast growing economies like those of South Korea, Taiwan, China and other South East Asian nations in relation to slow growing economies like the United States, the United Kingdom and Japan will amply demonstrate this point. Also, the 'Rule of 72' suggests that a growth rate of 12 per cent (China) doubles the income in 6 (72/12) years while that of 6 per cent (India) takes around 12 (72/6) years to double the income. Also if a high growth rate is achieved by over exploiting the resources, it would be unsustainable in future, which will be bad for the country. Similarly, the growth will have to be inclusive, lest it leads to more inequalities which would go against the social concerns and would thus be harmful in the long run.

Inflation Low and stable inflation is sought for various reasons. *One*, price fluctuations (inflation/deflation) negatively affect the real values of all variables denominated in money terms. For example, currency notes and bank deposits lose their real worth during inflation. Thus, inflation discourages households from holding financial assets and thereby hampers investment (which is financed largely through the mobilisation of financial savings) and therefore the growth. *Two*, inflation distorts income distribution in favour of debtors and business at the cost of creditors and fixed income earners, among others. *Three*, inflation distorts real foreign exchange rates and thereby the global competitiveness, unless it is uniform in various countries. *Four*, inflation affects the nominal interest rate, and thereby, the saving, investment and other important variables. *Five*, inflation distorts taxes through tax payers moving to higher tax brackets and paying taxes on apparent (not real) capital gains. There are several other consequences of inflation, which are dealt with in a later chapter

(Chapter 15). While a small degree of inflation is considered good for the economy as it encourages profits and thereby investment and growth, large doses of inflation are harmful. Deflation is worse than inflation. For, it harms the business, which impinges on investment and economic growth. Also, deflation tends to raise the real wage and thus discourages firms to hire labour. It is for these reasons that the developed countries like Japan, the United States and Germany were wary of deflation and had tried hard to avoid deflation during the beginning of the current century. In fact, avoiding deflation has become an important goal for several countries, lately. Details on this are discussed later in Chapter 15.

Unemployment Social justice has become a hot goal recently. It calls for growth with a 'human face', meaning universal/inclusive growth rather than lopsided prosperity. The extent of this is measured through unemployment, poverty and income inequality across households and regions. These have to be as low as possible, if not zero. The significance of this goal is obvious when a rich gentleman feels embarrassed on seeing a starving soul, and when one looks at the various causes of theft, terrorism and other social evils. Needless to say, the perusal of this objective does not necessitate equal income for everyone irrespective of the quantity and quality of their efforts.

Environment This has become an important goal for all countries in last about a decade. With an overwhelming emphasis on economic growth, countries have resorted to deforestation, land reclamation, over exploitation of natural resources, etc., which, in turn have led to global warming. This has adverse effects on climate, pollution, traffic hazard, etc. Groups of countries have met and they have unanimously resolved to foster clean environment.

Globalisation Globalisation is no more a choice but is inevitable. The experience of China and the South-East Asian nations over the last decade and longer has impressed all nations about the gains from being an open economy. India has been quite late in this aspect. However, there are bad examples of over dependence on other nations as well. Mexico, Indonesia, Russia and Argentina are some examples. Even assistance from the International Monetary Fund (IMF) and the World Bank has been questioned, for their conditions for aid have been termed as too stringent. Self-reliance or rather non-interference from others is an important objective for any country, lest the super powers impose restrictions on its pursuit of country-specific economic policies. With globalisation, interdependence is on the increase and it is now well known that international trade and investments have goodies to offer to all participating countries, provided they are carried out on mutually reasonable terms. However, if a country owes a lot to some other country/international financial institution, or depends on imports for essentials, it may not be able to enjoy freedom in its policy making. Thus, in order to enjoy non-interference, the country must avoid heavy external debt/debt servicing ratio (debt repayment plus interest to GDP ratio) and hence significant current account deficits for long. It must be noted that the external debt of a country is simply the cumulative sum of the deficits in the current account of the balance of payments. The bail out loans given by the IMF to Indonesia and Thailand during the financial crisis of 1997–98, and the resulting 'stringent' conditions on their policies provide ample proof of the significance of this objective. The United States is running into significant deficits in its current account for the last few years and therefore its external debt is quite high currently. Of course, the US is an economic powerhouse and thus its sovereignty is still intact. However, if it were some weak economy, it would have faced economic crisis and loss of sovereignty.

Unfortunately, the various economic goals are not always in harmony. While the rate of unemployment is consistent with the economic growth goal, no such unambiguous conclusion exists with respect to other goals. In this context, we may simply recall the following three famous curves/laws, the details of which would become clear only later in this text:

- Phillips' Curve
- Kuznets' Curve
- Okun's Law

The Phillips Curve describes a non-linear negative relationship between the rates of inflation and unemployment, and thus suggests that the goals of price stability and full employment (high level of output) are incompatible. The Kuznets' Curve outlines the inverted U-shaped relationship between the degree of income inequality and the level of per capita income, which implies that the goals of equality and high per capita income conflict in poor countries while they go hand in hand in rich countries. The Okun's Law suggests that there is a threshold level of growth (3% for USA) even for maintaining the current unemployment rate, which would only become worse if the economy grows at a rate below that minimum level. This happens because of the increasing population and rising workforce participation rate. For the economy of the United States, Okun's Law suggests that every one per cent increase in the unemployment rate, the growth rate in real GDP falls by about two per cent. The law thus argues in favour of the complementary nature of full employment and growth relationship. The Phillips curve and Okun's law are discussed in detail later in this book. Since the various goals are not complementary, prioritising them becomes essential, and different priorities would obviously call for different policies.

Leading Indicator and Intermediate Variables

The leading indicators, as the name suggest, are the variables changes in which precede the changes in the target variables. Thus, they signal whether we are getting closer to our policy targets, and accordingly serve the purpose of warning (barometer) to the policy-makers. These include variables like inventory levels, construction works; orders for plant and machines, and durable goods; lay-offs of workers; stock market indices; monsoon, political situation, fiscal and current account deficits, etc. Thus, if inventory levels are piling up, orders for durables are falling, workers are getting laid off increasingly, stock markets are signaling fall and/or deficits are growing high, there are signs of recession heading, and vice versa. The intermediate variables include variables like money supply, interest rate, wage rate, fiscal deficit, savings, investments, bank credit, foreign exchange rate, imports, exports, foreign investments, current account deficit and others. There is no hard line separating the indicators and intermediate variables but the unique factor distinguishing between the two is whether change in a variable precedes or coincides with the change in the target variables. All such variables are so called because they fall between the instruments and target variables and the former influence the latter through these.

Instrument Variables

The instrument variables exert influence on the intermediate variables, which in turn, affect the target variables. Instrument variables are variables whose values are set by policy makers. Thus, we have:

- **Stabilisation Policies:** Fiscal, monetary, trade and exchange rate and income policies
- **Structural Policies:** Agriculture, industry, trade, foreign investments, foreign exchange, competition policy, etc.

Stabilising Tools The major vehicle of **fiscal policy** is the **annual budget** and the instruments in India consist of changes in tax rates, disinvestments, heads of expenditures, financing of deficit through public debt (external and internal) and issuance of new money. The Central Government, state governments and local governments enjoy these powers and there is a clear-cut demarcation among these levels of government with respect to taxes and expenditure. The Central Government enjoys the power with regard to corporate income tax, personal income tax, expenditure tax, capital gains tax, customs duties, central excise taxes and other taxes, while sales tax, entertainment tax and stamp duty fall in the hands of state governments. Octroi, education cess and property tax are levied by local governments. Disinvestment in public enterprises is undertaken at all levels of government depending on the ownership of such undertakings. Defence expenditure is incurred fully by the Central Government and most other types of expenditure are made at the central, state, and local levels. Government run public enterprises and profits/ losses from them are other sources of income. How these instruments of fiscal policy affect the economy is explained in the later chapters.

Monetary policy, which is exercised by the Central Bank of the country—the Reserve Bank of India (RBI) in India—has instruments like bank rate, cash reserve ratio (CRR), open market operations (OMO), statutory liquidity ratio (SLR), interest rates' structure, selective credit controls (SCR) and moral persuasion. Currently, interest rates in India are basically market determined, barring the rate on saving deposits and some restrictions on the fixed deposit rates. As we shall see later in Chapter 8, RBI controls repo and reverse repo rates as well but these are basically to manage the liquidity in the system. Even the SLR is to manage the distribution of total bank credit and not to control the amount of bank credit per se. Various monetary instruments affect the reserves with banks and thereby the banks' ability to create deposits, which are part of the money supply. The money supply has a bearing on the level of economic activity. All this is detailed in the later chapters of the text. Foreign exchange rate is also managed by the RBI, but under the overall guidance of the Finance Ministry. Currently, in India, we have the managed floating exchange rate system, where the exchange rate is determined basically by the free interplay of the demand for and supply of foreign exchange, but if deemed desirable, the RBI intervenes in the market through selling/buying foreign exchange. While the bank rate, interest rate structure and foreign exchange rate are the **indirect tools**, the CRR, OMO, SLR and SCR are **direct instruments** of credit control.

Trade policy is handled by the Ministry of Commerce and Exchange rate policy is exercised by the country's Central Bank in consultation with the Ministry of Finance. The former deals with tariffs, quotas, laws, country-specific regulations and concessions, etc. The latter is concerned with the fixed or floating rate system. Also, there are varieties in each of these systems and the policy-makers have to opt for anyone at any time. The tools of the **incomes policy** include the wage-price guidelines, mandatory wage-price controls and tax-based incomes policy.

Structural Tools In addition to the above, governments are vested with some powers to regulate agriculture, industry, trade, banking, foreign investments, labour and other segments of their respective economies. These have bearings on the structure of the country's output and consumption, and thus impinge on the country's structure. These are basically direct tools in contrast to fiscal and monetary policies, which are indirect instruments in the hands of the government. For example, in India there are the agricultural policy, industrial policy, trade policy, foreign exchange management policy, restrictive trade practices acts, banking regulation acts, capital market regulations, price controls and subsidies of various kinds, among several other regulations. Governments formulate these policies, review them from time to time and make modifications. These tools affect the basic structure and institutions of the economy, and hence they together are also called as **structural policy** tools. Since the direct (quantitative) instruments tend to be negative ones, they are being replaced by the indirect (price) instruments, which form parts of monetary and fiscal policies. Besides, there is an emphasis on globalisation, privatisation and liberalisation. Accordingly, many of these direct instruments have been removed, some others softened, and yet others persist and perhaps will never be done away with completely.

SUBJECT MATTER OF MACROECONOMICS

Macroeconomics is a subject which has close ties with the real world. Accordingly its focus is on three aspects of national aggregates, which are:

- Measurement
- Stability
- Growth

This text covers all these aspects. While most macroeconomic variables are analysed, the emphasis lies on the three central variables, which are **(a)** national income, **(b)** price/inflation and **(c)** employment/unemployment. By understanding the measurement of such variables, readers are able to monitor the economy, both over time and space. Business cycles are facts of life. What could cause them and how to tame them to foster stability is the second area of macroeconomics. Economic growth is of prime importance and how some countries have grown faster than others in different time periods is the last aspect of this branch of economics. While stability is a short-term issue, growth is a long-term issue. The major macroeconomic issues that have confronted the world, viz., recession-depression-unemployment, hyperinflation, stagflation, deflation, fiscal deficit, saving investment gap, current account deficits and debt crisis, are well covered in the text. As usual, for macroeconomics' textbooks, only fiscal and monetary policies are dealt with in detail. The approach is integrative but first each of the major national aggregates is conceptually explained and then the methods of its measurement are presented, which is followed by an analysis of the time-series data on India and other selected countries. The behavioural and technological functions are then discussed through the cause-effect relationships in Part II. The historical developments in macroeconomic models are then traced in Part III to explain the economic fluctuations and the roles that stabilisation policies could have played in those periods. Causes, consequences and cures for unemployment and inflation are also covered in this part of the text. Theories of economic growth and growth experiences across countries are dealt in Part IV. The chapter on the state of macroeconomics concludes the text.

Indian Economy vis-à-vis the World Economy

Economists are known to be concerned more with relative than with absolute well being and, thus, it is imperative for the introductory chapter of a macroeconomics text to briefly outline the economic standing of India *vis-à-vis* the world. Accordingly, significant data has been collected and collated. These are presented in Table 1.1. The variables are selected on the basis of their importance to macroeconomic goals and the countries are selected to include a cross section of the developed world, developing world, good achievers and the neighbours of India. A group of countries, called BRIC (Brazil, Russia, India and China) have recently been identified by Goldman Sachs as the emerging countries in the world and accordingly the table includes all of them. Saving and investment rates are also important magnitudes, particularly to assess future well-being, and the data on them is provided later in Chapter 6, review question 7, for advanced readers. Though it is highly premature to analyse this data, a few observations are certainly warranted even at this stage:

(a) Per capita income (measured), which is a surrogate measure of the country's economic well-being, varies rather widely across countries. The extremes stand at a low of US \$1120 in Pakistan and a high of US \$48, 620 in United States in 2011. India's income at US \$1420 is close to the lowest. There are other economies, not included here, like Norway and Switzerland, whose per capita incomes are even higher than USA. And Bangladesh and Ghana who's said incomes are lower than Pakistan.

(b) Growth rate in income (real GDP: measured) during 2000-11 varied between a low of 0.7 per cent in Japan and a high of 10.8 per cent in China. India's growth rate, at 7.8 per cent, is among the highest and it is close to three times the world average of 2.7 per cent.

(c) Inflation rate during 2000-11 happens to be the lowest, at –0.2 per cent in Japan and the highest at 12.2 per cent in Nigeria. India's rate, at 6.4 per cent, is on the higher side.

(d) Unemployment rate during 2010 stood at the minimum of 2.9 per cent in China and the maximum of 9.6 per cent in USA. India's rate at 3.6 per cent is on a rather low side. However, it must be noted here that the unemployment rate definition is country specific and hence the data on it are not quite comparable.

Table 1.1 International Data on National Goal and Related Variables

Country	Population	Land area	GNP per capita		GDP growth rate	Inflation rate (CPI) (average)	Umemployment rate@	Below poverty line (% of population)	Share in GDP (%)		Total external debt	Gross int'l reserves	BOP current a/c balance
	(Million)	('000 Sq. kms)	Measured (US $)	PPP	(%)	(%)	(%)	Int'l (US $ 1.25/day)*	Poorest 20%	Richest 20%	(US $ Billions)	(US $ Billions)	(US $ Billions)
	2011	2011	2011		2000–2011	2000–2011	2010	2008–2010**	1993–2010**		2012	2012	2012
India	1241	3287	1420	3640	7.8	6.4	3.6	32.7	9	43	379	300	–60
USA	317	9831	48620	48820	1.6	2.3	9.6	—	5	46	—	574	–440
UK	63	244	48620	35950	1.7	2.5	7.8	—	6	44	—	105	–94
Japan	128	378	37780	35330	0.7	–0.2	5.0	—	11	36	—	1268	61
Singapore	5.2	0.70	42930	59380	6.0	1.8	5.9	—	5	49	—	266	51
Indonesia	242	1905	2940	4500	5.4	8.4	7.9	18.1	5	49	255	113	–24
Brazil	197	8515	10720	11420	3.8	6.5	8.3	6.1	3	59	440	373	–54
Republic of Korea	50	100	20870	30370	4.0	3.2	3.7	—	8	37	—	328	43
China	1344	9600	4940	8390	10.8	2.5	2.9	11.8	5	47	754	3388	193
Pakistan	177	796	1120	2870	4.9	9.4	5.0	21.0	10	40	62	14	–2.1
Sri Lanka	21	66	2580	5520	5.8	10.7	4.9	4.1	8	45	25	7	–4.6
Australia	22	7741	49790	38610	3.1	2.9	5.2	—	6	41	—	49	–57
Nigeria	162	924	1280	2290	6.8	12.2	—	68.0	4	54	10	48	20
Russian Federation	143	17098	10650	20410	5.1	11.7	7.5	<2	6	47	—	538	71
World	6974	134269	9514	11560	2.7	—	—	—	—	—	—	—	—

Note: * For OECD countries, the benchmark figure is US $14.40 at 1985 instead of US $1.00

** Data refers to the latest available year, —Not available, @ limited coverage for some countries

Sources: World Development Indicators, 2013, Human Development Report, UNDP, 2013; World Development Report 2013.

(e) The proportion of people below the poverty line, on the basis of international standard of US$ 1.25/day, during 2008-10 stands at zero in all developed countries, at the lowest level of 4.1 per cent in Sri Lanka and the highest level of 68 per cent in Nigeria. India's position in this regard is quite bad.

(f) The share of the poorest 20 per cent, with regards to national income, during the latest available year was a minimum of 3 per cent in Brazil and a maximum of 11 per cent in Japan. Also, in Brazil, the richest 20 per cent of the population takes away the highest proportion of the income (59%). Brazil appears to have the highest income inequalities. Income inequalities in India fall close to the average.

(g) External debt data are provided for developing countries only. In 2012, it varied between a low of US $10 billion in Nigeria and a high of US $754 billion in China. However, if one were to look at this debt in relation to national income, which is a more relevant figure, Sri Lanka (44 per cent) would be the most heavily indebted nation. India's external debt to GDP ratio stands at 21 per cent. Another yardstick would be external debt vis-à-vis international reserves. In this regard, China enjoys the best position, as her debt is just about 22 per cent of her international reserves. India is also quite comfortable with debt to reserves ratio of 1.13. Balance of payments' current account deficit in relation to GDP is yet another indicator of foreign intervention, and on this yardstick the Australia is perhaps in the worst position, as the said proportion stands at over 5 per cent. The current account deficit proportion stands at around 4, 3 and 3 per cent in the UK, US and India, respectively. Japan, China, Russia and several other countries are currently enjoying a surplus in their current account.

From the above, it is clear that while China seems to have performed the best, particularly in the last couple of decades, India is making excellent progress with regard to its macroeconomic goals. While India has been hit by the recent Great Recession (2007–09), it continues to enjoy the second highest growth rate (next to China) among the large countries. However, on global front in 2013, it has faced a significant fall in the value of its currency, high current account deficits and a stagnant foreign exchange reserve. Before closing the chapter, it may be mentioned that the external debt of developed countries is not seen as a problem, for such debts are either denominated in the debtor's own currency, or even if not, the debtor's currency is a hard/world currency. Thus, though the United States is considered the most indebted country, it faces no risk of involuntary default as it can always print dollars and repay any outstanding debt; of course, dollar printing may cause some other economic problems like inflation.

Keywords

Social science; Resources, Scarcity; Production possibility curve; Opportunity cost; Positive- Normative role; Deductive-Inductive approach; Post hoc fallacy; Economic system; Public goods; Externality; Fallacy of composition; Phillips curve; Kuznets curve; Okun's law; Stabilisation-Structural policy; Target-Intermediate-Leading indicator-Instrument variables; Fiscal-Monetary-Trade-Exchange rate-Incomes policy; Measurement; Stability, Growth.

REFERENCES

1. Allen R G D, *Mathematical Economics*, 2nd ed. (London: Macmillan, 1973).
2. Friedman Milton, 'Inflation and Unemployment,' *Journal of Political Economy* 85 (June, 1997): 451–72.
3. Marshall Alfred, *Principles of Economics*, (London: Macmillan, 1980).
4. Gupta G S, '*Economics, Economists and Economy: Facts, Fallacies and Feuds', Presidential Address,* Gujarat Economic Association, 35th Annual Conference, Bharuch, Gujarat, Feb 12–13, 2005.
5. Robbins Lionel, Essay on the Nature and Significance of Economic Science, (London: Macmillan, 1932).
6. Smith Adam, *An Enquiry into the Nature and Causes of the Wealth of Nations*, (New York: Edwin Cannan Max Lerner, 1776).

REVIEW QUESTIONS

1. Someone had once called economics a 'dismal science'. Do you agree with this view? Why?
2. Some choice is good but more choice is not necessarily better. Do you agree? Justify your answer.
3. Macroeconomics explains what is taken as given in microeconomics and *vice versa*. Discuss the validity of this statement.
4. Macroeconomics is useful in managing business organisations. How?
5. "You cannot solve a problem until you measure it". Explain.
6. Evaluate India's economic position and performance in relation to her declared high-level goals, viz., high and growing income, price stability, inclusive growth and globalisation with sovereignty intact, (see data in Table 1.1). Also, comment on India's performance in relation to that of other countries.

Chapter 2

National Income

Learning Objectives

After reading the chapter you should be able to:

1. Learn what are GDP and other related national income concepts and how they are measured.
2. Appreciate the pitfalls in the measurements of the GDP and the inevitability of the black/ parallel economy.
3. Know that the ex-post domestic investment need not equal ex-post national saving but the difference between the two must equal the trade deficit (imports minus exports).
4. Comprehend the significance of the GDP in relation to other comparable aggregate measures.
5. Get a feel of the data on various components of GDP by sectors of production, components of demand, and its distribution to the factors of production in India vis-a vis the other major economies.

National income—income of the nation during a period of time—provides a comprehensive measure of the economic activities of a nation. It denotes the country's purchasing power. It is considered as one of the few measures of country's size; the other important measures being population (residents) and geographical land area. Its annual magnitude divided by the nation's population, called the **per capita income**, is used as a measure of the standard of living of the people in the nation, and the distinction between rich, middle income and poor income countries is based on the magnitude of the per capita income. According to the World Bank Atlas method (Measured at the three years' average exchange rate), countries having per capita income (at the official exchange rate) in 2010, up to US $1005 were referred to as low income countries, those having between $1006 and $3,975 as lower middle income, between $3,976 and $12,275 as upper middle income and those whose income exceeds $12,275 as high income countries.

The growth rate of an economy is measured by the rate at which its real national income grows over time. Knowledge of the national income and its movements over time is of significance to a business organisation also, as this provides a measure of the nation's ability to buy goods and services, and, thus, business sales are dependent on its magnitude. The success/failure of policy makers is very often judged by the rate at which the real national income grows during their regime. National income thus serves as an instrument of economic planning. Further, national income is policy-maker's one of the three ultimate target macroeconomic variables, the other two being unemployment rate and inflation rate. Thus, a clear understanding of the meaning and measurement of national income is essential. Nobel laureate Simon Kuznets is considered as the inventor of the methodology for the measurement of national income.

Income Concepts

There are several versions of national income, though strictly speaking, only one of them is referred to as the national income. These include:

- Gross Domestic Product (GDP)
- Net Domestic Product (NDP)
- Gross National Product (GNP)
- Net National Product (NNP)
- Private Income
- Personal Income
- Personal Disposable Income
- Net National Disposable Income

Besides, some of these measures are defined both at the factor cost as well as at the market price. Thus, we have the GDP at factor cost (GDP_F), NDP at market price (NDP_M), NNP at the factor cost (NNP_F) and so on. Also, there are the nominal and real income, and the measured income and PPP income. Thus, income is classified on several grounds, viz., income at market price versus at factor cost, national versus domestic income, gross versus net income, national versus private personal and personal disposable incomes, nominal versus real income, and measured versus PPP income. All these are defined and distinguished in what follows. At this point it may be noted that it is the NNP at factor cost (NNP_F), which is globally referred to as the national income (NI). Of the various measures, GDP_F is the most popular and accordingly we start with this measure.

Gross Domestic Product

The GDP at factor cost stands for the monetary value of all goods and services that are

(a) Currently produced
(b) Not resold or used in further production during the measurement period
(c) Sold through the official market
(d) Produced on the nation's geographical territory
(e) Valued at factor cost.

A brief rationale and explanation of these factors follows.

GDP is *expressed in terms of money* (rupees in India) because the goods and services are non-additive in physical quantities due to differences in the units of measurements (tonnes of wheat, metres of cloth, number of cars, number of haircuts etc.) and the per unit values (one car is not equal to one haircut or even one scooter). It is said that 'you can not add apples and oranges'. By using the prices, the GDP is constructed. Quantities of various goods are multiplied by their respective prices, and then the various money magnitudes are added to give GDP.

Income (production) is a flow concept and so the GDP includes *only those items that are produced during the period of time for which the GDP stands*. Thus, the

GDP in 2011 includes the production of all goods and services between January 1, 2011 through December 31, 2011 only. The changes in **inventories** during the period are treated as positive or negative purchases by the producer for the purpose of reconciling the production measure with the end-use expenditure measure. Thus, if the inventory level goes up, the increase in inventory is added up to the end-use expenditure to give the current production data, and *vice versa*. In other words, increase in inventories is tantamount to positive production and decrease in inventories to negative production. The price (valuation) of the inventory is usually **imputed** on the basis of the cost of production. Incidentally, note that if some inventory is lost during the current period due to theft, fire, earthquake or such other reasons, it is considered as a *loss*, which reduces the current profit by the loss amount and thereby compensates for the cost of production of that lost inventory. Such produced but lost inventory is not a part of the output.

Transactions in **old goods** and the secondary **capital market**, barring commissions, if any, are excluded from the GDP. Even transactions in the primary capital market are ignored until they lead to purchase of goods and services. Thus, trade in old cars/houses/other items and equities/bonds are not part of the GDP, barring the commission, if any, by intermediaries. This is because the commissions alone constitute the current production. The second-hand sales either do not reflect current production (sale of an old car by one person to another) or they involve double counting (purchase of a new Maruti car by a household from Maruti Udyog and sale to another household). Similarly, purely financial transactions are mere exchanges between the parties and so are non-productive. **Capital gains/losses** are also ignored in the GDP as they are earned over a period of time and not usually during the current year. Thus, if an art collector sells his painting and makes a capital gain, the sales proceed does not enter the GDP as the painting was produced several decades ago. The year the painting was produced, it was a part of the national income but since it was not marketed then, it remained outside the national income.

Raw materials and intermediate goods and services (i.e., goods and services resold or used for further production during the measurement period) are not included in the GDP, so as to avoid double counting of production. Thus, wheat used in making bread, leather used in making shoes and tyres used in cars are excluded because these are contained in the values of bread, shoes and cars, respectively. Alternatively, one can think of recording 'value added' at each stage of production. Value added equals market value of the product/service minus the cost of inputs purchased from other firms and used in the production of the said product. Thus, if wheat used in the production of a loaf of bread is valued at ₹8, wheat flour produced by the miller is valued at ₹9, bread sold by the baker to the vendor is valued at ₹12 and that purchased by the household costs ₹14, then GDP due to this production is ₹14 and not the sum total of the values of wheat, flour and bread. If the value-added concept is used, then the farmer produces ₹8 worth of GDP, the miller Rupee one, the baker ₹3 and the vendor ₹2 worth of GDP. Therefore, only the value of the final goods (goods that are produced and sold for consumption or investment) are included in the GDP. Incidentally, note that business plants, factories and equipment, though used for further production, are final (investment), not resold, goods and so are included in the GDP. Houses, which produce dwelling services, are also final goods. These are capital goods which live long. Unlike raw materials and intermediate goods, plants, factories, equipment and houses are not consumed fully and hence do not disappear in the production process. Of course, the depreciation on them does take place but the same is taken out when the net national product is calculated. Similarly, recall that additions to inventories, though used for further production, are part of the GDP.

Also, some other market transactions, which are very much official, like transfer payments (payments which have no quid pro quo, like taxes, subsidies, gifts, unemployment compensations, bribes, robberies, made voluntary or involuntary) and capital gains/losses, as mentioned above, are not included in the GDP. This is because such transactions are one way, not exchange, and hence do not constitute current production. To appreciate this, consider the transfer payments, which are of two types: public and private. Public transfers are subsidies to producers or/and consumers (like those on fertilizer, food, fuel, interest rate) social security payments, relief payments, retirement and pension payments, and interest on public debt, which the government makes to households and firms. In these transactions, the recipients make no contribution to the current production in return for these benefits (retirement and pension payments are for the past work and not for current work). As such, they are excluded from the GDP. Private transfer payments, such as son paying father for his old age expenses, father's gift to son, and a rich households'/countries gift to poor persons/countries do not entail production but simply the transfer of funds from one household to another. Even taxes, both direct and indirect, that the government collects from individuals and corporations are transfer payments. Also, if someone works for others at a nominal salary (like Nandan Nilekan worked for the Indian government) then the foregone salary constitutes donation/transfer payment. Thus, not all the officially marketed transactions are included in the GDP. To sum up, the deliberately omitted transactions from GDP, barring commissions on their trades, if any, are grouped below by the reasons for the same:

- Non- Production
  - **(a)** Transfer payments, public or private, voluntary or otherwise
  - **(b)** Capital market (security) transactions
- Non-current production
  - **(a)** Old goods trades
  - **(b)** Capital gains
- Non-final goods
  - **(a)** Raw materials
  - **(b)** Intermediate goods production

GDP *accounts only for goods and services that are traded through the official market*. This is a limitation of the measure but it is resorted to internationally owing to the difficulties in measuring **non-marketed or not officially marketed** production. Thus, it ignores the 'do it yourself' activities (which are not paid for) as well as the un/under reported productions. For example, the household work, including babysitting, whitewashing of own house, and tutoring of own children and other *do it yourself activities are excluded*, while payments to maid-servants, loundry, paid babysitters, private tuitions and so on are included in the GDP. Also, activities like painting, drawing, photography etc, which are carried out for self-consumption (or even for sale but not in the current year), are left out of the GDP. Similarly, unreported productions (though a part of market transactions but not a part of official transactions) triggered by the desire to avoid excise duties or for other reasons, are not included in the GDP. These give rise to what is called as the **black (parallel/ underground) economy**, which has two components legal but un/under reported and illegal like corruption, gambling, drinking, prostitution and narcotics, which do not even warrant reporting. These are by all means parts of income but there is a problem in their valuation and information. This introduces a downward bias in the measurement of GDP.

There are three exceptions with regard to the exclusion rule of non-market transactions:

(a) Self-consumption of production by the producers is valued, and is included in the GDP. Thus, the farmers' consumption of their own food grains is a part of the GDP. This is included both in the income and expenditure of farmers.

(b) Rent on owner-occupied houses is imputed and included in the GDP. It is a part of both the income and expenditure of the home-owners.

(c) Expenditure on public administration, like national defence, police, fire-brigades, members of parliament, legislative assemblies and municipalities is included in GDP.

These three refinements in the GDP measures exist internationally, for these pose no serious difficulties in information gathering and valuation, and they are quite a large part of the GDP. The prices of the first two items are imputed on the basis of comparable market prices. Thus, the rule that only official transactions are considered in GDP is more of a convention than logic.

To sum up this part, the following productions, barring the three exceptions mentioned just above this, are **illegitimately omitted from GDP**:

- Non-marketed productions (and consumptions), known as "do it yourself activities".
- Non-official marketed productions (and consumptions), known as **black market part of the economy**, which are termed as
  - **(a)** Legal but un or under reported productions
  - **(b)** Illegal productions (and consumptions) such as gambling, prostitution, drugs, drinking and bribes

These omissions lead to under estimation of the true GDP.

The GDP is produced on the country's geographical territory. Further, it is produced largely by factors of production owned by the country, but a part of it is contributed by the factors of production owned by other nations (rest of the world) in the world. Similarly, some of the country's factors of production work abroad and thus they contribute to the GDP of the "rest of the world". It is so because some factors of production like labour, entrepreneur, and capital (equity and bonds) are globally mobile and we do have multinationals operating in many countries. A part of our GDP is thus produced by foreign owned factors and a part of foreign GDP is produced by the nation's factors of production on foreign territories. For example, if an Indian resident professor takes up a four-month's Visiting Professorship in a university in the United States, his income (production) in USA will be a part of US' GDP and similarly the profit that a foreign owned firm (say Citibank) makes in India is a part of India's GDP. Thus, for GDP, the ownership of factors of production is immaterial. To summarise, GDP is the production which is produced on the country's territory by factors of production owned by any country in the world.

GDP at factor cost (GDP_F), as the name indicates, is the production valued at the factor cost. This means at the cost of land, labour, capital, entrepreneurship, and the cost of raw materials and intermediate goods consumed by the production. Thus, it ignores, the taxes imposed as well as subsidies given by the governments on goods and services.

The GDP which includes such taxes and subsidies is known as GDP at market price (GDP_M), which represents the cost to the end user of the production. It is defined as follows:

$$GDP_M = GDP_F + T_i - S \quad \textbf{(2.1)}$$

Where, T_i stands for indirect taxes and S for indirect subsidies. The former includes excise duties, custom duties, sales tax, value added tax, service tax, etc. and the latter consists of subsidies on fertilizers, food, fuel, exports, interest rate, irrigation water, etc.

Gross National Product

The GNP refers to the value of the goods and services produced by the nation's factors of production, irrespective of the location (territory) where it is produced. Therefore, in the above examples, the professor's salary in USA is India's GNP while Citibank's income in India is USA's GNP. In view of this, while the GDP refers to income produced within the nation's territory, irrespective of the ownership of the resources that produced it, the GNP consists of income produced by the nation's owned resources, irrespective of the place of production. The difference between the two concepts is accounted for by the net factor income earned abroad (NIA), where, NIA stands for the incomes earned (by way of wages, interest and dividends) by the resident factors abroad minus the incomes earned by the non-resident factors in the home country. Thus,

$$GNP_F = GDP_F + NIA \quad \textbf{(2.2)}$$

$$GNP_M = GDP_M + NIA \quad \textbf{(2.3)}$$

From the point of the employment generation at home, GDP is more relevant than GNP, and hence, the former often receives greater attention than the latter.

Other Income Concepts

Corresponding to GDP and GNP, there are NDP and NNP. The difference between the gross and the net is the capital consumption, called depreciation (D). Thus,

$$NDP_F = GDP_F - D \quad \textbf{(2.4)}$$

$$NNP_F = GNP_F - D \quad \textbf{(2.5)}$$

It is the NNP_F, which is referred to as the **national income**. This is because depreciation is really the consumed part of the fixed capital in the production process and it is difficult to measure it accurately (what we have is the accounting and not the economic depreciation). Also, changes in the **indirect taxes** and **subsidies** are caused by government actions; they constitute transfer payments and represent no production. Moreover, this measure alone represents the income earned by domestically owned basic factors of production, namely, land, labour, capital and entrepreneurship.

In every country, there are the government and the private sectors. The former consists of the central, state and local governments, and the latter includes all households. Firms are owned both by the government and the households. The national income belongs to both the government and the households. There are three measures of households' income. They are, **private income** (Pvt. I) **personal income** (PI) and **personal disposable income** (PDI), and they refer to the income earned by, income received by and income available for disposition to the households, respectively. Personal income includes all incomes earned or unearned. The relationships between the national income and these households' income are described by the following identities:

$$\text{Pvt. I} = NNP_F - IAD - END + NDI + TAD + OTA \quad \textbf{(2.6)}$$

$$PI = \text{Pvt. I} - RE - CT \quad \textbf{(2.7)}$$

$$PDI = PI - HDT - MAD \quad \textbf{(2.8)}$$

where

Pvt. I = private income

IAD = income of government administration departments from entrepreneurship and property (e.g. railways, post and telegraphs departments)

END = earnings of government non-department enterprises (public sector units)

NDI = national debt interest on domestic debt

TAD = current transfers from government administration departments

OTA = other net current transfers from abroad

RE = retained earnings of nation's private corporate sector

CT = corporate tax

HDT = household direct tax

MAD = miscellaneous receipts of government administration departments (court fee, etc.)

The new items in equations **(2.6)** through **(2.8)** are of relatively small magnitudes and mostly self-explanatory. It would suffice to mention here that IAD and END are the government incomes from production and thus, while a part of the national income, they are not components of private income. NDI is a peculiar public transfer payment. It is the payment for the use of public debt incurred in past wars and other government programmes and as such does not represent a purchase of a current good or service. It is considered a transfer payment and hence not a part of the national income, but surely a part of the private income. Also, NDI is subject to tampering through more or less borrowings by the government and, hence, like depreciation, must be excluded from the national income. TAD (consisting of direct subsidies, social security payments, relief payments, pensions, etc.) represents the transfer payments financed from taxation and as such are a means of redistributing income. These are basically the means to re-distribute the income in the desired direction. They are, as stated above, not factor incomes for the current year and do not form a part of the national income. However, they are a component of private income. Similarly, OTA (including pensions from abroad) is a part of private income but not of the national income. It would thus be clear that it is the personal disposable income which the private sector has for using freely on consumption and saving. This is basically the national income (or NNP at factor cost) after adjusting for government/public income, corporate savings in the form of retained earnings and the direct taxes in the form of personal income tax and corporate taxes.

In macroeconomics, we usually assume that governments do not run enterprises by itself. If so, terms IAD and END in equation 2.6 above are ignored and the other three terms on the right side, viz., NDI, TAD and OTA, are summed up as transfer payments (TP). Under this adjustment, equation 2.6 above becomes

$$\text{Pvt. I} = NNP_F + TP \qquad \textbf{(2.6a)}$$

Macroeconomics ignores minor items including the miscellaneous receipts of government administration departments (MAD) and as such equation 2.8 reduces to

$$PDI = PI - HDT \qquad \textbf{(2.8a)}$$

Though improvements in the national income and production accounts are considered as a significant development in economics during the last century, it is obvious from the above description that the data are still far away from perfection. Nevertheless, they are good enough for a reasonable assessment, particularly for the purposes of comparison over time and across countries. To throw some light on the relative significance of the various items in India's national income accounting and their movements over time, data on them is provided for 1990–91, 2000–01 and 2011–12 (the latest year for which data was available) in Table 2.1.

Table 2.1 National Income and Related Aggregates (at Current Prices)

(₹ *Billion*)

Variable	*1990-91*	*2000-01*	*2011-12*
1. GDP at factor cost	4778	18920	83535
1.1 Indirect taxes	763	2408	9703
1.2 Subsidies	186	433	3489
2. GDP at market price (1+ 1.1 – 1.2)	5355	20895	89749
2.1 Net factor income earned abroad	-75	-181	-768
3. GNP at market price (2 + 2.1)	5280	20714	88981
3.1 Capital consumption	522	1979	8767
4. NDP at factor cost (1 – 3.1)	4256	16941	74768
5. NNP at factor cost (NI)(4 + 2.1)	4181	16760	73999
5.1 Income of govt. administration depts. from entrepreneurship and property	49	169	1558
5.2 Saving of govt. non-dept. enterprises	26	141	1371
5.3 National debt interest	202	1141	3801
5.4 Current transfers from govt. administration depts.	156	607	2642
5.5 Other net current transfers from abroad	37	588	3049
6. Private income (5 – 5.1 – 5.2 + 5.3 + 5.4 + 5.5)	4502	18785	80562
6.1 Retained earnings of nation's private sector	62	306	3203
6.2 Corporate tax	53	296	3327
7. Personal income (6 – 6.1 – 6.2)	4387	18183	74032
7.1 Household direct tax	76	529*	2391
7.2 Miscellaneous receipt of govt. admin. dept.	21		
8. Personal disposable income (7 – 7.1 – 7.2)	4290	17654	71641
9. NNP at market price (3 – 3.1)	4758	18735	80214
10. Net national disposable income (9 + 5.5)	4795	19323	83263

*Total for rows 7.1 and 7.2.

Source: National Accounts Statistics, CSO, various issues.

A careful study of the above data would reveal that the difference (positive) between the

- incomes at each of the market price and factor cost stands at about nine per cent.
- domestic and national incomes is around one per cent.

- gross and net incomes comes to around eleven per cent.
- private and national incomes approximates nine per cent.
- personal income and national income is shrinking and currently stands at little less than one per cent.
- national income and personal disposable incomes are currently close to three per cent.

Thus, the shares of the various items in national income stand approximately at, nine percent for net indirect taxes, less than one percent for net factor income earned from abroad, eleven per cent for depreciation, nine per cent for various items that distinguish private income from national income, and four per cent for each of corporate taxes, retained earnings, and for household direct taxes and miscellaneous receipts of the government administrative departments.

Economic Units and Circular Flow of Income

On the basis of the economic units, the nation could be studied through five sectors: **(a)** households, **(b)** firms, **(c)** financial institutions (banks and capital market), **(d)** the government and **(e)** the rest of the world. These five sectors interact, produce and circulate the income. There are three markets: (a) factor (labour and capital) market (b) product market and (c) financial (money and bond) market. The process of sources and uses of income is depicted in Fig. 2.1 and explained briefly below. In brief, the figure shows the flow of goods and services, and of money across the five sectors of the economy. The figure has a new notation, viz., TPA, which stands for net transfer payments from abroad and these are assumed to accrue to households only.

All the factors of production are assumed to be owned by households. Households supply these factors to firms (governmental, private and joint, domestic and foreign), who produce all the GDP. The firms pay factors' rewards (rent, wage, interest and profit) to households (residents and non-residents), corporate tax and indirect taxes net of subsidies to the government and maintain the balance as gross savings (retained profit and depreciation) with the financial institutions. The firms, in turn, receive payments for supplying consumption goods to households, governments and foreign residents (net exports = exports – imports). Firms raise funds for gross investments from financial institutions. GDP data can be obtained through either adding all the outflows from or inflows to the firms. The government receives indirect taxes and corporate tax from firms, and personal tax from households. It pays for its consumption expenditure (on goods and services) to firms, advances production subsidies to firms and transfer payments to households (residents and non-residents). Its savings (dis-savings) go to (come from) financial institutions. Financial institutions receive savings from all the three sectors (households, firms and government) and advance funds for all the investment goods to firms. Households receive payments for all the owned factors of production from firms (domestic as well as foreign) and transfer payments from the governments and abroad. It pays firms for consumption goods, personal tax to the government and puts its savings in financial institutions. The foreign sector (rest of the world) receives payments for its exports, and factor income and transfer payments from abroad. The said sector makes payments for its imports, and factor income and transfer payments to abroad. This process continues period after period and this is how the income is produced and circulated among

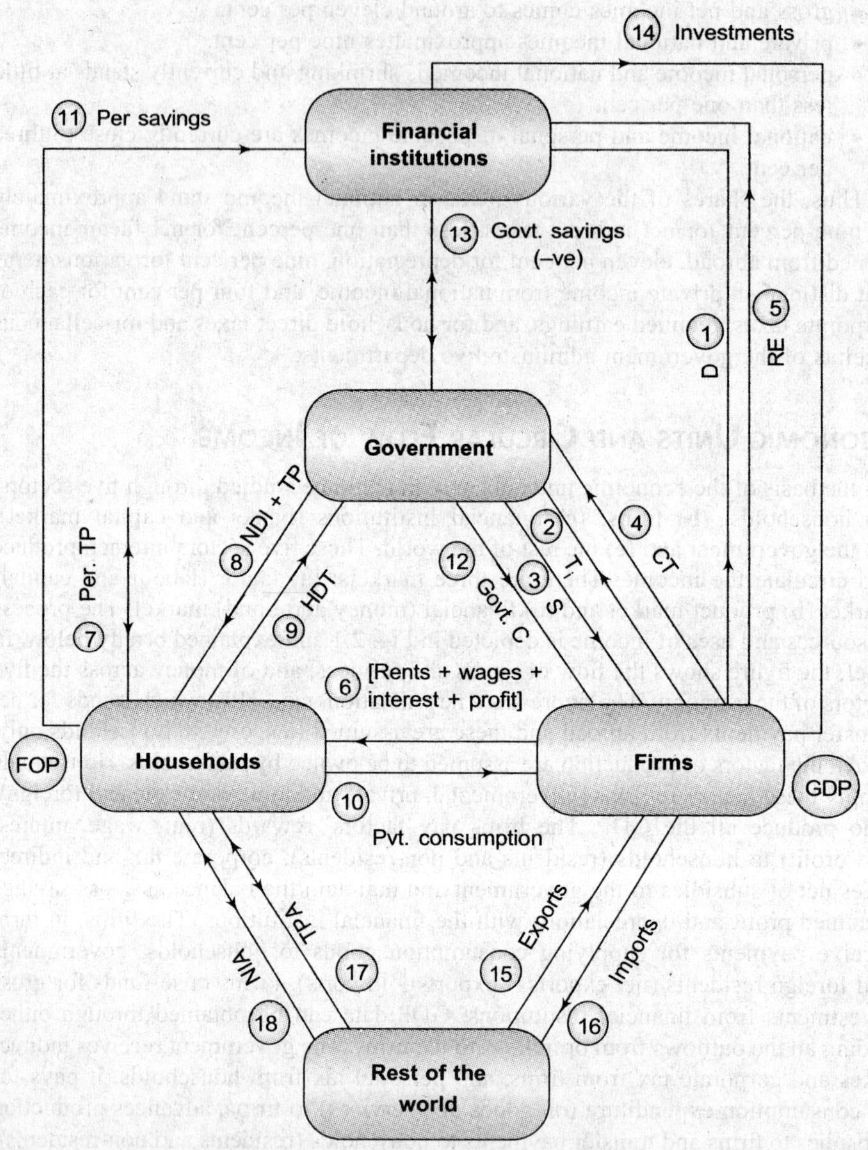

Fig. 2.1 Circular Flow of Income

the various sectors of the economy. Incidentally, note that this process assumes that all the production takes place at firms, all the investments are made by firms and all the savings go to financial institutions. These are merely simplifying assumptions and their relaxation does not pose any conceptual problem.

The circular flow of income shows leakages (withdrawals) from the national income, which does not form a part of the expenditure on national product. These are savings (S), taxes (T) and imports of goods and services (Z). Also, it indicates injections (additions) into expenditure on national product, which do not come from national income. These are investment (I), government expenditure (G) and exports of goods and services (X). These injections and leakages are related. Savings finance investment, partly or fully, as taxes finance government expenditure. Also, some of the expenditure on imports provides foreigners with the means to purchase our exports. Although the leakages may eventually finance the injections, they do not cause them. There is no reason for $S = I$, $T = G$ and $Z = X$, but the total planned leakages must equal the total planned injections for the equilibrium to hold:

$$S + T + Z = I + G + X \quad \textbf{(2.9)}$$

The above equation indicates that in an open economy there can be three gaps/imbalances:

- Investment-saving gap
- Fiscal deficit/surplus
- Current account (of balance of payments) deficit/surplus

However, the sum of the three gaps must equal zero. In India, investments have always exceeded savings and governments have often experienced fiscal deficits, and the two have been financed by the deficits (imports minus exports) in the current account. Incidentally note that the import-export gap is not exactly equal to the current account imbalance, for the current account of the balance of payments has two additional (though minor) items, viz., factor income and transfers.

INCOME MEASUREMENTS

As was implicit in the previous section, national income could be measured in three different ways:

- Production or value added approach
- Income approach
- Expenditure approach

And if done correctly, the following equation must hold:

Value of Domestic Production = Income of all factors of production

= Expenditure of all sectors on domestic production **(2.10)**

This is because the three approaches are circular in nature. It begins at production, through recruitments of factors of production, generating and going as incomes to factors of production, who expend it on production. GDP is produced (Production) at the firms, which is sold out (Revenue = Expenditure) to consumers for consumption (C), government for consumption (G), firms themselves for investment (I) and to foreigners as net exports (X – Z). The revenue so received are used up (Payment = Income) to pay wages to labour (W), interest and rent to capitalists (I + R), taxes to government (T_i – S + CT), dividend and proprietors' profit to owners and retained profit and depreciation allowance kept by firms themselves. A brief discussion of these approaches follows.

Production Approach

Under this approach, we get the GDP at the factor cost as the sum of the values of the flows of value added from various production centres or as the sum of the production of all final goods and services. Thus, the GDP at the factor cost is given by

$$\text{GDP}_F = P_1Q_1 + P_2Q_2 + \cdots + P_nQ_n \qquad \textbf{(2.11)}$$

where P_i = price of final good i

Q_i = output of final good i

n = number of goods and services produced in the economy

Incidentally, note that equation **(2.11)** assumes that all productions can be valued in money terms.

The production sectors are conveniently classified into **(a)** primary, **(b)** secondary and **(c)** tertiary. The primary sector includes agriculture, forestry and fishing and mining and quarrying. The secondary sector consists of manufacturing, electricity, gas and water supply and construction. The tertiary sector consists of all items under services. The contribution of each of these sectors and their sub-sectors to the GDP at the factor cost (at current prices) during 1950–51, 1990–91, 2000–01 and 2011–12 is reported in Table 2.2.

A distinction is also made between the agriculture, industry and services sectors. The first sector includes items 1 and 2 of the table, the second sector includes items 3, 4, and 5, and items 6 through 12 go in the third sector.

Table 2.2 Gross Domestic Product at Factor Cost by Economic Activity (at Current Prices)

(% share)

Sector	*1950–51*	*1990–91*	*2000–01*	*2011–12*
Primary	**56.5**	**33.5**	**27.3**	**20.0**
1. Agriculture	52.2	28.3	22.7	15.2
2. Forestry and fishing	3.6	2.7	2.2	2.4
3. Mining and quarrying	0.7	2.5	2.4	2.4
Secondary	**14.5**	**26.9**	**24.5**	**24.3**
4. Manufacturing	11.5	18.7	15.8	14.4
5. Electricity, gas and water supply	0.2	2.2	2.6	1.7
6. Construction	2.8	6.0	6.1	8.2
Tertiary (Services)	**29.0**	**39.7**	**48.2**	**55.7**
7. Trade, hotels and restaurants	6.5	13.0	13.8	18.0
8. Transport, storage and communication	3.5	7.1	7.3	7.1
9. Banking and insurance	0.8	4.4	6.2	5.7
10. Real estate, dwellings and business services	9.2	3.7	6.3	10.8
11. Public administration and defence	3.0	5.7	6.6	6.1
12. Other services	6.0	5.8	8.0	7.9
GDP at factor cost (₹ billion)	**90**	**4,778**	**18,958**	**83,535**

Source: National Accounts Statistics, CSO, various issues.

A careful examination of the data in Table 2.2 would reveal that in the last over 60 years, the share of both the secondary and tertiary sectors in GDP has increased substantially at the cost of the primary sector. Further, the role of the tertiary sector has grown at the fastest rate. This is a sign of prosperity, provided, of course, the requirements for wage-goods are met reasonably well! This will be obvious if one examines similar data for high and middle-income countries. In 2012, the share of agriculture, industry and services in GDP stood at about 1, 20 and 79 per cent in United States, and approximately at 10, 47 and 43 per cent, respectively in China. In the same year, the world average for the shares of these three sectors stood at about 3, 27 and 70 per cent, respectively. Thus, the production structure in India is still quite primitive. Incidentally, note that since the data in Table 2.2 is on productions from various sectors in the Indian territories, the sum total is domestic production. Since they are gross of depreciation, it is gross domestic product and since they are valued at the factor cost, it is the GDP at factor cost.

Indian government has been playing a significant role in the production of GDP. The relevant data are given below in Table 2.3.

Table 2.3 Share of Public Sector in GPD and Components: India

(% share)

Item	*1993–94*	*2000–01*	*2011–12*
GDP	25.9	24.8	20.5
1. Administrative departments	8.7	10.5	9.7
2. Departmental enterprises	3.7	3.5	2.1
3. Non-departmental enterprises	13.5	10.8	8.7

Note: The data are at current prices.
Source: CSO: National Accounts Statistics, various issues.

The data suggest that the government is currently producing about one-fifth of GDP in India. However, its contribution is falling over time. This is due to the policy of privatisation that the country is following particularly since 1991. Of the three components, the share of the administration departments enterprises has been the largest and of the departmental enterprises the least.

Income Approach

Under the cost or income approach, the national income equals the sum of the costs of production of final goods and services, which equals the incomes of labour and capital. Labour earns wages (W) for the services to the producers, profits (P) for entrepreneurship, and income for self-employment. Capital earns rental income (R) for renting out structures and equipment and interest (I) on money lending to producers. Thus, the NDP at the factor cost is given by

$$\text{NDP}_F = W + R + I + P \qquad \textbf{(2.12)}$$

Transfer payments/receipts, such as unemployment benefits and pensions are not included in income. Since there are self-employed people in all countries, and they rarely classify their incomes into the above four components, the functionally distributed national income data contains a mixed income category. Further, a significant proportion of the Indian people are self-employed and accordingly, the mixed income category is a dominant component here. Since the equation gives NDP at factor cost, it includes the incomes of both the Indian residents' factors as well as the non-resident factors accruing from the domestic production. Thus, the wages, interest and profits accruing to non-residents' labour, foreign capital and non-residents' entrepreneurship, respectively from the domestic production are included in it. Further, both the distributed profit (dividend) and the retained profit are included in it, and the included profits are before corporate taxes. Thus, in equation (2.12) above, P = dividend + retained earnings + corporate tax.

The Indian data on income by factors' share (functional distribution of income) for the selected few years is given in Table 2.4. Some columns in this table are blank as comparable data is not available. Remember that NDP data, which the table gives, include the incomes earned by the non-resident factors in India but exclude the incomes earned by the resident factors abroad. The data reveals that labour commands the maximum share in NDP (above 40 per cent) and that its share has fluctuated over time. The exact share in India can not be ascertained due to the significant share of mixed income (caused by the significant proportion of the unorganised sector and the self-employed persons). The labour share is over whelming in all countries. For example, in the United States in 1997, the share of employee compensation in national income stood at 72 per cent, the share of other factors were at 12, 6, 2 and 8 per cent for corporate profits, net interest, rental income and proprietor's income, respectively.

Table 2.4 NDP at Factor Cost by Factor Incomes (at Current Prices)

(% share)

Factor income	*1960–61*	*1974–75*	*1980–81*	*1990–91*	*1993–94*	*2003–04*
1. Compensation of employees	33.7	42.2	36.8	38.4	37.4	35.6
2. Operating surplus			7.7	11.5	12.9	
2.1 Rent		5.2	3.5			
2.2 Interest	3.2	8.6				
2.3 Profit and dividend	6.7	6.0				
3. Mixed income	51.2	39.7	55.5	50.1	49.7	64.4
4. NDP at factor cost (₹ billion)			1,103	4,256	6,513	22,661
5. Property incomes (₹ billion)				99	497	7,762
5.1 Rent				24	21.4	22
5.2 Interest				76	78.6	78

Note: Rent paid by an industry for land, structures, machinery, equipment etc. is treated as a factor payment. Except for residential buildings, no imputation for rent for using own buildings, machinery and equipment is made.

Source: National Accounts Statistics, CSO, various issues

Expenditure Approach

Under this method, national income is measured as the sum of all final expenditures. Final expenditure consists of private consumption expenditure on domestic goods (C), domestic gross investment expenditure on domestic goods/assets—both private and public (I), government (federal, state and local) consumption expenditure on domestic goods (G), foreigners' expenditure on domestic exports of domestic goods and services (X), net of domestic expenditure on imports of foreign goods and services (Z). Note that G does not include transfer payments and X and Z do not include factor income from/to abroad and transfer payment from/to abroad. Under this approach, GDP at the market price is thus given by,

$$GDP_M = C + I + G + X - Z \quad \textbf{(2.13)}$$

The equation gives GDP at market price because households, firms and governments buy consumption and investment goods and services at the market price only. The sum of the first three items of expenditure ($C + I + G$) denotes the domestic absorption of GDP, and net exports of goods and services ($X - Z$) the net foreign demand of GDP. It must be noted that what is not consumed is saving. Further, while saving equals investment in the world as a whole, the same is not necessarily true for a country. This is so because some countries save more and some less than they invest. The balance between the supply of savings and the demand for investments is met by financial flows between economies, the net of which is given by the difference between imports and exports of goods and services. Thus,

Domestic saving = domestic income – private consumption
– government consumption
= domestic investment + exports – imports.

This relationship as well as the one in equation **(2.13)** are similar to the leakages = injections equation (vide equation **2.9**). To see this, let us work on equation **(2.9)**. Note that

Private saving = Personal disposable income – personal consumption

or $S = (\text{NI} + \text{TP} - \text{HDT} - \text{CT}) - C$

Total taxes net of subsidies to producers and transfer payments) (T) is,

$$T = \text{HDT} + \text{CT} + \text{Indirect taxes} - \text{Subsidies} - \text{TP}.$$

Recall equation **(2.9)**:

$$S + T + Z = I + G + X$$

Substituting for S and T, and calling NI as Y, we get

$$(Y + \text{TP} - \text{HDT} - \text{CT} - C) + (\text{HDT} + \text{CT} + \text{Indirect taxes} - \text{Subsidies} - \text{TP}) + Z = I + G + X$$

On solving the equation and rearranging the terms, we get

$$Y = C + I + G + X - Z - (\text{Indirect taxes} - \text{Subsidies})$$

This is the GDP at factor cost version of equation **(2.13)** above. Note that in this equation, Y is GDP at factor cost. This is because I is gross (gross of depreciation) investment (S is also gross saving) and X and Z do not include factors' incomes from abroad. After necessary adjustments (subtract depreciation and add net factor income from abroad) it can be converted into national income or NNP at factor cost.

Equation **(2.9)** is an important one. It is written differently to mean several things. Three of its important versions are

$$I = S + (T - G) + (Z - X) \quad \textbf{(2.9a)}$$

$$S = I + (G - T) + (X - Z) \quad \textbf{(2.9b)}$$

$$(I - S) + (G - T) = (Z - X) \quad \textbf{(2.9c)}$$

Equation **(2.9a)** indicates that the domestic investments are financed through the private saving, government saving, and the foreign saving, the last being equal to the net imports of goods and services. Equation **(2.9b)** suggests that the private savings are used to finance the domestic investment, fiscal deficit, and to invest abroad (i.e.net exports of goods and services). The last equation implies that many countries like India have investment larger than saving and yet fiscal deficit, but then they must also be having imports in excess of exports. Recall that X and Z do not include factor income from/to abroad (and transfers from/to abroad), and thus S and I are domestic saving and domestic investment, and not the national saving and national investment, respectively. The several versions of equation **(2.9)** suggests that domestic saving need not equal domestic investment. However, if one examines the data across countries, it would be found that the correlation between S and I is positive and very high. This is referred to as the **S-I correlation puzzle.** The reasons for this are found in the governments' desire to limit the current account (of the balance of payments) imbalances and the limited access to the capital market that the firms enjoy. This point is elaborated later in Chapter 7.

Equation **(2.13)** is often referred to as the **income identity**. It also indicates that the difference between the gross domestic product and the gross domestic expenditure equals net exports of goods and services. It may be clarified that C includes all households' expenditure on non-durable goods and all durable goods, except land and buildings, which are included in gross investment. Government consumption, called government final consumption expenditure, includes government purchases of the services of its officials and non-durable goods/services from other suppliers to provide collective services (defence, justice, health, education etc.). The government renders these services free or at a token fee and they are not included in private consumption. Investment consists of expenditures on structures (residential and business), equipments and inventories.

The data on these components of expenditure on the final goods are provided in Table 2.5. The data reveal that while the share of private consumption declined significantly until 1990–91, it went up marginally in 2000–01, falling once again subsequently. Quite the opposite has been the trend for the share of investment in total expenditure. There was an upward trend in the share of the government expenditure until 2000–01, which has reversed after words. The share of the foreign trade in goods and services has witnessed an upward trend almost through out. The said share has more than trebled during the last over 60 years. Incidentally, note that the current (2011-12) structure of expenditure on (C), (I) and (G) in India differs significantly from the world average of around 61, 21 and 18 per cent, respectively. While our investment share is higher, the share of the other two is less than the world average. India's foreign trade in goods and services is now heading close to the world average of 31 per cent of GDP. It is instructive to note that India's trade has expanded at a relatively faster rate in last few years. In 2011-12, India's exports were at about 24 per cent and imports at 30 per cent of the GDP. Our country is marching ahead to be known as an open economy. It is known that the United States emphasises on consumption, while China on investment. Thus in 2012 the shares of consumption, investment and government consumption expenditure in the GDP stood at 72, 15 and 17 per cent in the United States, and 38, 48 and 14 per cent in China, respectively. Even in trade of goods and services, China enjoys a much larger relative share than the United States. In 2012, while the proportion of exports of goods and services to the GDP and import of goods and services to the GDP stood at 14 and 18 per cent in the United States, the said numbers in China were at 31 and 27 per cent, respectively. It is instructive to note that the sum total of the items in the above table is GDP at market prices, as investment here is gross, the various expenditures are on the domestically produced goods and services, and these are valued at the market price as they happen to be payments made by the final buyers. Also, note that the sum of C, I and G does not add to 100 per cent, because of the net exports, which is the fourth (net foreign) component of expenditure on domestic goods.

Table 2.5 GDP at Market Price by Expenditure (at Current Prices)

(*% share*)

Head of expenditure	*1950–51*	*1990–91*	*2000–01*	*2011–12*
Private consumption	83.9	61.7	64.2	56.3
Investment (gross)	10.2	25.2	22.9	35.4
Government expenditure	5.6	11.5	13.2	11.6
Exports	7.9	7.6	13.9	23.9
Imports (minus)	7.6	9.1	14.7	30.3
GDP at market prices (₹ billion)	94	5,355	20,880	89,749

Note: Sum may not add to 100% due to statistical discrepancies.
Source: National Accounts Statistics, CSO, various issues.

It would be interesting to discuss the contribution of the public sector to our gross domestic investment and gross domestic saving. The data on these are given below in Table 2.6.

Table 2.6 **Share of Public Sector in Gross Domestic Investment and Gross Domestic Saving: India**

(*% share*)

	1993–94	*2000–01*	*2011–12*
1. Gross Domestic Capital Formation	**38.8**	**29.3**	**24.0**
1.1 Administrative departments	8.6	10.8	11.2
1.2 Departmental enterprises	9.2	0.4	2.4
1.3 Non-departmental enterprises	21.0	18.1	10.4
2. Gross Domestic Saving	**2.8**	**–7.5**	**4.2**
2.1 Administrative departments	–13.4	–23.3	–6.6
2.2 Departmental enterprises	3.8	3.5	1.2
2.3 Non-departmental enterprises	12.4	12.3	9.7

Note: The data are at current prices.
Source: CSO: National Accounts Statistics, various issues.

The data suggest that the share of the government in investment has decreased significantly over time. This is no surprise as the country is pursuing the policy of privatisation. Since the share in investment exceeds that in saving by a significant margin, the government is a net user of the financial resources in the country. The bulk of public investment goes to administrative departments and non-department enterprises and bulk of its saving flows from non-departmental enterprises.

We may now turn to the **government budget constraint**, which is given by,

$$G + TP = T + GBD \qquad \textbf{(2.14)}$$

where

TP = all transfer payments from governments to households and firms
GBD = government budget/fiscal deficit
T = all taxes

Note that G (government expenditure) does not include transfer payments from the government, for they are not part of the GDP. Government income from departmental and public sector enterprises, and the proceeds from disinvestments are included in (T). GBD is financed through printing money (monetised deficit) and/or borrowing from citizens and/or abroad. This assumes that the government either makes no investments or it is included in (G).

The above three measures are used to generate income data. Since production must equal income, which must, in turn, equal expenditure, all the three approaches are expected to yield identical result. However, some statistical discrepancy might crop up due to the vast data and, thus, some allowance is often made for such errors.

Depending upon the state of perfection in the data collection, different countries use one or more approaches to arrive at the estimates of the national income. In India and most other countries, the production approach is used for incomes from the commodity producing sectors (primary and secondary, barring unregistered manufacturing and electricity, gas and water supply) and the income/cost approach is used for the rest. Since there is no unique measure of production in services, the income approach is used globally. Here it must be noted that since employees are not always paid equal to their contributions, the income remains an imperfect measure of output. For example, under the Fifth Pay Commission Report, the Government of India granted a big increase in the salaries of its staff while there was no corresponding increase in production. Thus, this is yet another shortcoming in the measurement of national income. The Central Statistical Organisation (CSO) is in charge of the national income accounts in India. The first official estimates were presented in 1956 and since then they have been presented on a yearly basis.

It may be worthwhile to indicate that while there are several versions of income and that they are really different, in the macroeconomic analysis of business cycles and growth, only national income (and personal disposable income) is commonly discussed. Thus, indirect taxes, subsidies to producers, depreciation and net factor income from abroad are often ignored to avoid complications. The present text would use the latter items only when they are unavoidable.

Nominal and Real Income

Income is measured in the nominal as well as real terms. The former is obtained when outputs are valued at their corresponding current prices and the latter is obtained when outputs are valued at their corresponding constant prices (prices prevailing in the chosen base year) or after nominal income is adjusted for inflation. Thus,

$$\text{Nominal income} = \sum_{i=1}^{n} P_i^c Q_i^c \tag{2.15}$$

$$\text{Real income} = \sum_{i=1}^{n} P_i^b Q_i^c \tag{2.16}$$

where

P_i^c = price of good i in the current year

Q_i^c = output of good i in the current year

P_i^b = price of good i in the base year

Both these concepts are useful. While nominal income is the true measure of income, a change in it over time is a poor indicator of the change in the economic well-being of the earner. This is because, this could change due to a mere change in prices or a change in it could be composed of changes both in the output as well as in the prices. As such, if an individual's income doubles and the prices of all the goods and services that he buys with all his income also double, there is no change in his purchasing power or economic well-being. Therefore, for judging the change in economic well-being, we need to remove the price-effect from the changed income. The real income concept achieves this by valuing all the goods and services at their corresponding prices in some base year, and thus, a change in it indicates a change in the purchasing power over the base year. In other words, the real income is like the actual physical volume of production. The ratio of the nominal to real income is called the **GDP income deflator**. Thus, in 2011–12 India's nominal GDP at factor cost was ₹83,535 billion and her real GDP at factor cost (at 2004–05 prices) was ₹52,436 billion and the GDP deflator stood at 1.59314. To separate the two effects, change in nominal income could be decomposed as

$$Y = QP$$

or, $$dY = QdP + PdQ \quad \text{(taking total differentiation)}$$

or, $$\frac{dY}{Y} = Q\frac{dP}{Y} + P\frac{dQ}{Y} \quad \text{(dividing both sides by } Y\text{)}$$

$$\dot{Y} = \dot{P} + \dot{Q} \quad \text{(noting that } Y = QP\text{)}$$

Thus, growth rate in nominal income = inflation rate + growth rate in real income.

Computation of the real income creates problems due to the emergence of new products and change in the quality of products over time, as those products have no price during the base year, when they did not exist. Approximations are made to take care of such difficulties. Also, in real income calculations, the choice of base year is significant, lest it gives distorted information. In this context, the controversy around the late Professor Raj Krishna's 'Hindu Rate of Growth' is well known. In the mid-1980s, the policy makers had argued that India had entered into a higher growth era, which the late Professor Raj Krishna denied on the grounds that they were basing their calculations on the 1979–80 base, which happened to be a negative growth year in the country. For this reason, the base year has to be a normal year, neither too good nor too bad and also not a year of significant events.

Measured and PPP Income

Gustav Cassel coined the concept of the purchasing power parity (PPP) income in 1923, though its intellectual origin could be traced to the early 19th century in the writings of David Ricardo. The concept is used to convert the country wise measured (at the official exchange rate) income data into the comparable (purchasing power equivalent) income data across countries. The national income data of different countries is constructed on the basis of the corresponding country's data on prices of goods and services. Further, those data are converted into a foreign currency (US dollars) at the official exchange rate. Since the official exchange rates do not normally represent the true relative purchasing power, the country-wise national income data is not comparable. To overcome this difficulty, the World Bank has designed a scheme of converting all individual country's income data into the PPP income data, by computing the PPP of each country's currency in terms of the US dollar. Under the law of one price theory, exchange rate must reflect the differences in price levels. Thus,

PPP of Indian rupee = number of Indian rupees required to purchase a representative basket of goods and services in India that one US dollar will buy in the United States.

Accordingly, PPP income of India = (Measured Income of India)

$$\times \left(\frac{\text{Official Rupee – Dollar Rate}}{\text{PPP of Indian Rupee}}\right)$$

Thus, referring Table 1.1 of Chapter 1 (also Table 2.5), while the measured (nominal) per capita income of India in 2011 was US $1420, its PPP counterpart was US $3640, giving a PPP correction of 2.56. This means the price in the United States is about 2.56 times the Indian price for a representative basket of goods and services. Thus, by the PPP theory, the Indian rupee is highly undervalued (by a factor of 2.56). On this same basis, it can be found through the data in Table 1.1 that the price in the United States was about 1.69 (8390/4970) times China's price, while Japan's price was only about 79 per cent (35380/44900) of the United States price in 2011. For international comparison, the PPP income is certainly a better measure of purchasing power than the measured income. The PPP income data of various countries are given later in Table 2.7 and analysed subsequently.

Income and Human Development Index

Human Development Index (HDI) is yet another measure used for the measurement of the extent of development across countries. It is based on three parameters:

- Per capita GDP-PPP (income)
- Life expectancy at birth (health)
- Mean years and expected years of schooling (skill).

These three ingredients are combined into an overall index called HDI by the United Nations Development Project (UNDP) and the UNDP publishes this data for various nations over time regularly. The above three variables are converted into indices and then geometric average is taken to give the HDI. This is not a place to go into details of its methodology but it may be noted that,

- For each of the three components, the minimum values are assigned and the observed maximum values are identified.
- Per capita GDP-PPP is adjusted through using its natural logarithm value so that the difference is compressed.
- Index for each variable is computed using the following formula:
  Index = (actual value – minimum value)/(maximum value – minimum value)
- The three indices are then combined into one (HDI) through geometric averaging.

Thus, HDI is more comprehensive than income for assessing the health of a country. The international data on this index is provided and compared later in this chapter. It may not be out of place to note that India's former Human Resource Development Minister, Murali Manohar Joshi, has challenged this measure as it ignores spirituality, morality, satisfaction and crime rate, which are integral parts of Human Resource Development.

INCOME AND WELFARE

Recall that national income is supposed to measure the material well-being of the nation. However, due to several measurement errors, it remains a misleading measure of material well-being and it is even less effective as a measure of welfare or happiness. This is because welfare is an economic concept and it is tantamount to happiness or quality of life and, thus, it is a much broader concept than income or even human development. It includes not only material well-being but also other aspects of economic welfare, such as leisure, education, health, environment, mutual respect, dignity, honour, respect for the family values, religion, culture, customs, traditions, habits, emotions and the like. The reason these factors are left out is that they have no price tags. Although our per capita income is only a fraction of that of North Americans, many of the latter think that Indians are happier than them. Even in India, the same is true regarding the rich when compared to their counterparts in middle income and happy families.

It is true that in the absence of a better measure, national income is taken as a surrogate measure of economic welfare. However, it is obvious that the per capita income (national income divided by the population) is a better indicator of the standard of living than national income. For example, the national income of India is over two times that of Indonesia but the standard of living in the former is much lower than that of the latter as the per capita income of the former is merely less than half of the latter. Thus, on the yardstick of per capita income, India emerges as one of the poorer countries in the world. Also, per capita income is subject to the uneven income distribution problem and it is said that "growth without social justice is inhuman and social justice without growth is impossible".

Thus, though it is undoubtedly true that ours is a relatively poor country, our poverty is perhaps exaggerated by the per capita income measure as it suffers from the twin limitations, viz. those due to errors in the measurement of national income, and those due to income being an imperfect measure of economic welfare. To summarise,

Measurement Errors in National Income

(a) Ignores the non-market and unofficial market (parallel/black/underground) economy. Thus, the measured income (data) underestimates the true income and thereby the material well-being.

(b) Measures the output of the service sector erroneously. Thus, material well being is poorly measured by income.

(c) Measures the values of the self-consumption of production and of the owner-occupied houses on the basis of imputed prices, which could differ from their real prices.

(d) Ignores the quality of products, which may not be accurately measured by their prices. Hence, income is an erroneous measure of material well being.

(e) Is valued at the official exchange rate. For international comparison, it is often over or under valued. For example, in July 1991, India devalued its currency by about 25 per cent and accordingly her national income, in terms of the US $, fell by 25 per cent. No output was destroyed and yet income fell! This is due to the somewhat arbitrary nature of the foreign exchange rate.

Income is an Imperfect Measure of Economic Welfare

Because of the absence of price tags on several items that have a bearing on economic welfare. This is because national income:

(i) Ignores the benefits due to leisure and the loss due to the human costs of employment in terms of the physical and mental strains associated with jobs. Leisure is valuable to everyone and thus considered as a normal good in economics while strain is unwanted.

(ii) Equates goods (education) and bads (weapons); public (defence), merit (education) and non-merit (air conditioner) goods' classification. Production of a gun is equated to that of wheat in equal value. However, such goods have varying values for the economy.

(iii) Ignores income distribution. Social welfare is perhaps the maximum when income is distributed equally among all the inhabitants.

(iv) Counts both addictions (drinking) and cures (medicines for drunks). The former are responsible for the latter.

(v) Ignores costs of growth, associated with traffic congestion, pollution, accidents, use of natural resources, environment degradation, crimes, increased stress on jobs and so on. These costs adversely affect economic welfare.

(vi) Ignores weather. Edward Denison once remarked that perhaps nothing affects national economic welfare so much as the weather. For example, people prefer to live in Bangalore over Delhi or Kolkata, other things being equal.

(vii) Includes incomes generated through non-productive activities such as defence, police and courts, which are considered 'regrettable' or 'necessary evil' goods. They may be necessary but do not contribute to the standard of living or quality of life.

(viii) Ignores the quality of life, which is influenced by education, health, living together, love to own land, human freedom and so on. All these factors contribute to social welfare.

(ix) Ignores ethics, values, customs, traditions, habits, religions, spirituality, emotions and so on. All these factors have positive values for economic welfare.

Robert Kennedy, in his 1968 US presidential campaign speech complained that GDP "counts napalm and counts nuclear warheads". Nicolas Sarkozy, the then France President in a speech in Sept 2009 said France will consider well-being, including factors such as time off, health care and family relationships, in addition to the classical measure of domestic product.

The relative size of these factors varies across countries and hence, they do affect the relative welfare of people. Due to this, efforts are on to develop indices to evaluate the quality of life by measuring the status of economic welfare. Currently, we have the 'Corruption Index', 'Competition Index' and so on. However, efforts towards a comprehensive welfare measure are still far from perfection and accordingly, per capita income (PPP) and HDI are still used as alternative measures of the standard of living over time and across countries. Recall that even these magnitudes do not include all the above variables and it is perhaps true that less developed economies are not as poor as revealed by their per capita incomes or HDI data alone.

What then is the **bottom line** for the measurement of economic well being? This is still debatable. However, internationally, GDP per capita (PPP) is considered as the one. To be more fair, it should be GNP per capita (PPP), adjusted in some way for non-market and parallel economy, average work hours (or leisure), quality and length of life (education, pollution and life expectancy) etc. as they alone determine the current consumption level and the saving-investment rate, which, as would be obvious later, determines future consumption levels. The message is that if one wants to be rich, not only he/she must work hard and smartly, but also save and invest productively. If everyone follows this principle, the country would be rich as well.

International Data and Compartaive Analysis

For international comparison, related data on the economic well-being and progress for selected countries are provided in Table 2.7, (saving-investment data are given later in Chapter 6). The data reveal the following:

- The United States happens to be the largest economy and this is true not only for countries included in the table but also for the world as a whole, both in terms of the measured as well as the PPP level of GNP. Furthermore, the United States GNP was around 23 per cent of the world GNP in terms of the measured income and 19 per cent in terms of the PPP income in 2011. This is so partly because the United States ranked 6th in per capita income (both measured and PPP) and third in population in the world in 2011, and countries ranking first and second in population (China and India, respectively) have rather low ranks in terms of per capita income. India takes the 3rd position in terms of the PPP GNP and the 7th position in measured GNP in the world. The same for China stand at 2nd both in measured and PPP GNP, respectively. The other high PPP GNP as well as measured GNP countries are Japan, Germany, France and United Kingdom, in that order.
- Norway enjoyed the highest measured per capita income (US $88,870), the 2nd rank being taken by Qatar ($80,440) in a sample of about 200 countries in 2011. The United States had the 6th highest PPP per capita income (US $48,820). India takes a rather low rank with 133rd for PPP and 140th for measured per capita income. Other countries with higher measured per capita income include the Luxembourg, Switzerland, United States, Japan, Germany, Singapore, France, and United Kingdom, in that order, while countries with higher PPP per capita income include Qatar, Luxembourg, Norway, Singapore, Switzerland, and USA, in the descending order.
- China has attained, among the large countries, the maximum growth rate (10.6 per cent) in GDP during 2000-2012. The other high growth economies include India, Vietnam, Nigeria, Indonesia, Sri Lanka and Russia. India's achievement at 7.7 per cent stands much above the world's average growth rate of 2.6 per ent.

Table 2.7 International Data on Income and Related Variables

Country	*GNP 2011*		*GNP per capita 2011*		*GDP growth rate 2000–2012*	*Life expectancy at birth 2012*	*Adult illiteracy rate 2005-2010*	*Human development index*
	(US $ billion)		*(US $)*		*(%)*	*(years)*	*(%)*	*(Max = 1)*
	Measured	*PPP*	*Measured*	*PPP*				*2012 (rank)*
India	1766	4525	1420	3640	7.7	66	37	0.554 (136)
United States	15418	15211	48620	48820	1.6	79	0	0.937 (3)
Canada	1571	1368	45550	39660	1.9	81	0	0.911 (11)
United Kingdom	2370	2256	37780	35950	1.6	80	0	0.875 (26)
Japan	5740	4516	44900	35330	0.7	84	0	0.912 (10)
Switzerland	604	416	76350	52530	1.9	83	0	0.913 (9)
Singapore	223	308	42930	59380	5.9	81	7	0.895 (18)
Indonesia	713	1091	2940	4500	5.5	70	10	0.629 (121)
Brazil	2108	2246	10720	11420	3.7	74	11	0.730 (85)
Republic of Korea	1039	1512	20870	30370	4.0	81	–	0.909 (12)
China	6643	11271	4940	8390	10.6	74	9	0.699 (101)
Pakistan	198	507	1120	2870	4.7	66	50	0.515 (146)
Sri Lanka	54	115	2580	5520	5.9	75	9	0.715 (92)
Australia	1111	862	49790	38610	3.1	82	0	0.938 (2)
Nigeria	207	373	1280	2290	6.8	52	–	0.471 (153)
Russian Fed.	1522	2918	10650	20410	4.8	69	1	0.788 (55)
World	66354	80624	9514	11560	2.6	70	20	0.694

Sources: *World Development Report 2006;* Human Development Report, UNDP, 2006—Not available.
World Development Indicators, World Bank, 2007 Norway tops 0.965 (1).

- Japan (84 Years) and Switzerland (83 Years) top the list in terms of life expectancy at birth rate. The other high achievers include Australia, Rep. Korea, Singapore and Canada. India's success in this regard is quite low at 66 years.
- Adult illiteracy is close to zero in most developed countries but it is still quite high in India, standing at 37 per cent.
- Norway tops the list in human development, with HDI of 0.955 (out of 1.00). India takes the 136th position out of about 200 countries. Countries with high HDI include Australia, USA, Netherlands, Germany and New Zealand, in that order. This ranking is given by the Human Development Report, which has a sample of about 200 countries and the latest available data are for 2012. According to this report, India's rank, in terms of the per capita income (PPP), is 133. This, together with India's HDI rank, implies that India's position is worse on the skills and health fronts than in per capita income alone.

For more detailed data and their analysis, readers may go through the original sources. However, it is rather clear from the above data that there are wide variations in income and other related variables across nations and India has a long way to catch up, even if it is able to accelerate its relative growth rate.

Keywords

National income; Per capita income; GDP-GNP-NDP-NNP; Depreciation; Factor cost-Market price; Indirect taxes; Subsidies; Net factor income earned abroad; Raw-materials; Intermediate goods; Value added; Double counting of production; Not marketed-not officially marketed; Do-it-yourself activities; Transfer payments; Black/Parallel/Underground economy; Legitimate-Illegitimate exclusions; Private-Personal-Personal disposable income; Circular flow of income; Injections to-Leakages from production; Saving-Investment correlation puzzle; Production-Income-Expenditure approach; Income identity; Nominal-Real income; GDP/Income deflator; Hindu rate of growth; Measured-PPP income; Human development index; Economic welfare, Price tag, bottom line.

References

1. EPW Research Foundation, 'National Accounts Statistics of India 1 and 2', *Economic and Political Weekly*, (November 18, 1995): pp. 2955–64 and (November 25, 1995): pp. 3021–36.
2. Ghosh, Arun, 'International Comparisons of National Income: A New Methodology', *Economic and Political Weekly*, (June 11, 1983).
3. Parker, R H and G C Harcourt (ed.), '*Readings in the Concepts and Measurement of Income*,' (Cambridge: Cambridge University Press, 1969).

Review Questions

1. Which of the following activities/transactions are included in GDP at factor cost and why?

(a) A father teaching his son

(b) A maid servant's work in her employer's house
(c) A vegetable vendor's profit
(d) A worker's wage on her employment
(e) Direct sale of an old car by Mohan to Mahesh
(f) Depreciation of machines due to wear, tear and obsolescence
(g) An excise duty
(h) Profits of a foreign company located in the country
(i) Pension payments to retired employees
(j) Pollution caused by a recently established factory
(k) Students' fees in a recently established primary school
(l) Earnings of a share broker
(m) Money received by Cronje from a bookie
(n) Monthly allowance that a child gets from his parents
(o) Travel Corporation of India purchases a new truck
(p) Pramod receives ₹5000 by selling his holdings of Reliance shares

2. Suppose the Happyland economy has the following national accounting data:

Personal consumption	19,500	Net exports of goods & services	0
Net domestic savings	9750	Retained profit	975
Capital consumption	1950	Corporate tax	5070
Government consumption expenditure	7800	Government transfer payments to households	3900
Indirect taxes net of subsidies	2730	Personal (direct) taxes	4875
Net factor income from abroad	0	Interest payments	3900
Wages of employees	26,000		

(a) Find the values of the following national aggregates in Happyland:
Gross national product at market price
Gross domestic investment
Personal income from production
Personal savings
Fiscal deficit (surplus)

(b) Make a sources and uses of income chart and enter the relevant data and the results of part (a) above on the chart.

3. The United States data on some national income and product accounts ($ billion) in 1992 are as follows:

Personal consumption	4140
Employees' compensation	3582
Gross private domestic investment	797
Proprietors' income	414
Net exports of goods & services	–30
Corporate profits	407
Government purchases of goods & services	1132
Net interest	442
Net factor income from abroad	7
Net Foreign investment	–55

Consumption of fixed capital	658
Subsidies	3
Indirect taxes	503

Determine the following magnitudes of the United States in 1992:

- GNP at market price
- GDP at market price
- National income
- Gross savings
- Rental income

4. Suppose the sources and uses of income with the production sector (all firms) of an economy were the following:

Sources of Income		**Uses of Income**	
Sales to households	500	Wages paid to residents	400
Sales to government	75	Wages paid to non-residents	20
Net (of imports) exports	20	Dividend paid to residents	40
Domestic gross investment	115	Dividend paid to non-residents	2
		Interest paid to residents	25
		Interest paid to non-residents	3
		Rent paid to residents	40
		Retained profit	45
		Corporate profit tax	60
		Net (of subsidies) indirect taxes	25
		Depreciation	50

Assume all other items, if any, as zero. Compute the economy's GDP at market price and national income.

5. GDP is a misleading measure of material well being. Is this true? How?

6. Nandan Niketan has worked for the Indian Government at a practically zero salary, as Narayan Murthy is working for Infosys currently (Jan 2014). Are their services a part of Indian GDP. Why or why not?

7. What is 'Black Money'? How it is created? Discuss its relevance to business.

8. India's GNP (PPP) is around one-fourth of that of the United States of America. Thus,

(a) India possesses about 25 per cent of the United States material well being.

(b) Economic welfare of the Indian people is about 25 per cent of that of people living in the United States.

Comment on the above observations.

9. If a chicken is born, the per capita GDP goes up but if a child is born, the per capita GDP goes down. How?

10. National income neither includes all the market transactions nor excludes all the non-market transactions in goods and services. Explain.

11. Given below are the data on the production structure in a cross-section of countries and the world.

(Per cent of GDP)

Country	*Value added by*							
	Agriculture		*Industry*		*Manufacturing*		*Services*	
	1990	*2012*	*1990*	*2012*	*1990*	*2012*	*1990*	*2012*
India	31	17	28	26	17	14	41	57
USA	2	1	28	20	20	13	70	79
UK	2	1	35	22	23	11	63	78
Japan	2	1	39	26	27	19	58	73
Malaysia	15	10	42	41	24	24	43	49
China	27	10	42	47	33	30	31	43
Australia	4	2	29	20	14	9	67	78
Nigeria	33	NA	41	NA	6	NA	26	NA
Russian Fed	17	4	48	37		15	35	59
Germany	2	1	38	28	28	21	60	71
Brazil	8	5	39	26	25	13	53	68
World	5	3	34	27	22	17	60	70

Source: World Development Indicators, World Bank, 2013.

(a) Examine the Indian data for 2012 and see whether the sum of the value added by various sectors equal the total output. If not, why? Repeat the exercise for a couple of other countries.

(b) Evaluate the above data in relation to the data given in Table 1.1 (Chapter 1) and Table 2.2 (Chapter 2), and suggest the relationships, if any, between the production structure and, each of standard of living and economic performance.

12. The table below presents the data on the structure of demand in some select countries and world:

(Per cent of GDP)

Country	*Household final consumption*		*Government's final consumption*		*Gross capital formation*		*Exports*		*Imports*	
							(of goods and services)			
	1990	*2004*	*1990*	*2004*	*1990*	*2004*	*1990*	*2004*	*1990*	*2004*
India	67	68	12	11	24	24	7	19	10	23
USA	67	71	17	16	18	18	10	10	11	14
UK	63	65	20	21	20	17	24	25	27	28
Japan	53	57	13	18	33	24	10	12	9	10
Malaysia	52	43	14	13	32	23	75	121	72	100
China	50	49	12	10	35	39	18	34	14	31
Australia	59	60	19	18	22	25	17	18	17	21
Nigeria	56	38	15	22	15	22	43	55	29	37
Russian Fed	49	50	21	17	30	21	18	35	18	22
Germany	55	59	19	19	22	17	29	38	25	33
Brazil	59	55	19	19	20	21	8	18	7	13
World	59	62	17	17	24	21	20	24	20	24

Source: World Development Indicators, World Bank, 2013.

(a) Verify the validity of the income identity for at least two countries and in two periods.
(b) Analyse the above data in relation to the data in Table 1.1 (Chapter 1) and Table 2.5 (Chapter 2), and infer the relationships, if any, between the demand pattern and each of standard of living and economic performance.

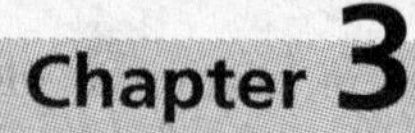

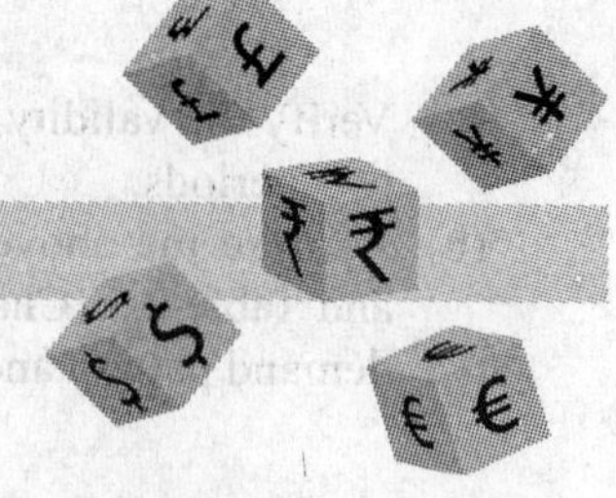

Chapter 3

Inflation, Unemployment, and Poverty

Learning Objectives

After reading the chapter you should be able to:

1. Understand what the inflation, unemployment and poverty (absolute and relative) concepts are and how each of them is measured.
2. Be aware of the various price indices that the country generates, their differences, limitations, and applications for different purposes.
3. Familiarise with the different kinds of unemployment and the limitations of their measurements.
4. Get a feel of the data on the rates of inflation, unemployment and poverty over time and across select major countries.

Inflation, unemployment and poverty belong to the group of the crucial endogenous macroeconomic variables. While a gentle, positive rate of inflation may be desirable, high as well as negative values of it pose serious economic problems (vide Chapter 1, Section on macroeconomic goals and instruments). Unemployment costs are heavy, not only in terms of the loss of income and output, but also in terms of human psychology. Poverty, both absolute (poor) as well as relative (income inequalities), are unwelcome as the former leads to deprivation from even the basic needs and the latter causes envy, jealousy and violence (thefts, loots, terror and wars). While these direct features are fairly well known, these concepts are not quite clear. Also, their measurements do not have international standards. The chapter therefore goes into details in terms of each of these three concepts and their measurements, particularly with reference to India.

INFLATION

Inflation is discussed under three broad heads: meaning and measurement, price indices in India and their measurement, and inflation rates across countries.

Meaning and Measurement of Inflation

Inflation means a continuous (not just once or in a few periods) increase in the general (macro) price level. Thus, if the general price was, say 100 (we do not denote this as ₹, the reason would be clear a little later) in 2000 and 110 in 2001, there is inflation at the rate of 10 per cent in 2001. However, if the price remains at 110 in 2002, which is higher than in 2000, there is no inflation in 2002. Before going further into the formal definition/formula, let us understand the meaning of this general price.

Price, in a monetary economy, is the *exchange value* of a unit of a commodity or service expressed in terms of money. Thus, if the price of a Maruti 800cc car is, say, ₹3,50,000, means a person could buy one car of this model for the said amount. Similarly, if the tuition fee of a college for one year is ₹30,000, a student could attend that college for a year for ₹30,000. In some other cases, like electricity, telephone or hotel accommodation charges, this price is often referred to as **tariff**. In still other cases, like payments for the purchase of irrigation water from government agencies, the price is referred to as **cess**; payment for services of professionals like consultants, doctors and advocates, is called **fee**; for the use of a house, price is called **rent;** and payment for transportation services, is called **fare**. However, in essence, all these terms are synonymous. The major difference in these terminologies is that while fee is often independent of the amount of use, the others pertain to a fixed utilisation. For example, college fees allows any level of utilisation of the corresponding facilities of the college, car price means the exact cost of a unit of the particularly well-defined (including accessories, free servicing, guarantee, if any) car.

Economists distinguish the **exchange value** from the **use value**, the latter refers to the utility or the satisfaction the consumer derives from the use of the commodity in question. The two values are very much different and Adam Smith cited the **water-diamond paradox** to explain the same. While water is highly useful, it has a small exchange rate. In contrast, diamond is of a little use but commands a very high exchange value. Further, while the exchange value is objective, the use value is highly subjective as it varies not only over time, as does the exchange value, but also from the person to person, place to place, and so on. Thus, while the car price of ₹3,50,000 is the same for all buyers at a point of time, the utility of water to a thirsty person or a person in a desert is much more than that for a not so thirsty one or for a person in a water rich place.

There are as many prices as there are goods and services. All these individual (micro) prices are combined into one, which is called the general (macro) price, price of a unit of all goods and services. General price is obtained as a weighted average of the individual goods' (micro) prices:

$$P_t = \sum_{i=1}^{n} w_i P_{it} \tag{3.1}$$

where P_t = General price in period t

P_{it} = Price of good i in period t

w_i = Weight of good i

n = Number of goods and services in the economy

$w_i \geq 0$

$\Sigma w_i = 1$

For example, if there were only three goods in an economy, with their prices in 2010 and weights as follows:

Goods	*Price*	*Weight*
Rice	₹30/kg	0.60
Shirt	₹400/piece	0.30
House (room)	₹2000/month	0.10

The general price in 2010 would be

$$P_{2010} = 0.6\ (30) + 0.3\ (400) + 0.1\ (2000)$$
$$= ₹338$$

Incidentally, note that there is nothing in particular which you could buy for ₹338. Thus, the general price is merely a concept, whose significance would be understood later.

The weights for the various component items are determined by the relative significance of that item in all the items during the base period

$$W_i = \frac{Q_{io}P_{io}}{\sum_i Q_{io}P_{io}} \tag{3.2}$$

where Q_{io} and P_{io} are the quantity and price of the commodity i in the base period, respectively. Weights in equation **(3.2)** are based on the relative monetary value, which is the most popular weighing scheme. However, there are price weighted and the equally weighted indices as well.

General price is the price of 'all goods' but since there is no one unit of 'all goods', there is nothing that could be purchased at this price. Thus, general price per se has little significance. Its only significance lies in the computation of the inflation rate, which is better approached through a price index. A price index expresses the current price in relation to its value in the base period. Thus, price index for period t (PI_t) is defined as

$$PI_t = \frac{P_t}{P_o} \tag{3.3}$$

Thus, if the price of shirt in the base year, say, 2005 was ₹120 and in 2010, it was ₹200, the price index for 2010 would be

$$PI_{2010} = \frac{200}{120} = 1.67$$

An index compares the data without worrying about the unit of measurement. Price index at 1.67 indicates that between 2005 and 2010, the shirt price has increased by 67 per cent. Index numbers are normally written with a base value = 100 and, if so, the above number must be multiplied by 100.

Equation **(3.3)** is good for the price of an individual item. For general price, which is a weighted average of various prices, the price index is computed as follows:

$$PI_t = \sum W_i \left[\frac{P_{it}}{P_{io}}\right]$$

substituting for w_i from equation **(3.2)**, we get

$$PI_t = \sum \left[\frac{Q_{io}P_{io}}{\Sigma Q_{io}P_{io}}\right]\left[\frac{P_{it}}{P_{io}}\right]$$

solution of this yield

$$PI_t\,(L) = \left[\frac{\Sigma Q_{io} P_{it}}{\Sigma Q_{io} P_{io}}\right] \qquad \textbf{(3.4)}$$

Since the weighing pattern in equation **(3.4)** was suggested by Laspeyre, it is known as the **Laspeyre's Index**. There is another index, called the **Paasche's Index**, which is defined as below:

$$PI_t\,(P) = \frac{\sum Q_{it} P_{it}}{\sum Q_{it} P_{io}} \qquad \textbf{(3.5)}$$

A comparison of equations (3.4) and (3.5) would indicate that the only difference between the Laspeyre's and Paasche's indices is that while the former takes the base year quantities the latter works with the current year quantities. Since quantities of various items do vary over time, the two methods of computation could very well yield different results. In practice, Laspeyre's method is more popular, though as we shall see later the Paasche's formula is used for computing the GDP deflator. To illustrate their calculations, consider the following three products economy:

Period	*Rice*		*Shirt*		*House (room)*	
	Price	*Quantity*	*Price*	*Quantity*	*Price*	*Quantity*
2005	20	10,000	240	400	1560	50
2013	30	12,000	400	500	2000	75

For this example, the price indices for 2013 would be

$$\text{Laspeyre's price index} = \frac{30 \times 10{,}000 + 400 \times 400 + 2000 \times 50}{20 \times 10{,}000 + 240 \times 400 + 1560 \times 50} = 1.497$$

$$\text{Paasche's price index} = \frac{30 \times 12{,}000 + 400 \times 500 + 2000 \times 75}{20 \times 12{,}000 + 240 \times 500 + 1560 \times 75} = 1.489$$

The two indices give different rates of price increase in eight years, viz., 49.7 per cent and 48.9 per cent. In this example, the difference is small but it could be large if the price/quantity of some product increases while that of other products decreases, or vice versa. The Laspeyre's index measures the changes in the cost of a **fixed basket** of goods from a base period and thus assumes **no substitution** due to the relative price changes, and thereby, it usually overestimates the true index. On the other hand, the Paasche's index assigns fixed weights by **current** consumption pattern and thereby tends to overstate the substitution and understate the price index relative to an earlier base period. Needless to say, the consumption basket does change over time and this can be well illustrated by recourse to the 1970s, during which period gas price rose significantly and hence consumers shifted to small cars, public transport, cut in travels, energy-saving machines, and resorted to other means of conserving gas. Such a big change obviously would have serious *repercussions* on the magnitude of the two weighing systems under discussion. Currently, we do have superlative indices like the **Fisher Ideal Index** and **Marshall-Edgeworth Index**, which try to approximate some of the substitution effect that separates a 'cost of living' index from a 'basket price' index such as the Laspeyre and Paasche indices. The former is the geometric mean (square root of the product) of the Laspeyre and

Paasche indices, and the latter uses the sum of the quantities of both the periods instead of the either. However, none of these two methods have yet become popular anywhere in the world, least of all, India.

Now we are ready to give a formal definition of **inflation**. It means the rate of change in the general price (P or PI) per year, expressed in percentages. Thus, the (simple) inflation rate in period t over the last one year is given by

$$\dot{P}_t = \frac{P_t - P_{t-1}}{P_{t-1}} \times 100 \quad \textbf{(3.6)}$$

if it is compounded once in a year only. However, if compounding is done on a continuous basis, the formula changes to

$$\dot{P}_t = \ln\left[\frac{P_t}{P_{t-1}}\right] \times 100 \quad \textbf{(3.7)}$$

where, ln stands for the natural logarithm. In case the gap between the two periods is more than one year, then the annual, continuous compounding annual and the semi-log (regression) trend rates of inflation become relevant and they are computed by equations **(3.8)**, **(3.9)** and **(3.10),** respectively:

$$\dot{P}_t = \left[\left[\frac{P_t}{P_{t-n}}\right]^{1/n} - 1\right] \times 100 \quad \textbf{(3.8)}$$

$$\dot{P}_t = \frac{1}{n}\left[\ln\frac{P_t}{P_{t-n}}\right] \times 100 \quad \textbf{(3.9)}$$

$$\ln P_t = a + bT_t + u_t \; (t = 1, 2, ..., n) \quad \textbf{(3.10)}$$

where T refers to the time period and n to the number of periods. Thus, $T_1 = 1$ for period 1, $T_2 = 2$ for period 2, ..., $T_n = n$ for period n.

Equation **(3.10)** is a simple regression equation, which calls for the estimation of the parameters a and b using the data on P_t and T_t. The estimate of the parameter b measures the annual semi-log growth rate.

Thus, if the general price index rises from, say, 150 in 2012 to 160 in 2013, the simple inflation rate during 2012–13 would be 6.67 per cent $\left(\frac{160-150}{150} \times 100\right)$ and the continuous compounded inflation rate would be 6.45 per cent $\left(\ln\frac{160}{150} \times 100\right)$. Similarly, the price increase of 48.9 per cent between 2005 and 2013 (as per the Paasche's index above) implies the simple annual inflation rate of 5.10 per cent $\left[(1.489)^{\frac{1}{8}} - 1\right] \times 100$ and continuous compounding inflation rate of 4.98 per cent $\left[\frac{1}{8}(\ln 1.489)\right] \times 100$. For computing the semi-log trend inflation rate, one needs data for each year of the period, viz. 2005 to 2013. Thus, if the price indices during 2005 through 2013 were 100, 105, 110, 120, 125, 120,130, 140 and 148.9, respectively, the semi-log growth function would be

$$\ln P = 4.56 + 0.0465\, T \quad \textbf{(3.11)}$$

$$R^2 = 0.952$$

and the semi-log annual inflation rate would be 4.65 per cent. Equation **(3.11)** was obtained by running a simple regression function on the natural log of price index data against the time period 1, 2, 3, ..., 9.

Incidentally, note that the continuous compound rate is always lower than the annual compounding rate of change. In practice, the annual compounding rate is often used. Between the compound rate and the semi-log rate, the latter is a better measure when the price data do not reflect a monotonous rising or falling trend. When the price changes are uni-directional, the two rates would be approximately equal.

Price Indices in India and their Measurement

In general, there are three price index series:

- GDP Deflator
- Wholesale Price Index (WPI)
- Consumer Price Index (CPI)

  The last series (CPI) is further classified into six sub-series
  - CPI for industrial workers (CPI-IW)
  - CPI for urban non manual employees (CPI-UNME)
  - CPI for agricultural labourers (CPI-AL)
  - CPI for rural India (CPI-RI)
  - CPI for Urban India (CPI-UI)
  - CPI for rural-urban combined (all India) (CPI-AI)

A discussion of each of these follows:

GDP Deflator Gross domestic product (GDP) deflator refers to the index of the average price of the goods and services produced in the economy. It includes the prices of all (only) final goods produced in the economy and thus excludes those of intermediate goods and raw materials. The producers and buyers of these goods are immaterial. Thus, whether they are produced by foreigners or locals operating in the country, and bought by local consumers, firms, the government, or even foreigners, all are included. It ignores the prices of imported goods, which enter our consumption basket and list of inputs in production. It is computed as the *ratio of the nominal (current price) GDP in a given year to the real (constant price) GDP of that year.* Since the nominal GDP is the value of the current production valued at the current price and real GDP is the value of current production valued at the base year price, the GDP deflator is based on the Paasche's method of computation (equation 3.5). To illustrate its computation, we could go back to the above example of the three-product economy. In that economy, the nominal and real GDP for 2005 and 2013, and hence the GDP deflator for the two years, would be as follows:

Year	*Nominal GDP*	*Real GDP*	*GDP deflator (base: 2005 = 1)*
2005	20 × 10,000 + 240 × 400 + 1560 × 50 = 3,74,000	20 × 10,000 + 240 × 400 + 1560 × 50 = 3,74,000	1
2013	30 × 12,000 + 400 × 500 + 2000 × 75 = 7,10,000	20 × 12,000 + 240 × 500 + 1560 × 75 = 4,77,000	1.489

For India, the time series data on GDP are available on an annual basis only and roughly on two years lag, and thus the GDP deflator data are also available on an annual basis only and on two years lag. Since the time lag is long and the frequency is just once in a year, this index is considered as a poor indicator for the true (current) inflation rate. Further, even from the policy point of view, it is the most up to date data, which alone can help formulate the appropriate policies to manage the same.

Wholesale Price Index The wholesale price index (WPI) refers to the index of the average price of all commodities produced and/or transacted in the economy at the first point of bulk sales in the domestic market. Only direct exports/imports from and to the factories alone are excluded. Thus, it includes the prices of raw materials and semi-finished goods, as well as of imported tangible goods, besides the prices of tangible goods included in the GDP, if they are transacted at the first point of bulk sale in the country. However, it excludes the prices of all services, such as education, health, banking, transport and communication. As this is the wholesale price, it is referred as the price that the producers of commodities get.

The WPI series is currently available for the base year of 2004–2005. This new series is an improvement over its old versions of 1993–1994, 1981–82, 1970–71, 1961–62, 1952–53 and August 1939 bases in terms of the appropriate weights and selection of products. In terms of the number of items and the number of price quotations, the 1981–82 series had the maximum coverage until the last base year (1993–1994). The 2004–05 base data have further improved on its coverage. The broad position in these respects is as given in Table 3.1. The comparable data for the 1981–82 base for significant items are also included in the table within parentheses.

The series since the 1981–82 are based mostly on the marketed surplus ratios for agricultural commodities in contrast to the use of the marketable surplus ratios for these commodities by earlier series. This was the major reason for a drastic reduction in the weight of the 'primary articles' group from 41.7 in 1970–71 to 32.295 in 1981–82, to 22.025 in 1993–94, and to 20.118 in the year 2004-05 series. A comparison of the weights assigned to the various items over time would reveal that while the weight for the primary articles has declined that for both fuel and manufactured products have increased over time. Currently, the primary articles occupy about 20 per cent; fuel, power, light and lubricants together account for 15 per cent and the remaining weight of 65 per cent is taken by manufactured products. Within the primary articles, the weights for all the three groups of products have declined over time. Under the manufactured products group, while the weights for textiles has gone down, that for chemicals, basic metals and machinery groups have gone up with time. The said trends obviously reflect the changing significance of these items in the wholesale market.

The weights are assigned on the basis of the relative value of wholesale transactions in various products in the economy. All major items are covered and price quotations are taken from a cross-section of markets all over the country. The weighted arithmetic mean and Laspeyre's formula are used for the computation. The series is prepared for the all-India level only. However, it is available for all commodities as well as for major groups, sub-groups and individual commodities, and is regularly published on a weekly basis by the office of the Economic Adviser, Ministry of Industries, Government of India. It is these characteristics that make WPI as an **ideal measure** of the inflation rate, particularly from the managerial point of

Table 3.1 Measurement of WPI with Base 2004–05

Major Group	*Weights*	*Number of items*	*Number of quotations*
1. Primary articles	20.118	102	579
	(32.295)	(93)	(519)
Food	14.337	55	431
	(17.386)	(44)	(320)
Non-food	4.258	29	108
	(10.081)	(28)	(132)
Minerals	1.521	18	40
	(4.828)	(21)	(67)
2. Fuel, power, light and lubricants	14. 910	19	72
	(10.663)	(20)	(73)
3. Manufactured products	64 .972	555	4831
	(57.042)	(334)	(1779)
Food products	9.974	57	406
	(10.143)	(45)	(231)
Beverages, tobacco and tobacco products	1.762	5	102
Textiles	7. 326	55	457
	(11.545)	(27)	(120)
Wood and wood products	0.587	10	64
Paper and paper products	2.034	18	138
Leather and leather products	0. 835	13	91
Rubber and plastic products	2.987	45	351
Chemicals and chemical products	12.018	107	1111
	(7.355)	(77)	(428)
Non-metallic mineral products	2. 556	26	225
Basic metals, alloys and metal products	10.748	69	696
	(7.632)	(57)	(235)
Machinery and machine tools	8. 931	107	903
	(6.268)	(44)	(266)
Transport equipment and parts	5.213	33	287
Other miscellaneous manufacturing Industries	0.0	0	0
	(0.972)	(4)	(30)
4. All commodities	100	676	5482
	(100)	(447)	(2371)

Note: Numbers in parentheses indicate the corresponding position as in 1981–82 based index.

Sources: *Economic and Political Weekly*, (September 18, 1993): 2015
Monthly Bulletins, Reserve Bank of India.

view. As the data is available for different commodity groups, policy makers can easily pin down the source of inflation and then suggest the policy measures to deal with it. Since the WPI ignores the prices of the non-commodity producing sectors (viz. services), which have tended to outgrow the commodity producing sectors in recent years (vide Chapter 2, Table 2.2) and which currently constitute close to 60 per cent of GDP, its use is questioned. However, the prices of services are influenced directly by the prices of inputs coming from the commodity sector, and vice versa. Further, there is no better measure for this purpose. Hence, variations in the WPI are considered as acceptable indicators of change in the general price in the Indian economy. Since, WPI stands for the index of prices received by producers, it is akin to the **Producers' Price Index** (PPI) of many countries, including the United States.

Consumer Price Indices A consumer price index (CPI) refers to the index of the average retail price of the goods and services contained in the consumption basket of the relevant group of consumers. It thus excludes the prices of capital goods (plant and equipment), raw materials and intermediate goods, and includes the prices of services as well as of imported goods. The consumption basket depends on the level of income/wealth, rural-urban living, type of work/profession the family is engaged in, habits, customs and so on. Thus, it varies practically from the family to family. However, no country could have too many CPIs and thus significant differences in the consumption pattern alone are considered in preparing CPIs. In India, as stated above, we have six of such indices, viz. CPI-IW, CPI-UNME, CPI-AL, CPI-R, CPI-U, CPI-AI. Of these, CPI-UNME has been discontinued since 2011, and the last three indices are new on which data are available only since 2011–12.

The Labour Bureau of the Ministry of Labour compiles and publishes data on CPI-IW and CPI-AL, while that on all the other CPI indices are carried out by the Central Statistical Organisation (CSO) of the Statistics Ministry. CSO makes use of the wide network of the Department of Posts to effectively reach out to rural consumers. Usually from each district in a state two villages are selected, from where data is collected from selected shops. Unlike WPI, which is prepared only at the all India level, CPI-AL is first prepared at the state level, CPI-IW, CPI-UNME, CPI-R, CPI-U and CPI-AI at the selected centres' levels, and then they are aggregated to all India levels. The aggregation is carried out as the weighted arithmetic average of the respective indices, with weights taken as proportionate to aggregate estimated expenditure of the state/centre in the all India figure. Lasperyre's formula is used for the computation. For deciding the weights for individual good/service, surveys of the relevant families are carried out in various centres spread out all over the country.

The CPI-IW is currently available at 2001 = 100 base. This series has succeeded the one at 1982 = 100 base and is constructed on the basis of the weights determined through a detailed consumer expenditure survey conducted by the National Sample Survey Organisation (NSSO) in 1999–2000 with the help of Labour Bureau, Simla. The weighing diagram, at the all India level, is the weighted average of the weights of 78 centres. The weights of 1982-based index were based on a comprehensive family living survey carried out in 1981–82 at 70 selected centres. The exact weights assigned to each group of items are provided in Table 3.2.

The CPI-AL series is currently published for the base 1986–87 = 100. These weights for the series were derived from the NSSO's 38th Round of Consumers Expendiuture Survey, 1983. There is yet one more price index in India, viz., CPI for rural labourers (CPI-RL). Since CPI-AL covers the household for agricultural labourers and the CPI-RL covers the households of rural labourers (including agricultural labourers) the former is a subset of the latter series.

Table 3.2 Weight Structure of Various CPIs

Product group	*CPI-IW 2001=100*	*CPI-AL 1986–87=100*	*CPI-Rural 2010=100*	*CPI-Urban 2010=100*	*CPI-Combined 2010=100*
Food, beverages and tobacco	48.47	72.94	59.31	37.15	49.71
Fuel and light	6.43	8.35	10.42	8.40	9.49
Housing	15.27	0*	0*	22.53	9.77
Clothing and footwear	6.57	6.98	5.36	3.91	4.73
Miscellaneous	23.26	11.76	24.91	28.00	26.31
Total	100	100	100	100	100

Note: * Less than one per cent
Sources: Economic Surveys and Documents from the Office of the Economic Adviser, Ministry of Commerce and Industry

The various CPIs indicate the cost of living index for the respective group of consumers. The time series data on various price indices are provided in Table 3.3.

Table 3.3 Price Indices in India

Year	*GDP Deflator 2004-05 =100*	*Wholesale price index (average of weeks) 2004-05 =100*	*Consumer price index for (annual average)*		
			Industrial workers 2010 = 100	*Agricultural labour 1986-87 = 100*	*All India (rural + urban) 2010 = 100*
1950-51	3.5	4.1	4.5		
1960-61	3.7	4.4	5.5	17	
1970-71	7.4	8.4	8.1	31	—
1980-81	17.3	21.5	17.6	69	—
1990-91	39.4	39.4	41.7	140	—
2000-01	84.9	83.1	96	305	—
2002-03	90.9	89.1	104	319	—
2003-04	94.4	93.9	108	331	—
2004-05	100.0	100.0	112	340	—
2005-06	104.2	104.5	117	353	—
2006-07	110.9	111.4	125	380	—
2007-08	117.3	116.6	133	409	—
2008-09	127.5	126.0	145	450	—
2009-10	135.2	130.8	163	513	—
2010-11	147.2	143.3	180	564	—

(*Contd.*)

2011-12	159.3	156.1	195	611	111.9
2012-13	172.4	167.6	227	672	123.3
Annual rate (%)*	6.5	6.2	6.5	7.3	10.2

Note: *Yearly compounded. —Not applicable

Sources: *National Accounts Statistics*, (CSO)
RBI Bulletins
Monthly Abstract of Statistics, (CSO)
Indian Labour Journal, Labour Bureau

The CPI-R and CPI-U data are given separately below.

Year	*CPI-Rural 2010=100*	*CPI-Urban 2010=100*
2011–12	113.1	110.4
2012–13	124.5	121.8
Growth rate (%)	10.1	10.3

The data in Table 3.3 and above table reveal a rather interesting phenomenon, viz., the annual inflation rate during the last 62 years comes to around 7 per cent in all the indices with long time series. Thus, no matter which index is used, one gets approximately the same rate of inflation. However, this is generally true when the time horizon is long. For year to year fluctuations, various indices could very well produce significantly different rates of inflation. For example, the inflation rate in 2012-13 over 2011–12 comes to a high of 16.4 per cent by CPI-IW and to a low of 7.4 per cent by WPI. In India, the official inflation rate hitherto used to be announced on the basis of WPI only, which gives the inflation rate at 7.4 for 2012–13. The said rate is lower than the one given by all other indices. Thus, it really underestimates the rate. For computing dearness allowances, CPI-IW is used, and this gives the rate of inflation at 16.4 per cent for 2012–13. The latter, thus, provides a rather higher compensation against inflation for the other classes of consumers.

A further analysis of the data in Table 3.3 would reveal that the long-term rate of inflation is the maximum under the CPI-AL and the minimum under the WPI. This implies that the services in the consumption basket, and particularly for agricultural labourers, have become relatively more costly than the commodities traded in the wholesale market during the period of the analysis.

Why do various indices yield different rates of inflation and which index is the most relevant for a particular purpose? The answer to the first part of this question could be found in the following factors:

(a) Prices of various items do not always change in the same direction and same proportion. For example, while the prices of most goods have gone up, those of computers and many other electronic goods have, in fact, fallen during the last decade.

(b) Prices of some items, like fruits and vegetables, are highly seasonal.

(c) Retail prices are generally more volatile than wholesale prices.

(d) Prices of commodities usually fluctuate more than those of services.

Since different indices represent different groups of people/geographical areas, cover different sets of items (though overlapping), use different weighing diagrams, based on different indexing formulas (Lasperyre's or Paasche's), and use prices at different sales' levels (wholesale versus retail), because of the four above factors, these indices yield different rates of inflation. Obviously, each of the indices is useful and the choice among them is dictated by the purpose.

Due to its high frequency (weekly), short time-lag (two weeks) and commodity/group-wise availability (which facilitates continuous monitoring for policy decisions), the WPI has been used to measure the official rate of inflation in the country. Lately, even retail inflation (on which data are available on monthly basis and by state) is being emphasized as the lag period in it has been reduced to just one month and it is more comprehensive than WPI., Thus, currently India has two official inflation rates, called wholesale and retail rates, which consists of those based on WPI and CPI-AI, respectively. Reserve Bank of India has been using wholesale rate but is slowly moving towards retail rate for its policy decisions/targets. Since industrial workers are the most organised group of people, CPI-IW is used for the purpose of measuring the cost of living, and thus, determining the dearness allowances, though each of the various CPIs is a measure of the cost of living for the specific group of consumers. The CPI-UNME, which has now been discontinued, had a limited use. It was used basically for determining dearness allowances of employees of some foreign companies working in India. Also, it was used under the Income Tax Act to determine capital gains and by the CSO for deflating selected service sectors' GDP at current prices to get the corresponding GDP at constant prices. The CPI-AL is basically used for revising minimum wages for agricultural labour in different states. Since the GDP deflator alone includes the prices of all commodities and services produced in the economy, and its weighing pattern reflects the implicit sector-wise shares of the nominal and real value added, it is the most general/ideal measure of the overall price situation in the economy. The new price indices (CPI-R, CPI-U and CPI-Combined) have come up only recently and thus have no long term rates for any meaningful uses so far. As WPI and all CPIs are based on Lasperyre's measure, they over state the true inflation rate in the country, and accordingly workers get over compensated through dearness allowance and investors gain through over stated indexation leading to lower capital gain taxation.

Incidentally, note neither any of the CPIs is a perfect measure of the cost of living, nor is the WPI a true measure of the inflation rate. This is because each of them is subject to the following four errors:

(a) They ignore the "new products", for these have no historical data which one needs to incorporate their effects on the price index.

(b) They ignore the changes in product quality, which happens on a continuous basis.

(c) They are based on **fixed weights** of the corresponding base year, which surely undergoes some change over time. Recall that WPI and all CPI indices are based on the Lasperyre's measure, which does not allow any substitution between goods when their relative price changes. This results in overstating of the inflation rate. In contrast, GDP deflator is based on the Paasche's measure, which also ignores substitution but as it uses the current output data, it understates the inflation rate.

(d) They are based on the sample data (barring the GDP deflator) and thus are subject to measurement error caused by the sampling and non-sampling errors.

The Boskin Commission has estimated that the effect of such factors on the measurement of inflation rate in the United States in 1996 was at plus 1.1 per cent, that is, true inflation was 1.1 per cent less than what was reported. For India, there is no such research study.

Inflation Rates in Select Countries

The data on inflation for select countries are provided in Table 3.4. There are three measures of inflation for each country, viz., based on the GDP deflator, CPI and Wholesale Price Index.

Table 3.4 Inflation Rate in Select Countries

(Percentage)

Country	*Inflation (annual average) rate based on*					
	GDP deflator		*Consumer price index*		*Wholesale price index*	
	1990–2000	*2000–2011*	*1990–2000*	*2000–2011*	*1990–2000*	*2000–2011*
India	8.0	5.9	9.1	6.4	7.4	5.6
USA	2.0	2.4	2.7	2.5	1.2	4.1
UK	2.4	2.4	2.5	2.3	2.4	2.3
Japan	0	–1.3	0.8	–0.2	–0.9	0.5
Singapore	1.4	1.6	1.7	1.8	–0.9	2.4
Indonesia	15.8	11.0	13.7	8.4	15.4	10.6
Brazil	212.0	8.1	200.0	6.5	205.0	8.9
Republic of Korea	5.9	2.3	5.1	3.2	3.7	2.8
China	2.9	4.6	8.6	2.5	NA	NA
Pakistan	11.1	10.0	9.7	9.4	10.4	10.6
Sri Lanka	3.9	3.1	3.8	2.8	2.4	3.2
Australia	1.6	3.9	2.1	2.9	1.1	3.2
Nigeria	29.5	13.8	32.5	12.2	NA	NA
Russian Federation	162.0	14.9	99.0	11.7	100.0	14.3

Source: World Development Indicators, World Bank, 2013.

A careful perusal of the above data would indicate that:

(a) The long-term inflation rate is about the same no matter which of the three price indices is used to measure it, barring Russian Fed for which CPI gives a relatively lower rate.

(b) The inflation rate was, in general, lower in 2000–11 than in 1990s. This suggests a downward trend in the said rate. Lately, some economists have even commented to this trend as "death of inflation".

(c) Japan has witnessed the lowest inflation rate (in fact the country has experienced deflation) during the last two decades among all the countries included here. Singapore comes next in this respect. The United States, UK and Australia take the next position on this criterion. The highest inflation rate countries would include the Russian Federation and Brazil. The only other countries in the table which experienced two-digit inflation rate sometime during the period are Indonesia and Pakistan. India's inflation rate has moved within a narrow range of 5.6 per cent to 9.1 per cent but the rate has consistently been larger than in China.

Before ending this section it would be instructive to mention that world over the inflation rate was rather high during the 1970s and it is somewhat tamed during the last decade. Though this is not the place to analyse its causes in detail, a few observations are in order. The formation of the Organisation of Petroleum Exporting Countries (OPEC) was the single most important factor for the former and the partial movement of production from the high cost countries to low cost ones was perhaps an important factor for the latter. A better understanding, and use of the fiscal and monetary policies, as discussed in later chapters, could be the other factor for controlling inflation.

UNEMPLOYMENT

Unemployment is discussed under four heads: meaning, kinds, full employment and measurement.

Meaning of Unemployment

Unemployment is perhaps the most worrisome macroeconomic problem in any country. The opposite of this viz. employment, is a must for a person to have some source of income for livelihood, and it is this which traditionally was deemed to distinguish the manhood of a man and the identity of a woman. While temporary unemployment may not be that bad (in fact, sometimes it may even be good, atleast psychologically), chronic unemployment is a luxury, which even a millionaire can ill afford. Furthermore, willful (voluntary) unemployment may be okay but forced (involuntary) unemployment is doubly bad leading to loss of income/output and feeling of desperation. Nevertheless, unemployment is a fact of life in the present world and this is considered as the worst example of both, market and government failures. Not only there exists a pocket of unemployed people in almost every country today, but there is also a great degree of unemployment of capital resources (structures and equipment) as well. We do see a host of residential, factory and office buildings, a large number of tools, equipment and machines, as well as inventories of raw materials, semi-finished and finished goods lying idle. Obviously, a reduction in such unemployment would go a long way in improving the well-being of the world. While all unemployment is bad, unemployment of manpower is the worst of all. Accordingly, unemployment is often equated to that of human beings only, and this is the major concern of macroeconomics.

Unemployment could be defined both in physical (U_P) as well as in economic ($U_E = U$) terms. In the former,

$$U_P = \text{Population} - \text{Employed people} \tag{3.12}$$

and in the latter,

$$U = \text{Work force} - \text{Employed people} \tag{3.13}$$

where

Workforce = Population – People not in workforce

People not in the workforce include children in the pre-school age group, full-time students in schools/colleges/universities, chronically sick people and retired persons. Accordingly, there is a concept called the work (labour) participation rate, which equals the workforce as a proportion of the population. It is alternatively defined as the workforce as a proportion of adult (15 years and above) population. Given these, the unemployment rate is defined as

$$u = \frac{U}{\text{Workforce}} \tag{3.14}$$

Thus, the **unemployment rate is given by the proportion of the unemployed persons in the total work force**. Conceptually, a person is (a) employed if he is working for a paid job, (b) unemployed if not employed and is looking for a job at reasonable (market) terms and (c) not in workforce if not employed and not looking for a job. A worthwhile point to note here is that if more people decide to go for higher education, *ceteris paribus*, both the workforce as well as the number of people employed falls by that number (assuming all new college students had jobs before), and since the unemployment rate is always positive, the unemployment rate goes up. This is true but the problem is temporary and it would be reversed (with better pay packets) soon those students graduate. There is one more method for a better measurement of unemployment rate. Since people employed in defence corps and such other services are always 100 per cent employed, to compute a more meaningful definition, such people are netted out from the work force and employed people for the purpose of computing the true unemployment rate. While equation **(3.14)** is good enough to define the (general) unemployment rate, there is a unique unemployment rate, called the **Natural Rate of Unemployment (U_n)**, which is also known as the Non-Accelerating Inflation Rate of Unemployment (NAIRU). This is a very relevant concept from the point of view of stabilisation policies and accordingly it is elaborated later in the text. Suffice to point out that NAIRU is that rate of unemployment which prevails in the long-run and the one that alone is consistent with a stable (constant) rate of inflation. If inflation in 2011 was at 5 per cent and it remains at 5 per cent in all years, say until 2015, then the inflation rate was stable between 2011 and 2015. However, if the inflation rate of 5 per cent in 2011 goes up to 6 per cent in 2012 and to 7 per cent in 2013, then we have the accelerating inflation rate and so on.

Kinds of Unemployment

Unemployment is distinguished as

- Voluntary and involuntary
- Open and hidden

Voluntary unemployment means willful unemployment while the **involuntary unemployment** means forced unemployment. To be more precise, a person who is willing and able to work, and is looking for a job but does not find one, is involuntary unemployed. The other unemployed people are voluntarily unemployed. The voluntary unemployment might arise due to the laziness, obsession with wealth and/or with leisure. Since this is voluntary, it poses no serious economic problem. Involuntary unemployment is caused by the paucity of employment opportunities and hence it is an economic issue. The distinction between these two kinds of unemployment is not that watertight as it is hard to define the term voluntary. Some people want jobs only of a particular kind, on particular terms and at a particular place, and unless this is forthcoming they may pretend to be involuntarily unemployed. Others may sincerely be seeking jobs, but if not found for long, may pretend to be voluntarily unemployed to save themselves from embarrassment. Also, there is genuine difficulty in terms of distinguishing the two. For example, consider an MBA from a fairly prestigious institution and assume that he/she receives just one offer, which carries a salary of say, ₹15,000 per month and the job is in a costly city. If this person declines the offer, is he/she involuntarily or voluntarily unemployed? The answer is clearly ambiguous. For this reason, some economists have argued that the distinction, which is due to John Maynard Keynes, is improper. Nevertheless, this is a very convenient and important classification and it would be respected through out this book.

Open unemployment is

- frictional
- structural
- seasonal
- cyclical

While **hidden unemployment** can be

- disguised
- underemployment

The **frictional** or **turnover unemployment** arises in between two jobs, the first job which a person has quit in order to find the second (better) job. Such unemployment is quite prevalent in developed countries where jobs are very demanding and are available in plenty for capable persons. People take off from their current jobs to be available full time to find more suitable jobs and thus remain unemployed during the course of such searches. It is obvious that his kind of unemployment is indeed healthy and it creates no serious economic problems. However, during recessions, like the one that started in 2007 and is still continuing, some workers are retrenched from their job and consequently join the group of frictionally unemployed persons. Also, in developing countries, many students do not find job soon after their graduation and thus they are frictionally unemployed during the period between graduation and joining the job. Such unemployment, though temporary, is universally bad.

Structural unemployment is caused by the mismatch of vacancies and skills of unemployed people. With the booming of information technology and sophistication in production of goods and services, and the changing structure of economies away from the primary sector and towards the secondary and tertiary sectors, traditional jobs are disappearing and jobs requiring 'new' training are emerging. This leads to structural unemployment until traditional workers are retrained and reemployed. Mismatch of locations of the unemployed and vacancies also cause the structural unemployment. The latter is compounded by poor infrastructure in rural and less developed areas.

Some occupations are **seasonal**. For example, farmers are occupied a lot during the Kharif (June—October) and Rabi (December—March) seasons and have a little work during the off (other) times. Unless, these farmers diversify and take up some other activities during the off seasons, they would be seasonally unemployed. Such off seasons arise even for industries based on inputs coming from agriculture, e.g., sugar, textiles, tea, coffee, food processing etc.

Cyclical unemployment is caused by business cycles and economic fluctuations. During droughts and floods, farmers may be left unemployed, and during strikes or lockouts, industrialists and workers may remain unemployed. When the economy slows down due to any such events, calamities or general recession, people lose their purchasing power, which reduces sales, and thereby production and employment. Quite the opposite happens during prosperity or upswings in business.

Disguised unemployment could arise when several people share a particular work at a given time and/or when such work is spread over time. For example, consider a 10-member farmer family which owns just one acre of land and none of its members has an outside job. All family members may share the work of farming that one acre of land, and thus technically all are employed. However, if one or two or even more members do not work on their farm, the production will remain the same. This means the marginal product of these withdrawn workers is zero, and hence their unemployment is hidden; this is called **disguised unemployment**. Various family members may work together but lightly all the time or they may take turns and work sincerely. In either case, such a case unemployment is disguised. For example, in the retail business in India, many fathers look after their respective businesses during early morning hours, late evenings and holidays, and the sons run the business during the peak hours.

Underemployment is the situation where the work available is for lesser than the full employment hours' or for periods lesser than the full working days in a given period (year/month/week) or is poorly paid. Part-time workers in industries and services, and the full time workers in agriculture under-paid workers suffer from this malady. Such unemployment is rampant in developing countries and among females and other racially discriminated people.

Full Employment

Full employment is an ambiguous concept and accordingly it has no unique definition. Literally, it means zero unemployment. But economists regard voluntary unemployment as no unemployment, and frictional and structural unemployment as 'not bad'. Thus, when the unemployment rate is close to, say 3-5 per cent, economists' call it a 'full employment' situation. Voluntary unemployment is hard to quantify, and the frictional and structural unemployment together is estimated to be around 3-5 per cent, particularly in developed countries. Since both the demand for and supply of labour are sensitive to the wage rate, full employment is also defined as the situation where the demand for labour equals the supply of labour in the economy at a given wage rate. This definition suffers from the problem of the immobility of labour as well as the non-uniform wage rates across occupations and places. The excess demand for labour in one occupation accompanied by the equivalent excess supply for labour in another occupation does not mean full employment in the economy. Similarly, the excess demand in one market or geographical place and the equivalent excess supply in another market or place may not mean full employment. Yet another definition, that defines full employment as a situation where the number of people unemployed equals the number of vacancies, is untenable. This is so because of the mismatch of skills needed and skills available, and such a situation exists in the present world. This is structural unemployment, and its correction calls for retraining and deployment.

Measurement of Unemployment

Measurement of unemployment is difficult and accordingly the unemployment data across nations and even time are not quite comparable. To appreciate their significance, we must discuss the various criteria suggested for the measurement of unemployment. These are

- willingness
- time
- income
- productivity

The willingness to work criterion will rule out a voluntarily unemployed person as an unemployed person. There are rules and regulations, which may vary over time and space, which define a certain number of hours per day/week as full employment. If a person works for hours less than this rule, he/she is partly unemployed. For example, if 40 hours a week is the norm and a particular person works for 30 hours a week, he is one-fourth unemployed. The income criterion could stipulate a certain minimum income per period and unless the income is no less than that stipulated figure, the person concerned is partly unemployed. Similarly, the productivity criterion would stipulate a certain minimum level of productivity (output per worker per period), and unless this is so, the employment would be less than full employment.

Income is difficult to measure by time in case of the self-employment and productivity is ambiguous in a highly specialised method of production. Thus, the unemployment data have ignored these two criteria and they rely merely on the willingness and time criteria. Though the measurement of any variable must be uniform in all countries, unemployment data remains an exception. In India, the National Sample Survey Organisation (NSSO) is the agency responsible for the collection and publication of the data on workforce, employment and unemployment. The NSSO has been conducting the periodical rounds of socio-economic survey since 1950–51. The first survey on employment and unemployment was conducted in the 27th Round (September 1972–October 1973) and the second quinquennial survey was carried out in the 32nd Round (July 1977–June 1978). More surveys have been carried out since then. In these surveys, the respondents are asked to indicate their employment status, viz. employed, unemployed and looking for or availability for job, or neither of these two categories (i.e., out of labour force). The respondents have to choose one of these three categories, and so it does create problems for those who belong to more than one status. To overcome this problem, two norms are followed:

- Priority Rule
- Three Reference Periods

Under the priority rule, in case of more than one status, 'employed' will have priority over 'unemployed', and the latter over out of work force. Thus, only one status gets reported in this regard. Further, the status is asked for each of the three reference periods, viz. 'usually' (one year), 'current weekly' and 'current daily' (in fact, half days). While it is difficult to identify a unique status over the long period (one year) and even over the week, it is easier to do so for half day. The majority time criterion is used to obtain estimates of unemployment/employment on the usual and weekly basis. Thus, for usual status, 183 days or more and for weekly basis 3.5 days or more is used as the cut-off period for classification. Further, for usual status, both principal and subsidiary activities are considered. For example, if a person is gainfully occupied for at least 3.5 days during the week preceding the date of the survey, the person is considered 'employed'. Under the daily status, if the interviewee works for four hours or more, he is considered fully employed and if he works for one to three hours, he is deemed half-employed.

Due to the above measurement procedure, and the relatively high proportion of under-employment and disguised unemployment in India, the reported Indian unemployment rate is quite low. According to the various NSSO employment-unemployment survey rounds, (the latest is 68th round conducted during July 2011–2012) the unemployment rates in India under different statuses for rural and urban categories, and separately for male and female are as shown in Table 3.5.

Table 3.5 Unemployment Rates in India

(Percentages)

Status	*Rural*		*Urban*	
	Male	*Female*	*Male*	*Female*
Usual (Current Year)				
July–June 1993–94	2.0	1.4	4.5	8.3
July–June 1999–00	2.1	1.5	4.8	7.1
July–June 2001–02	1.4	2.0	4.2	4.9
July–June 2011	1.84	1.6	4.0	5.2
Current Weekly				
July–June 1993–94	3.0	3.0	5.2	8.4
July–June 1999–00	3.9	3.7	5.6	7.3
July–June 2001–02	2.6	2.6	4.6	4.8
July–June 2011	3.3	3.5	3.8	6.9
Current Daily				
July–June 1993–94	5.6	5.6	6.7	10.5
July–June 1999–00	7.2	7.0	7.3	9.4
July–June 2001–02	NA	NA	NA	NA
July–June 2011	5.5	6.2	4.9	7.9

Sources: Economic and Political Weekly, December 31, 2005, 5523, and NSSO 68th round

The usual status projects our best labour market face and the daily status the worst face. This is so because, as per our definition, the former are subject to more serious underestimation than the latter. Obviously, the daily status data are more reliable than the other two. This puts the current unemployment rate in India between 4.9 and 7.9 per cent. According to our latest (2012–13) Economic Survey, the unemployment rate in all India in 2009–10 was 6.6 per cent on Current Daily status basis and 2 per cent on the Usual Principal and Subsidiary status basis. The cross-country data on unemployment were presented in Chapter 1, Table 1.1 and the readers may refer to them for a comparative look. A careful perusal of them would reveal a puzzle: the unemployment rate is higher in developed countries (USA, UK, Japan, etc.) than in some developing countries (India, China, etc), even though the per capita GDP and misery are less in the former than the latter. Why? The answer is easy to find. One could cite several reasons for the puzzle. First, developing countries have a larger proportion of their population engaged in agriculture than developed countries, and agriculture is more subject to seasonal, disguised and underemployment (which is hidden and thus not included in unemployment) than manufacturing or services. In this respect, it may be noted that the World Development Report (2002) of UNDP states "the concept of unemployment is not always meaningful in developing countries". Second, rich countries have strict minimum wage regulations, which induces less qualified and lazy persons to not to take up employment, and the firms to hire less workers as the minimum required marginal physical productivity is accordingly high. Third, social security benefits, including unemployment compensation exists only in the developed world and this makes unemployment a somewhat affordable luxury. Since European countries have a better social security system than the West, the unemployment rate is usually higher in the former than the latter. Besides, unlike most macroeconomic variables, the definition of unemployment is subjective as all countries do not define it uniformly. On these grounds one can conclude that the unemployment rate in India is not as low as indicated by the above data. Further, the low rate may be because the poor countries like India have little social security and thus can not afford unemployment.

The above data in comparison to data for earlier years suggest that the unemployment rate in India has only increased over the last decade.

To conclude this section,

The following points may be noted about the Indian labour market:

- Low open but high hidden unemployment
- Poor mobility across places and occupations
- Mismatch of skills between 'vacancies' and 'unemployed persons'
- Presence of domestic servants, bonded and child labour
- Low wages, no strict minimum wage regulations and hardly any social security system

India may not be the only country having such unwarranted facts and surely all these features are on decline over time.

Poverty

Poverty is the other economic problem facing most nations in the world. As for unemployment, there is no unique definition of poverty globally and accordingly international data give alternative figures for the proportion of the people below the poverty line. These are based on the national definition, as well as the international standards. Earlier US $ 1/day/person was deemed as the cut off line for the global definition of (extreme) poverty line. This has recently been revised to US $ 1.25/ day/person in 2005 PPP income terms, which represents the mean of the poverty lines found in the poorest 15 countries by per capita consumption. International data on poverty line are available even for its definition at US$2/day/person. It must be noted that the dollar figures are at the 2005 PPP rate and not at the official exchange rate. It is estimated that roughly one-fifth (1.4 billion) of the world population lives on up to US $1.25 per day/per person and one-half (3.5 billion) on US $2 per day. In general, the wealthier a country is, the lower the incidence of poverty. Education and health indicators are also better on an average for richer countries. In terms of its control, growth has served a powerful force, particularly during the 1980s through 2007. The world's poorest live in Africa and the progress in its reduction is also the slowest there. India and China also have larger proportions of poor people but poverty is falling fairly rapidly in these countries. Estimates suggest that in 1970, 11 per cent of the world's poor were in Africa and 76 per cent in Asia. In 2008, Sub-Saharan Africa had 49 per cent of them and South Asia 36 per cent.

In India, the subject of defining poverty was first posed at the Indian Labour Conference in 1957. The 'working' group of the planning commission recommended ₹25 per person per month for urban and ₹18 per person per month for rural areas at 1960–61 prices as the minimum consumption expenditure (called as monthly per capita expenditure-MPCE) for providing the minimum nutritional diet of calories (2100 for urban and 2400 for rural per person per day) intake as well as to allow for a modest expenditure on items other than food (barring health and education, which were expected to be provided by the government). This became the cut off amount and accordingly people having expenditure below this were bracketed as being 'below the poverty line'. These figures have since been revised from time to time to account for inflation. While there are other estimates as well, those of the Planning Commission are as follows:

Year	*Poverty line*		*People below poverty line*		
	Rural areas	*Urban areas*	*Rural areas*	*Urban areas*	*Combined*
	(₹ MPCE)		*(% of population)*		
1973–74	49	57	—	—	—
1993–94	229	264	37.3	32.4	36.0
1999–2000	327	454	27.1	23.6	26.1
2004–05*	447	579	42.0	25.5	37.2
2009–10*	673	860	33.8	20.9	29.8
2011–12*	816	1000	25.7	13.7	21.9

Source: Govt. of India, **Economic Surveys**: 2012-13 and earlier years

- Poverty line definition underwent a change as per the Tendulkar Committee Report 2009.

Thus, the urban people whose expenditure falls below ₹1,000 per person per month belong to the group of the people below the poverty line. Others whose expenditure exceeded this amount are above the said line. The NSSO data is used to classify people on this criterion and accordingly data is compiled and published on this variable. The table above indicates that the poverty ratio fell from 36 per cent in 1993–94 to 21.9 per cent in 2011–12 in all India; the fall being more pronounced in urban areas (from 32.4 to 13.7 per cent) than in rural areas (37.3 to 25.7 per cent). It is instructive to note that the statistics of poverty in India are full of controversy among economists, bureaucrats, politicians and social activists. However, most professionals subscribe to the view that the economic reforms of the 1990s have led to a radical improvement in the well-being of the bottom half of the population.

The United States government created the **poverty line** in 1960s. It is defined as the **amount of income necessary to buy basic necessities**. After adjusting for inflation, the 2002 poverty line is estimated at $8350 for a single adult and at $17,050 for a family of two adults and two children. On this criterion, roughly 11 per cent of Americans were poor then. The Census Bureau is responsible for designing/revising the poverty line. The time series data indicate that the poverty line rose steadily throughout the 1980s and thereafter and then drifted down in the 1990s. The poverty definitions of other countries and their data can similarly be analysed.

The above measure of poverty is known as the **Head-Count Ratio.** This measure ignores the size of the poverty gap as well as the relative inequality among the poor. To incorporate these factors, new measures have been designed, which include the **Poverty Gap**, **Squared Poverty Gap** and the **Sen Index.** The **Poverty Gap** is defined as the mean shortfall from the poverty line (counting the non-poor as having zero shortfall), expressed as a per cent of the poverty line. Thus, the said measure reflects both the depth of poverty and its incidence. The poverty gap in 2010 stood at 7.5 per cent in India, and it was at 2.8, 3.6, less than 0.5 in China, Brazil and Russia, respectively. The said gap was at the highest in Congo, Demo, Rep. standing at 52.8 per cent. The Squared Poverty Gap incorporates a squared coefficient of variation of the relative inequality; the Sen index uses the Gini coefficient among the poor population. The terms income inequality and the Gini coefficient are defined in the following section and for a detailed understanding of the new measures readers may refer to Sen (1976). Corresponding to the head count ratio, there is an interesting concept called the **Head Count Elasticity**. The said elasticity denotes the responsiveness of the head count poverty measure to the growth rate in the economy. It is expected to be negative, and its estimate for India is –1.3 and for the developing countries –2.[1]

INCOME INEQUALITY

In income inequality, one talks about the distribution of income among the inhabitants of the country. In a capitalist country, income is distributed not by needs but by contributions (efforts) to the production. Since different sections of society have varying abilities and desires to contribute, income differs across people. While income inequality may be a desirable feature of a modern capitalist society, particularly to encourage the acquisition of skills and to motivate the hard and smart work, too much

[1]Vide Revalian and Datt: *World Bank Economic Review* (January 1996): 1–25.

of it is considered bad on the ground of social justice. Reduction in it is obtained through programmes/facilities meant for the weaker sections of the society only and by progressive taxation. As mentioned in Chapter 1, this is an important activity of any government.

Income inequality is measured through the percentile distribution of national income *vis-à-vis* population, which is further reduced to one number, called the Gini coefficient. The data on these variables for a few countries are given below:

Table 3.6 Income Inequality in Selected Countries

(% share in income)

Country	*Survey year*	*Population*					*Gini coefficient*
		Poorest 20%	*Second 20%*	*Third 20%*	*Fourth 20%*	*Richest 20%*	
India	2010	9	12	16	21	43	0.34
USA	2000	5	11	16	22	46	0.41
UK	1999	6	11	16	22	44	0.36
Japan	1993	11	14	18	22	36	0.25
Canada	2000	7	13	17	23	40	0.33
Russian Fed	2009	6	10	15	21	47	0.40
China	2009	5	10	15	23	47	0.42
Pakistan	2008	10	13	16	21	40	0.30
Nigeria	2010	4	8	13	20	54	0.49
Australia	1994	5	12	17	24	41	0.35
Brazil	2009	3	7	12	19	59	0.55

Source: World Development Indicators/Report, World Bank, 2013.

The data reveal that in India, the poorest 20 per cent of the population receives just 9 per cent of the India's income, while the richest 20 per cent receives 43 per cent of the country's income, and so on. This data could be plotted on the Edgeworth's box diagram as follows:

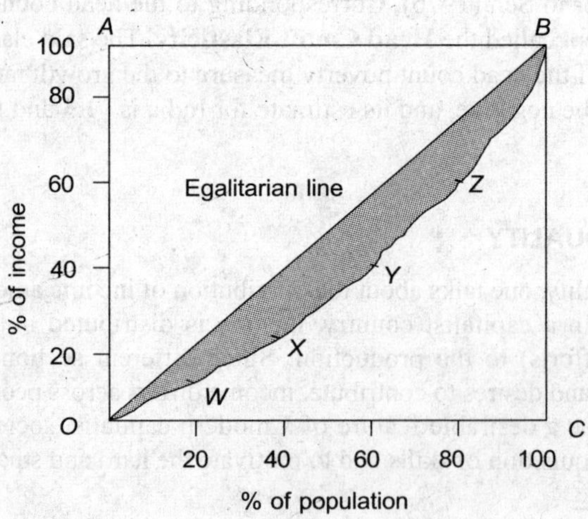

Fig. 3.1 Edgeworth's Box Diagram for India

The curve *OWXYZB* is drawn on the basis of the cumulative share of population in national income. Thus, the poorest 20 per cent of the population receives 9 per cent of the national income and gives us point *W*. The poorest 40 per cent of population receives 21 (9 + 12) per cent of income and gives point *X*, the poorest 60 per cent receives 37 (21 + 16) per cent of the income and gives point *Y*, the poorest 80 per cent receives 58 (37 + 21) per cent of income and gives point *Z*, and 100 per cent of the population receives 100 per cent of income and coincides with point *B*. Incidentally note that in case of India, the sum of the shares does not add exactly to 100 per cent and this could be due to rounding error. The straight line *OB* denotes the perfect equality (egalitarian) line, which is obviously the 45-degree angle on the graph. The farther the true line is from the egalitarian line, the more the income inequality. If all the income were pocketed by one person only, the income distribution curve will coincide with *OCB*, and the inequality will be the maximum.

Data in Table 3.6 measures income inequality but they are hard to compress so as to be able to judge the extent of inequality in one country as against another. For this purpose, the Gini coefficient (*G*) has been invented, which reduces this percentile distribution into one number. It is measured as

$$G = \frac{\text{Area of graph under } OWXYZB \text{ (shaded part)}}{\text{Area of } \Delta OCB}$$

$$= 0.34 \text{ (or 34 per cent) for India}$$

It is not easy to compute the areas of the two regions in the numerator and denominator of the above formula. Explanation of this is beyond the scope of this book and interested readers may refer to Gupta and Singh (1984) for this purpose.

The denominator is fixed and thus the larger the area under the numerator graph, the larger the inequality. Thus, *G* lies between 0 and 100 per cent; the former denotes perfect equality and the latter, perfect inequality. Of the 11 countries for which the data are provided in Table 3.6, India has the fourth lowest (0.34) and Brazil (0.55) the most income inequality. The Gini coefficient takes the lowest value of 0.25 both for Japan and Denmark and the highest value of 0.66 for Seychelles. These extreme values are rare outliers and thus Brazil is considered as having a rather high inequality and India as moderate inequality. Here mentioned must be made of the **Pareto Principle**, which is also known as the **80-20 Rule**, which states that a large percentage of the activity in a market (80) is always accounted for by a small percentage (20) of the operators. Thus, a large part of the national income is earned by a small part of the population, which is nothing but income inequality. Of course, as the data in the above table would reveal, the large part is less than 80 per cent (the highest is 59 per cent for Brazil) but the principle holds.

As mentioned above, efforts have been made to go into the detail on the extent of the poverty among the poor and to design a comprehensive measure of poverty and inequality (vide Sen 1976). However, such details are outside the scope of a macroeconomics textbook such as this one.

KEYWORDS

Exhange-Use value; Water-diamond paradox; Price index; Laspeyre-Passche index; Fisher Ideal-Marshall-Edgeworth index; GDP deflator- WPI-CPI; Industrial workers; Non-Manual urban employees; Agricultural labour; Rural; Urban; All

India/Combined; Base year; Fixed basket; New products; Quality improvements; Boskin Commission; Voluntary-Involuntary unemployment; Work force; Structural-Frictional-Seasonal unemployment; Cyclical-Natural (rate of) unemployment; Disguised unemployment; Priority rule; Usual-Weekly-Daily basis unemployed; Poverty line; Head count ratio; Poverty gap; Sen index; Edgeworth box diagram; Pareto principle, 80–20 rule.

REFERENCES

1. EPW Research Foundation, 'Wholesale and Consumer Prices', *Economic and Political Weekly*, (September 18, 1993): 2015–32.
2. Das, A and M Senapati, "GDP Deflator vis-à-vis Other Price Indices in India: An Exploratory Study, *Journal of Income and Wealth*, XXIX, No. 1 (Jan-June 2007): 3–15.
3. Ministry of Commerce and Industry, Office of Economic Adviser, Revision of Index Numbers of Wholesale Prices in India with base 2004–05 = 100 Methodology, Basket and Weights, 2010.
4. Reserve Bank of India 'New Series of Consumer Price Index Numbers for Industrial Workers (Base: 1982 =100)', *RBI Bulletin* (May, 1989): 435–37.
5. Gupta G S, R D Singh 'Income Inequality Across Nations Over time: How Much and Why', *Southern Economic Journal* LI, No. 1 (July, 1984): 250–7.
6. Sen A K 'Poverty: An Ordinary Approach to Measurement', *Econometrica* 44, No. 2, (1976): 219–31.

REVIEW QUESTIONS

1. Which price index (indices) in India contains the prices of the following goods?
   - Commodities
   - Services
   - Intermediate goods
   - Imports
   - New products

2. Dearness allowance and capital gains in India are over stated and as such while workers have undue gains, investors have undue losses. Comment.

3. Suppose the Freedesh economy produces only three goods and its production and price data for the two years are as follows:

Year	*Good A*		*Good B*		*Good C*	
	Prod.	*Price*	*Prod.*	*Price*	*Prod.*	*Price*
2008	100	10	50	100	200	30
2013	120	15	70	80	250	40

(a) Looking at the price data alone, compute the yearly-compounded annualised rate of inflation.

(b) Compute the GDP deflator and the corresponding yearly-compounded annualised rate of inflation.

(c) Compute the Laspeyre's Price Index and the corresponding yearly annualised rate of inflation.

(d) Compare the above three inflation rates and comment.

4. Analyse the various price indices in India in terms of the:
- Inclusion/exclusion of goods and services
- Weight structures
- Method of averaging
- Use in real life

5. Suppose your company has offices in Ahmedabad, Delhi and Mumbai, and you have the option of working in any one of these three cities on the same emoluments. If your decision was based purely on economic consideration, which location you would choose and why? Discuss the limitations of your answer.

6. Suppose the Greenpur economy shows the following statistics about its population, workforce and employment:

Population = 150 million
Workforce participation rate = 60%
Employment = 80 million

Compute the rate of unemployment in Greenpur.

7. Relative poverty is worse than the absolute poverty. Do you agree? Why?

8. Consider the following data on a cross section of countries and the world:

Country	*Labour force as % of Population (%)*		*Labour force as % of working people* (%)*		*Unemployment rate (%) (As % of population)*		*People below $1.25/ day (As % of poverty line)*	*Poverty gap at $1.25/ day*
	1980	*2011*	*Male 2011*	*Female 2011*	*Male 2008–11*	*Female 2008–11*	*2009–10*	*2009–10*
India	44	38	81	29	3	4	32.7	7.5
USA	48	51	70	58	9	9	—	—
UK	48	51	69	55	8	7	—	—
Japan	49	52	72	49	5	4	—	—
Malaysia	38	44	77	44	3	4	<2	<0.5
China	55	61	80	68	—	—	11.8	2.8
Australia	46	53	72	59	5	5	—	—
Nigeria	41	31	63	48	—	—	21.0	3.5
Russia, Fed	55	53	71	56	7	6	<2	<0.5
Germany	48	52	67	53	6	6	—	—
Brazil	39	52	81	60	6	11	6.1	3.6
World	46	47	71	51	—	—	—	—

Source: World Development Indicators, World Bank, 2003 and 2013.

* Population age group 15 years and older

(a) While the labour force proportion is fairly stable across countries, the unemployment rate varies widely. Why?

(b) Examine the above data in relation to the data in Table 1.1 (Chapter 1) and suggest the relationships, if any, among work force participation, unemployment rate, and poverty ratio, in terms of both economic well being and economic performance. It may be noted that working people are defined as all those who age 15–64 years.

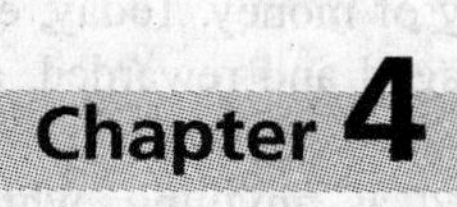

Chapter 4

Money, Fiscal and Foreign Sector Variables

Learning Objectives

After reading the chapter you should be able to:

1. Learn what the concepts like money, liquidity, interest rates, various fiscal variables, exchange rate, balance of payments and its components, and external debt mean and how they are quantified.
2. Comprehend the distinctions between the narrow and broad money; nominal and real interest rates; plan vs. non plan and revenue vs. capital expenditures and revenues, fiscal vs. revenue vs. primary deficits; bilateral vs. multilateral exchange rates, NEER vs. REER, fixed and floating exchange rate systems, current vs. capital account of balance of payments, merchandise vs. services vs. factor incomes, foreign direct vs. foreign portfolio investments, trade vs. current account vs. balance of payments deficits.
3. Value the reasons for holding the foreign exchange reserves.
4. Know the instruments of the monetary policy, fiscal policy, trade policy and the exchange rate.
5. Get a feel of the data on monetary magnitudes, fiscal variables, exchange rates and international transactions across select major countries.

The barter form of exchange is practically history and it has been replaced by exchange through money. Further, specialisation has become an inevitable engine of growth and this is facilitated by money. Also, price level and hence the inflation rate is influenced greatly by the quantity of money in the economy. Government role is recognised even by the strongest proponents of *laissez faire*, like Adam Smith, albeit the current move towards privatisation, liberalisation and deregulation. Monetary and fiscal policy tools play a significant role in taming business cycles and even in promoting growth. Thus, it is imperative to understand them thoroughly before dwelling on the theories of economic fluctuations and growth. Globalisation is no option and it is considered inevitable for survival and economic growth. This requires knowledge of various international transactions and the intricacies of the foreign exchange rate. Thus, no macroeconomics text could ignore clarification of concepts involved in money, fiscal and foreign sector variables.

Money and Liquidity Magnitudes

Money is considered one of the greatest inventions of modern society, the others being the wheel and fuel. To Noble laureate Milton Friedman, nothing in the system was as important as the quantity of money. Today, exchange of goods for goods is rare as specialisation is encouraged and rewarded, and the double coincidence of wants is impractical.

Initially, money was deemed as anything, which is generally acceptable in exchange of goods and services. Thus, anything that could buy any item became the money. Precious metals like gold and silver (commodity money) served as money in early periods. Currently, currency (fiat money) is money as it is the legal tender. If a bank cheque or any other instrument is accepted for payments, it is also money. Subsequently, the other roles of money were recognised and were considered a 'matter of functions four', which are **'a medium, a measure, a standard and a store'**. In these roles, money not only serves as the medium of exchange, but it also measures the worth of any item, serves as a standard for future payments and for comparing different assets, and acts as a 'temporary abode of the purchasing power'. Someone once commented that money was invented to determine as to how much one owes to others. While the medium of exchange role is universally recognised, the other roles enjoy varying degrees of acceptance. Most of these functions can be performed to a varying degree by a host of financial instruments (such as bank deposits, deposits with non-bank intermediaries, bonds and equity) and so there exists no unique measure of money. Due to lack of unanimity among economists and bankers as a single measure of many, we have several money magnitudes as well as liquidity aggregates.

Money is now considered as a financial asset that is universally accepted as a means of payment in transactions and settlement of debts. Accordingly, two basic measures of money are defined globally: **narrow** and **broad**. The former usually consists of the currency with the public and demand deposits with banks. The latter includes the time deposits with banks as well. While currency (notes and coins) is legal tender deposits are not so. However, their exact measurements may vary from country to country. In India, we have four different notions of money, sometimes referred to as the **old money measures**. Since the report of the Working Committee on Money Supply and Methodology of Compilation, 1998, we also have three **new money measures**. In addition, currently we also have three so-called, **liquidity aggregates.** The new measures are refinements of the old ones but the latter are more popular. Accordingly, all these measures are discussed in the following sub-sections.

Old Money Measures

The four old money measures are referred to as M_1, M_2, M_3 and M_4, and they are measured as

$$M_1 = \text{Currency with public} + \text{demand deposits with banks} + \text{'other deposits' with RBI}$$

$$M_2 = M_1 + \text{saving deposits with post offices}$$

$$M_3 = M_1 + \text{time deposit with banks}$$

$$M_4 = M_3 + \text{saving and time deposits with post offices.}$$

Various measures of money exist because the various kinds of deposits, which distinguish them, are close substitutes.

Bank deposits are usually classified as *current*, *saving* and *fixed* deposits. Demand deposits in the above definition consist of all current deposits and part of the saving deposits that can be withdrawn on demand. Also, note that travellers' cheques issued by banks and non-bank firms, and held by public are a component of money for these have been issued after debiting the amounts to the corresponding demand deposits. The travellers' cheques that are held by banks are not a part of money. Similarly, credit/debit cards are not a part of any definition of money. When used, they are merely temporary loans, which get cancelled on debits to the user's deposits' accounts. Time deposits consist of all fixed deposits and the part of saving deposits which have constrained on withdrawal. The "other deposits" with RBI are the deposits of quasi-government bodies, deposits/balances of foreign central banks and governments, and deposits/balances of international agencies like IMF with the RBI. Saving and time deposits with post offices are well known.

The data on the various components of money for the selected years are provided in Table 4.1.

Table 4.1 Old Money Stocks, Components and Reserve Money

(₹ billion)

Item	*At the end of financial year*			
	1990-91	*2000-01*	*2005-06*	*2012-13*
1. Currency with public	530	2096	4131	11447
2. Demand deposits with banks	392	1666	4052	7470
3. 'Other deposits' with RBI	7	36	69	32
4. Time deposits with banks	1729	9318	19043	64871
5. Time deposits with banks net of Resurgent India Bonds*	NA	9062	19224	NA
6. Post office saving banks' deposits	42	50	50	50
7. Post office time deposits	105	210	210	210
8. Narrow money (M_1) (1 + 2 + 3)	929	3798	8252	18949
9. Broad money (M_3) (M_1 + 4)	2658	13116	27295	83820
10. New broad money (NM_3)*	NA	12860	27476	NA
11. M_2 (M_1 + 6)	971	3848	8308	19000
12. M_4 (M_3 + 6 + 7)	2805	13376	27555	84080
13. Currency in circulation (public + banks)	553	2182	4307	11910
14. Bankers' deposits with RBI	318	815	1355	3207
15. Reserve Money (3 + 13 + 14)	878	3033	5731	15149

Note: *NM_3 is net of Resurgent India Bonds (₹256.62 billion) whose proceeds are deposited with State Bank of India since August 28, 1998.

Source: RBI Monthly Bulletin, various issues.

A brief analysis of the data reveals the following:

(a) post office savings and time deposits are a small component of M_2 and M_4 (less than 0.5 per cent), and their share has declined over time. Thus, the distinctions between M_1 and M_2, and between M_3 and M_4 are only conceptual.

(b) broad money (M_3) has been about 3–4 times that of narrow money (M_1) and the gap between the two has been expanding over time. This suggests the rather large and increasing size of time deposits with banks, which forms over thrice the size of narrow money.

(c) currency with the public constitutes about 60 per cent of the narrow and 15 per cent of the broad money. This indicates the dominance of deposit money in the money supply.

(d) in recent years, both the narrow as well as the broad money have grown at the rate of about 12 per cent per year.

Table 4.1 has also data on yet another concept of money, called **reserve money**. This is also known as the **government money** or **high-powered money** or **base money**. It equals the currency with the public and the banks (that is, currency in circulation), bankers' deposits with the RBI and 'other' deposits with the RBI. This is called 'high-powered' as it has the capacity to create more money in contrast to the other (low-powered) money (bank deposits), which enjoy no such power. This will be pursued in detail later, in the chapter on money demand and supply.

New Money Measures

The new measures are known as NM_0, NM_1, NM_2 and NM_3. NM_0 is exactly same as high-powered money and NM_1 as the old M_1. The other two are defined as follows:

$NM_2 = M_1$ + Time liabilities portion of savings deposits with banks + certificates of deposits issued by banks + Term deposits of residents with a contractual maturity of up to and including one year with the banks

$NM_3 = NM_2$ + Term (fixed) deposits of residents with a contractual maturity of over one year with banks + Call/term borrowings from non-depository financial corporations by banks

A comparison of the old and new measures would suggest three major changes, viz. **(a)** we now have something in between the hitherto narrow and broad money, that is, NM_2, **(b)** post office deposits have been dropped from the new moneys and **(c)** the old M_2 and M_4 concepts have been dropped. The new item (NM_2) is derived by bifurcation of fixed deposits into those up to and including one year and the rest. Post office deposits have been dropped as they always had a negligible share in money, and accordingly there is no M_4. Further, the new measures calculate money supply on residency basis, which is in tune with best international practices. The NM_2 version is a useful creation as it is a closer substitute to NM_1 ($=M_1$) than the old M_3. To see the statistical difference in the old and new series, three years data are provided in Table 4.2.

The difference between the old M_3 measure and the new NM_3 measure is small. The said difference is due to, to quote from an RBI publication, "the treatment of non-resident repatriable fixed foreign currency liabilities of banks in the money supply compilation. The difference owing to bank's call/term borrowings from non-bank sources is, at present, negligible on reporting Fridays as such liabilities are fully subject to reserve requirements. The divergence between the estimates of M_3 and NM_3 would, therefore, essentially depend on the magnitude of the non-resident

Table 4.2 Old and New Money Stock Measures

(₹ *billion*)

March 31		*Old series*		*New series*			
	Reserve money	M_1	M_3	NM_0	NM_1	NM_2	NM_3
1997	2000	2406	7018	2000	2406	4512	6700
2004	4365	5787	20057	4365	5787	11888	19602
2013	15149	18949	83820	15149	—	---	—

Source: RBI Monthly Bulletin, various issues.

inflows to the banking system in India." The difference between the growth rates of the two measures fall in the range of 0.1 to 1.7 per cent.

While there is no unique measure of money theoretically, in practice, the measure that bears the closest relationship with real national income is considered the appropriate one. Thus, this is an empirical issue. However, empirical studies across nations over time do not support any particular measure either.

Liquidity Measures

Liquidity refers to the case with which an asset can be converted to many at the reasonable (market) rate and thus money is fully liquid. The three liquidity measures have been designed recently and they are referred to as L_1, L_2 and L_3. These are broader than money and are defined as follows:

$L_1 = NM_3$ + Postal deposits

$L_2 = L_1$ + Liabilities of the financial institutions

$L_3 = L_2$ + Public deposits with non-bank finance companies

Postal deposits include all kinds of deposits with post offices. Liabilities of the financial institutions comprise of their term money borrowings, certificates of deposits and term deposits. To give a feel of the data, four years data are given in Table 4.3.

Table 4.3 Liquidity Measures

(₹ *billion*)

March 31	NM_3	*Postal deposits*	L_1	*Liabilities of Fin. Inst.*	L_2	*Public deposits With NBFCs*	L_3
2000	10,733	276	11,008	94	11,102	183	11,286
2001	12,265	344	12,609	129	12,738	201	12,940
2006	27,476	1038	28,514	29	28,543	217	28,760
2013	83,576	1399	84,974	29	85,004	106	85,110

Source: RBI Monthly Bulletin, various issues.

A comparison of the new broad money (NM_3) and the liquidity aggregates suggest that the various liquidity estimates are merely 2 to 5 per cent higher than the new broad money. This is precisely because the magnitudes of the three additional items in liquidity measures are insignificant components. Needless to say, the narrower the money, the more liquid it is and all money concepts are more liquid than all liquidity measures. Further, as one goes down on the liquidity measures, the degree of liquidity falls.

Interest Rates

Interest rate is an important macroeconomic variable as it affects saving and investment, money demand and flow of foreign funds, among other significant variables. Like the GDP, there are the nominal and the real interest rates. **Nominal rate is** the observed interest rate, which is paid by the borrower (issuer of debt instrument) and received by the lender (subscriber of debt instrument). Thus, there are nominal interest rates on:

- government bonds
- corporate bonds
- corporate deposits
- bank deposits
- bank loans

and so on. Various rates exist due to the differences in liquidity, risk (of default), maturity of debt instruments and such other factors. The more liquid assets earn lower interest rates than the less liquid ones. Generally, the higher the risk, the greater is the interest rate. However, there is no such unique theory for the maturity of the instrument. Instead, three theories have been put forth in this regard. The **liquidity preference theory** argues in favour of a positive relationship between the interest rate and maturity; for generally the shorter the maturity the more liquid the asset is and the greater the liquidity the less is the return, *ceteris paribus*. The **expectations theory** argues that the long-term rate is the geometric mean of the current short-term rate and the expected future short-term rates. Thus, the interest rate on a five year bond equals the geometric mean of the current actual interest rate on a one year bond and the expected rates on the one year bond next year, two years hence, three years hence and four years hence. Since expectations are dynamic, the theory is consistent with both the positive as well as the negative relationship between the interest rate and the maturity of the instrument. The **market segmentation** (between the markets for short-term and long-term debt instruments) **theory** postulates that since the market for different maturities are separate, there is no relationship between the short and the long-term interest rates. It thus suggests the independence of the two[1]. The relationship between the interest rate and the maturity of the instrument when plotted on a diagram is called the **yield curve**. Thus, the yield curve could be rising, falling or even flat. If one analyses the data across time and countries, one would discover that history has witnessed all the three shapes of the curve, and hence, there can be no unique theory for the **'term structure of interest rate'**. Since bank deposits are relatively more liquid and practically risk free, they command the lowest interest rate. In contrast, corporate deposits are, in general, the riskiest and hence, attract the highest interest rate. Government bonds have no default risk, and thus, command a lower interest rate than do corporate bonds. Within each category of the above financial assets, the interest rate varies with risk, liquidity and maturity.

In addition to the above rates, there are four other important rates as well. These are known as the

- Bank or discount rate
- Call money rate
- Repo rate
- Reverse repo rate

The **bank rate** is the rate at which the Central Bank of the country advances loans to other banks in the country. The **call rate**, on the other hand, is the money market rate at which banks borrow from other banks for overnight needs. In the United States, the latter rate is known as the *federal fund rate*. Repo rate is the rate at which the central bank of the country (Reserve Bank of India) advances loans to banks for overnight against government bonds under the liquidity adjustment facility. The last rate, viz., reverse repo rate is the rate at which banks can park their excess funds with the country's central bank for over night.

The real interest rate r is obtained by adjusting the nominal interest rate i to the change in the general price level (or inflation rate: $\dot{P}$)

$$r = i - \dot{P} \tag{4.1}$$

Equation **(4.1)** is referred to as the Fisher's equation in honour of the person who first hypothesised this relationship. There are a large number of interest rates in India and on some consistent time series data are not available. Data on selected nominal interest rates in India are provided in Table 4.4,

Table 4.4 Selected Interest Rates in India

(Percentages)

Item	*1970-71*	*1980-81*	*1990-91*	*2000-01*	*2010-11*	*2012-13*
1. Bank rate*	5-6	9.00	10.0	7.0	6.0-8.5	8.5
2. Call money rate (Mumbai/ average)	6.38	7.12	11.49	9.15	5.75	4.0
3. Commercial banks' deposit rate (1-3 years) (range)	6-6.5	7.5-8.5	9-10	8.5-9.0	8.25-9.0	8.75-9
4. Banks' Lending rate (range/ average)	7-8.5	16.5	16.5	11.5	8.85	9.95
5. Repo rate*	—	—	—	9.0	6.75	7.5
6. Central govt. Securities (weighted average/year) yield	—	7.03	11.41	10.95	7.92	8.36
7. Reverse repo rate*	—	—	—	6.75	5.75	6.5

Source: Handbook of Statistics on Indian Economy, Reserve Bank of India, various issues.
* Year-end rate

The data in Table 4.4 confirms that the interest rate varies over financial assets and the duration of the term. It is more on lending than on deposits. Needless to say, interest rate varies, not only from the asset to asset and maturity to maturity but also, to some extent, among public sector banks, private banks and foreign banks. For simplicity, such details have been avoided from the table. A careful look at the data would indicate that the interest rates have fallen rather significantly in the last few years and this is a worldwide phenomenon. In the United States, the federal fund rate was cut from 6.5 per cent in early January 2001, in several installments, to 1 per cent in June 2003, which was the lowest in the United States in 45 years (since 1958). Afterwards, the federal rate was revised upward several times until the great recession in 2007, after which it has reduced to around 1 per cent once again in several installments. Even in India and elsewhere in general, interest rates witnessed an upward trend until around 2008, then fell for a couple of years and is now fluctuating up and down occasionally. There is also a term known as the **neutral (nominal) interest rate** (the one which neither accelerates nor decelerates economic growth) is believed to be 6 to 7 per cent at the current inflation rate (about three per cent) in the United States. In addition there is another interest rate called the natural (nominal) interest rate as the one at which income equals its natural level ($Y = Y_n$) and inflation equals its desired level. The country is currently (Jan 2014) on a high (nominal) interest rate. This is partly due to the high inflation rate and thus the real rates have not risen to this extent.

Fiscal Magnitudes

Fiscal variables refer to the expenditures and receipts of the government at all levels, which are central (federal), state and local. Expenditure is classified into:

- Revenue and capital expenditure
- Plan and non-plan expenditure

Revenue expenditure consists of the government consumption expenditure and transfer payments, and capital expenditure is on the creation of assets. Government consumption expenditure includes expenditure on salaries and administration for the normal running of government departments (such as defence, police, postal deficits, economic, social, other general services and central plan). Transfer payments include expenditure on subsidies, interest payments on past debts and pensions to retired employees. Capital expenditure is expenditure on roads, structures and equipment used in the government sector and government investments in shares etc, as well as loans to PSUs. Plan expenditure is on new government initiatives, while non-plan expenditure is made to meet past commitments. Government receipts are likewise divided into **(a)** revenue and **(b)** capital receipts. The former are further classified into **(i)** tax and **(ii)** non-tax (interest, dividends from PSUs, fees, stamp duties, external grants etc.) revenue receipts. The latter (capital receipts) are grouped into **(i)** non-debt (loans and advances recovery, proceeds from PSUs disinvestments, etc.) and **(ii)** debt (public borrowings-internal and external and other liabilities) receipts to finance fiscal deficit.

Deficits

The differences between the different kinds of the expenditure and receipts are termed as the various types of deficits/surplus. Thus, there are concepts like:

- Fiscal deficit
- Revenue deficit
- Primary deficit

The **fiscal deficit** refers to the difference between the government total expenditure and the government total non-debt receipts. The **revenue deficit** stands for the difference between the government revenue expenditure and the government revenue receipts. The last, which is the **primary deficit,** is obtained by subtracting interest payments (a component of non-plan revenue expenditure) from the fiscal deficit. Therefore, the primary deficit is the deficit of the current year and it is accordingly triggered by an expansionary fiscal policy during the year. In addition, 'earlier' India used to have a **budget deficit**. This was defined as the fiscal deficit minus government borrowings and other liabilities (public debt receipts). This was considered close to the concept of **monetised deficit**, which meant the printing of the new money by the Reserve Bank of India (RBI) to part finance the deficit. In the Union Budget of 1997–98, the government came out with a slightly different version, which was named monetised deficit. Currently, budgets do not provide estimates either for the budget or the monetised deficit. The various concepts of expenditure, revenues and deficits will be clear if one looks at the data in Table 4.5.

Table 4.5 Union Budgets 1990–91 to 2013–14

(₹ billion)

Item	*1990–91*	*2000–01*	*2011–12*	*2012–13 Revised*	*2013–14 budget*
1. Total Expenditure	1067	3256	13044	14308	16653
1.1 Revenue expenditure	750	2778	11458	12631	14362
1.1.1 Plan	140	511	3337	3434	4433
1.1.2 Non-plan	609	2267	8120	9197	9929
1.1.2.1 of which interest payments	219	993	2732	3167	3707
1.2 Capital expenditure	318	478	1586	1678	2291
1.2.1 Plan	159	316	786	858	1121
1.2.2 Non-plan	158	162	799	819	1171
2. Total Receipts	959	3256	13044	14308	16653
2.1 Revenue receipts	574	1926	7514	8718	10563
2.1.1 Tax (net to centre)	443	1369	6298	7421	8841
2.1.2 Non-tax	131	557	1217	1297	1723
2.2 Capital receipts	386	1330	5529	5590	6090
2.2.1 Loans recovery	60	120	189	141	107
2.2.2 Other receipts	—	14	181	240	558
2.2.3 Borrowing and other liabilities	326*	504*	5160	5209	5425
3. Deficits					
3.1 Fiscal (1-2.1-2.2.1-2.2.2)	433	602	5160	5209	5425
	(8.3)	(5.4)	(5.7)	(5.2)	(4.8)
3.2 Revenue (1.1-2.1)	186	297	3943	3912	3798
	(3.5)	(2.7)	(4.4)	(3.9)	(3.3)
3.3 Budget (3.1-2.2.3)	107	98	—	—	—
	(2.1)	(0.9)			
3.4 Primary (3.1-1.1.2.1)	231	102	2428	2043	1718
	(4.3)	(0.9)	(2.7)	(2.0)	(1.5)

Note: Numbers in parentheses are percentages of GDP

* Excludes budget deficit (= 91 days treasury bills)

Source: 'Budget at a Glance', Budget document, Ministry of Finance, Government of India, various issues

It must be noted that the above data is strictly for the central government only and, thus, it is exclusive of state and local government data. A scrutiny of this data would reveal the following:

(a) Revenue expenditure constitutes roughly 87 per cent of the total expenditure in the budget 2013-14. The said proportion has almost steadily gone up from around 70 per cent in 1990-91 and 85 per cent in 2000-01 to this latest 87 per cent. As such, capital expenditure has been reduced to a small proportion, which speaks poorly for the size of public investment.

(b) Non-plan expenditure (both revenue and capital) forms about 70 per cent of the total expenditure and this fraction has remained stagnant over time. Thus, the proportion of the plan expenditure, which is on new initiatives, has remained almost invariant at below 30 per cent over time.

(c) Though the revenue receipts have always dominated total receipts, public borrowings (fiscal deficits) have witnessed distressing magnitude. However, the share of debts in total receipts has gone down from 40 per cent in 2011-12 to 33 per cent in the latest budget. This is in line with the Fiscal Responsibility and Budget Management (FRBM) Act.

(d) In tune with the FRBM Act, the fiscal deficit was tamed during the post 2000 until 2007-08, but it moved up again thereafter due to the worldwide recession and it stands at 4.8 per cent of GDP in the last budget. As per the said Act, it was to be reduced approximately by 0.3 per cent per year and finally to settle at the IMF prescribed rate of 3 per cent of GDP. In spite of the best efforts, the target has remained unmet so far.

(e) Revenue deficit (which is like current account deficit), as a proportion to the fiscal deficit, had steadily increased from 43 per cent in 1990-91 to 75 per cent in 2012-13. It is heartening to note that this has declined to 70 per cent in the budget 2013-14. Further, the primary deficit, which is the one caused by the corresponding year's budget, had steadily fallen to below zero in 2007-08 but again it has gone up to 1.5 per cent of GDP in the last budget.

It must be emphasised that the revenue deficit is the worst, as capital deficit is for public investment, which leads to the creation of public assets that supplements the long-term growth. Similarly, interest payments are past legacy and hence hard to handle. Thus, primary deficit alone is the true indicator of the current fiscal stance.

It would be of interest to note that transfer payments (interest, subsidies and pension) account for about 60 per cent of the total non-plan revenue expenditure and that this share is on rise over time. Also, it would be instructive to note the combined deficits of the central and state governments as per cent of GDP. Data on the three relevant deficits for the selected years are as follows:

Item	*1990–91*	*2000–01*	*2010–11*	*2011–12*
Gross fiscal deficit	9.1	9.2	6.9	7.2
Gross revenue deficit	4.1	6.4	3.2	3.1
Gross primary deficit	4.9	3.4	2.4	2.6

Source: RBI Monthly Bulletin, various issues.

Over the last two decades, all the three deficits have fallen, though not monotonically. This means the government at all levels is getting fiscal prudent, which is an encouraging feature.

Before closing this section, it is instructive to note that economists, unlike the accountants, are not sticklers for balanced budgets. In fact, as would be seen in the later chapters, economists prescribe a moderate deficit during recession, a modest surplus during prosperity and a balanced budget only in the long run. Unfortunately, India's budgets have revealed deficits even over a long period of time. The United States economy also turned into a surplus budget only around the turn of the century and it is back again to a deficit budget. Most other countries are in similar circumstances.

Yet another important factor to consider here is the size of the government. Recall that the data in table above refers to the central government alone. An analysis of this data relative to the GDP would suggest that central government expenditure forms about 15 per cent of GDP in India. The said expenditure in the US and UK, Japan, France and Russian Federation stands at about 26, 44, 20, 48 and 25 per cent respectively. Thus, the Indian (Central) government is relatively small.

Foreign Sector Magnitudes

Foreign or international macroeconomic variables consist of foreign exchange rates and various items that form part of the country's balance of payments and balance of indebtedness (external debt).

Foreign Exchange Rate

A foreign exchange rate measures the price of one currency in terms of the price of another currency. For example, exchange rate of Indian rupee in terms of the US dollar equals ₹62/$ or $0.01613/rupee on Jan 02, 2014. Just as there are individual prices of various goods and services, as well as general price of all goods and services, there are two kinds of foreign exchange rates, viz.,

- Bilateral exchange rates
- Multilaterial exchange rates

The two are discussed below.

Bilateral Exchange Rates The bilateral exchange rates denote the price of a currency in terms of some other currency. Thus, the current exchange rate of the Indian rupee in terms of the United States' dollar (about ₹62 per dollar) measures the dollar's price in Indian rupees and the inverse of it measures the Indian rupee's price in terms of the US dollar. Accordingly, there are two ways of quoting the exchange rate:

- Direct method (E)
- Indirect method $\left(\frac{1}{E}\right)$

In the former, the domestic currency is expressed as the number of units of the currency per unit of the foreign currency (e.g, ₹62/US $) while under the latter it is expressed as the units of the foreign currency per unit of the domestic currency (e.g, US $0.025/Re). We denote the former as E and the latter as $\frac{1}{E}$. An increase in E or a decrease in $\frac{1}{E}$ means the depreciation while a decrease in E or an increase

$\frac{1}{E}$ means the appreciation of the domestic currency in relation to the foreign currency. Therefore, if the exchange rate changes from ₹62 per US dollar to ₹65 per US dollar, E goes up from 62 to 65 and the rupee is depreciated by about 4.8 per cent, and $\frac{1}{E}$ goes down from $\frac{1}{62}$ to $\frac{1}{65}$, which also implies the depreciation of the rupee by about 4.8 per cent. The terms depreciation and appreciation of a currency are the appropriate terms when the exchange rate system is a floating one. Under the fixed exchange rate system, as under the Bretton Woods system, these terms were referred respectively, to as the devaluation and revaluation of the currency in question. Accordingly, depreciation and appreciation of a currency are caused by market forces which devaluation and revaluation are caused by policy actions.

Just as there are the nominal GNP and real GNP, there are

- Nominal exchange rate
- Real exchange rate

The above was the definition of the **nominal exchange rate**. The **real exchange rate** (e) adjusts the nominal exchange rate (E) to the relative inflation rate in the two countries. Thus,

$$e_1 = E\left(\frac{1+\dot{P}_1}{1+\dot{P}_0}\right) \quad \textbf{(4.2)}$$

$$e_2 = \frac{1}{E}\left(\frac{1+\dot{P}_0}{1+\dot{P}_1}\right) \quad \textbf{(4.3)}$$

where e_1 and e_2 denote the real exchange rates under the direct and indirect quotations, respectively, and $\dot{P}_0$ and $\dot{P}_1$ denote the inflation rates in the domestic and foreign country, respectively. From these definitions, it must be clear that while the nominal exchange rate is the rate at which people trade one currency for another, the real exchange rate is the rate at which people trade goods and services of one country for those of another country. In other words, the real exchange rate is the price of domestic goods relative to foreign goods. The relationship between the magnitudes and the rates of change in the real and nominal exchange rates may be expressed as follows as well:

$$e = E(P_1/P_0) \quad \textbf{(4.2a)}$$

Differentiating the above with respect to time would give

$$\dot{e} = \dot{E} + (\dot{P}_1 - \dot{P}_0) \quad \textbf{(4.2b)}$$

where the dot indicates the rate of change over time. Thus, the real rate is simply the nominal rate multiplied by the ratio of the foreign price to domestic price, and the rate of change in the real rate equals the rate of change in the nominal rate plus the difference between the inflation rates of foreign and domestic countries.

Just as in E, an increase in e_1 means the depreciation and a decrease in it means the appreciation of the real exchange rate of the domestic currency. Quite the opposite is true for e_2. Note that if the inflation rate at home exceeds that abroad, E remaining the same, the real exchange rate under the direct quotation, goes down, indicating an appreciation in the real exchange rate. Thus, if the exchange rate = ₹62, the inflation rate in India = 10 per cent, and inflation rate in the United States = 5 per cent, then

$$e_1 = 62(1.05/1.10) = 59.18$$

Since the new rate is below the earlier one, it indicates that the real exchange rate of the rupee has appreciated with regard to the US dollar. Similarly, if indirect quotation were used, we would have

$$e_2 = 1/62(1.10/1.05) = 0.01690$$

which is more than 1/62, and therefore, the real exchange rate again shows appreciation of the rupee. For this reason, high inflation countries usually adjust their nominal exchange rates upward to maintain a stable real exchange rate against the currencies of low inflation countries, so that their competitive position remains unaltered. Here and below, the subscript 1 with the exchange rate stands for those under the direct quotation and 2 for those under the indirect quotation.

Exchange rates exist for each currency in terms of every other currency and, thus, theoretically there are $n \times n$ exchange rates, where n stands for the number of currencies (countries). However, half of these are just duplicates and some more can be obtained through the corresponding cross rates, leaving just $n - 1$ as the independent (basic) exchange rate. Thus, for example, in a four country (currency) world, out of the 16 (4 × 4) rates, only 3 (4 – 1) rates are independent ones:

	US $	*£*	*¥*	*₹*
US $	1	0.5	100	50
British £	0.5	1	200	100
Japan ¥	100	200	1	0.5
Indian ₹	50	100	0.5	1

In the above table,

US $1 = £0.5 or £1 = US $2

= ¥100 or ¥1 = US $0.01

= ₹50 or ₹1 = US $0.02

are the three basic exchange rates. Diagonal unitary terms are not really the exchange rates as they value a currency in terms of itself, the six off-diagonal terms on either side of the diagonal are simply duplicates of the other, and the remaining three rates, which are

£1 = ¥ 200

= ₹100 and

¥1 = ₹0.5

can be derived from the above three basic rates:

$$£/\$ = 0.5,\ ¥/\$ = 100 \Rightarrow ¥/£ = \frac{100}{0.5} = 200$$

$$£/\$ = 0.5,\ ₹/\$ = 50 \Rightarrow ₹/£ = \frac{50}{0.5} = 100,$$

$$¥/\$ = 100,\ ₹/\$ = 50 \Rightarrow ₹/¥ = \frac{50}{100} = 0.5$$

The above calculations assume that the various exchange rates are consistent, which must be true at least approximately lest there are opportunities for arbitrage. If the rates are inconsistent across currencies, arbitrageurs would enter the market and restore equilibrium.

The number of the independent exchange rates equals one less than the number of the currencies. Since the number of countries in the world is in hundreds, every currency has hundreds of exchange rates. These are the *bilateral exchange rates.*

Multilateral Exchange Rates As prices of individual goods and services are combined into a general price, the bilateral exchange rates are merged into a multilateral exchange rate, called the effective exchange rate. The latter are further distinguished as the **Nominal** and **Real Effective Exchange Rates** (NEER and REER). The NEER is obtained as the weighted average of the bilateral nominal exchange rates:

$$\text{NEER}_1 = w_1E_1 + w_2E_2 + \cdots + w_nE_n \quad \textbf{(4.4)}$$

$$\text{NEER}_2 = w_1\left(\frac{1}{E_1}\right) + w_2\left(\frac{1}{E_2}\right) + \ldots + w_n\left(\frac{1}{E_n}\right) \quad \textbf{(4.5)}$$

where w_i = weight attached to the bilateral exchange rate E_i, and n = number of the bilateral exchange rates, which equals one less than the number of countries.

The weight could be assigned on the basis of the share of the total trade (trade weighted NEER) of the country whose NEER is obtained with the country in terms of whose currency the bilateral exchange rate is. Alternatively, instead of the total trade, exports could be used as the criterion, and thus, there are *trade weighted* as well as the *export weighted NEERs*. For example, in computing the trade weighted NEER for India, w_1 could be the share of India's trade with the United States in India's total international trade, and E_1, the bilateral exchange rate between the Indian rupee and the US dollar. In practice, we have 4 countries, 8 countries and so on, trade (export) weighted NEERs, where the share of the top 4 or 8 countries trade share alone are used after proportionately raising their shares to a total of 100 per cent. To illustrate this, consider the following example of four countries. Suppose the Indian data were as follows:

Country	*Bilateral exchange rate*		*Share in India's trade*		*Inflation rate*
	Direct quote	*Indirect quote*	*Actual*	*Proportional*	
US	₹50/$	$0.02/₹	40%	47.06%	5%
UK	₹100/£	£0.01/₹	15%	17.65%	4%
Japan	₹0.5/¥	¥2/₹	20%	23.53%	3%
Germany	₹25/Euro	Euro 0.04/₹	10%	11.76	7%
Total	—		85%	100%	—
India	—	—	—	—	8%

From the above data, the two values for NEER could be computed, one each on the direct and indirect method of quoting the exchange rates:

$$\begin{aligned}\text{NEER}_1 &= ₹0.4706\ (50) + 0.1765\ (100) + 0.2353\ (0.5) + 0.1176\ (25)\\ &= ₹44.23765\end{aligned}$$

$$NEER_2 = ₹0.4706\ (0.02) + 0.1765\ (0.01) + 0.2353\ (2) + 0.1176\ (0.04)$$
$$= 0.486481$$

While the $NEER_1$ is in rupees, $NEER_2$ has no unique currency. Also, note that for each exchange rate the direct quoted rate = the reciprocal of the indirect quoted rate $NEER_1 \neq \frac{1}{NEER_2}$ because of the differential weights. Only if the weight for each exchange rate were the same, one weighted average would equal the reciprocal of the other. *Like inflation* refers to the change in the general price level, the *appreciation/depreciation of a country's currency* is defined as change in the NEER. Increase in $NEER_1$ or decrease in $NEER_2$ would mean depreciation of the domestic currency and *vice versa*. Thus, if the $NEER_1$ of the Indian currency increased from ₹44.2376 in 2002 to ₹47.50 in 2003, the depreciation of the Indian rupee during 2003 would equal 7 per cent. Similarly, a fall in $NEER_2$ from 0.486481 to say 0.45, would mean depreciation of Indian currency by 7.5 per cent.

Just as there is a bilateral real exchange rate, there is a Real Effective Exchange Rate (REER), which adjusts NEER to the relative inflation rates in foreign countries. Thus, REERs for India come to

$$REER_1 = ₹0.4706\ (50)\left(\frac{1.05}{1.08}\right) + 0.1765\ (100)\left(\frac{1.04}{1.08}\right) + 0.2353\ (0.5)\left(\frac{1.03}{1.08}\right)$$
$$+ 0.1176(25)\left(\frac{1.07}{1.08}\right)$$
$$= ₹42.89767$$

$$REER_2 = 0.4706\ (0.02)\left(\frac{1.08}{1.05}\right) + 0.1765\ (0.1)\left(\frac{1.08}{1.04}\right) + 0.2353\ (2)\left(\frac{1.08}{1.03}\right)$$
$$+ 0.1176\ (0.04)\left(\frac{1.08}{1.07}\right)$$
$$= 0.5262021$$

When the inflation rate at home exceeds the inflation rate abroad, the nominal exchange rates having remained constant, $REER_1 < NEER_1$ and $REER_2 > NEER_2$. This means an appreciation of the real exchange rate.

Thus, a comparison of the values of the NEER and REER would indicate that the real exchange rate of the Indian rupee has appreciated due to a relatively high inflation rate in India. The algebraical formulas for the REERs are as follows:

$$REER_1 = w_1 E_1\left(\frac{1+\dot{P}_1}{1+\dot{P}_0}\right) + w_2 E_2\left(\frac{1+\dot{P}_2}{1+\dot{P}_0}\right) + \ldots + w_n E_n\left(\frac{1+\dot{P}_n}{1+\dot{P}_0}\right) \quad \textbf{(4.6)}$$

$$REER_2 = w_1 \frac{1}{E_1}\left(\frac{1+\dot{P}_0}{1+\dot{P}_1}\right) + w_2 \frac{1}{E_2}\left(\frac{1+\dot{P}_0}{1+\dot{P}_2}\right) + \ldots + w_n \frac{1}{E_n}\left(\frac{1+\dot{P}_0}{1+\dot{P}_n}\right) \quad \textbf{(4.7)}$$

where, $\dot{P}_0$ = inflation rate in the domestic country, $\dot{P}_1$ = inflation rate in the foreign country 1, *w*s are weights and so on. Recall that E_i is defined in terms of direct quotation while $1/E_i$ in the indirect quotation. The arithmetic average sometimes creates ambiguities, and thus, geometric averaging is often preferred. However, we do not go into such perfections here.

Like the general price level, the multilateral foreign exchange rate represents the price of the domestic currency in terms of none of the foreign currencies but of all the foreign currencies, which have gone into its computation. Further, as seen above, if the multilateral exchange rate is based on the indirect quotations of the bilateral exchange rates, then the former is not even in any particular currency's units. Therefore, the multilateral rates' only use is in terms of computing the rate of the currency's appreciation/depreciation rate, which can be handled better through the index numbers. To illustrate this, suppose the foreign exchange rates in the table above were for period 2, the trade shares in that table were the same for both, periods 1 and 2, and the foreign exchange rates (indirect quotation) for period 1 were as follows:

₹45 = US $1	₹0.6 = ¥1
₹90 = UK £1	₹25 = Euro1

Then if the index for NEER in period 1 were 1.00, the index of NEER in period 2 would be given by:

$$0.4706\left(\frac{50}{45}\right) + 0.1765\left(\frac{100}{90}\right) + 0.2353\left(\frac{0.5}{0.6}\right) + 0.1176\left(\frac{25}{25}\right) = 1.03202$$

This implies that the NEER has depreciated by 3.202 per cent in period 2, when compared to period 1.

Similarly, if the index number of the REER for period 1 were 1.0, then that for the REER for period 2 would be given by

$$0.4706\left(\frac{50}{45}\right)\left(\frac{1.05}{1.08}\right) + 0.1765\left(\frac{100}{90}\right)\left(\frac{1.04}{1.08}\right) + 0.2353\left(\frac{0.5}{0.6}\right)\left(\frac{1.03}{1.08}\right) + 0.1176\left(\frac{25}{25}\right)\left(\frac{1.07}{1.08}\right) = 1.00073$$

This means that the REER in period 2 has depreciated by 0.073 per cent over period 1. Since the inflation rate at home (India) exceeds that in all foreign countries, the depreciation of the REER is less than that of the NEER.

Foreign Exchange Rate System/Data A country may either have the fixed or the floating exchange rate (nominal) system. Under the former, the exchange rate of the country's currency is fixed in terms of one or more of the foreign currencies, while under the latter the exchange rate floats over time. Also, the float may be clean or managed (dirty). Under the clean system, the exchange rate is determined simply by the market forces of the demand for and the supply of the currencies in question. In contrast, under the managed system, the Central Bank of the country intervenes in the market to influence the demand and/or supply of the currency through buying/selling of foreign exchange, and thereby, ensures the desired level of exchange rate. There are both pros and cons of each of these systems, and in the real world the system has varied, both, over space (country) and time. India was on the fixed exchange rate system until March 1993, when it entered into the managed floating rate system. The details are discussed in Chapter 7.

The data on the foreign exchange rates are given in Table 4.6.

Table 4.6 Foreign Exchange Rates (Nominal) of Indian Rupee

(Rupees/Foreign currency/Index: year average)

Exchange rate	*1980*	*1990*	*2000*	*2005*	*2010*	*2012*
1. US dollar	7.9	17.5	44.9	44.1	45.7	53.4
2. British pound	18.3	31.3	68.1	80.3	70.7	84.7
3. Japanese yen (100)	3.8	12.2	41.7	40.1	41.7	52.2
4. Deutsche mark	4.3	10.9	NA	NA	NA	NA
5. SDR	10.3	23.8	59.2	65.1	69.8	81.8
6. Euro	NA	NA	41.5	54.9	60.7	68.7
7. NEER index (36 country trade weighted)	228.1	154.3	92.1	101.9	93.8	79.8
8. REER index (36 country trade weighted) (2004–05 = 100)	158.0	114. 7	99.1	102.7	102.9	95.5

Sources: Monthly Bulletins, Reserve Bank of India, various issues.
International Financial Statistics, IMF, various issues.

The above data reveal that the exchange rate of the Indian rupee has devalued considerably over time in its all versions, though at different rates. For instance, between 1980 and 2012, the Indian rupee has depreciated by over 85 per cent (on the current rate base) in terms of the US dollar. While the NEER of the Indian rupee fell by over 50 per cent, its REER depreciated just by about 40 per cent between 1985 and 2012. The difference in the latter two was due to the differential inflation rate in India versus her trade partners. It would be instructive here to mention that the calculation of the rate of depreciation (like any other rate of change) is ambiguous, for it depends on whether the first period or the second period value is used as the base value. Thus, if the first period value were taken as the base value the rate of depreciation of the Indian rupee in relation to the US dollar between 1980 and 2012 would come to 575 per cent and not 85 per cent as just mentioned. Also, note that in the table above while the bilateral rates are in direct quotations the multilateral rates are in indirect quotations.

Balance of Payments

Balance of payments (BOP) is a set of accounts, which records the flows of all the economic transactions that take place during the specified period between the residents of the country and their counterparts in the rest of the world. Conceptually, it is divided into three accounts, which are further classified into sub-accounts as follows:

I Current account

- Merchandise
- Invisibles
  - — Services
  - — Factor Incomes
- Unilateral Transfers

II Capital account

- Foreign Investment
  - — Foreign Direct Investment
  - — Portfolio Investment
- Loans
  - — External Assistance
  - — Commercial Borrowings
  - — Short-term Borrowings
- Banking Capital
  - — Commercial Banks
  - — Others
- Rupee Debt Service
- Other Capital
- Errors and Omissions

III Monetary Movements
Changes in

- Reserve Position with IMF
- Foreign Exchange Reserves

The *merchandise* section records all the transactions in commodities. The *invisibles section records the transactions* in (non-factor) services (like tourism, education, shipping, insurance, banking and government not included elsewhere (GNIE)), and (factor) incomes (viz. investment income, repatriation of profits and dividends, and interest on debts, and compensation of employees). Incidentally, note that the net factor income earned from abroad, which distinguishes the national from the domestic income (Chapter 2) is the item that becomes the credits minus debits entries under "factor incomes" in the BOP account. Factor income is not taken as a part of exports/imports of goods and services, the latter consists of trade in merchandise and non-factor services. Transfers also considered as a part of invisibles, constitutes NRI remittances, and private and official gifts, donations, grants and pensions. Thus, on the whole, the *current account* reflects the difference between the incomes that we earn from the rest of the world (ROW) and the incomes that ROW earns from us. The bulk of this income comes from trade in goods and services. Further, as a thumb rule, the current account deficit is treated as the net inflow of capital from abroad.

The *capital account* records transactions in money and capital. It is divided into five sub-sections and an item called *errors and omissions*. *Foreign investments* are classified into direct and indirect, the latter better known as portfolio. *Foreign direct investment (FDI)*, consists of all capital investment that is owned and operated by a foreign entity, and foreign portfolio investment (PI) is capital investment that is financed with foreign money but operated by domestic residents. Since this distinction is difficult to practice exactly, it is separated through another convention. Under this convention FDI includes all foreign equity/factory investments that constitute 10 per cent or more of the voting equity holdings by any individual investor (individual or company) of any domestic company. Foreign investments that form less than 10 per cent of voting equity investment owned by an investor constitute foreign portfolio investment (PI). The cut-off rate of 10 per cent is fixed somewhat arbitrarily on the belief that this signifies the distinction between *the* 'operated role' and 'not operated' or 'played' or 'not played' a role in the management of a company. Basically, FDI comprises equity investments while PI includes foreign institutional investments (FIIs), funds raised through ADRs/ GDRs (American/Global Depository Receipts) by Indian companies and through offshore funds. From the point of view of a country receiving such capital, FDI is more stable than the PI as the former is harder to reverse than the latter. Loans are divided into three categories: one, *external assistance* denotes aids extended by India to other foreign governments under various agreements and repayment of such loans, and the external assistance received by India through multilateral and bilateral loans under the agreements with foreign governments and international institutions and their repayments. The loan repayment to erstwhile "rupee area" are excluded from external assistance section and are shown separately under rupee *debt service* section. Two, *commercial borrowings* includes all medium/long-term loans by and to India taken on commercial terms. Three, *short-term loans* refer to loans with a maturity of less than one year.

Banking capital has two components. The *commercial banks* have assets and liabilities. Foreign assets of commercial banks consist of foreign currency holdings and rupee overdrafts to non-resident banks. Foreign liabilities of these banks consist of non-resident (NRI) deposits and liabilities other than NRI deposits which comprises rupee and foreign currency liabilities to non-resident banks and official and semi-official institutions. *The* second item under banking capital is "others", which includes movements in balances of foreign central banks and international institutions (like World Bank, Asian Development Bank, International Financial Corp.) maintained with RBI as well as movement in balances held abroad by the embassies of India in London and Tokyo. *Rupee debt service* includes repayments on account of civilian and non-civilian debt in respect of Rupee Payment Area (RPA) and interest payment thereof. *Other capital* comprises mainly the leads and lags in export receipts, that is, the difference between the custom data and the banking channel *data.* Besides these, other items included are funds held abroad, India's subscription to international institutions, quota payments to IMF, remittances towards recouping the losses of branches/subsidiaries and residual item of capital transactions not included elsewhere. *Errors* and *omissions* (balancing entry) exist due to differences in accounting practices (exports are recorded on FOB (free on board) while imports on CIF (cost, insurance, and freight inclusive), fluctuations in exchange rates, timings of recording differences, smuggling, and so on).

Monetary movements or changes in the official reserves' position are referred to as the **compensating/accommodating or financing** transactions to distinguish them from the current account and capital account transactions, which are carried out for their own sake on business incentives considerations. All countries who are members of the International Monetary Fund (IMF) are required to maintain a certain amount of reserves with the IMF, they could of course, keep more. Such reserves are partly in foreign exchange, including SDR (special drawing rights) and partly in the member country's currency. Only the first part of this forms the item under the reserve position with IMF. Gold and foreign currency reserves, which are like household jeweler, are maintained partly to facilitate foreign transactions, particularly during bad times and partly to maintain the foreign exchange rate at its desired level.

The items held under the official reserves account are part of the world money and they could be used to finance deficits in the balance of payments (BOP). Since the Jamaica Agreement of 1976, gold, however, is not international money any more.

The degree of globalisation of a country is measured in two ways, viz.,

(a) Common measure = (Export + Import)/GDP

(b) Expanded measure = (Gross current account + Gross capital account)/GDP (where gross means the sum of credits and debits).

The BOP records all international transactions on a **double entry** basis, as does the balance sheet of any corporation. Further, all transactions that result in the **inflow of money** into the economy enter as **credit** items while others, which cause **outflow of money**, as the **debit** item. Thus, import of any product like vehicles, plants or machines are entered as the debit item under the merchandise part of the current account and the payments made for them get entered in the official reserves account as the corresponding reduction in the foreign exchange reserves. Similarly, borrowings from abroad are entered as the credit items under the loans part of the capital account and as a corresponding increase in the reserves in the official reserves account. Likewise, NRI deposits go as the credit item under the banking capital part of the capital account and as the corresponding increase in the foreign exchange reserves in the official reserves account. Since FDI, NRI deposits and borrowings bring money into the economy, they enter as credit items in the capital account of the BOP.

Balance of Payments' Deficits/Surpluses Balance of payments may not balance and it may contain one or more of the following deficits/surpluses:

- Merchandise trade deficit (surplus)
- GDP trade deficit (surplus)
- Current account deficit (surplus)
- Capital account deficit (surplus)
- BOP deficit (surplus)

The *merchandise trade deficit (surplus)* refers to the excess of merchandise imports (exports) over merchandise exports (imports). The excess of both the merchandise as well as the invisibles' (non factor services) imports over their counterpart exports is called the *GDP trade deficit (surplus)* or the *GDP net imports (exports)*. In the literature, this is often simply called as the *trade deficit (surplus) or net imports (exports)*. This is so because both the merchandise and the invisibles' transactions are components of the GDP. Current account deficit is the overall deficit in all the three components of the current account and similarly the capital account deficit is the sum of the deficits in all the five components of the capital account plus that in errors and omissions. The *balance of payments deficit (surplus)* is defined as the sum total of the current account deficit (surplus) and the capital account deficit (surplus). Accordingly, the **fundamental BOP equation** is defined as:

$$\text{current a/c deficit} + \text{capital a/c deficit (including errors and omissions)} = \text{BOP deficit} \quad \textbf{(4.8)}$$

Alternatively, *BOP deficit* is given by the decrease in the "official reserves account". Obviously, the sum of the BOP balance (deficit/surplus) and changes in the "official reserves account" necessarily equals zero. While putting the BOP of a country on paper, it is customary to put all the items but the "monetary movements/ changes in official reserves account" above the line and the latter account below the line, and thus, the BOP deficit/surplus is also referred to as the deficit/surplus "above the line".

The various deficits/surpluses are distinguished because they have varying significances. *Trade deficit* (balance of trade) is relatively easier to control by the countries, and hence, it is the most transparent value and talked about by business and labour spokesmen while lobbying with the government. The GNP net export affects the GNP and reveals the gap between the domestic investment and saving, and hence its importance in financing the country's investment through foreign saving. *Current account deficit* indicates increase in the indebtedness of the nation to the rest of the world. Therefore, international bankers look at this while considering loans to such countries. In contrast, the *capital account's surplus* reveals the extent to which the country is using its assets (equity, bonds and factories) to meet with its current expenditures over and above its current earnings, thereby revealing the long-term health of the country. In other words, the capital surplus refers to the net sale of domestic assets to foreigners, which is not always desirable. *Changes in the official reserves* indicate decrease or increase in the liquidity position of the nation, and thus, indicate the short-term ability of the nation to sustain various imbalances in international transactions as well as its ability to tamper (manage) the foreign exchange rate. Increase in official reserves means investing in foreign currency.

Economists are not particularly against any one or more of the various deficits/ surpluses in international transactions. In fact, they believe that the current account deficit (which is normally associated with the capital account surplus) can be a sign of strength as money pours into the country that shows potential for future growth. However, if a country is simply importing more than it exports without making investments that will raise future output, then the problem may arise. The issue could be illustrated with an example of students. If a student borrows and gets a good degree, his future is bright. However, if he borrows and squanders the money without getting a degree, he is in deep trouble. Is current account deficit good or bad? Good, because it allows a country to consume and invest more than her GDP. It is bad, for it adds to external debt or/and amounts to sale of domestic assets to foreigners. Thus current account deficit may be good for a country which has good investment opportunities but in short of investment funds in a given period, however, it is bad as it is not sustainable in the long run.

The United States was running a current account deficit in the order of over 5 per cent of her GDP in 2006 and yet the then Finance Secretary of the country, Mr Paul O'Neill, called this as a triumph and not a problem for the country. He would argue that it is sustainable! Why? May be because, it is financed by the rise in the demand for the US dollar abroad. And the latter, may be for the purpose of just holding it as a foreign exchange reserve for any reason, including drug trafficking and criminal activities. Some people prefer the US dollar even to gold.

Foreign Exchange Reserves Lately many countries are building on their foreign exchange reserves and taking pride in such an achievement. Nevertheless, it must be noted that their pride is highly beneficial for countries whose currencies (called hard currencies) are serving the purpose of such reserves. This is because the latter group of countries just prints their currencies at hardly any cost, and with that they buy goods and services from the former group of countries, who merely hold such hard currencies to build their reserves. Thus, the United States, Europe and Japan are beneficiaries in this respect. This is known as **seigniorage**, which is discussed further in later chapters. Suffice to say here that it stands for the profit that the issuers of such currencies make due to their monopoly powers. It is instructive to note here that though the Euro is slowly gaining significance, the US dollar happens to be the main component of the foreign exchange assets held by various countries.

There is an ongoing debate as to what is the optimum amount of foreign exchange reserves. There are two approaches to determine the optimum level of foreign exchange reserves: positive and normative. Under the former, the country projects her requirements and decides on the level of the reserves. Under the latter, one compares the marginal benefits of holding the reserves and its marginal cost, and then computes the optimum size for reserves. The foreign exchange reserves are needed for four purposes:

- **(a)** to finance imports of goods and services
- **(b)** to honour the external debt obligations
- **(c)** to manage the exchange rate at the desired level
- **(d)** to face threats from capital flights
- **(e)** to speculate/invest in the foreign exchange market

Earlier it was thought that the reserves must approximate about three months' equivalent of imports. This is so because imports may be essential while exports depend not only on our ability to export but also on the demand for them from the rest of the world, which can hardly be assumed. Around the beginning of this century, Pablo Guidotti, the then Deputy Minister of Finance of Argentina, had impressed the world with his views wherein he suggests that the reserves should be sufficient for the country to live without any foreign borrowing for one year. Thus, the reserves should not only be able to finance the difference between the expected imports and exports but also be sufficient to meet with the external amortisations due in the next one year. To this we need to add further the need for reserves to maintain the foreign exchange rate at the desired level to face the threat of impending capital flight, if any and to be able to speculate/invest in foreign exchange market if seemed appropriate. Further, history reminds us that foreign exchange crises have come from capital account volatility, not from the current account deficits. Countries like Panama and Ecuador, which have adopted the US dollar even for local currency, of course, need more of such reserves. Other countries, like Hong Kong, who are on the currency board of the exchange rate system, also need more of these reserves as their local currency is fully or heavily backed by these reserves. Also, countries, which are on the fixed exchange rate system, like China and UAE, obviously need more of such reserves than others who are on the floating exchange rate system. Such views and facts have led many countries, including India, to build more and more of such reserves. However, there is a cost to them as well. These reserves are practically income barren (may earn approximately equal to the rate on US treasury bonds) but they have high opportunity cost for they could be used to repay costly external debts and/or to upgrade infrastructure etc. For this reason, many economists and others are already complaining of 'excess reserves'. In India, the foreign exchange reserves stood at $80.9 billion in June 2003. Of this, $29.8 billion were held in foreign securities, $36.9 billion as deposits with other central banks and the remaining $14.2 billion as deposits with foreign commercial banks. Currently (December 2013) our foreign exchange reserves stands at around $300 billion. Obviously the average returns on these (about 2-3 per cent a year) must have been less than the average cost of our external borrowings. There are optimization models which could incorporate all these factors and determine the optimum size of foreign exchange reserves. However, this is out of the scope of this text.

Trends in Foreign Transactions India's foreign trade and investments have expanded more in last decade than ever before. This is because since 1991, India is moving towards globalisation in a big way. Most of the quantitative restrictions on the movement of goods and services have been removed and tariffs have been slashed gradually. Goods of strategic significance alone are being banned or have quotas and most items are on the open general license (OGL) list. Though we do not still have capital account convertibility, restrictions on the movement of capital have been eased considerably. Several Indian companies are now listed even on important foreign bourses. This is not the text for such details on foreign trade and investment but the data on India's BOP, given below in the available format in Table 4.7, would confirm the policy stance and changing pattern. Some entries are blanks, as the data in this format for earlier years are not available.

The following major trends emerge from the data on India's BOP:

(a) India has almost always experienced trade as well as current account deficits, and these have increased substantially during the eighties and recently during the last decade. However, if one were to look up the yearly data, one would notice that while the trade balance has always been negative, the current account has revealed positive balance in some years (viz. 1950–51, 1973–74, 1976–77, 1977–78, 2001–02, 2002–03 and 2003–04).

(b) Invisibles have usually witnessed a net credit in India and they have recorded a significant upward trend in the nineties and thereafter. The net proceeds from private transfer payments have always enjoyed the dominant place within the invisibles. Since there is a lot of net foreign investment in India and it has been increasing over time, factors' income has usually been negative and upward moving.

(c) Capital account has almost always served the function of financing the current account deficits but this role has been overwhelming during the sixties and thereafter. In the recent past, the surplus in this account has exceeded the deficit in the current account, and thus has led to the building up of the foreign exchange reserves in the economy.

(d) BOP deficit was the most alarming during the eighties when it was financed both by drawing down the international reserves as well as the position with the IMF, culminating in a fall of India's foreign exchange reserves to a level of just around US dollar one billion on the eve of the economic reforms in June 1991. The said position has reversed post 1990s, though the rising trend of BOP surplus has been arrested post the great recession of 2007–08.

Table 4.7 India's Balance of Payments: Past Trends

(₹ *billion*)

Items	*NET (Credits-debits) during*					
	1950 –51	*1970* –71	*1990* –91	*2000* –01	*2010* –11	*2012* –13
1. Current Account	0.39	–4.45	–174	–116	–2197	–4796
1.1 Merchandise	–0.04	–4.08	–169	–567	–5805	–10645
1.2 Invisibles	0.42	–0.37	–4.3	–451	3608	5848
a. Services	0.29	0.08	17.6	79	2006	3532
a. Transfer payments	0.37	2.09	45.4	600	2421	3484
b. Factors' income	–.24	–2.54	–67.3	–227	–818	–1168
2. Capital Account	–0.04	5.02	126.6	392	2912	4857
2.1 Foreign investment				267	1935	2547
a. Foreign direct investment				149	541	1082
(i) In India				184	1324	1470
(ii) Abroad				–35	–783	–388
b. Portfolio Investment				118	1394	1465
(i) In India				126	1447	1513
(ii) abroad				–8	–53	–48
2.2 Loans				245	1327	1691
a. External assistance				20	225	53
b. Commercial borrowings				202	554	461
c. Short term				23	549	1177
2.3 Banking Capital				–91	220	903
2.4 Rupee debt service				–28	–3	26
2.5 Other capital				13	–567	–279
2.6 Errors and Omissions	–.07	–0.67	2.3	–14	–121	146
3. Balance of Payments	0.28	–0.10	–44.7	276	595	207
4. Official Reserve Account Change*	–0.28	0.10	44.7	–276	–595	–207
4.1 IMF Position	0	–0.79	21.8	–1.2	0	0
4.2 Foreign Exchange Reserves	0.28	0.89	22.9	–275	–595	–207

Note: *Decrease +; increase -
Sources: Monthly Bulletins, RBI, various issues.
Statistical Abstracts of India, CSO, various issues.

(e) Our official reserve account is becoming healthier since the beginning of the economic reforms in 1991 and India is now in a position to be proud of its foreign exchange reserves, which have even crossed a figure of US $300 billion.

Tables 4.8 and 4.9 contain similar data for the selected countries.

Table 4.8 Balance of Payments' Current Account of Select Countries

(US $ billion)

Country	*Goods and Services*				*Net Primary income*		*Net Secondary Income*		*Current Account balance*	
	Exports		*Imports*							
	1980	*2012*	*1980*	*2012*	*1980*	*2012*	*1980*	*2012*	*1980*	*2012*
India	11	437	17	540	0.4	–18	2.9	61.6	–2.9	–60
USA	272	2212	291	2747	29.6	224	–8.0	–129.7	2.2	–440
UK	146	765	134	825	–0.4	3	–4.6	–36.4	6.9	–94
Japan	147	911	157	1015	0.8	179	–1.5	–14.3	–10.8	61
Singapore	24	555	25	494	–0.4	–3	–0.1	–6.7	–1.6	51
Indonesia	24	211	22	540	–3.1	–18	0.3	61.6	–0.6	–60
Brazil	22	282	28	304	–7.0	–35	0.1	2.8	–12.8	–54
Korea, Rep.	20	664	25	622	–0.5	5	0.5	–2.8	–5.3	43
China	24	2167	19	1935	0.5	–42	0.5	3.4	5.7	193
Pakistan	3.0	31	6	48	–0.3	–3	2.2	18.4	–0.9	–2
Sri Lanka	1.3	14	2	22	–0.03	–1	0.3	4.6	–0.7	–5
Australia	26	311	27	328	–2.7	–39	–0.4	–1.4	–4.4	–57
Nigeria	27	98	20	77	–1.3	–22	–0.6	21.9	5.2	20
Russian Fed	NA	590	NA	445	NA	–68	NA	–6.1	NA	71
World	NA	22354	NA	21738	NA	NA	NA	NA	NA	NA

Source: World Development Indicators, World Bank, 2013 and earlier issues.

Table 4.9 International Financial Flows and Rates: Select Data

Country	*Gross int'l reserves*	*Total external debt*	*Foreign direct Investment Inflow (net)*	*Portfolio Equity inflow (net)*	*Bonds and net lending**	*Interest rate (Lending)*
	2012	*2012*	*2012*	*2012*	*2012*	*2012*
	(US dollar billions)					*Lending (%)*
India	300	379	24.0	22.8	27.5	10.6
USA	574	NA	203.8	232.1	NA	3.3
UK	105	NA	56.1	-27.6	NA	0.5
Japan	1268	NA	2.5	34.9	NA	1.4
Singapore	266	NA	58.7	2.9	NA	5.4
Indonesia	113	255	19.6	1.7	6.92	11.8
Brazil	373	440	76.1	5.6	25.4	36.5
Korea, Rep.	328	NA	5.0	16.9	NA	NA
China	3388	754	253.5	25.0	3.0	6.0

(Contd.)

Table 4.9 (*Contd.*)

Pakistan	134	62	0.9	0.2	–0.2	13.5
Sri Lanka	7.1	25	0.9	0.3	0.6	13.3
UAE	47	NA	9.6	NA	NA	NA
Australia	49	NA	56.6	15.1	NA	7.0
Nigeria	48	10	7.1	10.0	0.4	19.2
Russian Fed	538	543.0	50.7	1.2	—	11.4
World	—	—	1509.6	776.0	—	—

Lending is from commercial banks and others
Source: World Development Indicators, World Bank, 2013.

The above data reveal the following:

(a) Trade in goods and services not only constitute the major component of the current account across all the countries but the balance in it also dominates the current account balance in most countries. The net primary factors' income dictates the current account balance in countries like the United Kingdom, Japan and Australia, where the balance of trade in the goods and services does not dominate.

(b) Trade in goods and services has expanded during the last over three decades in all countries. It has increased the most in China (95 times), Republic of Korea (28 times) and Singapore (21 times), in that order, and the least in Indonesia (16 times) and the United Kingdom (6 times) during the last about three decades.

(c) Trade volume (export + import of goods and services) is the most in the United States. The other high trade volume countries, in descending order, are China, Japan, the United Kingdom, the Republic of Korea, Singapore and so on. Of course, the trade volume must be seen in relation to the GDP and if that is done, Singapore would take the first position as its trade volume is roughly four times of its GDP. This ratio of trade volume to GDP stands at about 56 per cent in India and 32 per cent in the United States.

(d) United States is the leading country in foreign trade, as it is in national income. Its current share in the world export of goods and services approximates 10 per cent and that in the world import of goods and services is around 13 per cent. In contrast, the said proportions stand at around 1.95 and 2.48 for India, and 9.7 and 8.9 per cent for China, respectively.

(e) Currently, China leads in terms of surplus in the current account. The other countries with current account surplus include Japan, Singapore, Rep. of Korea and Nigeria in the descending order. Further, China and Nigeria alone have witnessed this surplus in both 1980 as well as 2012. Among the countries having the worst deficit in this account are the United States, UK, India and Indonesia. It is interesting to note that the United States had witnessed a surplus in this account in 1980. The countries facing chronic deficits include Australia, Brazil, Pakistan, Australia and Sri Lanka. The major source of current account surplus for Japan is net income while that for China, is trade in goods and services. Trade happens to be the principal source of deficits in the United States, and India, while the net income takes this position in Australia and

Indonesia. India, Indonesia, Pakistan and Nigeria are the major recipients of secondary income while the United States, UK and Japan are major donors in this regard.

Before closing this section, some discussion on total international transactions is in order. The data in Tables 4.8 and 4.9 represent genuine transactions only. These are believed to form less than five per cent of the total transactions in foreign exchange. Estimates suggest that the total international transactions stand at around two trillion per day, the ones not included in the tables consist of foreign exchange transactions carried out for arbitrage and speculation purposes. This volume is so large that James Tobin, a Nobel laureate, has gone to the extent of even recommending a tax at the rate of 0.5 per cent on them, and use of the proceeds for financing some global needs.

External Debt

External (foreign) debt refers to the debt a country owes to non-residents repayable in foreign currency, goods or services. It is sum of public, publicly guaranteed and private non-guaranteed long-term debt, use of IMF credit and short-term debt from the rest of the world. It is a stock variable and the corresponding flow variable is the current account deficit in the BOP. From another angle; external debt is the cumulative fiscal deficits that have been financed through net foreign debts. External debt provides a source of funds to a nation but a large size of it, particularly in relation to the GDP, adversely affects the country's credit worthiness. Also, servicing of it through interest aggravates the current account deficit, and thereby, the size of the external debt itself. In 1982, Mexico fell into an external debt crisis when she was unable to service her external debt obligations. Subsequently, several other Latin American countries, some African countries, several countries in South East Asia (1997–98 Crisis), the Russian Federation and more recently Argentina, have suffered such a difficulty. Fortunately, India has never faced such a crisis, though she was on the verge of this in 1991 when a part of her gold holdings had to be kept in the custody of foreign governments. The data on external debt for select countries in 2012 are included in Table 4.9. They warn Sri Lanka of having a relatively high debt-GDP ratio, which stands at around 44 per cent (for country wise GDP/GNP data, readers must look at Table 2.7, Chapter 2). It is pertinent to mention here that India and China have foreign exchange assets that are quite comparable to their respective external debts. Although the debt tables do not provide data for industrially advanced countries, it is reported that the United States of America happens to be the most heavily indebted nation in the world.

Foreign Investments and Interest Rates

Table 4.9 includes data on foreign investments and nominal interest rates in select countries. The sum of foreign direct investment and portfolio investment gives the net foreign investment in the country. While FDI usually comes with a more long-term commitment, portfolio investment is the short-term. When capital flights occur, it often leaves behind an economic mess, requiring billions of dollar rescue packages to straighten things out. An analysis of the data in Table 4.9 would suggest that China and United States are the major recipients of FDI. USA and Japan are the major recipients of portfolio investment; and the major portfolio capital flight is from UK. China alone attracts over 16 per cent of the world's FDI, and the United States about 14 per cent. India has a net inflow of foreign capital, but her share in FDI remains below 2 per cent. If one looks at the worldwide capital flow one would notice that richer countries attract most (70 per cent) of the international investments and this is so because they have high income consumers, well-educated workers and extensive infrastructure. As regards to the level of interest rate it is the lowest in UK and second lowest in Japan. Other countries with a relatively lower interest rates are, the United States, the United Kingdom, Singapore, China and Australia. Interest rate is the highest in Brazil and the other countries with a relatively higher rates include Nigeria, Indonesia, and the Russian Federation, in that order. India has an interest rate at 10.6 per cent which falls around the world average. Capital goes where it earns the most, but it must be noted that earnings are to be seen in terms of the real rate rather than the nominal one and also in relation to the risk involved. Japan, the United States, China and the United Kingdom have experienced relatively low inflation rates and perhaps low risk as well.

This completes the measurement of the macroeconomic variables' section and we will move to the section on behavioural functions in the next chapter.

Keywords

Narrow-Broad money; M_1-M_2-M_3-M_4; L_1-L_2-L_3; High-powered/Reserve/Base/Government money, Liquidity preference-Expectations-Market segmentation theory; Bank rate; Call rate; Federal Fund rate; Revenue-Capital Expenditure/Receipts, Plan-Non plan expenditure; Fiscal-Revenue-Primary deficit; Monetised deficit; Bilateral-Multi lateral exchange rate; Direct-Indirect method of quotation, Nominal –Real exchange rate; NEER-REER; Currency Depreciation-Appreciation; Fixed-Floating exchange rate system; Pure/Clean-Dirty/Managed floating rate; Balance of Payments; Current-Capital-Official reserves/Monetary movements/Compensating/Accommodating/Financing account; Double entry basis; Merchandise-(GDP) Trade-Current account-Capital account- BOP deficit/surplus; Fundamental equation of BOP; Foreign exchange reserves; Seigniorage.

References

1. EPW Research Foundation India's Balance of Payments, *Economic and Political Weekly*, (November 13–20, 1993), 2551–60.
2. EPW Research Foundation Money, Banking and Finance, *Economic and Political Weekly*', (January 16–23, 1999): 218–40.
3. Ministry of Finance, Government of India. *Union Budget*, various issues.
4. Fisher Irving, *The Theory of Interest*, (New York: 1930).
5. Reserve Bank of India, *RBI Bulletins*, various issues.

Review Questions

1. Some of the current macroeconomic data for the Wonderdesh economy are as follows:

GDP = 6500 Merchandise exports = 550
Consumption expenditure = 4550 Imports of goods and services = 950
Government expenditure = 1120 Credits on invisibles = 240
Tax revenue = 450
(exports of invisibles)
Proceeds from PSU dis-investments = 5 Net unilateral credits = 50
Government interest payments = 325 Capital account surplus = 90
Currency in circulation = 650 Time deposits with bank = 2250
Narrow money supply (M_1) = 950 Banks' deposit with the Central
Bank of Wonderdesh = 250 Government non-tax revenue = 180

Determine the magnitudes of the following variables:

- Broad money (M_3)
- Fiscal deficit
- Current account deficit
- High-powered money
- Primary deficit
- Balance of payments deficit

2. Fiscal deficit must be minimised, for it pre-empts future tax revenues. Analyse.

3. Revenue deficit is worse than the fiscal deficit. Explain.

4. The spot foreign exchange rates (direct quotation) of the Goodland economy's currency, with the currencies of her three major trade partners in two periods, are as follows:

Country	*Period 1*	*Period 2*
1	10	12
2	20	18
3	0.10	0.15

The trade shares of the three countries in Goodland's total trade remain the same in the two periods at 35 per cent, 20 per cent and 25 per cent for countries 1, 2 and 3, respectively and the inflation rate between the two periods in Goodland and countries 1, 2 and 3 happened to be 6 per cent, 10 per cent, 5 per cent and 2 per cent, respectively.

Compute the values of the trade weighted nominal effective exchange rate for each of the two periods and of the trade weighted real effective exchange rate for period 2 for the Goodland's currency. Has the Goodland's currency devalued? Use the geometric averaging system as well as the arithmetic averaging system and see if the two methods yield significantly different results.

5. Trade deficit is an inevitable consequence of foreign investment. Comment.

6. While some current account deficit may be a sign of strength, a chronic deficit is necessarily bad. Why?

7. Holding of foreign exchange reserves is a necessary evil. Do you agree? Why?

8. The table below presents some relevant data on a cross section of countries and the world:

Country	*Central government*				*External debt*		*Interest rate spread*	
	Total Expenditure		*Overall budget balance*				*(Lending-Borrowing)*	
	(As per cent of GDP)				*(US $ billion)*		*(Per cent)*	
	1990	*2011*	*1990*	*2011*	*1990*	*2011*	*1990*	*2012*
India	16.3	15.3	–7.6	–3.7	83.6	334.3	—	NA
USA	22.7	26.1	–3.8	–9.3	—	—	—	NA
UK	37.5	44.3	0.6	–7.7	—	—	2.2	NA
Japan	15.3	19.7	–1.5	–8.3	—	—	3.4	0.9
Malaysia	29.3	20.4	–2.0	–4.8	15.3	94.5	1.3	1.8
China	10.1	NA	–1.9	NA	55.3	685.4	0.7	3.0
Australia	23.3	26.1	2.0	–3.7	—	—	4.5	3.1
Nigeria	—	7.2	—	–1.7	33.4	13.1	5.5	8.4
Russian Fed	—	–25.2	—	3.3	59.3	543.0	—	3.6
Germany	26.3	29.7	–1.4	–0.4	—	—	4.5	NA
Brazil	34.9	26.3	–5.8	–2.6	120	404.3	—	28.7
World	25.8	29.2	–2.8	–5.5	—	—	—	—

Note: *1999 data.
Source: World Development Indicators, World Bank, 2013.

(a) Examine the trend in the size of the government and the budget deficits across countries.

(b) Assess the above data in relation to the data in Tables 1.1 (Chapter 1) and 2.5 (Chapter 2), and see if the size of the government, budget (fiscal) deficit, external debt and interest rate spread have any relationship with either economic well being or the economic performance. It may be noted that the total expenditure of the Central Government includes non-repayable current and capital expenditures.

PART 2

BEHAVIOURAL AND TECHNOLOGICAL FUNCTIONS

Economic growth, unemployment, inflation and current account imbalance are the four major concerns of any economy. The levels of the first two are governed by the real national income, of the third by the general price level and of the last by the international transactions on the current account of the balance of payments. The real national income and the general price, in turn, are determined by the interactions of the aggregate demand and aggregate supply functions, just as the quantity and price of an individual commodity are determined by the interactions of the demand for and supply of that commodity. Behind the aggregate demand (AD) are its components, which are private consumption, investment, government expenditure and net exports of goods and services. Each of these components is governed by different sets of variables, and thus, there is a need to understand the functions for all these components. Behind the aggregate supply (AS) are the production function and the demand for and supply of the various factors of production (inputs). The current account balance is governed by the sum of net exports of goods and services, net factor income from abroad and net transfer payments. This section deals with all these behavioural/technological functions.

Before proceeding to dwell on various functions, it is imperative to note that all macroeconomic functions are basically derived from their corresponding microeconomic functions, which are founded on the postulate of the optimum behaviour of individual decision makers. Thereby, an individual households' decision on the division of its disposable personal income into consumption and saving and summation of that over all households yields the macroeconomic consumption function. Similarly, an individual firm's decision on the amount of its investment and the summation of that over all firms gives the macroeconomic investment function. Likewise, an individual firm's demand for labour and the summation of that over firms provides the macroeconomic demand for labour function; and the individual worker's supply of labour function [derived through the maximisation of his/her utility (satisfaction) from leisure and work, subject to the budget (time) constraint] summed over workers gives the macroeconomics labour supply function. This is what is referred to as the microeconomic foundation of macroeconomics. While the production function is a technological function—as it is the technology that determines the required inputs for a given output—all other functions are behavioural—as they are hypothesised on the basis of the behaviour of the decision makers. Behavioural functions, in general, are formulated on the basis of the:

- Observed facts
- Potential causes
- Econometric verification

The potential causes include:

- Scale/source/finance variable
- Opportunity cost
- Yield

Econometrics helps in estimating the functions using the observed facts (data) and the postulates of the theory, and thus, determines the most appropriate function. Also, it helps to segregate the individual effects of the various cause variables on the effect variable.

It is customary in economics to start with the demand side of the market, and accordingly, the consumption (saving) function is discussed first, and this is followed by the investment function, government sector functions, foreign trade functions, money demand and supply functions, production, labour demand and supply functions, in that order. Transformation of these functions into the AD and AS functions is carried out in the next section of the text.

Chapter 5

Consumption Function

Learning Objectives

After reading the chapter you should be able to:

1. Understand the general concept of the consumption expenditure and the meaning of the private (or households) saving, sum of which two equals the disposable personal income.
2. Learn the various factors which affect the consumption spending, the direction of their effects and the rationale behind them
3. Know about the application of the utility theory (indifference curve technique) in allocating disposable income between consumption and saving.
4. Comprehend why some relatively high per capita income countries save less vis-à-vis some low per capita income countries.
5. Get a feel of the data on the share of the consumption spending in GDP and the national saving rate across select major countries over time.

The interaction of aggregate demand and aggregate supply determines the GDP, employment/unemployment and general price. Consumption expenditure is the most dominant component of the aggregate demand in all countries. In India, it currently accounts for 60 per cent of the gross domestic product, which compares well with the world average of 61 per cent. In general, the said fraction has actually fluctuated between around 41 (Singapore) and 72 (USA) per cent of the respective GDP. Barring some consuming countries like USA and thrifty countries like China, relatively poor countries have this share at a relatively higher level and rich countries at a lower level. Thus, countries enjoying a relatively higher consumption share (around 100 per cent) include Afghanistan, El Salvador, Guyana, Liberia, Tajikistan and Zimbabwe, and those with a low share (around 50 per cent or less) include Angola, Bahrain, China, Norway, Singapore, Saudi Arabia, Norway and Sweden. This proves the significance of the consumption function in macroeconomics and the need to understand its behaviour rather carefully.

The disposable personal income is used for consumption and saving. While consumption brings immediate benefits by way of satisfaction of the human needs, saving serves the needs of old age, a rainy day, bequest and charity. Both are useful and, thus, every household has to decide on them on the basis of rational behaviour. Needless to say, what is not consumed from the personal disposable income is saved and vice versa, and thus, given the consumption function, the saving function is available simply by subtracting the consumption function from the disposable personal income. Symbolically, this could be expressed as follows:

$$Y^d = C + S \tag{5.1}$$

now if

$$C = a + bY^d$$

then

$$S = Y^d - C$$
$$= Y^d - a - b\,Y^d$$

$$\Rightarrow \quad S = -a + (1 - b)Y^d$$

where Y^d = disposable personal income
C = consumption by households
S = saving by households
a, b = parameters

Disposable personal income is defined as

$$Y^d = Y - \text{retained profit} - T + TP$$

where Y = national income, T = direct taxes (corporate tax, income tax, etc.) and TP = (direct) transfer payments; government income from departmental and public sector enterprises is ignored for simplicity. The difference between direct taxes and transfer payments ($T - TP$) is often referred as the net direct taxes, and retained profit is the saving by the corporate sector. Thus,

Private sector saving = S + retained profit

In addition, there is saving by the government. In this chapter, we are explaining the personal consumption and thus the relevant income variable is the personal disposable income. To avoid complications, notation Y would be used to denote the personal disposable income in this chapter. Alternatively, one can think of this as the national income if we ignore government income from departmental and public sector enterprises, direct taxes, transfer payments and retained profits.

Components of Consumption

To appreciate the consumption function, it is useful to divide the consumption into the following three categories:

- Non-durable goods
- Durable goods
- Services

Non-durable goods are short-lived goods like all foods, drinks, clothes, lighting, heating and entertainment. All these disappear (or become useless) on consumption, and are hence called non-durables. In contrast, **durable goods** are long-lived consumer goods, which consist of furniture, entertainment equipment, kitchen appliances, washing machines, cars, scooters, air conditioners, jewellery and other such goods. All these have long lives and are consumed gradually (again and again) over time. They are subject to depreciation (wear and tear and obsolescence) and never disappear. Incidentally, note that household expenditure on real estate (land) and housing (residential) are treated as parts of investment, and are therefore not a part of the consumption of durable goods. The last item, which is services, is all nondurable and it consists of haircut, laundry, parleys, transport, banking, insurance, health, education, legal and such other services.

Of the three categories, expenditure on durable goods is the most volatile and that on the non-durable goods the most stable. The former takes place only after the need for the latter is met and thus it goes up during good times and falls during bad periods. The latter being the most essential and belonging to the almost fixed need category, stays stable during all times. Since some services are quite essential while others are partly or fully luxury, the expenditure on them falls between the two. Accordingly, the expenditure on services is only partially pro cyclical. Some people consider the expenditure on durables as a saving/investment. However, in economics, all the above kinds of expenditure are treated as consumption. This is mainly because, as mentioned above, durable consumer goods are consumed over time and the consumed amount (depreciation) is hard to estimate. For example, I have a car, which I have been using (consuming) for the last 7 years. What is the yearly depreciation on it? Is there a good way to measure it? The use of car varies significantly across owners and its price has an upward trend. The same is true for all other durable consumer goods.

Although the relative significance of the various determinants (causes) varies with the kind of the consumption expenditure, it is usual to lump all these into one while analysing the consumption function. Another point to mention here is that while consumption is measured in nominal terms only (as various consumption items, like GDP, are not additive in their physical terms); here it is measured at constant prices or deflated by the price index (CPI) to reflect consumption in real terms. Similarly, income and wealth variables referred to below are in real terms (at constant prices).

Determinants of Consumption

Like any other behavioural variable, consumption expenditure depends on the scale/finance/source variable, and on its yield and opportunity cost, among others. About the appropriate scale variable, there have been significant developments and these will be reviewed shortly. It would suffice to point out here that one or the other kind of income measure serves this purpose. The yield variable is not relevant here as the consumption yields the satisfaction of human needs, which does not warrant measurement. Interest rate denotes the opportunity cost as it reflects the earning on the income not used for consumption (saving).

The most comprehensive consumption theory would include the following factors in the consumption function:

- Income (current, life time average or permanent)
- Wealth (real balance)
- Relative income
- Interest rate (real)
- Credit availability
- Consumers' expectations
- Income/wealth distribution

The rationale for each of these and their relative significance in the various types of consumption expenditure follows.

Income

Income is the major source for financing consumption, and thus, it is a direct determinant of consumption. Also, consumption is the most dominant component of income (from expenditure side) and is therefore a determinant of income. Thus, there is a two-way causation. This is a feedback mechanism, which is found in several other economic variables as well. Further, the literature on consumption function distinguishes between the three kinds of incomes, viz.

- Absolute income
- Life-cycle income
- Permanent income

Accordingly, there are three alternative theories of consumption, one for each income category, and the same are discussed below.

Absolute Income Hypothesis The absolute income hypothesis (AIH) is due to John Maynard Keynes. He was the first to recognise income as the main determinant of consumption. In his 1936 book, *The General Theory of Employment, Interest and Money*, he advanced a behavioural (as opposed to the optimisation) theory wherein consumption has two components, viz., autonomous (C_0) and induced consumption. While the former is a constant, the latter varies directly with the current income (recall that this is personal disposable income) through a linear function, with no influence from any other factor, including the interest rate:

$$C = C_0 + b\,Y \qquad \textbf{(5.2)}$$

$$C_0, b > 0$$

He further stated that due to the, 'fundamental psychological law', the increase in consumption is less than the increase in income:

$$b < 1$$

Under this theory, which is referred to as the **absolute income hypothesis** (AIH), to distinguish it from the others like the relative income and permanent income hypotheses, the marginal propensity to consume (MPC) is a constant (b) while the average propensity to consume (APC) falls as the income increases:

$$\text{MPC} = \frac{\partial C}{\partial Y} = b$$

$$\text{APC} = \frac{C}{Y} = \frac{C_0}{Y} + b$$

and APC tends to MPC as the income tends to infinity. Geometrically, the theory can be described as in Fig. 5.1.

In part (A), the straight line C denotes the consumption function. Its intercept gives the autonomous part of the consumption and its slope, which is less than one, measures the MPC. In part (B), the straight line denotes the MPC. This is horizontal at point 'b', which equals MPC, for the MPC is independent of the level of income. The APC is given by the downward sloping curve leveled as APC. As income increases, the APC tends to approach the MPC.

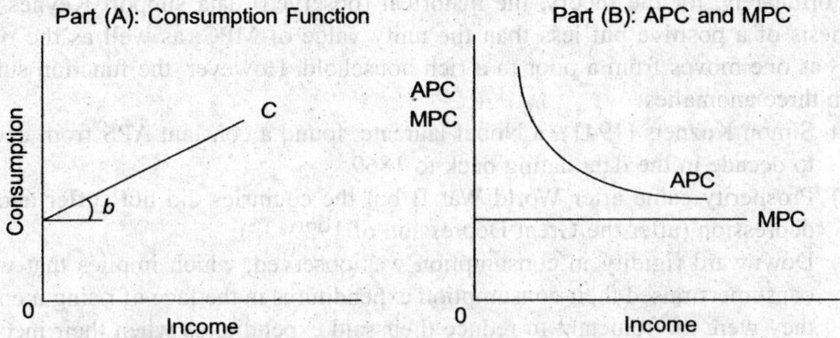

Fig. 5.1 Keynesian Consumption Function

The corollary of the above provides the saving function, and it suggests that the marginal propensity to save (MPS) is a constant (= 1 – *b*) and the average propensity to save (APS) increases as the income increases:

$$S = Y - C$$

$$= Y - C_0 - bY$$

$$\Rightarrow \quad S = -C_0 + (1 - b)Y \qquad \textbf{(5.3)}$$

Thus,

$$\text{MPS} = \frac{\partial S}{\partial Y} = 1 - b$$

$$\text{APS} = -\frac{C_0}{Y} + (1 - b)$$

and APS tends to MPS as the income approaches infinity. It would be easy to see that

$$\text{MPC} + \text{MPS} = 1$$

$$\text{APC} + \text{APS} = 1$$

Function **(5.2)** has two significant implications:

(a) Current consumption depends on current income and thus there is no inter-temporal dependence. In other words, current saving/dis-saving has no bearing on future consumption.

(b) APC can be greater than unity. This means APS can be negative.

According to this theory, as the economy prospers over time, the income goes up and so the saving rate (S/Y = APS) witnesses an upward trend over time. Also, rich people and rich countries have high saving rates in comparison to poor people and poor countries. Therefore, the prosperity leads to high saving rate, which as argued below, leads to stagnation. The latter result arises because as income grows, APS goes up and APC comes down, thereby consumption expenditure falls. The fall in consumption, *ceteris paribus*, suppresses the total expenditure, and thereby, the aggregate demand. The resulting increase in saving does not automatically lead to increased investment and there may not be adequate opportunities for investment. In the absence of sufficient demand, inventory becomes excessive and consequently producers cut their production. The fall in production is tantamount to stagnation. Thus, it is alleged that the Keynes consumption theory implies the **secular stagnation hypothesis**.

Fortunately, for the theory, the historical (observed) data support Keynes' hypothesis of a positive but less than the unity value of MPC, as well as the rising APS as one moves from a poor to a rich household. However, the function suffers from three anomalies:

(a) Simon Kuznets (1941), a Nobel laureate, found a constant APS from decade to decade in the data dating back to 1869.

(b) Prosperity came after World War II but the countries did not suffer another depression (after the Great Depression of 1929–33).

(c) Downward rigidity in consumption was observed, which implies that while consumers raised their consumption expenditures in the face of rising incomes they were too reluctant to reduce their said expenditures when their incomes fell. This is known as the **ratchet effect**.

In addition, the rationality theory suggests that consumption also depends on past and expected future incomes, and thus consumption function is dynamic and not static as postulated by Keynes.

Thus, while the Keynesian hypothesis of a rising APS was found good over the cross-section data (short-run), it was not so over the time-series data (long run); the so-called **consumption puzzle**. This together with the non-validity of the secular stagnation theory and the downward rigidity of consumption, among other factors has led economists to rethink and develop the alternative explanations for consumption spending.

Life Cycle Income Theory Franco Modigliani, another Nobel laureate and his collaborators, Abbert Ando and Richard Brumberg have advanced the **life cycle** theory (LCT) for the consumption function. They borrowed Irving Fisher's idea that consumption depends on the person's lifetime income rather than on the current income alone. According to Fisher, if borrowing and lending were accessible to a person at a given interest rate (which is true in a perfect capital market), then the person could choose any combination of consumption over time, subject to his/her **inter-temporal budget constraint** given by the equality of the discounted value of all consumptions and that of the lifetime income. In a two-period framework, this would mean choosing the values of the present consumption (C_1) and the future consumption (C_2), subject to the budget constraint:

$$C_1 + \frac{C_2}{1+i} = Y_1 + \frac{Y_2}{1+i} \qquad \textbf{(5.4)}$$

where i = interest rate (real) on the borrowing/lending (assumed same on both)

Equation **(5.4)** gives the present value of the total income (wealth) as well as the present value of total consumption. The consumer would have its own preference function such as the following:

$$U = f(C_1, C_2) \qquad \textbf{(5.5)}$$

The rational consumer would choose the values of C_1 and C_2 such that the value of function **(5.5)** is maximized subject to the budget constraint **(5.4)**. This can be explained geometrically using the indifference curve approach, where one draws the budget constraint and a family of the consumer's indifference curves between C_1 and C_2. To get the budget constraint line, let us first get the extreme points. If the consumer's income in each of the first and second periods were ₹10,000 and the interest rate were 10 per cent, the present value of the total income would equal ₹19,091 and the compound value would be ₹21,000. This means the concerned individual could consume a maximum worth of ₹19,091 in the first period (but nothing in the second period) and a maximum worth of ₹21,000 in the second period (but nothing in the first period). For attaining the first position, the individual would borrow in the first period and pay back the loan with interest in the second period. Quite the opposite would have to be done to achieve the second position. Of course, the individual could use any other combination of consumption and borrowing-lending according to the budget constraint. His preference function between the present and future consumptions (indifference curves) would dictate the choice. Diagrammatically, the equilibrium could be explained as in Fig. 5.2.

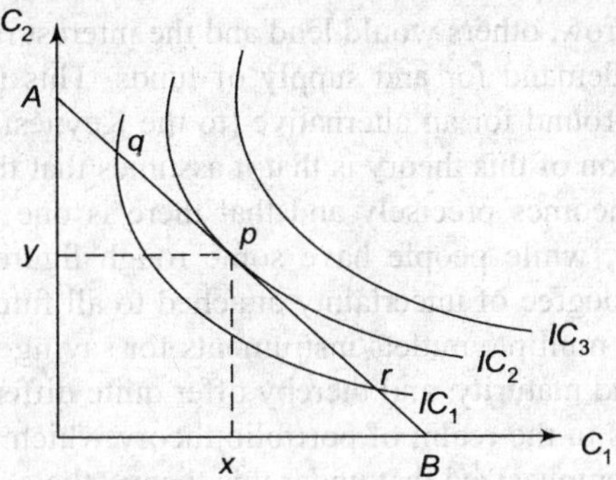

Fig. 5.2 Consumption-Saving Decisions

The linear line *AB*, the counterpart of equation 5.4, denotes the households' inter-temporal budget constraint. Its slope ($OA/OB = 1 + i$), gives the market rate of time preference. The point *A* denotes the maximum possible consumption in the second period, which for the numerical example, equals ₹21,000 and point *B* gives the maximum possible consumption in the first period, which here equals ₹19,091. Its slope at point *B* (= 21,000/19,091= 1.1) gives (1 + interest rate). Various indifference curves (IC_1, IC_2 and IC_3) denote the individual's preference between present and future consumptions or his/her time preference. Note that indifference curves are subjective and they are convex to the origin. This means that the individual's marginal rate of time preference decreases as one moves downward along the curve, i.e. as C_2 decreases and C_1 increases. The various indifference curves are parallel to each other. Obviously, the higher the *IC*, the happier is the consumer. The point of tangency at point *p* gives the optimum choice for the household. While the consumer has the option of choosing the combination at point *q* or that at point *r*, each of these points lies on a lower indifference curve and thus is inferior to the combination at point *p*. Any point to the north-east of point *p* is unattainable due to the budget constraint. Thus, the best choice for the household is to consume the amount *x* in year 1 and amount *y* in year 2, which equals ₹11,000 and ₹8900, respectively. The household in this case borrows ₹1000 in year 1 and repays the loan in year 2 with interest, totaling ₹1100. Other households would choose similarly.

Each household would have its own inter-temporal budget constraint as well as indifference curves. Since incomes vary across households, different households would have different budget constraint. Various households are not alike in their preferences between present and future consumptions. Those who are thrifty (high propensity to save) would have indifference curves that would be steeper around the y-axis and flatter around the x-axis. Quite the opposite would be true for extravagant (impatient/myopic) individuals. In consequence, while the former would tend to save more, the latter would tend to consume more in the current period.

Incidentally, note that the interest rate is determined by borrowing-lending by all persons. It goes up if the demand for borrowing exceeds the supply of lending and vice versa. The theory can easily be extended to more than two periods. The theory suggests that consumers are free to borrow or lend and thus they need not decide on their current consumption levels on the basis of current income levels alone. While some would borrow, others would lend and the interest rate would be so determined as to clear the demand for and supply of funds. This is quite appealing and thus became a background for an alternative (to the Keynesian) theory of consumption. A major limitation of this theory is that it assumes that the person/household knows his/her future incomes precisely and that there is one and only one interest rate. Needless to say, while people have some rough figures of their future incomes, there is a great degree of uncertainty attached to all future values. Also, in the real world, there are multiple outlets/instruments for saving which differ with regard to liquidity, risk and maturity, and thereby offer quite different rates of return/interest. The subject falls in the realm of portfolio theory which is beyond the scope of this text. It must be emphasized that under this theory, the current consumption depends not only on the current income but also on the past and future incomes, and also on the interest rate and the consumers' preference function between the present and future consumptions (i.e. on time preference).

Taking a clue from the above theory, Modigliani and others postulated that consumers have a smooth consumption even if the income fluctuates during their lifetime. Income is usually low on the first job/occupation and then it rises until retirement, when it drops substantially. However, consumption and standard of living usually follow a smooth path. It may rise as the income grows but does not decline as the income falls (ratchet effect). This is made possible through borrowing, when the income falls and savings when the income goes up. Therefore, households spend more on consumption than they earn when their incomes are below the average and less on consumption than incomes when their incomes are above the corresponding average. Thus, while the young tend to borrow, the middle-aged tend to save and retirees live off their savings. The large up and down spikes in income generate only modest consumption responses. To explain this further, consider an illustration. Suppose a person starts working when he is 25 years old, works until the age of 65, earns an average annual income of ₹200,000 and expects to die when he is 75 years old. Then by the LCT, his consumption in any year between the ages of 25-75 years (his consumption between the ages of 0-25 is determined by his parents/guardian) would be:

$$₹\frac{65-25}{75-25}(200{,}000) = ₹0.8\ (200{,}000) = ₹160{,}000/\text{year}$$

In this example, the person has uniform income throughout his working career and zero income after the retirement. However, this need not always be the case. All that this theory indicates is that the consumer divides his/her lifetime income into his/her lifetime consumption, uniformly. Thus, if the above person earns, say, ₹150,000 annually when he is 25-35 years, ₹200,000 annually when he is 35-50 years and ₹300,000 annually when he is 50-65 years, his annual consumption would be:

$$₹\frac{65-25}{75-25}\left[\frac{1,50,000\times10+2,00,000\times15+3,00,000\times15}{10+15+15}\right] = ₹0.8\ [225,000]$$

$$= ₹180,000$$

Thus, though the person's income fluctuates, his consumption is held constant through his lifetime. This is achieved through borrowing during the first ten years, saving during the next 30 years and then using the past savings during the retirement years. Real life examples are even more complicated than those given above. However, the approach is the same. In essence, there are periods when incomes are low and when they are high. Also consumption, instead of remaining uniform through the lifetime, may rise over time, though it rarely falls. To generalise this theory, let us resort to the graph in Fig. 5.3.

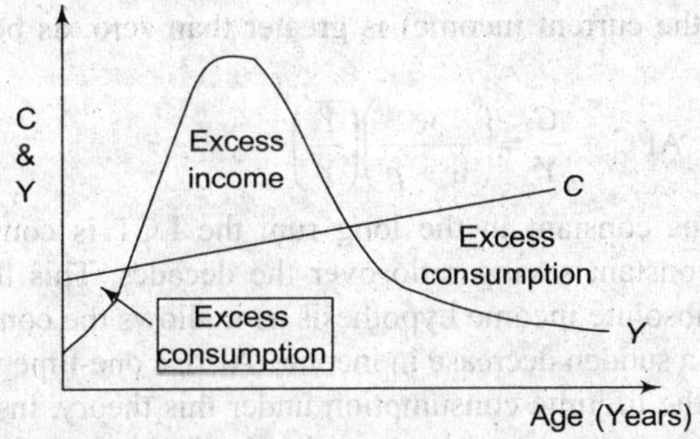

Fig. 5.3 Life Cycle Theory Consumption Function

In Fig. 5.3, the horizontal axis denotes the age (in years) of the consumer and the vertical axis his/her income and consumption. The origin point is at the age when the concerned consumer becomes independent with regard to his/her consumption decision. The bell (hump)-shaped curve Y denotes the income and the upward sloping line C denotes the consumption over the lifetime. The positive gap between Y and C gives the saving/lending and the negative gap between the two, the lack of saving/borrowing at different ages. Thus, though the representative household has a fluctuating income, the consumer enjoys steady consumption throughout his/her lifetime. He/she borrows while young and when retired, and lends during the prime part of his/her life. Also, consumers borrow to maintain their consumption levels in the face of falling incomes. Incidentally, note the area of the curve Y above the line C (marked as excess income) and that below the said line (marked as excess consumption) differ only by the interest differential on payments towards borrowings and the earnings on lending, if any. Since generally people are rich in their prime age, they enjoy a relatively high saving rate. In contrast, the young and retirees are poor and so have low saving rates. It then follows that the greater the proportion of senior peoples in the population, the lesser the saving rate in the country, and vice versa.

Going back to the above simple (first) numerical example and translating the same in algebra, we have the following consumption function under the LCT:

$$C = \left(\frac{w}{w+p}\right)\bar{Y} \qquad \textbf{(5.6)}$$

where, w = number of working years

p = number of post retirement years of living

$\bar{Y}$ = average annual income during the working period

Alternatively, the function could be written as:

$$C = \frac{1}{w+p}(\Sigma Y)$$

where, ΣY = total lifetime income

As in the Keynesian theory, under the LCT:

$$\text{MPC} = \left(\frac{w}{w+p}\right)\left(\frac{\partial \bar{Y}}{\partial Y}\right) < 1$$

and it (MPC out of the current income) is greater than zero, as both w and p are non-negative.

Further $$\text{APC} = \frac{C}{Y} = \left(\frac{w}{w+p}\right)\left(\frac{\bar{Y}}{Y}\right)$$

Since $\bar{Y}/Y$ remains constant in the long run, the LCT is consistent with the historical fact of a constant saving ratio over the decades. This theory is an improvement over the absolute income hypothesis as it allows the consumption not to decline in the face of a sudden decrease in income. Also, a one-time windfall income would be used over the lifetime consumption under this theory, instead of it being used for that period's consumption alone as in the absolute income hypothesis. Thus, if the person in the above example gets an award of ₹50,000, when he is 50 years, his annual consumption would increase by rupees

$$\frac{50{,}000}{75-25} = 1{,}000$$

and not that the consumption in the year when he is 50 years would go up by ₹40,000, if his MPC = 0.8. In contrast, instead of the one-time award of ₹50,000 if he gets a promotion when he is 50 years and his salary goes up by ₹50,000 each year, his consumption each year would go up by rupees

$$\frac{50{,}000 \times 10}{75-25} = 10{,}000$$

Thus, while there could be spikes in income, there is no such thing in consumption. For this reason, the theory belongs to the smoothing **theory of consumption** group. Incidentally, note that for simplicity, the interest rate has been implicitly assumed to be zero in the above numerical example.

Under the LCT, consumption is affected by the wealth of the consumer as well. The consumer may inherit some wealth from his parents, which may appreciate/depreciate due to capital gain/loss and he may like to leave a bequest for his children. The net (difference) of these he would consume during his lifetime. Thus, if the net wealth were ₹1,00,000, he could have had an additional consumption of ₹2,000[1,00,000/75-25] each year of his adult life. Thus, if some of the wealth were in the form of company stocks annual consumption would fluctuate with the ups and downs of the stock market. Incorporating wealth (W), the LCT consumption function becomes

$$C = \frac{1}{w+p}(W) + \frac{w}{w+p}\,\bar{Y} \tag{5.7}$$

and the *APC* comes to

$$APC = \frac{1}{w+p}\left(\frac{W}{Y}\right) + \frac{w}{w+p}\left(\frac{\bar{Y}}{Y}\right)$$

The consumption function (Equation 5.7) contains the life cycle theory of consumption. The main feature of this is that consumption depends positively on the lifetime average income rather than on the current income as in the Keynesian AIH. In addition, the new theory recognises the positive role of wealth in consumption as well. The theory marks an improvement over the AIH in explaining past behaviour. To see this, we need to analyse the average propensity to consume. Since neither the wealth-income ratio nor the lifetime average income to the current income ratio varies from person to person or from year to year, we must note through the APC equation above that a high income corresponds to a low APC when looking at the data across individuals or over a short period of time. However, since the wealth and income grow together (*W*/*Y* is a constant) and the average to current income remains invariant over a long period of time, the APC is constant in the long run. Thus, the LCT in this form is consistent with the historical fact of a variable APC across the households and a constant APC over the long run. Further, since APC is constant in the long run, it follows that APS is constant as well, and this rules out the stagnation hypothesis of the absolute income theory. Consequently, the life cycle theory is free from both the shortcomings of the Keynesian theory. However, the theory suffers from the following limitations:

(a) Future incomes are unknown and thus the lifetime average income is uncertain.

(b) Capital market is not quite perfect, and so borrowing and appropriate use of saving cannot be assumed. In other words, the theory's assumption of liquidity may not hold good. If the liquidity constraint is binding, the individual may be forced to consume less than otherwise. For example, if the individual can not borrow at all but can lend, he (under the two period case) would face an additional constraint $C_1 \leq Y_1$ and his inter-temporal budget constraint would become vertical at $C_1 = Y_1$. Even if the liquidity constraint is not binding, the fact that it may bind in future restricts current consumption.

(c) The bequest motive is quite prevalent particularly in the primitive societies and this renders the life cycle theory less reliable.

Permanent Income Hypothesis The LCT is a forward-looking expectations advance', as it requires the consumer to form expectations about his/her lifetime income to decide on the consumption expenditure. Yet another forward-looking consumption theory is due to Milton Friedman (1957), another Nobel laureate, who advanced the Permanent Income Hypothesis (PIH). The theory could be expressed in the following three equations:

$$C = k\,Y^P \tag{5.8}$$

$$Y = Y^T + Y^P \tag{5.9}$$

$$Y^P = \alpha Y_{-1} + (1 - \alpha)\,Y^P_{-1} \tag{5.10}$$

where, Y^P = permanent income

Y^T = transitory income

k and α are parameters such that $0 < k,\ \alpha < 1$

Milton Friedman divides income into two parts, which are permanent and transitory (equation **5.9**). Under his theory, consumption is governed by the permanent income (equation **5.8**) and not by the current or the lifetime average income as in the AIH and LCT, respectively. Though the permanent income is unobserved, Friedman has suggested an approach by which its magnitude could be derived, as the weighted average of the current and past incomes, weight declining geometrically. Thus,

$$Y^P = \alpha Y + \alpha(1 - \alpha)Y_{-1} + \alpha(1 - \alpha)^2\,Y_{-2} + \cdots$$

and so,

$$(1 - \alpha)\,Y^P_{-1} = \alpha(1 - \alpha)Y_{-1} + \alpha(1 - \alpha)^2\,Y_{-2} + \cdots$$

Subtracting the second equation from the first equation yields equation **(5.10)**, given above. This is known as Koyck's transformation, which is very popular in economics/econometrics. Alternatively, permanent income may be defined as the annuity (constant income stream) of the life-time income. In terms of the Fisher model, a permanent increase in income is an increase in both the current and future incomes, where as a transitory increase in income is an increase in current income alone with no change in future incomes. Accordingly, a permanent one-unit increase in income has a greater impact on life time income than a temporary increase in the same amount.

Under the PIH,

$$APC = k(Y^P/Y)$$

$$= \text{constant, if } Y^P/Y \text{ is a constant.}$$

In the long run, Y^P/Y is a constant, and hence, the theory is consistent with a constant APC and, thereby, has a constant saving rate, as found in the long-term historical data. Also, like in the Keynes AIH, here the rich have higher saving ratios than the poor do. This is so because rich people have a positive transitory income (all of which goes into savings) through such sources as bonuses to executives, extra reward to movie stars on their popular films or to athletes on their performances and so on. In contrast, poor people have a negative transitory income (leading to lack of savings) as they may be farmers whose crops were damaged by a bad monsoon or employees who were laid off their jobs, etc. Similarly, transitory incomes are positive during prosperity and negative during recessions. Therefore, the saving ratios are high during the boom period and low during the depression. As would be seen through the APC function above, when the transitory income is positive, $Y > Y^P$ and $Y^P/Y < 1$; accordingly APC $< k$, and vice-versa. Thus, the permanent income theory is consistent with the historical facts of a constant long term APC or APS and a variable APC or APS across cross sections of households and during the short term. Accordingly, like the life cycle theory, it is free from the limitations of the absolute income hypothesis.

The permanent income theory is quite close to the life cycle theory and, in fact, the distinction between the two is disappearing. Nevertheless, a technical point of difference is seen in that while the former requires the past incomes, which are known, the latter needs the future income, which is unknown. Thus, the PIH removes the uncertainty part of the limitations of the LCT. Incidentally, note that while Friedman did provide a method to compute the permanent income, the said method can at the most be an approximate one only. This is because the future is always uncertain and so are future incomes. Thus, if future incomes differ drastically from past incomes, the Friedman method would give a very wrong result. Further, the permanent income is dynamic. This is because, for example, tomorrow is future today, and it would become current tomorrow and past the day after. Thus, if future incomes keep changing, the permanent incomes would keep changing over time. Also, it is not always easy to decide as to which part of the income is current and which is transitory. We know this for a professor, his salary is a permanent income but what part of his consulting income is permanent is hard to decide. So is the case of a sales person, who receives a commission over and above his salary, and also of a senior manager who may get stock options besides the salary. This renders the PIH an incomplete theory of consumption. Yet another distinction between the two theories is that while LCT assumes finite life, PYH assumes infinite life span.

To conclude this part, under all the above hypotheses, the current income is a determinant of the current consumption, which in some theories depends on the past and/or expected future incomes as well. While the LCT and PIH are attractive in view of their emphasis on the smoothness of consumption over time, the AIH is useful as it lays emphasis on the sensitivity of the current consumption to the current income. The validity of the LCT and PIH depends on the existence of perfect capital market, i.e. no borrowing or liquidity constraint. Under these theories, a temporary cut in taxation or increase in transfer payments during recession may fail to boost current consumption, for the increase in disposable income will be transitory, and thereby reduce the force of stabilization policies.

All these three theories ignore uncertainty, which is a fact of life. To incorporate uncertainty in the consumption theory, we have Hall's consumption function (vide Robert Hall, Journal of Political Economy, December 1978). This is a modern version of the LCT and PIH, which emphasises the link between income uncertainty and changes in consumption. It takes a formal approach of maximising the utility from consumption in all years, subject to the lifetime income constraint and uses the rational expectations theory to project expected future incomes. The approach is too complicated to dwell on in this intermediate text. Suffice to mention here that ultimately it leads to the famous Hall's **random walk model** under which the consumption next year simply equals the current year consumption plus a random term, which could take either a positive or a negative value and it is not predictable. Thus, current consumption is a good predictor of the next period's consumption. Under the random walk model, information is very quickly incorporated into income, prices, etc., and also in economic actors' decisions.

An implication of the later theories of consumption (LCT, PIH, Hall's theory) is that they reduce the effectiveness of stabilization policies. For example, a temporary cut in taxation or an increase in transfer payments to cure recession may fail to boost consumption, for the increase in disposable income will be transitory! Also, a reduction in current taxation financed by borrowing will fail to stimulate consumption.

Consumers have some sets of thumb rules, which they usually use as guide in making their consumption decisions. Three of these are as follows:

(a) Individuals usually find it worthwhile to spend their current income fully or partly but resort to using assets only under exceptional circumstances.

(b) Households are unwilling to risk the very low consumption that would occur if they were in debt or future incomes were low. This follows from the law of diminishing marginal utility, which indicates that the said utility approaches infinity as consumption gets smaller and smaller. The guideline thus suggests that consumption rarely exceeds current income in prudent households.

(c) Welfare programmes provide insurance against very low levels of consumption. This discourages savings of those who could fall into the trap and partly explains the poor saving rates in most of Europe, the United States and so on.

The above discussion fully justifies the role of income in consumption decisions.

Wealth

Wealth is a stock of the net physical and financial assets owned by the consumer and it could also serve as a source of finance for consumption, among other uses. However, it is a source that, if used, gets exhausted fast, leaving nothing to fall back on, particularly in difficult times. For this reason, people rarely use wealth for consumption. Though the income from wealth does add to a person's total income; the latter governs his/her consumption expenditure. Also, ups and downs in the property/stocks/durables' market bring ups and downs in the nominal values of wealth and these do influence the consumption. Thus, during the stock market booms, like the ones during the early and late 1990s, 2003, 2008, and so on, which created a lot of wealth for households, consumption went up. Similarly, the stock market crash of 1929 and subsequent bank failures eroded the wealth of the consumers, and accordingly consumption fell and that, inter alia, led to the Great Depression. Even the South-East Asian crisis of the 1997–98 and the Great Recession of 2007–09 seem to have been triggered by a fall in the stock and property prices. Recall that the role of wealth in consumption was recognised even by the life cycle hypothesis.

A C Pigou, a prominent neoclassical economist, had drawn our attention to the significance of real money balances with households in their consumption expenditure. As product prices fall and consequently real money balances rise, consumers get wealthier and consume more. Similarly, a relative rise in the stock's prices or real estates' price gives a boost to the nominal and real wealth of those who own them, and in consequence, they tend to increase their consumption expenditure. Quite the opposite holds good when the general price rises or stock/property prices fall, for both of them are wealth destructive for the households.

Relative Income

Two types of relative income may exert influence on consumption expenditure:

- Current income relative to the past peak income
- Own income relative to the average income in the neighbourhood/nation

Consumption determines the standard of living and by habit people enjoy raising their standard but hate letting it slide downwards. This implies a somewhat asymmetric behaviour of consumers. When their incomes rise, they raise their consumption but they refuse to reduce their consumption in the face of falling incomes. This behaviour suggests that the ratio of the household's current income to its peak income achieved in the past acts as an additional determinant of its current consumption. If this ratio falls, *ceteris paribus*, the current consumption goes up, and *vice versa*. Algebraically, this can be expressed as follows:

$$C = a + bY - cY/Y_{mp} \quad \textbf{(5.11)}$$

where a, b and c are positive parameters, and Y_m is the maximum past income of the concerned consumer. To get the expression for the average propensity to consume, we divide both sides of the above equation by Y:

$$C/Y = a(1/Y) + b - c(1/Y_{mp}) \quad \textbf{(5.12)}$$

The equation suggests that the APC varies positively with the past peak income of the concerned consumer. Recall that $S/Y = 1 - C/Y$, and substituting this in the above equation gives,

$$S/Y = (1 - b) - a\,(1/Y) + c\,(1/Y_{mp}) \quad \textbf{(5.13)}$$

The above equation indicates that the saving rate is a negative function of the peak income. Thus, if income continues to rise, the ratio Y/Y_{mp} goes up and thereby consumption falls and saving increase. Quite the opposite holds good when income tends to fall.

Summing the consumption function over all households would give the macro consumption function, which would have the relative income as an additional argument. The algebra is complicated due to the aggregation problem and so it is avoided here. However, as would be evident from equation (5.13) above that the theory will make the nation's saving ratio to rise slower than the otherwise during the prosperity and to fall slower than otherwise during the depression. This feature will help explain why prosperity does not lead to recession (stagnation hypothesis), which was seen as a weakness of the Keynesian theory.

It is well known that if a person's neighbour has a car and he does not have one, his children will persuade him to buy one. This is called the **bandwagon effect** in economics. Thus, to some extent there is interdependence of consumption among different households. Recognition of this gives the ratio of one's own income to the average income of other households in the vicinity/country as an additional determinant of one's consumption. The algebra would be similar to that in equations (5.11) to (5.13) above, with the only difference being the average vicinity/country income instead of the maximum past income. The higher this ratio, *ceteris paribus*, the lower the consumption and vice versa. Summing the various consumers' consumption function would yield the macro consumption function. The latter would have relative income as an additional determinant of national consumption. This would also refute the stagnation hypothesis and thereby rationalise the constancy of the saving rate in the long run.

James Duesenberry (1944) hypothesised the role of relative income in consumption and through this he was able to explain the stability of the saving rate.

Interest Rate

Irving Fisher's theory dominated classical thinking about the consumption function. For them, the interest rate (real) was the reward for saving, and the opportunity cost of consumption—note that it is the real and not the nominal rate that is relevant here. Accordingly, an increase in interest rate would increase saving and reduce consumption. Not only this, classical economists considered interest rate as the primary (sole) determinant of consumption or saving. Furthermore, as will be explained in the macroeconomic models later, the classical economists gave interest rate the role of bringing equilibrium between saving and investment, and thereby, in the product market too.

The above theory suggesting a positive relationship between real interest rate and saving is flawed. As in the consumer demand theory of microeconomics, a change in the interest rate affects savings (and hence consumption) through two sources, which are:

- Income effect
- Substitution effect

Under the former, as the interest rate goes up, the income of the creditor (lender) goes up while that of the debtor (borrower) goes down. Recognising the fact that both consumption and savings are normal (superior) goods, will cause the creditor's consumption and saving to increase while that of the debtor's to decrease. Thus, through the income effect, while the consumption and saving of the creditor will increase, those of the debtor will decline when the interest rate goes up. Quite the opposite would happen in the event of a fall in the interest rate.

Under the substitution effect, an increase in interest rate will make savings more attractive, and therefore, hamper consumption of all the creditors as well as debtors. The two effects do not always work in the same direction. For the creditors, the two effects reinforce each other for saving but they work in the opposite direction for consumption. Quite the opposite is true for debtors. This can be summarized as follows:

Effects of Increase in Interest Rate on Saving and Consumption

	Saving		*Consumption*	
	Creditor	*Debtor*	*Creditor*	*Debtor*
Income effect	Increase	Decrease	Increase	Decrease
Substitution effect	Increase	Increase	Decrease	Decrease
Total effect	Increase	?	?	Decrease

Therefore, while an increase in the interest rate unambiguously reduces the consumption of the debtors, it may either increase or decrease (or even leave unaffected, if the two effects cancel out exactly) the consumption of the creditors. Its effect on savings is positive for creditors and ambiguous for debtors. The private sector in most countries is a net creditor. Thus, the effect of the interest rate on the private consumption is ambiguous in theory. This has prompted economists to go for empirical findings on this matter. However, such findings are also weak.

The relationship between the interest rate and consumption/saving can also be examined through geometry using the Fisherian framework on Fig. 5.2. A change in the interest rate would change the inter-temporal budget constraint. If the interest rate goes up, the said constraint would rotate through the point where $C_1 = Y_1$ and $C_2 = Y_2$ in a clock-wise direction, making the constraint steeper than before. This is shown in Fig. 5.4.

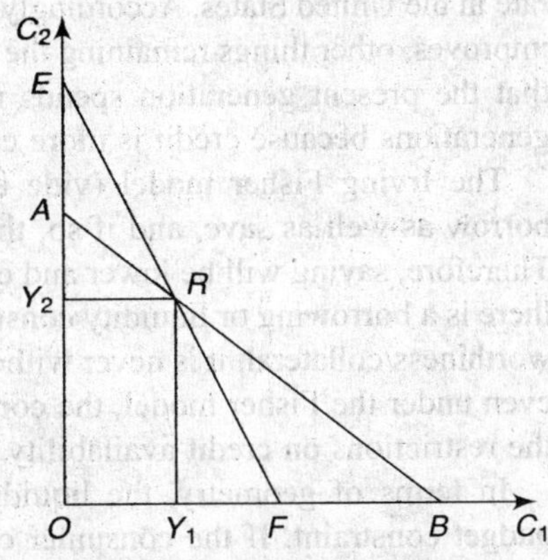

Fig. 5.4 Budget Constraints

The initial constraint is shown by line *AB*. As the interest goes up, the constraint changes to line *EF*. If the interest rate goes down the constraint would rotate again through the same point but in an anti-clock-wise direction, making it flatter than before. This so happens because an increase (decrease) in the interest rate would reduce (increase) the discounted value of Y_2 and thereby of the maximum possible consumption in the first period, increase (decrease) the compounded value of Y_1, thereby of the maximum possible consumption in the second period, and would be of no consequence if the individual consumer neither borrows nor lends. Depending upon the individual's indifference curves, the new equilibrium could be at more, less or even at the same consumption/saving levels. This rationalizes interest rate as a potential determinant of consumption and saving.

There is yet another view on the relationship between consumption/saving and interest rate. This is through the role of target savers. **Target savers** are defined as persons who save in order to earn a fixed income from their savings. Such persons may include retirees and widows who depend largely on the income from their savings for their livelihood. For such persons, as the interest rate goes up, the target saving amount goes down, and vice versa. Thus, these persons would save less when the interest rate is high and more when the said rate is low. Consequently, the effect of the interest rate on savings is negative for such persons.

Due to the above conflicting theories and the weak empirical findings, the interest rate is considered a weak or irrelevant determinant of consumption (and saving). Recall that Keynes did not even consider interest rate as an important determinant of consumption expenditure. Given this, it is no wonder that different groups of people talk differently about the consequences of the current low real interest rates on the saving rate.

Credit Availability/Liquidity Constraint

Households save partly for contingencies (rainy days) and partly for the old age and bequests. To the extent they save for rainy days, saving depends negatively on the ease with which credit is available (liquidity constraint). In fact, the easier availability of finance in the United States in contrast to Japan and other high saving rate countries is considered as one of the factors responsible for the relatively low saving rate in the United States. Accordingly, consumption increases as the credit availability improves, other things remaining the same, and vice versa. Thus, many people argue that the present generation spends relatively more on consumption than the past generations because credit is more easily available today than perhaps ever before.

The Irving Fisher model (vide equation 5.4) assumes that the consumer can borrow as well as save, and if so, the households need not save for contingencies. Therefore, saving will be lower and consumption higher under this model than when there is a borrowing or liquidity constraint. However, since borrowing requires credit worthiness/collateral, it is never without a constraint even in the United States. Thus, even under the Fisher model, the consumption expenditure is adversely affected by the restrictions on credit availability.

In terms of geometry, the liquidity constraint would affect the inter-temporal budget constraint. If the consumer can not borrow but lend, then his/her liquidity constraint would be the same up to the point where $C_1 = Y_1$ and would become vertical at this point ($C_1 = Y_1$). In Fig. 5.4, at the initial interest rate, the relevant budget constraint under the 'lending but no borrowing' constraint would be given by the curve ARY_1. This would affect the consumer's allocation between consumption and saving only if his/her equilibrium with no liquidity constraint were on that part of the then inter-temporal budget constraint which is no longer available. Thus, the liquidity constraint would be binding if the consumer's optimum position required borrowing in the first period.

Consumers' Expectations

While some consumption is essential, the more of it is merely desirable. In particular, the consumption of most durable goods falls in the latter category. Purchase of these goods is undertaken, inter alia, when the consumer expects his income to rise and/or the prices of those goods to go up in the future. Quite the opposite is the case when his/her expectations are just the reverse. This is easy to understand and calls for no explanation. Even the consumption of non-durable goods and services, to some extent, is governed by the consumer's expectations. We see MBA students spend beyond their income constraints on non-durables like clothing, transportation and outings and this is primarily because their expected future incomes are high. This factor is partly covered in the life cycle and permanent income theories. In general, expectations vary from consumer to consumer, and if so, the variable is of little significance in a macro-function. Nevertheless, there are situations, like the one during the Great Depression, when almost all the persons have identical expectations. Needless to say, under condition of uniform expectations, the expectations play a dominant role in macro-consumption decisions. Many economists argue that the pessimistic expectations, accompanied with uncertainty, were responsible for the fall in consumption as well as investment expenditure during the early 1930s, which led to that all time worst depression in the world.

Income/Wealth Distribution

Since the marginal (and average) propensity to consume is higher for low-income people than for the high-income people, the income distribution across households in a country affects that country's total consumption expenditure. In consequence, the more equal the income distribution, *ceteris paribus*, the higher the total consumption, and vice versa. Since the progressive income tax system, the social security system and the minimum wage regulations, among others, tend to favour the poor against the rich, all such regulations exert a positive influence on the macro consumption. Some of these provide yet another reason as to why saving rates are low in Europe, the United States and other nations.

Incidentally, recall that the macro consumption function is obtained through the summation of micro consumption functions of various households in the country. The aggregation theory, dealt with briefly in Chapter 1, suggests that if income distribution undergoes a significant change in favour of rich people, an increase in the national income could lead to a decline in the national consumption even if the marginal propensities to consume were positive for all households (vide Chapter 1, section 1.4). Needless to say, this is true only in an extreme situation, which is highly unlikely to arise. However, the message is clear, that is, income distribution across households has a bearing on the national consumption.

This completes the list of the determinants of consumption. However, it must be noted that since human behaviour is sometimes random, no list can be exhaustive. Besides, customs, traditions, habits and emotions often dictate consumption but these factors are not measurable and are hence ignored. Even demographic factors (age profile of the population) exert some influence on macro consumption/saving.

Consumption Function

Collecting all the above hypotheses together yields the following consumption function:

$$C = f\left[Y, Ys \text{ (past)}, Y_s \text{ (future)}, W, \frac{Y}{Y_{mp}}, i, CA, CE, IWD, u\right] \qquad \textbf{(5.14)}$$

$$f_1, f_2, f_3, f_4, f_7 > 0 > f_5, f_9$$

$$f_6, f_8, f_{10} \gtreqless 0$$

where, C = personal consumption

Y's = personal disposable incomes (current, past and expected future)

Y_{mp} = maximum past personal disposable income

W = wealth

i = interest rate (real)

CA = ease of credit availability/liquidity

CE = consumers' expectations

IWD = inequality in income/wealth distribution

u = unknown factors

f_i = partial derivative of function f with respect to the ith factor.

In general, the current income would be a major determinant, and thus, would have a larger coefficient than any other income (past or future) variable. The corresponding saving function will have the same arguments but in the reverse relationships, barring the income and wealth variables. While income/wealth enjoy a positive causal relationship both with the consumption and saving, the interest rate, liquidity constraint, consumers' expectations and the income/wealth inequality exert differential directional effects on consumption and saving.

Conclusion

The various consumption function hypotheses suggest that the current measured income is the most dominant determinant of the current consumption. Past income levels also affect the consumption, as consumption habits and the standard of living are somewhat irreversible. Even future expected income influences current consumption through the capital market which allows borrowing and lending, and the desire to smoothen consumption inter-temporarily. The classical theory, which had assigned a dominant role to the interest rate, has been questioned through the principle of optimisation. A change in the interest rate affects consumption and saving through the so-called, income and substitution effects, which do not always work in the same direction, thus, producing an ambiguous relationship. The credit availability, consumers' expectations about prices of durable consumer goods and income distribution are the other factors causing fluctuations in consumption/saving.

The relatively low saving rates in countries like the United States and United Kingdom, as well as in Europe, in comparison to those in the South-East Asian countries, Japan and China are explained through the differences in the per capita income, cost and easiness with which the credit is available, the social security provisions, the minimum wage regulations, demographic profile, taxation system, culture (attitude towards bequest), political stability, fiscal deficits, among other factors. Also, the saving rate tends to be low in countries with frequent wars, revolutions, coups and poor political institutions like corruption. Of course, each of these factors does not always tend to support the differences in the saving rate across countries but on the whole they provide a good explanation. For example, in spite of the high per capita income, the saving rate is low in USA because its people practice consumerism, they have fairly good social security, loans are easily and cheaply available, its population is aging and the country runs large fiscal deficits and so on. If one looks at United States data, he/she would discover that there is hardly any households' saving in the country. The readily available 1998 United States data suggests that, of the gross saving rate of 18.8 per cent, 13 per cent came from the business (retained earnings), 3 per cent from the government and only the remaining 2.8 per cent from households. In contrast, Indian data would reveal that about two-thirds of the country's saving comes from the household sector. As a post script, it must be emphasized that the saving rate in India, which had remained about stagnant for over a decade, had gone up remarkably from 23.5 per cent in 2001-02 to 36.8 per cent in 2007-08, and then declined to 30.8 per cent in 2011-12 (vide Economic Survey, 2012-13). The share of the household, private corporate and public sector in 30.8 per cent stood at 22.3,7.2 and 1.3 per cent, respectively.

Keywords

Aggregate demand-Aggregate supply, Durable-Non durable goods, Keynesian theory of consumption; Absolute income -Life cycle-Permanent income hypothesis; Smoothing theory of consumption; MPC-APC; MPS-APS; Secular stagnation hypothesis; Ratchet effect; Consumption puzzle; Inter-temporal budget constraint; Indifference curve; Hall's function; Random walk model; Relative income; Bandwagon effect; Income-Substitution effect; Target savers; Liquidity constraint; Consumers' expectations; Income/wealth distribution; Classical theory of consumption; Demographic profile; Consumption function.

REFERENCES

1. Duesenberry James S, *Theory of Consumer Behaviour* (Cambridge: Harvard University Press, 1944).
2. Fisher Irving, *Theory of Interest* (New York, 1930).
3. Friedman Milton, *A Theory of the Consumption Function* (New Jersey, Princeton University Press, 1957).
4. Keynes John Maynard, *The General Theory of Employment, Interest and Money* (London: Macmillan, 1936).
5. Koyck L M, *Distributed Lags and Investment Analysis* (Amsterdam: North-Holland Publishing Company, 1954).
6. Kuznets Simon, *National Income and its Composition* (New York, 1941).
7. Modigliani Franco, Abbert Ando, R E Brumberg, 'Utility Analysis and the Consumption Function', in *Post-Keynesian Economics* ed., KK Kurihara (New Brunswick, New Jersey: Rutgers University Press, 1954).
8. Pigou A C, 'The Value of Money', *Quarterly Journal of Economics*, Vol. 37, pp. 1917-18.

REVIEW QUESTIONS

1. The saving rate varies significantly across households in a country as well as across countries in the world, and yet it is sluggish over time. Why?

2. Govind has estimated the following consumption function for the Wonderland economy:

$$C = 50 + 0.75\,Y - 8.5\frac{Y}{Y_{mp}} - 0.50\,i$$

$$R^2 = 0.85$$

where the variables have the same notations as in the chapter, the interest rate is measured as a percentage and all the other variables are in billions of the currency of Wonderland. The current values of the determinants of consumption are

$$Y = 500,\ Y_{mp} = 540 \text{ and } i = 11$$

(a) What is the autonomous consumption?

(b) Determine the values of the average and marginal propensities to consume.

(c) Derive the expression for the saving function.

(d) Comment on the reliability of the estimated function.

3. The table below gives the data on the private (household final) consumption expenditure as a percentage of the gross domestic product and on the gross saving rate for selected countries, for 1980, 1990 and 2012:

(Percentages)

Country	*Private consumption (% of GDP)*			*Gross saving rate*		
	1980	*1990*	*2012*	*1980*	*1990*	*2012*
India	73	66	60	17	22	31
Australia	59	59	54	24	18	25
Brazil	70	59	62	21	19	15
China	51	50	36	35	39	49
France	59	55	58	23	20	18
Germany	NA	55	58	NA	23	24
Japan	59	53	61	31	34	22
Korea (Rep.)	64	53	54	24	37	31
Malaysia	51	52	49	33	30	32
Nigeria	56	56	NA	31	19	NA
Russian Fed	62	49	48	NA	36	30
Singapore	52	47	41	38	45	46
UK	59	63	66	19	15	11
USA	64	67	72	19	15	12
World	59	60	61	25	22	21

Source: World Development Indicators, World Bank, various issues including 2013

(a) Which consumption-income hypothesis, if any, is consistent with the above data? Why?

(b) Account for the variations in consumption and savings rates over time and across countries.

Note that the savings rate includes all savings in the respective country. Thus, it consists of savings by households, businesses and governments. In India, the household sector is a major contributor to savings while in United States that position is taken by the business sector.

4. According to the life cycle theory, while the young tend to borrow, working people save and retirees live off their savings. If so, what impact will the changing age structure towards older people of the Indian population have on the aggregate saving rate in the country? What will the impact be of the increase in the retirement age?

5. Temporary cuts in tax rates have much smaller effects on consumption and saving than do the permanent ones. Do you agree? Why?

6. Saving is both a private as well as a social virtue. Comment.

7. Jagdish Bhagwati wrote "Saving is a sin, consumption is virtue". Do you agree? Why or why not?

8. While explaining the 2003 Bill to cut taxes, US President George Bush said "When people have more money, they can spend it on goods and services". Under which ones of the consumption theories, if any, his statement may not be valid? Why?

Chapter 6

Investment Function

Learning Objectives

After reading the chapter you should be able to:

1. Learn the general concept of the capital expenditure, called investment, its three components, viz., fixed business investment, inventory investment and fixed residential investment.
2. Understand the link between investment and capital and the saving-investment correlation puzzle.
3. Know various factors which affect investments, the direction of their effects, and the rationale behind them.
4. Comprehend the dubious relationship between the government/public investment and private investment.
5. Get a feel of the data on the saving and investment rates across select major countries and over time.

Investment is spending done by firms, governments and households on final goods and services, primarily capital goods. Note that investment for the economy, which is the subject matter here, means spending on physical capital, not financial capital (equity and debts). It is most volatile component of GDP on the expenditure/demand side. It is high during prosperity and low during recession and is thus pro-cyclical. As will be seen later in the chapter on economic growth, investment is a major determinant of economic growth and this distinguishes a high growth economy from a low growth one. Countries across the world compete to attract foreign investments in their own lands so as to supplement the domestic investment, which is limited by their own savings. One of the reasons for the tiger and baby tiger economies (Singapore, Hong Kong, Taiwan, Malaysia, Thailand and Indonesia) and China achieving high growth rate over several years in a row has been their ability to attain high investment rates, partly through foreign investments. The United States and UK, among other nations, suffer from low investment rates, and hence, their performances have been below their potential. To provide some statistics, the current (2012, the latest year for which cross-country data are available) rate of investment (gross investment as a per cent of GDP) is 36 per cent in India, which is quite above the world average rate of 21 per cent. The said rate stands at 20, 15 and 48 per cent in Japan, the United States and China, respectively. It ranges broadly between 15 and 40 per cent globally. Countries having a relatively high rate (over 30 per cent) include China, India, Bhutan, Indonesia and Tanzania. The rate is low (below 20 per cent) in USA, UK, Brazil, Germany and France, among others.

Investments are financed from savings. Since capital flows across countries in all open economies, domestic saving need not equal domestic investment in such economies. But the two must for the world as a whole. However, there is a puzzle, called the **saving-investment correlation puzzle**. It states that though theoretically domestic saving needs not equal domestic investment, the empirical studies find that the correlation between the two across countries is very high and positive. The rationale for this comes from two factors:

(a) Foreign investment in any country is limited because it tends to increase the capital account surplus (in balance of payments) in that country which, in turn, results into foreign exchange inflow unless there is a current account deficit. Foreign exchange inflows have bearing on the exchange rate and/or money supply which may not be desirable for the economy. The persistent current account deficit worsens the current account sustainability constraint, which is discussed later in Chapter 10. Accordingly, the capital mobility across countries is not very high.

(b) Firms' access to capital markets is limited by the need for collaterals and the viability of their projects, among other factors. This justifies the significance of retained profit in financing investments; retained profit is a component of domestic saving.

Fluctuations in investments are largely responsible for business cycles. The stabilisation policies, which are mainly fiscal and monetary policies, operate basically through investment. Increase in the government expenditure crowds out private investment and this limits the effectiveness of the fiscal policy in stabilising the economy. The monetary policy operates through regulating investments via the interest rate to exert influence on the level of employment, output and inflation.

Investment expenditure has a dual role. Like consumption expenditure, it creates new demand, thus, leading to an increase in the aggregate demand (AD). But unlike consumption, investment adds to the productive capacity, thereby, enhancing the aggregate supply (AS). Therefore, investment positively affects both the AD as well as AS, leading to an increase in the output (real GDP), though its effect on the price level is ambiguous. This aspect would be dealt in detail later in the chapters on macroeconomic models and policies.

Yet another point to note here is that investments, unlike consumption, are self-terminating and self-financing. The former because investment means the acquisition (or building up) of assets and when this is complete investment stops. The latter because, if an investment is well conceived, returns from it will generate enough revenue to pay for its cost and even bring some profit to the shareholders. Neither of these is the characteristic of consumption expenditure as they tend to continue forever once you get used to them and they create no assets or returns to finance them. To appreciate all these virtues of investments, one needs to understand their meaning better.

Components of Investments

Investment expenditure is classified into three categories:

- Fixed non-residential (business) investments

- Inventory investments
- Fixed residential investments

The first category consists of the firms' expenditure on non-residential structures and durable equipment (plant and machinery), which form the largest component of all investments. These include business expenditure on factory buildings, residential buildings for employees, all kinds of machinery needed for operations, computers, fax machines, furniture, cars and the like, and expenses incurred on their installations. The second group includes the firms' investments in raw materials, supplies (intermediate goods, spare parts etc.), semi-finished goods (goods in process) and finished goods lying in warehouses and on shelves. This component is small, particularly due to an emphasis on the just-in-time (JIT) approach, but it happens to be the most volatile of the three parts. When the economy is booming, firms build on their inventories in the anticipation of large demands for their products and when recession sets in they cut their inventories, as their order books turn thin. Also, when there is a sudden surge in the demand for their products (caused, say, by an expansionary fiscal policy or a stock market boom), firms take the advantage of the opportunity by selling beyond their productions through cuts in inventories. In contrast, during a recession, particularly if it is expected to be temporary, firms enlarge their inventories. The last category of investment consists of expenditure by households on new houses for their own dwellings and by rental firms on the construction of the new residential buildings for rental purposes. This component is gaining in significance recently and it is fairly volatile pro-cyclically. House construction involves heavy expenditure and so households go for it when their economic position is good, and the credit is relatively easy and cheap. In contrast, during the down swing of business cycles, residential investments suffer. While all fixed investment is for building up the capital that stays at least for a while, the inventory investment is used up or sold out shortly after.

Investments of all three kinds are undertaken both by the private sector (firms and households) as well as the governments. Governments invest in infrastructure, defence services, offices, even in business to some extent, residential accommodations for its officers and staff, etc.

It must be emphasised that buying an existing (old) house from its seller does not amount to be an investment for the economy as it constitutes an investment by the new owner and disinvestment by the old owner, and thus, cancels out. Similarly, buying of old machines/factories and stocks and debentures from the secondary capital market does not qualify as investment. However, payments for brokerages on these transactions, which add to the price of these assets, are investments. Even mere purchases of stocks and debentures in the primary capital market are not national investments, unless and until they go into the purchase of fixed assets and/ or inventories. Thus, all investments are produced means of production to distinguish them from land and human capital, which are the other means of production.

Like all other components of the GDP, investments are measured in nominal terms. However, the inflation component in them must be removed for the purpose of analysing their determinants. Accordingly, in what follows, investments will be referred to in real terms, that is, nominal investments deflated by appropriate price indices.

The three kinds of investments are motivated by different factors. It is imperative to understand these specific motives before proceeding to discuss their determinants.

Motivation for Investment

Why do businesses go for investment? The reasons vary across the three investment categories discussed above. Business fixed investments are undertaken by production firms as well as by rental firms. Very often these roles are combined in a single firm, but this distinction is convenient here. Since production requires factories and equipment, firms engaged in the production of goods and services must invest in these assets. The more these firms desire to produce, the more they would need to invest in fixed assets, unless there is some idle capacity. Also, firms tend to invest more in fixed assets when the labour cost relative to the capital rental goes up and when they wish to emphasise innovations. Rental firms invest in such assets as they are in the business of renting out these assets to production firms. Again, the more the renting business, the more the investment in fixed assets.

Firms hold inventories for four reasons:

- Production smoothing
- Factor of production
- Stock out avoidance
- Work-in-process

At any point of time, a firm has a given capacity to produce its goods. However, its sales vary over time depending on the market. When the demand falls short of its capacity output, the firm may either under use its capacity or use it fully but store the difference as an inventory of finished goods. Idle capacity is costly and therefore it may be prudent to build on inventories. Quite the opposite is the case when the demand exceeds the production capacity. The firm produces less than it sells and the deficiency is made up through reduction in inventories. Thus, the holding of inventories of finished/semi-finished goods allows the firm to have smooth production in the face of fluctuating demands for its products.

Though inventory is not a basic factor of production, it does aid production. Holdings of raw materials, intermediate goods and spare parts avoid production shut downs due to the non-availability of such items or break down of machines. This, to some extent, makes the production vary positively with the stock of inventories.

Firms hold inventories of the finished goods on shelves and godowns. This helps them to show their goods to prospective buyers and make deliveries instantly. In the absence of these stocks, a firm may lose customers to its rivals. When you are indifferent between, say, a Maruti car and an Indica car, the one that is in stock for quick delivery is often preferred.

Heavy items like machines, cars, scooters, computers and kitchen appliances take a considerable amount of time to produce, and their production goes through several steps or processes. This entails holdings of semi-finished goods, and thus, the inventory.

Another way to look at inventory investment is to look at it like the demand for money. Inventory is held for three purposes, which are (a) transactions, (b) precautionary and (c) speculative. Smooth production requires inventory of raw materials and intermediate goods, which are not acquired on a daily basis due to the transaction cost and risk of their non-availability. Spare parts are stored to repair machines if and when they break down, and the other inventory is held for rainy days. Inventory is also held to guard against, and to take advantage of inflation. If firms fear shortage of raw materials in the future or/and expect their prices to go up, they find it prudent to accumulate inventories. The transaction demand for inventories has also been explained through the method of optimisation, which links this demand positively with the output and the shortage cost, and negatively with the cost of holding inventories. In particular, the relationship is expressed by the so-called **square root formula**, which means that each of the three concerned elasticity equals 0.5. The said function is the same as the transaction demand for money, which is explained in detail in Chapter 8.

The last category of investments, which is the fixed residential investment, like the fixed non-residential investment, is undertaken by households to own and live in their own houses and by the landlords who are in the house renting business. The reasons for both are obvious, and thus, they need no further rationalisation.

The above is the basic rationale for induced investments. Such investments are undertaken not only by private entrepreneurs but also by the government. In India, there is a large public sector as well as the joint sector, where some investments are governed by the same motives as in the private sector. For example, we have many public sector enterprises (like Oil and Natural Gas Commission, Indian Oil Corporation, Air India and Indian Airlines Corporation, Steel Authority of India Limited, Bharat Aluminium Corporation, State Bank of India and several other public sector banks, hotels and so on), which essentially run like private business units. In addition, there are autonomous investments, which are made largely by the governments. These consist of investments in physical infrastructure (transport, power, and communication networks), human infrastructure (health and education), public goods (defence), irrigation and such other sectors. Public sector investments are governed both by the profit as well as social motives.

Public investments are strategic investments, which are governed by economic policies. They cannot be explained by the private benefit-cost analysis kind of approach. They are rationalised, if at all, on the principle of social benefit-cost analysis. Examples would include national highway projects, river linkage projects, the Narmada Dam project etc. Both induced as well as autonomous investments by the government are found in all countries including the developed world. Lately, in a quest for efficiency and liberalisation, governments all over the globe are slowly withdrawing from such activities.

Investments and Capital

Investment is related to the capital. While the former is a flow, the latter is a stock. To be precise, the capital is cumulative net investments:

$$K_t = \sum_{i=1}^{t} I_i \qquad \textbf{(6.1)}$$

where K_t = capital at time t

I_i = net investment made during time period i

Net investment is the gross investment less the depreciation of capital (wear, tear and obsolescence of structures and equipment). Since the capital is measured at a point of time, there is a point to clarify. If it is measured at the beginning of the period, then it does not include the investment made during that period. However, if it is measured at the end of the period, as assumed in equation (6.1) above, it is inclusive of the current investment.

Investment is a serious economic activity, for it has significant repercussions on the welfare of the investor and his/her future generations. Also, it requires support from suppliers of equipment, contractors and financial institutions, among others. For these reasons, economists distinguish between the actual and desired investments or stocks of capital. The former denotes the true value of this variable, while the latter denotes its value which the investor desires or prefers to have. The two concepts are linked through the **stock (partial) adjustment model**, as follows:

$$I_t = K_t - K_{t-1} = \lambda(K_t^* - K_{t-1}) \quad \textbf{(6.2)}$$

where * denotes the desired level and λ the coefficient of adjustment, such that $\lambda \leq 1$. The function **(6.2)** suggests that investment varies directly with the deviation of the desired stock of capital from its actual level in the previous period. Further, it states that the rate of change does not exceed the said deviation. When $\lambda = 1$, $K_t = K_t^*$, means the investment desires are fully implemented. However, due to hurdles in investment and conservatism on the part of the investors, investment may adjust slowly to its desired level. If so, $\lambda < 1$, and accordingly $I_t < (K_t^* - K_{t-1})$ and $K_t < K_t^*$.

The theory of investment, whose discussion follows, obviously rationalises only the desired level of capital stock and thus equation **(6.2)** is needed to supplement the theory to explain the behaviour of the actual investment. To simplify the matter, equation **(6.2)** implies

$$I_t = f(K_t^*, K_{t-1}) \quad \textbf{(6.3)}$$
$$f_1 > 0 > f_2 \quad .$$

This means, we merely need to take K_{t-1} as an additional determinant of investment over and above the ones that determine the desired stock of capital or investment.

DETERMINANTS OF INVESTMENT

Induced investment expenditure, like any other behavioural variable, depends positively on the scale/financing/source variable and its yield, and negatively on its cost, among some other peculiar variables. Output is the appropriate scale variable; profitability of investment is the yield, and the interest on investment funds and depreciation of capital items are the cost variables. The other determinants found in the literature include the wage rate, Tobin's *Q*, tax laws, financing constraints, technology, business expectations and government strategies for investments. Various theories have been advanced to rationalise these factors, though they are largely complementary. At the cost of seeming repetitive, remember that the following theories are for induced investments only, as autonomous investment is largely an exogenous (policy determined) variable.

Output

No production is possible without capital and more production entails more capital. This is a technological relation, and can be expressed as follows:

$$K^* = AY \tag{6.4}$$

where K^* = desired capital stock
Y = expected output
A = capital–output ratio, called the 'accelerator'.

The expected output is taken as the actual output in the **acceleration theory**. The first difference of this function yields

$$\Delta K^* = A\ \Delta Y$$

or,

$$I^* = A\ (Y - Y_{-1}) \tag{6.5}$$

The above equation is referred to as the acceleration (output) theory or principle and is attributed to J M Clark (1917). Under this, the desired net investment is governed positively by the change in (expected) output (not the level of output). Since past production was made possible by the past stock of capital, it is only the increment in output that requires the additional capital. When there is acceleration in the business and expected output increases, the net investment is positive. If the expected output stops increasing, the net investment falls to zero. Further, if the expected output declines, the net investment becomes negative. It may be recalled that net investment equals gross investment minus depreciation. Thus, net investment would be negative when gross investment is positive or zero (gross investment could rarely be negative) and the latter is less than the depreciation.

The acceleration theory in equation **(6.5)** (as well as the partial adjustment model of equation **6.2**) is too naïve as it suffers from the following limitations:

(a) It assumes no excess capacity. If some of the capital was lying idle earlier, more could be produced simply through an improvement in capacity utilisation.

(b) If the increased demand for its product was considered temporary, the firm may not like to add to its capacity. This is so because idle capacity is a big burden (overhead cost) to any organisation.

(c) Net investment does not respond instantaneously to changes in output growth due to hurdles in implementing such decisions. For instance, investment requires funds and the availability of construction material, machines, technical personnel, among other things, which may not be readily available. Construction of factories, acquisition of capital equipment, and training of workers, etc. require time.

(d) Net investment behaviour is somewhat asymmetric. It can increase unboundedly but its decline is usually limited by the extent of depreciation. Firms can decide not to replace worn out or outdated machines but would rarely entertain off-loading their stock of capital. This is so because it is not generally possible to sell capital items at their reasonable prices so promptly, particularly for sick firms and firms do suffer from inertia.

To avoid these problems, the acceleration theory has been modified as follows:

$$I^* = A\ (Y_{-1} - Y_{-2}) \tag{6.6}$$

The revised acceleration principle makes the desired net investment vary directly with the change in output in the previous (instead of the current) year. This is for net investment. However, even replacement investment is governed by change in output, for even depreciation is more if more is produced, which involves greater use of fixed assets.

The acceleration theory holds good practically for all three kinds of investments. Fixed non-residential investment is directly used in production and so the theory is clearly applicable. More inventories are needed to support more production and vice versa. Fixed residential investment is incurred to meet the new and replacement demands for housing. Like any other consumption demand, housing demand directly depends upon the disposable income. That is, the increased demand for housing (net investment in housing) varies directly with the change in income at the aggregate level.

The profit theory of investment also argues for output as a determinant of investment. Under this, firms invest more when their profits rise and vice versa. This is so because a part of the profit is retained in the business, which adds to the internal funds. Internal funds definitely provide an incentive as well as a source of funds for investments, thereby encourage investments. Since the level of profit usually varies directly with the level of output, investments are influenced positively by the output. The **theory of business confidence** further reinforces the output (or incremental output) theory of investment, for the firm gets more and more optimistic when its market, and thus, output boom.

The **neoclassical** (optimisation/profit) **theory** provides yet another rationale for the output as a positive factor in the investment function. Under this, every firm tends to maximise its production, subject to the budget (cost) constraint (or minimise the production cost subject to a given output constraint) as follows:

Production function: $Y = f(K, L)$ **(6.7)**

Total cost equation: $C = R\,K + W\,L$ **(6.8)**

where Y = output
K = capital
L = labour
C = total production cost
R = capital rental (nominal)
W = wage rate (nominal)

This is a constraint optimisation problem and can be solved through the Lagrangian multiplier technique. Thus, the Lagrangian expression (L) would be:

$$L = f(K, L) + \lambda(C - RK - WL)$$

The partial derivatives of the above function with respect to each of K and L, and equating each results to zero gives

$$MPP_k = \lambda R \text{ and } MPP_L = \lambda W$$

Solution of the above two equations results in

$$MPP_k/R = MPP_L/W = \lambda = 1/MC \qquad \textbf{(6.9)}$$

where MPP_K and MPP_L = marginal physical productivity of capital and labour, respectively,

MC = marginal cost

The partial derivative of the Lagrangian term (L = output) with respect to total cost (C) equals λ, and thus, the inverse of λ equals marginal cost.

It must be noted that the MPPs are the partial derivatives of the production function with respect to capital and labour, and so they are in terms of Y, K and L, and parameters of the production function. Solution of equation **(6.7)** and of the first part of equation **(6.9)** would give the demand for capital and that for labour functions. The capital demand function so obtained would be,

$$K = f(Y, R/W) \tag{6.10}$$

Under function **(6.10)**, K is a positive function of Y and W, and a negative function of R. This leads investment to vary directly with a change in output. Thus, there are various approaches to explain the positive role of output in investment decisions. Note that the production function **(6.7)** assumes labour and capital as substitute inputs. If they were not substitute (as in Leontief production function), function **(6.10)** would not have R and W as determinants of K and thus it would be as per the acceleration theory.

Interest Rate

The negative role of interest rate in investment decisions is well known since the time of classical economists, to whom the investment was solely governed by interest rate. However, it is made popular by the just explained neoclassical theory of investment behaviour, which is due to Dale Jorgenson (1963). The optimising firm would like to undertake more and more investment so long as the return from the investment exceeds the cost of investment. For the production firm, the return from investment is the marginal physical product of capital (or the **marginal efficiency of capital**, as it was called by Keynes) while that for the capital rental firm is the real capital rental, R/P, where R is the nominal rent per unit of capital and P is the general price level. By the microeconomics' law of diminishing return and also by virtue of limited investment opportunities, the MPP_K declines as the investment increases, and vice versa. Also, the capital rental firm will be able to rent out more and more capital only at lower and lower real capital rental in an imperfectly competitive market. The cost of investment for the production firm would equal the real capital rental under the assumption of perfect competition in the product market. This as well as the equilibrium position of such a firm can be ascertained through equation **(6.9)** above. In perfect competition, MC = product price (P). Substituting this in the select part of equation **(6.9)** would give

$$MPP_k/R = 1/P$$

the solution of which gives

$$MPP_K = R/P \tag{6.11}$$

Thus, a maximum profit seeking production firm would invest up to the point where its MPP of capital equals the real capital rental. Since MPP_K declines as capital increases, more investment would be undertaken at the lower capital rental, and vice versa. The capital rental is the charge on the use of capital by the production firm and this would be determined by the optimum behaviour of the rental firm.

The rental firm would receive the capital rental and pay for the cost of acquiring the capital. The latter, called the cost of capital to the rental firm, will have three components:

- Nominal interest rate (i)
- Depreciation rate (d)
- Capital loss (gain) ($-\dot{P}$)

Investment requires funds, which come from borrowing or/and own sources. The nominal interest rate denotes the cost of these funds as it denotes the rate of interest on borrowings or the opportunity cost of the firm's own funds. The wear and tear of capital assets (structures, equipment and inventories), and their becoming obsolete over time at some rate is called the depreciation rate, which denotes the second component of the cost of capital. Prices of capital assets change over time. When there is inflation their prices go up, and they fall during deflation. This generates capital gains during inflation at the inflation rate ($\dot{P}$) and capital loss during deflation. Thus, the cost of capital (COC) is given by;

$$\text{COC} = i + d - \dot{P}$$

or

$$\text{COC} = r + d \tag{6.12}$$

(r = real interest rate)
for, according to the Fisher's theory

$$i = r + \dot{P}$$

In equation **(6.12)** inflation rate has one-for-one effect on the nominal interest rate, and this is known as the **Fisher effect**.

Integrating the above arguments together, the optimisation principle suggests that the rental firm would attempt to achieve:

$$R/P = r + d$$

Further, if the same firm performs the two roles of production and rental, as is commonly found, its optimum position would be governed by

$$MPP_K = r + d \tag{6.13}$$

Since the MPP_K declines as the investment increases, more investment would be forthcoming at the lower ($r + d$) level, and vice versa. Depreciation is covered up through replacement investment, and therefore net investment is a negative function of the real interest rate. If this is so for investment by a firm, it is so for all the firms in the economy, and hence, the desired investment in a country varies inversely with the real interest rate, other things remaining the same.

The interest rate affects not only the fixed non-residential investment but also the other two kinds of investments. Inventories have a carrying cost, which is the same as *COC* in equation **(6.12)**. Inventories are made possible through funds, which are raised at a nominal interest rate. Their nominal value is subject to inflation/deflation and they depreciate through the loss of weight, spoilage, storage cost and so on. The case of the fixed residential investment is similar. Low mortgage rates have certainly encouraged the private sector to go for more and more investments in housing. Thus, all kinds of net investments are affected negatively by the real interest rate. Inventory investment, in addition, is positively affected by the shortage cost of inventory, which is influenced by the supply conditions of inventories and the profitability of investment. The relationship between investment and interest rate can be depicted geometrically as in Fig. 6.1.

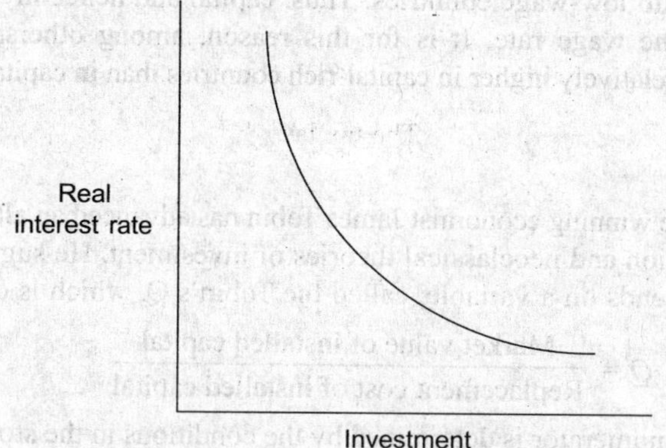

Fig. 6.1 Investment Schedule/Curve

The graph is downward sloping, indicating the inverse relationship between investment and the real interest rate. Further, the curve is convex from below, which suggests that the sensitiveness of investment to the interest rate increases at an increasing rate as the interest rate falls. This is generally true.

The above theory is unanimously accepted. However, empirically inclined economists and management experts argue that interest payments are a small fraction of the total investment cost, and the interest rate is an insignificant determinant of investment. Thus, there is a serious policy dilemma in this regard. Currently, the world over, there is a move towards low rate of interest and this is basically to promote investments and thereby economic growth. But this strategy is being questioned on the premise of low interest sensitivity of investment and on its adverse effect on the saving rate, which is the only long-term source for investments. Though the debate is never-ending, the significance of the shape of the investment schedule/curve or the interest elasticity of investment demand in macroeconomics can not be exaggerated, for as would be seen later in the chapters on the theories of business cycles, the effectiveness of both fiscal and monetary policies hinges a great deal on this elasticity.

Wage Rate

As would be evident from the demand for capital function (vide equation **6.10**), the optimum stock of capital that a firm should have depends on the capital rental relative to the wage rate. This is so because capital and labour are substitutes in production to some extent. Thus, when capital becomes cheaper relative to labour, firms tend to substitute capital for labour and vice versa. We have relatively capital abundant and labour scarce countries like Japan, the United States and Germany, where we find more capital-intensive production technology than in other countries, where the opposite is true. India and China, for example, have relatively cheap labour and expensive capital and so they use more labour per unit of capital in their production. Currently, due to the intense international competition and easy mobility of capital relative to labour, we are witnessing production/investment shifting from high-wage countries to low-wage countries. Thus, capital and hence investment depends positively on the wage rate. It is for this reason, among others, that the labour productivity is relatively higher in capital-rich countries than in capital-poor countries.

Tobin's Q

The Nobel prize winning economist James Tobin has advanced an alternative/addition to the acceleration and neoclassical theories of investment. He suggests that the net investment depends on a variable, called the Tobin's Q, which is defined as:

$$Q = \frac{\text{Market value of installed capital}}{\text{Replacement cost of installed capital}} \tag{6.14}$$

The equation's numerator is determined by the conditions in the stock market and its denominator by the current market prices of capital assets. If $Q > 1$, the stock market values the installed capital more than its replacement cost. Thus, the firm can raise the market value of its stocks by buying more capital assets, and accordingly, the net investment goes up. Quite the opposite is true when $Q < 1$. This is true for all the firms. Thus, the Q (**stock market**) theory suggests a link between the fluctuations in investment and those in the stock market. Earlier, in the chapter on the consumption function, we had seen that fluctuations in the stock market cause direct fluctuations in the consumption expenditure as well. This explains why firms and policy makers pay so much attention to the stock market.

The Q theory is consistent with the neoclassical theory. According to the latter, a firm likes to invest when its marginal physical product of capital exceeds its real cost of capital, that is, when it makes a profit on the new investment. The profits will ultimately influence the dividend paid out by the firm, which will tend to raise the price of the firm's stock. The latter would push up the Tobin's Q, which means more investment. Thus, both the Tobin's Q as well as the neoclassical theory suggest that the investment would be forthcoming when the profit rate (i.e. $Q > 1$ or $MPP_k > COC$) is positive.

Tax Laws

Tax laws have a bearing on investment. This is due to three reasons: one, the corporate tax is on business profits, which are net of the depreciation cost. However, depreciation is calculated on the basis of the historical costs of the capital assets, and thus, is underestimated during inflation. This leads to an underestimation of the cost of capital, and thereby, an overestimation of profits, which influences investments positively. Two, personal income tax rules permit interest on housing loan (as well as the repayment of the principal amount) up to a certain amount as deductible from income for computing taxable income, but not the rent paid out on renting out residential accommodations. This encourages the households to have more fixed residential investments. Three, most governments, including India's, have explicit policies to encourage investments. These include investment tax credit, capital subsidy, tax concessions/holidays and so on. Under the investment tax credit, which is very popular across the globe, companies get tax credit for each rupee of new investment that they make. It is through this route that the many growing and profitable companies (like Reliance) enjoyed the status of 'zero tax paying' companies in the past. However, this role is now modified, at least in India, and currently investment tax credit is also subject to **minimum alternative tax**.

The tax laws have, thus, favoured investments and they have, perhaps consciously, been designed to do so. Even the monetary policy exerts its influence on investment through its regulation of the nominal interest rate and credit availability and the power to monitor the inflation rate.

Financing Constraints/Firm's Balance Sheet

The neoclassical theory of investment behaviour assumes that firms can raise any amount of funds at a given interest rate for investment that they deem fit. This is not always the case, particularly for new entrants and in capital-scarce countries. During recessions, when profits fall and expectations are poor, firms may not be able to raise funds even if they expect the recession to be a short lived one. New entrants have a hard time in demonstrating the expected viability of their projects to financial institutions. Also, some firms do not have adequate collaterals to support their loan applications and if the balance sheet of the firm is not sound enough, no financial institution may agree to provide the requisite finance. Further, capital- scarce countries have more investment opportunities than their finance would permit. All these put a constraint on investments just as liquidity constraints forbid households from enjoying their genuine consumptions. This **credit rationing theory**, therefore, reinforces the role of profits, particularly retained profits in investments, as they provide readily available funds for investment.

Technology

Technology breeds investment. With the emergence of computers, the internet, wireless communication, and nuclear explosions, among others, investments all over the world have grown significantly. Computers have replaced or supplemented labour to boost up the production, and thereby, investments. Even teaching is no more limited through chalk-blackboards and classrooms as it has spread through audio-visual and distance learning. Technological breakthroughs have reduced the cost of capital relative to labour, and therefore, boosted investments. New methods of production have considerably replaced manual work through speed and have even reduced the cost of production. Thus, a lot of recent investments have been triggered by fast developing technology. The present emphasis on knowledge-based industries has also led to new types of investments. All these could be rationalised to some extent even by the neoclassical and other theories of investment behaviour.

Business Confidence/Stock Market Behaviour

It is well known that optimism encourages all economic activities while pessimism discourages them. Investment is no exception. When firms are optimistic, they expect the marginal products of the new investment projects to be higher and the cost of capital to be lower than otherwise, each of which, *ceteris paribus*, encourages investment through their sales, and hence, output is higher than otherwise, leading to more investment under the acceleration theory. Quite the opposite is true when there is pessimism among firms. Economists argue that the pessimistic outlook of households and firms was partly responsible for the Great Depression of the early 1930s. While all firms may not always have uniform expectations, they often tend to think alike. Thus, business confidence, called animal spirits, has a role in investment behaviour.

Government/Other Factors

Besides tax laws, governments influence investments through several other means/ schemes/strategies. The Narmada dam project in Gujarat, the Prime Minister's High-way project to link Kashmir with Kanyakumari by a well-developed road network, airports' up-gradation projects, proposed linking of various rivers, etc. have not only created new investments in the public sector but have also triggered private investments in related industries, business and housing. Public investment is both a substitute as well as complimentary to private investment. It is a substitute in as much as it competes for the scarce physical and financial resources that would otherwise be available to the private sector. It is complimentary in so far as it provides infrastructure and public goods which raise the productivity of the private capital. Liberalisation of rules governing foreign direct and portfolio investments is attracting more and more of these investments in the country, and more often than not, these are serving as complements to domestic investments. 'Own your own house', kind of schemes are also rendering a helping hand in improving the investment rate in the country. Even the stability of the government and its policy, social harmony and the absence of corruption contribute positively to the size of investment. Also, the inflation rate (a measure of economic uncertainty) and fluctuations in output (a measure of volatility of demand) affect investment negatively.

Investment Function

Firms do not behave rationally all the time, and if so, no theory could explain that behaviour. However, increasing market competition and professionalisation of management is forcing firms to be objective. Believing in the latter, we could take courage to hypothesise the investment function, which is based on the theories of the last section:

$$I = f(Y, r, w, Q, FMP, F, T, BC, Y_{-1}, K_{-1}, u) \qquad \textbf{(6.15)}$$

$$f_1, f_3, f_4, f_7, f_8 > 0 > f_2, f_6, f_9, f_{10}$$

$$f_5, f_{11} \gtreqless 0$$

where
I = net investment
Y = output (income)
r = real interest rate
w = real wage rate
Q = Tobin's Q
FMP = fiscal (tax) and monetary (credit) policies
F = financial constraints
T = technology

BC = business confidence
Y_{-1} = output in the previous year
K_{-1} = stock of capital in the previous year
u = 'other' factors

Function **(6.15)** contains all the theories of investment behaviour. However, it must be noted that the various theories are not independent or exclusive as they have overlapping elements. For example, as noted above, the Tobin's Q theory has components of both the acceleration theory and the neoclassical theory. Business confidence and even the technology are contained in each of these two theories. Since production changes only gradually from year to year, the effects of Y and Y_{-1} on investment partly cancel out. This observation has repercussions on the estimation of the investment function, on the basis of the historical data. To be precise, it may cause the problem of multicollinearity. To minimise this problem, researchers have to consider alternative combinations of various determinants and choose the best function on the basis of the received theory and econometric tests. Also, the above function ignores the determinants of foreign investment, which is a component of total investment in the country. These factors are discussed in the next chapter, which deals with all international transactions. It may be noted that all the determinants, other than the real interest rate, are known as the shifters of investment curve. This is because the said curve denotes the relationship between investment and real interest rate, *ceteris paribus*. Let us recall before concluding that all kinds of investments do not depend on each of these factors. To sum up the differences, following points may be noted:

(a) Public investments are largely autonomous and thus policy determined. They are based on some kind of social benefit-cost analysis and security-infrastructure–technology-innovation–political considerations.

(b) Private/induced fixed non-residential business investments depend on almost all the factors in investment function (6.15) above.

(c) Business Inventory investments are influenced basically positively by expected sales and inventory shortage/transaction cost (transport, inflation, availability, etc.) and negatively by inventory carrying cost (interest rate, storage, deflation, etc.).

(d) Fixed residential investments are governed directly by income/wealth, inflation rate in real estate pricing, and tax incentives and negatively by interest (mortgage) rate and return on non-housing investments (stock market, precious metals, etc.).

Conclusion

The investment schedule/curve (vide Fig. 6.1) is expressed as a relationship between investment and real interest rate. Obviously, this assumes that all the other (other than the interest rate) determinants of investments remain constant. Thus, while the investment curve slopes downward, it shifts up (signifying increase in investment) and down (signifying decrease in investment) due to changes in the 'other' factors. The shift is upwards when either any one of the positively affecting factors goes up or any of the negatively affecting factors goes down. Accordingly, upward shifts in the investment curve are caused by increases in any one of the following:

- current output
- wage rate
- Tobin's Q
- technology up-gradation
- improved business confidence

or decreases in any one of the following:

- financing constraints
- previous year output
- previous year stock of capital

or some favourable changes in the:

- fiscal-monetary policies/government's investment projects.

Further, the curve will shift downward if quite the opposite happens. If more than one factor changes simultaneously, the nature of the shift will depend on the strength of the relationships and the degree of those changes. As a post script, it must be noted that the investment rate (gross domestic investment as a per cent of GDP) in India, which hovered around 23 per cent until 2000, has increased significantly from 22.9 per cent in 2001-02 to 3.5 per cent in 2011-12 (vide Economic Survey, 2012-13).

Keywords

Saving-investment correlation puzzle; Induced-autonomous investment; Inventory investment; Square root formula; Capital; Stock-flow variables; Stock (Partial) adjustment model; Acceleration principle; Profit theory of investment; Theory of business confidence; Neo-classical theory; Constraint optimisation; Lagrangian expression; Capital demand function; Leontief production function; Marginal efficiency of capital; Capital rental; Opportunity cost; Depreciation rate; Capital gain/loss; Law of diminishing marginal returns; Fisher theory; Fisher effect; Investment curve; Tobin Q; Nobel prize; Minimum alternative tax; Firm's balance sheet; Stock market behaviour; Fiscal-monetary policy; Animal spirits; Investment function.

References

1. Clark J M, 'Business Acceleration and the Law of Demand' 1917, *Journal of Political Economy* 25 (March, 1917): 217-35.
2. Fumio Hayashi, 'Tobin's Marginal Q and Average Q: A Neo-classical Approach', *Econometrica* 50 (January 1982): 213-24.
3. Hirshleifer J, 'On the Theory of Optimal Investment Decision', *Journal of Political Economy* 66 (1958): 329-52.
4. Jorgenson Dale, 'Capital Theory and Investment Behaviour', *American Economic Review* 52 (May, 1963): 247-57.

REVIEW QUESTIONS

1. The investment rate in the Indian economy is low. Suggest ways to improve it.
2. If output increases, so will investment; if investment increases, so will output. Explain.
3. The 'Q theory' captures the link between fluctuations in investment and the stock market. Comment.
4. Investment depends on the real interest rate and not on the nominal interest rate. Do you agree? Why?
5. Investment is the most volatile component of national expenditure. Why?
6. The table below gives data on the gross domestic saving and investment rates in selected countries for 1980,1990 and 2012:

Percentages

Country	*Gross domestic saving*			*Gross domestic investment*		
	(as per cent of GDP)					
	1980	*1990*	*2012*	*1980*	*1990*	*2012*
India	17	22	31	20	24	36
Australia	24	18	25	25	22	28
Brazil	21	19	15	23	20	18
China	35	39	49	35	35	48
France	23	20	18	24	22	20
Germany		23	24		24	17
Japan	31	34	22	32	33	20
Korea (Rep.)	24	37	31	32	38	28
Malaysia	33	30	32	30	32	25
Nigeria	31	19	NA	21	15	NA
Russia Fed		36	30	22	30	26
Singapore	38	45	46	46	36	27
UK	19	15	11	17	20	14
USA	19	15	12	20	18	15
World	25	22	21	24	23	21

Source: World Development Indicators, World Bank, 2013.

Using the knowledge of the saving and investment functions, and relevant data (like interest rate and income) from this textbook and other sources, explain the differences in the

(a) saving and investment rates across countries over a period of time.
(b) saving-investment gap across countries over a period of time.

Chapter 7

Government, Foreign Trade and Foreign Exchange Rate Functions

Learning Objectives

After reading the chapter you should be able to:

1. Understand that the government sector variables are largely autonomous, political or policy variables except that the tax revenue are subject to the inverted U-shaped Laffer curve, which depicts a relationship between the tax revenue and the average tax rate.
2. Learn the trade theories which hypothesise the net exports as a negative function of the domestic income and a positive function of both the world income and the real exchange rate (relative price), besides the effects of the trade policies.
3. Appreciate that the trade policies, restrictive or otherwise, while have bearings on the trade, result in the dead weight (social) loss. Also, note the J-curve phenomenon, which suggests that depreciation could worsen the trade deficit in the short-run but improve it in the long run.
4. Know how net capital inflows, if unrestricted, vary directly with the domestic interest rate and inversely with the interest rate abroad, and how they are affected by the expectations about the change in the exchange rate and the country risk.
5. Comprehend the difference between the fixed and floating exchange rate systems and their different versions.
6. Learn how the exchange rate between any two currencies is determined and why the PPP theory fails to explain the actual exchange rates.

Government expenditure and net exports are the two components, apart from the private consumption and investment expenditures of the GDP from the expenditure (demand) side. Government expenditure is basically a fiscal instrument but the net export is amenable to economic explanation. These, together with the foreign exchange rate and international capital flows, are explained in this chapter.

Government Sector

Governance is indispensable to any system. This is because the government performs the functions that no other institution can undertake. These include framing and executing law and order; granting and protecting property rights; provision of public goods (internal and external security, police and defence services, light houses in sea, basic research, etc.) and common resources (public park, beach, picnic spots, etc.)

and encouraging production of merit and essential goods; ensuring justice; correcting situations when the free market creates undesirable externalities; redistributing the wealth when deemed desirable, promoting economic growth, taming business cycles, etc. In addition, many governments undertake commercial activities to supplement their incomes and/or to promote long-term development. Performance of these functions does involve expenditure, which are both, capital and consumption types. Recall that the capital expenditure of the government is a component of total investment in the country and this was discussed in detail in the previous chapter. Thus, the government expenditure analysed here is merely the consumption expenditure of the government at all levels—centre (federal), state, and local bodies. Recall that government consumption expenditure does not include transfer payments. It merely consists of the money the governments at various levels spend on food, clothing, and other commodities for the military, hospital, legislators (MPs, MLAs), and other staff; on salaries and allowances to government employees, including the bureaucrats and politicians, and such other items. Transfer payments consist of the interest payments on public debt, pensions to its retired government employees, social security payments, subsidies (on fertilizers, food, fuel, etc.) to encourage production and consumption, and so on. The size of government expenditure varies across countries. In India, the general government consumption expenditure takes a value of 12 per cent of the GDP, which is lower than the world average of 18 per cent. It generally varies between 10 and 25 per cent globally. High proportion (20 per cent and over) countries include UK, Japan, Brazil, France, Israel, Sweden, and Netherlands; and the low share (10 per cent and below) ones are Bangladesh, Singapore, Cambodia and so on. It accounts for 22, 17, 20, 21 and 19 per cent of the GDP in the United Kingdom, the United States, Japan, Brazil and Russian Fed., respectively. All the data here refer to 2012, the latest year for which data are available.

Though there has been a lively debate over the size of the government, no economic models have yet been developed to explain government consumption behaviour (general government expenditure) and transfer payments. Accordingly, both the government consumption expenditure and its transfer payments are assumed as autonomous expenditures. By the virtue of this, all government expenditure serves as a fiscal policy instrument in macroeconomic models. To meet its expenditure, government raises funds from various sources. It is endowed with the unlimited powers of collecting revenues through taxation (direct and indirect). Though taxation is the ultimate source of income to the government, it supplements this income through some profits from government run enterprises (such as railways and post and telegraphs services) and public sector undertakings (such as banks, oil companies, electricity suppliers, road transport services, steel manufacturers, and hotel); fees on public services (courts, schools, and colleges); grants from donors (domestic and foreign); disinvestments in public sector units; and so on. In addition, the government could and does incur fiscal deficits, which are financed through printing money and borrowings, both from domestic and external sources. What determine these various sources of revenue?

Taxation represents a leakage/withdrawal from the system. Taxes, unlike government spending, cannot be treated as autonomous since the revenue from them bears a direct relationship to income. Direct taxes are a compulsory withdrawal of income from firms and households. Indirect taxes cause spending at market price to exceed spending at factor cost. Subsidies (indirect) cause the market price to be less than the factor cost, and hence, can be regarded as negative taxes. Thus, the net tax collection (T) is given by:

$$T = tY \tag{7.1}$$

where,

t = tax rate (average)

Y = national income

The tax rate (net of subsidies) is a fiscal policy instrument, and the national income and tax collection are the endogenous variables. Transfer payments (TP) are treated as autonomous. Tax revenue minus transfer payment ($T - TP$) is referred to as net tax revenue.

Laffer Curve

The Laffer curve, known so after its founder Arthur Laffer, is an important concept that should be taken into consideration in this context.

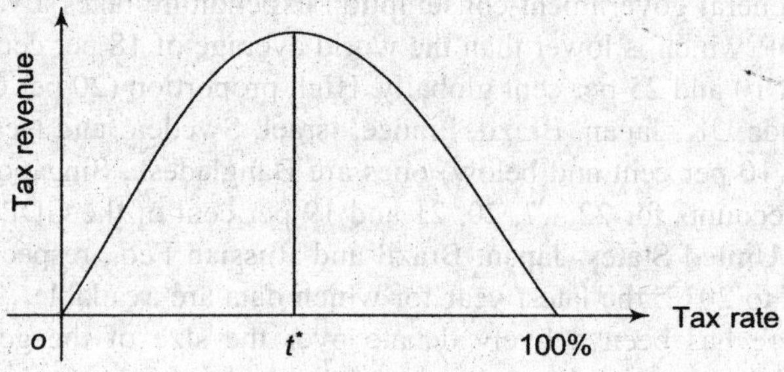

Fig. 7.1 Laffer Curve

The curve indicates that the tax collection is zero when either the tax rate is zero or it is 100 per cent. The former is obvious and the latter is due to the fact that when the tax rate is 100 per cent there would be no incentive for people to work and earn any income, and hence, the national income would be zero. Under the non-extreme situations, tax collection would be positive. However, though the relationship between tax collection and the tax rate is positive, the relationship is non-linear and the Laffer curve is inverted U-shaped. To understand this somewhat unique curve, we need to relax the basic assumption of a multivariate function, called the *ceteris paribus* assumption. Normally, when a curve is drawn from a multivariate function, the variables, other than the two of the curve, are treated as constants. In the Laffer curve this is not so. In particular, the tax rate and income are interdependent and thus when the tax rate changes income does not remain invariant. This is the **fallacy of *ceteris paribus***. When the tax rate is raised, the take home (after tax) income decreases and so the incentive to work and, hence, the national income goes down, and vice versa. Further, as the tax rate goes up, people shift from paid work to "do it yourself" activities (which is not included in national income, Chapter 2), thus, the income goes down. However, the opposite holds good when the tax rate is lowered. Since the tax rate and income move in the opposite direction, the product of the two could increase, stay constant, or decrease. Initially, when the tax rate is small, increase in the tax rate dominates the fall in income and the product of t and Y goes up, and hence the Laffer curve slopes upward for low tax rates. As the tax rate keeps going up, a point is reached when the tax rate is such that it (t^*) ensures the maximum possible value of tY and thus the top of the Laffer curve. Any further increase in the tax rate beyond that point (t^*) makes the fall in income to dominate the rise in the tax rate, and accordingly the tax collection falls. The latter explains the falling part of the said curve. Hence, the Laffer curve is inverted U-shaped. Incidentally, note that the Laffer curve is similar to the behaviour of the total revenue curve under imperfect competition in the face of a price fall. A fall in price is accompanied by an increase in quantity and the product of price and quantity (= total revenue) may thus increase, decrease, or remain constant, depending upon whether the price elasticity of demand (absolute value) is greater than, equal to, or less than (minus) unity. This is so because price and quantity are not independent in imperfect competition. This is due to the fallacy of *ceteris paribus*. It is a fallacy because the economics assumption of *ceteris paribus* in a multivariate function is no longer true in this case.

The tax collection is the maximum at the tax rate of t^*, as shown in Fig. 7.1. Unfortunately, the value of t^* is not known and it varies over time and across countries. In the late 1960s when Arthur Laffer advanced this hypothesis, most countries had high income tax rates and he recommended that a reduction in the tax rate would fetch larger tax revenues than otherwise. This is partly through improved incentives to work and earn and partly through better compliance to tax rules as the reward for tax evasion would be reduced. Ronald Reagan the then President of the United States, Margaret Thatcher the then Prime Minister of the Great Britain, and Rajiv Gandhi the then Prime Minister of India, among others, were convinced by this logic and the world over tax rates have fallen since then.

The profits of government run enterprises and of the public sector undertakings (PSUs) have been too little, and these units have slowly been going in to private hands over time. Fees from public services depend on the various fee rates and the sales of those services; the latter varying directly with the level of economic activity (i.e., national income). These charges are also relatively small and though very different from taxes, can be combined with taxes as far as model building is concerned. Grants depend on the donors and economic conditions in the country, and thus, could be taken as a non-policy exogenous variable. The proceeds from the disinvestment of PSUs have been highly political and are hard to rationalise on economic grounds. The size of the fiscal deficits and means of financing the same is largely a mix of economic-political-social decision, and is not quite amenable to explanation through economic models. This leaves the tax collection alone as the endogenous (behavioural) variable in government finances. At the cost of being repetitive, note that all government consumption expenditure, transfer payments and the various tax rates are exogenous (given or autonomous) variables in macroeconomics. The profits from government departments and PSUs, fees from publicly rendered services, grants, and donations are minor elements, and so are ignored in macroeconomic models. Public borrowing (both internal and external) and money printing are also treated as policy variables.

The annual budget (union, state and local government) sets out the planned revenue and expenditure of the government for the year ahead together with a statement on the actual (revised) revenue and expenditure for the past financial year(s). The budget is used as a major instrument of economic policy and a budget (fiscal) deficit or surplus may be deliberately planned in order to bring about the desired structural and anti-cyclical changes in the economy.

The size of government, besides the ratio of government consumption expenditure to GDP, is judged by the proportion of total tax revenue in gross domestic product. The said proportion (tax revenue for central government only) for India stood at 10.1 per cent in 2010 and 10.4 per cent in 2011, and it has fluctuated between the low of 7.0 per cent in 1970 and high of 11.9 per cent in 2009. A comparison of this proportion across countries reveals that the said ratio is relatively low in India. In 2011, it was 27.0 per cent in UK, 21.3 per cent in France, 20.5 per cent in Australia, 15.7 per cent in Brazil, 15.3 per cent in Malaysia, 15.0 per cent in Russian Fed, 11.7 per cent in Germany, 9.8 per cent in Japan and 9.7 per cent in USA. The said proportion stood at 10.5 per cent for China in 2010, at 9.8 per cent for Mexico in 2000 and at 11.86 per cent for Japan in 1993-94, the latest years for which data are available on the Google. Oil rich countries like Kuwait have the lowest figure (0.8 per cent in 2011) for this ratio. The said ratio takes the top and the second highest value in Algeria at 37.4 and Denmark at 33.8 per cent in 2011. The other high tax-GDP ratio countries include New Zealand, Ireland, Italy, Hungary, Netherlands, Norway, Sweden, among others. Thus, the Indian government is relatively small and there is a large scope for increasing the tax ratio in India.

Net Exports and Globalisation

Net exports, a component of the total expenditure (aggregate demand), is an aggregate that equals the difference between the exports and imports of goods and services. It thus, represents the net foreign demand for domestic goods and services, which equals the gap between domestic production and domestic demand (ignoring changes in inventory). An increase in it, like that in the private consumption, investment, or government expenditure, leads to an increase in the aggregate demand, and vice versa. The latter affects production, employment, and inflation, among other important macroeconomic variables. Since macroeconomics is concerned with macroeconomic variables, a text on the subject must discuss the behaviour of net exports. Further, the foreign exchange rate happens to play a dominant role in the determination of both exports and imports, among all other international transactions and, hence, foreign exchange rate models, too, have a place in the text. Capital movements across countries together with current account transactions determine the balance of payment situation and thus they too are dealt with in this chapter.

India has been a relatively closed economy, but it is slowly and steadily opening up with the spread of globalisation and the integration of the world markets in goods and services, money and capital, and labour. To cite the relevant data, as a proportion to the GDP our exports currently (2012) stands at 24 per cent and imports at 32 per cent, which are lower than even the world average of about 31 and 31 per cent, respectively. In contrast, the said proportions for exports and imports in 2012 stood at 31 and 27 for China, 14 and 18 for the United States, 32 and 34 for the United Kingdom, 87 and 76 for Malaysia, 224 and 224 for Hong Kong (China), 57 and 53 for Korea Rep., 52 and 48 for Germany, 40 and 36 for Nigeria, 29 and 22 for Russian Fed., 75 and 74 for Thailand, and 13 and 14 for Brazil, respectively. As the global movement of money and capital is the mirror image of the current account balances, the relative situation of India is similar with regard to international flows of investments. Many countries, including the South East Asian nations and China, have prospered in the last couple of decades and their growth has been attributed partly to their relatively open economic policies. It is argued that while specialisation promotes productivity and productivity enhances economic growth, free trade ensures the most efficient use of the world resources. There are evidences of unfavourable consequence as well. For example, the world has faced the OPEC crisis in the 1970s; India has faced foreign exchange crisis in 1990-91, Mexico and several Latin American and African countries have faced the external debt crisis in the 1980s; and Mexico, Argentina, the Russian Federation and several South East Asian nations (Indonesia, Thailand, and Malaysia) have suffered the foreign exchange crisis in the 1990s. Oil price fluctuations are creating havoc across most countries even currently. Even the unexpected changes in the foreign exchange rates are causing serious economic ills across nations. Thus, there are both pros and cons of globalisation. Incidentally, note that the principle of rational choice suggests that resources tend to gravitate towards their most valuable uses, particularly if voluntary exchanges are permitted. Thus, if the transactions are carried out on fair terms, they are win-win situations to all the partners. Unfortunately, the transactions are not quite free and fair and so the gains from them may not have been distributed properly among the trading partners. It is said "you get not what you deserve but what you negotiate". In any case, the fact remains that globalisation is causing a perceptible impact on the macro economy.

Open Economy

Literally, an open economy is the one that has non-zero flows (inflows/outflows) of goods, services, and/or capital (stocks, bonds, and money) from/to at least one other nation. On this criterion, all countries are currently open economies. However, the extent of the openness varies greatly across nations. As seen in Chapter 4 and also in the previous paragraph, on the one extreme there are countries like Singapore, Hong Kong, Taiwan, Malaysia, among others, whose total foreign trade (exports and imports), as a percentage of the GDP (a measure of the degree of openness), stands at around 100 per cent or more, while on the other extreme there are countries like India, USA, Pakistan, Japan, among others, whose said percentage stands around or below 40 per cent. With regard to capital flows, rich countries like the United States, UK, Germany, France, Canada etc. command a much larger proportion than relatively poor countries like India, Pakistan, and Mexico. Even China attracts much larger foreign capital flows than India. The pertinent questions are "why do such significant differences exist?" and "what are its consequences?"

The degree of openness is partly due to the economic policies followed by the respective governments and partly due to their absolute/comparative advantages/ disadvantages, innovations, return on capital, foreign exchange and country risks, etc. This is no place to go into such details but it would suffice to point out here that it is partly because of the attitude and partly because of the resource endowment and opportunities in the respective country. Until 1991 or the early 1980s, India had adopted '**inward looking**' policies in this regard, where she laid emphasis on export and import substitution. South Asian countries, in contrast, adopted '**outward looking**' policies right through the 1960s or even earlier. Developed nations, including the United States, Japan, the United Kingdom, among others, have generally favoured open economy policies. Countries have also differed with regard to the international movements of money and capital. In general, developed nations have favoured free movement while developing nations have had restrictions on such flows. India opted for full **current account convertibility** in the early 1990s and her capital account is only gradually being opened since then. This means all transactions in the current account of the balance of payments are free for execution so far as foreign exchange is concerned (subject, of course, to trade restrictions, if any) but some of the transactions that fall in the capital account of the balance of payments still need approval from the competent authority for the inflow/outflow of foreign exchange. Besides such policy differences, capital flows are based both on the 'push' as well as 'pull factors'. The former includes factors such as low interest rates, low return on capital (direct) investments and instability of currency and government, which push capital out to countries promising higher returns and better environments. The latter are the factors that serve to attract capital into particular host countries, and these comprise of low wages, tax incentives/havens, level of financial market developments, protection of property rights etc.

Openness causes interdependence, which produces mixed blessings. On the positive side, households can consume what is not produced in the country and firms can invest more than the domestic saving, besides the advantage of better prices and qualities. On the negative side, there is the '**contagion effect**', which plagued Asian economies in the late 1990s (South Asian financial crisis) and the globe during 2007-08 (great recession), and the 'infancy' argument, which is often cited to enact the protectionist policies. In addition, the foreign exchange rate risk and political instability pose their own problems. Over and above all this is the role of the monetary and fiscal policies, which change dramatically as the country moves from a closed to an open economy. The extent of this change depends upon whether the country is freely (totally) open or there are restrictions (sanctions) to international transactions and whether the economy is a small or a large one. All such issues will be discussed partly in this chapter and partly in later chapters.

Net Exports, Income Identity and Saving Investment GAP

Recall the national income identity (Y = GDP at factor cost) of Chapter 2:

$$Y = C + I + G + (X - Z) - (T_i - S)$$

Using the definition of net exports of goods and services ($NX = X - Z$), adding and subtracting the net direct taxes (T_d) and transfer payments (TP), and rearranging the terms, we get

$$(Y + \text{TP} - C - T_d) + (T_d - \text{TP} + T_i - S - G) - I = NX$$

The first term on the left denotes households' and business (private sector) savings, the second term, government savings, and the sum of the two gives the domestic savings (S), therefore,

$$S - I = NX \tag{7.2}$$

Equation 7.2 indicates that the net export of goods and services simply equals the difference between the domestic saving and domestic investment. Accordingly, if a country saves more than it invests (like Russia, China, Singapore and Malaysia), it has positive net exports, and if it invests more than its savings (like India, the United States, Sri Lanka and Nigeria) it has negative net exports. This implies that the determinants of net exports are the same as those of the domestic savings and investment. Also, note that

$$I - S = \text{Net Foreign Investment} = \text{Net Capital inflow}$$

In terms of the balance of payments (vide Chapter 4), net exports are used for remittances and other transfers, capital account deficit (i.e., buying foreign bonds, equities and deposits) and/or for increasing the official reserves' position, all of which means investing abroad in foreign bonds/equity, direct investment, and in foreign currencies. Equation (7.2) suggests that a country can have larger investments at home than her savings, through having net imports of goods and services, and vice versa. However, for the world as a whole $I = S$ as the world has to have a fully balanced current/capital/balance of payments' account. India, generally, has been importing more than her exports. Thus, she has a net inflow of foreign investment in the country. Looking at it this way, the net exports are governed by the attractiveness of foreign investments. Incidentally, note that exports and imports here mean those of both goods and services, thus, they are different from merchandise exports and merchandise imports, which refer to trade in goods/commodities only. Also, note that the current account (of balance of payments), in addition to exports and imports of goods and services, and transfer payments, has the net factor income from abroad (NIA). However, NIA is not a part of GDP and accordingly this is excluded from the derivation of equation **(7.2)**.

Determinants of Trade/Exports and Imports

There are two ways of looking at the trade, i.e., exports, imports and net exports of goods and services. One, through analysing the export and import functions. Two, by explaining the foreign investment function. The latter involves dealing in bonds, equities and money, and it is difficult to explain the remittances and foreign exchange reserves. In contrast, the export and import functions have been well explored. Accordingly, the first approach is followed here.

As in all economic models, there are two sides of all behavioural variables, viz. demand and supply sides. However, in each of exports and imports, the literature assumes the supply is perfectly elastic at the ruling price. This is so because "the rest of the world" is rather large relative to any one country and thus the supplies of exports and imports to any country should not be a constraint. Accordingly, there are merely demand for export function and demand for import function, which are referred to as the export and import functions, respectively.

As in other functions, exports (and imports) vary positively with the scale/financing variable, that is, income and negatively (positively) with the relative price, that is, the domestic versus the foreign price. Besides, they are governed by the restrictions (sanctions), if any, placed on them. In what follows, trade restrictions like bans (total prohibition) and quotas (quantity restrictions) are ignored and custom duties/tariffs (import-export duties) are incorporated in the prices. This is a reasonable assumption, for most countries are now members of the World Trade Organisation (WTO), which is striving for the elimination of all quantitative restrictions. Incidentally, note that tariffs are generally better than quotas, for one can achieve the same results under the former as under the latter and, in addition, while tariffs give revenue to the government, quota puts the resulting price difference into the pockets of the importers or exporters lucky enough to get a permit or import license. Also, tariffs only encourage/discourage trade instead of forcing it to zero or to a certain pre-specified level, as under quotas. To understand all this, consider the following graph in Fig. 7.2.

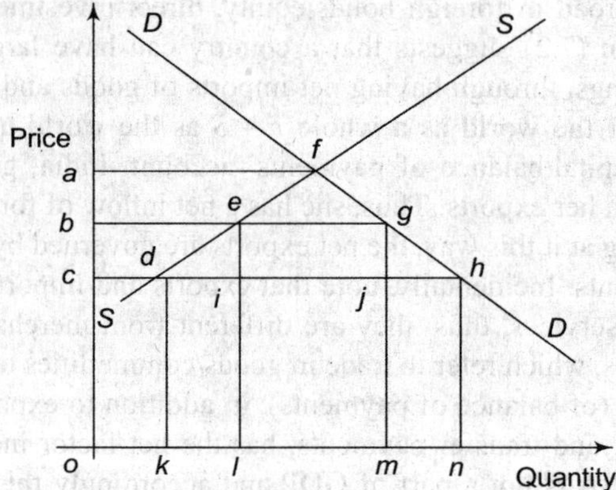

Fig. 7.2 Tariffs *versus* Quotas

Figure 7.2 describes the equilibrium positions, for both, a closed economy (autarky) and an open economy with no barriers, with tariffs and with a quota. The domestic demand and supply curves for the product under illustration are assumed linear and marked as *DD* and *SS*, respectively. The closed economy would have the equilibrium at point *f*, with the price at *o a* and quantity at *a f*. The world price could be lower or higher than the domestic price. If lower, the country would tend to import and if higher it would export. Let us consider the case where the world price is lower at *o c*. Under the free trade, the price at home would equal that in the world, and the domestic demand would equal *o n*, domestic supply *o k*, and the difference *k n* would be met by imports. The consumer surplus goes up by the area *c a f h*. Thus, free trade leads to a fall in the domestic price and supply, and a rise in consumption and consumer surplus. However, if trade was constrained by a specific tariff at the rate of *c b* per unit of import, the price at home would go up to *o b*, and accordingly, the domestic demand and supply would equal *o m* and *o l*, respectively, and consumer surplus would fall by the area *c b g h*. Imports would then equal *l m* and the government revenue from tariffs equal the area of the rectangle *e g j i*. In comparison to the free trade, the price and production at home are up, and demand and consumer surplus down. Next suppose, instead of tariff, the government restricts imports by way of quota on import, equal to *e g* (= *l m* = import under tariff), then the price at home would equal *o b*, and demand, supply and import would equal *o m, o l* and *l m*, respectively. The new results are identical to those under tariff barring the fact that while under tariff the government collects the tax revenue, under quota the advantage of trade restrictions is taken by the persons/firms who can manage to grab the quota. Thus, tariff is superior to quota on social consideration. Another significant result is that though tariff (in comparison to free trade) may be good from the point of the infant industry argument, it (as well as quota) leads to economic inefficiency. This is reflected in increased production (= *k l*) and decreased consumption (= *m n*), both of which are inefficient. This gives rise to what is called "dead weight loss", which equals the loss of economic (sum of the producer and consumer) surplus caused by distortions (tariff/quota) to market functioning. The dead weight loss would equal the sum of two little triangles, viz. *d e i* and *g h j*. This is the subject matter of micro-economics and so we leave it here. With this we move on to the determinants of trade.

Income

Income denotes the purchasing power, and thus, is a determinant of the demand for goods and services. Accordingly, income was taken as an important factor in the consumption function in Chapter 5. However, there are two differences here. One, export of a country denotes the demand for that country's products by foreign residents. Thus, the relevant income is the income of all foreign residents. There is no ready data on it but it can be approximated by the world income (Y^w), for a country's income would be merely a small fraction of the world income[1]. Two, import of country signifies the demand for foreign goods by the residents of the nation. These residents include the households, firms and the government. Thus, the relevant income variable in the import function would be the country's total national income and not the personal disposable income, as in the consumption function. Obviously, income affects the demand positively, and thus, exports vary directly with the world income, and imports directly with the national income.

Relative Price

The relevant relative price in foreign trade is the price abroad versus the price at home. Obviously, the two prices have to be in terms of a common currency. Thus, if we measure the prices in domestic currency, the foreign price in foreign currency (like in dollars) would have to be multiplied by the appropriate exchange rate. For example, if the price of a Big Mac (Mc Donald's big sandwich) is $2 in the United States and ₹100 in India, and the rupee-dollar exchange rate equals ₹60 per dollar, then the relative price would be ₹(2 × 60)/100 = ₹120/100. In view of this, the price

[1]There are exceptions to this, for a few large economies like those of the United States, Japan and China, enjoy a sizable share of the world income.

of goods abroad relative to that in India (called the real exchange rate) becomes the relevant relative price in the export-import functions. There are multiple bilateral exchange rates but the relevant one is the macro exchange rate, which is called the real effective exchange rate, REER (Chapter 4). Similarly, the price of import/export goods abroad is also not unique because a country usually has many trade partners. The macro world price is not yet designed and instead the unit value concept is used to serve the purpose. Accordingly,(P^wE/P^d) is the relevant relative price in export-import functions.

where E = nominal (effective) exchange rate (measured on the direct quotation, e.g, ₹62 per US $)

P^d = domestic price in national currency

P^w = world price in foreign currency

Incidentally, note that the depreciation of the Indian rupee would cause E to rise and vice versa. The principle of optimisation suggests that exports would be more when the relative price (real exchange rate) is high and vice versa, ceteris paribus. Quite the opposite would be true for imports. Since the relative price contains the nominal exchange rate on the numerator, net exports vary directly with the nominal exchange rate. Remember that the relative price here is the foreign price relative to the domestic price, and hence the direction of the relationship between export/import and the relative price as suggested above. If the relative price were instead defined as the domestic price relative to the foreign price, the direction of the relationship would exactly be the reverse of what is argued here.

Other Factors

In addition to the above two factors, quantitative trade barriers (bans, quotas and other non-tariff barriers) would affect net exports. Non-tariff barriers have become a big issue as these have been adopted by USA, Europe and Japan, among others. They take the form of new standards of safety and technical regulations for chemical products and food, import licensing, most favoured nations status, discriminating subsidies, "buy local", government procurements, voluntary export restraints, orderly market arrangements, regional cooperation, etc. Incidentally, note that the role of the custom duties/tariffs is contained in the relative price, if the prices were inclusive of such duties. As any behaviour could be partly random, the firms, households and government may well import/export even if their economics were unsound. This means the said function needs "a catch all" variable as well.

Net Export Function

Combining the above hypotheses would yield:

$$X = f\left[Y^w, \left(\frac{P^wE}{P^d}\right), U\right] \tag{7.3}$$

$$Z = F\left[Y, \left(\frac{P^wE}{P^d}\right), V\right] \tag{7.4}$$

Hence, the net export function is:

$$NX = \phi\left[Y^w, Y, \left(\frac{P^w E}{P^d}\right), U, V\right] \qquad \textbf{(7.5)}$$

where U and V are the unknown (catch all) factors, and

$$f_1, f_2 > 0$$
$$F_1 > 0 > F_2$$
$$\phi_1, \phi_3 > 0 > \phi_2$$

A nation has hardly any control over the world income (barring the exception of the last footnote). Therefore, Y^w is taken as exogenous (autonomous) and, correspondingly there is some autonomous net export. The other (induced) part of the net export moves negatively with the national income and positively with the relative price.

Also, remember that the nominal exchange rate is a part of the relative price, and it affects the net export positively. Incidentally, note that if the foreign exchange rate were defined through its indirect quotation method (like US \$0.02 = Indian rupee 1), the exchange rate would be on the denominator of the relative price instead of numerator, the relative price would be in dollars instead of in rupees and the effect of the exchange rate on the net export would be negative instead of positive. All these relationships can be explained graphically as shown in Fig. 7.3.

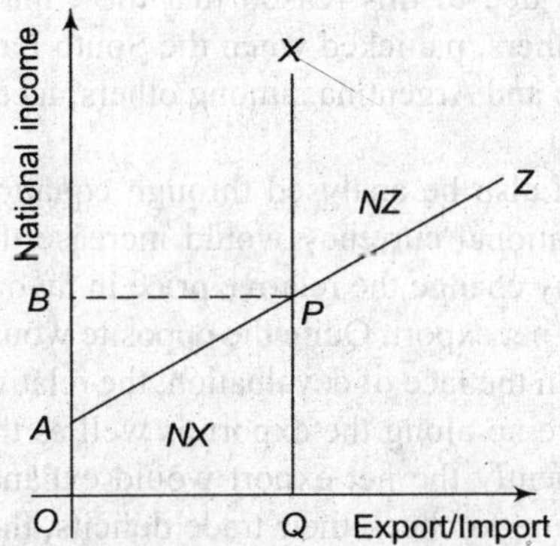

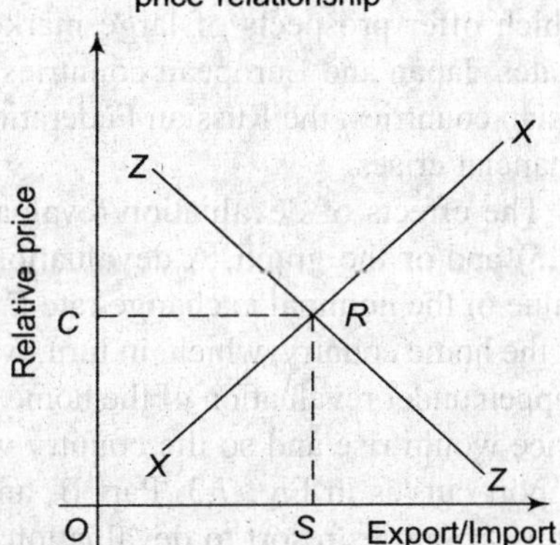

Fig. 7.3 Export-Import Function

Part A of Fig. 7.3 describes the relationship between export and national income and import and national income. Since exports are independent of the home income, the export curve marked as QX is vertical. The level of the world income positively governs the distance OQ. The curve AZ gives the import function for a given relative price and other determinants of imports. The point of intersection P denotes the equilibrium position. When imports are less than OQ, there is net export, which is given by the area between the export and import curves (marked as NX); and when imports exceed exports, there is net import, which is indicated by the area above point *P* between the export and import curves (marked as *NZ*). The figure suggests that if the domestic income grows, the world income remaining the same, the trade deficit goes up and vice versa. Thus, the relative home prosperity, *ceteris paribus*, is harmful from the viewpoint of trade balance, and vice versa. In contrast, if the world income grows, *ceteris paribus*, the export line *QX* shifts to the right and consequently net export expands and trade deficit contracts, and vice versa. Thus, prosperity abroad is good for net exports of goods and services.

Part B of the above figure describes the role of the relative price in the import and export functions for given values of other determinants. The import curve *ZZ* is negatively sloped as imports vary inversely with the relative price and the export line *XX* is positively sloped due to the direct relationship between exports and the relative price. The point of intersection of the two curves *R* is consistent with zero trade balance. The figure suggests that the lower the relative price, the more is the trade deficit, and vice versa. It is important to mention here that the various curves in the figure above have been drawn as linear simply for convenience while, in general, they are non-linear.

The interdependence of the various countries can be gauged, to a certain extent, through equation **(7.5)** and Fig. 7.3. If the 'rest of the world' gets richer, the nation's export goes up and so does the net export, and so does GDP, and vice versa. It is because of this that it is said, "if America sneezes, countries like India get fever". (Recall that the United States has the largest purchasing power [national income] in the world). Also, it is because of this that even rich countries care for the prosperity of poor and developing countries, particularly of large ones like China and India, which offer prospects of large markets. It was due to this reason that the United States, Japan and European countries, among others, panicked when the South East Asian countries, the Russian Federation, Mexico and Argentina, among others, faced financial crises.

The effects of devaluation/revaluation could also be analysed through equation **(7.5)** and/or the graph. A devaluation of the national currency would increase the value of the nominal exchange rate E and thereby change the relative price in favour of the home country, which, in turn, would boost net export. Quite the opposite would happen under revaluation of the home currency. In the face of devaluation, the relative price would rise and so the country would move up along the export as well as the import curves in Fig. 7.3, Part B, and consequently the net export would expand. Thus, countries resort to devaluation as a measure to check their trade deficits, that is, to reduce or eliminate net imports (i.e., negative net export). However, this result is conditional. A further analysis of equation **(7.5)** or/and the Fig. 7.3, Part B would indicate that the success of this would depend on three factors, which are:

(a) Price elasticity each of exports and imports
(b) Size of external debt and its repayment schedule
(c) Reactions of trade partners

Price Elasticities: To the extent imports are essential either for domestic consumption (like oil and food grains) or/and for domestic production (like oil, machines, technical know-how, gold ingots for jewelers, intermediate goods and spare parts for automobiles), they are not quite sensitive to the relative price. If so, imports do not fall or fall too little in the face of devaluation or increase in the relative price.

Also, though devaluation would cause export volume (quantity) to increase, the rate of actual increase depends on the price elasticity of exports. Normally, exports are highly price elastic, as several countries compete in exports. Thus, devaluation leads to a significant increase in export volume. Since each decrease in imports and increase in exports tends to help reduce trade deficit, it is argued that devaluation provides a solution to attack the trade deficit. However, this is not always the case. To fully understand the effect of devaluation on the trade balance we have to distinguish between the quantity of imports/exports and the value of imports/exports. **Pass through devaluation** (from devaluation to inflation, that is when the effect of devaluation is passed on to the prices of export and import) raises the price of imports (in domestic currency) and thereby increases the relative price (makes imports dearer than before), thus causing the quantity of imports to fall. Therefore, while the quantity of imports falls, the price of imports increases, and hence the product of the two (i.e. value of imports) may rise, remain constant or even fall. Recall the Laffer curve (and the example of the total revenue curve under the imperfect competition in that section), which is inverted U-shaped because the assumption of *ceteris paribus* does not hold. Therefore, only if imports were price elastic (i.e., elasticity greater than unity), would devaluation (increase in import price in domestic currency) decrease the value of imports. In the situation where the said elasticity exactly equals unity, the value of imports would remain unchanged, and when the elasticity is less than unity, the value of imports would rise.

Considering next the effect of devaluation on the value of exports, we note that pass through devaluation makes exports cheaper for foreigners and so the quantity of exports would increase so long as exports were somewhat price sensitive. Note that the price of exports in the domestic currency would remain the same even after devaluation and accordingly an increase in the quantity of exports would always mean an increase in the value of exports in domestic currency. Thus, devaluation would lead to an increase in the value of exports to the extent they were price elastic.

It must be noted here that all exports and imports of goods and services that takes place after devaluation are not negotiated at the exchange rate which has passed through the devaluation. Thus, those contracts which were signed before the devaluation happened, are not affected by the devaluation. This further reduces the effect of devaluation on net export in the short-run.

Since the trade deficit/surplus is in terms of the value, it follows that devaluation would reduce the deficit (or increase the surplus) whenever the price elasticity of imports is no less than unity and export were somewhat price elastic. To generalise, devaluation would help correct the trade deficit if the (absolute) sum of the price elasticity of imports and the price elasticity of exports exceed unity. This is known as the **Marshall-Lerner Condition**. Since the price elasticity of exports and that of imports had have the opposite signs, the absolute sum of the two is relevant here. For example, if the price elasticity of imports was minus 0.5 and that of exports was plus unity, the sum of the two would be 1.5 and the Marshall-Lerner condition would hold good. The said condition normally holds good in the long run but not in the short run due to:

(i) sluggish quantity adjustments caused by poor-substitutability of foreign and domestic goods in production and consumption.

(ii) some export-import contracts being signed prior to devaluation, i.e. at pre-devaluation exchange rate.

Therefore, it is argued and verified empirically that devaluation is a cure for trade deficit only in the long run. The short run solution to the trade deficit is found in import substitution, where the country substitutes its homemade products for the erstwhile imported products.

Before we proceed further, it may be mentioned that imports and exports could be measured either in the domestic or in the foreign currency. In the above example we had assumed them to be measured in the domestic currency. However, our result holds even if they were expressed in foreign currency. Under the latter, the import price would not change and thus decrease in the quantity of imports would imply decrease in the value of imports. But the export price would undergo a change opposite to the change in the quantity of exports and thus the change in the value of exports would depend on the magnitude of the price elasticity of exports.

External Debt: If the trade deficit country has external debt, then devaluation would increase the nominal debt burden as well as its servicing through enhanced interest and dividend obligations, which would adversely affect the net export (as interest and dividend are outflows in the invisibles' part of the current account). Thus, the presence of external debt, which is often the case for the trade deficit countries, limits gains from devaluation.

Trade Partners: The 'beggar-thy-neighbour' policy could lead to reactions from foreign countries whose trades are affected by someone else's devaluation. In such a situation, when a country, like India devalues its currency, its neighbour, China may lose its competitive advantage at least partly to India. To combat such consequences, China may respond through devaluation of its own currency. This may prompt India to institute a further devaluation, to which China may react again by devaluation, and the process may continue till both countries realise the superficiality of their actions. Between 1929 and 1933, several countries participated in competitive devaluations. Fortunately, such is usually the case only when the neighbouring country (or other countries) is in a similar boat, that is, the net exports being negative and unsustainable. Since all the countries cannot simultaneously be in the current account deficit (or negative net imports), devaluation is very often effective at least through this angle. Furthermore, devaluation is the recommended measure, when the trade deficit country devalues its currency in terms of the currency of the country having the trade surplus.

Due to the above factors, economists have coined the **J-curve phenomenon** (Fig. 7.4) to describe the effects of the devaluation on the trade deficit.

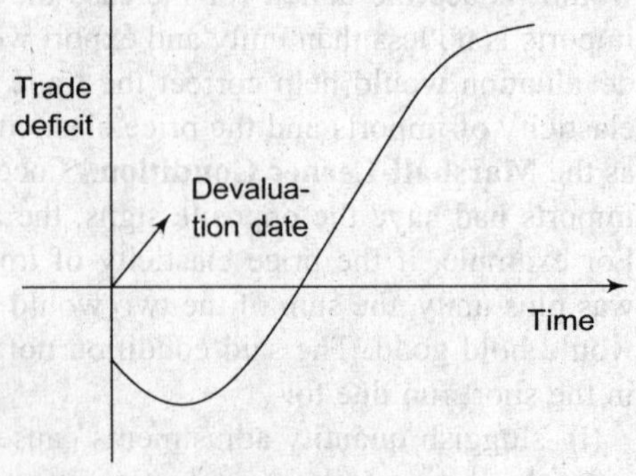

Fig. 7.4 The J-Curve

Initially, devaluation worsens the trade balance as debt servicing goes up immediately while import and export hardly adjust due to inertia and some pre-devaluation contracts. Subsequently, substitution takes place and imports and exports respond, thereby exerting pressure on the trade deficit and even turning it into its positive magnitudes. Hence, the deficit first goes up and then reverses to larger and larger positive values over time. This is what the J-curve describes. Thus, devaluation is expected to serve the purpose of curbing the current account deficit, though only in the long run. It is because of this belief that many countries, including the crisis-ridden South East Asian nations, Mexico, Argentina, among others, have resorted to devaluation in the face of unsustainable deficits; and devaluation has remained as one of the prescriptions of the International Monetary Fund (IMF) to countries seeking bail out financial assistance.

Equation (7.5) implies that relatively high inflation at home will harm the net export. For this reason, high inflation countries often allow their currencies to depreciate (in nominal terms) to save the erosion of their purchasing powers. Before we close this section, it may be noted that the current account of the balance of payments provide a source for the interdependence of nations, the other sources for this are found in the savings-investment gap and the capital account of the balance of payments. The former has been discussed earlier and the latter is explained below.

DETERMINANTS OF CAPITAL FLOWS AND THE FUNCTION

Like goods and services, capital also flows across countries both ways, and thus there are capital inflows (credits) and capital outflows (debits) for any country. Recall from Chapter 4 that capital inflows are the purchases of Indian financial and physical assets (like purchases of Indian bonds—both government and private, shares—both of PSUs and private corporations, bank deposits, and foreign direct investments in factories) by foreign residents and capital outflows are the purchases of such foreign assets by Indian residents. In essence, capital inflows represent the borrowings by the country from abroad and capital outflows her lending abroad. The principle of optimisation suggests that money goes where it earns (return on investment) the most, assuming that

(a) there are no restrictions on cross border capital movements, and

(b) domestic and foreign assets are homogenous or perfect substitutes.

The former assumption does not hold good in countries not having the full capital account convertibility, which is true in India. However, with the realisation of the gains from free movements and the presence of WTO, most countries have already opted for the free capital mobility and India is moving fast on it. The latter assumption with regard to the degree of substitution, is also gaining popularity among the investors and the process is speeding up with the spread of information technology, increasing proportion of both foreign investment and the cross listing of bonds and stocks globally. Given these two assumptions and assuming further that

(c) there is either no transaction cost or it is the same both for domestic as well as foreign investments, and

(d) exchange rate is either on the fixed exchange rate system or the investors expect it to remain fixed during the reference period.

Movements of capital across borders is explained simply by the difference in the rates of interest at home (i^d) versus abroad/world (i^w). Thus, net capital inflow (NKI) in a country would be governed by the following function:

$$NKI = f(i^d - i^w) \qquad (7.6)$$
$$f > 0$$

Please note that if exchange rate were a variable, the changes in it would also affect NKI; an appreciation of the domestic currency would tend to increase NKI and vice versa. According to equation (7.6), the net capital inflow would be positive if the domestic interest rate is higher than the foreign interest rate, and vice versa. The free movement of capital would ensure that the two interest rates are equal, and if so, NKI would be zero. Thus, under the four assumptions in the last two paragraphs, the equilibrium would be where

$$i^d = i^w$$

However, in a floating exchange rate system, the exchange rate is highly unlikely to remain invariant over time and accordingly no prudent investor would assume it to remain constant even during any reference period. Under such a system where all four but one of the assumptions does not hold, the two interest rates would not be equal and the difference between them would be given by the following popular **Covered and uncovered interest rate parity theorems:**

$$\text{Covered Interest Rate Parity: } i_{rupee} - i_{dollar} = (F - S)/S \qquad (7.7)$$
$$\text{Uncovered Interest Rate parity: } i_{rupee} - i_{dollar} = (E - S)/S \qquad (7.8)$$

where, i_{rupee} and i_{dollar} are (nominal) domestic (India) interest rates in India and the abroad (say, USA), respectively

F = forward foreign exchange rate

S = spot foreign exchange rate and

E = expected foreign exchange rate

Also, note that the time period for the interest rates and the F and E are uniform. The first theorem is prefixed the "covered" because it involves no risk of loss due to changes in the exchange rate. This is so as the forward contract is made at the same time as the capital transaction. The latter theorem is prefixed "uncovered" because the gain from foreign investment is affected by the movements in the exchange rate, for the expected rate could well deviate from the spot rate. The first theorem suggests that the interest rate differential between the two countries must equal the discount/premium on the currency in the forward market. The second theorem suggests the said difference must equal the investors' expected depreciation/appreciation of the exchange rate. To explain how these theorems hold, consider you as an investor has ₹10 million to invest and your options are to deposit the amount in India at i_{rupee} or to deposit in USA at i_{dollar}, then for the two alternatives to have the same yield (law of one price), the following must be true:

$$₹10 \text{ million } (1 + i_{rupee}) = ₹10 \text{ million}/S\,(1 + i_{dollar})\,E$$

The left hand side denotes the amount on maturity if invested in India, and the right hand side the amount if invested in USA; under the latter the money is first converted into dollars at the spot rate (S), deposited in USA at i_{dollar}, received in dollars on maturity, and then converted into rupees at the expected exchange rate (E). Solution of the above equation gives,

$$(1 + i_{\text{rupee}})/(1 + i_{\text{dollar}}) = E/S$$

Subtracting 1 from each side and solving, yields

$$(i_{\text{rupee}} - i_{\text{dollar}})/1 + i_{\text{dollar}} = (E - S)/S$$

Since $1 + i_{\text{dollar}}$ is small, the above equation approximately results into equation (7.8) above. Similarly equation (7.7) can be derived. The theorem indicates that international differences in interest rates are approximately equal to the expected proportional change in the exchange rate.

To illustrate its applications, assume the interest rates for 3 months in India and United States are 4 and 2 per cent, respectively, and the spot exchange rate is ₹60 per US dollar. Substitution of these values in equation (7.6) above gives

$$0.04 - 0.02 = (E - 60)/60$$

solution of which gives $E = 61.2$

This means the expected (forward) rate (3 months) should be two per cent higher than the spot rate or that the rupee must be on two per cent discount against the dollar in the three months forward market. If the market had these rates exactly matched, there would be no scope for arbitrage (profits from trading in the foreign exchange market without investment and risk). However, if the rates were different, profitability would exist in such opportunities. Thus, for example, if the Indian interest rate were 5 per cent, *ceteris paribus*, an arbitrator could make a riskless profit as follows:

- Borrow $1000 for 3 months at 2 percent to pay $1020
- Sell, $1000 into rupees at the spot rate and get ₹60,000
- Invest the proceeds of ₹60,000 at 5 per cent for 3 months and get ₹63,000 at the end of 3 months
- Sell ₹63,000 in the 3 months forward market at ₹61.20/$ and get $1,029.4 at the end of 3 months

In this process the arbitrator makes a profit of $9.4 (1029.4 – 1020) without bearing any risk! Obviously, the foreign exchange transactions are in large amounts and so the profits could be exorbitant. In this example, we have implicitly assumed zero transaction cost. The unit transaction costs are small and in any case it suggests that the interest rate differential could differ by the forward market discount/premium only by the cost of transaction lest there would be arbitrage activities, which would ultimately wipe out the difference, if any. These parity conditions provide a link between the interest rates and the foreign exchange rates globally. Thus, in essence, they serve as the **monetary link** across nations through the capital account of the balance of payments (financial markets).

If there are restrictions on the movements of capital across countries, the domestic and foreign interest rates could differ by any extent and any direction. NKI would then be regulated by policies and accordingly it would cease to be a behavioural variable. Further, if domestic and foreign assets were not perfect substitutes, the two interest rates would differ, as they would contain the corresponding rewards for risk besides for waiting. In general, foreign assets are riskier than domestic and so the relevant variable in equation **(7.6)** above would be $((i^d + k) - i^n)$, where k is the premium attached to the domestic assets and it is positive ($k > 0$). Accordingly, the relevant determinant of NKI in equation **(7.6)** would be $((i^d + k) - i^n)$. In addition, foreign investments are subject to country risk, while domestic ones are free of this risk. The said risk consists of political risk (investors fortune is controlled by the relationships between own country and the concerned foreign nation) and social-cultural risk.

Foreign Exchange Rate System

The exchange rate regime is concerned with the method of determining the exchange rate between a particular currency and every other currency in the world. This is significant to ensure the liquidity and stability of the currency. Liquidity is essential for carrying out international transactions smoothly and stability is needed for their efficiency. Even essential and profitable transactions are constrained by the availability of foreign exchange (liquidity). Fluctuations in the foreign exchange rate affect the profitability of international transactions through the so called foreign exchange (economic) risk and, thus, the latter are encouraged by the stability of the former. When the exchange rate is fluctuating significantly, the foreign exchange risk is large and the otherwise highly profitable transactions could become unprofitable. The cases like the closure of the 125-year-old Baring Bank of England due to the speculation in foreign exchange transactions by its senior officer Mr Nick Leeson in 1997 and the troubles faced by Kodak film in competition with Fuji film during the 1980s, among many others, are well known. Even the foreign exchange risk management techniques offer no panacea to absolve firms from this risk. The case of Lufthansa provides an interesting example for the latter situation. Lufthansa ordered Boeing aircrafts in 1985, price contracted in US dollars, payment was to be made in US dollars after a few months and it covered the foreign exchange risk to 50 per cent through a forward contract to buy the US dollars against the Deutsch Mark (DM) on a date closer to the due date. Subsequently, and until the maturity of the contract date, the US dollar fell in relation to the DM and, consequently, the foreign exchange risk hedge turned unfavourable to Lufthansa. The purpose of the foreign exchange rate is to promote international transactions while facilitating adjustments to shocks and disequilibria.

Systems of Foreign Exchange Rate

There are essentially two systems of the exchange rate. These are:

(a) Fixed exchange rate system
(b) Floating exchange rate system

Under the first, the exchange rate is fixed while under the second it is floating or flexible. There are alternative versions of both.

Types of Fixed Rate System Under the fixed rate system, there are two kinds, viz.

(a) Hard peg
(b) Soft peg

The hard peg includes the **dollarisation** (euroisation), currency/monetary union, and currency board systems. Some small countries like Panama, Ecuador in 2000 and El Salvador in 2001 have adopted the US dollar as their own currency (dollarisation) and have essentially done away with the problem of fixing an exchange rate. This system allows the adopting country to inherit the price stability of the foreign country but at the cost of sacrificing the revenue from Seigniorage. Eleven (one more later) European countries (viz. Austria, Belgium, Finland, France, Germany, Greece, Ireland, Italy, Luxembourg, Netherlands, Portugal and Spain—all members of the European Union except Britain, Denmark and Sweden) have formed the **currency union** since 1999, where they have adopted the Euro as the universal currency in all member countries. Thus, they have done away with the exchange rate among them, though they have a floating rate system with the rest of the world. In addition, there are other currency unions as well, like the East Caribbean Currency Union, Western African Monetary Union, and Central African Exchange Monetary Coop. Some other countries like Hong Kong, Bulgaria, Estonia, Lithuania, and until December 2001 Argentina have opted for the **currency board** under which their home currencies are backed fully or largely by US dollar reserves (dollar standard) and the exchange rate between the two is fixed. Under this system, the domestic high-powered (not all money components) is fully convertible into the foreign currency and vice versa by the Central Bank of the country.

Under the Bretton Woods Agreement of 1944 among all the member countries of IMF, the adjustable fixed rate (soft peg)/limited flexibility system prevailed between 1944 and 1971. Under this system, the United States set the dollar-gold parity (United States had emerged as the only economically powerful country after the World War II), and offered to convert the dollar into gold on demand, and other member nations set the gold parity with their currencies and accordingly the exchange rate with the dollar. The exchange rates were thus fixed but were allowed to adjust by plus/minus one per cent. Further, if the member nations had serious balance of payments problem, they could change the exchange rate up to 10 per cent in either direction without the consent of IMF, for changes beyond this limit the member nations were obliged to seek IMF approval. This was considered as the golden period for foreign trade as it grew exponentially then. This system got into trouble in August 1971 when the then United States President, Richard Nixon, decided unilaterally to withdraw the conversion of the US dollar into gold, triggered by the meager stock of gold with the United States, relative to the dollar holdings outside the United States, due to the heavy burden of the Vietnam War (1964-1975). Efforts were made during 1971-73 to restore the system, but in vain. Ultimately, the Bretton Woods system collapsed. However, some countries still peg their currencies to the currency of their major trade partner or to a common currency in a group of countries (like Euro) or to some composite unit like SDR (special drawing rights) or to a basket of currencies. These countries change the exchange rates as and when they so deem appropriate and thus they are on soft pegs. Malaysia and UAE, among others, are currently on the fixed peg with the US dollar. While some countries have pegged rates within horizontal bands (e.g. Denmark), others follow some other band arrangements (for example Egypt and Hungary), and still others (Bolivia, Costa Rice and Nicaragua) enjoy crawling pegs. Under the latest system, the exchange rate moves slowly over time to either direction.

Types of Floating Rate System Even within the floating rate system, there are two kinds, which are:

(a) clean, pure, free or independent float
(b) dirty or managed float

Under the independent float rate system, the exchange rate is determined freely by the market forces of the demand for and supply of the currency in question. In contrast, under the latter the Central Bank of the concerned country intervenes in the market to influence the demand/supply of the currency in order to ensure the desired level of the exchange rate. No country in the world is currently on a pure flexible rate system, for no central bank allows its currency to fluctuate with complete freedom. However, the degree of the flexibility varies across countries. The interventions are generally more in the developing countries than in developed ones. The US dollar vis-à-vis the Japanese yen has fluctuated significantly in the past and this had caused panic not only in these two countries but in the whole group of G-7 countries, besides other nations, leading to meetings and the enforcement of interventions to the market forces. Recently, the Euro-US dollar rate has fluctuated violently and interventions have been enforced. Yet, developed countries like the United States, the United Kingdom, Canada, Japan and Australia are considered to be on independent floats.

Under the managed/dirty float system, the Central Bank must have an adequate reserve of foreign exchange to be able to maintain the desired level of the exchange rate. For, if the foreign exchange reserves were plenty, the central bank could sell foreign exchange reserves when their demand exceeds the supply and succeed in holding the exchange rate. However, if the foreign exchange reserves were inadequate, the bank would be unable to manage the exchange rate. It is this inadequacy of the foreign exchange reserves with the Central Bank of Mexico that forced Mexico to devalue her currency in 1995. The same was true for Argentina when it gave up the currency board and floated her currency. Also, it is because of this that the central banks of countries having the dirty exchange rate system endeavour to build their foreign exchange reserves. India has been comfortable in this regard in the last few years and accordingly the Reserve Bank of India (RBI) has quite successfully achieved a fairly stable exchange rate. In fact, currently, India is perhaps having the problem of too much reserves and she is struggling hard to avoid excess appreciation of her currency, in terms of the dollar, through sterilisations. India is on the managed float rate system since March 1993 and so are the most developing/emerging countries. Thus, Singapore, Indonesia, Pakistan, Sri Lanka, among others, are on the managed float system. Under this system, the exchange rate is market determined but the central bank of the country acts as a major market participant. Our Indian system has been criticised as being asymmetric, for the Reserve Bank of India fights much harder to prevent appreciation than the depreciation of the rupee. The developed world is basically on the free float rate system ever since the failed efforts to restore the Bretton Woods system in 1993. The Central Banks of such countries only rarely operate in the currency market significantly. Within the dirty floating rate system, while some countries have crawling bands, the others have no pre-announced path for their exchange rates. Note that the success of the managed float system depends on the adequacy of foreign exchange reserves.

Why the government intervenes the foreign exchange rate? Some of the reasons are as follows:

(a) To manage trade flows and thereby inflation and hence GDP and unemployment

(b) To manage expectations about the exchange rate and thereby the capital flows and hence the interest rate and GDP
(c) To apply the exchange rate policy to meet its other goals, like joining a trade block or currency union.

The intervention could be sterilised or non-sterilised. Under the former, the Central Bank buys foreign currency and issues domestic money, which is then reversed through open market sales of government bonds, thereby leaving the domestic money supply unchanged. Under the latter, the domestic money supply changes directly and proportionately with the amount of intervention. Also, a mix of the two can be practiced.

Ideal Foreign Exchange Rate System

Which system of the forex rate is the best? Unfortunately, both systems have pros and cons. Under the fixed rate system, the Central Bank is committed to the maintenance of a fixed exchange rate and thus the uncertainty of the exchange rate is removed. However, the fixed rate system offers no protection against shocks originating abroad. Under the system, the country sacrifices its role in other economic goals like economic growth, stable prices and so on. When there is an excess demand for foreign currency, resulting in an upward pressure on the value of that currency, and correspondingly, into a downward pressure on the country's currency (depreciation), the Central Bank would sell some foreign exchange, which would lead to a given contraction of the money supply, irrespective of its desired level on other considerations. Quite opposite would be the case when the currency faces an upward pressure (appreciation), caused by the excess demand for its currency over its supply. Thus, under the fixed rate system, the central bank of the country is unable to regulate the money supply to any desired level. In this respect there is a famous trilemma, known as the **international trilemma** or the **impossible trinity**. The trilemma was first noted by Mundell and Flemming, and hence it is also called as the Mundell-Flemming Model. This is how it works. Of the three options, viz., integration, regulation and sovereignty, a country can choose only any two and all three are not possible simultaneously. Integration here refers to the free flow of goods, services and capital across countries (that is, both the current as well as capital account convertibility); regulation to the freedom of deciding the exchange rate (fixed rate); and sovereignty means the independence of the Central Bank to choose the supply of money. Thus, for example, if a country chooses the integration and the fixed exchange rate system, then it cannot have the luxury of independence in the matter of the money supply. To explain this, let a country that has these two and tries to increase the money supply, *ceteris paribus*. As the money supply increases, the interest rate comes down, which triggers capital flight (for capital goes where it earns more), which, in turn, increases the demand for foreign currency and thereby puts pressure on the domestic currency to depreciate. Since depreciation cannot be allowed under the fixed rate system, the above event would force the Central Bank of the country to sell the foreign exchange, which, in turn, would mean less foreign exchange and more of domestic money with the Central Bank, and thus, less money supply with the public, including banks. Ultimately, the initial increase in money supply would have to be rolled back! Quite the opposite would happen if the Central Bank tries to reduce the money supply. However, this assumes that the Central Bank has enough of foreign exchange reserves for the purpose. But if it does not have, it would fail to maintain the fixed exchange rate itself.

Similarly, the other combinations of the three options can be explained. In addition, the fixed exchange rate system suffers from the fact that it forbids the depreciation/appreciation of the exchange rate to correct the imbalances (through affecting net exports and imports of goods and services-vide equation 7.5 above) in the current account as well as in the over-all balance of payments. The adverse imbalance in the current account, in turn, could worsen the country's inter-temporal budget constraint (i.e. the sustainability of her current account balance). Several countries have fallen into such a trap.

Example: South East Asian countries (Thailand, Malaysia, Indonesia, etc) faced a financial crisis during 1997-98 and Argentina faced it in 2001 due to over valuation of their currencies. It has been argued that China's currency is under valued currently and its major trade partners like USA are having large trade deficits due to this factor mainly.

As against the said two disadvantages, the fixed exchange rate system has the advantage of no foreign exchange risk, for the change in exchange rate, which alone causes the foreign exchange risk, is zero under such a system. The fixed rate system thus promotes foreign trade and investments. Incidentally note that under the fixed exchange rate system, the exchange rate is a tool in the hands of the Central Bank, though its use is subject to the "beggar thy neighbour" issue.

Needless to say, the disadvantages of the fixed exchange rate system become the advantages of the floating rate system, and vice versa. Thus, a free floating exchange rate allows the country to set its own money supply and to immune the country from external shocks. Under the system, there is no imbalance in the current account or the over-all balance of payments and thus it avoids the dilemma of internal balance and external balance. But under such a system, the exchange rate may over-shoot and cause suffering to speculators in foreign exchange market from foreign exchange risk. Due to these mixed consequences, neither system is universally the best. Accordingly, different countries have different systems and most are on the hybrid system, viz. the managed or dirty float. Also, some countries have moved from one system to the other over time. Further, no definite indicator appears from the IMF in this regard. To substantiate this assertion, literature shows,

The IMF urged Asian nations to devalue/float their currencies in 1997, lent billions of dollars to Russia and Brazil to help them maintain their exchange rates in 1998, praised Hong Kong for its super strict currency board in 1998, and feted Singapore for its managed float in 1998. Nevertheless, some guidance is available on this count.

The fixed rate system is usually suitable to countries having a harmonious inflation rate, concentrated trade both geographically and commodity wise, small size, low economic development and/or a relatively open economy, while the floating rate system is suited to countries with the opposite features (Rogoff, et al 2004). This is so because inflation rate differentials affect competitiveness. Thus, for example, if the inflation rate in India exceeds that abroad, *ceteris paribus*, India's competitiveness is harmed. This is apparent from the purchasing power parity theorem (explained in the following section). If so, the fixed rate system would harm the economy through losses in foreign trade. However, if the inflation rate were nearly the same in all competing countries, then this disadvantage would not be there at all. Similarly, if the trade is largely with one country (or invoiced in one currency), the foreign exchange risk is the minimum if the exchange rate is tied to the currency of that country than if it were freely floating. Also, if the trade was basically in a few commodities/services, the fixed rate with the major trade partner would minimize the foreign exchange risk. Further, if the country happened to be a small one, the foreign exchange risk would easily kill it while the large countries would have the cushion to survive such a phenomenon. The less developed countries can only ill afford the foreign exchange risk and thus it should go for a fixed rate system. Also, the more open an economy is, the more the foreign exchange risk, *ceteris paribus*, and thus, openness favours the fixed rate system. Needless to say, all these statements assume *ceteris paribus*. Lately, most economists believe that only radical solutions will work, i.e., either currencies must float freely or they must be tightly tied through a currency board or currency union. Some argue that floating rates make no sense for small emerging economies. It is such facts and opinions that have prompted the launch of a common currency in Europe (the Euro, in 11 European countries, since January 1, 1999) and the formation of trade blocks like the North American Frontier of Trade Agreement (NAFTA) between US, Canada and Mexico, among others. The latter strategies are expected to promote intra-regional trade, and thereby, try to achieve the outcomes of the fixed exchange rate system in the midst of the worldwide floating exchange rates.

Before moving to the next section, it would be instructive to cite some real life experiences with the international trilemma. The East Asian crisis is believed to have been caused basically by this trilemma. These countries had the fixed exchange rate system and free movements of capital, goods and services. After years of capital inflows, capital fled these countries in mid-1997. The affected countries could not maintain the exchange rates, and hence were forced to float their currencies. In consequence, these countries faced sharp drops in their exchange rates and declines in the GDPs, among other economic troubles. By adopting the Euro as a single currency in 1999, eleven countries in Europe have given up their power to maintain independent control of domestic monetary policies. The latter role is now played by the European Central Bank. Inspired by the above macroeconomic trilemma, Dani Rodrik of the Harvard University has come out with a political version of it. According to him, **deep international economic integration, a strong nation-state and mass politics cannot coexist**. A country has to pick two of the three. Argentina's financial crisis in 2001 illustrates the new trilemma. France has globalised, maintained a strong nation-state and retained vibrant domestic politics. However, in recent years even France has been ceding greater powers to the European Union. India enjoys a strong government and an independent country status but it is facing problems in integrating with the world. During 2012-13, Indian economy has experienced significant depreciation in its exchange rate due to fall in foreign investment flows, excessive current account deficit, low growth rate, scams and political issues.

Determinants of Foreign Exchange Rate

Recall from Chapter 4 that the foreign exchange rate has fluctuated significantly over time. In particular, the variations have been much more after the breakdown of the Bretton Woods System in 1973, than ever before. To cite our own example here, the rupee-dollar rate was at ₹4.76/$ until June 1966, ₹7.5 between June 6, 1966 and mid-December 1971, below ₹10 until the end of 1983, below ₹20 until the end of 1991, below ₹30 until the end of 1993, below ₹40 until the end of 1998, had crossed ₹65 by mid-2013 and stands at around ₹62 currently (January 2014). The story of other foreign exchange rates is similar. What causes these variations? Needless to say, the fixed rate (both the hard and soft peg) is set by the authorities, the government and/or the Central Bank of the concerned country. Accordingly, it becomes a policy variable. The managed floating rate is partly market determined and partly a policy variable. The freely floating rate is truly market determined and could be explained through analysis. However, in the long run, even the authorities can not ignore the market factors while setting the exchange rate. In what follows, we dwell on the various theories which attempt to explain the exchange rate.

Demand and Supply of Currencies/Balance of Payments Theory

Irrespective of whether the foreign exchange rate system is fixed, managed or free float rate one, the exchange rate of a currency, in the long run, is basically determined by the demand for and supply of that currency in relation to the other pertinent currency. Therefore, the rate, for example, between the Indian rupee and the United States' dollar is governed by the foreign exchange need, i.e., by the supply of the US dollars (= demand for the Indian rupee) and the demand for the US dollars (= supply of the Indian rupee) in exchange for the India rupees (United States' dollar). The supply for the US dollars stems from two sources, viz.

(a) exports of goods and services from India (X_{g+s}), and
(b) imports of capital (capital inflows) into India (Z_k)

Under the former, foreigners buy Indian goods requiring payments to India and thus they supply the US dollars in India. Under the latter, foreigners invest (and lend) in (to) India, thereby they buy Indian capital (bonds, equity, factories, etc.) and hence supply the US dollars in India. Similarly, the demand for the US dollars is created by the

(a) imports of goods and services by India (Z_{g+s}) and
(b) exports of capital (capital outflows) (X_k) from India.

Recall from the last three sections that while exports and imports of goods and services vary with the exchange rate (exports positively and imports negatively), exports and imports of capital are independent of the exchange rate. Accordingly, the supply and demand curves for the US dollars with respect to the exchange rate would be upward and downward sloping, and these would shift parallel to the right with the size of imports and exports of capital, respectively. The remaining components of balance of payments (BOP), viz., factor income (dividends, interest and labour remunerations) and transfer payments (pensions, grants and gifts) are independent of the exchange rate. Inflows of such payments would shift the supply of the US dollars curve to the right and outflows of such payments would shift the demand curve for the US dollars to the right. Since their effects on the demand and supply of foreign currency are same as those of imports and exports of capital, and they form a relatively small component of BOP, they are here included in imports and exports of capital.

Equilibrium exchange rate is given by the point where demand for a currency equals its supply:

Demand for \$ = Supply of \$

Or, $Z_{g+s} + X_k = X_{g+s} + Z_k$

The interplay of the supply and demand curves for the US dollars determines the real exchange rate between the Indian rupee and US dollar. If the supply of the US dollar goes up, demand remaining the same, the US dollar depreciates (and Indian rupee appreciates) and vice versa. Also, if the demand for the US dollar increases, supply remaining constant, the US dollar appreciates (and Indian rupee depreciates). Thus, any factor that affects the demand or supply of the currency exercises an influence on the exchange rate. These factors include the world income, national income, relative inflation rate and relative interest rate, among other factors. Similarly, all other bilateral exchange rates are determined. For example, the exchange rate between the Japanese yen and British pound would be set by the demand for yen with respect to pound and the supply of yen vis-à-vis pound. This demand-supply theory is alternatively known as the **balance of payments theory**. Graphically, the theory can be illustrated as shown in Fig. 7.5.

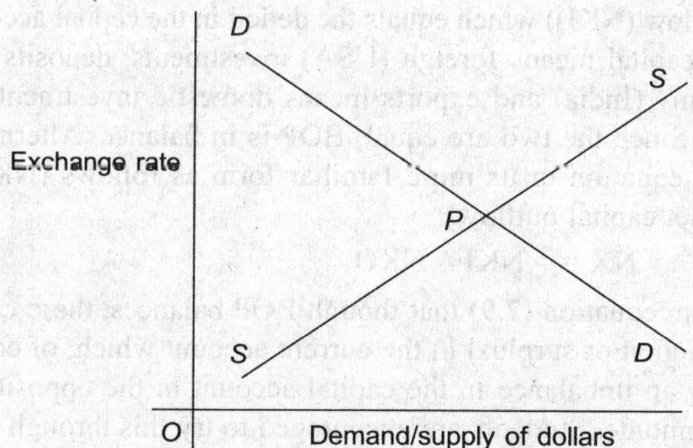

Fig. 7.5 BOP Theory of Forex Rate

In the above graph, the exchange rate (E) is in direct quotation (i.e. rupees per dollar), the real exchange rate is defined as $e = P^w E/P^d$, and the relationship between each of the supply of and the demand for the US dollars with the real exchange rate is assumed to be linear. The lines *SS* and *DD* denote the supply and demand curves for the dollar (or the demand and supply curves for the rupee, respectively). The point of intersection *P* denotes the equilibrium exchange rate under no intervention by the government. If the country was on the fixed nominal exchange rate and the corresponding real exchange rate was below *P*, the demand for dollars would exceed their supply. In that situation, the Government/Central Bank must defend the rate and it can do so only through selling dollars to meet the excess demand, rationing the dollar via controls on capital movements, and/or the dollar black market. Quite the opposite would happen when the exchange rate was above the equilibrium level *P*. Further, if the demand for dollar goes up (say, because India's imports of goods and services increase due to changes in any variable other than the exchange rate or India's exports of capital increases), *ceteris paribus*, the *DD* curve would shift to right and the exchange rate would increase, meaning a depreciation of the rupee in relation to dollar. Quite the opposite would happen when the demand for dollars falls (due to, say, an increase in India's exports of goods and services caused by non-exchange rate factors or India's imports of capital increases). Similarly, the consequences of changes in supply could be analysed. Incidentally note that the exchange rate as determined by the DD and SS curves is the real rate and the nominal rate is then determined by the relative inflation rate as per equation (4.2), Chapter 4.

It must be noted here that under free movements of goods, services and capital, and the freely floating exchange rate system, there would be no imbalance in the BOP. This can be shown through re-arranging the above equation of demand for dollars equals supply of dollar as follows: The above equation can be re-written as

$$X_{g+s} - Z_{g+s} = X_k - Z_k \tag{7.9}$$

The left hand side (LHS) of the above equation denotes net exports of goods and services (NX) which means surplus in the current account of the BOP (remember that here we are assuming that factor income and transfers are part of the capital account). Its right hand side (RHS) gives net exports of capital (net capital out flow = — net capital inflow (NKI)) which equals the deficit in the capital account; remember that imports of capital means foreign (USA) investments, deposits and lending in domestic economy (India) and exports means domestic investments, deposits and lending abroad. Since the two are equal, BOP is in balance. Alternatively, we can write the above equation in its more familiar form as follows (NKI = net capital inflow, NKO= net capital outflow):

$$\text{NX} = -\text{NKI} = \text{NKO} \tag{7.10}$$

It is obvious from equation **(7.9)** that though BOP balances, there can be an imbalance (of either deficit or surplus) in the current account which, of course, would be accompanied by an imbalance in the capital account in the opposite direction and in the same magnitude. Students are encouraged to try this through geometry using the approach of Fig. (7.5).

Relative Interest Rate

Exports and imports of goods and services change only gradually, over time. However, changes in the capital inflows (i.e. exports of capital) and outflows (i.e. imports of capital) could be significant even in the short run. Since the foreign exchange rate changes frequently and sometime even drastically, the changes in it are attributed largely to the changes in the net capital flows across countries. The latter are caused by the changes in investment opportunities. Thus, if the interest rate (and correspondingly, the profitability of investment) goes up in India, without a corresponding increase in the interest rate in the United States, capital will flow into India, leading to an increase in the demand for the Indian rupee, and thereby, to an appreciation in the value of the Indian rupee in terms of the US dollar. Quite the opposite will hold if the differential in the two interest rates goes in favour of the United States. As mentioned in the previous paragraph, this comes through appropriate shifts in the *SS* and *DD* curves of Fig. 7.5. Accordingly, the interest rate differential is an important determinant of the exchange rate. The greater the positive difference between the Indian and US interest rates, the lesser number of rupees will equal a US dollar, *ceteris paribus*, and vice versa.

Purchasing Power Parity/Relative Inflation Rate

The famous law of one price suggests that an identical commodity cannot sell for different prices in different locations at the same time. The purchasing power parity (PPP) theory extends this law to the pricing of currencies. Thus, if a commodity (or a basket of goods) sells for, say, ₹100 in India, and $10 in the United States, the exchange rate between the two currencies would be:

$$(₹100) = \$10$$

or, $$E = ₹10/\$.$$

i.e., $$E = \text{Price at home/Price abroad} \quad \textbf{(7.11)}$$

where, E = Units of the domestic currency per unit of the foreign currency

Thus, the exchange rate is given by the ratio of the price at home to the price abroad. The said rate E is referred to as the nominal exchange rate (vide Chapter 4). Just as there are the nominal GDP and real GDP, there are the nominal exchange rate and real exchange rate. The latter is obtained by adjusting the nominal rate to changes in the relative inflation rate in the two countries. Thus, the real exchange rate e is given by:

$$e = E(1 + \dot{P}_1/1 + \dot{P}_0) \quad \textbf{(7.12)}$$

or, $$E = e(1 + \dot{P}_0/1 + \dot{P}_1) \quad \textbf{(7.13)}$$

where,

$\dot{P}_0$ = inflation rate in India

$\dot{P}_1$ = inflation rate in the United States

If the inflation rate in the two countries during the period of reference were the same, E = e. A relatively higher inflation rate causes the real exchange rate to go down (i.e, appreciation) and vice versa. Thus, if the inflation rate in India was 10 per cent and that in the United States 2 per cent, the nominal exchange rate remaining unchanged at ₹10 per dollar, the real exchange rate will be:

$$e = ₹10\ (1.02/1.10)$$
$$= ₹9.272$$

Therefore, the real exchange appreciates by about 8 per cent. Since the real exchange rate affects net export (vide equation 7.5), the nominal rate is often adjusted to neutralise the effect of the differential inflation rate. If this were done here, the nominal rate would need to come down to:

$$e = ₹10 = E\ (1.02/1.10)$$

$$\Rightarrow \quad E = ₹10.784$$

This implies a depreciation of the nominal exchange rate of the Indian currency by about 8 per cent (from ₹10 to ₹10.784) Thus, by the PPP theory, while the real exchange rate varies inversely, the nominal exchange rate varies directly with the gap between the domestic and foreign inflation rates. The formula for the new nominal exchange rate (E_t), given the earlier rate (E_{t-1}), and the current inflation rates is given by

$$E_t = E_{t-1}(1 + \dot{P}_0 / 1 + \dot{P}_1) \quad \textbf{(7.14)}$$

It is obvious from equation **(7.11)** that the nominal exchange rate varies directly with the inflation rate at home and inversely with that abroad. Thus, while the BOP theory determines the real exchange rate, the nominal exchange rate is obtained by multiplying the real rate by the corresponding relative price of the two countries. It must be noted that the PPP theory assumes that all goods are homogenous and tradable, that there are no restrictions (tariffs, quotas etc.) on trade across countries, and that there is no transaction cost. Of course, the theory could be modified to incorporate tariffs. However, there are non-tradable goods (like structures which carry rents, haircut and other services), all the tradable goods are not perfect substitutes to their counterparts in the other countries, and trade barriers and transaction costs do exist. Thus, the PPP theory does not describe the real world perfectly. The PPP rate differs from the actual rate for its assumptions do not hold exactly in the real world. The PPP refers to the long-run tendency of exchange rates to offset divergent trends in national price levels. The theory is useful and it does provide a reason to expect that the fluctuations in the real exchange rate will typically be small or temporary, lest it affect the net export. If exchange rates follow PPP, nominal exchange rate movements have no effects on relative competitiveness.

To assess its relevance in the real world, Mc Donald's Big Mac's price comparison across nations is often cited, for the product is of standard quality and is available in over 100 countries globally. A few years ago an article in the *Times of India* reported that the average price in the United States and Euro areas were same, at $2.71. Thus, if the PPP theory was true, the forex rate should have been Euro 1 equal to US dollar 1. The true exchange rate then was Euro 0.91 = $1. The Euro was thus only marginally over-valued. In case of other currencies the difference, of course, could be high.

Incidentally, note that the PPP theory provides the link across nations through the current account of the balance of payments. Since the balance in the current account is a component of the aggregate demand, this link is known as the multiplier link.

Relative Growth Rate

Since the domestic income affects imports and the world income the exports, the growth rates in the two incomes play a role in the demand and supply of the foreign exchange, and thereby on the exchange rate. Thus, if the domestic country grows faster than the world economy, *ceteris paribus*, imports would increase more than the exports, and so there would be an extra demand for foreign currency, which, in turn, would cause a depreciation of the domestic currency. Quite the opposite would hold when the relative growth rate in the country is weak. By this factor, China and India should have had depreciating currencies over time.

It is obvious that the balance of payments theory contains all the determinants of the exchange rate. Integration of these theories suggest that if, for example, India experiences a lower interest rate, a higher inflation rate and/or a higher economic growth rate than the United States, then the Indian rupee would tend to depreciate in terms of the dollar over time. From this it follows that the four important rates for international transactions are

- Exchange rate
- Interest rate
- Inflation rate
- Economic growth rate

In essence, interactions among economic and financial variables across relevant nations determine the exchange rate. As noted in Chapter 4, the bulk of the foreign exchange transactions are carried out not for the genuine need of exports/ imports/ productive investments, but for currency speculations and arbitrage. Thus, expectations play a significant role in the determination of the exchange rate. After the breakdown of the Bretton Woods System in 1973, the exchange rate fluctuated rather violently, more than the fluctuations in the inflation or the economic growth rate. Dornbusch (1976) then developed the **Overshooting Theory**. The new theory suggests that, to quote from Stanley Fisher's recent article in *Economic Times*, "since both the price as well as output levels are 'sticky', and thus when a shock hits the economy, it is initially absorbed by the interest rate and exchange rate. In the process, the exchange rate typically overshoots its long-run value". Since shocks are largely unpredictable and expectations are hard to explain, no theory can do real justice to explain exchange rate behaviour. In view of this, though a number of empirical studies have been carried out on the determination of the exchange rate in various countries, unfortunately none has succeeded in predicting this variable with any meaningful degree of accuracy (vide Gupta and Keshava, 1994). Perhaps the naive method (where the future exchange rate = present exchange rate) or some such pure statistical method serves as a better tool than a theory based tool for this purpose. Nevertheless, theory alone offers an explanation of changes and thus its significance is beyond doubt.

International Financial Institutions

Recall that the Bretton Woods Conference of 1944 led to the establishment of the International Bank for Reconstruction and Development (IBRD), better known as the World Bank, and the International Monetary Fund (IMF). The former was charged with the responsibility of advancing loans for the purpose of reconstruction and development, and the latter with the supervision of the exchange rate system and the balance of payments (BOP), and advancing loans if the deficits in BOP were otherwise unmanageable. The World Trade Organisation (WTO) was founded later in 1995 to regulate trade, which was hitherto regulated through the General Agreements on Tariffs and Trade (GATT). These institutions have been helping member nations with respect to their responsibilities and their role was fairly well appreciated until the Asian Crisis of 1997. In particular, the Bretton Woods fixed exchange rate system during 1945 to 1971 is credited with significant advancements in foreign trade and investments. However, since the said crisis, some academicians as well as politicians have sounded warnings against seeking their advice and assistance. During the crisis, IMF had put forth rather stringent conditions for advancing loans, which included cutting of fiscal/budget deficits to 3 per cent, opening the economy and balancing the trade and going for the floating exchange rate system, among others. While such aids have generally rescued several countries (like Mexico in 1982 and in the 1990s and Russia in the 1990s), some have fallen into trouble as well. The latter responded to the tough conditions and got into still deeper trouble, and those who did not accept those conditions were fairly successful in handling the crises. Examples for the first group includes Indonesia, Thailand and Argentina, and for the second, Malaysia. Malaysia was on the fixed exchange rate system with a peg to the US dollar before the crisis and she floated the currency soon after the crisis. To cite some concrete data, before the crisis the peg was at around ringgit (Malaysian currency) 2.55 per US dollar. On floatation in July 1997, the ringgit started falling, hitting almost ringgit 5 per US dollar by early 1998. The then Prime Minister of Malaysia, Dr Mahathir Mohammed, who happens to be a vocal critic of IMF policies, refused the bailout loan from IMF and instead imposed selective restrictions on the capital account of the BOP and reverted to the currency peg with the US dollar, of course, at a lower level of ringgit 3.8 to one dollar. The country revived thereafter and the peg remains intact even today. The Indonesian rupiah and Thailand baht were also floated and their rates too were violent during and after the crisis. The baht fell from 25 baht per dollar to about 50 baht per dollar during the crisis. The IMF role in coping with the crises faced by Mexico in 1995, Russia in 1998, Brazil in 1999 and Argentina in 2001, among others, has been criticised by some and praised by others. Kapur and Webb (2007) have recently argued that the IMF is not fulfilling its role well and accordingly a variety of initiatives and developments are taking place which complement or supplement the IMF's efforts towards financial coordination, insurance and surveillance.

Conclusion

While concluding this chapter, we must note that economists make distinctions between:

- a closed economy and an open economy
- a small open economy and a large open economy

Openness is measured by the share of the international trade and capital flows in the national income, and thus, an economy is closed if she has no international movements in goods, services and capital. In the present world, perhaps, no country will qualify as a closed economy. All economies that are not closed are open economies. Thus, all the economies are the open ones. The distinction between small and large open economies is not that precise. It is suggested that a country is a large open economy if it exerts influence on the world's interest rate and inflation. However, this is not easy to determine. Alternatively, it could be assessed on the basis of the country's foreign transactions' share in the total worldwide transactions. The United States of America enjoys the top position with regard to the size of GDP, a significant share in the world trade in goods and services (about 11 per cent in 2012), and her currency happens to be the most important currency for invoicing international transactions (about 50 per cent) and holding foreign exchange assets (about 60 per cent). Besides USA, in general, enjoys the free movements of goods, services and capital (though not of people). Thus, the United States is surely a large open economy. In contrast, India's share in the world trade currently approximates merely 2.2 per cent in 2012 and the Indian rupee is hardly used for international invoicing and foreign exchange reserves. On the basis of the above criterion, India could be bracketed as a small open economy. However, even this may also not be true because India does not yet have free movement of capital internationally. While the rupee is convertible on the current account, there are restrictions on the capital account convertibility, besides some restrictions on trade in selected items. Thereby, India could not be termed even as a small, pure open economy. An open economy is characterised by perfect capital mobility, which means the residents of the country have full access to the world's financial markets and the government does not restrict international borrowing or lending. A small open economy would be practically open for all trade in goods and capital, and its share in international transactions will be small or insignificant. China's share in world trade, currently (2012) stands at around 11 per cent, her GDP assumes number two ranking, growth rate stands at the top among all large economies for last nearly two decades, and its currency value is believed to be the cause of US persistent current account deficit. However, China does not have free capital movements. Accordingly, it is hard to say if China qualifies to be called as a large open economy.

A closed economy is totally insulated from the happenings in the 'rest of the world', and consequently, the material of this chapter is irrelevant to the understanding of its working. In contrast, a small open economy is highly sensitive to what goes on in the world and, in fact, product prices and interest rates in such economies tend to equal those in the world. By itself a small open economy can have only a negligible effect on world prices and interest rates, just as a firm has little influence on the price of its product if it operates in a perfectly competitive market. A large open economy falls somewhere in between these two extremes. While such an economy is affected by what goes on outside, it does enjoy considerable control over product prices and interest rates under its territory. Today, most economies are fairly open or opening up, and they are neither too big nor too small. Therefore the material of this chapter is inevitable for understanding their working.

Keywords

Laffer curve; Fallacy of ceteris paribus; Open economy; Current account convertibility; Measures of the degree of openness; Tariffs–Quantitative restrictions/ Quotas/Bans; Dead weight loss; WTO; Currency Devaluation-Revaluation; Export-Import-Net export function; Price elasticity; Pass through devaluation; Marshall-Lerner condition; J-curve phenomenon; Covered-Uncovered interest rate parity condition; Fixed-Floating exchange rate system; Hard-Soft peg; Dollarisation; Currency/Monetary union; Currency Board; Bretton Woods system; Horizontal band; Crawling peg; Crawling band; Pre-announced path; Pure/Clean/Free/Independent-Dirty/Managed floating exchange rate system, Ideal foreign exchange rate system, International trilemma, Impossible trinity, Mundell-Fleming model, BOP theory – PPP theory of exchange rate, Overshooting theory, GATT, IBRD, IMF.

REFERENCES

1. Bhagwati J N, 'The Pure Theory of International Trade: A Survey', *Economic Journal* 74 (1964): 1-84.
2. Chipman J S, 'A Survey of the Theory of International Trade: Part 3, The Modern Theory', *Economica* (1960): 18-76.
3. Dornbusch Rudi, 'Expectations and Exchange Rate Dynamics', *Journal of Political Economy,* (December 1976): 1161-76.
4. Gupta G S and H Keshava, 'Income and Price Elasticities in India's Trade', Vikalpa 14 (April–June 1994): 13-19.
5. Gupta G S and H Keshava, 'Exchange Rate Determinations: Models, Verification and Findings', *Journal of Foreign Exchange and International Finance,* 8 (July–September 1994): 178-94.
6. Kapur D and Richard Webb, 'Beyond the IMF', *Economic and Political Weekly* (Feb 17, 2007):581-589.
7. Lerner A P, *Essays in Economic Analysis*. London: Macmillan and Company, 1953.
8. Rogoff K S, Husain A M, Mody A, Brooks R and N Oomes, 'Evolution and Performance of Exchange Rate Regimes', Occasional Papers, International Monetary Fund, Washington DC, 2004.

REVIEW QUESTIONS

1. The table below gives the data on general government consumption and exports and imports as proportions of the gross domestic product in the selected countries for 1980 and 2012:

(Percentages)

Country	*General government consumption*		*Exports*		*Imports*	
	(% of GDP)		*(of goods and services as % of GDP)*			
	1980	*2012*	*1980*	*2012*	*1980*	*2012*
India	10	12	6	24	9	32
Australia	18	18	16	21	18	21
Brazil	9	21	9	13	11	14
China	15	14	8	31	8	27
France	18	25	22	27	23	30
Germany	NA	19	NA	52	NA	48
Japan	10	20	14	15	15	16
Korea (Rep.)	12	16	33	57	41	53
Malaysia	17	14	58	87	55	76
Nigeria	12	NA	29	40	19	36

Russian Fed	15	19	NA	29	NA	22
Singapore	10	10	215	210	224	178
UK	22	22	27	32	25	34
USA	17	17	10	14	11	18
World	16	18	22	31	21	31

Sources: World Development Indicators, World Bank, 2013.
International Financial Statistics, IMF March, 2013.

(a) Account for the differences in the size of the government consumption over time and across countries.
(b) Which country is more open? How and why?
(c) Compare the above data with the saving-investment data in question 6 of Chapter 6 and comment.

2. In the light of the data in above table (vide review question 1), discuss the role of the fiscal policy in the aggregate demand.

3. What roles, if any, does the following variables play in the aggregate demand?
(a) Foreign trade
(b) International price
(c) Foreign exchange rate

4. The table below gives the data on all the three components of the net private capital flows internationally for the select countries for 1990 and 2012:

($ billions)

Country	*Foreign direct investments (net inflows)*		*Portfolio equity (net inflows)*		*Bonds and lending (net inflows) PTCF**
	1990	*2012*	*1990*	*2012*	*2012*
India	0.24	24.0	0.15	22.8	27.5
Australia	8.11	56.6	NA	15.2	NA
Brazil	0.99	76.1	0.23	–0.01	46.4
China	3.49	253.5	–0.05	29.9	3.0
France	13.18	28.1	NA	36.1	NA
Germany	3.01	27.2	NA	–3.7	NA
Japan	1.78	2.5	NA	34.9	NA
Korea (Rep.)	0.79	5.0	0.67	16.9	NA
Malaysia	2.33	9.7	–1.24	NA	8.0
Nigeria	0.59	7.1	0	10.0	0
Russia Fed	NA	52.7	NA	1.2	NA
Singapore	5.58	56.7	NA	2.9	NA
UK	33.50	56.1	NA	27.6	NA
US	48.49	203.8	NA	232.1	NA
World	201.41	1509.6	NA	776.0	NA

*PTCF stands for Personal transfers and compensation of employees received
Source: World Development Indicators, 2006.

(a) Analyse the relative destinations for foreign investments and the trend in the same.
(b) Do foreign investments have any relationship with the growth rate (Table 1.1, Chapter 1)?

5. The move towards increasing business process outsourcing (BPO) is mutually beneficial. Do you agree? Why?
6. Devaluation is a sure remedy for balancing the current account of the balance of payments. Comment.
7. Tariffs are superior to quotas in regulating foreign trade. Explain.
8. Briefly explain the following concepts/theorems and their significance in macroeconomics:
    - Dollarisation
    - International trilemma
    - Covered interest rate parity condition
    - Fallacy of ceteris paribus
9. The table below gives data on the integration of a cross-section of countries with the world economy:

Country	*Merchandise trade (% of GDP)*	*Net private capital flows (% of GDP)*	*Net official capital flows (% of GDP)*	*External debt (% of GDP)*
	2012	*2012*	*2012*	*2012*
India	40.5	4.0	0.08	20.8
USA	25.0	2.8	NA	NA
UK	45.4	1.2	NA	NA
Japan	28.6	0.6	NA	NA
Malaysia	144.0	5.8	0.20	35.5
Brazil	19.9	5.7	0.12	19.9
China	49.8	3.5	0.03	9.2
Australia	37.3	4.7	NA	NA
Nigeria	71.3	6.6	0.25	4.2
Russian Fed	45.5	2.6	NA	NA
Germany	75.8	0.7	NA	NA
World	51.8	3.2	NA	NA

Source: World Development Indicators, 2013

It may be noted that the data on capital flows in the table are on the net flows, meaning inflows minus outflows.

(a) What is the difference between net private capital flows and net foreign direct investments?
(b) Examine the degree of globalisation of various countries and comment.
(c) Evaluate the relationship between globalisation and, both, standard of living and economic performance. (Hint: refer to Table 1.1, Chapter 1 and Table 2.5, Chapter 2).

Chapter 8

Money Demand and Supply Functions

Learning Objectives

After reading the chapter you should be able to:

1. Learn the functions of money, the reasons for its versions, and their components.
2. Appreciate why people/business hold money (liquidity), and that the size of their holdings varies positively with their income/business size and negatively with the interest rate.
3. Comprehend the system through which the monetary authority of the country, the country's Central Bank, prints the currency notes and the way the commercial banks create the deposit money.
4. Understand the fundamentals of deposit and money multipliers, and appreciate the roles of the public (including the business) and the commercial banks in affecting the actual quantity of the money supply.
5. Know the goals and the instruments of the monetary policy and their workings, besides their actual uses and priorities particularly in India.

Money is considered one of the three great inventions of the world, the others being the wheel and the fuel. Today, it is an essential tool of civilization, not only to carry out transactions, to measure the value of all goods and deferred payments and to serve as a store of value, but also to lubricate production. Some economists (like James Tobin) have, thus, even called it a factor of production. However, money is not a component of the real wealth of the nation, which consists of the stock of material goods only. And as such, it is not a determinant of material welfare. For individuals, of course, money is a part of wealth, just as foreign exchange reserves are wealth for the nation. Before the invention of money, barter trade prevailed, but it is practically out today and is replaced by the trade through the media of money. Whether the entry of this media influenced macroeconomic variables like the magnitude and growth of the GDP, employment and unemployment, as well as the inflation rate is an important question that requires analysis and deliberation. An answer to this question would throw some light on the issue of whether the 'central bank' of the country, which conducts the monetary policy, enjoys any power to regulate the economy.

Money happens to be an intermediate variable between the ultimate goal variables and the instruments (Chapter 1). Further, recall that the interest rate is a determinant of both the consumption and investment expenditures and, as would be explained later, money plays an important role in the determination of that rate. Quantity of money in the economy obviously has bearing on the price level as it is used to buy all goods and services. Through these links, money occupies an important place in macroeconomics. While some economists and policymakers consider money as neutral or a veil over the real magnitudes, there are others who argue otherwise. Accordingly, economists differ in their views on the role of monetary policy. An understanding of this lively debate and the true role of money in the economy requires a deep insight into the factors that determine the demand for money and the mechanism through which money supply is created and regulated in the economy. Though there is no unique measure of money anywhere, its two definitions, viz., **narrow and broad money**, are universal. Accordingly, these two measures alone would be referred to in this chapter and thereafter. Recall from Chapter 4 that in India, we have four 'old' measures and three 'new' measures of money, besides this there are three liquidity aggregates. Though the new measures mark an improvement over the old ones, they have yet to be internationalised and there is no long-term data series available on them. However, the old versions of the narrow and broad moneys are in use, they approximate the new measures NM_I and NM_3 and are referred to as M_I and M_3, respectively.

Demand for Money

John Maynard Keynes proposed that people hold money for three reasons:

(a) Transactions motive
(b) Precautionary motive
(c) Speculative motive

Money serves as the medium of exchange, and the receipts of money (income and the borrowing) and the payments of money (expenditure and lending) lack perfect synchronisation. This gives rise to the holding of money to carry out day-to-day expected transactions. The precautionary need is to finance expenses on rainy days, like accidents, sickness, and entertaining guests, which are not quite predictable. The last motive is due to the uncertainty regarding the monetary yields on the non-money assets. Money is an asset, which serves as a store of value or as the "temporary abode of purchasing power" to use Milton Friedman's terminology. However, there are other assets (like bonds, stocks, house) which also serve as stores of value. The yields on money and alternative assets are dynamic, and thus peoples' expectations about this relative yield give rise to a specific type of demand for money, which is referred to as the speculative demand for money, or as a candidate in the portfolio of assets. While money is the only asset which has a fixed monetary value, has zero (or near) risk of default, and yet some part of it (time deposits) earns a positive rate of (nominal) interest. Accordingly, money reduces the risk associated with the portfolio of assets and so people holds money for speculative purpose. Thus, if a person expects the bond price to fall or the interest rate to increase, he/she would like to keep ready cash to take the advantage of the emerging situation, should his expectation turns out to be true. While there are no alternative assets to satisfy the first motive (as money is the only universally acceptable means of payment), the other two motives could be met even with other assets, called the near money (bonds) or to some extent even by durable goods. The latter assets, though, may not be as liquid as money (**liquidity** refers to the ease with which an asset can be converted into money at its reasonable price); they attract yields (generally larger than bank deposits) in the form of interest rate or as a hedge against inflation.

Currency enjoys the status of **legal tender** and, therefore, it is universally acceptable for all the payments. Cheques enjoy this power in most cases around the world, though less in India and some other nations. Thus, bank deposits, which can be withdrawn through cheques, could also be held for transaction motives. In contrast, the 'other' bank deposits (not subject to cheques, like fixed deposits), which are the components of money, are held to serve the other two motives. Lately, almost all bank deposits have become withdrawable on demand/through cheques, and thus, the above distinction is somewhat blurred[1]. Since the currency is interest barren and can be lost or stolen, it is not a good means to hold wealth or as a store of value. Thus, while currency serves the medium of exchange function better and bank deposit serves as stores of value better than the other components of money, basically all money components could serve all the functions with varying degree of convenience.

Determinants of Money Demand

The demand for money varies directly with scale variables (income and wealth) and negatively with the returns on alternative assets. Since money earns nothing (or a low interest rate), other than the convenience (or liquidity), which is not measurable, yield on it is irrelevant. The alternative assets, which could serve as a store of value, include bonds, equity and even the durable goods. However, durable goods are only a rather poor substitute for money and, thus, the return on them (capital appreciation or inflation) is often ignored. Therefore, the interest rate on bonds (and return on equity) is considered as the negative factor in the money demand function.

Income Money is needed to carry out transactions and the value of the transactions a person would have obviously varies directly with his/her income. Rich people buy more valuable goods for consumption than the poor do. Recall the consumption function of Chapter 5 where the consumption expenditure was hypothesised to vary directly with the income. Also, even the precautionary need for money is more among richer people than among poorer people. This is because, in general, rich people tend to spend more on entertaining unexpected guests, on sickness and on accidents than poor people. Recognising these facts, classical economists, who did not accept that money serves the speculative motive, hypothesised the **quantity theory of money**, which is expressed alternatively as the Irving Fisher's equation and Cambridge's equation:

Fisher's equation: $MV = PT$ **(8.1)**

Cambridge equation: $M = k\,PY$ **(8.2)**

where M = money supply (nominal)
V = velocity of circulation (rate of turnover) of money
P = general price
T = volume of transactions (= real income)

[1]In India, fixed deposits can be withdrawn at any time, though premature withdrawals result some loss of interest on them.

k = proportion of nominal income held in money
Y = output (real income)

In these versions, the demand for real money is a positive function of the real income.[2] Classical economists believed, as would be discussed in detail later in chapters on business cycles, that the economy always operated at the full employment level and accordingly they considered the real income as a constant (given). Further, they assumed the velocity of circulation of money (that is, the number of times an average unit of money is used to transact goods and services during a given period) as a constant. On these premises, the classical economists argued in favour of a direct and proportionate relationship between the quantity of money and the price level. Keynes, who was the first to articulate the three motives behind holding money in his 'General Theory' in 1936, postulated that the transaction and precautionary demands for money vary directly with the level of income. Income, thus, has been treated as an important positive determinant of the money demand in all the models. Figure 8.1 describes the relationship graphically:

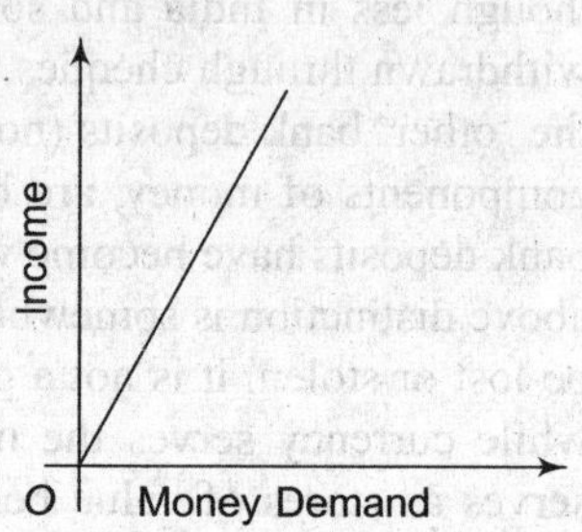

Fig 8.1 Classical Money Demand Function

The graph is drawn linear, though the relationship between the money demand and income need not be so. In particular, as we shall see later under the square root formula (equation **8.6**), there may be economies of scale in money holdings. That is, as the income goes up, people hold more but proportionately less and less money. If so, the said curve would still be upward sloping but convex to the money demand axis.

Wealth James Tobin (1958) and Milton Friedman (1956) have imparted money demand a portfolio theory approach. According to them, money is one of the assets in the form of which people could hold their portfolios of assets. The size of this portfolio depends positively on the wealth of the people. The more wealth a person has, the more he/she would save, and the larger would be the size of his/her portfolio. Thus, wealth is a positive factor in the money demand function. However, since income includes the income from wealth, it is often taken as a 'surrogate' measure of the asset holding power of individuals. Also, if wealth was used along with income in the function, there could be an econometric problem, called multicollinearity, in the estimation of the function. Due to these factors, wealth is often ignored as a determinant in the money demand function.

Interest Rate Recall that under the narrow definition M_1, money is interest barren, or almost so (Chapter 4). Therefore, the interest rate on bonds represents an opportunity cost of holding the money. Interest rate denotes the payment made for the use of the services of money. According to the broad definition (M_3), a part of the money (savings and fixed deposits) earns interest but usually the rate of interest

[2]While equations **(8.1)** and **(8.2)** are generally treated as the money demand functions, they are sometimes referred to as the price functions. The particular reference is subject to the belief as to whether the price causes money, or vice versa. Since the direction of the causation is in dispute, either identity is appropriate.

on bank deposits is less than that on the corporate and government bonds. Thus, even in a wider definition, the difference in the interest rate on bonds over that on the money happens to be the yield on alternative assets. Accordingly, to the extent the money is held as a store of value (i.e., to satisfy the speculative motive), the demand for it varies inversely with the rate of interest. Recall from Chapter 4 that there is a vast array of interest rates, depending on the asset, its liquidity, maturity period and risk. For simplicity here we lump all those assets into just one, and call it the non-money asset or bond, and assume that it earns the said (excess) interest rate. James Tobin (1953) suggests that money alone is a risk-free asset and even in the Markowitz- Sharpe return-risk optimisation theory, money is a potential asset for a position in the portfolio. The returns on non-money assets have negative effects on the holding of money even in that theory. It is instructive to note here that the interest rate relevant in the money demand function is the nominal rate (not the real interest rate), as it is the nominal rate alone that clearly measures the yield on bonds. Both money and bonds are financial assets, whose real value erodes equally with inflation.

Milton Friedman (1956) has gone a step further in this regard. According to him, even the return on equity and that on human capital represents yields on alternative assets, and accordingly, they have negative effects on the demand for money. In addition, the inflation rate is argued to affect the real money holdings inversely. This is because people could hold their assets even in durable goods, which provide a hedge against inflation. According to this logic, the inflation rate becomes the yield on durable goods (assuming they have zero wear and tear and storage costs) and, thus, an argument in the money demand function.

It is true that there are many alternatives to money as a store of value. But returns on all of them may not really be included in the money demand function. This is because most yields usually move in the same direction and roughly in the same proportion. Thereby, if all of them were included in the function, the estimation of the function would be subject to multicollinearity, yielding wrong estimates. To avoid this problem, the yield on the closest substitute of money alone is considered. Since bonds happen to be the closest alternative to money in the portfolio, the interest rate on bonds alone is considered as the opportunity cost of holding money.

The interest sensitiveness of money demand, like the interest sensitiveness of investment, assumes special significance in macroeconomics. This would be seen in the later chapters. In view of this, the relationship may be explained graphically, as shown in Fig. 8.2.

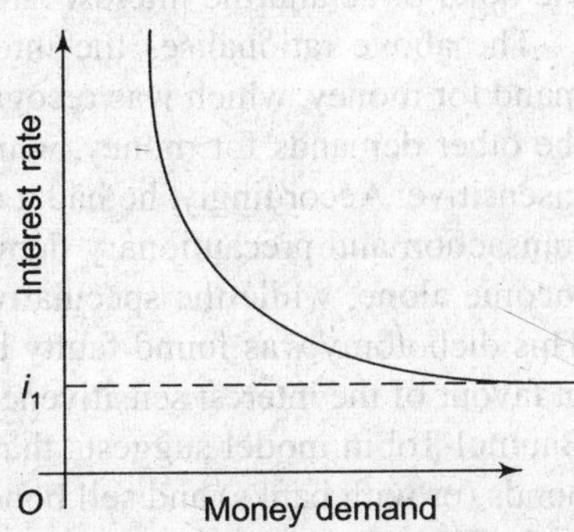

Fig. 8.2 Interest Sensitiveness of Money Demand

The curve in the figure is generally referred to as the liquidity preference curve. It is falling and convex to the money demand axis. When the interest rate is too high, the bond price is too low and people hold most of their assets in bonds and a little in money, so the curve is steep. In contrast, at a very low interest rate the bond price is prohibitive and people put most of their assets in money, accordingly, the curve is flat. Further, when the interest rate is too low (i_1, in Fig. 8.2) it is expected to rise in future and thus people do not hold their assets in bonds but only in money. This is referred to as the **Liquidity trap**. At $i = i_1$, the curve is totally flat, meaning all assets are held in money only, and this is because the convenience/benefits of holding money exceeds the low interest rate at i_1. At the intermediate interest rates, the liquidity preference curve is downward sloping, and its slope increases as the interest rate falls. The negative relationship between the bond price and interest rate follows from the discounting principle. To show this, let us express the bond price equation:

$$BP = \frac{I}{1+i} + \frac{I}{(1+i)^2} + \frac{I}{(1+i)^3} + \dots$$

where BP = bond price
I = interest amount on bond each period
i = interest rate in the market

If the bond was a perpetuity (that is, never redeemed) like a console, then the interest is received indefinitely and the bond never matures. If so, the right hand side of the equation goes on infinitely and is in geometric progression with common ratio equals 1/1 + i. Accordingly, the sum would give

$$BP = \frac{I/1+i}{1-\frac{1}{1+i}}$$

or, $$BP = \frac{I}{i} \tag{8.3}$$

Thus, if the annual return from a bond was ₹1,000 and the market interest rate was at 8 per cent per annum, the bond price would be ₹1000/0.08 = 12,500. Further, if the interest rate was at 5 per cent, *ceteris paribus*, the bond price would be ₹1000/0.05 = 20,000 and so on. This proves the inverse relationship between the interest rate and the bond price. If the bond was not a console, the right hand side of the above equation would be finite, going up to the bond maturity period and having the redemption amount at the maturity. In that case also, the relationship between the bond price and the interest rate would be negative.

The above rationalises the interest sensitiveness of the speculative (asset) demand for money, which was recognised even by Keynes (1936). Keynes considered the other demands for money, which are, transaction and precautionary, as interest insensitive. Accordingly, he had a dichotomised money demand function, where the transaction and precautionary demands were deemed to depend (positively) on the income alone, while the speculative demand on the interest rate (negatively) only. This dichotomy was found faulty by Baumol (1952) and Tobin (1956), who argued in favour of the interest sensitiveness of even the transaction demand for money. The Baumol-Tobin model suggests that people could keep their transaction balances in bonds (or with banks) and sell bonds (withdraw from banks) as and when they need cash. They earn interest on bonds, but on going from bonds to money they incur transactions cost. A rational person would decide this on the basis of the optimisation principle. To explain this, let us study the following example.

Suppose a person has an income of Y per period (say month) and he/she spends all this on transactions during the next period. Income is received at the beginning of the period and transactions are spread uniformly throughout the period. If the person keeps all the income in cash, and the cash holdings = Y at the beginning of the month, reducing everyday by 1/30th (assuming month = 30 days) each day, going to zero on the 30th day. The average cash holdings will then be *Y*/2:

$$\text{Average cash holdings} = \frac{1}{30}\left[Y + \frac{29}{30}Y + \frac{28}{30}Y + \frac{27}{30}Y + \cdots + \frac{2}{30}Y + \frac{1}{30}Y\right]$$

$$= \frac{1}{30}\left(\frac{Y}{30}\right)[30 + 29 + 28 + 27 + \cdots + 2 + 1]$$

$$= \frac{1}{30}\left(\frac{Y}{30}\right)(465)$$

$$\approx \frac{Y}{2} \text{ (if data were continuous)}$$

The advantage of cash holdings is convenience, and the cost is the loss of interest, which the person could earn if the balances were held in bonds or kept as bank deposits. Also, if the balances were held in bank, the person would need to visit the bank as and when he needed the cash for carrying out his transactions. This would involve the transaction cost, called the **shoe-leather cost**, each time he visits the bank for the purpose. A rational person would weigh the benefits and cost of holding the cash balances and then decide on how many visits he must make to the bank per period.

Let *N* be the number of bank visits. Then, his average cash holdings would equal *Y*/2*N*, which equals the amount of money he withdraws from the bank each time he visits. His total cost would then be given by

$$C = \left(\frac{Y}{2N}\right)(i) + aN \tag{8.4}$$

where C = total cost of cash holdings
i = interest rate on bank deposits
a = transaction cost per visit (shoe-leather cost)

The first term on the right of equation **(8.4)** represents the loss of interest on his cash holdings and the second term the total transaction cost. Further, the first term indicates the downward (and rectangular hyperbolic) relationship between the cost and the number of bank visits and the second term the upward (and linear) relationship between the two. Figure 8.3 illustrates these relations.

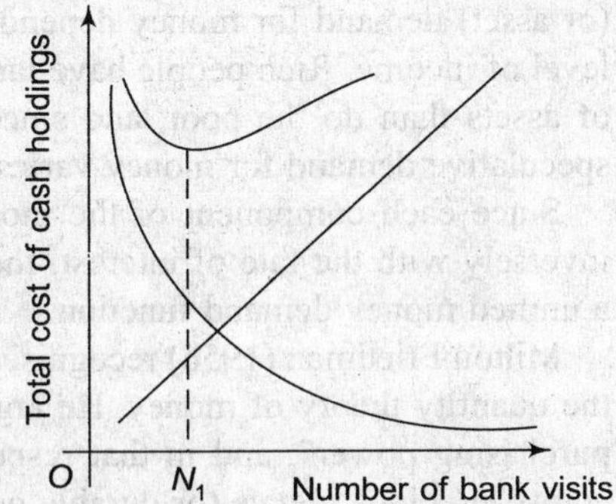

Fig. 8.3 Cost of Cash Holdings

In Fig. 8.3, the downward sloping curve maps the first term of the cost function (8.4) and the linear upward sloping line the second term of the said function. The vertical sum of these two curves gives the total cost. The same is contained in the U-shaped curve in Fig. 8.3. A rational person would choose the minimum point on the U-curve, thus N_l indicates the optimum value for N. The diagram is simple to understand but less precise for those who are well versed in mathematics. If we could use the calculus of optimisation, the optimum value for N would be obtained by setting the first derivative of function (8.4) with respect to N to zero and ensuring that the second derivative is positive. Thus

$$\frac{\partial C}{\partial N} = -\frac{Y\,i}{2N^2} + a = 0$$

$$\Rightarrow \qquad N = \sqrt{\frac{Y\,i}{2a}} \tag{8.5}$$

and $$\frac{\partial^2 C}{\partial N^2} = \frac{Y\,i}{N^3} > 0$$

Equation (8.5) gives the optimum value for N. Substitution of this in the average cash holdings yield:

$$\text{Average cash holdings} = \frac{Y}{2N}$$

$$= \sqrt{\frac{aY}{2i}} \tag{8.6}$$

Equation (8.6) is known as the **square root formula**. By this, the average cash holdings, that is, the demand for money for the transactions' purpose depends positively on the income and the transactions' cost, and negatively on the interest rate. Calculation of elasticity, would, show that the income elasticity of the demand for money = 1/2, transactions cost elasticity = 1/2 and the interest rate elasticity of the demand for money = –1/2. Since the income elasticity is less than unity (as also the other two), it is said that there are economies of scale in the transactions' demand for money. In this model, the income elasticity is under-estimated and interest elasticity over-estimated, and this is because the model treats N as a continuous variable, which in fact, is an integer in the real life.

Equation (8.6) clearly indicates that the transactions' demand for money is interest sensitive, besides being responsive to income. It is easy to see that the speculative (or asset) demand for money depends not only on the interest rate but also on the level of income. Rich people have larger savings, and accordingly, larger portfolios of assets than do the poor, and since money is a candidate for the portfolio, the speculative demand for money varies directly with income.

Since each component of the money demand varies directly with income and inversely with the rate of interest, the Keynes dichotomy is discarded in favour of a unified money demand function.

Milton Friedman (1956) recognised all the above developments and yet favoured the quantity theory of money. He argued that "money is a temporary abode of the purchasing power", and in that respect money has several substitutes like bonds, equity, precious metals (or durable goods), and even human capital (education and health). Returns (risk-adjusted) on each of these alternative assets would, thus, affect the demand for money. Return on the human capital is not known, and thus, has to be left out on empirical grounds. Return on durable goods is the rate of expected inflation as they are a hedge against inflation. The returns on bonds and equity (as well as on the other assets) are highly correlated and they create a multicollinearity problem in estimation. The expected inflation rate affects the nominal interest rate directly through Fisher's relation (vide equation 6.6, Chapter 6), and thus, it is contained in the interest rate. Also, the opportunity cost of real cash balances is really the return on bonds only as bonds alone are the closest substitute of money. Milton Friedman estimated the money demand function for the United States economy and he found that the coefficients of the various interest rates were insignificant. On this basis, he suggested that, though theoretically interest is a determinant of the money demand, empirically it is an insignificant factor. Thus, he favours the quantity theory of money for the money demand function.

Money Demand Function

The above discussion yields the following function:

$$\frac{L}{P} = f(Y, i) \qquad \textbf{(8.7)}$$

$$f_1 > 0 > f_2$$

where L = money (liquidity) demand in nominal terms
P = price level
Y = real income
i = interest rate (nominal)

The function is in real terms, because inflation must be neutral for the money balances out of income: if the general price level doubles, *ceteris paribus*, money income doubles and so would the nominal money demand. This assumes the absence of **money illusion**, that is, decision makers are assumed to be guided by real magnitudes and not by nominal ones.

The above demand for money function performed reasonably well until about the early 1970s. However, beginning 1974, the said demand function began to seriously over predict the demand for money—the 'case of missing money'. Later, during the 1980s, the situation was reversed; the function began to under predict the money demand. The explanations offered for its poor performance include innovations in the financial sector, problems in measuring the opportunity cost of holding money, and low inflation and interest rates. While the said innovations (like automatic teller machines, ATM, electronic transfer of money and proliferation of near-money assets), which were concentrated in the 1970s, have reduced the money demand, falls in the inflation and interest rates, which have been significant in the 1980s and 1990s, have increased the said demand. Due to these factors, the function has proved unstable and accordingly there has been a gradual loss of support for monetarism. Nevertheless, since the world is dynamic, no function can guarantee validity for all times and the above function is still considered as the standard one. Appropriate modifications would have to be made as and when required. The other determinants of money demand would include:

(a) ease and certainty of getting loan

(b) expectations about future income receipts
(c) nature and availability of substitutes for money
(d) popularity of purchases on credit.

The more favourable each of these factors are the lesser would be the demand for money. Since these factors are difficult to measure, they are rarely used in any empirical work.

Equation (8.7) indicates that the real income and the interest rate are governed by the money demand function as well, besides the ones seen under the consumption and investment functions. The significance of this will be clear when all such relations are combined into a macroeconomic model of income and price determination.

SUPPLY OF MONEY

Money, to serve as a medium of exchange, first came into human history in the form of commodities such as cattle, olive oil, beer or wine, copper, iron, gold, silver, diamonds and cigarettes. These products were non-divisible and so created problems in small exchanges. By the 19th century, commodity money was almost exclusively limited to metals like silver and gold. Since money had intrinsic (real) value, there was no need for government guarantee. Further, as the supply of money was regulated by the supply of those precious metals, there was no need to regulate its quantity either. However, as trade expanded, money supply became insufficient and it posed a major constraint to further growth. Thus, token/fiat money (money by government declaration) in the form of paper money and coins was invented. The former consists of currency printed by the treasury and/or the central bank of the country, and the latter is coined by government owned agencies/mint. In addition, there are bank deposits, which also form a component of money. Thus, money supply in reality consists of debts of the money creating agencies (government, central bank and commercial/cooperative banks). Both the currency and deposit moneys are, however, controlled by the central bank of the country. On what bases the two kinds of money are created and how these are regulated is explained in this chapter. The methods are basically similar all over the world, but here India's position is explained in detail.

Recall from Chapter 4 that there are two components of money supply in India, viz., currency with the public and bank (and postal) deposits. Further, since globally only narrow and broad money concepts are common, we will restrict the discussion to these concepts only. Before we go into the details on them, it would be appropriate to discuss the sources of money supply in India. The sources of broad money supply in India, for some selected years, are presented in Table 8.1.

Table 8.1 Sources of Broad Money Supply in India

(₹ billion/end of period)

Source	*1990–91*	*2000–01*	*2012–13*
1. Net bank credit to government	**1,402**	**5,120**	**27,072**
• RBI's	888	1539	5,906
• Other banks'	514	3,581	21,166

(Contd.)

(*Contd.*)

2. Bank credit to commercial sector	**1,718**	**6,792**	**56,647**
• RBI's	63	133	31
• Other banks'	1,655	6,659	56,616
3. Net foreign assets of banking sector	106	2,498	16,367
• RBI's	80	1,972	15,581
• Other banks'	26	526	786
4. Government currency liabilities to public	**16**	**54**	**153**
5. Banking sectors' net monetary liabilities other than demand & time deposits	**583**	**1,331**	**16,418**
• RBI's	270	793	6925
• Other banks'	313	538	9,493
6. Broad money (M3) (1 + 2 + 3 + 4 – 5)	**2,658**	**13,132**	**83,820**

Source: Monthly Bulletins, RBI.

From the above table, it is clear that RBI's and other banks' credit to the government and commercial sector, their holdings of foreign assets and currency issued by the government constitute the sources of money supply. Since the demand and time deposits' alone are part of banks' liabilities in the money supply, other liabilities (viz net worth, etc.) are subtracted from the banks' total credit (item 5 in Table 8.1). Against these credits/assets, the RBI issues currency and other banks create deposits, which alone are the components of money supply, and how this is done is explained in what follows. Incidentally, note that the RBI's share is less in all components barring foreign assets, and that the relative share of foreign assets has grown considerably (106/2658 = 3.99% in 1990–91 to 16367/83820 = 19.52% in 2012–13). If one looks at full time series data, it would be seen that the said share was even higher than the current one a few years back. These aspects would be analysed later.

Currency

Currency is issued by the central bank of the country and the Ministry of Finance. In India, all the currency notes in the denominations of rupees two and above are issued by the Reserve Bank of India (RBI) and the one rupee currency notes and all the coins are issued by the Ministry of Finance. This is all token (face value > intrinsic value) but the fiat money. The respective issuers have the monopoly power granted by the Constitution/Cabinet. The profit that the central bank of the country makes through its monopoly power of printing the currency is called **seigniorage**. The word "seigniorage", which is derived from the French word "seigneur", means lord who used to charge fee to finance kings' expenses.

The RBI maintains the issue department for the purpose of currency issue. The issued currency (currency in circulation and notes held in Banking Department of RBI) is the liability, and the assets against them are in terms of gold (coin and bullion), foreign exchange/securities, rupee coin and government of India rupee securities (credit to central government). Thus, all currency issues have to be backed by these four asset items. Since 1957 or so, the RBI is required to have a minimum of ₹2000 million in the form of gold and foreign exchange assets, of which ₹1150 million must be in gold. The entire remaining amount could come from government securities. This is called the fixed reserve system in contrast to the earlier proportional reserve system, under which 40 per cent of the issued currency was required to be backed by gold and foreign reserves.[3] Under the present system, the RBI and government enjoy flexibility as they could issue any amount of currency deemed appropriate from time to time. Today, the currency issue system in all countries is similar to the Indian one, though the fixed reserve requirements (stipulations) vary from country to country. Until 1967, the United States had the system where the currency was backed by 25 per cent gold holdings. Gold reserves fell and so the system could not be maintained. There is no such gold backing requirement since then. Thus, the onus of issuing currency rests with the central bank and the government. Since the behaviour of these decision makers are difficult to explain, currency is considered as an autonomous (exogenous/policy) variable.

The balance sheets of the RBI's issue department in selected two years were as shown in Table 8.2.

Table 8.2 Issue Department of RBI

(*₹ Billions*)

Item	*1990–91*	*2012–13*
1. Liabilities		
* Notes in circulation	537.84	11772.18
* Notes held in banking dept	0.23	0.08
2. Total liabilities/Assets	538.07	11772.26
3. Assets		
* Gold coin and bullion	66.54	740.85
* Foreign securities	2.00	11019.02
* Rupee coin	0.29	1.92
* Govt. of India rupee securities	469.24	10.46

Source: RBI Bulletin, Nov. 2013

From the above data, it would be clear that while the government rupee securities dominated the assets in 1990–91, the foreign securities have assumed that position in 2012–13. This change has occurred mainly because of the enhanced autonomy the RBI has been given since around 1994 and the need to sterilise the increasing flow of foreign exchange into the country. Note that the RBI's holdings of gold and foreign securities have always been in good excess over the respective legal requirements.

Bank Deposits

Currency is held partly by the public and partly by the banks, on behalf of the public, in the form of bank deposits. If banks were merely cloakrooms, they would maintain 100 per cent reserves against their deposits and the money supply would just equal

[3]Initially, the fixed reserve system required ₹4000 million worth of gold and forex reserves, which was reduced subsequently to ₹2000 million due to the foreign exchange crisis.

the supply of the currency. However, banks are commercial entities and they not only do not charge cloakroom fees on deposits but also pay interest on most of them. This is possible through the **fractional reserve system** that banks follow against their deposits in the form of cash, using the rest for making loans to the public and for investing in some financial assets like bonds and equities. Banks know from experience and the theory of probability that not all depositors come simultaneously to withdraw their deposits and not usually in full amounts, and that while some come to withdraw, the others come to deposit. This enables banks to maintain only a part of their deposits in the form of currency (cash) and yet be able to honour the claims of all the depositors on time. This allows banks, what is known as, the creation of deposits' power or the **multiple creation of credit**, and accordingly, bank deposits are some multiple of the currency held by them.

Before going further on the multiple creation of credit, it is imperative to note that banks are required by law (from the central bank of the country) to maintain a certain fraction of their deposits in the form of cash balances with the Central Bank of the country. This law is designed partly to safeguard the interests of depositors and partly to provide an instrument in the hands of the Central Bank. This is an instrument of monetary control because the required fraction is subject to change (though within prescribed limits) at the discretion of the Central Bank. In India, the required reserves against the deposit liabilities, called the cash reserve (requirement) ratio, could vary between 3 and 15 per cent. Currently, it stands at 4.0 per cent (since Feb. 9, 2013), and this instrument was heavily used during the 1980s and the 1990s.

Over and above this reserve requirement, banks keep some reserves (called the **excess reserves**) to honour the claims of the depositors, as well as for other uses. Thus, the actual reserve ratio (reserve/deposit) is the sum total of the required reserve ratio and the excess reserve ratio. It is instructive to note here that while the fractional reserve system offers advantages in terms of permitting multiple credit creation, among others, it opens the possibility of bank panics, 'run on banks' and even bank failures. If depositors learn that their bank is not doing well, they would rush to withdraw their deposits and the bank, which is on the fractional reserve system, would not be able to honour the claims. It is this source, which has led to the failure of several cooperative banks in India, particularly in Gujarat, recently. However, the danger has been limited, and there are usually deposit insurances for large depositors and the Central Bank of the country is obliged to rescue the failing entity, thereby making the risk worth the advantage.

Multiple Creation of Deposits

Banks are financial intermediaries who accept deposits from those who save and advance loans to those who invest. In general, households earn more than they consume, and hence, they are the net savers. They have several outlets for their savings. They could invest directly in stocks and bonds or could go indirectly through financial institutions by holding bank deposits. Since the various outlets are only imperfect substitutes, households hold a mix of all such assets. Firms invest more than they save, and they cover the difference through public issues of stocks and bonds and borrowings from financial institutions, including banks. In this process, banks create new deposits, which are a part of the money supply. To illustrate this process, consider an example.

Mr Goyal puts ₹1,000 as a deposit with, say, the State Bank of India (SBI), which has just been registered. The balance sheet (BS) of SBI would then look like this:

Liabilities	*Assets*
Deposits ₹1,000	Reserves (cash) ₹1,000

The money supply will be unaffected by this transaction. Currency with the public is reduced by ₹1,000 and bank deposits show an amount of ₹1,000. All the deposits are in 100 per cent reserves.

The SBI is on a fractional reserve system, with a fraction, of say, 20 per cent. Remember that this 20 per cent has to meet with, both, the cash reserve requirements' condition as well as the need for excess reserves. The SBI pays some interest on its deposits and it earns nothing on its reserves. Prompted by this situation, the SBI will be eager to advance loan in the amount of ₹800, retaining ₹200 as reserves to meet the stipulated 20 per cent requirement. Therefore, when a borrower (Mr Sharma) comes, the SBI will advance a loan of ₹800, and its balance sheet then would change to:

Liabilities	*Assets*
Deposits ₹1000	Reserves ₹200
	Loans ₹800

After this loan is made, the money supply is up by ₹800! This is because the erstwhile currency of ₹1000 is replaced by bank deposits of ₹1000 and, in addition, Mr Sharma has ₹800 in currency, which he gets on loan from the SBI. Thus, money has been created. Further, the creation of money does not stop here. Mr Sharma will spend ₹800 on buying some goods/services from, say, Mr Patel, who, in turn, would deposit the proceeds with the SBI or some other bank, say, the Bank of Baroda (BoB). The BoB would keep ₹160 (20 per cent of 800) in reserves and advance loan in the remaining amount to, say, Mr Shah. The BoB balance sheet would then look like this:

Liabilities	*Assets*
Deposits ₹800	Reserves ₹160
	Loan ₹640

Mr Shah has now ₹640 in currency, besides deposits worth ₹1,000 with the SBI and ₹800 with the BoB. Thus, the money supply is further up by ₹640. Mr Shah may then spend his loan proceeds on buying goods from, say, Mr Shukla, who, will in turn, go and deposit the amount with his bank, which could be the SBI, the BoB or a third bank, say, UTI. The recipient bank will keep 20 per cent of the new deposit in reserves and advance a loan from the remaining amount to some borrower, say, Mr Gandhi. Consequently, Mr Gandhi will have cash of:

$$₹(640)\ (1 - 0.2) = ₹512$$

with the total bank deposits in the amounts of:

₹1000 (SBI) + ₹800 (BoB) + ₹640 (UTI).

Thus, the money supply is again up by ₹512. This process goes on continuously. With each deposit and loan, more money is created. Although this process of money creation can continue forever, it does not create an infinite amount of money. Since money creation reduces at every stage, it tends towards zero at some stage. The total money creation would be given by:

$$₹1000\,[1 + (1 - 0.20) + (1 - 0.20)^2 + \cdots]$$

$$= ₹1000\left[\frac{1}{1-(1-0.20)}\right] = 1000\left[\frac{1}{0.20}\right]$$

$$= ₹5000$$

In general, rupee one of the first deposit (called the primary deposit) would create the total deposits (primary + secondary) of rupees $1/r$, where r = the fraction of deposits held as reserves by the banks. In turn, the money supply due to the fractional reserve system would increase by the additional deposits of rupees $[(1/r) - 1]$, which is referred to as the secondary deposits of banks. In the above example, the primary deposit of ₹1000 created secondary deposits of ₹4000, and increased each of the bank's deposits and money supply by ₹5000. This process reduces the currency with the public by ₹1,000 and increases the bank deposits by ₹5000, giving a net increase in the supply of money by ₹4000. The amount of increase varies inversely with the fractional reserves maintained by the banks. This is how banks create deposits and thence the money supply. This happens because the loss of reserves of one bank becomes gain of reserves in the same amount of other bank. Incidentally, note that the above description assumes:

- No leakage of cash from the system
- Fixed reserve ratio maintained by banks

If the money leaks out even partly, that is, held in the form of currency by bank borrowers, the creation of money will be reduced accordingly. Also, if banks change their reserve ratio, deposit creation will be affected. It must be noted that banks create money through primary deposits (reserves) and not out of thin air. An individual banks' capacity to create deposits/money, is limited to the extent of its excess reserves. For the banking system as a whole, the said capacity is limited by the ratio of all banks excess reserves and their average reserve ratio (ER/r). When a bank makes a loan or invests in government and private bonds, it creates deposits and hence money. Also, this power of creating money rests merely with the banking system. Other financial intermediaries like non-bank financial institutions, both at the centre (like National Industrial Development Corp., Industrial Reconstruction Bank of India, Shipping Credit and Investment Corp. of India, Tourism Finance Corp. of India, National Small Industries Corp., etc.) and state (State Financial Corps., State Industrial Development Corps., Technical Consultancy Organisations, etc.), and the stocks/bonds' market and the other non-finance companies do not enjoy this power. In fact, it is this power that distinguishes banks from other financial institutions and non-finance companies. This unique role of banks, as explained in Chapter 4, is due to the fact that only banks' (and postal) deposits are a part of the money supply.

The above system of money creation merely increases the supply of money and the liquidity, and not the wealth in the economy. Against this new money (assets), there are new bank loans (liabilities) of an equal amount, and thus, there is no change in the wealth of the economy. Incidentally, it may be noted that the Indian banking system is like the British, where there is branch banking, in contrast to the American system of unit banking. Currently, India has many banks, some in the public and others in the private (including foreign) sector, each of which has multiple branches spread in various parts of the country.

Money Supply Function

The system of deposit creation under the fractional reserve system can be extended to delineate the determinants of the money supply. This is done through the definition of monetary aggregates and algebraically:

$$M = C + D \quad \textbf{(8.8)}$$

$$H = C + R \quad \textbf{(8.9)}$$

where M = money supply
C = currency with the public
D = bank deposits
H = high-powered money
R = bank reserves

Equation (8.8) does not distinguish between bank deposits of different kinds and is thus applicable both to narrow and broad definitions of money supply. **High-powered money**, also known as the **reserve money, government money**, and **monetary base**, is so-called because it has the capacity to create more money and it represents the liabilities of the government (including the Central Bank of the country). As seen in the previous sub-section, bank reserves do enjoy the power of creating money, and if deposited with banks, currency is able to create more money. Note that bank reserves are partly kept with the Central Bank (RBI) (that is, bankers' deposits with RBI) and partly held in their own vaults by banks (which is referred to as currency in circulation).The data on the components of reserve money for selected years are given in Table 8.3.

Table 8.3 Components of Reserve Money

(₹ billion/end of year)

Component	*1990-91*	*2000-01*	*2012-13*
1. Currency in circulation	553	2,182	11,910
• With public	531	2,095	11,447
• With banks	22	87	463
2. 'Other' deposits with RBI	7	36	32
3. Bankers' deposits with RBI	318	815	3,207
4. Reserve money (1 + 2 + 3)	878	3,033	15,149

Source: Reserve Bank of India, Monthly Bulletins, Various Issues.

It may be noted that currency with banks and bankers' deposits with banks together constitute banks' reserves. Similarly, 'other' deposits with banks are considered as a part of the currency with the public. A careful look at the data would suggest that the currency part enjoys the dominant share in the reserve money.

To derive the money multiplier function, divide equation (8.8) by equation (8.9):

$$\frac{M}{H} = \frac{M}{C+R} = \frac{1}{\frac{C}{M} + \frac{R}{M}} = \frac{1}{\frac{C}{M} + \left(\frac{R}{D}\right)\left(\frac{D}{M}\right)}$$

From equation (8.8), $D = M - C$. Substituting this, we have:

$$\frac{M}{H} = \frac{1}{\frac{C}{M} + \left(\frac{R}{D}\right)\left(1 - \frac{C}{M}\right)}$$

Note that C/M is the currency ratio (c) and R/D is the reserve-deposit ratio (r). Making these substitutions, and taking H to the right, we get:

$$M = \left[\frac{1}{c + r(1-c)}\right] H$$

or

$$M = \left[\frac{1}{1-(1-c)(1-r)}\right] H \qquad \textbf{(8.10)}$$

Equation (8.10) indicates that the supply of money depends on three variables, which are:

- High powered money
- Currency ratio
- Reserve ratio

Money supply varies directly with the high-powered money and inversely with each of the currency ratio and the reserve ratio. Further, the relationship between M and H is proportional, and the factor of proportionality, denoted as m is called the **money multiplier**.

$$m = \frac{1}{1-(1-c)(1-r)} \qquad \textbf{(8.11)}$$

$$M = mH \qquad \textbf{(8.12)}$$

Each rupee of the high-powered money produces m rupees of money. This is called the multiplier, for $m > 1$, as c and r each is generally less than unity. Note that if either $c = 1$ or $r = 1$, $m = 1$. The lower the c or r, the higher the money multiplier. As money multiplier is greater than one, quantity of money is larger than the size of high-powered money. This holds because deposits are larger than the reserves that banks hold to back those deposits, which is the outcome of fractional reserves system which banks follow. Also, note that the banks' power to create money hinges on two factors, which are:

(a) currency ratio, which is less than unity, implying that people hold bank deposits.

(b) reserve ratio, which is less than unity, meaning banks follow the fractional reserve system.

While the Central Bank of the country (and the governments) determine the size of the high powered money, the currency ratio is the prerogative of the public and the reserve ratio of the banking system. Accordingly, the stock of money is determined jointly by the Central Bank of the country, banks and the public. However, there is a caveat to it. As noted above, banks are subject to some cash reserve requirement ratio (CRR) by the country's Central Bank, and thus, they are not totally free to choose the value of the reserve ratio; the higher is the CRR, the higher the r. Nevertheless, banks choose the excess reserve ratio (over and above the CRR). Banks hold excess reserves for the same purpose that households hold money. While the required reserves serve the purposes of the monetary policy instrument and insurance against bank failures, excess reserve serve the liquidity needs of banks. Banks enjoy borrowing facilities from the Central Bank of the country. The difference between the excess reserves and banks' borrowing from the Central Bank is called **free reserves**.

Both the currency with the public and the excess reserves with the banks are interest barren, and the alternative assets (bank deposits, bank's loans and investments, respectively) have positive returns. Thus, rational behaviour would suggest that both the currency ratio and the reserve ratio are negative functions of the (nominal) interest rate.[4] Since the money multiplier is a negative function of both c and r, it becomes a positive function of the interest rate, which, in turn, makes the money supply vary directly with the interest rate. In addition, in all behavioural functions, there is always a 'catch all' variable, defined here as u. Collecting all the above hypotheses together, we get the money supply function as follows:

$$M = f(H, CRR, i, u) \quad \textbf{(8.13)}$$
$$f_1, f_3 > 0 > f_2$$

Equation **(8.13)** refers to just one side of the money market. The other side is the demand for money. The two sides together determine quantity of money and interest rate, given the real income. Further, since demand for money comes from public and banks, the Central Bank can set either the quantity of money or the interest rate but not the both, as the former also has a role in choosing the residual variable. To explain the role of high-powered money vis-à-vis the money multiplier in the supply of money in India, the relevant data on them for a few selected years are presented in Table 8.4.

Table 8.4 Money Multipliers

(₹ *billion/Ratios*)

Item	*At the end of financial year*			
	1970-71	*1980-81*	*1990-91*	*2012-13*
1. Narrow money supply (M_1)	74	234	929	18,949
2. Broad money supply (M_3)	110	558	2,658	83,820
3. High powered money (H)	48	195	878	15,149
4. Narrow money multiplier (1/3)	1.54	1.20	1.06	1.25
5. Broad money multiplier (2/3)	2.29	2.86	3.03	5.53

Source: Monthly Bulletin, RBI, various issues

[4] The currency ratio also depends (negatively) on the popularity of the cheques and the credit cards, as well as on the laws governing the defaults through cheques' bounces, etc.

Corresponding to the narrow M_1 and broad money M_3 (vide Chapter 4), there are two multipliers, which are, M_1/H and M_3/H. The data suggest that while the narrow money multiplier has varied between 1.06 and 1.54, the broad money multiplier has fluctuated between 2.29 and 5.53 during the last over 40 years. Further, the data indicate that while the broad money multiplier has increased monotonously over time, the narrow money multiplier first fell during 1970 through 1991 and then went up. These fluctuations have been caused by changes in the cash reserve requirement ratio and the nominal interest rate, among some unknown factors (u).

To appreciate the determinants of reserve money, the sources for the same in India during the selected years are provided in Table 8.5:

Table 8.5 Sources of Reserve Money

(₹ billion/end of year)

Source	*1990-91*	*2000-01*	*2012-13*
1. RBI's claims on			
• Government	888	1,539	5,906
• Commercial & cooperative banks	69	64	403*
• National bank for agri. & rural dev.	31	66	
• Commercial sector	63	133	31
2. Net foreign exchange assets of RBI	80	1,972	15,581
3. Govt. currency liabilities to public	16	54	153
4. Net non-monetary liabilities of the RBI	270	793	6,925
5. Reserve money (1 + 2 + 3 — 4)	878	3,033	15,149

* includes claims on NABARD

Source: Reserve Bank of India, Monthly Bulletins, Various Issues.

From Table 8.5 we can see what determines reserve money. Since the RBI has claims on the government in the form of government bonds, it can sell and even buy them in the open market, thereby affecting the level of reserve money. This is called an open market operations tool in the hands of the central bank. However, the power of the RBI with regard to the open market sales is relatively very little currently as its relative holding of government bonds has declined considerably over time – RBI's holding of government bonds was at ₹888 billion out of ₹878 billion (101%) of reserve money in 1990–91, which fell to ₹81 billion out of ₹5731 billion (1.4%) in 2005–06, and rose again to ₹5906 billion out of ₹15149 billion (39%) in 2012–13. Further, the RBI has claims on banks, which, as we shall see later under the section on monetary policy instruments, exist partly due to the reserve requirements on the part of banks and partly for the borrowing privilege that banks enjoy from the RBI. Thus, by tempering such rules again the central bank can affect the reserve money. In addition, the stock of foreign exchange assets with the RBI is a major factor in the stock of reserve money, and thus, ups and downs in that have bearings both on the reserve money and on the money supply. As one-rupee notes and all coins are issued by the federal government (Ministry of Finance), they are also a component of the reserve money. Non-monetary liabilities of the RBI constitute largely its net worth.

Since the RBI is the monetary authority in India, it is obvious from the table that the reserve money is government money. The decreased share of RBI's claims on government and the increased share of foreign exchange assets in the reserve money, as noted above, has been due to (a) net inflow of foreign assets into India and (b) lest this change lead to over expansion of money supply in the economy, the RBI has been countering it through selling government bonds in the open market (to banks and public). This strategy is known as **sterilisation** in monetary literature. This is the act by which the central bank of the country buys excess foreign assets so that the foreign exchange rate is not impinged and, to nullify its impact on the reserve money and money supply, it sells government bonds to banks and public. Under this approach, banks hold excess of government bonds, which is appropriate from their point of view, particularly because these bonds now (since banks' reform beginning mid 1990s) earn the market rate. However, this has preempted banks' assets to some extent, thereby reducing banks' credit to the commercial sector. Rakesh Mohan, one of the then Deputy Governors of the RBI, has gone to the extent of even alleging banks as 'lazy bankers' on this count.

Function (8.13) indicates that the money supply is basically determined by the monetary authorities, who regulate both H and CRR. Thus, to the extent the money supply's sensitiveness to the interest rate is insignificant, money supply is a policy variable. It is for this reason that most macroeconomic models consider money supply as being directly controlled by the country's central bank. Incidentally, note that even the size of the high-powered money is subject to the government budget constraint and to borrowings' by banks from the central bank. This renders the money supply as an endogenous variable. However, such complications are often ignored in macroeconomics.

Regulation of Money Supply and Instruments of Monetary Policy

Recall that earlier we have stated that the central bank of the country controls the quantity of money in that country. How this is done is the subject matter of this section. However, before we go into it, a little of history may be recalled. Under the erstwhile commodity money, the money supply was restricted by the availability of that particular product and so the need for control did not even arise. Even when the **pure gold standard** came into existence, only gold coins and, thus, intrinsic money was in circulation. The replacement of this by **gold bullion standard** created token money. However, since money had to then be backed fully by gold, there was no artificial need to control it. It was largely because of this that money supply did not expand during the Great Depression. The gold bullion standard was subsequently replaced by the **gold exchange standard** (Bretton Woods System), under which the token money circulated, which, in turn, was backed by gold, foreign exchange assets and government bonds, and was convertible at a fixed exchange rate into US dollars, which, in turn, was convertible into gold. This imparted some flexibility with regard to the quantum of money supply, particularly through government bonds, and accordingly the need to manage the same. Today, even the latter system does not operate anywhere in the world and so there is a need to regulate the money supply. However, even today, some countries do not have this need and these are the ones who are on **dollarisation, currency board or common currency**. Recall from Chapter 7 that, the countries like Panama, Ecuador and El Salvador, who have adopted the US dollar as their home currency, have voluntarily given up the right to create their own money and thus have no power to even control it. The inflows of US dollar through their international transactions in goods, services, labour and capital determines the quantity of money available in those countries. Under the currency board, which exists in Hong Kong and in a few other countries, there is domestic currency but the same is backed fully or largely by a chosen foreign currency like the US dollar. Accordingly, the money supply in such countries is regulated by their holdings of US dollars. A group of countries in Europe are currently on the euro, the so called common currency, whose supply is regulated by their common central bank, known as the European Central Bank, and thus individual member country enjoy no power to regulate their own money supply. The rest of the countries (including India) have their own money, each one of which is backed only a little by gold and foreign exchange assets, and mostly by their own government bonds/treasury bills. Accordingly, such countries enjoy the power of regulating the supply of money in their respective country. This function is carried out by the central bank/monetary authority of the country and how this is done is explained below.

Recall from Chapter 7 that countries that are not on dollarisation, currency board or common currency, could be either on some other form of **currency peg** or on **floating rate system** that is either free or managed. This distinction is important here because the central bank's power to regulate the money supply is somewhat more limited under the peg than without it. If the exchange rate is fixed (and the country is integrated with the world, that is, it has no restrictions on the international flow of goods, services and capital), the central bank has to give up other objectives, if any (like maintaining price stability or/and promoting economic growth), and manage the money supply such that the peg is maintained; the other objectives become subordinate to maintaining the peg. Thus, for example, if the central bank decides to increase the money supply, ceteris paribus, the interest rate falls (interest rate equates the demand for money and supply of money; thus, demand remaining constant, increase in supply reduces the interest rate), which renders money and capital less attractive to the home country than before. The latter leads to capital flight (or fall in the net inflow of capital into the home country), that is, people wanting to convert the home currency into foreign currency. Thus, the demand for foreign currency goes up, which would force the home currency to depreciate. Since the country is on the fixed exchange rate system, the central bank is forced to intervene and stop the impending depreciation, which it can do only through selling the foreign currency (if it has it, if not, the peg would be challenged and ultimately the currency would float). When the central bank sells the foreign currency, it receives the domestic money back, thereby causing the stock of money supply in circulation to fall. Under full equilibrium, this reduction in money supply would equal the earlier increase in money supply, and thus, the exchange rate peg forces the central bank to roll back its attempt to increase the money supply. Quite the opposite sequence takes place if efforts are made to curtail the money supply. Thus, under the fixed rate system and free movement of capital globally, while the central bank is empowered to manage the money supply, its efforts to change the money supply beyond the market needs only lead to frustration. However, recall the **international trilemma** (vide Chapter 7) that if capital movements are curbed, the country can have, both, a fixed exchange rate as well as an independent monetary policy. But since the world is progressively opening up, the latter two remain incompatible.

Under the floating exchange rate system, either the free or managed, which alone prevails in most of the countries today, the monetary authority (Central Bank and the Federal/Union Government/treasury) enjoys significant power, if not total monopoly, to decide on the quantity of money supply in the economy. For, money consists of currency with the public and bank deposits, both of which are regulated fully or largely by it. Thus, currency is issued by the monetary authority alone, and it is backed only marginally by gold holdings and foreign exchange assets, and mostly by the treasury/central government bonds, which can be increased or decreased to any level if the government so wishes. Bank deposits are controlled by the central bank through monetary instruments that are bestowed on it by the Parliament/law makers. How this is done is explained below through a discussion of monetary policy instruments and their application in India, and with the aid of the monetary multiplier (vide equation 8.10).

Instruments of Monetary Policy

The monetary authority is empowered with both direct as well as indirect instruments to regulate the quantity of money supply. The former includes open market operations (OMO) and the cash reserve ratio (CRR) and the latter the bank rate. In addition, in India, the Reserve Bank of India (RBI), the country's monetary authority, is bestowed with some additional powers of regulating the selected interest rates (like the saving deposit rate at banks and repo and reverse repo rates), the banks' liquidity (through its stipulation on the statutory liquidity requirements (SLR) by banks and now prevailing Liquidity Adjustment Facility and Marginal Standing Facility) and the quality/direction/ sector allocation of bank credit through its empowered selective credit control (SCC) instrument. Besides, of course, all monetary authorities always have the instrument of moral persuasion in their armoury to advice banks about their intentions formally or informally. In addition, since the beginning of the 21st century, the central banks of several advanced countries have resorted to an unconventional tool, called the Quantitative Easing, particularly in difficult times. A discussion of policy instruments and their workings follows.

Open Market Operations The open market operations (OMO) refer to purchases and sales of the government bonds by the central bank from/to the banks and primary dealers. When the RBI buys bonds, the rupees it pays for the bonds increase the high-powered money (currency with the public or/and bank reserves), thereby increasing the money supply through the money multiplier (equation 8.10). Similarly, when the RBI sells bonds, the rupees it receives reduces the high-powered money, and thus, decreases the money supply. Since these operations directly affect the reserve money, the OMO is considered a direct instrument of the monetary policy. The central bank always has some stock of government bonds (which, among other securities, backs its currency issues) and it is authorised to buy/sell them in the open market. As would be seen under the sources of reserve money in Table 8.5, the RBI possession of government bonds has depleted in relative term. In 2012-13, the share of government bonds in reserve money stands at about 39 per cent, where as in 2000-01, the share stood at 51 per cent and in 1990-91 at above 100 per cent. In fact, if one looks up at data in 2005-06, the said share had gone below 2 per cent. The trend is so as the instrument was used heavily in India until mid-1990s, particularly, as stated above, to nullify or reduce/sterilise the effect of increasing foreign exchange assets with the RBI on the money supply. Also, in OMO, the RBI has yet another tool (other than bank rate and repo rate) to manage the interest rates in the country. When it sells bonds in the open market, the bond price tends to fall and the interest rate goes up, and *vice versa*.

Cash Reserve Ratio Recall that the central bank enjoys the power to set the cash reserve requirement ratios (CRR) within the prescribed limit against deposits for the banking system. In India, the prescribed limit is 3 to 15 per cent of deposit liabilities. An increase in the CRR, *ceteris paribus* (banks' excess reserves remaining constant), raises the reserve-deposit ratio, and thus, lowering the money multiplier and, therefore, the money supply. Quite the opposite happens when the CRR is lowered. Further, the use of CRR also, alters the level of the RBI claims on banks, which have a bearing on the level of reserve money (vide Table 8.5). Thus, if CRR is raised, banks have to put additional money with the RBI and accordingly the RBI's claims on banks fall, and so does the reserve money and thence the money supply. Quite the opposite happens when CRR is lowered. The two effects work in the same direction and thus CRR is a strong tool. Thus, if the RBI desires to expand the money supply, one way it can do so is through lowering the CRR. Like the OMO, this is a direct instrument of the monetary control as a change in CRR directly affects the banks' capacity to create credit (money). Currently CRR stands at 4 per cent in India since February 2013. It had stood at its maximum permissible level of 15 per cent in the past (during 1991-1993 and 1995) and has fluctuated both ways, though always in small doses. It was lowered from 11 per cent in August 1998 on several occasions until it came down to 4.5 per cent in August 2003, which was followed by upward revisions to 9 per cent by August 2008 and so on. Due to uncertainty, all policy changes are usually gradual all over the world, and the said instrument was no exception; the maximum change in CRR at any time was within one per cent in India. In USA, the CRR varies by the size of bank and the kind of deposits. It used to vary between 8 per cent for the smallest bank and 18 per cent for the largest bank for the demand deposits, and from 1 to 6 per cent for the time deposits depending on the ease of withdrawal.

The RBI is additionally empowered to set the **statutory liquidity requirements** (SLR), which banks are required to maintain against their deposit liabilities. Under this, banks are obliged to invest a specified percentage of their deposit liabilities in government and other approved securities/bonds. Obviously, this preempts the banks' ability partly to advance loans to the private sector, which has bearings on business investment and banks' profitability (if the risk adjusted yield on government bonds was less than that on business loans). However, it has no direct effect on the volume of bank credit and money supply. In India, the SLR was as high as 38.5 per cent for a few years until 1992 and that was viewed as one key reason for the poor performance of banks in those days; the yield on government bonds was kept low lest fiscal deficit gets worse. Fortunately for banks, and even the public, on the implementation of the Chakravorty and Narsimham Commitees' reports, among others, the interest rate on government bonds is now the market determined one and SLR has been reduced gradually since 1993, currently standing at 22.5 per cent since June 17, 2014. Of course, as hitherto mentioned, the attractive interest rate on the risk free government bonds and the pressure on banks to reduce the non-performing assets (NPAs), has led banks to over invest in government bonds, which exceed the prescribed requirement fairly significantly.

Bank Rate The Bank (discount) rate is the rate at which the central bank lends money to other banks. Incidentally, this is also the rate which the RBI pays, exactly or a given per cent of it, on the required reserves held by member banks with it under the CRR rule. Of course, banks do have alternatives to raise funds (like inter-bank loans at the call money rate) but the RBI is the last resort for banks to borrow money from when their reserves fall short of the requirements or below their appropriate level. The lower the discount rate, the cheaper it is to borrow from the RBI, and the more the banks borrow from the central bank and vice versa. Thus, by changing the discount rate, the central bank can influence the banks' borrowings from the RBI, and thereby, the banks' reserves and, thence, the high-powered money (Table 8.5) and the money supply. The discount rate is, however, an indirect instrument as "one can lead the horse to the water but cannot make it drink". Low or high Bank rate only encourages banks to borrow more or less, respectively, but it does not force them to do so. In other words, the commercial banks may not use the discount window even if the discount rate is reduced when their fund position is favourable, and they may borrow from the central bank even though the discount rate is up when their fund position is too tight and the call money rate is relatively high. Hence, the instrument is an indirect one only.

Currently, the Bank rate stands at 10.25 per cent since July 15, 2013. It has fluctuated widely in the past, going up to 12 per cent and then falling to a low of 6 per cent in April 2003, stayed at that level until it was raised to 9.5 per cent in Feb 2012. Basically, the rate has followed the world wide trend, though it is somewhat higher in India than most part of the world. Accordingly, the Bank rate was revised downward several times during mid-1990s through 2003 or so though all the revisions have been within the range of one per cent. Lately, owing to the sub mortgage loans crisis and high inflationary trend, the rate has witnessed upward revision. Further, with the lead from the Federal Reserve Bank of the United States, bank rate along with the repo rate (the rate at which the RBI lends to banks against government bonds for over-night) has lately become an important tool for the RBI, to at least, signal its policy stance. Since banks borrow from the RBI in difficult times, a change in it causes a revision of all other interest rates in the stipulated direction. Raghuram

Rajan, the current Governor of RBI, has opined that **interest rate is the main tool of the central bank and its main target variable is the inflation rate, growth rate being the secondary target variable**.

For example, if the Bank rate is reduced, all other rates fall, and vice versa. If so, a reduction in the Bank rate leads to an all-round fall in interest rates. Recall the money multiplier equations (8.10 through 8.12), which state that the money multiplier, which affects the money supply positively, depends negatively on the reserve–deposit ratio and the currency–money ratio, both of which, in turn, depend, among other factors, negatively on the interest rate. Accordingly (and as can also be seen through the money supply function (8.13), as the interest rates fall, both the reserve ratio as well as the currency ratio rise, and the money multiplier falls, thereby leading to a decline in the money supply. Quite the opposite would happen when the bank rate is raised.

> The RBI enjoys a dual role in the Bank rate to control the money supply: one, through the effect of the bank rate on banks' borrowings and thereby on their reserves, which are a component of high-powered money; two, via the effect of the Bank rate on other interest rates, which affect reserve and currency ratios, and thereby the money multiplier. Accordingly, though surely an indirect tool, Bank rate is a powerful tool in the hands of the monetary authority to regulate money supply.

In addition to other functions (like issuance of currency, bank to governments, bankers' bank, regulation of money, credit and foreign exchange), the central bank acts as a lender of last resort to banks and primary dealers in the country. In this role, it is the responsibility of the central bank to help the participants tide over temporary mismatches of funds. Hitherto, banks had access to borrowings from the RBI at the Bank rate for normal purposes and at the penalty rate (2 per cent above the bank rate) for extra liquidity needs. These fixed rates were largely divorced from the cost of equivalent short-term funds in the market. Further, the borrowing was limited to a preset level. To improve on this system, the RBI has introduced **Liquidity Adjustment Facility** (LAF) in the country, effective June 5, 2000. Under the LAF, the RBI conducts auctions in both ways, called the repos (RBI lends to banks and primary dealers for overnight to help them at the **repo rate** primarily against government bonds) and reverse repos (the RBI borrows from banks and primary dealers at the **reverse repo rate**) to inject and suck out liquidity, respectively, on a daily basis. The exact quantum of liquidity to be absorbed or injected is decided by the Financial Markets Committee of the RBI, which meets every day. The transactions could be one (same) day or 14 days with, of course, different repo and reverse repo rates. Thus, the facility ensures unlimited liquidity at variable interest rates to banks and primary dealers in the country. Further, the LAF has imparted much needed stability to the short-term interest rate, which now has a corridor between the repo and reverse repo rates. Before the LAF came into operation, besides borrowings from the RBI, inter-bank borrowing/lending was a major source to manage the short-term liquidity needs and the rate on them, the call money rate, was highly volatile. Currently, LAF is quite popular and the short-term interest rates, including the call money rate, are fairly stable. Since both the quantum of liquidity as well as the repo and reverse repo rates are finalised by the RBI committee, and on the consideration of the policy stance, among other factors, LAF could be seen as an additional weapon in the hands of the RBI. RBI changes the repo and reverse repo rates to manage the liquidity. Currently (June 2014) the repo rate and reverse repo rates stand at 8.00 and 7.00 per cent since Feb. 11, 2014, respectively. Since May 03, 2011, the repo rate has become the **single independent policy rate** to signal the monetary policy stance. The reverse repo rate continues to be operative but it is now pegged at a fixed 100 basis (= 1%) points below the repo rate and is thus no longer an independent rate. In addition to LAF, effective since May 9, 2013, RBI has introduced yet another window called **Marginal Standing Facility** (MSF), under which it lends money to scheduled banks up to 2 per cent of their demand and time liabilities during acute cash shortage for overnight. The MSF rate is pegged at 1 per cent above the repo rate, and the former currently stands at 9 per cent. Thus, repo rate retains its status as the single independent policy rate.

Selective Credit Controls The . tools, as hitherto mentioned, are for regulating the total quantity of bank credit and money supply in the economy. In India, we have the selective credit control (SCC) tool as well with the RBI and this one is to direct/distribute bank credit to certain sectors in the economy in the way deemed fit by the RBI. Under this, the RBI could stipulate differential margin requirements for bank loans against different products, as well as the differential interest rates on different borrowings/borrowers. Thus, if the RBI feels that the high groundnut oil price and/or its shortage is due to business hoarding of the commodity through loans from banks, it could raise the margin requirements and/or advice banks to raise interest rates for banks' loans against groundnut and/or groundnut oil and thereby restrict bank credit against that product and hopefully ease the situation. Quite the opposite may be done if there is a glut of some commodity. By this measure, the RBI is affecting the distribution of total bank credit to various sectors and not the total availability of banks' credit in the economy, thus this is the selective credit control tool. It is a direct tool as the regulation is binding on banks. The RBI has used this instrument quite often but going into details is beyond the scope of this macroeconomics text.

Moral Persuasion As the supervisor of/boss to the banking system, the RBI governor could just tell the banks formally in its periodic credit policy announcements, frequent formal releases or even informally on occasional meetings/phone calls, to go slow/fast in credit creation to all/select sectors. If the banks follow the instructions, which they better do than not, the bank credit and money supply is affected. Since it operates through advice only, the instrument is referred to as moral persuasion. Obviously, it could be used to control both the quantity as well as the quality/distribution of bank credit and money supply. This is surely an indirect tool as advice can never be enforced scientifically.

Quantitative Easing The Quantitative Easing (QE) is an unconventional tool of monetary policy. It was first used by Bank of Japan in 2001 to fight domestic deflation. Subsequently, it has been applied by the US Federal Reserve Bank several times beginning November 2008 and by the Central Banks of UK, Japan, Euro Area and others to tame the USA's sub-mortgaged triggered Great Recession of 2007-09 and the Euro zone financial crisis of 2007-12. This instrument is also known by other names such as **"Credit Easing"**, **"Printing Money"** and **"An Expansion of a Central Bank's Balance Sheet"**. Under this instrument, the Central Bank of a country buys long-term government bonds as well as long term private bonds and equities (like mortgaged backed securities and equities) and pays for them through printing its own currency. Thus, the process leads to an increase in the reserves of banks as well as an increase in the prices of government and private bonds and thence in a decrease in the long-term interest rate. Unless banks decide to sit on their enlarged reserves, banks credit would increase, which, in turn, would lead to more investments and thereby more production, more employment, less unemployment and more growth. Thus, it would stimulate the economy which is otherwise suffering from recession. After the economy recovers, the QE instrument can be reversed.

The QE instrument differs from the OMO's tool, as the former deals in the long term bonds, which could include both the government as well as the private bonds, and its objective is to tamper the long term interest rate as compared to the latter which operates through the government bonds only and its target is to affect the short term (inter-bank) interest rate. Note that while the government bonds are free from the risk of default, the private bonds are subject to this risk. Incidentally note that since it leads to the granting of additional credit by banks, it is known as credit easing; involves the printing of additional currency, its other name is printing money; and it tends to increase the size of the central bank's balance sheet, its yet other name is an expansion of a central bank's balance sheet.

Notwithstanding these instruments, the central bank of the country does not enjoy the full powers to control the money supply exactly. The currency ratio is inversely related to the interest rate and is a public prerogative. Accordingly, the public can frustrate the efforts of the RBI through changing the currency ratio, which adversely affects the money supply (vide equation 8.13). Similarly, excess reserves, which affect the reserve ratio, and in turn affect the money supply inversely (vide equation 8.13), happen to be a banks' prerogative. Thus, banks can also limit the role of the RBI in managing the money supply.

Further, banks have a right to borrow from the RBI and their borrowings are a part of their reserves. Reserves, in turn, are a component of the reserve money, which directly affects the money supply (vide equation 8.13). The higher the currency ratio, the lower the money multiplier and the money supply. The higher the excess reserves, the higher the reserve-deposit ratio, and thence lower the money multiplier and thereby lower the money supply (vide equation 8.12). The higher the banks' borrowings from the RBI, the more the banks' reserves, the reserve money and the money supply. Since each of these is at least partly a behavioural variable, the monetary authority does not enjoy absolute power to control the money supply. Further, the RBI's power to regulate even reserve money is constrained by the governments' budget constraint (vide equation (2.14), Chapter 2). The said constraint indicates that the fiscal deficit has to be financed through a mix of borrowings, both internal and external, and monetisation, i.e., issuance of currency. Until around the mid-1990s, the RBI was obliged to buy ad hoc treasury bills from the government and to issue the equivalent amount of currency (that is, simply swap bills for currency) to partly finance the fiscal deficit, and thereby increase the money supply. Accordingly, the RBI was not quite independent in its power to regulate the money supply. However, this system of automatic monetisation has since been replaced by the Ways and Means Advances (WMA), where the government enjoys access to funds from the RBI to meet its short term needs through this tool, but to a limited extent and temporarily only. Such independence of the RBI from the government has been progressive with time. The change has thus imparted the missing teeth to the RBI to manage the money supply. In many advanced countries, including the United States, the central banks enjoy reasonable independence in this regard. If so, the government budget constraint does not pose serious issues.

There is yet another factor that inhibits full control over money supply by the central bank. This is the desired level of interest rate. As said above, the money market largely, if not exclusively, determines the interest rate. If so, demand for money and supply of money determines the interest rate. Money demand comes from households, firms and banks, which are largely independent of the central bank of the country. Recall the microeconomics theory which states that a monopolist can choose either its products' output or the price, the remaining will be determined by the consumers' demand function. Accordingly, **RBI can choose/target either quantity of money supply or the interest rate but not the both**, the remaining of the two will be determined by the money demand function on which RBI has no power. Thus, controlling the money supply to a chosen level, *ceteris paribus*, would lead to a particular level of interest rate and if the RBI does not like the latter, it can not choose the former. Thus, due to all these factors, the money supply sometimes moves in ways the RBI does not intend it to be. Nevertheless, in macroeconomic analysis, the money supply is usually treated as the policy/autonomous/exogenous/target variable, and this is so partly for simplicity, and partly because the limited role that the public, firms and banks enjoy in its regulation, and the increasing independence of the monetary authority from the governments' budget constraint. As stated above, lately the RBI (as also the Federal Reserve Bank of USA) is setting the interest rate (Repo rate) and letting the market determines the money supply. Of the two, the interest rate is considered as a better policy tool when the money demand function is more unstable than the investment demand function, and the quantity of money is the preferred policy tool when the opposite is true. This is particularly recommended if unemployment is to be eliminated (vide Poole 1970). Before we close this section a quotation from John Kenneth Galbraith is in order.

"Overall history, **money has oppressed people in one of two ways: either it has been abundant and very unreliable, or reliable and very scarce**". This would be pursued later when we discuss inflation in detail in Chapter 15.

CONCLUSION

Money demand and money supply offer yet another link between income, interest rate and prices, and thus, form an integral part of macroeconomics. It will be seen later that it is the equilibrium in the money market (i.e., demand for money = supply of money) which yields the famous LM curve; the shifting LM curve, caused by the changing product price, maps the aggregate demand AD curve. The AD curve together with the aggregate supply AS curve determines the level of output, price, employment and unemployment, the crucial macroeconomic variables. The analysis of the money demand and supply of this chapter would also be helpful when the role of the monetary policy in stabilising and boosting the growth of the economy is discussed.

Keywords

Quantity theory of money; Irving Fisher-Cambridge equation; Liquidity; Velocity of money; Temporary abode of purchasing power; Liquidity trap; Shoe-leather cost; Square root formula; Money illusion; Economies of scale; Money demand function; Seigniorage; Fixed-proportional reserve system; Fractional reserve system; Multiple creation of credit; Excess reserves; Free reserves; Primary-Secondary deposit; High-powered money; Money multiplier; Reserve ratio; Currency ratio; Money supply function; Sterilisation; Pure gold-Gold bullion-Gold exchange standard; Dollarisation-Currency board-Common currency-Currency peg-floating rate system; Open market operations; Cash reserve ratio; Bank rate; Lender of last resort; Liquidity adjustment facility; Marginal standing facility; Repo-Reverse repo rate; Quantitative easing-Credit easing-Balance sheet expansion; Selective credit controls; Moral persuasion, Government budget constraint.

References

1. Baumol William J, 'The Transactions Demand for Cash: An Inventory Theoretic Approach', *Quarterly Journal of Economics* 66, (November, 1952): 545-56.
2. Friedman Milton, ed, 'The Quantity Theory of Money—A Restatement in Friedman', Studies in the Quantity Theory of Money, (Chicago: University of Chicago Press, 1956): 3-21.
3. Friedman Milton, Anna Schwartz, *A Monetary History of the United States*, 1867-1960, (Princeton: Princeton University Press, 1960).
4. Gupta G S, 'Money Supply Determinants and their Relative Contribution to Monetary Growth in India', *Indian Economic Review* (7 April, 1972): 33-52.
5. Gupta G S, 'Demand for Money: An Examination of the Unsettled Issues for India', *Prajnan* 16, (October-December, 1987): 463-76.
6. Keynes John Maynard, 'General Theory of Employment, Interest and Money', (London: Macmillan, 1936).
7. Poole William, 'Optimal Choice of Monetary Policy Instruments in a Simple Stochastic Macro Model', *Quarterly Journal of Economics*, May 1970.
8. Tobin James, 'The Interest Elasticity of the Transactions Demand for Cash,' *Review of Economics and Statistics* 38, (August, 1956): 241-47.
9. Tobin James, 'Liquidity Preference as Behaviour Towards Risk', *Review of Economics Studies* 25, (February, 1958): 65-86.

Review Questions

1. The table below gives the recent international data on some important monetary aggregates:

(Percentages)

Country	*Broad money* (as % of GDP)	*Domestic bank credit*	*Ratio of Broad money to reserve money*	*Interest rate@ %* Nominal	*Real***
	2011	*2011*	*2012*	*2012*	*2012*
India	77	74	5.2	10.6	2.3
Australia	106	145	25.6	7.0	5.3
Brazil	74	98	7.0	36.5	29.7
China	180	146	3.9	6.0	2.4
France	NA	134	NA	NA	NA
Germany	NA	125	NA	NA	NA
Japan	239	342	8.3	1.4	2.3
Korea (Rep.)	78	103	20.8	5.4	4.4
Malaysia	139	129	12.5	4.8	4.0
Nigeria	34	38	4.5	16.8	14.1
Russian Fed	53	40	3.3	9.1	0.6
Singapore	136	94	9.8	5.4	3.2
UK	166	213	7.6	0.5	–0.9
USA	90	235	5.3	3.3	0.9

Note: @ Lending rate
**adjusted by GDP deflator
Sources: (a) World Development Indicators, World Bank, 2013.
(b) International Financial Statistics, IMF, 2013.

(a) Compute and analyse the income velocity of money across countries (income data are available in Table 2.7, Chapter 2)
(b) Comment on the role of banking across countries
(c) Explain the variations in the money multiplier across countries
(d) Discuss the degree of monetary controls in different nations.

2. While the real interest rate is the appropriate determinant of consumption/saving and investment, the nominal interest rate is the relevant one in the money demand function. Discuss.

3. The supply of money is a monetary policy instrument. Examine the validity of this statement.

4. Money market is an integral part of macroeconomics. Explain.

5. While the relationship between the quantity of money and the price level is direct and proportional in the classical money demand function (vide equation 8.1 and 8.2), it is not so in the Keynesian demand function (vide function 8.7). Comment.

6. While the demand for nominal money balances goes up as price goes up, that for real money balances goes down as inflation happens. Explain.

7. Money supply is backed by foreign exchange assets, among others. Yet, while the foreign exchange reserves have multiplied by over 500 times during 1990-91 through 2012-13 in India, money supply (broad) has grown just by about 30 times during the same period in the country (vide Table 8.1). Explain the said phenomenon.

8. On September 20, 2013, magnitudes (₹ billions) of some money related variables in India were as follows:

RBI's claims on	
(a) Government	6798
(b) Banks	424
(c) Commercial sector	38
Net foreign exchange assets of RBI	17023
Government currency liabilities to public	162
Net non-monetary liabilities of RBI	8856
Net credit to government by RBI and other banks	29040
Credit to commercial sector by RBI and other banks	59979
Net foreign exchange assets of RBI and other banks	17226
Non-monetary liabilities of RBI and other banks	18452

Source: RBI Bulletin, Nov. 2013.

(a) Compute the magnitudes of broad money and reserve money. (b) Compute the value of the money multiplier.

(c) Compare these values with those of the end of 2012-13 (vide Ch 8 Tables 8.1 and 8.5) and comment.

9. The table below gives the data on income velocity of money (V = income/money), both for narrow money as well as broad money, for three select countries, for select years:

End of year	*India*		*USA*		*China*	
	VNarrow	*VBroad*	*VNarrow*	*VBroad*	*VNarrow*	*VBroad*
1950	5.3	4.4	2.4	NA	NA	NA
1960	5.3	3.8	3.5	1.6	NA	NA
1970	6.3	4.3	4.6	1.5	NA	NA
1980	6.6	2.7	6.3	1.3	3.9	3.1
1990	6.3	2.2	6.4	1.3	2.6	1.3
1995	6.3	2.2	6.4	1.6	2.4	0.96
2000	6.0	1.8	8.8	1.4	1.6	0.66
2005	4.4	1.3	8.2	1.5	1.7	0.61
2012	5.2	1.2	6.3	1.5	1.7	0.53

Source: International Financial Statistics, IMF, various issues.

(a) Evaluate the income velocities across countries over time.

(b) Which money demand theory, Classical or Keynes, if any, is consistent with the above data? Why?

(c) What light, if any, does the above data throw on the stability of the money demand function as represented by function (8.7) above in this chapter?

10. The decade-wise data on money multipliers (m) and currency ratios (c), both for the narrow (n) as well as the broad (b) money, and on the banks' reserve ratio (r) for India and the United States are as given below:

Year end	*India*					*USA*				
	m_n	m_b	c_n	c_b	r	m_n	m_b	c_n	c_b	r
1950	1.29	1.57	0.72	0.59	0.11	6.16	NA	NA	NA	NA
1960	1.23	1.77	0.74	0.51	0.11	3.24	7.07	0.17	0.078	0.068
1970	1.51	2.22	0.60	0.41	0.07	3.76	11.49	0.13	0.043	0.046
1980	1.18	2.91	0.62	0.25	0.13	4.51	21.22	0.12	0.025	0.023
1990	1.08	3.08	0.59	0.21	0.15	2.48	12.00	0.35	0.072	0.012
1995	1.06	2.94	0.60	0.22	0.16	2.56	10.32	0.33	0.077	0.016
2000	1.25	4.20	0.58	0.17	0.077	1.73	11.16	0.52	0.081	0.009
2005	1.38	4.55	0.54	0.17	0.065	1.87	9.97	0.49	0.092	0.016
2009	1.31	5.16	0.56	0.14	0.062	0.85	6.44	0.48	0.064	NA
2010	1.28	5.01	0.55	0.14	0.066	0.93	6.29	0.48	0.070	NA
2011	1.22	5.18	0.58	0.14	0.063	0.84	5.16	0.44	0.072	NA
2012	1.24	5.51	0.60	0.14	0.049	0.93	5.29	0.42	0.074	NA

Source: International Financial Statistics, IMF, various issues

(a) Examine the time variability of multipliers, currency ratios and the reserve ratio in two countries.

(b) On the basis of the above data, what you think about the monetary authority's power to regulate the money supply in each of these two countries?

Chapter 9

Production Function, Factor Market and Aggregate Supply Function

Learning Objectives

After reading the chapter you should be able to:

1. Review your understanding of the production function and appreciate why the labour productivity varies significantly across capital rich and capital poor countries.
2. Appreciate the relationship between the production function and the demands for labour and capital, as well as that in the trade-off between the income and leisure and the supply of labour, and that in the trade-off between consumption and saving and the supply of capital.
3. Comprehend the various implications (shapes) of the aggregate supply (AS) curve including long run aggregate (LAS) curve, short run aggregate supply (SAS), and very short run aggregate supply curve.
4. Learn about the models which rationalise how the people form their expectations about the future prices and the Friedman's concept of the natural rate of unemployment and the corresponding natural rate of output.
5. Recognise the consolidated Lucas AS function/curve and the factors that affect its slope and position. Understand the famous Phillips curve and see its relationship with the AS curve.

The output and price level are governed by the demand for and the supply of the good(s) in question. Microeconomics deals with the outputs and prices of individual goods, while macroeconomics deals with those of all goods and services in the economy. The determinants of each of the four components of the macro (aggregate) demand (that is, the demand for all goods and services in the economy), viz., private consumption expenditure, domestic investment expenditure, government consumption expenditure and net exports of goods and services, have been dealt with in the earlier chapters. The summation of the four parts of the aggregate demand (AD) would yield the AD function. This is deferred to Chapter 11 for convenience. Accordingly, we now turn to aggregate supply, that is, the supply of all goods and services in the economy.

As in microeconomics, the aggregate supply (AS) function is derived through the analysis of the production function and the factor market. The production function is a technological relationship between the inputs, called the factors of production and the output (that is, production of goods and services). The factor market has the suppliers of the factors of production, like workers supplying labour and capitalists (savers and the financial institutions) supplying capital; and the producers of goods and services demanding those factors for production. While in microeconomics we deal with the production function for a particular product/industry, and the demand and supply of factors of production pertaining to that product/industry, in macroeconomics we study these factors for all goods and services in the economy as a whole. The economy-wide production technology and the factor markets interact and generate the AS function. How this AS function is derived and how it behaves is the subject matter of this chapter. In particular, unlike AD function, there is no unique AS function. The AS function varies with the time period under analysis. It will be shown that the said function is **horizontal** (at the fixed price) up to the full employment level of output (due to resource constraint) under price rigidity which is true in very short run, **upward sloping** (at and above the shutdown price) up to the full employment under fixed nominal wages/information barriers/some fixed, some flexible prices, which is true in the short (intermediate) run and **vertical** at the full employment level of output under wage-price flexibility, which happens in the long run. That is, the aggregate supply

(a) is infinitely price elastic up to the full employment level of output and perfectly price inelastic thereafter in the very short-run

(b) increases as the general price increases (until the full employment) in the short-run (intermediate period), and vice versa

(c) is fixed at the full employment level of all resources no matter what the general price level is in the long run.

The essential difference between the short, intermediate and long run is that while the price is sticky in the short run, it is flexible in the long run. Before proceeding to the derivation of the AS function, it would be useful to highlight the differences between the industry (micro) supply curve and the aggregate supply curve.[1] The industry (say, the sugar industry) supply curve (IS) represents the locus of the various minimum prices at which the industry (all firms producing sugar) is both willing and able to supply the various quantities of the industry's product (sugar), given the magnitudes of all the other determinants of the industry supply. In contrast, the aggregate supply curve (AS) gives the various minimum levels of the general price (say, the GDP deflator) at which all the industries in the economy (say, India) are willing and able to supply the various hypothetical levels of aggregate output, holding the other determinant of the aggregate supply constant. Thus, the two are similar in their definition, the only difference being that in the former the industry determines the price and in the later the economy. An important point to note here is that the price being referred to in both the cases is the minimum one. This is so because the producer (firm, industry or all industries) is the receiver of the price (consumer is the payer of the price) and obviously it always welcomes a higher price. For example, if Maruti Udyog is currently selling its 800 cc ordinary car for ₹2,50,000 to whomsoever wishes to buy, it would always be happy to sell the same quantity or possibly more at prices higher than ₹2,50,000. However, at prices below the said price, it may not sell to all or some potential buyers, that is, the firm

[1]Note that while a function usually has several determinants, a curve represents only a bi-variate relationship between a dependent variable and one of the independent variables, assuming all other determinants take the given values.

may sell a lesser number of cars than otherwise. The supply curve thus denotes the minimum price for each supply quantity and if it is upward sloping, as it usually is, it indicates that more is supplied at higher prices. Both the IS and AS curves normally slope upward from left to right. However, their slopes differ a great deal, particularly when considering different time periods. In general, the

(a) AS curve is flatter than the IS curve in the short run

(b) AS curve is steeper than the IS curve in the long run

It should be noted that the above statements are in relative terms and not in an absolute sense. They hold because, in the short run, the industry's production capacity is fixed (by the plant size or the stock of capital in the forms of structures, equipment, and inventories that cannot increase in the short run) and the law of diminishing returns operates (that is, increase in labour without increasing the capital tends to increase the production at the diminishing rate), each of which limits the industry's flexibility to change the production in response to changes in its product's price. However, in the long run, the capacity is flexible, and the law is irrelevant (in the long run, labour increase and capital increase can go hand in hand). Thus, if the product's relative price increases, the industry's relative profitability improves, which, in the long run, will attract resources (factors) from the other industries whose profitability's have been eroded. Consequently, while the output of the industry whose product price has increased would expand and of that industry whose price has fallen would contract, resulting in a positively price sensitive supply function. To drive the point home, one may simply be reminded of the current situation where the production of knowledge-based industries ('sunrise' sector), in general, is expanding while that of the traditional ones ('dog' and 'cow' sectors) is contracting. Needless to say, the short run IS curve can still be upward sloping, for the industry can stretch its fixed resources somewhat and/or use more variable resources(labour), and produce and supply a little more if the price is high. The point under emphasis here is simply that the long run IS curve is relatively more price elastic than the short run one. In contrast, the economy has some flexibility in the short run as it could induce workers to work overtime, substitute work for leisure, attract immigrants and foreign capital, make extra use of the non-renewable resources, operate extra shifts for production, and so on, and thus produce more in the face of rising prices. However, in the long run, the production in the economy as a whole is constrained by its possession of the factors of production (natural, and even human and human made resources), which, though capable of being expanded to a certain extent, may not be very flexible as it is hard to attract/import from the rest of the world. While an industry can easily attract resources from other industries, an economy may not be able to attract factors from other countries so easily. Recall that we are talking in the relative terms and not in an absolute sense, that is, the IS supply curve versus the AS curve, and their slopes in the short run vis-a-vis the long run. Further, the said distinction is losing its significance as the world gets increasingly integrated.

Another important point to note here is that prices and the corresponding quantities supplied denote the movements along the corresponding IS and AS curves. The two curves shift up or down if and when some non-price determinant(s) of the corresponding (industry/aggregate) supply undergoes a change. As would be seen later, the availabilities and productivities of the various factors of production, factor prices and technology in a given industry cause shifts in the industry supply curve. The economy-wide factor availabilities and productivities, factor prices and technology bring shifts in the aggregate supply function. The details of the former are the subject matter of microeconomics, and those of the latter would be demonstrated in this chapter.

Aggregate supply depends basically on two forces:

(a) Potential output

(b) Inputs' prices

The firms' ability to supply is constrained by the potential output and their willingness to supply is dictated by the profitability of the production. The potential output, in turn, depends positively on the quantities and qualities (productivity) of the resources/inputs (factors of production) at their command. Thus, the only ways the potential production could expand is either through increase in the quantity of one or more of the factors of production or through increase in the productivity (output per factor unit) of one or more of those inputs. The profitability of the production is governed by the cost of production, among other factors, which, in turn, varies directly with the prices of inputs (and negatively with the productivity of inputs). Input prices are determined in the factors' markets by the demand for and supply of those inputs. The higher the input prices, the higher the cost of production, *ceteris paribus* and the lesser would be the output the firms would like to supply, and vice versa. Thus, supply essentially hinges on the available quantity and quality of inputs and their prices. The higher the quantity and quality of resources, the higher the potential output; and the lower the input cost, the more firms would like to supply and the greater will be the aggregate supply, and vice versa. The former relationship is contained in the production function and the latter in the factor market, to which we will soon proceed. At this point, we need to note an important concept, that is, the **shutdown price**. It is the cut-off level of price, below which the firm is better off by shutting up the production than producing any output. Thus, if a firm finds that the price of its product is below its shut down price, it would supply nothing. Similarly, if the general price is below the macro shut down price, the AS would be zero. At the prices above the shutdown price, the supply would vary positively with the price. Since inputs' prices are paid by the firms, they affect the cost of production directly, which, in turn, affect the shutdown price positively.

Production Function

The production function describes the technological relationship between the inputs, called the factors of production, and the output. The output of an economy is represented by the real income or real GDP (Y) and the economy's factors of production are the quantities of land (Ld), labour (L), capital (K) and entrepreneur ship (E) that the economy possesses and uses in production. Besides, the qualities of the various inputs, surrogatively called the technology (T), affect the production. Since the land, which stands for the natural resources, is fixed, it ceases to be a factor in explaining the changes in output.[2] Further, entrepreneurship is a kind of

[2]Discovery of natural resources does lead to increase in production. However, it is only rare or insignificant, and thus, ignored here.

labour and, for simplicity, it is often combined with the labour input, both unskilled and skilled. Thus, the economy's production function may be expressed as follows:

$$Y = f(L, K, T) \tag{9.1}$$
$$f_1, f_2, f_3 > 0$$

No prudent enterprise (economy) would employ an extra unit of any input (which has price tags) unless its output expands and, thus, the first two partial derivatives are positive. Technology is defined in terms of improved skills of labour and/or quality of capital (structures, equipment and inventories), and accordingly, the third partial derivative is positive as well. Also, the microeconomics' **law of diminishing marginal returns** applies not only to the production of any good but also to that of all the goods and services. This means that the marginal physical product (MPP) of each factor declines as more and more of that factor is used in the production, the other factors remaining constant. As the second (direct) partial derivative (that is, for example, the derivative of MPP of labour with respect to labour) denotes the change in MPP as the input itself changes, *ceteris paribus*, all the three second partial derivatives are accordingly negative. Further, since both labour and capital are useful for production, an increase in one increases the productivity of the other. Thus, if capital increases, the productivity of labour goes up and if labour increases, the productivity of capital goes up, and vice versa. It is essentially for this reason that labour productivity is relatively higher in developed countries having relatively more capital per unit of labour and capital productivity is relatively higher in developing countries having relatively more labour per unit of capital. In terms of calculus, this means that the second cross partial derivatives (that is, for example, the derivative of the MPP of labour with respect to capital) are all positive. This has an important implication for the production theory. According to the production function, the only two ways to expand the production are by either increasing some inputs or expanding some inputs' productivity. The former option is constrained by the supply of inputs. The second option, as just mentioned, requires that if you want a particular factor's productivity to go up, the employment of some other input must increase. India could thus attain a higher labour productivity only through ensuring larger capital per worker, besides, of course, through skill development (technology). The other implication of this would be that more capital per worker, given the technology, would render capital less productive, and hence less attractive, and the same is true for labour. Needless to say, a factor is hired/employed for its productivity. Thus, if the productivity declines, the firm would surely like to hire less of that input, and accordingly, production would suffer. This suggests that efforts to attract more and more foreign capital would fail miserably unless they are accompanied by an increase in the quantity and/or quality of the labour. For the developed world the message is that the mere attraction of foreign labour would be frustrating unless they simultaneously ensure improved technology and/or additional capital. This is the dilemma every country faces and the only solution to it appears in improved technology on a continuous basis. Geometrically, the production function may be described as in Fig. 9.1.

Figure 9.1 draws the output as a function of labour, holding the capital and technology as constants. The function can similarly be drawn for capital and technology. In Fig. 9.1, the production function would shift upwards if either capital

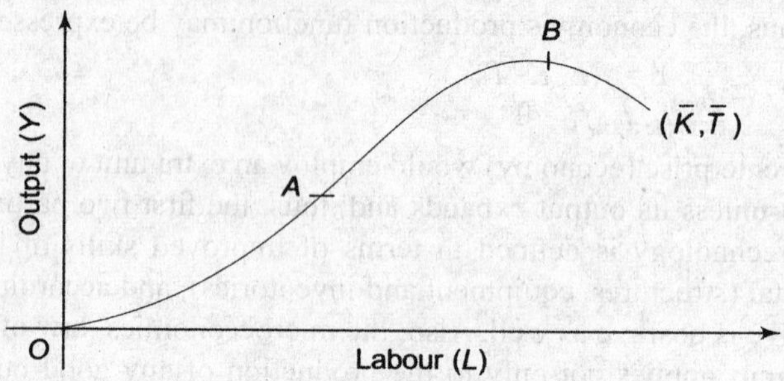

Fig. 9.1 Production Function

input goes up or technology improves. The curve would shift downward if either capital falls or technology retards. The curve is first concave (up to point A), then convex from below, and thereafter it hits the saturation point B and subsequently falls. This shape is due to the law of diminishing marginal return, under which the MPP of the variable input first rises, then falls, hits zero and turns negative thereafter. The height of the curve denotes the production and the length the labour input, and thus the ratio of the two at any given level of labour gives the labour productivity at the corresponding level. The labour productivity goes up if more capital is available, for we would then have shifted to the higher production curve. (For details, refer to any good microeconomics text.)

The production function, as mentioned above, describes the technology only. That is, it tells what is and what alone is possible technically. It does not tell what ought to be done or how much the producers with given inputs would actually produce/supply. The actual supply decisions depend not only on the production function but also on the profitability of the same. To be able to appreciate this, one needs to understand the factor market, to which we now proceed. Incidentally, we are using the term production and supply interchangeably, but they need not be the same. A firm can produce more than it supplies, and vice versa. In the former case it builds on the inventories of its product and in the latter it scales down the inventories. Such steps are not uncommon but for simplicity we are merely ignoring the difference.

Demand for Factors of Production

Factor demands are derived from the behaviour of firms, given the production function and factor prices. Assuming economics' rational behaviour on the part of the firms, they would choose the factor employment such that they attain the maximum possible profits. A firm and also the economy as a whole could face one of these three possibilities:

(a) It faces a given demand for its products and chooses the technology such that the total cost of producing that quantity is the minimum.

(b) It faces a given production budget and chooses the technology such that the output is the maximum possible.

(c) It faces neither the demand nor the budget constraint and chooses the technology such that the profit is the maximum possible.

Microeconomics/optimisation theory suggests that the first two cases are (equality) constraint optimisation issues while the third is the problem of unconstrained optimisation. Thus, if the production function and the cost equation were like:

$$Q = f(L, K) \tag{9.2}$$

$$C = LW + KR \tag{9.3}$$

where, C, W and R are the total cost, nominal wage rate and nominal capital rental (vide Chapter 6), respectively, the profit function would be:

$$\begin{aligned} \text{Profit} &= TR - TC \\ &= f(L, K)\,P - LW - KR \end{aligned}$$

where

TR = total revenue

$TC(C)$ = total cost

P = price of the product(s).

Solution of the optimisation problem in any of the three cases (viz. points a, b and c above) would yield

MRP of labour = Marginal cost of labour

MRP of capital = Marginal cost of capital

Equations 9.2 and 9.3 imply that the producers would go on hiring more and more of a factor until its MRP (marginal revenue product) (the benefit of hiring it) is larger than its marginal cost (the cost of hiring it), and would stop at a point where the two are exactly equal. This is what economics always means. Further, it is known from microeconomics that under the assumption of perfect competition in the product market, MRP of a factor equals its MPP (marginal physical product) times the product price, and under the assumption of perfect competition in the factor market, marginal cost of a factor equals the price of that factor (that is, W or R). These assumptions are becoming more and more valid as competition is increasing not only within an economy but also in the global world. Incorporating these features in the above two equations, we get

$$\text{MPP of labour} = \frac{W}{P} \tag{9.4}$$

and

$$\text{MPP of capital} = \frac{R}{P} \tag{9.5}$$

Note that while the nominal wage rate and the nominal capital rental refer to actual factor prices, their real counterparts are the corresponding actual deflated by the aggregate product price. Some explanation on the capital rental is also needed here. It may be recalled from Chapter 6, that a firm (or all firms in the economy) either could be merely producers of output and take the capital on rental basis or combine the two functions into one unit entity itself. In the former case, the capital rental would be the correct capital price variable here. However, in the latter case, the correct capital price would be the interest rate, nominal interest rate for nominal capital rental and real interest rate for real capital rental. Another point worth noting here is that the capital stock in the production function is the net capital (gross capital minus depreciation) and thus the depreciation rate is a relevant component of the capital cost.

Equations **(9.4)** and **(9.5)** suggest that firms would hire a factor until their MPP exceeds their real cost and stop when the two are equal. This comes from the necessary conditions for optimisation. If one were to go into the sufficient conditions of optimisation, one would discover that these require the said MPPs to be falling. Accordingly, though MPP first rises and then falls as more of a factor is employed (by the law of diminishing marginal return); only the downward sloping MPP is relevant for the demand function of a factor. In other words, the falling part of the MPP of labour denotes the demand curve for labour and that of capital, the demand curve for capital. These are shown in the in Fig. 9.2(a–b).

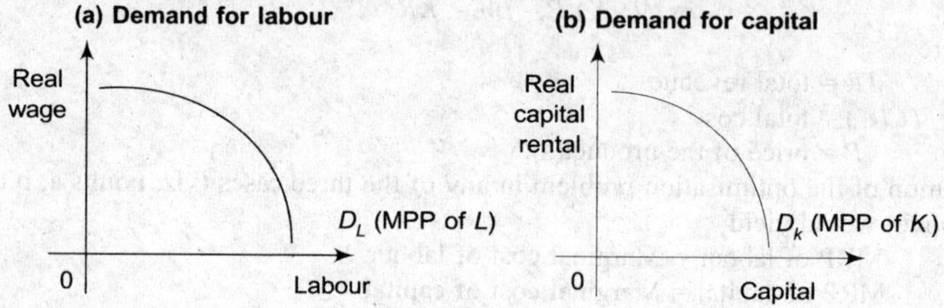

Fig. 9.2 Factors' Demand Curves

Note that the labour demand curve is same as the MPP of labour curve and the capital demand curve is same as the MPP of capital curve. The positions (intercepts) of these curves are determined by the availability of other inputs, including the technology, and their slopes are governed by the law of diminishing marginal return. Thus, if capital input goes up, the MPP of labour goes up, and so the labour demand curve shifts up to the right. Similarly, if labour input increases, MPP of capital increases and the capital demand curve shifts upwards. Along these curves, the corresponding factor demand expands or contracts as that factor's real price falls or rises, respectively. Thus, the higher the real wage, the lower the labour demand, and vice versa, and the higher the real capital rental, the lower the capital demand, and vice versa. This is because the higher factor price requires the higher MPP of that factor [vide equations **(9.4)** and **(9.5)**], which means the lower factor demand (due to the law of diminishing marginal return). Thus, it is clear that the factor demand curves follow from equations **(9.4)** and **(9.5)** above.

If one were to solve the optimisation problem step by step, he/she would have got the full labour and capital demand functions. Instead of going into the detailed derivation for an unspecified production function, we illustrate below for a Cobb - Douglas production function with constant returns to scale. Let the said function be:

$$Q = A\, L^{a}\, K^{1-a} \qquad \textbf{(9.6)}$$

The first partial derivatives of this with respect to labour and capital, and substitution of the results into the division of equation **(9.4)** by equation **(9.5)** would give

$$[(1 - a)\ (Q/L)]/[a\ (Q/K)] = W/R$$

The solution of the above two equations for L and K, treating Q, W and R as constants and remembering that a and A (measure of technology) are parameters, would give:

$$L = [(1 - a)/a]^{a}\ [R/W]^{a}\ [Q/A] \qquad \textbf{(9.7)}$$

and

$$K = [a/(1 - a)]^{1-a}\ [W/R]^{1-a}\ [Q/A] \qquad \textbf{(9.8)}$$

The last two equations denote the labour and capital demand functions, respectively. The first one suggests that the labour demand varies directly with output and the capital rental, and negatively with the wage rate. The second equation indicates that the demand for capital is a positive function of output and wage rate, and a negative function of capital rental. These are quite obvious, for more output obviously needs more labour and/or capital (given the technology, which, in the Cobb-Douglas function **(9.6)**, is contained in parameter A). The own price is the cost and hence negatively influences the factor's demand, and since labour and capital are substitutes to each other in the production, the cross factor prices have positive effects on factor demands. The factor demand functions imply that if the output expands or the capital rental goes up, the demand for labour would increase and the labour demand curve in Fig. 9.2(a) would shift up, and vice versa. Similarly, if the output contracts or the wage rate falls, the demand for capital would fall and the capital demand curve in Fig. 9.2(b) would shift down, and vice versa.

Thus, it is clear that the factor demand functions follow from the production function, and the optimum behaviour of producers of goods and services. Any change in the production function would cause a shift in the factor demand functions. For instance, if the technology improves (that is, A goes up in our Cobb-Douglas function **9.6**) or a new natural resource is discovered, the production function curve (Fig. 9.1) would shift up, and through it the labour and capital demand curves (Fig. 9.2(a) and (b)) would shift up. What is true for an individual enterprise is true for the economy at large as well. The only difference will be in terms of the prices and MPPs. For the firm, P, W and R are its product price, the wage rate it pays to its workers and the capital rental on its capital, respectively. In the case of the economy, P = general price, W = nominal money wage rate in the economy and R = nominal capital rental in the country. The MPPs for the firm are those it reaps in its production, while those for the economy are as per its experience.

Supply of Factors of Production

Labour is supplied by the workers (households) and capital by the capitalists. If capital rental and production are combined into a single entity, then capital suppliers are savers and financial institutions, who supply funds in terms of contribution to the equity, bonds and loans of/to the investors/firms for buying the capital in the forms of structures, equipment and inventories. The behaviour of households with regard to the supply of labour, and the behaviour of savers (households, firms and governments) with respect to the saving behaviour thus determine the factor supply functions.

Under the free play of the market, the workers decide on their supply of labour (working hours or days) by maximising their utility (satisfaction), which depends positively on the income from work and leisure (that is, free time, which equals total hours available less the hours worked, leisure is a normal good in economics), subject to the constraint that income from work equals the wage rate times the hours worked. Mathematically this can be shown as follows:

Maximise $U = f(Y, F)$ **(9.9)**

Subject to $Y = (T - F)\,(W/P)$ **(9.10)**

where, U = utility enjoyed by the labour
Y = real income of the labour
T = total time available to the labour
F = leisure (free time) enjoyed by the labour
W/P = real wage rate per unit of time

Thus, the workers face the trade-off between the income and the leisure; the more income they want the less leisure they get, and vice versa. Thus, leisure has an opportunity cost in terms of the loss of the wage/income and the supply of labour has costs in terms of the loss of leisure/utility. The above is a constrained optimization problem. The solution of this would yield the following familiar condition:

$$f_F/f_Y = W/P \qquad \textbf{(9.11a)}$$

The term f_F stands for the marginal utility of leisure and f_Y for the marginal utility of income. Accordingly, the left hand side of equation **(9.11a)** stands for the marginal rate of substitution between leisure and income ($MRS_{F,Y}$). Thus, equation **(9.11a)** which is the necessary condition for the optimisation by the labour, suggests that labour would equate its marginal rate of substitution between leisure and income to the real wage rate that it receives. The law of diminishing marginal utility holds even for leisure and income. Equation **(9.11a)** suggests that as the real wage rate goes up, $MRS_{F,Y}$ must go up to retain the equilibrium position. The latter would happen only if the labour supply goes up because f_F/f_Y would increase if its numerator increases and denominator falls. The said changes in the numerator and denominator, by the law of diminishing return, would come true when the labour supply goes up which would be associated with a decrease in leisure (causing f_F to rise) and an increase in income (causing f_Y to fall). Accordingly, the labour supply curve slopes upward on the labour supply and real wage rate graph. However, there is a need for one qualification on this statement. This has to do with the marginal utility of income. Thus, like the price effect, increase in the wage rate produces two effects, viz., **substitution and income effects**. Under the former, as the wage rate increase, leisure becomes relatively more expensive than before, and so workers take less leisure and supply more labour. Under the latter (income effect), as the wage rate increase, the worker becomes richer than before, and desires to have more of leisure and supply less labour. The two effects thus work in the opposite directions and the sum of the two becomes ambiguous. Further, it is believed that initially, when the wage rate is relatively low (the marginal utility of income is relatively high), the substitution effect dominates the two and so an increase in the wage rate leads to an increase in the supply of labour. However, after the wage rate hits a critical high level (when the marginal utility of income becomes relatively small) and the labour supply hits an upper boundary (marginal utility of leisure becomes relatively high), the income effect gets stronger than the substitution effect and consequently, an increase in the wage rate results in a decrease in labour supply. Integration of both the arguments, thus, suggest that when the wage rate is relatively low, labour supply responds positively to the wage rate, and when the wage rate is relatively high, the said response is negative. Under this, the labour supply curve is non-linear, it is upward sloping up to a point, and beyond that point it bends backward. It is the so-called **backward bending labour supply curve**, as shown below in Fig. 9.3 (a) below:

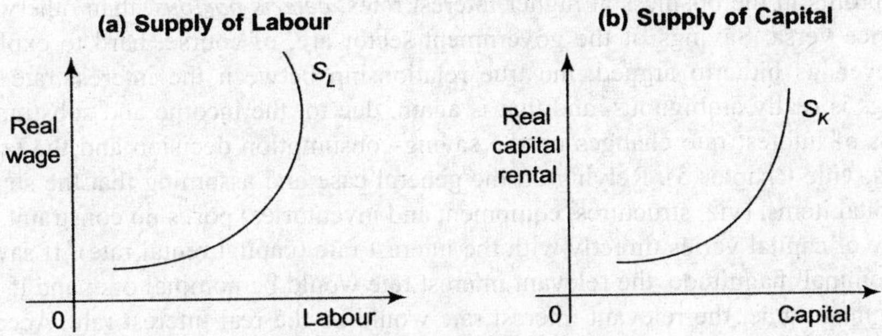

Fig. 9.3 Factors' Supply Curves

Economists agree on the shape of the labour supply curve, though they are not sure about when it starts bending backward and how sharp it bends. The labour supply, of course, responds to some non-wage variables as well. For the economy as a whole, which is our concern in macroeconomics, such factors would include **(a)** population size **(b)** workforce participation rate **(c)** working hours/day **(d)** retirement age **(e)** over-time wage rate vis-à-vis the regular wage rate **(f)** unemployment benefits **(g)** leisure-work preference of workers **(h)** minimum wage rate and **(i)** immigration rules.

It is easy to see that an increase in any one of the first five factors, *ceteris paribus*, would increase the labour supply, and vice versa. Since the Americans work for longer hours and retire late, the supply of labour in the United States is relatively high. If the over-time wage rate is higher than the regular rate, workers would have incentives not only to work for full-time but also to put in some overtime efforts. In contrast, an increase in any one of the next three factors, *ceteris paribus*, would decrease the labour supply, and vice versa. For example, when the unemployment benefits go up, *ceteris paribus*, some lazy workers might just withdraw from the workforce. When the minimum wage rate goes up, the target income seeker workers may cut on their working hours. Similarly, if the workers' preference changes in favour of leisure, *ceteris paribus*, they would work for shorter hours. European countries, in general, have better unemployment packages and relatively high preference for leisure, and therefore the average working hours are relatively low there. It is obvious to see that the easier the immigration rules, other factors remaining the same, the more foreign workers would enter the country and the more would be in the labour supply. As the United States immigration rules are becoming easier over time, more and more foreign workers are entering the United States and the supply of labour is increasing there. A change in any one or more of the above nine factors would shift the labour supply curve downward or upward depending on whether its/their net effect is positive or negative. Incidentally, remember that a downward shift in the supply curve implies an increase in supply and an upward shift a decrease in supply. Also, note that all the nine factors above affect the size of the labour/workforce and, accordingly, together for convenience, they would be referred to as the labour force in what follows.

Moving next to the capital supply, savers, in general, save more as the interest rate goes up, and vice versa. Thus, households save more and firms retain more of their profits in the business at higher interest rates, *ceteris paribus*, than otherwise, and vice versa. Savings of the government sector are, of course, hard to explain. However, as hitherto argued, the true relationship between the interest rate and savings is really ambiguous, and that is again, due to, the income and substitution effects of interest rate changes on the saving-consumption decision and the target savers (vide Chapter 5). Relying on the general case and assuming that the supply of capital items, (viz. structures, equipment and inventories) poses no constraint, the supply of capital varies directly with the interest rate (capital rental rate). If saving is a nominal magnitude, the relevant interest rate would be nominal one; and if it is a real magnitude, the relevant interest rate would be the real interest rate. Accordingly, the capital supply curve would be as shown in Fig. 9.3(b) above.

The factor supply curves slope upwards, because the more a factor receives, *ceteris paribus*, the more it will like to work/supply the capital, and vice versa. Like the supply of labour, the supply curve of capital depends on some non-interest rate variables as well. These include: **(a)** propensities to save and invest; **(b)** return-risk preference of savers and investors/firms; **(c)** tax incentives on savings and investments; **(d)** foreign investments' regulations; and **(e)** legal aspects governing capital (property rights).

Obviously, the higher/better any one of the above five factors, *ceteris paribus*, the more the supply of capital in the economy, and vice versa. Some of these factors are referred to as the **supply side economics**, which became popular in the late 1970s and 1980s. Recall from Chapter 7 the **Laffer curve** that Arthur Laffer introduced, which suggests that tax cuts could be expansionary not only in terms of the work effort, saving, investment and output but also in terms of higher tax revenue. The details on this are pursued further in Chapter 13. Thus, the governments of most countries are trying to have larger and larger supplies of capital in their respective countries through providing larger tax breaks, liberalising the capital flows and strengthening property rights. The developed countries, in general, are better placed in these regards and that is the reason they have the larger capital supply than the developing world. Further, the South East Asian nations and China have opened up their economies earlier and faster than India, and it is because of this that they have attracted more foreign capital than India. A change in any one or more of the above factor, *ceteris paribus*, would cause a shift in the supply curve of capital, and the shift would be downward if the factor becomes more favourable to supply and upward if the factor gets less favourable to the supply. With this, we now move to the factor market equilibrium.

FACTOR MARKET EQUILIBRIUM

The factor prices and factor quantities, like other variables, are determined by the interactions between the corresponding demands and supplies. Under the flexible wage-rental-price theory, the real wage rate and employment, for instance, will be determined as shown in Fig. 9.4.

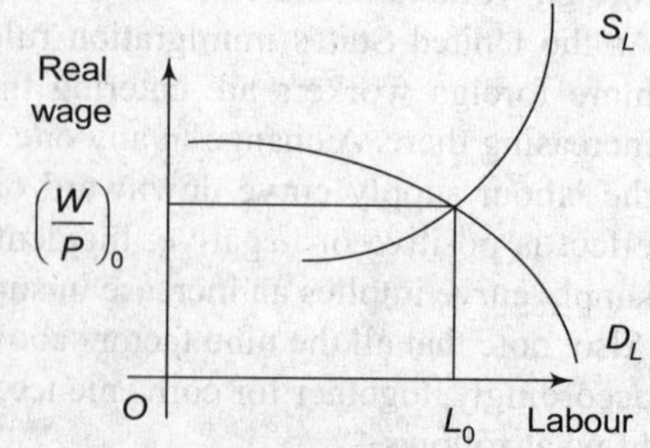

Fig. 9.4 Labour Market Equilibrium

The free play of the market forces will ensure the employment L_0 and the real wage rate $(W/P)_0$. There will be no unemployment and no vacancy. All the workers seeking jobs would get the job at the ruling wage rate and all the firms looking for workers would get the workers at the ruling wage rate. Any attempt on the part of either the workers or firms for higher/lower wage rate would only be frustrating. Thus, if the wage rate were lower than $(W/P)_0$ the demand for workers would exceed their supply, which, in turn, would force the wage rate to go up, and vice versa. This would rule out any unemployment of workers as well as the vacancy for them at any firm, ensuring the full satisfaction of both the parties as well as the full employment of labour. The equilibrium of the capital market under the full flexibility of the capital rental/interest rate can similarly be shown. Instead of the labour on the horizontal axis, there would be capital and instead of the real wage rate on the vertical, there would be the real capital rental. All those who need capital at the equilibrium level of capital rental would get it and all those who supply capital at the said rental would find a buyer. The capital market would thus be in full equilibrium, ruling out any unemployment of capital and any shortage of that. When both the labour and capital markets are in equilibrium, the output would be a constant at its full employment level of all resources. It is on this basis of full flexibility of the wage-price and assumption of perfect knowledge on the part of all decision makers (workers, savers and firms) that classical economists argued for full employment equilibrium and fixed output level.

The later economists have questioned the classical assumption of the wage-price flexibility and/or perfect information, and accordingly have suggested alternative demand and/or supply functions of labour and capital. We would discuss them in the next section under the aggregate supply function. Nevertheless, it is better to talk of an interesting case even under this section.

Keynesian economists argue that the price and wage rate are rigid in the short run, owing to several factors, which are discussed later in this text. Thus, if the products' prices were fixed, the firms would supply any quantity of output of their goods and services until their full capacities at these fixed prices. Consequently, they would hire the required quantity of labour no matter what the real wage rate was. In other words, the employment level of workers and the real wage rate would then be governed simply by the supply of labour and the product prices; the demand for labour would be of no consequence. Under the situation of the fixed money wage rate, the situation would be quite the opposite. Thus, if the money wage rate was fixed for a given period (say at W_o), may be through negotiations between trade unions and managements, the labour force would supply any quantity of labour until their full employment that the firms would like to hire at that fixed wage rate. Under such a situation, there would be no labour supply curve, and the real wage rate and the employment of workers would be governed exclusively by the labour demand curve and the product price. Figure 9.5 illustrates the nominal wage rigidity situation graphically.

The falling curve is the labour demand curve, which is nothing but the falling part of the MPP of the labour curve. If the money wage rate was fixed at W_o and the general price was equal to P_o, the employment of labour would equal L_o and the real wage = W_o/P_o. Further if the price level were at $P_1 (P_1 > P_0)$, the employment = L_1, and the real wage = W_o/P_1 and so on. The higher the price, the more the employment and the less would be the real wage rate. According to this theory, it is obvious that

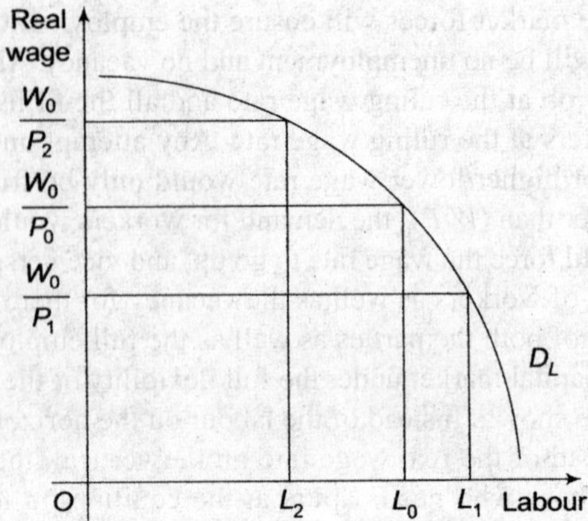

Fig. 9.5 Labour Market under Fixed Nominal Wage Rate

while firms operate on their labour demand curves, workers have no role in fixing their real wage and employment barring receiving a fixed nominal wage rate. For this reason, Milton Friedman has named this theory as the **Labour Fooling Theory**. This topic is discussed in detail in a later section.

AGGREGATE SUPPLY FUNCTION

The supply function, as stated above, follows from the production function and the factors' demands and supplies. The factor market generates real factor prices and the factors' employments. The factors' employments, in turn, with the aid of the economy's production function, give the quantity of output that the country will produce/supply. The real factor prices, would give the corresponding nominal factor prices for a given general (product) price. This will give one point on the aggregate supply curve *AS*. Repeating this for some other chosen value of the general price will give the second point on the *AS* curve. Carrying out this exercise further for the different values for the aggregate price would yield the full *AS* curve. The derivation of the supply curve thus appears straight forward. However, as seen above, the factor market is complicated due to the **varying beliefs about the flexibility or otherwise of price and wage rate, and about the perfect or imperfect information** of the market with the workers and firms. For this reason, the supply side of the product market is not as straight forward as its demand side.

The stock of capital is fixed at a point of time and it is invariant even in the short run as per the economics' definition of the short run. The technology changes gradually and it can safely be assumed as given in the short run. Accordingly, the output varies simply by the size of the labour employed only in the short run. The short run production function is thus fully described in Fig. 9.1.

There are four alternative AS curve hypotheses, depending upon the assumptions about the wage-price flexibility/rigidity:

(a) AS curve under the wage-price flexibility;

(b) AS curve under the fixed price;

(c) AS curve under the nominal wage rigidity; and

(d) AS curve under the imperfect information (misperception) or when both fixed and flexible prices coexist.

Since the wage rate and price are flexible in the long run and rigid in the short run, the first AS curve is in the long run while the other three are the alternative short run AS curves. Also, as per their assumptions, the first one is referred to as the classical supply curve, the second and third as the Keynesian supply curves and the last as the Friedman-Lucas supply curves. In contrast to the last curve, the first three curves are based on the full/perfect information assumption among the workers and firms. The derivation of the AS curve under all the four situations and their rationalisations are provided in what follows.

Aggregate Supply Curve under Wage-Price Flexibility (Long run AS Curve)

The wage-price flexibility assumption is tantamount to the frictionless auction market like assumption. Under this assumption, the labour market would have both the demand for and supply of labour curves in full relevance. The production function would have the given capital and technology in the short run, but their varying levels in the long run. Given these the derivation of the AS curve is illustrated below in Fig. 9.6.

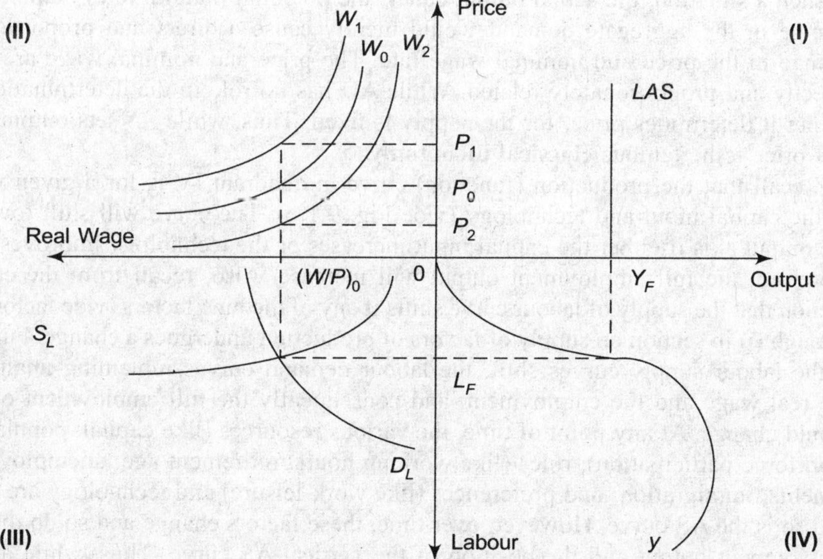

Fig. 9.6 AS Curve under Wage-Price Flexibility

In Fig. 9.6, and in all other four-quadrant graphs in this chapter, the quadrant III determines the level of employment L_F and the real wage rate $(W/P)_0$. Given the level of employment so determined, the quadrant IV determines the level of output Y_F. These values are irrespective of any values of the general price and the nominal wage rate. Incidentally, note that the shapes of the various curves in the above figure are interdependent. The production curve in quadrant IV is first convex to the labour axis and then to the output axis, due to the law of diminishing marginal returns. The slope of the labour demand curve follows from that of the production curve, for the falling part of the marginal physical product of labour curve is the labour demand curve. The labour supply curve is backward bending, implying the convexity towards the units of labour axis. The nominal wage rate curves in quadrant II are rectangular hyperbolas, for the product of the real wage rate and product price equals the nominal wage rate.

If the general price level is P_o (determined by the intersection of the AD and AS curves, which will be explained later), the nominal wage rate corresponding to the above determined real wage rate $(W/P)_0$ will be W_0. If the general price goes up to P_1 due to an increase in the aggregate demand, the nominal wage rate would be W_1, the other real magnitudes (viz. real income, employment and the real wage rate) remaining unchanged. Similarly, if the price falls to P_2 due to a decline in the aggregate demand, the nominal wage would equal W_2, and so on. Thus, the supply of output is fixed (at the full employment level), no matter what the general price level is, giving a vertical LAS curve. Since there is a flexibility in the labour market, there will always be full employment, giving a constant level of output (= full employment output = Y_F). This is the classical theory of full employment equilibrium. Note that the equilibrium in the labour market is consistent with many different price levels but with only a single level each for the real wage rate, employment and output. In such a situation, the actual output equals the potential (natural rate) output. Any change in the aggregate demand would merely cause a direct and proportionate change in the price and nominal wage rate. The price and nominal wage are thus directly and proportionately related. While AD has no role in the determination of output it determines price, for the supply is fixed. Thus, while *AS* sets output, *AD* sets price – the famous **classical dichotomy**.

Recall that the production (function) curve in quadrant IV is for a given value of the capital input and technology (vide Fig. 9.1 e). The curve will shift towards the output axis if either the capital input increases or the technology improves and, therefore, the full employment output will increase. Also, recall from the earlier section that the supply of labour curve shifts if any of the nine factors (vide factors **(a)** through **(i)** in section on supply of factors of production undergoes a change. Further, if the labour supply curves shift, the labour demand curves remaining unaltered, the real wage and the employment, and consequently the full employment output would change. At any point of time, the various resources (like capital, population, workforce participation), rules (like working hours, retirement age, unemployment benefits, immigration) and preferences (like work-leisure) and technology are fixed and so is the AS curve. However, over time, these factors change and so do the full employment output and the position of the vertical AS curve. Thus, while at any point of time, the output is fixed under the wage-price flexibility, over a period of time, the output is variable, though both are given by the full employment level of all the resources.

Since the wage rate and product price are flexible in the long run, the above supply curve is the long run one. Also, the real wage rate is at its equilibrium and thus it is a long run AS curve. Therefore, the long run AS curve is vertical at the full employment level of output, and the full employment output level depends positively upon population, labour force participation, capital and technology, among other factors pertaining to the relevant rules and preferences. In the long run, the output supply is determined by the amounts of labour and capital and the available technology, and it does not depend on the price level. In contrast, the general price is solely demand determined under such a situation, for LAS curve is vertical at full employment level at any point of time and AD curve slopes downward, as usual. Further, there is no involuntary unemployment.

Aggregate Supply Curve under Fixed Price-Flexible Wages

A group of the Keynesian economists suggests that firms enjoy some market power (i.e. they operate in imperfectly competitive markets) and in reality they play a significant role in setting the prices at which they want to sell their outputs. Further, they bring out their price catalogues only once in a while as it is costly to issue (and circulate) new ones. Thus, firms are reluctant to change their product prices until they are ready to release their next catalogues or there are significant changes in their costs of production. Also, the releases of these catalogues is staggered rather than coordinated by all firms at any fixed time period. These factors and the fear of stiff competition on the price front lead to fixed product prices in the very short run. Under such a contractual market assumption, firms supply any quantity of their products, within their production capacities, at a fixed price, to meet their customers' demands and hire the required labour to produce the amounts so demanded. This makes the AS curve horizontal at the fixed general price level up to the point of full employment of all the resources (factors of production) and vertical at the full employment level of output. Accordingly, the AS curve is inverted L-shaped. Some Keynesians who support the horizontal AS curve throughout ignore the resource constraint, which happens to be the core of economics.

In such a scenario, the product market is imperfectly competitive; and while workers operate on their labour supply curve, firms ignore their demand for the labour curve. When the AD increases, firms expand their production, if it is below the full employment level, to meet the increased demand without raising the price. They do this by employing more labour, by paying them a higher nominal as well as a higher real wage and, thus, lowering their mark up (difference between the price and marginal cost), which exists due to market imperfections. Quite the opposite happens when the AD falls. Thus, under the fixed price model, the **mark up** moves counter-cyclically, that is, it falls when output expands and rises when output contracts. The equilibrium is illustrated graphically in Fig. 9.7.

If the fixed price = P_o and the full employment level of output = Y_F, the AS curve would be P_0AB. As the full employment output expands due to improved technology and/or increased labour force and/or capital inputs, the P_0A part of the curve extends beyond point A, like A′ and the AB part shifts to the right like $A'B'$. If aggregate demand (AD) is less than Y_F (say, Y_0), the nominal wage rate would be W_0, and the real wage rate = $(W/P)_0$ and employment = L_0. If AD equals Y_F, the nominal wage rate goes up to W_1, the real wage goes up to $(W/P)_1$ and employment increases to L_F, and so on. The product price remains invariant at P_0 under all situations. Note that both the nominal and real wage rates are pro-cyclical in this model.

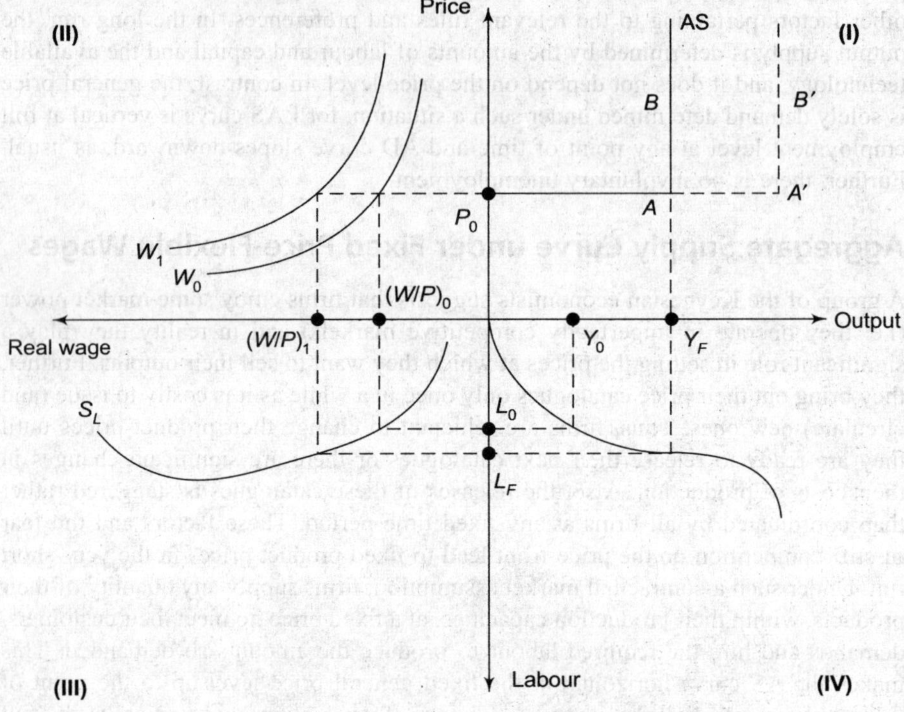

Fig. 9.7 AS Curve under Fixed Price

The above is obviously a very short run AS curve as it assumes the fixed price, which could be a reasonable assumption merely for the very short run and not for the long run. Under this model, there is no guarantee that the real wage rate is at its equilibrium, and if it is not, changes will occur in the long run.

In the real world, in the short-run, while some prices are flexible (like prices of fruits and vegetables), others are sticky (like prices of cars, kitchen gadgets, plants and machines). Since the former gives the vertical AS curve and the latter the horizontal AS curve, a mix of the two would generate an upward sloping AS curve.

Aggregate Supply Curve under Nominal Wage Rigidity, Flexible price (Short-Run AS Curve)

Another group of the Keynesian economists argue that the nominal wage rate is often negotiated between the labour unions and the management, such settlements/contracts are made once in a while, they remain valid until the next settlement/contract dates, and that those may not even be indexed to inflation. Also, there is no perfect coordination among various groups and thus such agreements are staggered. Money wage may be rigid also because of the minimum wage law and efficiency wage theory (Vide Chapter 14). Further, the workers are guided by the nominal wage rate alone or rather their relative (to other workers) nominal wage rate, and thus they ignore the real wage rate. Under such a contractual market assumption, workers refuse to accept any cut in their nominal wage rate as they think other workers may not have any such cuts. However, they take the cut in real wages! This suggests that the workers suffer from **money illusion**. Thus, the labour market is subject to nominal wage rigidity, though the product market is competitive with fully flexible prices. In such a scenario, the labour market operates as discussed in two earlier sections. Accordingly, the AS curve in such a situation would be as shown in Fig. 9.8.

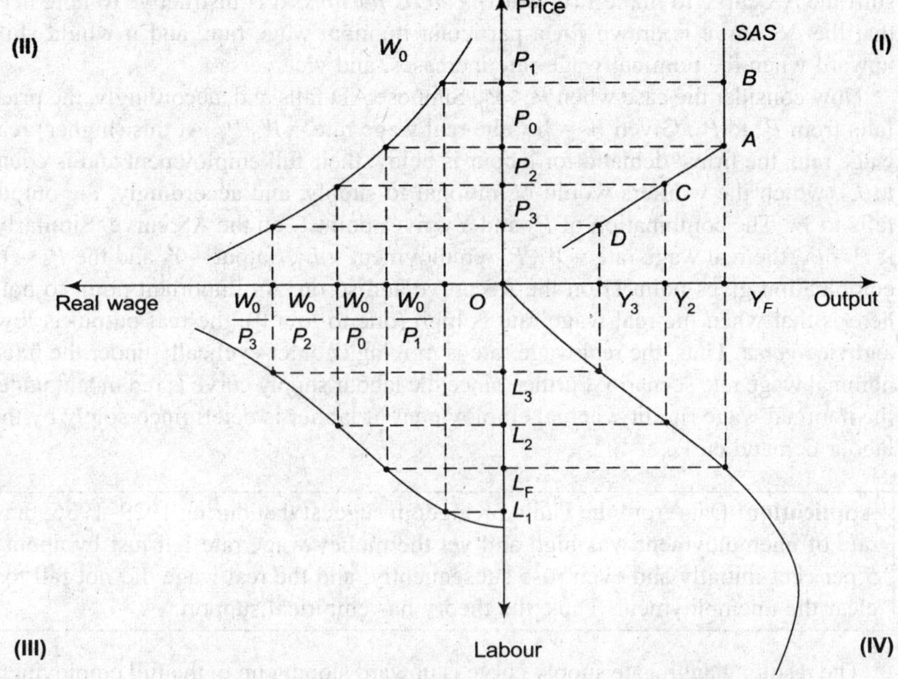

Fig. 9.8 AS Curve under Nominal Wage Rigidity

Like in Fig. 9.6, quadrant I has the AS curve, quadrant II the rectangular hyperbolic nominal wage curve, quadrant III the labour market and quadrant IV the production function. As the nominal wage is fixed *a priori*, the labour supply curve is redundant. The labour market, thus, functions through the labour demand function only. The nominal wage rate is assumed to be fixed at W_0, say, on the basis of some expected inflation rate. At this rate, the workers supply any quantity of labour to meet the firms' demand for it until their full employment and no more beyond that. Thus, if $P = P_0$, the real wage rate is W_0/P_0 ($W = W_0$ fixed), at which the firm's demand for labour = L_F, which is associated with the output = Y_F. The combination of P_0 and Y_F gives point A on the AS curve. Now assume that the price level increases to P_1 due to an increase in AD. Corresponding to $P = P_1$, the real wage rate is lower at W_0/P_1($W = W_0$ fixed), at which the firms' demand for labour = L_1. Now $L_1 > L_F$ (full employment level), but the workers are unable to supply any labour beyond L_F. Accordingly, the firms end up hiring L_F quantity of labour only. In effect, the output becomes Y_F. Thus, at $P = P_1$, $Y = Y_F$, giving point B on the AS curve. From this, it would be clear that for $P > P_0$, the AS curve will be vertical at $Y = Y_F$. Increase in AD brings about an increase in the price (and decrease in the real wage rate) without causing any change in employment (and nominal wage rate) and output. It must be noted here that if $P > P_0$, the workers would find to their dismay that the real wage rate has fallen. This will encourage the workers to ask for a higher nominal wage at the next round of the wage settlement. This, if granted at $W = W_1$ ($W_1 > W_0$), will shift the AS curve to the left (upward), *ceteris paribus*. It is instructive to note here that the AS curve is drawn for a particular nominal wage rate, and it would shift upward when the nominal wage rate increases, and vice versa.

Now consider the case when $P < P_0$. Suppose AD falls and, accordingly, the price falls from P_0 to P_2. Given $W = W_0$, the real wage rate $= W_0/P_2$. At this (higher) real wage rate, the firms' demand for labour is below their full employment and is equal to L_2, which the workers would be rational to supply, and accordingly, the output falls to Y_2. The combination of P_2 and Y_2 gives point C on the AS curve. Similarly, if $P = P_3$, the real wage rate $= W_0/P_3$, employment $= L_3$, output $= Y_3$ and the $P_3 - Y_3$ combination gives point D on the AS curve and so on. An important point to note here is that when the real wage rate is high (due to low P), the real output is low, and vice versa. Thus, the real wage rate is moving counter-cyclically under the fixed nominal wage rate scenario. Further, since the labour supply curve is redundant under the nominal wage rigidity; actual employment of labour is determined solely by the labour demand curve.

Application: Data from the United Kingdom suggest that during 1929–1936, the rate of unemployment was high and yet the money wage rate fell just by about 5 per cent initially and even rose subsequently; and the real wage did not fall to clear the unemployment. Thus, the theory has empirical support.

The resulting aggregate supply curve is upward sloping up to the full employment level of output (Y_F) and vertical thereafter at $Y = Y_F$. This curve is a short run AS curve, because the nominal wage rigidity, on the assumption of which it is based, is a short-term phenomenon. In the long run, the wage contracts do change and, thus, the assumption of the rigid nominal wage rate is untenable in the long run. Note that the real wage rate will be at its equilibrium level if and only if the price $= P_0$. Also, note that this short run AS curve, like those in Figs. 9.6 and 9.7 would shift to the right, if and when the production curve in quadrant IV shifts towards the output axis due to the improvement in the technology and/or increases in the quantities of capital and labour force, among the other labour supply determinants. In the event of a retardation in technology or a fall in capital or/and labour force, the SAS curve would shift to the left. The slope of the SAS curve is dependent on the nature of the labour demand curve, which is linked to the production function of quadrant IV. The faster the MPP of labour falls as more and more workers are added, the steeper is the SAS curve, and vice versa. In general, the SAS curve is flatter the lower the output, and this is because labour is relatively abundant when there is relatively more unemployment. The upward slope may continue even beyond the potential (full employment) output, if the labour could be stretched any further but it would be fairly steep in that region.

Friedman-Lucas Aggregate Supply Curve/ Keynesian AS Curve under Variable Money Wage, Flexible Price

Milton Friedman has proposed the **Fooling of Workers Model** for the SAS curve. He does this on the contention that while firms have the perfect knowledge about the market, workers do not, and hence the latter are fooled. In this model, the money wage rate is not fixed and, yet the short run AS curve is an upward sloping one. This is so because as the general price level increases due to an increase in AD, *ceteris paribus*, the real wage rate goes down but this is known to the firms only and not to the workers (**asymmetric information**—further developed into the Lemon theory by the Nobel laureates Joseph Stiglitz and George Akerlof). Friedman argues that since the workers buy a lot of goods for consumption and even during inflation all prices do not go up, they do not realise that the general price has gone up. In contrast, firms are aware of the price increases, if any. Accordingly, the labour demand and supply functions under such a scenario are as follows:

Labour Demand: $D_L = f(W/P)$

$f_1 < 0$

Labour Supply: $S_L = F(W/P^e)$

$F_1 > 0$

where, P^e = expected price.

While labour demand varies inversely with the real wage rate, labour supply varies positively with the expected real wage rate. Thus, when the general price increases, the ex post (actual) real wage rate falls, and so firms demand more workers. Since workers are not aware of the price increase, they continue holding their price expectations as before and do not know that their relative wage rate has fallen. Accordingly, workers do not cut the supply of their labour at the hitherto money wage rate. If workers are reluctant to supply additional labour at the old money wage in the face of the increased demand, firms could attract them to work longer through offering a little higher nominal wage (i.e. by raising the ex anti real wage), keeping the ex post real wage rate still lower than hitherto. Thus, an increase in price would raise the employment and output. Of course, the expansion continues until there is some unemployment of workers. When the general price falls, *ceteris paribus*, the ex post real wage rate goes up while the ex anti real wage rate goes down. Accordingly, firms demand for workers falls. Supply of labour may not increase due to workers not being aware of the price decrease. Anyway, the employment of labour would fall and so would the aggregate supply.[3] Thus, the SAS curve is upward sloping up to the full employment level of output under Friedman's theory. At the full employment output, the AS curve remains vertical even under this model.

Robert Lucas argues that the information about the general price changes is imperfect not only among workers but also among firms. The information barriers arise due to the time lag and inaccuracies in data collection and publication, cost of

[3] Economists distinguish between a decrease in 'quantity supplied' and a decrease in 'supply', where the former refers to a downward movement along the supply curve and the latter to an upward shift in the supply curve. All through this section, by decrease (fall) in supply we mean decrease (fall)/ upward shift in supply/supply curve and by increase in supply we mean increase/downward shift in supply/supply curve.

information gathering, lack of education and interest, among other factors. Therefore, when the general price level increases, *ceteris paribus*, neither the workers nor the firms realise that and each firm thinks that the price of its product alone has increased. This leads firms to demand more labour even through a small (relative to the price increase) raise in the nominal wage rate, for the higher prices/lower real wage rate make their productions more profitable. The workers happily supply more labour as their money wage has increased and they do not realise that their real wage has gone down. Accordingly, employment of labour increases and so does the aggregate supply of goods and services. Thus, an increase in the general price level leads to an increase in the aggregate supply. Similarly, when the general price level falls, each firm notices a fall only in its own product's price, and accordingly cuts its production and employs fewer workers. In consequence, the aggregate supply falls. Thereby, a fall in the general price level, *ceteris paribus*, results in a fall in the aggregate supply due to information barriers. Hence, the short-run aggregate supply curve slopes upward from the left to the right by the Lucas theory of **'information barrier'** or **'imperfect information'**. Incidentally note that, like that under the Friedman model and for the same reason, the SAS curve is vertical at the full employment level even under the Lucas model. Further, since this upward sloping supply curve results due to the incorrect expectations about the price, it is also called as the **mistaken expectations AS curve**.

The Friedman-Lucas theory is based on the Keynesian contention that wage contracts between firms and labour are negotiated on the basis of the money wage rate and not the real wage rate. Since workers know the money wage and not the price, they are not aware of their real wage. Further, in this (Friedman-Lucas) model, the money wage is flexible and yet we have the upward sloping AS curve. On these grounds, the said theory is also known as the Keynesian AS curve under variable money wage rate theory. However, the two SAS curves of the nominal wage rigidity and nominal wage flexibility, though both upward sloping, would be different as for as their exact slopes are concerned. The former would be flatter than the latter. This is because the change in employment of labour and hence in the level of output due to a given increase in the general price would be larger under wage the rigidity than under the wage flexibility. The said outcome happens because the increase in the money wage in the flexible wage case dampens the effect on employment and output from an increase in the price level, which is absent in the fixed money wage case. In what follows, we would often ignore this difference. Under the Friedman theory as well as the Lucas theory, workers or/and firms take decisions under imperfect information, and hence these models of short run supply curve together are known as the **misperceptions theory**.

There is yet one more theory for upward sloping AS curve. This happens when wage is flexible but some firms have fixed and others flexible prices. Under such a situation, macro price will be a weighted average of the fixed and flexible price and accordingly AS curve will have a mix of horizontal and upward sloping curves yielding a somewhat more elastic (than under imperfect information) but upward sloping AS curve.

A full grasp of the above discussion would suggest that the short run AS (SAS) curve slopes upward basically for two reasons:

(a) law of diminishing marginal returns, resulting into a falling marginal physical product of labour as output expands

(b) increasing upward pressure on the money wage rate as employment and output expands

Both these factors push the production cost up as output expands and hence the SAS curve slopes upward. These factors are absent in the long run, and accordingly LAS curve is vertical at the potential level of output.

Short and Long Run Aggregate Supply Functions

The discussion of the above four sub-sections suggests the following shapes for the short and long run AS curves, illustrated in Fig. 9.9 .

At the current price = P_0 and the current full employment = Y_F or at the natural rate of output = Y_N, the AS curves are as follows:

(a) $P_Q BC$ is the very short run AS curve under the fixed price

(b) *ABC* is the short run (medium term) AS curve under the nominal wage rigidity/ fooling of workers/information barrier/ mix of fixed and flexible price/misperceptions

(c) $Y_F BC$ is the long run AS curve under the full wage-price flexibility and perfect information

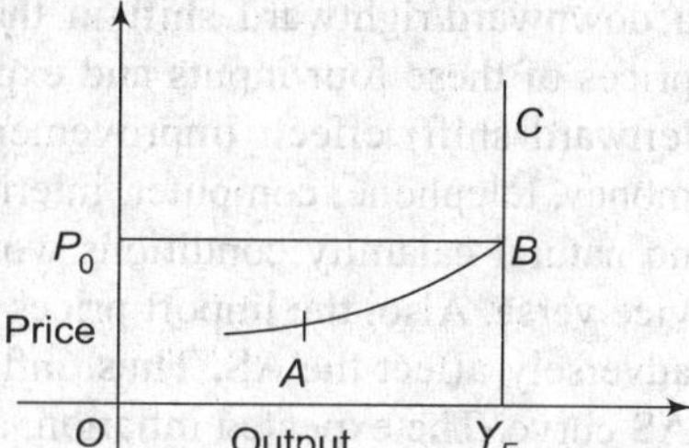

Fig. 9.9 Short and Long Run AS Curves

Thus, the apparent puzzle, that while the long run AS curve is vertical (at the full employment level or at the natural rate of output), the very short run AS curve is horizontal (at the fixed general price level) and the short run (or medium term) AS curve upward sloping (beyond the shutdown price and up to the full employment level of output), is due to the varying behaviour of the product prices and input costs (wage rate), and variations in the availability of full information over different time horizons. The short run AS (SAS) curve would become steeper and steeper as the price increases and thus it is convex to the output axis.

All the above supply curves indicate the quantities of the national output, which all the firms in the economy would jointly be willing and able to supply at the various hypothetical minimum prices, other things remaining the same. A change in any of the other things (factors) would cause a shift in these AS curves. The list of these other factors would include the sizes and the prices of the country's factor resources, such as:

(a) labour force

(b) capital (structures, business equipment and inventories)

(c) materials and supplies

(d) energy resources

and the level of

(e) technology (factor productivities)

(f) weather/natural calamities/industrial relations condition

and, as we shall see later

(g) expected inflation

The labour force could expand through an increase in population, work participation rate, working hours/day or/and retirement age; higher over-time wage rate relative to the regular rate; or/and liberal immigration; and by a decrease in minimum wage or/and unemployment benefits; or/and by a favourable change in leisure-work preference. Capital could increase through the discovery of new reservoirs/ mines, increase in risk preference, increase in tax incentives for investments, increase in the propensity to save/invest, strengthening the property rights, or/and liberalisation of capital flows from abroad. The energy resources could be augmented by discovering new sources like the windmill and solar energy, among others. While an increase in the supply of any of the first four factors (viz. **(a)** through **(d)** above) would cause a downward/rightward shift in the AS curve, and vice versa, an increase in the prices of these four inputs and expected inflation would have the reverse (upward/ leftward shift) effect. Improvements in the technology (like discovery of wheel, money, telephone, computer, internet, *i*pad) and good weather, industrial peace and no natural calamity conditions would cause the AS curve to shift to the right, and vice versa. Also, the import prices of significant import items, like crude oil, would adversely affect the AS. Thus, inflation abroad would cause an upward shift in the AS curve. The expected inflation, affects supply through the holding of inventories. If the firms expect the price to go up, they would accumulate more inventories and reduce the supply, and vice versa. Price expectations are influenced by fiscal and monetary policies, among other factors and, thus, the latter play a role in the aggregate supply as well. The incorporation of the role of price expectations in the AS function has made the said function dynamic (that is, interdependent with time).

To distinguish the short run AS curve from the long run AS curve, it must be noted that the assumption of the fixed price is untenable even in the short run. If the cost of production rises significantly due to, say, an increase in the prices of raw materials or the price of fuel (like OPEC oil price hike), no firm would be able to hold the price of its product. In contrast, the fixed nominal wage model in the short run is quite appealing as wage contracts do exist and the nominal wages change only infrequently, like once in a year or even once in 2–3 years. Also, even if the nominal wage rate were not fixed, the Friedman-Lucas theories of 'fooling of workers' and 'information barriers', which are highly credible in the short run, argue for an upward sloping SAS curve. Accordingly, we conclude that the short run aggregate supply curve is upward sloping and it tends to become vertical as output closes towards the full employment level. This assumes that the resources (factors of production) are limited, which is the foundation of economics. However, if there was no resource constraint, the AS curve would be upward sloping throughout, and not limited up to the point of full employment of all resources. Also, since no prudent firm would operate if the price of its product is below its shutdown price, the AS curve would also start from the general (macro) shutdown price level. Further, since the wage rate and price are flexible in the long run, and no one can really fool any group (all workers—Milton Friedman, or all workers and all firms—Robert Lucas) for all the time, the long run supply curve is vertical at the full employment level of output. However, remember, the full employment level of output is dynamic—it is fixed at any point of time but flexible over time. Also, remember that both the short run as well as the long run supply curve shifts as any one of the above first six non-price supply determinants changes, and the last factor (viz. expected inflation) causes change in the short run AS curve only.

We may now express the aggregate supply function algebraically as follows:

$$Y = Y_n + \alpha(P - P_e) \qquad \textbf{(9.11)}$$
$$\alpha > 0$$

where, Y = actual output/real income

Y_n = real income (output), corresponding to the full employment/natural rate of unemployment (U_n) level of output

P = general price

P_e = expected price and α is a (positive) parameter

The natural rate of unemployment concept is explained below in the next section. It would suffice to say here that $U_n > 0$ and its size is not constant over time, and $Y_n < Y_F$. Economists believe that some amount of involuntary unemployment is inevitable in any economy (besides the voluntary unemployment) in the long run, and this (not the full employment) sets the upper limit to the actual output. Alternatively, the natural level of output may be called the '**speed limit**' level of output. Also, there could be a situation, where actual unemployment falls below U_n, and if so, the SAS curve will continue sloping upward beyond Y_n and the economy then is described as "**overheated**".

In the long run, the actual price = expected price ($P = P^e$) and, accordingly, the long run aggregate supply function reduces to

$$Y = Y_n \qquad \textbf{(9.12)}$$

However, in the short run, $P \neq P^e$ and, accordingly, the short run supply function take the form of equation **(9.11)**. This is easy to see from the derivation of the short run AS curve under the nominal wage rigidity. As mentioned earlier, the nominal wage rate is fixed on the basis of the expected inflation rate, expected by the workers and management. At this fixed rate, workers supply all the labour the firms find profitable to hire so long as there is any unemployment. Thus, if the actual price turns out to be higher than the one given by the expected inflation, the real wage rate is below its expected value, and so the firms, who learn quickly about the new price, will hire additional labour and produce more than the natural level of output. Consequently,

$$Y > Y_n$$

In this case the workers are fooled, for $P > P^e$, and they would ask for the higher nominal wage rate subsequently. Thus, if $Y > Y_n$, there is an upward pressure on the nominal wage rate. However, the wage rate will go up slowly only due to the longer term wage contracts and their staggering nature.

In contrast, if the actual price is less than the expected price, the real wage rate would be higher than its expected value and, accordingly, profit maximising firms will hire less workers and produce an output below their natural level. In consequence,

$$Y < Y_n$$

This would cause a downward pressure on the nominal wage rate. Only when $P = P^e$, would the firms hire the workers as planned and have

$$Y = Y_n$$

and the stable money wage rate.

If the deviations of the actual price from the expected price were assumed to have a symmetric effect on the actual output and if this effect was given by the parameter α, the aggregate supply function would be as in equation **(9.11)**.

Function **(9.11)** states that the supply of output depends positively on the actual price and negatively on the expected price. In addition, it varies directly and one-to- one with the natural level of (potential) output, which is governed by the factors **(a)** to **(f)** above. Further, it states that the output deviates from its natural rate when the price level deviates from the expected price level. In terms of the short run AS curve, three points are worth noting:

(a) The short run AS curve slopes upward ($\alpha > 0$).

(b) The slope of the short run AS curve (α) is governed by the sensitiveness of the supply to the changes in the difference between the actual and expected price (called the **price surprise**). The higher this sensitiveness, the flatter the AS curve is.

(c) The position (intercept) of the short run AS curve depends, besides the slope parameter (α), on two crucial variables, which are, the natural rate of output Y_n and the expected price P^e level, positively on the former and negatively on the latter. Thus, if the natural rate of output goes up, the supply curve will shift downward, indicating an increase in the supply, and vice versa. Further, if the firms' expected price goes up, the supply curve will shift upward, signifying a decrease in the supply, and vice versa.

Function **(9.11)** is usually called as the **Friedman-Lucas AS curve**, in honour of these economists' contribution to the AS function.

PHILLIPS CURVE

Phillips (1958) introduced the price function to the erstwhile fixed price IS-LM model (to be explained later in Chapter 11) of real income and interest rate determination and, thus, triggered the AD-AS model of income and price determination. He carried out an empirical study on British annual data for the period 1861 through 1957 and found a negative relationship between the rate of change in the nominal wage rate and the rate of unemployment. Incidentally, the finding of the negative relationship between the two rates is consistent with economic theory and this can be shown as follows. The money wage rate (W) is expected to move directly with the gap between the aggregate demand (AD_L) for and aggregate supply of labour (AS_L):

$$W = f(AD_L - AS_L)$$

$$f_1 > 0$$

Further, AD_L = Labour employed + Vacancies, and AS_L = Labour employed + Unemployment. There are no data on vacancies and if we ignore these and substitute the remaining, we would get the nominal wage rate as a negative function of unemployment. When the said relationship is changed to the rate of change, it would imply that the rate of change in the money wage rate is a negative function of the rate of unemployment. Hence the Phillips curve.

The newly found Phillips relationship proved very appealing as it provided an explanation of price determination, which was missing in the erstwhile macroeconomic models. Accordingly, it was quickly adopted by the orthodox Keynesians.

Since the nominal wage rate is positively related to the rate of inflation and the unemployment rate negatively to the real income, the said relationship was subsequently extended to the ones between the rate of inflation and the rate of unemployment (negative), and the rate of inflation and the real income (positive). In honour of the founder, all such relationships are known as the Phillips Curve.

The original Phillips curve had the rate of change in the nominal wage ($\dot{W}$) rate as a linear function of the inverse of the rate of unemployment (u). On the United States data for 1950 to 1966, the Phillips curve was found as follows:

$$\dot{W} = -1.43 + 8.27(1/u)$$
$$R^2 = 0.38$$

The positive slope confirms the trade-off between the nominal wage inflation and the rate of unemployment. Further, it suggests that if the nominal wage rate was to be kept stable (i.e., $\dot{W} = 0$), the unemployment rate had to be at 5.8 (= 8.27/1.43) per cent; and if the former was to be maintained at 2 per cent, the latter would have to be at 2.4 [= 8.27/(2 + 1.43)] and so on. If the above equation was used to draw a graph in W and u, the Phillips curve would be downward sloping and convex to the origin. At the low level of unemployment rate, wage inflation would be too high; and at $\dot{W} = -1.43$, the said curve would be flat, indicating very high unemployment rate. Thus, the Phillips curve indicates that full employment is not practical and there is a floor to the fall in money wages (consistent with subsistence wage theory) at 1.43 per cent.

On the introduction of the natural rate of unemployment (vide Milton Friedman 1968), the following formulation of the Phillips curve became popular:

$$\dot{W} = -\beta(u - u_n) \tag{9.13}$$

where, $\dot{W}$ = rate of change in the nominal wage rate (w)

u = actual unemployment rate

u_n = natural rate of unemployment

$\beta > 0$

The term "**natural rate of unemployment**"(due to Milton Friedman) is defined as the rate of unemployment at which the inflation rate is non–accelerating, or it is the rate of unemployment to which the economy always returns in the long run. Accordingly, it is alternatively known as the non-accelerating inflation rate of unemployment (NAIRU) or the lowest sustainable unemployment rate (LSUR). Incidentally, the non-accelerating inflation means the inflation whose rate is not increasing. Thus, if the inflation rate was, say, 5 per cent last year, and if the current inflation rate is also to 5 per cent or less, the inflation is non-accelerating; and if the current inflation is exactly at 5 per cent then the inflation is stable. The lowest sustainable unemployment rate, as the name implies, is the floor to the rate of unemployment in the long run. While efforts to reduce the unemployment rate below LSUR may succeed in the short run, they would be frustrating in the long run. There is nothing "natural" in the "natural rate of unemployment" and Milton Friedman called it so in order to separate the real forces from the monetary forces. Natural unemployment has four components, which are:

(a) Frictional (or turnover) unemployment

(b) Structural (or mismatch) unemployment

(c) Seasonal unemployment
(d) Wait unemployment, if there is wage rigidity

Turnover unemployment occurs in the normal process of job search by individuals who voluntarily quit their jobs, are entering the labour force for the first time or are re-entering the labour force. In contrast, the mismatch unemployment occurs when there is a mismatch between the skills or location requirements of the job vacancies and the available skills or the location of the members of the labour force. Seasonal unemployment is caused by the paucity of work during off-seasons. Wait unemployment occurs when the workers are waiting for a fall in the wage rate to open employment opportunities for them. An economy would have moderate amounts of such unemployment at any point of time. However, these types of unemployment are structural and the 'no serious problem' kind and, thus, their existence have no impact on the nominal wage rate. To this extent, the natural unemployment rate is like a zero unemployment rate. However, if the true unemployment rate exceeds these, it is called the cyclical unemployment (= $U - U_n$), the existence of which obviously adversely affects the nominal wage rate. This is what equation **(9.13)** tells. Incidentally, note that in equation **(9.13)**, the parameter β represents the response of the nominal wage rate change to the change in cyclical unemployment. The subject of unemployment would be pursued again in detail in Chapter 15.

Paul Samuelson and Robert Solow (1960) have popularised the Phillips relation **(9.13)** in the United States and extended it to the rate of inflation. They argue that price inflation is merely a mark-up over the nominal wage inflation, and if the mark-up is a constant, the two would have a one-to-one relationship. Hypothesising so, they transformed the Phillips curve in terms of inflation and unemployment rate. Accordingly, the new relationship was formulated as follows:

$$\dot{P} = -\beta(u - u_n) \tag{9.14}$$

where, $\dot{P}$ = inflation rate

In this function and others below, parameter β indicates the response of inflation to the changes in the cyclical unemployment rate; u = total unemployment rate and u_n= non-cyclical (structural)/natural unemployment rate.

Equation **(9.14)** indicates the famous trade-off between the inflation rate and the unemployment rate. If the one is low, the other is high and vice versa. Thus, if policy makers desire to reduce the unemployment rate, they would succeed only if they are willing to accept a higher inflation rate; and if they like to check inflation, they could do so only by having a higher rate of unemployment. Geometrically, the Phillips curve could be described as a falling curve SP_0, illustrated in Fig. 9.10 .

The above relationship was observed in several countries until about the late 1960s and accordingly economists were convinced that there was really a trade-off between inflation and unemployment (vide USA data in Chapter 14, Review Question 1, indicate that in 12 out of the 16 years data, from 1953 through 1969, the inflation rate and unemployment rate moved in the opposite direction). However, beginning around the late 1960s, the two rates started moving hand in hand in several countries (like France, UK and Malaysia) and in a mixed pattern in others, signifying either a positive or an insignificant rather than a negative correlation. The positive relationship became stronger after the formation of the Organisation of Petroleum Exporting Countries (OPEC) in 1973, which lead to a significant increase in the

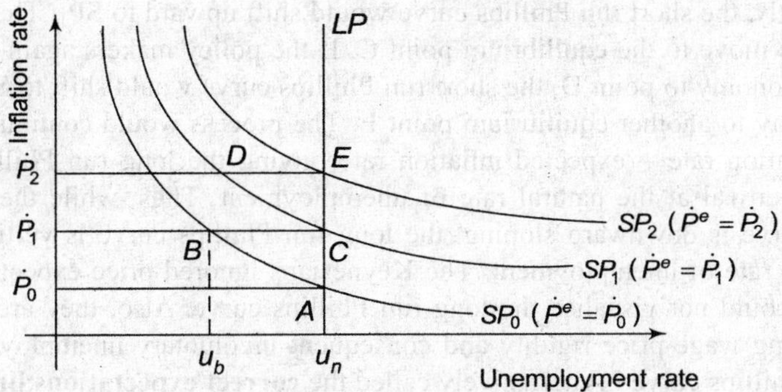

Fig. 9.10 Phillips Curve

crude oil price, triggering worldwide inflation and unemployment. The credibility of the erstwhile Phillips curve thus went down the hill. Economists got the new job to explain both the trade-off as well as the positive relationship between inflation and unemployment. This inspired Milton Friedman (1968) and Edmund Phelps (1967) to introduce the inflation expectations in the erstwhile Phillips curve. They argued that the above Phillips curve was mis-specified, as both the workers as well as the firms are interested in the real wage rate rather than the nominal one (absence of money illusion). They argued that the money wage contracts are negotiated on the basis of the expected inflation rate, and thus, affects the nominal wage rate and, thereby, the inflation rate. Incidentally, note that if all people expect inflation, there would surely be inflation, for buyers would like to buy more and sellers would prefer to supply less. This is referred to as the **self-fulfilling prophecy**. Accordingly, they hypothesised the said function in terms of the real wage by incorporating the expected inflation rate in the erstwhile function. The so hypothesised, inflation augmented Phillips curve is expressed as follows:

$$\dot{P} = \dot{P}^e - \beta(u - u_n) \quad \textbf{(9.15)}$$

where $\dot{P}^e$ = expected inflation rate.

In equation **(9.15)**, there is a family of the Phillips curve, now renamed as the short run Phillips curves (SPs), one for each value of the expected inflation rate. In Fig. 9.10, the short run Phillips curves are denoted as SP_0, SP_1 and SP_2. The long run Phillips curve [denoted as LP in Fig. (9.10)], which is vertical at the natural rate of unemployment $u = u_n$, is defined as the one on which the actual inflation rate = expected inflation rate. To understand it well, assume that currently the economy is at SP_0 on the equilibrium point A, where the expected and actual inflation rates are the same. The policy makers, through the liberal demand management (monetary and fiscal) policies, could take the economy to, say, point B, where the unemployment rate is less ($u_b < u_n$) and the inflation rate higher than before. On finding the higher inflation rate, the people will revise their inflation expectations upward[4] and

---

[4]Milton Friedman has advanced the adaptive theory of expectations' formation under which the expected inflation is a weighted average of the current and past inflation rates. For details, see below the section on Price Expectations Model. Under this theory, if $a = 1$, $\dot{P}^e = \dot{P}_{-1}$.

consequently, the short run Phillips curve would shift upward to SP_1. The economy would thus move to the equilibrium point C. If the policy makers again attempt to take the economy to point D, the short run Phillips curve would shift to SP_2, taking the economy to another equilibrium point E. The process would continue until the actual inflation rate = expected inflation rate, giving the long run Phillips curve, which is vertical at the natural rate of unemployment. Thus, while the short run Phillips curve is downward sloping, the long run Phillips curve is vertical and at the natural rate of unemployment. The Keynesians ignored price expectations and thus they could not visualise the long run Phillips curve. Also, they are criticised for assuming wage-price rigidity and consequent involuntary unemployment. The long run Phillips curve is alternatively called the **correct expectations line**. The LP curve will shift to the right if the natural rate of real income increases and to the left if the latter decreases.

The rationale for the co-existence of the short run and the long run Phillips curve provided the necessary explanation for the observed two way relationship between the inflation rate and the rate of unemployment. The relationship was negative in the absence of adverse supply shocks in the form of increase in oil price and/or bad weather, etc. However, the adverse supply shocks caused people to revise their price expectations upward, shifting the Phillips curve itself rightward, resulting in higher inflation as well as higher unemployment. Thus, the apparent contradiction of the late 1960s and early 1970s was resolved by the inflation augmented Phillips curve.

The long run Phillips curve suggests that policy makers could reduce the unemployment rate below the natural rate, only temporarily, and market forces would ensure the return to the natural level over time. Some countries like Singapore and Malaysia did succeed in this direction during the early 1990s but today they are back to the natural or even a higher rate of unemployment. When the unemployment rate falls below this sustainable level (or when the aggregate demand exceeds the potential aggregate supply/supply constraint), the concerned economy is referred to as an **overheated economy**.

Supply shocks, which represent exogenous events such as changes in the world oil price, monsoon failure, or/and the discovery of significant natural resources, do exercise an impact on the product price. If these shocks are favourable (e.g, fall in the oil price or discovery of resources), the price will fall and if unfavourable (e.g, rise in the oil price or drought), the price will go up. Incorporating this into the function on the one-to-one basis, the Phillips curve becomes

$$\dot{P} = \dot{P}^e - \beta(u - u_n) + v \tag{9.16}$$

where v = adverse supply shocks.

According to the Phillips curve in **(9.16)**, which, in fact, is the price equation, the inflation rate depends positively and one-to-one on the **(a)** expected inflation rate, and **(b)** adverse supply shock; and negatively on **(c)** deviation of the unemployment rate from its natural rate (= $u - u_n$ = cyclical rate of unemployment). Recall that β is a parameter measuring the response of inflation to cyclical unemployment.

PHILLIPS CURVE VIS-À-VIS AGGREGATE SUPPLY FUNCTION

The Phillips curve equation **(9.16)** is, in fact, the same as the aggregate supply function **(9.11)**. To demonstrate this, we derive the former from the latter. Solving the AS equation **(9.11)** in terms of P, we get

$$P = P^e + \frac{1}{\alpha}(Y - Y_n)$$

Since the Phillips curve is in terms of the inflation rate, we need to convert the above function in the inflation rate as well. To do this, we subtract P_{-1} from both the sides,

$$P - P_{-1} = (P_e - P_{-1}) + \frac{1}{\alpha}(Y - Y_n)$$

The difference between the current and previous periods' prices denotes the price change, and if the price was in the logarithm, it would be the inflation rate. Assuming it so, the above function can be rewritten as

$$\dot{P} = \dot{P}^e + \frac{1}{\alpha}(Y - Y_n)$$

The above function is in outputs while the Phillips curve is in terms of the unemployment rate. To bring them into the common format, we have to know the conversion factor, which is known as Okun's law. According to one version of the Okun's law, the deviation of output from its natural rate (Y_n) is inversely related to the deviation of the unemployment rate from its natural rate.[5]

$$(Y - Y_n) = f(u - u_n)$$
$$f_1 < 0$$

The exact form of this relationship is not known. However, if we assume this to be given by:

$$\frac{1}{\alpha}(Y - Y_n) = -\beta(u - u_n)$$

We could demonstrate the equivalence of the Phillips curve equation and the AS curve equation. Before we go further into it, note that the fluctuations in the unemployment rate are a mirror image of the fluctuations in the output. As the economy expands, output increases and the unemployment rate falls, and vice versa.

Substituting the above relationship into the previous function yields:

$$\dot{P} = \dot{P}^e - \beta(u - u_n)$$

If we add the supply shock term, *v*, to the above equation, we will get the Phillips curve as in equation **(9.16)**. Thus, the Phillips curve and the aggregate supply function are just one and the same function. The result is amazing, for Phillips perhaps never thought in this way as he simply analysed the statistical relationship between the nominal wage rate change and the change in the unemployment rate. Further, as stated at the beginning of this section, Phillips provided the price function to the erstwhile rigid price IS-LM model and, thereby, brought the supply side to play an

---

[5] For the United States economy, Okun (1962) found that for every 2 per cent fall in the GDP relative to the potential GDP, the unemployment rate goes up by about 1 per cent point. Alternatively, the cost of one per cent additional unemployment rate was the loss of 2 per cent growth in GDP.

active role in the price-output determination model, in which both the price and output are the endogenous variables.

The Phillips curve equation **(9.16)** in terms of output can similarly be written as

$$\dot{P} = \dot{P}^e + \frac{1}{\alpha}(Y - Y_n) + v \qquad \textbf{(9.17)}$$

This is similar to the AS function (vide equation 9.11), incorporating the supply shock variable v. Under the function, the inflation rate equals the expected inflation rate if there is no supply shock ($v = 0$) and output is at its natural level. The resulting rate is thus called the **core rate of inflation**. Function **(9.17)** indicates that there is a positive relationship between the rate of inflation and the level of output. This, in turn, suggests that the growth rate in output and inflation move hand in hand. In other words, high economic growth is accompanied by high inflation rate, and vice versa. Thus, the Phillips curve also implies that policy makers face a tradeoff between growth and price stability, as striving for the one would harm the other goal.

PRICE EXPECTATIONS' MODELS

The expected price plays an important role in the aggregate supply function. However, this is not an observable variable and, thus, there is a need to determine its value through some appropriate procedure. Two models have been advanced for this purpose, **(a) Adaptive Expectations Theory** (AET); and **(b) Rational Expectations Hypothesis** (REH).

The first is credited to Milton Friedman and the second to Robert Lucas, Thomas Sargent and others. Under the AET, the expected price in the next period is given by the weighted average of the current price (P_t) and the past prices $P_{t-1}, P_{t-2}, \ldots$ Therefore,

$$P^e_{t+1} = w_1 P_t + w_2 P_{t-1} + w_3 P_{t-2} + \ldots$$

where w_1, w_2, w_3, are the weights; all positive, less than unity and sum equals unity.

The role of the current and past prices varies negatively with the time. Thus, $w_1 > w_2 > w_3$, and so on. The above relation is based on the contention that there is inertia in the economy caused by some nominal rigidities. The lagged variables capture some such sluggishness and this is the reason for their introduction in all macroeconomic functions, including the AET. The above function is simplified by assuming that the weights (roles) fall geometrically as we move from the current period to the distant past. Assuming the weight of the current price as 'a' ($a < 1$) and the geometrically declining weights, the above equation becomes

$$P^e_{t+1} = a\,P_t + a\,(1 - a)\,P_{t-1} + a\,(1 - a)^2\,P_{t-2} + \cdots \qquad \textbf{(9.18)}$$

Note that the sum of all the weights is unity:

$$S = a + a\,(1 - a) + a\,(1 - a)^2 + \cdots$$

$$= \frac{a}{1-(1-a)}$$

$$= 1$$

On the basis of the relation **(9.18)**, we have

$$P_t^e = aP_{t-1} + a(1-a)P_{t-2} + a(1-a)^2P_{t-3} + \cdots$$

Multiplying the above equation by $(1 - a)$ and subtracting the result from equation **(9.18)**, we get:

$$P_{t+1}^e - (1-a)\,P_t^e = a\,P_t$$

which implies:

$$P_{t+1}^e = aP_t + (1-a)\,P_t^e \qquad \textbf{(9.19)}$$

Equation **(9.19)** thus states that the expected price in the next period is simply a weighted average of the current true price and the expected price for the current period. This helps us to generate the data on P_{t+1}^e from the actual price data. The AET was thus found neat and useful. In the extreme case when a = 1,

$$P_{t+1}^e = P_t \qquad \textbf{(9.20)}$$

Equation (9.20) describes a naïve model for estimating/forecasting the future values. Alternatively, equation **(9.19)** could be written in another familiar way:

$$P_{t+1}^e = P_t^e + a\,(P_t - P_t^e) \qquad \textbf{(9.21)}$$

These equations suggest that inflation has inertia, i.e. it keeps going unless something stops it. Robert Lucas and others, however, saw the above theory faulty on the ground that it is subject to some systematic error. According to this theory, if the price has had either the positive or the negative trend, it would never give correct predictions. For example, if the price has been rising all through in the past, the expected price on the basis of the AET will be biased downward, and vice versa. To show this let us assume the historical prices were the following:

Year:	*1995*	*1996*	*1997*	*1998*	*1999*	*2000*	*2001*	*2002*	*2003*
Price:	10	12	13	15	16	19	20	21	23

If we apply the above formula and take any weighted average of all the prices in 1995 through 2002 to predict the 2003 price, we would surely under predict, and thus would be biased downward. The under prediction is certain, for an average, weighted or otherwise, would always be somewhere between the lowest and the highest number. Thus, the average of all prices during 1995 through 2002 would be less than 21, which would necessarily be below the 2003 price, given the assumption of the upward trend. Quite the reverse would be true if the trend in price was downward.

The above errors are avoidable and are hence called the systematic. They render the theory wrong. It must be emphasised here that under the AET, the expected value of a variable depends solely on the current and the past values of that variable alone. This is very restrictive as will be clear on a review of the alternative theory, which is, known as the rational expectations hypothesis (REH). In particular, we know that so many factors impinge on the movement of any variable and, thus, the AET is inappropriate even if the variable under forecasting is not moving monotonously.

The **rational expectations hypothesis** is also known as the **full information theory.** Under this the expected price is obtained through an intelligent use of the: **(a)** Current price; **(b)** Past prices; **(c)** Current and past values of all the variables that impinge on the price; and **(d)** Expected/systematic policy actions and non-policy events that have bearings on the future price.

To apply this theory, one should not only have the historical data on the variable whose expected future value is to be estimated but also on all its other determinants, including the future policy and non-policy variables/parameters. Besides, the enormous data would have to be analysed intelligently, which would call for a good grasp of the relevant theories, techniques and computer skills. This is thus a tedious, difficult and long-drawn procedure. Further, even the above procedure (and in fact, any other) will offer no guarantee for an accurate forecast for the next period's price. This is because the future is uncertain. Techniques and good analysis can help minimise the forecast error but can only rarely eliminate the same. However, proponents of the REH argue that the practice of this would surely eliminate avoidable systematic error of the AET mentioned above. In other words, **REH make errors but no predictable or systematic ones**. This by itself is a significant factor in favour of REH. This suggests that the optimising behaviour of a rational decision maker will entail the use of all the available relevant information rather than be content with the history of the variable alone for estimating future values. Under the REH, people make the best forecast they can with the available data and make no consistent errors in forecasting. Under this, people do not repeat their mistakes. In contrast, under the AET, people could end up repeating mistakes, period after period. The central implication of the REH is that people may not always get forecasts right but they know that they make no systematic error. Under the AET, predictions are based on historical data alone and thus it has been labelled as the **backward looking theory**; in contrast to the REH, which is **forward looking** as it considers both the historical facts as well as likely future events.

The REH obviously marks an improvement over the AET. However, it is subject to limitations as well. The foremost of all is that unlike the AET, the REH has no formula that could be applied mechanically. Besides, the intelligence level varies from person to person and the information collection is a costly affair. It is the last factor, which recognises the value of the information, and the REH endorses that information is valuable. Those who have better information, reap better dividends than the others do, *ceteris paribus*.

Needless to say, while the different people may obtain similar forecasts under the AET (to the extent they use the same weights and same data), they are unlikely to get the same under the REH. Thus, the chances of the self-fulfilling prophesy are more under the former than the latter. Incidentally, note that both the models, AET and REH, are available for estimating the next period's value of any variable rather than being limited to the price variable alone. As we shall see later, these models have enriched the debate on the role of the stabilisation policies in the economy.

Conclusion

The aggregate supply (AS) function represents the supply side of the market. In the long run, the supply is constrained by the quantity and quality of the resources (factors of production) and the LAS curve is vertical at the full employment level of output. Increases in price are accompanied by increases in the wage and other input costs, and so supply does not respond to the price changes. However, as the supply of the factors of production and technology are augmented period after period, the vertical LAS curve keeps shifting to the right. In the very short run (called the market period), the price is fixed and the AS curve is horizontal at the fixed price level up to the full employment level of output. In the medium term (normally referred to as the short run), the nominal wage rate is sticky, so an increase in price induces firms to increase supplies of their products to take advantage of higher profits. Even if the nominal wage rate were flexible, 'fooling of worker' or the 'information barriers' causes the SAS curve to be upward sloping. Thus, while the long run aggregate supply curve is vertical at the full employment level of output/natural output level, the short run aggregate supply function is upward sloping.

The original classical economists believed in the wage-price flexibility and market clearing and, thus, hypothesised the vertical AS curve. To them, the national output was purely supply determined and the price was to regulate the aggregate demand to equate it with the fixed AS. In contrast, old Keynesians hypothesised a horizontal AS curve and to them the national output was to be determined primarily by the aggregate demand at the fixed price. Therefore, while the **suppliers set the price, the consumers set the output**. Currently, neither theory is believed to be correct. Both the supply and demand play a role in deciding, both, the quantity and price of the national output. In this chapter we have analysed this role for the supply side. The role of the demand side, as well as of both sides simultaneously, is discussed in the following chapters through the alternative macroeconomic models.

Keywords

Sticky-Flexible prices; Potential output; Shut down price; Law of diminishing marginal returns; Net capital; Cobb-Douglas production function; Constant returns to scale; Marginal rate of substitution between leisure and income; Substitution-Income effect; Backward bending labour supply curve; Supply side economics; Laffer curve; Labour Fooling theory; AS–AD curve; Classical dichotomy; Long run AS curve; Very short run AS curve; Pro-Anti-cyclical; Mark up; Money illusion; Asymmetric information; Information barrier; Mistaken expectations AS curve; Short run/Medium term AS curve; AS curve puzzle; Friedman-Lucas AS function; Phillips curve; Price function; Natural rate of unemployment; Natural level of output; Price surprise; Self-fulfilling prophesy; Inflation augmented Phillips curve; Short-Long run Phillips curve; Correct expectations line; Overheated economy; Okun's law; Core rate of inflation; Adaptive expectations-Rational expectations theory; Full information theory; Backward looking-Forward looking theory.

References

1. Friedman Milton, 'The Role of Monetary Policy', *American Economic Review* 58, (March, 1968), Pp. 1-17.
2. Lucas Robert E, 'Some International Evidence on Output Inflation Tradeoffs', *American Economic Review* 63, (June, 1973), Pp. 326-34.

3. Okun Arthur, 'Potential GNP: Its Measurement and Significance', Proceedings of the Business and Economics Statistics Section, American Statistical Association, (Washington, DC, 1962), Pp. 98-103.
4. Phelps Edmund S, 'Phillips Curves, Expectations of Inflation and Optimal Unemployment Over Time', *Economica* 34, (August, 1967), Pp. 254-81.
5. Phillips AWH, 'The Relation Between Unemployment and the Rate of Change of Money Wage Rates in the United Kingdom, 1861-1957, *Economica* 25, (November 1958), Pp. 283-99.
6. Samuelson Paul, Solow Robert, 'Analytical Aspects of Anti-Inflation Policy', *American Economic Review* 50, (May, 1960), Pp. 177-94.

REVIEW QUESTIONS

1. What is the role of the shutdown price in the aggregate supply curve?
2. While the long run aggregate curve is vertical at the potential level of output, the short run aggregate supply curve is upward sloping with the increasing slope. Why?
3. While the real wage rate is counter-cyclical in the sticky nominal wage rate model, the mark up (of price over marginal cost) is so under the sticky price situation. Discuss.
4. Consider the model of aggregate supply under price rigidity:
   (a) Suppose that AD at $P = P_0$ equals Y_F (full employment output). Show the resulting situation in the labour market.
   (b) Suppose that AD at $P = P_0$ equals Y_1, which is less than Y_F. What would then be the situation in the labour market?
5. Suppose the production function is $Y = f(L, K, T)$ and T (technology) falls. How would this negative technology shock affect the AS curve under all the four cases of AS function (vide pages 232–241).
6. The aggregate supply function is still in infancy. Why?
7. The Phillips' curve is the price function of macroeconomics. Do you agree? Why?
8. Significance of the supply side during the post-Keynesian era has been highlighted by the works of Arthur Laffer, AW Phillips, Milton Friedman and Robert Lucas, among others. Analyse.
9. Assume an economy faces the following production function:
   $$Q = (0.3)\, L^{0.5}\, K^{0.7}$$
   where, Q = output (NDP in ₹ billion at 1993-94 prices), L = labour (hours in billion), and K = capital (net capital in ₹ billion at 1993-94 prices).
   (a) Does the law of diminishing marginal returns holds good in this economy? How?
   (b) Show that the MPP of labour goes down as labour increases but it goes up as capital increases. What does this imply for a factor's productivity?
   (c) If the nominal wage rate was ₹10/hour, the nominal capital rental ₹0.15 per rupee of the capital (i.e., 15%), and the general price index 1.7 (base = 1), determine the demand functions for labour and capital. Show that the

demand for an input varies inversely with its own price and directly with the price of other input(s).

(d) Does the production function ignore the technology factor? Give reasons for your answer.

10. Suppose an economy is characterised by expected inflation rate = 5%, unemployment rate (u) = 3 %, natural rate of unemployment (u_n) = 5% and speed of inflation adjustment to the employment gap = 0.4. Determine the actual annual inflation in that country, using the expectations augmented Phillips curve.

PART 3

ECONOMIC FLUCTUATIONS AND STABILISATION POLICY: MACROECONOMIC MODELS

The previous part of the text has provided a discussion of all the received theories behind the various components of aggregate demand and aggregate supply. This part of the text will combine these theories into alternative macroeconomic models, each of which explains the determination of national income and price, among other macroeconomic magnitudes, in the short run. These models would account for the economic fluctuations (trough, recovery, peak and recession) that the world has experienced, and suggest the roles of fiscal, monetary exchange rate, trade and income policies in dampening business cycles.

Recall that one of the significant aspects of macroeconomics is to explain the periods of prosperity and recession, the so-called business cycles, and therefore this is rather an important part of this text. Needless to say, while history should not be ignored, it can at best serve as a poor guide for the future. Events rarely repeat in exact form and every successive event may need a new theory. Fortunately, economics is a live subject, it has evolved slowly, and it is still developing. This part of the text would take up all major economic events/ups and downs faced so far and try to explain them through the received economic models. Also, the policy actions/inactions would be analysed. The approach would be model building.

This part of the text has six Chapters. Chapter 10 introduces and narrates business cycles, stabilisation policies and their constraints, and models and their special features. Chapter 11 covers the (old) classical model and the fixed price versions (Keynesian cross and *IS-LM* models) of the (old) Keynesian model. Chapter 12 presents the Keynesian open economy (Mundell–Fleming) model and Chapter 13 the

Keynesian flexible price (AD-AS) model. Chapter 14 covers the remaining models, viz. New Classical, New Keynesian and the real business cycle models. A bird's eye view of the comparative features of all these models is included at the end of Chapter 14. Chapter 15, the last in this part, goes deep into the economic maladies of unemployment and inflation.

Chapter 10

Business Cycles, Stabilisation Policies and Economic Models

Learning Objectives

After reading the chapter you should be able to:

1. Appreciate the prevalence of business cycles and the key facts about them.
2. Study the fluctuations in our GDP during 1950 through 2013 and note the lengths and depths of business cycles in India.
3. Learn the various stabilisation policies, their tools and operating constraints.
4. Comprehend what an economic model is, their ingredients, variety and shocks to them.

An important area of macroeconomics is to explain the short run fluctuations in the real GDP, unemployment rate and inflation, all of which are macroeconomic instabilities. In addition, the discipline offers some guidelines to policy makers for countering the said fluctuations through the appropriate use of the fiscal, monetary trade, exchange rate and income policies. It is therefore imperative to first understand the basics of these aspects before we go into a full-fledged discussion of the theories of business cycles and the application of stabilisation policies to tame the said fluctuations. Model building is an important methodology in economics. These are built on the principles of economics and used to explain/predict economic events. Needless to say, history has witnessed different events of varying magnitudes over time. For example, the world faced the Great Depression during 1929–33, the capitalists' Golden period during the 1950s and most of the 1960s, Stagflation during the 1970s and early 1980s, Great Moderation during 1986–2007, the Great Recession during 2007–09, Financial Crisis in some part of Europe (PIIGS: Portugal, Ireland, Italy, Greece and Spain) during 2009–10 and some recovery happening since then. Economists have responded to such events through developing more and more appropriate theories to account for such economic realities and to predict the future. This has been done in the form of models. This chapter, therefore, includes some discussion on the significant features of macroeconomic models. Suffice to mention here, the subject has witnessed enormous developments.

Business Cycles

Economic fluctuations/business cycles are ups and downs in economic variables over time. Recall that the core macro-economic variables include real national income, unemployment and price level. Though the real national income is really the one that provides a better measure of economic well-being than any other measurable variable, the real gross domestic product (GDP at factor cost), which is relatively a better measure for the level of employment, is used globally for this purpose. Accordingly, the level and growth rate in the real GDP are used to denote economic standing and performance/progress in this text. Recall that the general price *per se* has little usefulness and its significance lies in measuring the inflation rate. Accordingly, inflation rate is the right price variable in macroeconomics. Though the GDP deflator is the most appropriate price variable, the global practice is in favour of the consumer price index. For the last variable of interest, viz., unemployment, again the level is of little significance as the workforce varies widely across countries and even over time. Thus, the rate of unemployment is analysed in macroeconomics.

While an analysis of all the three magnitudes is relevant in discussing economic fluctuations and this text deals with all of them, the business cycles· analysis confine to variations in the real GDP or its growth rate over time only. Thus, a business cycle is defined as ups and downs in the real GDP or its growth rate.

Cycle of Recession and Recovery

Since history has witnessed downs even in terms of the falls in real GDP (or negative growth rates), and, of course, ups in it even to a fairly high growth rates in real GDP, a business cycle is referred to as a cycle of recession and recovery or a cycle of prosperity and recession around the smooth trend (growth) line for a few quarters to several years. Accordingly, a business cycle is described by four phases, viz., trough, recovery, peak and recession. The first is the phase where the real GDP reaches its floor level within a cycle. The turning point to that bottom, where the real GDP starts and continues growing, is referred to as the recovery/prosperity phase. Once the recovery stops and hits the local top/hill, the cycle is at the peak. The turning point from the top, where the real GDP starts and continues descending, marks the recession phase. Once the recession ends, the next bottom is hit, and the next business cycle begins. A business cycle length is counted from trough to trough or peak to peak. Alternatively, a business cycle can be gauged by examining the growth rates in the real GDP. Thus, so long as the growth rate is positive, there is the recovery phase. When the growth stops, the GDP reaches the local top and that is the peak point on the cycle. The negative growth rate denotes the recession phase. When the negative growth ends, we have the trough point of the local cycle. The ensuing positive growth marks the new recovery phase. The year(s) in which the growth rate is negative is the recession year(s).

To illustrate these concepts of the business cycle, we consider India's real GDP and its growth rate over a period of time. The data for the same are given in Table 10.1, and the graphs in Figs. 10.1 and 10.2.

Table 10.1 Real GDP (at Factor Cost at 2004–05 Prices) and its Growth Rates (India)

Year	*Real GDP (₹ bill.)*	*Growth Rate (%)*	*Year*	*Real GDP (₹ bill.)*	*Growth Rate (%)*	*Year*	*Real GDP (₹ bill.)*	*Growth Rate (%)*
1950–51	2796	—	1971–72	5957	1.0	1992–93	14405	5.4
1951–52	2861	2.3	1972–73	5938	–0.3	1993–94	15223	5.7
1952–53	2943	2.8	1973–74	6209	4.6	1994–95	16197	6.4
1953–54	3122	6.1	1974–75	6281	1.2	1995–96	17377	7.3
1954–55	3254	4.2	1975–76	6846	9.0	1996–97	18763	8.0
1955–56	3338	2.7	1976–77	6932	1.2	1997–98	19570	4.3
1956–57	3528	5.7	1977–78	7450	7.5	1998–99	20878	6.7
1957–58	3485	–1.3	1978–79	7860	5.5	1999–00	22549	8.0
1958–59	3749	7.5	1979–80	7451	–5.2	2000–01	23485	4.1
1959–60	3832	2.2	1980–81	7985	7.2	2001–02	24750	5.4
1960–61	4103	7.1	1981–82	8434	5.5	2002–03	25709	3.9
1961–62	4230	3.1	1982–83	8681	2.6	2003–04	27757	8.0
1962–63	4320	2.1	1983–84	9363	7.8	2004–05	29715	7.1
1963–64	4538	5.1	1984–85	9734	3.8	2005–06	32531	9.5
1964–65	4882	7.5	1985–86	10139	4.2	2006–07	35644	9.6
1965–66	4704	–3.7	1986–87	10576	4.3	2007–08	38966	9.3
1966–67	4752	1.0	1987–88	10950	3.5	2008–09	41587	6.7
1967–68	5139	8.1	1988–89	12062	10.2	2009–10	45161	8.6
1968–69	5273	2.6	1989–90	12802	6.1	2010–11	49370	9.3
1969–70	5616	6.5	1990–91	13479	5.3	2011–12*	52436	6.2
1970–71	5898	5.0	1991–92	13672	1.4	2012–13**	55036	5.0

Sources: (a) *National Accounts Statistics of India,* CSO, (b) Economic Intelligence Service, Centre for Monitoring Indian Economy, (c) Economic Survey, Government of India, 2012–13. * Revised ** Advance

Components of a Time Series

A time series, like the real GDP in Table 10.1, has four components, viz. trend, seasonal, cyclical and irregular (random). The trend is secular and is caused by secular changes in factors like population, resources, technology and inflation. Thus, the GDP has a secular tendency to grow over time due to increase in population, improvements in technology etc. Seasonal variations are due to seasons; busy and slack, summer and winter, etc., which cause changes in seasonal data. Thus, the demand for woolen clothes is higher in winter than in summer. Cyclical fluctuations are ups and downs in economic variables due to elections, wars, weather, technical breakthrough, and significant changes in government, economic structure, economic system, economic policies, etc.

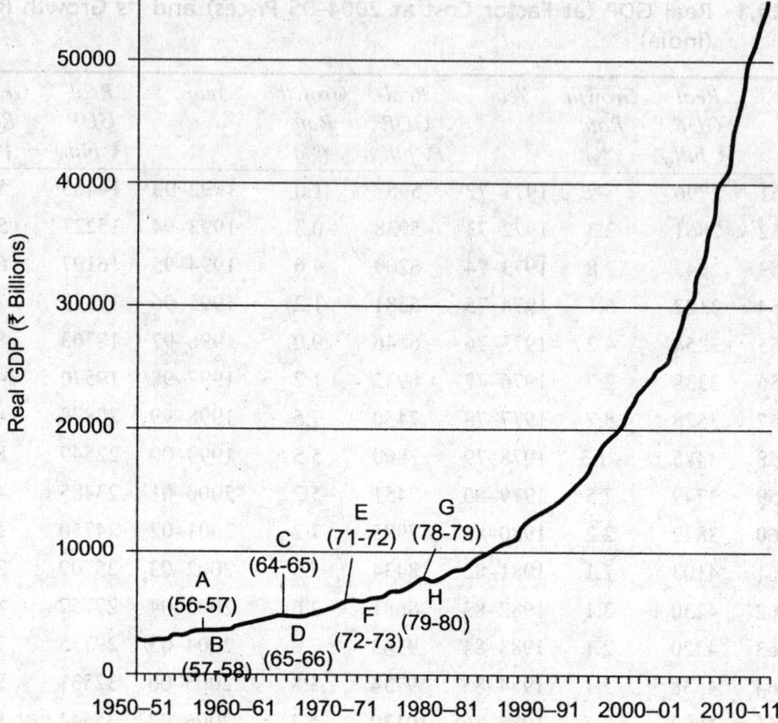

Fig. 10.1 Time Series of Real GDP

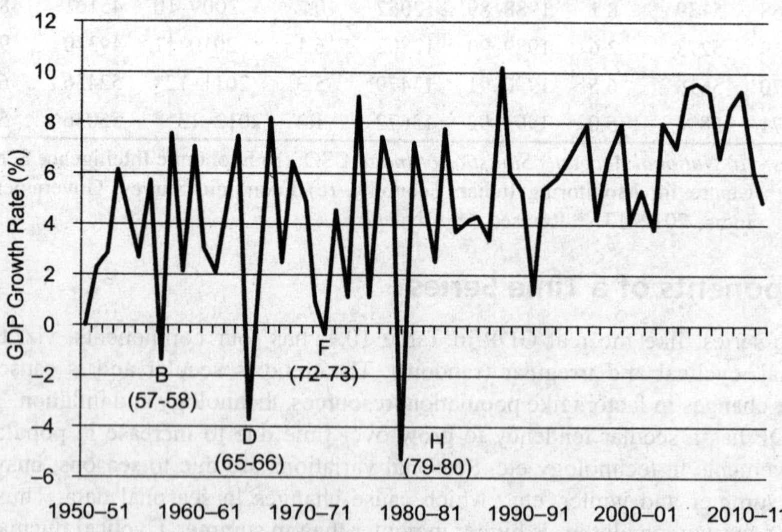

Fig. 10.2 Real GDP Growth Rates

Thus, there was the Great Depression during 1929–33, large oil price fluctuations in 1970s, information technology bubble during the second half of the 1990s, and subprime lending collapse in 2007–09. The last component of a time series, viz., random variations, is caused by minor events like strikes and lockouts in a few firms/ industries, earthquakes, epidemics and minor variations in factors like weather and political instability. Our real GDP data are annual and, thus, free from seasonal fluctuations. They have a strong secular upward trend and that is why the curve in Fig. 10.1 is steady. They contain the cyclical variations but the same are hidden due to their insignificance in relation to the trend. The graph in Fig. 10.2 is more explicit in this regard as the rates of annual changes are all within almost a digit. Nevertheless, the cycles can still be identified. A careful review of the above data and graphs would suggest the following:

Trends

Long-term trends in India's GDP are best observed through decade-wise changes in it. These are as follows:

Decade	*Incremental Real GDP (₹)*	*Decade-wise Growth rate (%)*
1950–51 to 1960–61	1307	
1960–61 to 1970–71	1795	37.3
1970–71 to 1980–81	2087	16.3
1980–81 to 1990–91	5494	163.2
1990–91 to 2000–01	10006	82.1
2000–01 to 2010–11	25885	158.7

These numbers indicate that the decade of the 1980s turned out the best for our growth rate and that of the 1970s the worst. The differences in these rates are highly significant. The trend is interesting as it shows how fast the size of Indian purchasing power is accelerating in consecutive decades. This is the miracle of compounding. The increase in growth rate appears modest but the absolute increase in real GDP over decades is astonishing.

Cycles

- From the initial year until 1956–57, the real GDP grew monotonically. The phase accordingly marks the (first) recovery, its starting point is not known. In Fig. 10.1, this is the phase where the graph is upward moving (until point A on the graph); and in Fig. 10.2, it is the phase where the growth rate line is above the zero growth rate axis (until just before the point A).
- Real GDP falls in 1957–58, and so this is the (first) recession year. The previous year accordingly marks the peak of the first cycle. In Fig. 10.1, it is the first top and in Fig. 10.2, it is the last year of the first cycle when the growth rate was positive.
- Real GDP starts rising beginning 1958-59. Thus, the trough of the first cycle falls in 1957–58. In Fig. 10.1, this is the first bottom (marked as point B) and in Fig. 10.2, this is the first time when the growth line is below the origin (point B).

- Real GDP continues its upward march in a row during 1958-59 through 1964–65, becoming the next (second) recovery phase. The trend is reversed in 1965–66. Thus, 1964–65 happens to be the second top point on the business cycle. In Fig. 10.1, this is the second phase (from point A to point C) where the real GDP line slopes upward in a row, and in Fig. 10.2 it is the second phase where the growth line is above the X-axis (between points B and D).
- Recall that the first top was hit in 1956–57 and the next one in 1964–65. The duration, which comes to eight years, gives the length of the first cycle. Alternatively, the duration could be measured from the first trough to the next, i.e., from 1957–58 to 1965–66, which also gives an eight years cycle. In Fig. 10.1, the length of the cycle is seen from the first bump to the next (from point A to point C) or from the first bust to the next (from point B to point D). In Fig., 10.2, the said length is measured from the first point below the X-axis to the next point below the X-axis (from point B to point D).
- Year 1965–66 marks the second turning point of the business cycle. This is the second recession year and since the trend reverses immediately thereafter, this also marks the second trough of the business cycle. The same is reflected in point D in Fig. 10.1 and point D in Fig. 10.2.
- Beginning 1966–67 until 1971–72 is the third recovery phase. This phase is halted in 1972–73, when the real GDP falls once again. 1971–72, thus, gives the third peak (point E in Fig. 10.1) and 1972–73 the third recession year (point F in Fig. 10.1 and point F in Fig. 10.2). From the second peak (1964–65) to the third peak (1971–72)(distance between points C and E or D and F in Fig. 10.1, or that between points D and F in Fig. 10.2), that is, seven years, is the length of the second cycle.

Similarly, the other cycles can be examined. It would be found that the fourth recovery period falls during 1973–74 through 1978–79, the fourth (and the last) recession year in 1979–80 and the fifth (and the last) recovery period, which still continues, runs from 1980-81 onwards. The third (and the last) cycle, measured from the third peak (1971–72) to the fourth peak (1978–79)(distance between points E and G in Fig. 10.1) or from the third bottom to the fourth bottom (distance between points F and H in Fig. 10.1) has a length of seven years. It must be noted that the real GDP is generally moving up over time, and thus each successive trough/peak is at the higher level than the previous trough/peak. The global (overall) trough is at ₹3,845 billion in 1957–58 (point B in Fig. 10.1) and the global peak (so far) is at ₹7,860 billion in 1978–79 (point G in Fig. 10.1); all other troughs and peaks are local (within a particular cycle) ones only. Note that the real GDP is rising monotonously since the last trough in 1979–80 but since the trend continues unabated there is yet no peak after 1978–79. Further, the real GDP graph has become steeper over time which clearly demonstrates an accelerating rate of growth.

Amplitude

Business cycles are also distinguished on the basis of the amplitude (depth), that is, the gap between the top and the bottom values of the variable during a particular cycle. For the first cycle, this comes to ₹1,176 billion (₹3,528 billion in 1956–57 and ₹4,704 billion in 1965–66, or the vertical distance between points A and B in Fig. 10.1). The amplitudes for other cycles can similarly be calculated.

Needless to say, the various elements of a cycle depend on the frequency of the data—the lesser the data periodicity, the more observed fluctuations there are; the more the cycles, the lesser the amplitude and the cycle duration, and so on. This is so because the yearly data hides quarterly, monthly or weekly variations and the quarterly those of monthly and weekly fluctuations and so on. This would become obvious if one compares the above facts on cycles with the cycles found on the basis of the quarterly or monthly data. In India, we do have monthly data on industrial production and if that can be used as a proxy for GDP, more elaborate business cycles can be delineated.

Recession

While business cycles have plagued practically all countries, its various phases do not have unique technical definitions. In the United States, for example, a **recession is declared when the real GDP falls for two quarters of a year in a row**, and a recession year is declared when the GDP is lower than it was in the previous year. However, developing countries like India face time lags in the GDP data, which runs beyond two quarters, and their GDP is contributed significantly by agriculture, which is seasonal in character. This precludes India and many other countries from adopting the United States definition of recession. Again, there is no exact definition of recovery but it usually refers to the period immediately after recession, when growth in the real GDP is restored.

Depression

Depression is a familiar term with regard to business cycles. Yet, there is no hard and fast definition for it. It is a term reserved for deep recession that lasts for several years and is spread well across the globe. The recession of 1929-33 is the only one which is considered as the Great Depression.

In general term, recession is the period when one's neighbor loses the job and depression is the period when one own-self loses the job. The recession of 2007–09 was fairly well spread and it lasted for over two quarters in several countries, and accordingly it has been labeled as the **great recession** as well as the **global recession**.

Stylised Facts about Business Cycles

Business cycles have several interesting facts. These include

- These occur and recur in all countries across the globe.
- Unlike seasonal fluctuations, cycles are irregular in timings of occurrence, duration they last, amplitude/depth/severity they have, and the turning points they have; and hence are rarely predictable.

- Most macroeconomic variables fluctuate together, in known directions and in varying magnitudes.
- While Great Depression was well spread across countries, Great Recession fairly spread across globe, many other recessions/prosperities did not occur simultaneously in all countries.

Why cycles have these features and how economic policies counter them is the subject matter of this and the next four chapters.

It may not be out of place here to provide some comparable data on business cycles that have occurred in India and other appropriately selected countries. At the cost of repetition, let us look again at the growth rate in the real GDP in India during the last over 60 years. Note that the growth rate has fluctuated between a negative of 5.2 per cent in 1979–80 and a positive of 10.5 per cent in 1988–89. Further, during the over 60 years of its history, the growth rate was negative in four years (1957–58, 1965–66, 1972–73 and 1979–80), it was a one digit positive value in all the other years but one year (1988–89), and the magnitude varied widely over years. The average growth rate comes to around 5.5 per cent with a standard deviation of around 3 per cent. Thus, cycles did exist and their periodicity and amplitude have shown no fixed pattern. A study by the RBI (vide RBI Occasional Papers, winter 2000) attempted to identify the cycles in India on the basis of the monthly data on the index of industrial production in the country. It finds that during the second quarter of 1971 and the second quarter of 2000, there were as many as 13 cycles; the duration (trough to trough) varying between 15 and 42 months, with an average of 27 months. The expansion phase lasted anywhere between 7 and 20 months, having an average length of 12 months; and the contraction phase between 7 and 30 months, with an average duration of 16 months. The situation has been similar in other countries. The relevant summary data on a few selected countries for various calendar years are provided in Table 10.2 and more are used for the business cycle analysis, which follows:

Table 10.2 Real GDP Growth Rates in Selected Countries

(Percentages)

Year	*India*	*USA*	*Japan*	*China*	*UK*	*Germany*	*Malaysia*	*Brazil*	*Russian Fed*	*World*
1950	NA	8.5	NA	19.0	3.6	NA	NA	NA	NA	NA
1960	7.0	2.2	13.3	–1.4	4.6	31.5	NA	NA	NA	5.4
1970	5.2	–0.1	10.3	19.4	2.4	5.1	6.0	8.8	NA	4.3
1980	7.5	–0.6	3.5	7.8	–1.9	1.0	7.4	9.1	NA	1.8
1985	5.5	2.9	5.1	13.5	3.7	2.1	–1.1	8.0	NA	3.6
1990	5.7	1.1	4.8	3.8	0.5	4.9	9.0	–4.3	–3.0	2.9
1995	8.0	2.3	1.5	10.5	2.8	1.9	9.8	4.2	–4.1	2.8
2000	5.2	3.1	2.8	8.0	3.8	2.8	8.9	4.4	10.0	4.0
2001	5.5	1.1	0.4	8.3	2.9	1.6	0.5	1.3	5.1	1.4
2002	4.0	1.8	0.3	9.1	2.4	NA	5.4	2.7	4.7	1.8
2003	8.1	2.5	1.7	10.0	3.8	–0.4	5.8	1.2	7.9	2.8
2004	7.0	3.5	2.4	10.1	2.9	0.7	6.8	5.7	7.2	5.1
2005	9.5	3.1	1.3	11.3	2.8	0.8	5.3	3.2	6.4	4.3
2006	9.6	2.7	1.7	12.7	2.6	3.9	5.6	4.0	8.2	5.1
2007	9.3	1.9	2.2	14.2	3.6	3.4	6.3	6.1	8.5	5.0

(Contd.)

(*Contd.*)

2008	6.7	–0.3	–1.1	9.6	–1.0	0.8	4.8	5.2	5.2	2.3
2009	8.6	–3.1	–5.5	9.2	–4.0	–5.1	–1.5	–0.3	–7.8	–1.3
2010	9.3	2.4	4.7	10.3	1.8	4.0	7.2	7.5	4.3	4.5
2011	6.2	1.8	–0.5	9.4	1.0	3.1	5.1	2.7	4.3	3.3
2012	5.0	2.2	2.0	7.8	0.3	0.9	5.6	NA	NA	2.6

Source: *International Financial Statistics*, IMF, various issues

United States

In the United States, the growth rate has been generally positive, with an average of 2.6 per cent and standard deviation of 2.1 per cent during 1953 through 2012 (vide Ch. 14, Review Question 1, table). The growth rate took a negative value in several years. The worst recession (after the Great Depression) occurred in 2009 when the GDP fell by 3.1 per cent. The other years of the negative growth include 1954, 1958, 1970, 1974, 1975, 1980, 1982, 1991 and 2008. The growth rate was the maximum at 6.0 per cent in 1984. A study of business cycles in the United States during August 1929 through March 1991 finds that there were as many as 11 cycles, with the length (peak to peak) varying between 18 and 109 months, having an average of 66 months (vide Dornbusch, Fischer and Startz, 2001). During the four years of the Great Depression (1929–1933), the real GDP fell by about 30 per cent (and the rate of unemployment rose from 3.2 to 25.2 per cent).

Japan

In Japan, the best year was 1960 when its real GDP recorded a growth rate of 13.3 per cent. Through most of the 1960s, Japan witnessed the double-digit growth rates. However, 1971 and onwards it has never experienced such a double-digit rate. The situation was bad during 1997–2002, with growth of less than one per cent, positive or negative, barring the year 2000 when it achieved a 2.8 per cent growth rate. During 2003–2007, it performed reasonably well, landed into recession during the next two years, did rather well in 2010, suffered recession again in 2011 and recorded a two percent growth rate in 2012. The last two decades have been termed as the "lost decades" for Japan.

China

The story of China, is this regard, is quite interesting. China recorded its top rate at 19.0 per cent in 1950, and double-digit rates in several years in a row during most of the mid- and late-1960s, 1980s through mid-1990s, again during 2003–2007, also in 2010, and in high one-digit rates in all other post 1980 years. Nevertheless, the country could not escape the negative rate, which she experienced during a few years in 1960, 1962, 1967, 1968 and 1976. The average growth rate between 1964 and 2012 comes to around 9.2 per cent with a standard deviation of about 6.5 per cent. It must be noted that China is credited with the attainment of the highest growth rate among the large countries in the last couple of decades.

If we look at the world as a whole, there was, of course, never a negative growth rate (barring perhaps the Great Depression period as it was well spread) but the rate varied between a low of 0.2 per cent in 1982 and a high of 6.2 per cent in 1964; and the average rate and the standard deviation standing at 3.8 and 1.4 per cent during 1964–2012, respectively. The data of other countries may similarly be looked into. Suffice to say here, the story of ups and downs in the economy is universal and we need macroeconomics to explain this phenomenon.

The observed economic fluctuations, please note, have been in the midst of stabilisation policies and surely they would have been even more severe in the absence of these policies. Explanation of these fluctuations is one of the core areas of macroeconomics and the stabilisation policies are designed to counter these fluctuations. The next section focuses on these issues.

Stabilisation Policies

All economies are subject to business cycles, but there is no perfect automatic mechanism to counter them. Yes, we do have some built-in system (called **automatic stabilisers**) that works against the cycles, and this consists of the progressive income taxation and other transfer payments (social security system, unemployment compensation, etc.). When the economy is under recession, income tax proceeds fall and transfer payments rise. Consequently, the disposable income increase, which, in turn, tend to push up consumption expenditure and thereby the aggregate demand and, thus, help counter the downswing. Quite the opposite happens when the economy is under unsustainable prosperity. However, history suggests that these automatic stabilisers are grossly inadequate to avoid cycles. The cycles are bad and they get worse as their depth, length and spread increases. Thus, economists have suggested some policy actions on the part of governments to tame business cycles. These are accordingly called stabilisation policies, and they are basically the fiscal and monetary policies. The other minor such policies are the trade and exchange rate (only if the country is on a fixed or managed exchange rate policy), and incomes (carrot-stick) policies. These are called stabilisation policies, for they aim at reducing the severity of short-run economic fluctuations in GDP, unemployment and inflation so the latter variables stay as close to their natural levels as possible. While economic fluctuations are considered bad, they have some good side effects as well. For example, if bad times do not come, people may become complacent which would harm growth. If business cycles are removed, there would never be booms!

Tools of Stabilisation Policies

The tools of fiscal policy are government expenditure, taxation, subsidies and other (non-tax non-subsidies) transfer payments. However, in macroeconomics, government expenditure alone is usually treated as the policy variable. This is because (a) government merely decides the tax rates and not the tax collection amount, which varies not only according to the tax rate but also by the tax base, which is hardly under government control, and tax collection (including non-tax revenues) and subsidy disbursements, net of other transfer payments, can deviate from government expenditure only marginally and temporarily (vide government inter-temporal budget constraint); (b) subsidies on production and consumption are basically past legacy or currently inevitable, and government decides them mainly on the need/political ground; (c) transfer payments referred to here are pensions, interest on past debts and social security payments which are mainly obligatory.

As discussed in detail in Chapter 8, the tools of monetary policy are open market operation, cash reserve requirements, Bank rate, selective credit controls, moral persuasion, statutory liquidity requirements, repo rate, marginal standing facility and the like. These help the Central Bank to regulate (nominal) money supply and or the (nominal) interest rate, its quantity and distribution. However, as seen in Chapter 8, the money supply is largely under the control of the monetary authority (RBI) and, accordingly macroeconomics takes the money supply (instead of the various instruments of monetary policy that regulate it) as the only monetary policy instrument. Alternatively, though neither there is a unique interest rate in any country nor the Central Bank of the country fully regulates the interest rate structure, some economists suggest the use of interest rate as the monetary policy tool. The said position may be appropriate, particularly if the Central Bank uses a given interest rate, which it controls, as the signal rate for its policy stance. Lately, the Federal Reserve Bank in the United States and the Reserve Bank of India, among others, are using the interest rate under their respective commands, viz. the federal fund rate, and the repo rate (and reverse repo and bank rates), respectively for this purpose. Thus, interest rate could be taken as the monetary policy vehicle. Nevertheless, we would follow the usual system and use the money supply as the monetary policy tool. Incidentally, recall from Chapter 8 that the monetary authority could control either the availability (money/credit supply) or the cost of credit (interest rate) but not both (just as the monopolist could set either the quantity or the price of its product, but not both) and, thus, one of the two magnitudes would have to be left to the market.

If the country is under the freely floating exchange rate system, it has no exchange rate policy. But if she is under any other system, it has the exchange rate tool as well. Further, exports and imports could be controlled through bans and quotas (sanctions), besides the tariffs and tax breaks. In addition, the policy makers have the incomes (also called **carrot-stick**) policy, whose components are wage-price guidelines, mandatory wage-price controls and tax based incentives and disincentives. Under the first, government merely issues the guidelines within which the wage and prices have to be set, while in the second government sets these rates itself. Under the third and last component, government declares tax breaks for well-defined good behaviour and penalties for unexpected behaviour. Such policy actions obviously have bearings on the production, employment and prices.

Types of Policy Stance

Two kinds of policy stance are distinguished, viz., easy, liberal or expansionary; and dear, tight or restrictive. The said distinction is relevant for fiscal and monetary policies only. The former for the fiscal policy would mean an increase in government expenditure (or/and decrease in tax rate or increase in fiscal deficit) and for the monetary policy an increase in money supply (or a reduction in the interest rate). Quite the opposite would mean the respective tight policy. Further, an increase in government expenditure, not accompanied by an increase in taxes (and other sources of revenue), leads to an increase in fiscal/ budget deficit, and vice versa. There are only three avenues to finance fiscal deficit; these consist of public borrowings, internally and externally, and monetisation (issuing of new money, currency, against government bonds). All the three add to the public debt. Thus, fiscal deficit is a flow to public debt and therefore increase in the former leads to an increase in the latter, and vice versa. In view of this,

> while the monetary policy stance could be judged by the rate of change in money supply or in interest rate (assuming the demand for money is stable), that in the fiscal policy could be assessed by the proportion of government expenditure in the GDP, that of fiscal deficit in the GDP, or that of public debt in the GDP.

Expansionary policies tend to create new demands in the economy and push up the aggregate demand. The mechanism through which this effect is created depends on the model under operation; the details are discussed in the following chapters. Suffice to say here that the fiscal and monetary policies exert varying effects on the economy, and therefore the government must choose one or the other, or a mix of the two judicially. The two policies are, however, often complementary and thus the government may opt for both, and in the same stance (direction) if the situation is tough or/ and urgent. For example, a recession may be attacked by an expansionary fiscal as well as an expansionary monetary policy. Further, when the two policies affect a variable differently, policy makers could be tough on one and liberal on the other policy, or vice versa. As we shall see later in this part of the book,

> while an expansionary fiscal policy, *ceteris paribus*, causes the interest rate to rise; an expansionary monetary policy, *ceteris paribus*, triggers a fall in the interest rate.

Thus, if the government does not wish to tamper the interest rate while it wishes to tame the recession, it may combine an expansionary fiscal with a restrictive monetary policy, or vice versa. The detailed uses and consequences of all such policies would be dealt with in detail in what follows. However, we must note here the difference between a pure fiscal or pure monetary policy and a mix of the two. In case of a pure policy, only one instrument, fiscal or monetary, is used; while in case of a mixed policy, the two may be combined in any combination. Thus, if government expenditure increases without any increase or decrease in money supply, we have a pure fiscal policy. In contrast, if the former is accompanied by an increase in money supply (as under monetisation of fiscal deficit), we have a mix of the two expansionary policies.

Demand Management Policies

Fiscal, monetary, exchange rate, trade and income policies exert influence on the economy basically through the aggregate demand and, therefore, they are also known as the demand management policies. When policy makers find that the demand is lacking threatening recession/ unemployment, they could boost it up through fiscal (government expenditure) expansion, monetary (money supply) expansion, devaluation of the currency, trade liberalisation, and/or easy income policies. In contrast, when there is excessive demand in relation to the capacity to supply, threatening inflation, policy makers would cut government expenditure, slow the growth in money supply, revalue the currency, and so on. The monetary policy is handled by the monetary authority (the Central Bank of the country) and the fiscal and other policies by the Ministry of Finance/Treasury. Since both are parts of the government, they generally work in tandem. They are largely independent, though some interdependence does exist. They not only help counter business cycles but also help promote growth (thus, containing unemployment) and check inflation/deflation. How these are achieved depend on the underlying model. Also, each policy has its unique strengths as well as limitations, which again are subject to the model specifications. However, each of the fiscal and monetary, as well as the exchange rate policy faces some constraint, independent of the model. These are now discussed.

Fiscal Policy Constraints

The constraints to fiscal policy emanate from the politics of government expenditure, and the sustainability of fiscal deficit and public debt. All government expenditures have to be approved by the Parliament/budget authority and the Parliaments' political representatives. Due to political differences, even the most urgent expenditure may not get approved on time. Further, the trouble gets worse if a cut in expenditure is proposed. While people welcome increases in salaries, perquisites, subsidies, and support staff, they vehemently oppose any cut in them. This is obvious from the fact that in spite of the best efforts to downsize the government departments in almost every country, hardly any significant success is seen in practice. In India, we are witnessing currently (January 2014) that while Finance Minister is working hard to adhere to his declared level of fiscal deficit, several politicians are taking holiday trips abroad for fun, calling them study tours. This tells that the **fiscal policy is asymmetric**, meaning you can have an expansionary policy relatively easily but a restrictive one is hard to put into practice.

With regard to the sustainability of deficits and debt, recall that expansionary fiscal policy leads to increases in fiscal deficit and public debt. Any debt is bad and public debt is no exception. The moot question then is, "is public debt sustainable to any level"? Or, to put it differently, "is public debt/fiscal deficit free from the solvency constraint"? Recently (October 2013), we have seen USA's shut down for about a fortnight due to fiscal cliff.

The answer is clearly "no" but to appreciate this we must first understand the meaning of debt sustainability. All debts to any one is subject to servicing by way of interest and principal and on time. Government debt is no exception to this rule. In view of this, economists and policy makers believe that government faces an **inter-temporal budget constraint.** This means that over time, government would like to retire all its debt or at least not face the prospects of default. However, this does not mean that debt can not go on increasing with time. To appreciate this, we must first understand that what is at stake here is not the absolute size of debt but the debt relative to GDP to indicate the debt burden – to take the point home, think of a debt of ₹10,000 on a person below the poverty line and compare it with a debt of ₹10 billion on a person like Laxmi Nivas Mittal and see which one is more burdensome. Currently our government, like most others, has a significant debt to GDP ratio and it has not suffered any debt crisis to date. This suggests that the current level of the debt to GDP ratio is sustainable. Let us next look at a relevant paradox, called the **paradox of debt.** It states that even fairly large fiscal deficits may not endanger the debt to GDP ratio. Since the debt is normally measured in nominal terms, the relevant GDP here is the nominal (at current prices) GDP. The nominal GDP of a country rises on two counts, viz., growth in real GDP ($\dot{y}$) and growth in general price-inflation ($\dot{P}$). Therefore, if the growth rate in the public debt (d) just equals, ignoring the insignificant interaction term, the sum of the above two rates, i.e.

$$d = \dot{y} + \dot{P} \tag{10.1}$$

there is no change in the public debt to GDP ratio. To show its significance, let us consider an example. Suppose a country's current debt outstanding is ₹10,000 billion and its current GDP is ₹20,000 billion, giving a debt to GDP ratio of 50 per cent. Further, assume that this country has a real GDP growth rate of 6 per cent and inflation rate of 5 per cent. Then, according to equation (10.1), if this country's public debt grows by 11 per cent; its GDP to debt ratio will remain unaltered at 50 (= 11,100/22,200) per cent. The 11 per cent of the total debt of ₹10,000 billion comes to ₹1100 billion. Thus, a fiscal deficit of ₹1100 billion, which equals 5.5 per cent of the GDP (1100/20,000), would leave the debt-GDP ratio constant. The 5.5 per cent is fairly large on the current standard and the assumption of the 50 per cent debt-GDP ratio is fairly reasonable, looking at those numbers for various countries today. The example, thus, illustrates an interesting paradox, which is a good help in supporting the use of the fiscal policy, for stimulating the economy, particularly if it is facing a recession.

A corollary of the above paradox would take us to the constraint under which the debt to GDP ratio is a constant, if the primary deficit is zero:

$$\dot{Y} = i \tag{10.2}$$

where

$\dot{Y}$ = growth rate in nominal GDP (= $\dot{y} + \dot{P}$)
i = nominal interest rate

Recall that if the public debt increases at the rate equal to the sum of the growth rate in real income and the inflation rate, which equals the rate of growth in normal GDP ($\dot{y} + \dot{P} = \dot{Y}$), the debt-GDP ratio remains constant. Thus, the public debt could increase by the rate of growth in nominal income, and yet the said ratio would remain constant. The nominal interest rate i measures the interest rate applicable on public debt. If $\dot{Y} = i$, all increases in debt D on account of the interest obligations on it ($i\,D$) could be served through increases in the nominal GDP ($\dot{Y}$) without altering the debt-GDP ratio. To clarify this, let us take the above numerical example again, and assume a nominal interest rate of 11 per cent.

- Annual interest obligations of public debt = ₹10,000 billion × 0.11 = ₹1100 billion
- If all interest is paid through new debt, the extra debt = ₹1100 billion
- Cumulative debt = ₹10,000 billion + ₹1100 billion = ₹11,100 billion

- Nominal GDP after one year ($\dot{Y}$ =11 per cent) = ₹20,000 × (1.11) = ₹22,200 billion
- New debt-income ratio = ₹11,100/22,200 = 50 per cent

Thus, the government would be able to honour its interest obligations simply through fresh borrowings if the condition **(10.2)** is met without any increase in the debt-GDP ratio. Recalling from Chapter 4 the definition of primary deficit, which equals fiscal deficit minus interest on public debt, it means that so long as the primary deficit is zero, fiscal deficit would never endanger the debt to the GDP ratio. Further, it implies that if the primary deficit were negative, the said ratio would fall and if it were positive, the ratio would go up. Further, if a country has faced no solvency constraint in the past, then it is unlikely to experience one so long as its debt to GDP ratio does not rise. The implication of this is that the expansionary fiscal policies up to a limit (zero primary deficits) are sustainable. Further, the debt could last forever so long as the government is able to raise sufficient revenue to cover the non-interest obligations. The earlier loans due for repayments could be paid off with interest simply through the fresh issues of bonds.

The constraint in equation **(10.2)** however may not hold. If so, what would be the condition for the debt to GDP ratio to remain stable? To get this, we need to use algebra and calculus. Let FD denote the fiscal deficit, D the public debt, G the non-interest government expenditure, T the government tax and other non-debt revenues net of transfer payments, Y the nominal GDP, i the nominal interest rate on public debt, $\dot{Y}$ the growth rate in nominal GDP, and D the first difference operator. Recalling the various definitions from Chapter 4 and here, we have

$$FD = (G - T) + i\,(D) = \Delta(D)$$

Division of both the sides by D, and rearrangement of the terms gives,

$$\Delta(D)/D = [(G - T)/D] + i \quad \textbf{(10.3)}$$

Next, taking the first difference of the debt to GDP ratio (vide calculus of derivation), we get

$$\Delta(D/Y) = [Y\Delta D - D\Delta Y]/Y^2$$

Dividing and multiplying the right hand side by D, we get

$$\Delta(D/Y) = D/Y\,[\Delta(D)/D - \Delta(Y)/Y] \quad \textbf{(10.4)}$$

Substitution from equation **(10.3)** in **(10.4)** and solution of the result, gives

$$\Delta(D/Y) = D/Y\,\{[(G - T)/D] + i] - \Delta(Y)/Y\}$$
$$= [(G - T)/Y] + (D/Y)\,[i - \Delta Y/Y]$$

or,

$$\Delta(D/Y) = [(G - T)\,/Y] + (D/Y)\,[i - \dot{Y}\,] \quad \textbf{(10.5)}$$

Equation **10.5** is the **fundamental equation of public debt**. It is also known as the inter-temporal budget constraint of the government. It gives the conditions for debt sustainability and hence is also known as the public debt/fiscal sustainability constraint. It assumes that the debt/fiscal deficit is sustainable so long as the debt to GDP ratio does not increase from its current level. The first term of the right hand side of the above equation is simply the primary deficit to GDP ratio and the second term is the debt-GDP ratio multiplied by the difference between the nominal interest rate and the growth rate in the nominal GDP. Thus, it indicates that the debt-GDP ratio is constant under the following two conditions:

(i) Primary deficit $(G - T)$ is zero

(ii) Nominal interest rate on public debt (i) equals growth rate in the nominal GDP($\dot{Y}$)

These are identical to those in equation **(10.2)** above. Further, the said equation indicates that the debt to GDP ratio would rise if there is a primary deficit and the nominal interest rate is not less than the growth rate in the nominal GDP. Thus, for insuring a non-accelerating debt-GDP ratio, a country has to see that if it is running any primary deficit, it must ensure that its nominal GDPs growth rate is higher than the nominal interest rate applicable to its debt; the extent of the difference in the two rates could easily be calculated through equation **(10.5)**. To see it unambiguously, setting the left hand side of equation **(10.5)** equal to zero gives the condition for a stable debt ratio:

$$(G - T)/Y = (D/Y)[\dot{Y} - i] \qquad \textbf{(10.6)}$$

or,

$$D/Y = [(G - T)/Y]/[\dot{Y} - i] \qquad \textbf{(10.7)}$$

The above equation suggests that the debt ratio can be maintained at the erstwhile level if the ratio of the primary deficit to GDP exactly equals the difference between the growth rate in nominal GDP and the nominal interest rate applicable to public debt. Further, it suggests that a country can aspire even to reduce the GDP ratio through ensuring a certain level of primary surplus and/or achieving a certain growth rate in its nominal GDP in excess of the nominal interest rate.

If one were to look at the Indian data, we would discover that the country (at the Central government level) is facing a yearly average primary deficit of about 2.0 per cent in the last three years (ending 2013–14). This by itself is a cause for an increase in the debt-GDP ratio by the same number. During the same period, the average growth rate in nominal GDP stands at around 15 per cent, the average central government debt to GDP at around 48 per cent, and the average of the weighted average interest rate on central government securities at 8.36 per cent. Putting these values in equation **(10.5)** would suggest that our debt to GDP ratio would go down by 1.19 [= 2.0 + 0.48(8.36 – 15.0) = –1.19] per cent yearly. The future scenario looks even better. This is because as per the **Fiscal Responsibility and Budget Management (FRBM) Act**, the government has been targeting to hit a zero revenue deficit and 3 per cent fiscal deficit within five years of the said Act, first by 2006–07, then by 2008-09, which has delayed partly due to the Great Recession of 2007–09 and subsequent economic and political hurdles in the country. Accordingly, there is no expectation for any significant change either in the debt ratio or in the difference between the nominal magnitudes of the interest rate and the GDP growth rate.

A study by Rangarajan and Srivastava (2003) has examined the relevant data for the Indian economy. The study finds that the debt (central government only, but including all the monetised and non-monetised internal debt as well as the external debt) to GDP ratio had gone up from 28.84 per cent in 1950–51 to 55.36 per cent in 2001–02; the primary deficit to GDP ratio gone up from 0.073 to 1.840 per cent, nominal GDP growth rate up from 6.362 to 9.112 per cent and the effective nominal interest rate on debt from 1.361 to 10.242 per cent during the same period. The study concludes that while in the past the growth rate in nominal GDP has usually exceeded the effective nominal interest rate on public debt, the last three years have witnessed a reverse situation. Further, the study states that the positive difference between the said growth and interest rates "may not be expected on a sustained basis—the prospects are that the difference will remain in a narrow range, even if the growth rate remains higher than the interest rate." Under such a prediction, the debt-GDP ratio theory suggests that the primary deficit ratio would basically govern the said ratio. However, as noted above, Rangarajan and Srivastva's predictions about narrowing of the difference between the growth rate in nominal GDP and nominal interest rate have not been upheld by the data in the last decade.

What does the above analysis imply for the sustainability of public debt? The main message is that it is no problem if the primary deficit is under control or/and the growth rate in nominal GDP exceeds the nominal interest rate on public debt. Countries around the world have become increasingly careful regarding the level of their fiscal deficits. For example, Chile and Brazil have set strict limits of their fiscal deficits. In Chile, the rule calls for a structural surplus of one per cent of GDP. In Brazil, the government is required to adhere to a pre-announced primary budget balance. However, if such conditions do not hold and the said debt ratio increases over time, the debt does not automatically become unsustainable or risky for the country's solvency. To cite some live examples, the debt to GDP ratio of the United States shot up to its peak at 114 per cent in 1946 and to a recent peak at 82 per cent in 2011, but still, the country has always remained solvent. Japan's public debt to GDP ratio stood at 214 per cent in 2012 and yet the country remained solvent. To derive the point home, note that there is nothing sacrosanct about a particular level of the debt ratio. The solvency is always in relation to the ability to honour a debt claim when due. Yes, Mexico in 1982 and many countries thereafter have defaulted (external) debt servicing but that by itself does not mean the debt ratio beyond a level inevitably endangers solvency. To see this clearly we have to consider other relevant factors as well, which follows.

Public Debt Concerns

Besides the above arguments, there are other factors which warrant consideration for judging the size of public debt. These are dealt with under this head.

(a) The solvency of a public debt depends on whether it is owed internally or externally. This is so because an internal debt of a country is a debt to itself and hence it poses no threat to solvency. All internal debts are held internally in the form of government bonds by public, and so they cancel out. Further, an internal debt can always be paid back on demand through more taxes or simply through printing its own currency; note that **governments have unlimited power to tax its people/business and to issue own currency/money**. These methods would, of course, have repercussions on the economy in terms of causing recession or/and inflation but they do not threaten the solvency. Developed countries like the United States do not have a problem even in the case of an external debt. For, the currency of such a country is usually a hot one, which is accepted world over for all kinds of payments and in many cases the external debt itself is contracted in such a currency. In case of the United States this is surely true, and hence, the country is never threatened with her solvency. But developing countries like India surely have a solvency constraint against their external debts. For, if the country is short of foreign exchange and foreign lenders refuse to roll over or forgive the debt, it would face a financial crisis, which may have serious repercussions on its economy. Such was the trouble faced by Thailand in 1997, causing significant depreciation of its currency, bankruptcies of many debtors, bank failures, and financial crisis in the country. Similar problems were faced by PIIGS group of European countries recently (2008–10).

(b) There are arguments that suggest that public debt per se is not bad and, hence, not a burden at all. Firms borrow through bonds and invest the proceeds in structures, equipment, and inventories. They keep doing this time and again, and go on adding to their debt. Most of them have not suffered any debt crisis and rather have prospered through this. Check the financial statements of successful companies around the world to verify this. On similar grounds, if a government takes a loan and invest the proceeds in good projects it would not only be able to service such debts on time but also yield extra returns for other uses. Thus, the purpose behind the debt is significant here. In other words, if public debt is incurred to finance capital account deficits (government capital expenditures), it is not an issue; but if it is to finance a current account deficit (government consumption), it may cause a servicing problem.

(c) The **Barro-Ricardo Equivalence Theorem** (1974) has advanced yet another reason as to why deficits and public debt do not really matter.[1] Their theorem states that the financing of the government expenditure by debt is equivalent to financing it by taxes and, therefore, debt financed tax cuts have no effect on national savings and investments. This is because, in such a case, individuals increase their personal saving to exactly offset the increase in the fiscal deficit. Further, if private saving goes up one for one with any government fiscal deficit, government bonds in the hands of the private sector are not wealth and accordingly the fiscal deficit have no real effect on the economy. The theorem assumes that the decision makers (a) are forward looking (b) have perfect foresight (c) have the **bequest motive** (i.e. they save partly to leave some assets (bequest) for their children/grandchildren and/or for charity) and (d) face no liquidity constraint. In addition, it assumes that (e) government budget is inter-temporally balanced. The argument goes as follows: The forward-looking consumer understands that government borrowing today means higher taxes in the future, for government budget is assumed to balance inter-temporarily. If so, a tax cut financed by government debt does not reduce the tax burden, it merely reschedules it. Accordingly, the father, who likes to leave some bequests for his children, would offset the government action of borrowing today instead of taxing today (and thus increasing future taxes) by increasing his saving by the amount of future taxes. Assumption of perfect foresight would ensure the equivalence of the two amounts. The government action would thus leave the father's consumption unchanged. On these assumptions, the equivalence

[1]It is known as the Barro-Ricardo theorem because David Ricardo (1817) had originally proposed this theme and it was later developed by Robert Barro.

theorem is easy to prove: consider just two periods: present (1) and future (2), and just two persons, father (F) and son (S), and assume the two alternative ways of financing the government expenditure are taxes T and debt D ($T = D$). If the government taxes at present, then

(i) $B_1 = (1 + i)\,[Y_F - T - C_F)$

(ii) $C_s = Y_s + B_1$

If the government borrows today and taxes in the future, then

(iii) $B_2 = (1+ i)\,[Y_F - D - C_F] + (1 + i)\,D$

$= B_1 + (1+ i)\,D$, for $D = T$

(iv) $C_s = [Y_s - (1+ i)\,T] + B_2$

$= Y_s + [B_2 - (1 + i)T]$

$= Y_s + B_1$, on substitution from relation (iii).

where

B = bequest

C = consumption expenditure

Y = income

i = interest rate

The above implicitly assumes (vide bequest motive) that in either case, the father's consumption spending is the same. If so, the above proves that the consumption spending of the son is also the same under both situations. Hence, the two ways of financing the government expenditure are equivalent. This, in turn, implies that the debt financed tax cuts or tax hikes to finance debt have no effect on the solvency of the government and accordingly they exert no influence on the real magnitudes, like real GDP, real interest rate. Of course, there are critics of this theorem. They argue that bequests and concern for children are not equivalent, and many parents do not even care for their descendants and some even do not have any. Also, the assumption of no liquidity constraint is not valid, for the capital market is far from being perfect and the rate of lending differs from that of borrowing. Even perfect foresight under such a dynamic world is unimaginable and several governments across countries have been running into fiscal deficits year after year. Many people are myopic and their time horizon for decision-making is about a year. Such people tend to ignore the potential tax burden of government debt. Also, historical data do not reveal any positive relationship between the private saving and fiscal deficit. Thus, it is generally believed that the equivalence theorem is not quite valid and, accordingly, fiscal deficits and public debt do impinge on national savings. Nevertheless, the theorem does undermine the solvency concern of public debt. The said theorem is regarded as the most coherent **critique of the public debt inducing deficits**.

(d) During recession both the GDP and net (of transfer payments) tax revenues fall, and during prosperity they tend to rise. This implies that if government expenditure does not change much (or rise, as happens usually during recessions), fiscal deficits tend to increase during recessions and decrease during prosperities. Thus, during recessions, while fiscal deficits increase (means public debt rise), GDPs fall and hence the debt to GDP ratios tend to go up. Quite the opposite would happen during periods of prosperity. For this reason, economists distinguish between actual fiscal deficits (AFD), structural fiscal deficits (SFD) and cyclical fiscal deficits (CFD). They are defined as

$$\text{AFD} = G + TP - t(Y) \quad \textbf{(10.8)}$$

$$\text{SFD} = G + TP - t(Y_F) \quad \textbf{(10.9)}$$

$$\text{CFD} = t(Y_F - Y) \quad \textbf{(10.10)}$$

where Y_F = full employment output and Y = actual output. The difference between the actual and structural deficits is cyclical deficit. The cyclical deficit is the result of the actual output being less than the potential output. Thus, note that the actual fiscal deficit has two components: One, viz. cyclical deficit, which is caused by the state of the economy (business cycles) and two, viz. structural deficit, which is caused by the fiscal policy. Note that SFD is independent of the position of the business cycle, i.e. boom or recession.

Sometime government undertakes massive investments in the public sector or spends money to fight wars or such other events, and, if so, the debt-GDP ratio goes up. These are facts of life and they do not pose serious trouble in the long run. While structural fiscal deficit is bad, cyclical fiscal deficit is not only not bad, it is even recommended to counter recession. The Keynesian message is that **budget deficits must be operated counter-cyclically**.

(e) There are arguments against deficits and public debt that we are spending our children's money. This is not quite right, for we are also leaving larger assets in the public sector for their use, assuming, of course, that the government expenditure is not wasteful. Even if wasteful, future generations would have more government bonds in any case. Also, the posterity would benefit through the technical progress as well as the bequests left by the past generations, and surely they could well expect a better standard of living over their forefathers.

One can go on further with such arguments. However, the main point is that while the government does have an inter-temporal budget constraint, fiscal deficits and public debt need not be an overriding issue in formulating and executing prudent fiscal policy. What is relevant is the cause of such deficits. Further, as we shall examine in later chapters, government expenditure or fiscal policy often influences the real GDP, unemployment, and inflation—the factors of major concern in macroeconomic policy making—and these are more relevant in deciding the size of the policy action rather than the debt ratio, etc. In other words, there is practically no solvency constraint for the fiscal policy. Needless to say, a large debt preempts a significant part of the public revenue and, thereby, restricts the government's ability to spend on social, educational and infrastructure projects. Also, large borrowings lead to significant increases in the interest rate, inflation, etc., which may not be good for the economy. Thus, the constraints to the fiscal policy come less from its effect on the debt ratio and more from its economic consequences. In particular, if fiscal deficit/public debt is high, governments have little room for expansionary fiscal policy – which is called as **Fiscal Drag**. All such consequences would be dealt with in detail in the next four chapters. Since contractionary fiscal policies only result in fiscal surpluses, which reduce public debt, they are always sustainable.

Monetary Policy Constraints

Monetary policy has fewer constraints than fiscal policy. Firstly, unlike the fiscal policy, it has to do little with politics. The Governor and the most other senior officers at the country's Central Bank, though appointed by the government, are usually academicians and professionals. Besides, the monetary authority is usually independent of the government in decision-making. Recall from Chapter 8 that since the mid-1990s, there has been no automatic monetisation of any fiscal deficit in India. The monetary authority is practically free to decide on the rate of interest or the rate of monetary expansion year after year. The same holds good currently in most countries/European common currency area. Secondly, unlike the fiscal policy, the monetary policy is close to being symmetric. The RBI does not face any threat from the voters and its actions are hardly understood by the common people. It is thus fairly in equal ease both in accelerating the rate of increase in money supply (or the interest rate at its command) or in decelerating the same. Nevertheless, it is always easier to ease than tighten and, thus, some degree of asymmetry does exist even in case of the monetary policy. In addition, the monetary authorities face certain other constraints, which are as follows:

(a) Currently, certain countries are on dollarisation, some on currency boards, and some others on the fixed exchange rate system. As argued in Chapter 8, the ones on dollarisation, have no monetary powers; those on currency boards are subject to the corresponding currency reserves condition; and the last, which are on the fixed rate system, can only use their monetary power to maintain the fixed foreign exchange rate, unless they restrict capital flows (vide international trilemma). These days, the world is going fast on globalisation and therefore, unless a country has a floating exchange rate, its monetary policy is restrained in its options in any given exchange rate system.

(b) Countries that are on the floating exchange rate system, of either the pure or managed type are free to exercise their monetary powers. Since such countries have given up the regulation of exchange rate, they enjoy both the integration as well as the monetary sovereignty. Most advanced countries, barring the group of the European countries who have gone for a common currency, and even a good number of developing countries, including India, are on the floating rate system and, accordingly, they face practically no constraint in operating their monetary policy. It is for this reason that the monetary policy has become so popular lately.

(c) Central Bank's power to control money supply can be countered through public changing the currency to money ratio or/and banks changing the (the (excess) reserves to deposits ratio, each of which affect the money multiplier (vide Chapter 8).

(d) Monetary policy works through interest rate, directly or indirectly, and, as will be seen in later chapters, it has little/no effect on the real economy when the economy has low interest rate, which leads its decision makers to fall under liquidity trap.

(e) Recall from Chapter 8, that the country's Central Bank can control either the money supply or the interest rate but not the both. Accordingly, monetary authorities could choose either the money supply or the interest rate as its tools to regulate the economy. Also, since the two versions of money, viz. narrow (M_1) broad (M_2) money, do not usually have the proportionate relationship, the Central Bank has to decide which one of these to target if it chooses to target the money supply. Currently, many Central Banks, including RBI, are operating basically through interest rate and leaving money supply to be determined by money demand given the target for the interest rate. If one looks at the history, initially interest rate was the target variable but sometime around and after 1960, many countries shifted to target money supply. Once again, around mid-1980s, countries reverted back to interest rate target and many are now practicing an **eclectic approach** to monetary policy.

It will be interesting to see as to which of the two (viz. money supply and interest rate) is a better target under a given situation. The appropriate target variable depends basically on factors, viz. **(a)** which of the potential target variables' the policy makers could control exactly and **(b)** which of the potential target variables' has stable relationship with the ultimate goal variable (growth and inflation rates). Obviously, the better is the control and better is the relationship, the better is the candidate. Since such situations vary over time and space, the appropriate target variable varies from situation to situation. Lately, due to innovations like internet banking, ATMs, credit cards, etc., money demand function has become more unstable [illegible] investment function (the two main functions which happen to be the yardsticks for the effectiveness of stabilization policies vide Chapters 11–14) and hence interest rate has become a popular target variable for Central Banks. However, no Central Bank can afford to ignore the money supply as it bears a fairly strong relationship with inflation, which happens to be a top priority for it. Accordingly, RBI and most other Central Banks have eclectic approach to monetary policy.

Trade and Exchange Rate Policy Constraints

Recall from Chapter 7 that the trade policy and exchange rate exert influence both on exports and imports of goods and services (and not on capital flows) and thereby on the current account (of BOP) imbalances. The latter has to tally with the capital account imbalances in the same magnitude and opposite direction to ensure the BOP equilibrium. For example, if there is a current account deficit, say, in the amount of ₹100 billion then there must be a capital account surplus in the amount of ₹100 billion. Further, a surplus in the capital account means net capital inflow (NKI) in the economy through selling of domestic bonds, equity and bank deposits, taking loans from abroad, or drawing down our holdings of foreign exchange reserves. These, in turn, leads to increase in the country's external debt, which poses the issue of servicing (interest, dividend and repayments) in future. Quite the opposite would be true in the face of a surplus in the current account. The question therefore is, what is the sustainable current account imbalance, or alternatively known as the **national inter-temporal budget constraint**?

Just as a fiscal deficit adds to public debt and fiscal surplus cuts public debt, a current account deficit adds to external debt and current account surplus reduces external debt. Just as a fiscal surplus poses no problem for debt sustainability, current account surplus creates no issue for current account/external debt sustainability. Thus, the issue at hand is the current account deficit only. As seen above, the said deficit is associated with external debt and thereby with interest burden. The latter is a part of the current account and thus it worsens the deficit in question. While a country can live with such a deficit in the short run, it has to be retired sometime in future. This can be done only through additional exports which would reduce domestic consumption. Thus, current account deficit has undesirable consequences and hence it is a constraint. Further, as discussed above under the fiscal policy constraint, it is the external debt relative to GDP rather than debt per se which matters for the current account deficit/external debt sustainability. As before, we assume that the said sustainability would remain intact so long as the external debt to GDP ratio does not increase.

The external debt to GDP ratio depends on a number of factors. First, it depends (positively and in one to one relationship) on the previous value of this ratio. Second, it would increase by the magnitudes of the current account deficit to GDP ratio in the current year. Third, it would change by the servicing cost of the external debt to GDP ratio of the previous period. The last term need not be positive, for while there would be a cost of external debt, there would be growth in GDP. The exact formula for this would be as follows:

$$\mathrm{ED}/Y = (\mathrm{ED}/Y)_{-1} + \mathrm{CAD}/Y + (\mathrm{ED}/Y)_{-1}\,(i - g) \qquad \textbf{(10.11)}$$

where, ED = external debt (nominal), Y = nominal GDP, CAD = current account deficit net of payments on (interest cost of) external debt (nominal), i = nominal rate of interest on external debt and g = growth rate in domestic nominal GDP. Subscript –1 is for the previous year (t – 1) and no subscript means for the current year (t).

The above equation is just like equation **(10.5)** above and it can be derived similarly. The equation assumes that either the whole debt is denominated in domestic currency or there is no change in the exchange rate during the year (vide Callen and Cashin 1999). From equation **(10.11)**, it would be clear that *ED/Y* would remain constant if the following condition is met:

$$\mathrm{CAD}/Y = (\mathrm{ED}/Y)_{-1}\,(g - i) \qquad \textbf{(10.12)}$$

Equation **(10.12)** gives the condition on which the current account imbalance would be sustainable. Thus, if the country's external debt to GDP ratio were 0.208, nominal growth rate in GDP 14.3 per cent (as in 2012) and the interest rate on external debt, say 5 per cent, then current account deficit to GDP ratio of 1.93 [=(0.208)(0.143 — 0.05)= 0.0193] per cent would be consistent with the sustainable current account imbalance. India's present (2012) CAD to GDP ratio stands at 3.2 per cent and thus it is above this number, and accordingly the country is in the danger region on this count.

If the exchange rate is used as a policy tool, either under the managed or the fixed rate system, its application must ensure that it does not violate the national inter-temporal budget constraint as given in equation **(10.11)**. Recall from Chapter 7 that there could be current account deficit even under the freely floating exchange rate system. The said constraint is thus relevant even then.

Income Policy Constraints

The income (carrot-stick) policy basically deals with the wage-price regulations/ guidelines, tax cuts, tax surcharges, and social programmes—incentives/disincentives to producers and consumers. These are normally the short-term measures and they are rolled back as soon as the purpose is served. They would have bearing on fiscal deficit and thus they are subject to the same constraint as the fiscal policy. The policy is typically used as a supplement to traditional fiscal and monetary policies. Further, it is well known in economics that any distortion to market economy, including the exercise of income policy, is accompanied by **dead weight loss**.

To conclude the section, though there is an inter-temporal budget constraint facing the government, the only real constraint to an economy is the current account (or external debt) sustainability one. Accordingly, governments are free to apply the various stabilisation policies within the said constraint. However, for good of the economy, there uses have to be prudent on various grounds, which are hard to verify. This is a significant matter and it would be dealt with in detail in the next four chapters under varying hypotheses.

Macroeconomic Models

Various macroeconomic models have been advanced to explain the past and the emerging economic scenarios in the world. Since it is imperative for any worthwhile economic model to be consistent with history, newer and newer models have emerged when the existing model(s) have failed to explain the past or the current scenario. Economic models have evolved over time to face the new challenges. However, none of the models discussed later in this part can be called useless even now. While each successive model hopefully marks an improvement over the earlier one, each model offers useful insights for managing the economy. Further, no model is perfect even today, and we do not expect a perfect model ever. This is because the world is highly dynamic and new issues keep on cropping up, inspiring new developments and new models. Also, economics is an inexact science. Thus, model building in economics happens to be an ongoing activity.

It is instructive to note that true models are unobtainable in practice and perhaps also in principle. Besides, for a model to be manageable, one must avoid trivial things, lest it becomes too complicated to understand and apply. Thus, a model is merely a simplification of the complicated reality. As such it cannot have all the details on its various components and, thus, may contain distortions. However, a good model must possess the salient features of all its constituents and be neat, lest it remains incomplete and leaves avoidable ambiguities. It is on the basis of this spirit that various models have been advanced in the literature, and will be discussed under this part of the text.

Before we proceed to macroeconomic models, it is important to note the salient characteristics of a complete model:

- **(a)** A model could be a general equilibrium model or a partial equilibrium one.
- **(b)** A model has variables that are classified into those that are endogenous and those that are exogenous.

(c) A model has equations, which are classified into behavioural, technological, institutional and identities.
(d) A model is complete (exactly determinable) when the number of endogenous variables exactly equals the number of equations.
(e) A model could be either an analytical or a policy model.
(f) A model could be subject to dichotomy (segmentation) or otherwise.

General Equilibrium and Partial Equilibrium

The general equilibrium model is the one which considers all segments/markets of the economy simultaneously and thus it incorporates the effects of a change in any one market on all other markets in the economy. In contrast, the partial equilibrium model focuses on the determination of equilibrium in one market at a time (or even the market for a single good, like automobiles market), ignoring the interdependence among the various markets of the economy. Macroeconomic models fall in the former group while microeconomic models belong to the latter category. As seen in the earlier chapters of this text, an economy consists of five markets, viz.

(a) Factors market
(b) Products market
(c) Money market
(d) Bonds/financial market
(e) Global (Foreign exchange) market

The various markets are interdependent and accordingly, a macroeconomic model must include all these markets. However, there is a Walras' law which states that if there are 'n' number of markets and 'n – 1' of them are in equilibrium, then the remaining one market is also in equilibrium. In view of this, one can develop a macroeconomic model ignoring any one of the above five markets. As usual in this field, the bonds market is left out in this text and all the remaining four markets are considered simultaneously to understand and analyse the macroeconomic relationships, and significance of stabilisation policies.

Endogenous and Exogenous Variables

Endogenous (also known as dependent/explained/effect) variables are the ones whose values are determined by the model while the exogenous (also called independent/explanatory/cause) variables· values are available outside the model. In other words, while the values of the exogenous variables are inputs, those of the endogenous variables are the outputs of the model. The exogenous variables are further classified into policy and non-policy variables. While the policy variables are the instruments whose values are decided by the policy makers, the non-policy variables are outside the control of even the policy makers. The former inrludes government expenditure, tax rate, money supply or interest rate, etc., and the latter, variables like weather and war. If the model is dynamic, it would have lagged endogenous variables as well among the independent variables, which together with the exogenous variables are called the predetermined variables.

Types of Equations

As the name implies, behavioural equations are inferred from the rational behaviour postulate of the concerned decision makers (like the consumption function); technological equations are based on the prevailing technology (like the production function); institutional equations are founded on the postulates of the institutions (like the tax equation: Laffer curve); and identities (like income identity) are mere definitions. It is a mathematical property that the system of equations is exactly solvable if the number of equations (E) equals the number of the unknowns (endogenous) variables (V); and it is over-determined if $E > V$; and under-determined if $E < V$.

Types of Models

An analytical model has behavioural variables (like consumption, saving, investment and import levels) as the endogenous ones and policy variables (like government expenditure and tax rate) as exogenous, while quite the opposite is true for a policy model. A segmentable model is one that can be divided into two or more independent models, while a non-segmentable model is not subject to such a compartmentalisation.

The various macroeconomic models discussed in this text are general equilibrium, analytical, and, of course, complete. Further, barring the classical and the Keynesian cross model, all are non-dichotomised models. The list of endogenous and exogenous variables varies from model to model. The simpler the model is, the fewer the endogenous variables, and, generally, the more the exogenous variables. However, some variables are exogenous by their very nature and thus they remain exogenous in all models. For example, government expenditure and the tax rates are the fiscal instruments, and the money supply the monetary instrument, and these are all exogenous variables.[2] Similarly, there are other truly exogenous variables, such as business expectations, weather conditions, political factors, events in the rest of the world (like OPEC formation, IT revolution, sub-prime lending crisis), etc. Changes in exogenous variables are called **(a)** demand shocks and **(b)** supply shocks.

Demand and Supply Shocks

The demand shocks includes changes in all the policy and other exogenous variables that affect the aggregate demand (AD) like **(a)** Government expenditure, **(b)** money supply, **(c)** wars **(d)** political crisis/elections **(e)** propensity to consume/save, and **(f)** business confidence and attitude to risk. The supply shocks consists of changes in all the policy and non-policy exogenous variables that command influence on the aggregate supply (AS) like **(a)** tax rate **(b)** labour force (that is, population/labour participation rate/working hours) **(b)** discovery of new resources/reservoirs **(c)** technology **(d)** prices of oil (energy) and raw materials/import prices **(e)** changing role of trade unions **(f)** regulations on effluents and pollutions affecting the production cost and **(g)** weather, natural calamities and industrial relation conditions.

[2] Recall that in Chapter 8, the money supply was argued to be an endogenous variable. However, since the effect of the non-policy variables (currency and excess reserve ratios) is small or insignificant, the money supply is treated as the monetary policy instrument in all the macroeconomic models.

Since the above variables could change in either direction the demand and supply shocks could be either favourable or adverse. A shock is favourable if it increases the AD or AS, and adverse if it decreases AD or AS.

Business Cycle Models

The various economic models can be grouped under the following categories chronologically: **(a)** Classical model; **(b)** Keynesian model; **(c)** New Classical model; and **(d)** New Keynesian model. These models differ in their assumptions and implications for business cycles. Suffice to point out here the two (old and new) classical models assume full flexibility of the wage rate (input prices) and product price and, thereby, market clearing; the two Keynesian models assume some degree of Wage-price rigidity and, thus, are market disequilibrium models. The details on each of them are presented in this part of the text. For each model, essential ingredients are first presented through the underlying assumptions/doctrines and equations; this is followed by a discussion regarding the interactions among the relations to give the equilibrium values for national income and general price. The factors responsible for economic fluctuations (business cycles) and the role the stabilisation policies (fiscal, monetary and trade and exchange rate) play in taming business cycles are then analysed before moving on to the next model.

Recall that a full-fledged macroeconomic model has four markets, viz. the factor, product, money and the foreign exchange markets. The factor market consists of the demand and supply of labour and capital, production function, and the so determined wage rate, capital rental, and quantities of labour, capital and the national output. If the factor prices were fully flexible (as in long-run), there would be no unemployment and the output would be at its potential full (or natural) employment level (vide Chapter 9, AS function). Under the condition of fixed price/wage rate (short-run), the factors market may not have equilibrium and thus may have some unemployment of labour and capital. The product market contains consumption, investment, export and import functions, which results into the Keynesian cross or the IS equation. The money market has money demand and supply functions and is contained in the LM equation. The foreign exchange market consists of export, import and capital flow functions and is compressed into the BP (balance of payments), also called as FE-foreign exchange market equilibrium condition. The interactions of these markets determine the levels of GDP, price, unemployment, interest rate, exchange rate, wage rate, etc.; for the regulated values of the policy variables like government expenditure, money supply, trade restrictions, etc.

KEYWORDS

Business cycles; Cycle of recession and prosperity; Recession-trough-Recovery-Peak; Length-Depth/Amplitude of business cycle; Depression; Automatic stabilisers; Fiscal-Monetary policy; Monetisation of fiscal deficit; Pure-Mixed fiscal-monetary policy; Unsustainable fiscal deficit; Governments inter-temporal budget constraint;

Paradox of debt; Debt to GDP ratio; Fundamental equation of public debt; Public debt/Fiscal sustainability constraint; Fiscal responsibility and budget management (FRBM) act; Barro-Ricardo equivalence theorem; Forward looking; Perfect foresight; Bequest motive; Actual/Total-Structural-Cyclical fiscal deficit; Trade and exchange rate policy; Fiscal drag; Sustainable current account balance; National inter-temporal budget constraint; Income policy; Dead weight loss; General-Partial equilibrium; Endogenous-Exogenous variables; Behavioural-technological-institutional-Definitional/Identity equations; Complete model; Analytical/Structural-Policy model; Segmentable model; Demand-Supply shocks.

References

1. Barro Robert J, 'Are Government Bonds Net Worth,' *Journal of Political Economy* 81, (November-December, 1974), Pp. 1095-1117.
2. Callen, Tim and Paul Cashin, 'Assessing External Sustainability in India', *IMF Working Paper* 99/181,1999.
3. Dornbusch R, S Fischer, R Startz, *Macroeconomics,* 8th ed. (McGraw-Hill, 2008).
4. Feldstein Martin, 'Budget Deficits and National Debt', *Reserve Bank of India Monthly Bulletins*, (February, 2004).
5. Gupta G S, 'Economic Fluctuations and Stabilisation Policies', *Vikalpa* 28, No. 1 (January-March, 2003), Pp. 1-10.
6. Poole William, 'Optimal Choice of Monetary Policy Instruments in a Simple Stochastic Model', *Quarterly Journal of Economics*, May 1970.
7. Rangarajan C and Srivastava D K, 'Dynamics of Debt Accumulation in India: Impact of Primary Deficit, Growth and Interest Rate', *Economic and Political Weekly* (November 15 2003), Pp. 4851-4858.
8. Reserve Bank of India, RBI Occasional Papers, (Monsoon and Winter 2000).
9. Ricardo David, *Principles of Political Economy and Taxation*, (J M Dent, Reprint).

Review Questions

1. Business cycles occur and recur but have no fixed periodicity. Explain.
2. Name a couple of variables that decline, and other couple of variables that rise when the economy goes into recession.
3. Name a few variables that have large fluctuations, and other few variables that have small fluctuations, during business cycles.
4. What are the tools of the fiscal and monetary policy? When a particular policy is expansionary? Consider the following data and infer the policy stance that you think each of the three countries adopted in various years.

(Percentages)

Year	Money supply@ growth rate			Govt. expenditure* (as % of GDP)			Fiscal/Cash deficit# (as % of GDP)		
	India	USA	China	India	USA	China	India	USA	China
1970	10.8	3.8	NA	9	20	NA	3.2	1.1	NA
1980	12.3	6.3	24.8	13	22	27	6.5	2.5	2.85
1990	18.9	3.8	3.4	17	22	17	8.1	4.1	0.81
1995	11.1	6.1	29.5	11	19	11	5.0	2.0	1.56
2000	15.2	8.8	12.3	13	18	13	5.2	–2.6	3.10
2004	16.7	5.7	14.9	11	15	14	3.7	3.5	2.10
2005	15.6	8.2	16.7	11	15	14	3.2	2.7	NA
2006	21.6	9.0	22.1	10	15	14	2.2	1.8	NA
2007	22.3	11.7	16.7	10	15	14	0.5	2.2	NA
2008	20.5	8.2	17.8	11	16	13	4.9	5.2	NA
2009	18.0	4.7	28.4	12	17	13	5.4	10.2	NA
2010	17.8	–2.8	18.9	11	17	13	3.6	10.0	NA
2011	16.1	6.6	17.3	12	16	13	3.7	9.0	NA
2012	11.0	4.8	14.4	12	16	14	NA	NA	NA

Note: @ Broad Money

\# Data are on fiscal deficit for 1970-2000 and cash deficit for other years

* For USA, it is consumption plus investment and for other countries it is consumption only.

Sources: International Financial Statistics, IMF, various issues

World Development Indicators, various issues.

5. Public debt, no matter how large it is, is free from the risk of involuntary default/insolvency. Do you agree? Why?
6. Public debt is sustainable so long as the rate of growth in the GDP does not fall short of the real rate of interest. Explain.
7. Distinguish between the items under each of the following pairs:
   (a) Endogenous and exogenous variables
   (b) Behavioural and technological equations
   (c) Policy and non-policy models
   (d) Segmentable and non-segmentable models

Chapter 11

Classical and Keynesian Fixed Price Models

Learning Objectives

After reading the chapter you should be able to:

1. Understand the classical model of the full employment equilibrium and see that it is valid in the long run only when the prices and wages are fully flexible and the decision makers have the full and timely information.
2. Comprehend the Keynesian fixed price Cross model, its very elementary nature and how it illustrates the unusual paradox of thrift and suggests that the fiscal policy could cause or even tame output fluctuations, while the monetary policy can only cause or tame inflations.
3. Learn about the IS-LM model of a closed economy—a very short run model—and how it demonstrates that economic fluctuations could spring from the actions of the private sector including business confidence, and the wrong fiscal and/or monetary policy.
4. Know that at least one of the two stabilisation policies is always available to counter business cycles in the very short run. The Great Depression of the 1930s could at least be partly rationalised through this model.

The classical model happens to be the first full-fledged macroeconomic model and its implications were well accepted as the reality until the outburst of the Great Depression of the early 1930s. The experience of the Great Depression (1929-33) had left serious doubts regarding the classical theory, and this inspired Lord John Maynard Keynes to give a new twist to macroeconomic theory and policy. In fact, most economists regard **Keynes as the founder of macroeconomics and the mixed economy, and the saviour of capitalism**.

Before we move to present individual macroeconomic models, it is appropriate to highlight what the various models attempt to do and how. In essence, each model consists of aggregate demand (AD) and aggregate supply (AS) which together determine real GDP (output), employment-unemployment and price-inflation rate. However, these demand and supply functions and their roles in the values of real GDP and other core variables differ from model to model. In general, in the long-run (classical models), at any point of time, output is fixed at its full employment level (thus vertical AS curve determines the output and employment), and price in then determined by falling AD curve. In contrast, in the very short run (Keynesian models of fixed price and horizontal AS curve), falling AD curve determines the output – employment, price is fixed and AS plays a passive role. In the intermediate period when both price and output are flexible, upward sloping AS curve and downward sloping AD curve together determine output-employment and price. In addition, it is instructive to note that the fixed price models, called as the Keynesian cross model, IS–LM model and open economy IS–LM model are relevant in the very short run only; the flexible wage-price model, called as the classical model is relevant in the long-run; and the flexible price and fixed money wage (Friedman) or flexible price and information barrier model is the relevant one under the short or medium term.

CLASSICAL MODEL

The term 'classical' was coined by Karl Marx, who used it to cover the theories of Adam Smith, David Ricardo, John Stuart Mill, J B Say, among others. Keynes extended the term to include the followers of Ricardo, namely, Alfred Marshall, F Y Edgeworth and Arthur C Pigou, who are regarded as "neo-classical" economists.

In his "General Theory", Keynes used the term classical economics to refer to all the writers who preceded him. Accordingly, the term is now synonymous with the pre-Keynesian theory of income determination. The classical theory was an accepted theory for macroeconomic phenomena for well over a century, lasting until the late 1920s. Prior to it, the Mercantilists' thoughts dominated macroeconomics, under which the accumulation of precious metals was considered as the over-riding goal of every economy. Favourable international trade was accorded high priority as this alone could ensure the greatest possible holdings of precious metals. The government was accorded the role of promoting foreign trade and developing colonies for exports. Subsequently, Physiocrats began emphasising agriculture as the only surplus generating sector. Franco Quesnay (1694–1774), the leader of the Physiocrats, created the first economic model, called the Tableau Economique, which explained the distribution of income among different sections of the community. Classical ideas embodied significant departures from those thoughts and are thus considered the first revolution in macroeconomic theory and policy. Under this theory, we have the first lessons from the Father of Economics, Adam Smith (1723–1790), who saw **(a)** labour and division of labour as the principal sources of all wealth, **(b)** self-interest of all individuals and competition among them to lead to increasing capital and welfare and **(c)** *laissez faire*, the way to best progress through capitalism. Unlike the mercantilists, Smith considered free trade as the most efficient system, with the government not interfering in the free market working. David Ricardo discovered the **principle of comparative advantage** in foreign trade. These ideas were followed primarily by those of Karl Marx (1818–1883), bracketed as a revolutionary, who foresaw that competition would lead to more and more capital intensive ('round about') production, driving out of production all those who fail to cope up with this strategy, leading to a larger and larger 'reserve army' (unemployed people), and ultimately to the collapse of capitalism. During the Great Depression of 1929-33, the world was on the verge of such a predicament. Robert Malthus advanced the law of diminishing marginal returns and thereby visualised the danger of the population growth to outstrip the food supply. Alfred Marshall (1842-1924) came forward with the concepts of demand-supply, elasticity, and partial equilibrium, among others. Leon Walras is known for the general equilibrium notion and his law, known as the Walras law.

Assumptions and Beliefs

The classical theory was founded on two basic postulates, which are

(a) Wage-price flexibility

(b) Perfect (accurate and timely) information about the market among all players—workers, firms, and consumers.

The first assumption ensured market clearing, which means all workers who wanted jobs at the prevailing wage rate got jobs, all firms found enough workers at the ruling wage rate and adequate customers to buy their products at the prevailing prices, and all households could buy as much of all goods as they wished at the going product prices. The second assumption guaranteed that no one was fooled by any unreasonable deals.

Classicalists believed in the: **(a)** Optimisation theory; **(b)** Laissez faire; and **(c)** Say's law. They thought that the people are rational and act optimally. They had faith in the free market mechanism; and wanted the government to simply look after the defence, law and order, and provision and maintenance of certain public works (like roads, bridges, canals and harbours), institutions (like schools, hospitals) and ambassadors abroad to promote free trade. They saw no role for the government to run business and/or to counter business cycles or promote growth. J B Say had promulgated the now famous Say's Law, "supply creates its own demand", to which all classicalists subscribed. On the basis of this, the demand was given no role in determining income/output, which was considered purely supply determined.

Description of the Model

The classical model is segmentable, i.e., it is made of parts, each of which is independent. First, the assumption of the flexible wage would ensure that the wage rate was so determined as to leave no worker (involuntary) unemployed and no firm without the labour that it wanted. Accordingly, **full employment** equilibrium was the rule and equilibrium below full employment was regarded as abnormal. At any point of time, capital and technology are fixed, and thus the full employment of workers would give a **fixed level of output**. Second, as per the Say's Law, the demand is restricted to the supply of output. The distribution of national output into its various demand components was governed merely by the rate of interest. Under the classical model, consumption/saving and investment depended merely on the interest rate. The classicalists believed that people save in order to earn interest and, therefore, they postulated saving to be a positive function of the rate of interest (and consumption as a negative function of the interest rate). Investment was guided by its marginal productivity and, thus, depended negatively on the interest rate (vide Chapter 6). Variation in the interest rate was assigned the role of bringing equilibrium between saving and investment. Accordingly, the interest rate was determined by the demand for loanable funds (investment) and the supply of that fund (saving). In effect, the interest rate played the crucial role of ensuring no deficiency of aggregate demand. Government expenditure was exogenously determined on policy considerations. Variations in the interest rate would thus ensure the equilibrium (no pressure to change) in the product market.

Changes in government spending would cause changes in the opposite direction and in equal amounts in the other components of the aggregate spending. For example, if the government were to enforce an expansionary fiscal policy, it would increase its expenditure and finance the same through borrowing. Note that if the additional increased government expenditure was financed through increased taxes, it would not be an expansionary fiscal policy; and if it were financed through monetisation (increased money supply), it would not be a pure fiscal policy but a mix of the expansionary fiscal and expansionary monetary policy. For the government to be able to expand its expenditure through borrowing, it must sell its bonds to the public. This would require the bond price to fall (and the interest rate to go up) so as to encourage the private sector to subscribe to them. The increase in interest rate, in turn, would cause the national savings to go up, and private consumption as well as investment to go down. The decrease in private consumption and investment, called the **crowding out**, would exactly equal the increase in government expenditure, and thereby, the crowding out would be (exactly) full. If the consumption/saving were not sensitive to the interest rate, investment alone would change in the opposite direction and in equal amount to change in government expenditure. Quite the opposite would happen if the pure, restrictive fiscal policy was applied. Thus, the sum total of the private consumption, investment and government expenditure would always equal to the level of output governed by the full employment of all resources. Accordingly, the fiscal policy's role was seen merely in the distribution of total output among its demand components, and thereby the said policy was considered totally ineffective with respect to output and even price (as we would see below).

In the classical system, price was determined using Irving Fisher's **quantity theory of money** equation (vide Chapter 8), which also represents their AD function:

$$MV = PT$$

or

$$MV = PY$$

Recall that in this equation, M refers to the quantity of money in circulation; V the income velocity of circulation of money (i.e., the number of times a unit of money changes hands during the given period or the turnover of money); P the general price level; and T or Y the real income or output. The left hand side of the above equation indicates the value of what is spent and its right hand side, the value of what is purchased; the two are equal and thus the equation was even thought of a truism. However, it has serious implications. The velocity of money (V) depends on the community's income and payment habits, which change slowly, and is thus like a constant. The level of output, as mentioned above, is governed by the real resources, and is a constant at the full employment level of output. Thus, both V and Y are independent of the money supply. Further, classicalists argued that causation runs from money to price. Given these, the **price moves directly and proportionately with the quantity of money *M***. Thus, the higher the money supply, the higher the price, and vice versa. Accordingly, the quantity theory of money equation becomes the **price equation**. Given the constant values of V and Y, the quantity of money determines the price level through the above (price) equation. Obviously, government expenditure has no influence on the price level and, thus, the fiscal policy is neutral to the price, as stated above. In the framework of the *AD* and *AS* curves, the income and price determination could be shown as in Fig. 11.1.

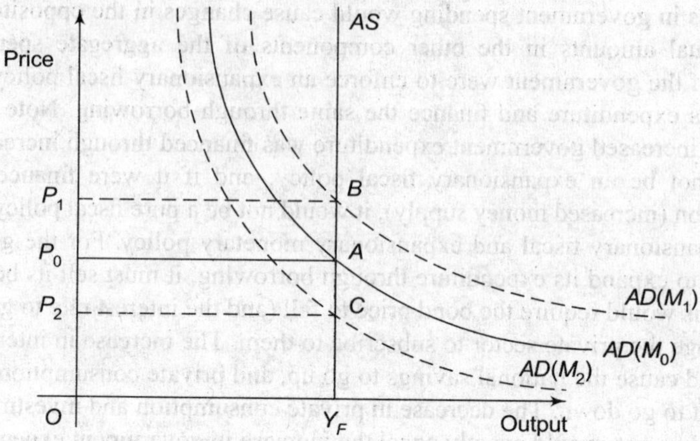

Fig 11.1 AD-AS Curves in the Classical Model

The *AD* curve is a rectangular hyperbola. For, given the quantity of money and the velocity of money, the product of *Y* and *P* is a constant = *MV*. Further, the larger the supply of money, the higher the *AD* curve. Thus, if $M = M_0$, the *AD* curve would be $AD\ (M_0)$; if $M = M_1$, *AD* will be $AD\ (M_1)$, and so on ($M_1 > M_0 > M_2$). The *AS* curve is vertical at the full employment level of output (Y_F). Thus, if $M = M_0$, *AD* will meet *AS* at point *A*, and the equilibrium price would equal P_0. The equilibrium price will be P_1 if $M = M_1$, and P_2 if $M = M_2$, and so on.

The above is a full description of the classical model. The model is dichotomised as:

(a) Production function and the factor market independently determine the (full employment) level of output, and the real wage rate and real capital rental

(b) Product market determines the rate of interest, private consumption/saving and investment, given the government expenditure (fixed by the government) and the total expenditure (full employment output)

(c) Money market determines the price level, given the quantity of money, which is set by the monetary authority (Reserve Bank of India) and the level of output (Y_F).

Economic Fluctuations and Stabilisation Policies

In the classical model, all resources are always fully employed and so there is no scope for any involuntary unemployment. The fluctuations in output (business cycles) can come only through changes in the supply of factors of production and technology, called the real factors or the supply shocks. An adverse supply shock (vide Chapter 10) would reduce the output through a decline in factor supply and/or factor productivities (but not through an increase in unemployment) while a favourable supply shock would raise the output through an increase in factor supply and/or factor productivities (but not through a decrease in unemployment). Accordingly, to the classicalists, business cycles were purely a real phenomenon. However, this is true under the assumption that the adjustments are instantaneous. The sluggishness in adjustments, if any, could cause temporary cycles. How?

Some economists believe that the quantity theory of money ($MV = PY$) offered the first theory of business cycles. To see this we have to assume that decision makers do not adjust instantaneously to policy changes. Recall that under the quantity theory, causation runs from money to price. Thus, when the money supply is increased under an expansionary monetary policy, the price starts rising and the real interest rate falling, but only slowly until the full adjustment is reached when the price has increased proportionately and there is no change in the real interest rate. Though the classicalists believed in flexible price-wage and interest rates, they thought that the price and interest rate were relatively more flexible than the wage rate. In view of this contention, when the money supply increases, initially the increase in the money wage rate is less than the proportionate increase in the money supply, and so the profits go up for the time being. This induces firms to borrow more and invest more; and, if so, the aggregate demand goes up. If resources could be stretched a bit (or since money wage has not yet adjusted fully, the real wage falls and the labour supply increases), production goes up. Thus:

An increase in money supply could cause an upward movement in output, hence the upswing in business cycle. Quite the opposite would happen when the money supply is decreased. As the money supply falls, price falls, interest rate goes up, money wage rate falls less than proportionately, profits fall, investment falls and output falls, and recession occurs.

However, such a cycle would be purely temporary. As adjustments proceed, firms would find that the wage rate, interest rate and other production costs have changed in proportion to the price (and money supply) change (for there is no unemployment), and there are no incentives/disincentives to invest and produce more/less. Thus, until the adjustments are complete, the monetary policy can cause cycles but as soon as the adjustments are complete the cycle would disappear. To conclude:

The only permanent cause of business cycles under the classical model of wage-price flexibility and perfect information lies merely in the supply shocks, or the real factors.

Role of Fiscal/Monetary Policy in Stabilising the Economy What is the role of the fiscal and monetary policies in stabilising the economy? The fiscal policy has no role at all in this regard. For, the output and employment, which cause cycles, are, as shown above, governed entirely by the factor market and the production function. Further, the said policy has no influence whatsoever even on the price level, which is given exclusively by the quantity theory of money. Its only effect is felt on the interest rate and the distribution of total output among private consumption, investment and government expenditure. The role of the monetary policy is a limited one. Under the full adjustments, the said policy has no influence on the level of output, employment and the other real magnitudes (real consumption, real investment and real interest rate), but it exerts influence on the price and nominal magnitudes (nominal consumption, nominal investment and so on). As noticed earlier, the money supply and the general price are directly and proportionately related. Thus, if the RBI increases M, P goes up proportionately and so do the other nominal magnitudes, and vice versa. It is because of this role of the monetary policy that the money is said to be neutral (just a veil) under the classical system. Thus, like the fiscal policy, monetary policy has no stabilisation role. Accordingly, the classicalists accorded the' non-interventionist' (laissez faire) role to the government.

Applications: The classical model could be applicable even today if its assumptions of wage price flexibility and perfect information were true. Its implied direct and proportionate relationship between money supply and price level was fairly valid during the hyperinflations in Germany and Hungary. Germany faced the hyperinflation between August 1922 and November 1923, when the money supply increased by 314 per cent/month and the price level by 322 per cent/month. Hungary experienced hyperinflation during August 1945 to July 1946. The rate of inflation in Hungary during that period averaged 12,200 per cent per month, which was caused basically by a 19,800 per cent per month growth in money supply (vide Chapter 15).

Case Study: Great Depression

The best-known macroeconomic event that has ever happened in the world was the Great Depression during 1929-33. During the four-year period, the world production fell by about 30 per cent, the world trade in volume by about 25 per cent and the world trade in value fell by over 50 per cent. The United States data on some relevant macroeconomic variables during the Great Depression and thereafter for a few years are given below:

Table 11.1 Great Depression and After: USA

Year	*GNP at 1958 prices*	*Unemployment rate*	*GNP deflator*	*Nominal interest rate*	*Government expenditure at 1958 prices*	*Narrow money supply (Nominal)*	*Stock market index (S and P)*
	($ billion)	*(%)*	*(1958 = 100)*	*(%)*	*($ billion)*	*($ billion)*	*(Sept. 1929 = 100)*
1929	204	3.2	50.6	5.9	22.0	26.6	83.1
1930	184	8.9	49.3	3.6	24.3	25.8	67.2
1931	170	16.3	44.8	2.6	25.4	24.1	43.6
1932	144	24.1	40.2	2.7	24.2	21.1	22.1
1933	142	25.2	39.3	1.7	23.3	19.9	28.6
1934	154	22.0	42.2	1.0	26,6	21.9	31.4
1935	170	20.3	42.6	0.8	27.0	25.9	33.9
1936	193	17.0	42.7	0.8	31.8	29.6	49.4
1937	203	14.3	44.5	0.9	30.8	30.9	49.2
1938	193	19.1	43.9	0.8	33.9	30.5	36.7
1939	209	17.2	43.2	0.6	35.2	34.2	38.5
1940	227	14.6	43.9	0.6	36.4	39.7	35.8

Source: Mankiw, N G, *Macroeconomics*, (Worth Publications 2000), pp 296-97.

Using the above data, try and answer the following questions:

(a) Examine the validity of the Classical model in USA during 1929 through 1940.

(b) Which of the above years were the recession years in the United States? How?

(c) Examine the relationship between the rates of economic growth and unemployment. Comment.

(d) Study the relationship between the rates of unemployment and inflation. Comment.

(e) Are money supply and interest rate related? How?

(f) Check the relationship between the rate of unemployment and government expenditure. Do you think the two have moved in the expected way? How?

(g) How the inflation rate and money supply are related? Does the relationship appear reasonable? Justify your answer.

(h) Study the relationship between the stock market index and real GNP and comment.

(i) Comment on the United States use of stabilisation policies during the period 1929-40.

KEYNESIAN CROSS MODEL

The Great Depression of 1929 through 1933 was world-wide. The most severely hit was the USA, where the stock market crash began on October 24, 1929 and continued for four years. It led to enormous unemployment all over the world. In the United States, the unemployment rate shot up from a low of about 3 per cent in 1928 to a high of about 25 per cent in 1933, and the real GDP fell by about 30 per cent during the period. Although the recession was not so deep in most other countries, it was well spread throughout the world. For example, during 1929-32, the real GDP fell by 5.8, 15.7, 11.0, 22.5, 8.2, 8.0, 18.2 and 11.5 per cent in the United Kingdom, Germany, France, Austria, Netherlands, Spain, Czechoslovakia and Hungary, respectively. Thus, Karl Marx's prediction of the collapse of the capitalism was well in sight. Further, it provided sufficient proof for the inappropriateness of the classical theory of output, employment and price, which is characterised by the full employment equilibrium. Since no theory is good unless it explains the historical and current facts, Keynes was prompted to come out with an alternative theory, which later became the Keynesian theory of income determination, which he outlined in his famous book "General Theory of Employment, Interest and Money", published on February 4, 1936. This marked the second revolution in macroeconomics. Keynes is now regarded as the **father of macroeconomics**. The Keynesian model, as understood currently, has two versions, which are **(a)** Fixed price model and **(b)** Flexible price model.

In order to clearly demonstrate the role of the fiscal policy in stabilising an otherwise fluctuating economy, the fixed price model is further presented in three versions, which are the: **(i)** Keynesian cross model, **(ii)** IS-LM model and **(iii)** Open economy (Mundell-Fleming) model.

The present section deals with the first of these models. It is pertinent to note at the outset that:

> The Keynesian model in all its versions assumes some degree of wage-price rigidity, which reverses the classicalist Say's Law philosophy to the Keynesian's

belief that demand creates its own supply, which in turn, demonstrates the possibility of Unemployment or Non-market clearing equilibrium, and suggests an active role for the **(a)** Fiscal policy, **(b)** Monetary policy and **(c)** Exchange rate and trade policy in stabilising the otherwise fluctuating economy.

The wage-price rigidity was taken merely as a fact of life, which was explained much later by the new Keynesians only. Further, the Keynesian fixed price model postulates that the volume of output is determined by the aggregate expenditure/demand and firms were expected to supply any quantity of their products at the fixed price to meet the consumers, governments and investors demand. If the spending on the current output falls short of the current income (i.e., if sale proceeds from current production fall short of the costs of producing it), income must fall to the level of expenditure, via a reduction in output and employment (vide the fixed money wage rate). Thus, the real income or output is purely demand determined. Since the Keynesian model marks a significant departure from the classical model, it could be labeled as a revolution in macroeconomics. As would be seen below, Keynes provided a **new consumption theory** and a **new money demand function** besides **new labour demand-supply functions** (vide Chapter 9).

Description of the Model

The Keynesian cross model is very simple and the simplest form of this model could be expressed in just two equations:[1]

Consumption function: $C = C_0 + b\,(Y - T_0)$ **(11.1)**

Income identity: $Y = C + I_0 + G_0$ **(11.2)**

where C = consumption expenditure,
Y = real income,
T = taxes net of transfer payments,
I = investment expenditure and
G = government expenditure

The subscript 0 (zero) indicates that the concerned variable is autonomous (exogenous), for example, C_0 = autonomous consumption. The b is a parameter. Unlike the classicalists, Keynes believed that investment expenditure was not quite sensitive to variations in the rate of interest. The cross model equates this insensitivity to zero and, thus, treats all investments as autonomous. Since here, as well as in all versions of the fixed price model, the price is constant, it is immaterial as to whether the various variables are in nominal or in real terms. Note that the Keynesian consumption function **(11.1)** hypothesizes that (current) consumption (and thus, saving) has two parts, viz. autonomous and induced, the latter varies directly with (current) income, as explained in Chapter 5. Keynes, thus, ignored the interest rate as a determinant of consumption, which happened to be the only factor determining private consumption/saving in the classical model. Further, the said equation indicates that if income goes up by one unit, *ceteris paribus*, consumption would go up by b.

[1]In all these models, just the personal direct taxes (net of direct personal transfer payments) are considered. All other taxes, like the corporate tax and indirect taxes, are ignored. Also, the economy is assumed to be a closed one and so exports and imports are ignored.

Thus, note that the parameter b denotes the Keynes' famous marginal propensity to consume. Equation **(11.2)** is the equilibrium condition, which equates income to planned expenditure, where the latter equals the sum of the planned private consumption; planned investment and planned government expenditure.

The solution of the above two-equation model for income would give:

$$Y = \frac{1}{1-b}(C_0 - bT_0 + I_0 + G_0) \qquad \textbf{(11.3)}$$

Since the marginal propensity to consume is less than unity (vide Chapter 5), $b < 1$, and accordingly $\frac{1}{1-b} > 1$. The last term is referred to as the **autonomous expenditure (or Keynesian or fiscal) multiplier** k. As will be apparent from equation **(11.3)**, if government expenditure goes up by one rupee, all other variables held constant, the income would increase by rupees $\frac{1}{1-b}$, which equals rupees five, if $b = 0.8$. Also, if investment or autonomous part of private consumption expenditure increases by rupee one, *ceteris paribus*, real income goes up by ₹5. The higher the b (marginal propensity to consume), the larger is the multiplier (k), and vice versa. In this model, investment always drags saving along with it at an equal pace. The equilibrium requires income to be equal to all expenditures ($Y = C + I_0 + G_0$), which means national saving ($= Y - C - G_0$) equals national investment (I_0). When investment increases, savings fall short of investment and the restoration of equality requires saving to go up. Further, corresponding to the consumption function, the saving function is given by:

National saving = private saving + government saving.

This means,

$$S = (Y - T_0 - C) + (T_0 - G_0) = Y - C_0 - b\,(Y - T_0) - G_0$$

or,

$$S = -(C_0 + G_0) + b\,T_0 + (1 - b)Y$$

This suggests that, given the exogenous variables and the marginal propensity to consume, saving can increase only if income goes up. Further, since increase in saving must equal increase in investment, income must increase by a multiplier equal to $\frac{1}{1-b}$. The question is how this much increase in income comes through. This is explained a little later, after the geometric explanation of the model, through the example of an increase in autonomous expenditure, which amounts to the same as increase in investment, as investment in this model is all-autonomous. In the above equation, marginal propensity to save (MPS) equals $(1 - b)$ and thus MPC + MPS $= b + (1 - b) = 1$.

An important application of the above model is found in the **balanced budget multiplier**. The said multiplier states that if the government expenditure goes up by rupee one, and at the same time tax revenue goes up by rupee one (leaving the budget balance unchanged), equation **(11.3)** would indicate that the income would also go up exactly by rupee one. This is so for:

$$\frac{\partial Y}{\partial G_0} = \frac{1}{1-b} \quad \text{and} \quad \frac{\partial Y}{\partial T_0} = -\frac{b}{1-b}$$

and thus

$$\frac{\partial Y}{\partial T_0} + \frac{\partial Y}{\partial G_0} = \frac{1}{1-b} - \frac{b}{1-b} = 1$$

This result is interesting because it indicates that the government can increase national income, say, by ₹10 billion, simply by increasing its expenditure by ₹10 billion and financing the same through an equivalent increase in tax revenue. How this is possible? In this rather simple model, this so happens because income is solely demand (expenditure) determined, and while the government spends all its revenues (MPC for government = 1), consumers spend only 80 per cent (MPC = 0.8) of the increase in their income (the rest they save). As G_0 increases by ₹10 billion, *ceteris paribus*, income is up by ₹50 (10 k = 10 × 1/(1 – 0.8) billion through the just explained multiplier process; and as T_0 increases by ₹10 billion, income is down by ₹40 billion (10 × 0.8/(1 – 0.8), giving a net increase of ₹10 billion in national income. Incidentally, note an important point here. The pure government expenditure (i.e. not accompanied by increase in taxes) multiplier is 1/(1 – b) (which is greater than unity) while the balanced budget (government expenditure financed through increased taxes) multiplier is unity. This means that government expenditure financed through public debt is more expansionary than the one financed through taxation. This so happens because while taxes reduce disposable income of the private sector, buying government bonds (or lending to government) by them does not. The said observation contradicts the Barro-Ricardo Equivalence theorem, which in any way, as argued in Chapter 10, is not really valid due to its unrealistic assumptions. The cross model could be described geometrically as in Fig. 11.2.

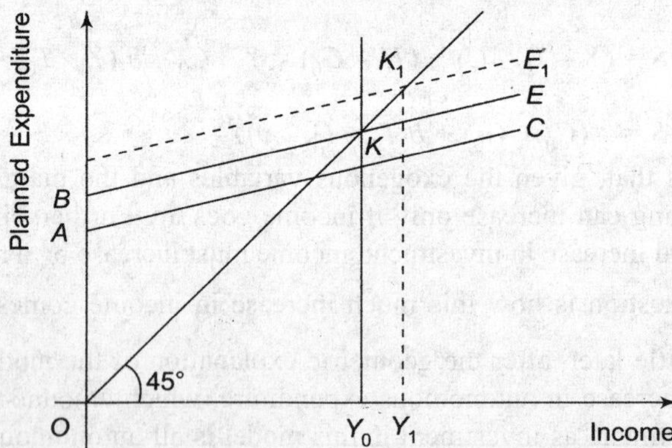

Fig. 11.2 Keynesian Cross Model

In the figure, the line C denotes the consumption function, E the total planned (or desired) expenditure function, and the 45° line transforms Y into E, and vice versa. The distance OA = autonomous consumption its (C_0) and OB = autonomous total expenditure. The slopes of both the C and E lines = b < 1. The equilibrium is given by point K, where income = expenditure (or saving = investment) or where the E line crosses the 45° line, hence, the name the Keynesian cross model. If any of the autonomous expenditure increases, the E line would shift up to, say, the E_1 line, the cross would move to point K_1, and the income would increase to Y_1 and so on. The increase in income would be a multiplier of the increase in the autonomous expenditure. The said multiplier is the most important element of the Keynesian magic. It ignores, as we shall see later, the crowding out effect and the financing problems of government expenditure.

How does the multiplier work? When the autonomous expenditure (investment and/or government expenditure) increases by, say, ₹10 billion, *ceteris paribus*, the income goes up by ₹10 billion, as the total expenditure, which determines the income, has increased by that amount. Now, since income is up by ₹10 billion, private consumption goes up by ₹8 billion (assuming $b = 0.8$), which causes a ₹8 billion increase in total expenditure and, hence, in the income by the same amount. In the third round, ₹8 billion increase in income would lead to a ₹6.4 billion (8×0.8) increase in private consumption and, therefore, in income as well by the same amount. The process would continue until the stimulus exhausts. The total increase in income would thus be given by rupees:

$$= 10 + 8 + 6.4 + 5.12 + \dots \text{ billion}$$
$$= 10 + 10(0.8) + 10\,(0.8)^2 + 10(0.8)^3 + \dots \text{ billion}$$
$$= 10/(1 - 0.8) \text{ billion}$$
$$= 50 \text{ billion}$$

Further, savings would increase by ₹10 (= 2 + 1.6 + 1.28 + ...) billion, just equal to the increase in autonomous expenditure, so that the new equilibrium is established exactly. The process is taken to work instantaneously in the Keynesian model, and hence the said multiplier is called a "**static multiplier**". This is the Keynesian multiplier theory. In reality, the adjustments happen through time lags, which are ignored here. Three relevant time lags are

(a) Gestation period, is the time lapse between (autonomous) spending and production

(b) Output-income gap, is the time lapse between receipts of revenues from output to the payments to the factors of production

(c) Robertson lag, is the time lost between change in income and consequent change in consumption expenditure

How the above process affects the production? Initially, when the autonomous expenditure increases, the demand exceeds the production, and the additional demand is met through reduction in inventories of finished goods. Consequently, the inventory level falls below the desired level. Subsequently, production will be increased to replenish **inventories**. Quite the opposite holds when the demand is short of production. If the government expenditure or investment falls, *ceteris paribus*, the total expenditure becomes less than the value of the output, the firms are thus not able to sell all of their production, and accordingly firms add the difference to their stock of inventories. When the inventory level is above its desired level, firms cut down their production. The production falls and the process continues until the balance between the total demand and the output is re-established. In a static model, this process is instantaneous, but it may take some time if the model is dynamic.

In this model, output is governed solely by expenditure as firms supply all that customers' demand at the fixed price (set either by firms or through a contract between firms and customers). Therefore, there is no guarantee that the expenditure determined income (Y_e) equals the full employment level of output (Y_F). If:

$$Y_e < Y_F, \text{ there is unemployment}$$

$$Y_e = Y_F, \text{ there is full employment}$$

And, $Y_e > Y_F$ is not possible due to constraints on the production, caused by the available factor supplies and technology. Thus, the Keynesian model is consistent with both under-full and full employment equilibrium, and also with the near full employment until around 1928 and massive unemployment during 1929–33. This is how Keynes explained the Great Depression, which according to him was due to the lack of **effective demand**. The stock market boom of the 1920s busted in 1929 and so wealth was eroded. As a result, banks could not recover their loaned amounts and many of them failed. There was no insurance on bank deposits and so the public could not get their deposits back. In consequence, private consumption suffered and investors lost confidence. Governments then were not aware of the fiscal policy miracle (vide the Keynesian multiplier theory) and were instead practicing balanced budgets. The effectiveness of the monetary policy in countering the recession was also not quite known. Further, money supply could not even be expanded as it was constrained by the availability of gold under the then prevailing gold standard. Accordingly, the shortage of demand could not be remedied. The result was the Great Depression.

Some important concepts are relevant at this point. When $Y_e < Y_F$, there is an income (GDP) gap due to the shortage of effective demand, called the **deflationary (recessionary) gap**. Recall the autonomous expenditure multiplier, the recessionary gap can be met through an increase in the autonomous expenditure by the amount equal to $(Y_F - Y)/k$. If $Y > Y_F$, there is excess demand, called the **inflationary gap**, which can be corrected by decreasing the autonomous expenditure by $(Y - Y_F)/k$. Thus, as stated above, the Keynes model suggests that the Great Depression could have been avoided through an appropriate increase in the government expenditure, i.e., pure fiscal expansion.

An important paradox, called the **paradox of thrift**, also deserves our attention here. This states that as the people become more thrifty,[2] the national savings decrease rather than increase. This is true in the Keynesian cross model, basically because saving and investment, though equal, are independent of each other. Thus, as people get thriftier, they save more and spend less; and as the total spending falls (note that investment and government expenditure remain same as before, and increased saving go into hoarding), firms are not able to sell all their outputs and so their inventory holdings increase. Consequently, firms cut on their production and so the output or real income falls. Fall in income leads to low savings, that is, savings come back to their original level so that savings still remains equal to investment. In this case, increased thriftiness leads to no change in saving and not to a fall in saving as the paradox of thrift suggests. However, if investment depended (positively) on income as per the profit/accelerator theory (vide Chapter 6), the said paradox would hold. To show this, let us resort to algebra. Let the Keynesian model be as follows:

$$C = 150 + 0.8\,(Y - T_0)$$

$$I = 50 + 0.1\,Y$$

[2]Increase in thrift means decrease in either autonomous consumption or in the marginal propensity to consume.

$$Y = C + I + G_0$$
$$G_0 = 100,\ T_0 = 80$$

Solution of the above model for Y would give

$$0.1\ Y = [150 - 0.8\ T_0 + 50 + G_0]$$

On substitution of the values for G_0 and T_0, we get, $Y = 2360$

Further substitution of the value of Y in I and C functions would give

$$I = 286 \text{ and } C = 1974$$

Private saving is defined as $S = Y - C - T$, which, on substitution, would give

$$S = 306$$

Note that $S + T = I + G = 386$

Next, suppose people become thriftier, *ceteris paribus*. This means either autonomous consumption declines or/and the marginal propensity to consume (MPC) falls. Let MPC fall from 0.8 to 0.7, *ceteris paribus*. Solution of the model, as above, would give

$$Y = 1,220;\ I = 172;\ C = 948;\ S = 192 \text{ and } S + T = I + G = 272$$

A comparison of the two sets of results would indicate that the saving has fallen from 306 to 192 due to just one change, viz, MPC falling from 0.8 to 0.7, hence the paradox of thrift. Incidentally, note that there is a catch here, which is that the increased saving does not result in more investment. Where does the saving go then? There is no automatic relationship between saving and investment. Though saving is a source for investment, saving could well go into hoarding. Households could leave their saving as cash in lockers. Alternatively, they could put it in banks or/and in stocks and bonds of firms. If the banks kept these saving in their vaults instead of lending to businesses, the saving still remains hoarded and not invested. Also, if banks lent those savings to business or even the government, but the business and government kept such loan proceeds and/or the proceeds from bonds and stocks as idle funds instead of using them to acquire capital items (like structures, equipment or inventory), the saving is still hoarded and not invested. Such a situation often arises when the economy is facing a recession. Business is pessimistic and so it shies away from investment. If this happens, saving remains a private virtue but does not become a social virtue. Please note that under the classical model of full employment, saving and investment are not independent (they are linked through interest rate), and hence the paradox of thrift does not hold in it.

The above two equations model (vide equations **11.1** and **11.2**) could be expanded through endogenising the tax revenue as follows:[3]

Consumption function: $C = C_0 + b(Y - T)$ **(11.1)**

Tax function: $T = T_0 + tY$ **(11.4)**

Income identity: $Y = C + I_0 + G_0$ **(11.2)**

Substitution of the first two equations into the last equation, and the solution of the resultant equation for income would give:

$$Y = \frac{1}{1 - b(1 - t)}[C_0 - bT_0 + I_0 + G_0] \quad \textbf{(11.5)}$$

which reduces the value of the Keynesian multiplier (k) to:

[3]Equations' numbers are retained from the earlier ones if they are repeated in the chapter.

$$k = \frac{1}{1 - b(1-t)}$$

This is less than the value of the said multiplier in the earlier two equations model, for:

$$t, b < 0$$

Thus, if $b = 0.8$ (as before) and $t = 0.1$, the new multiplier is

$$k = 3.57$$

Since taxes are leakages from expenditure (vide Chapter 2), the multiplier varies inversely with the tax rate.[4] The inverse of the multiplier is accordingly called the **marginal leakage rate**. In its implications for unemployment, this model is similar to the above two-equation model. We may now conclude that in the above Keynesian models.

- **(a)** Price is determined exogenously
- **(b)** Output is determined in the product market by the aggregate expenditure
- **(c)** Employment-unemployment, not shown here, are determined in the factor market (with production function) by the output level determined in the product market (vide Chapter 9)
- **(d)** Interest rate, not shown here, is determined in the money market by the demand for and supply of money. Interest rate is thus purely a monetary phenomenon in the model

The model is thus segmentable. In terms of the AD-AS curves, the model would look like in Fig. 11.3.

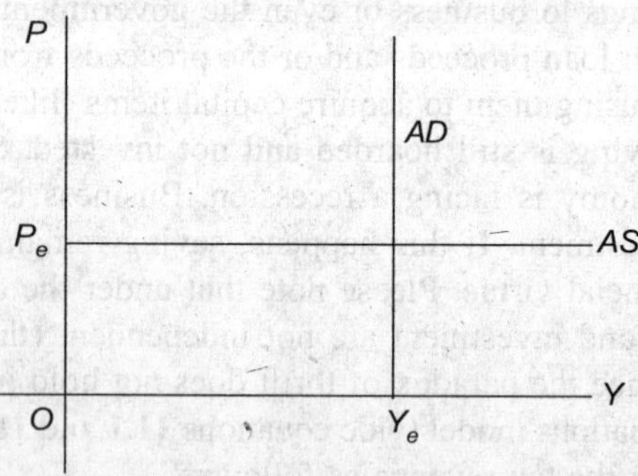

Fig 11.3 AD-AS curves in the Keynesian Cross Model

In the above graph, Y_e is given by the total expenditure and P_e by the fixed price nature of the model. Y_e may or may not equal Y_F, the full employment output. Thus, the Keynesian model is consistent with both full employment as well as the under full employment equilibrium. Further, unemployment, if any, is involuntary in

[4] If investment was hypothesised as a function (positive) of income, the marginal propensity to invest would affect the Keynesian multiplier positively, as investment, like consumption, is an injection to the aggregate demand.

character as it arises because the firms hire less workers than the supply of workers at the ruling wage rate; and they hire less not because the real wage rate is above the marginal productivity of workers, but because they are unable to sell more of their product due to the lack of effective demand. While workers, operate on their supply curve, firms are off their labour demand (MPP of labour) curve (vide Chapter 9—fixed money wages) and, hence, the involuntary unemployment.

It needs to be emphasised that unlike the classicalists, Keynes thought that the motive behind saving was not interest income and that savings need not flow automatically into investment (it could be hoarded). The Keynes' theory assigns the role of bringing saving = investment to income and not to the interest rate, as in the classics. This can be seen explicitly if we derive the saving function under this model. Private saving (S) is given by

$S = Y - T - C$, substitution for C gives,
$= Y - T - C_0 - b\,(Y - T)$, substitution for T yields,
$= Y - T_0 - t\,Y - C_0 - b\,(Y - T_0 - t\,Y)$, rearranging gives,
$= -C_0 - (1 - b)\,T_0 + (1 - b)\,(1 - t)\,Y$

Accordingly, marginal propensity to save (MPS) = $(1 - b)\,(1 - t)$, which is positive as both b and t are positive fractions. This means as income goes up, private saving increases and vice versa. Marginal propensity to consume (MPC) in the model represented by equations **(11.1)**, **(11.2)** and **(11.4)**, is given by

$$C = C_0 + b\,(Y - T) = C_0 + b\,(Y - T_0 - t\,Y)$$
$$= C_0 - bT_0 + b\,(1 - t)Y$$

Thus, MPC = $b\,(1 - t)$

In addition there is marginal tax rate (MTR) which equals = t. It can easily be proved that the sum of the three marginal terms equals one:

$$MPC + MPS + MTR = b\,(1 - t) + (1 - b)\,(1 - t) + t = 1$$

Let us next look at government saving, which is same as budget or fiscal surplus (FS). It is given by (recall here T is net of transfer payments)

$$FS = T - G = T_0 + tY - G$$

The above equation suggests that fiscal surplus varies positively with income, if G, T_0 and t stay constant. Next let us look at how fiscal surplus varies as **(a)** government expenditure alone change **(b)** tax rate alone change, and **(c)** both government expenditure as well as tax rate change. In the first case, the partial derivative of FS with respect to G gives,

$$\frac{d(FS)}{dG} = 0 + t\frac{dY}{dG} - 1 = t\,(k) - 1$$ (Recall k = autonomous expenditure multiplier)

Or, $$\frac{d(FS)}{dG} = \left[\frac{t}{1 - b(1 - t)} - 1\right]$$, on substitution for k

$$= -\left[\frac{(1 - b)(1 - t)}{1 - b(1 - t)}\right] < 0$$, since both b and t are positive fractions

Thus, as government expenditure goes up, *ceteris paribus*, fiscal surplus falls, and vice versa. Similarly, it is easy to see that the relationship between fiscal surplus and autonomous tax (T_0) would be given by (take partial derivative of FS with respect to T_0)

$$\frac{d(FS)}{dT_0} = 1 + t\frac{dY}{dT_0} = 1 + t\left[\frac{b}{1-b(1-t)}\right]$$

$$= \left[\frac{1-b}{1-b(1-t)}\right] > 0, \text{ since both } b \text{ and } t \text{ are positive fractions}$$

It shows that, as expected, increase in autonomous tax, *ceteris paribus*, leads to increase in fiscal surplus. Further, the two results can be combined to determine the effect of an autonomous tax financed government expenditure on fiscal surplus. This is given by the sum of two above effects:

$$-\left[\frac{(1-b)(1-t)}{1-b(1-t)}\right] + \left[\frac{1-b}{1-b(1-t)}\right] = \frac{t(1-b)}{1-b(1-t)} > 0, \text{ for both } t \text{ and } b \text{ are positive fractions}$$

The said policy thus raises fiscal surplus. In other words, government expenditure financed through autonomous tax is more than self-financing! This comes through the fact that the fiscal expenditure multiplier is larger than the fiscal (autonomous) tax multiplier, which happens because, as seen hitherto, balanced budget multiplier is positive! A consequence of this is that fiscal policy is more effective with respect to output if it is applied through enhanced government expenditure than through a cut in tax, both being of equal size in terms of their impact on fiscal deficit. We leave it to the readers to check on the effects of a change in tax rate on fiscal surplus and further such analysis.

Economic Fluctuations and Stabilisation Policies

The business cycles in the Keynesian cross model could be caused, only, by some disturbance in the product market, that is, expenditure or aggregate demand. If investors become pessimistic, autonomous investment falls, and then through the multiplier process, income falls by a multiple of the fall in autonomous investment. Similarly, consumers' pessimism would reduce the autonomous consumption and a fall in the world income would reduce autonomous exports (vide Chapter 7) and so on. A fall in government expenditure or a rise in autonomous tax, *ceteris paribus*, would similarly reduce the total autonomous expenditure. Such events would cause a recession and fall in income, again through the multiplier process. The reverse events would trigger recovery and prosperity. As stated above, the Keynesians attribute the Great Depression to the lack of effective demand; caused by the stock market crash, bank failures, poor business confidence, contagion effect through the "rest of the world's" falling income adversely affecting the net exports, etc. Instead of sitting passively, if the government had increased its expenditure (financed through borrowing—internally or externally—or even taxes or monetisation), it could have softened or even avoided the Great Depression. The extent of the required increase in government expenditure or decrease in taxes to raise income to a given level depends on the size of the fiscal multiplier, which, in turns, depends on a number of factors including the marginal propensity to consume and the method by which government finances the resultant fiscal deficit. Thus:

Unlike the classicalists, Keynes advocated an interventionist fiscal policy.

Paul Samuelson (1939) has shown that the interaction of the Keynesian multiplier and the acceleration principle (vide Chapter 6) could cause business cycles.

In this simple model, the monetary policy has no role in stabilising the economy, as neither the quantity of money nor even the rate of interest enjoy any influence on the aggregate demand, which alone is the sole determinant of the output, employment and unemployment. However, the fiscal policy is significant in this regard as any change in government expenditure and/or taxes exerts significant effects on the real income through the multiplier. Further, the effectiveness of this policy varies directly with the Keynesian multiplier or directly with the marginal propensity to consume b and inversely with the tax rate t (and, as will be demonstrated later, inversely with the marginal propensity to import y if the economy is an open one (vide Chapter 12). In the above models, investment does not depend on the interest rate and, thus, there is not even a crowding out of private investment due to government expenditure. The recessions can be softened or even eliminated through an appropriate increase in government expenditure and/or a cut in taxes. The only constraint to this would come from the government budget constraint, which may go haywire unless the government is able to raise funds through additional money supply and/or public borrowings, which may be associated with their own problems. Nevertheless, the Keynesians think that the Great Depression could have been softened if the various governments around the world had played active roles.

Incidentally, note that if taxes depend on income, as they do, the tax revenue (= tY) goes down during the recessions due to fall in income and it goes up during the prosperity when income rise. Similarly, the transfer payments (social security, unemployment compensation, etc.) are more during recession and less during prosperity, for they vary inversely with the income. Taxes and transfer payments affect disposable income and there by private consumption and investment. Thus, both of these are counter cyclical in nature and dampen the effects of recession and prosperity on the economy. Further, they are built in the system rather than come through any policy initiative. Accordingly, they check business cycles to some extent automatically and hence they are called the **automatic stabilisers** in the economy. Unfortunately, they are not adequate to avoid the business cycles altogether and hence we need stabilisation policies.

Keynesian Cross Model—An Illustration

The working of the Keynesian cross model may now be illustrated through a hypothetical example. Note that the theoretical model is good only for analyzing the directions of the relationships and for measuring the sizes of the relationships one needs to quantify the model using the historical data on the variables involved and the econometrics techniques to estimate the model. Suppose an economy is characterised by the following estimated (econometric) structural model:

Product Market:

$$C = 150 + 0.8\,(Y - T)$$
$$T = 100 + 0.1\,Y$$

$$I_0 = 200,\ G_0 = 300$$
$$Y = C + I + G$$

Money Market:

$$\frac{L}{P} = 0.4Y - 100\ i$$
$$M_0 = 800,\ P = 1 \text{ (fixed)}$$

Production Function and Factor Market:

Full employment income = 2100

The above model is segmentable. The product market will determine the real income *Y*, and other real magnitudes, which are consumption *C*, investment I and tax revenue T. At the so determined income level, the money market will determine the internal rate i. The gap between the so determined income level and the full employment income, if any, would indicate if the economy is at full employment, under-full employment or over-full employment equilibrium. Remember that output level gets determined in the product market and the employment of labour is then determined simply by the requirement of labour as per the production function. In other words, the labour market plays the passive role. Recall from Chapter 9, that under price rigidity, firms surrender their labour demand function, and demand as much labour as required to produce the output demanded. To show this, let us work on the product market model first.

Substitution of the various equations in the income identity yields:

$$Y = 150 + 0.8\ (Y - 100 - 0.1\ Y) + 200 + 300$$

or, $Y(1 - 0.8 + 0.08) = 150 - 80 + 500$

or, $Y = \dfrac{1}{0.28}[570] = 2035$

Further, at $Y = 2035$, tax revenue equals

$$T = 100 + 0.1Y$$
$$= 100 + 0.1\ [2035]$$
$$= 303.5$$

The government budget surplus (BS) is given by:

$$BS = T - G$$
$$= 303.5 - 300 = 3.5$$

Private consumption is given by:

$$C = 150 + 0.8\ (Y - T)$$
$$= 150 + 0.8\ (2035 - 303.5) = 1535$$

Private saving (*S*) is given by

$$S = Y - T - C$$
$$= 2035 - 303.5 - 1535 = 196.5$$

National saving = $BS + S = 196.5 + 3.5 = 200$

Which equals the autonomous national investment ($I_0 = 200$).

Marginal propensity to save = $(1 - t)\ (1 - b) = 0.9 \times 0.2 = 0.18$

Marginal propensity to consume = $b(1 - t) = 0.8 \times 0.9 = 0.72$

Marginal tax rate = $t = 0.1$

Thus, if income goes up by 100, tax revenue goes up by 10, and the remaining disposable income = 90 is used partly as increased private consumption = 72 and partly as increased private saving = 18. Further, if government expenditure goes up by one rupee and it is financed by one rupee increase in autonomous tax, the increase in fiscal deficit would $= \dfrac{t(1-b)}{1-b(1-t)} = \dfrac{0.1(1-0.8)}{1-0.8(1-0.1)} = 0.0714$

Thus, if G and T_0 each go up by ₹100, *ceteris paribus*, fiscal surplus would go up by ₹7.14.

$$\text{The Keynesian multiplier} = \frac{1}{0.28} = 3.571$$

$$\text{The marginal leakage rate} = \frac{1}{3.571} = 0.28$$

To determine the interest rate, we must move to the money market given the income level, as determined in the product market. Thus,

$$\frac{L}{P} = 0.4\ Y - 100\ i$$

$$L = M_0 = 800,\ P = 1$$

And so,

$$800 = 0.4\ (2035) - 100\ i$$

$$\Rightarrow \qquad i = 0.14, \text{ or } i = 14\%$$

Since the equilibrium output (2035) falls short of the full employment output (2100), the quantity of labour employed will be below the full employment, causing under-full employment equilibrium. The deflationary gap equals:

$$\frac{2100 - 2035}{3.571} = 18.2$$

Therefore, if the total autonomous expenditure (i.e., $C_0 + I_0 + G_0 - T_0$) increases by 18.2, the full employment level of income would be attained. As Keynes argued, the under-full employment equilibrium is entirely due to the lack of effective demand. Note that as income is first determined in the product market itself and then at the so determined income, interest rate is determined in the money market, the above model is dichotomized.

KEYNESIAN IS-LM MODEL

The Keynesian cross model treats investment as autonomous or as dependent merely on income. This is considered very unsatisfactory, for the rational behaviour of firms would cause investment to vary inversely with the real interest rate (vide Chapter 6). Recall that even the classical model hypothesised investment as a negative function of the interest rate. Also, Keynes did recognise the role of interest rate in the investment function; he merely thought this was insignificant. With this role, the Keynesian cross model becomes the famous IS-LM model. The said model dominated macroeconomics and the theories of business cycles until the late 1960s, and is fairly popular in the classrooms even today.

Description of the Model

John R Hicks (1937) transformed the Keynesian model into a simultaneous equations (IS-LM) model, referred to by some as the **portable model**. The model retains the Keynes' assumption of the fixed (aggregate) price. Thus, even here firms are postulated to supply any quantity of their products at the fixed price to meet demands from their customers. Accordingly, the AS curve is horizontal at the fixed price, implying a perfectly price elastic supply curve.

The demand for the product side has behavioural functions for the various components of the demand. For simplicity, we continue with the assumption of a **closed economy,** and thereby ignore imports and exports, which we would incorporate in the open economy model, dealt in the next chapter. Also, for simplicity, taxes are assumed autonomous/exogenous. Government expenditure remains autonomous, as always, and the other relations would be as follows:[5]

Consumption function: $C = C_0 + b\,(Y - T_0)$ **(11.1)**

Investment function: $I = I_0 - d\,i$ **(11.6)**

Income identity: $Y = C + I + G_0$ **(11.7)**

Substitution of the first two equations in the last equation, and solution of the resultant for income would yield[6]:

$$Y = \frac{1}{1-b}(C_0 - bT_0 + I_0 + G_0) - \left(\frac{d}{1-b}\right)i$$

or,

$$Y = kA_0 - d\,k\,i \qquad \textbf{(11.8)}$$

Where $k = \dfrac{1}{1-b}$ (autonomous expenditure parameter)

$A_0 = C_0 - bT_0 + I_0 + G_0$ (autonomous expenditure)

Equation **(11.8)** relates income negatively to the interest rate and, thus, if the interest rate is a variable, Y is undetermined. To determine Y and i, we need another equation in these two variables, which comes from the money market.

Recall from Chapter 8 that in the Keynesian theory, money is demanded not only for carrying out transactions but also as a store of value (as a candidate in the portfolio). Accordingly, the demand for real money balances varies directly with the real income and inversely with the rate of interest. Therefore,

Money demand function: $\dfrac{L}{P} = eY - f\,i$ **(11.9)**

where L = nominal amount of money demanded (liquidity demand)

e, f = parameters, denoting sensitiveness of the money demand to changes in income and interest rate, respectively.

Equilibrium in the money market requires that the money market identity holds:

$$L = M_0 \qquad \textbf{(11.10)}$$

where M_0 = money supply, fixed autonomously

---

[5] For simplicity, all equations are assumed to be linear.

[6] Note that if the tax revenue is endogenous and the economy was an open one, the Keynesian multiplier would be given by $k = 1/[1 - b\,(1 - t) + c]$ and the autonomous expenditure by $A_0 = C_0 - bT_0 + I_0 + G_0 + X_0 - Z_0$, as in the above model (c = marginal propensity to import and Y^w is world income).

Solution of equations **(11.9)** and **(11.10)** for *Y* gives

$$Y = \frac{1}{e}\left(\frac{M_0}{P}\right) + \left(\frac{f}{e}\right) i \qquad \textbf{(11.11)}$$

Equations **(11.8)** and **(11.11)** are the two equations in just two endogenous variables, which are Y and *i*, and can be solved. Thus, rewriting equation **(11.11)** in terms of *i* gives

$$i = \frac{e}{f}\left[Y - \frac{1}{e}\left(\frac{M_0}{P}\right)\right]$$

Substituting this value of *i* in equation **(11.8)**, we get:

$$Y = kA_0 - d\,k\left[Y - \frac{1}{e}\left(\frac{M_0}{P}\right)\right]\left[\frac{e}{f}\right]$$

or,
$$Y\left[1 + \frac{d\,e\,k}{f}\right] = k\left[A_0 + \frac{d}{f}\left(\frac{M_0}{P}\right)\right]$$

Dividing both the sides by *k* and solving for *Y* gives:

$$Y = \frac{A_0 + \dfrac{d}{f}\left(\dfrac{M_0}{P}\right)}{\dfrac{1}{k} + \dfrac{d\,e}{f}} \qquad \textbf{(11.12)}$$

To solve for *i*, subtract equation **(11.11)** from equation **(11.8)** and get

$$0 = kA_0 - d\,k\,i - \frac{1}{e}\left(\frac{M_0}{P}\right) - \left(\frac{f}{e}\right) i$$

or,
$$i\left[dk + \frac{f}{e}\right] = kA_0 - \frac{1}{e}\left(\frac{M_0}{P}\right)$$

or,
$$i = \frac{kA_0 - \dfrac{1}{e}\left(\dfrac{M_0}{P}\right)}{\dfrac{f}{e} + dk}$$

Multiplying and dividing both the numerator and denominator by *e*/*f k*, we get:

$$i = \frac{\left(\dfrac{e}{f}\right) A_0 - \dfrac{1}{f\,k}\left(\dfrac{M_0}{P}\right)}{\dfrac{1}{k} + \dfrac{d\,e}{f}} \qquad \textbf{(11.13)}$$

Equations **(11.12)** and **(11.13)** represent the solution of the macroeconomic model contained in equations **(11.8)** and **(11.11)**, which, in turn, denote the solution of the model in *Y* and *i* contained in the analytical macroeconomic model expressed in equations **(11.1)**, **(11.6)**, **(11.7)**, **(11.9)** and **(11.10)**. In equations **(11.12)** and **(11.13)**, *Y* and *i* are expressed in terms of parameters and exogenous variables and, thus, given the values of the latter, numerical values for income and interest rate could be obtained. In view of this, equations **(11.12)** and **(11.13)** provide a complete solution of how income and the interest rate are determined. A mathematically inclined reader will be able to see that the effect of a given increase in government expenditure (which is a component of A_0 in equation **(11.12)**) on income under the IS-LM model, which is given by the partial derivative of Y with respect to A_0 in equation **(11.12)**, is smaller than the one in the Keynesian cross model, the former = $[k\,f/(f + k\,d\,e)]$ and the latter being just equal to k. **Incidentally note that the fiscal (or government expenditure, or autonomous expenditure) multiplier in the IS-LM model is [k f /(f + k d e)] and not *k*.**

The above explanation involves heavy algebra and, thus, it may now be cast in simple language and geometry. The product market has three equations (11.1, 11.6 and 11.7) in four endogenous variables, which are, C, I, Y and i. Similarly, the money market has two equations **(11.9)** and **(11.10)** in three endogenous variables, which are, L, Y and i. However, the interest rate and income are common in both these sub-models. Thus, while neither part of the model is a complete model, the combination of the two parts would make a complete model: five equations in five endogenous variables. This means that the model is not segmentable/dichotomized.

Equation **(11.8)** is referred to as the **equation of the *IS* curve**. This is because, by definition the IS curve is the locus of all the combinations of income and interest rate at which investment I equals savings S. However, $S = I$, only when the product market is in equilibrium. To understand this, we need to rewrite the income identity, equation **(11.7)**, which ensures the equilibrium in the product market.

$$Y - C = I + G_0$$

or,

$$S_{pvt} + T = I + G_0$$

The unconsumed income $(Y - C)$ is used by the private sector for paying personal and corporate taxes (T) and private savings (S_{pvt}). Since $T - G_0$ denotes government savings S_G, we could write the above equation as

$$S_{pvt} + S_G = I$$

or,

$$S = I$$

Thereby, equation **(11.8)** is the equation of the *IS* curve. Equation **(11.11)** was obtained by equating the demand for money L with the supply of money M and accordingly it is called the **LM curve equation**. It represents all the combinations of the income and interest rate at which the money market is in equilibrium.

It is easy to see that the IS curve is a downward sloping one. It is apparent in equation **(11.8)**, for the coefficient of the interest rate has a negative sign.[7] Also, it is so because while consumption (or saving) is not related (or it is also negatively related) to the interest rate, investment happens to be a negative function of the interest rate. Thus, when the interest rate falls, *ceteris paribus*, investment increases, consumption remains the same (or increases), the total expenditure goes up and, hence, the income goes up, and vice versa. Alternatively, one could argue that as income goes up, both private consumption and saving go up, for $S = I$, I must go up, which would happen if interest rate falls; and vice versa. The derivation of the IS curve is illustrated in Fig. 11.4.

[7]Note that the parameters d and k in equation **(10.8)** and, in fact, all the parameters in this text, are defined to be non-negative.

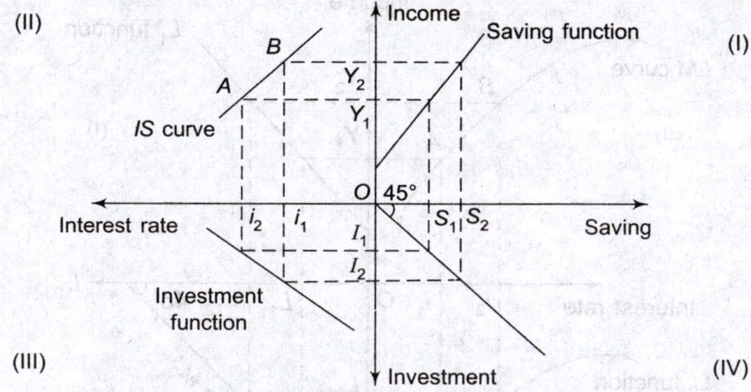

Fig. 11.4 Derivation of the *IS* Curve

The saving curve/function in quadrant I starts from a positive income (i.e., saving is negative at zero income), for there is some (minimum) consumption even at the zero income, and it is steep, as saving is a fraction of income. The 45° line in quadrant IV ensures $S = I$. The investment function in quadrant III is downward sloping due to the negative relationship between the investment and the rate of interest. To understand the derivation of the *IS* curve, start with an income level, say, Y_1. At this income, saving = S_1, and if so, the saving-investment equality requires, $I = I_1$, which is possible if and only if the interest rate equals i_2. The combination of Y_1 and i_2 gives point A on the IS curve. Repeating this procedure for $Y = Y_2$ yields the combination of Y_2 and i_1, which gives point *B* on the *IS* curve. If the *IS* curve is linear, the two points on this gives the entire curve. However, if it is non-linear, the other points on it could be generated by the above procedure.

The *LM* curve is an upward sloping one and accordingly the coefficient of the interest rate is positive in the *LM* equation **(11.11)**, and while money supply is exogenous, the demand for money function **(11.9)** postulates a positive relationship between the income and the interest rate. Thus, as the interest rate falls, *ceteris paribus*, the demand for real money balances (*L*/*P*) increases. However, this can not happen, for the equilibrium in the money market requires real money balances to be equal to real money supply, which is constant due to the fixed nominal money supply and fixed price level. To reverse the increase in real money balances, income must fall. Thus, a fall in interest rate leads to a fall in income. Quite the opposite would be true if interest rate rises. *LM* curve is accordingly, upward sloping. Fundamental to the Keynes' theory of money is his belief that money supply affects income through interest rate. The derivation of the *LM* curve is illustrated in Fig. 11.5.

Keynes dichotomised the money demand into the transaction and precautionary (transaction) demand L_1 and the speculative (portfolio) demand L_2, the former depending positively on the income and the latter negatively on the interest rate. Accordingly, quadrant I maps the L_1 function (which is steep as L_1 is a fraction of *Y*) and quadrant III the L_2 function. Also, Keynes argued that the L_2 function is non-linear, being less sensitive to the interest rate when the interest rate is high and more sensitive when it is low. In fact, he argued for the liquidity trap at a very low

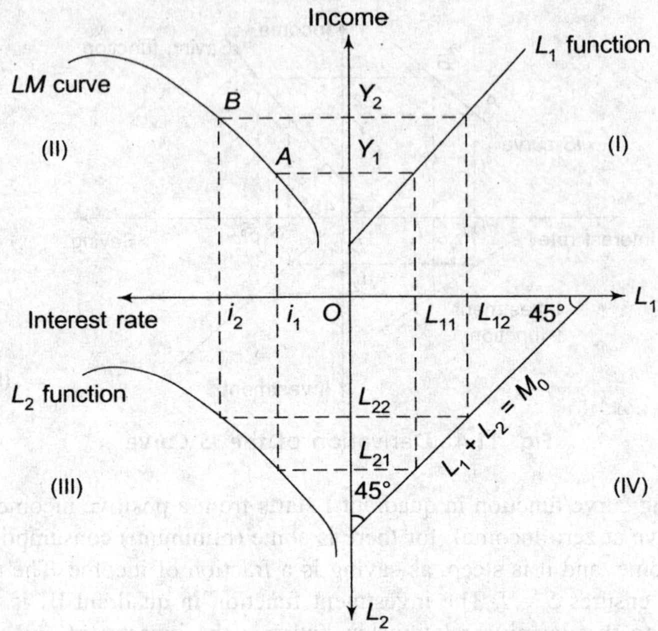

Fig. 11.5 Derivation of the *LM* Curve

interest rate. The 45° line in quadrant IV ensures equilibrium in the money market, where the total demand for money ($L_1 + L_2$) equals the money supply M_0.

To understand the derivation of the *LM* curve, start with an income level, say, Y_1. At this income, the transaction (and precautionary) demand for money = L_{11}. Given the money supply equals M_0, the money market equilibrium requires the speculative demand for money to be equal to L_{21}, which requires the interest rate to equal i_1. The combination of Y_1 and i_1 yields point *A* on the *LM* curve. Repetition of this process for income = Y_2 would yield point *B* on the *LM* curve. Since the L_2 curve is non-linear, the *LM* curve would be non-linear as well. The other points on this curve can be mapped similarly. Incidentally, note that the *LM* curve in the above graph is almost horizontal at very high interest rate (corresponding to the near zero interest elasticity of money demand at very high interest rate) and vertical at the very low interest rate (corresponding to the **liquidity trap**). It is interesting to note that the *LM* curve is independent of the fiscal policy (government expenditure and taxes) and the *IS* curve is free of the monetary policy (money supply).

The *IS* and *LM* curves can now be superimposed on one graph to explain the simultaneous determination of income and interest rate. For simplicity, the curves are assumed linear, and they are plotted below in Fig. 11.6. It is interesting to note that when the interest rate is zero, income takes a positive value on the *IS* curve (vide equation 11.8) and, hence, the *IS* curve starts with a positive income on the horizontal axis. Similarly, when the interest rate is zero, income is positive on the *LM* curve (vide equation 10.11) and, hence, the *LM* curve has a positive intercept on the income axis.

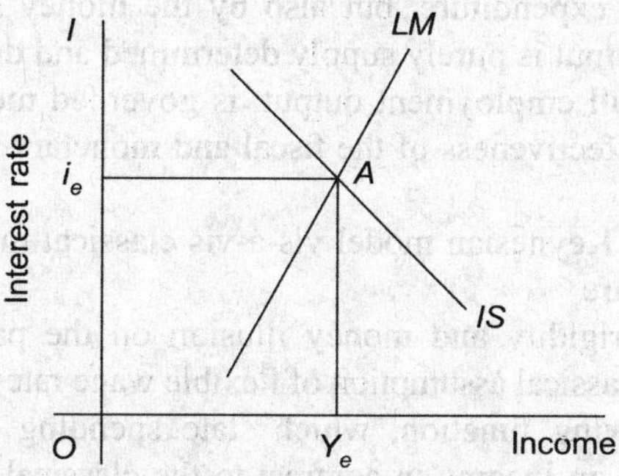

Fig. 11.6 IS-LM Model

Along the *IS* curve, the product market is in equilibrium and along the *LM* curve the money market is in equilibrium. Accordingly, the point of their intersection (point *A*) denotes the equilibrium in both the markets simultaneously. Also, the said equilibrium is stable, meaning that if there is any disturbance to this position, the market forces would operate to bring it back to this point. We do not take space here to prove this. Thus, the equilibrium values for income and interest rates are given by Y_e and i_e, respectively. The income so determined may or may not equal the full employment level of income, and thus the model is consistent with

- Full employment equilibrium, if $Y_e = Y_F$
- Under-full employment equilibrium, if $Y_e < Y_F$
- Over-full employment equilibrium, if $Y_e > Y_F$

The exact position hinges on the level of effective (aggregate) demand given by private consumption, investment and government expenditures (and net exports if the economy is an open one). For this reason, Keynesians attribute the Great Depression to the lack of effective demand. The remedy to cure unemployment, as a corollary, lies in increasing the aggregate demand. How this is done is examined in the next section.

At this point it will be useful to compare the IS-LM model with the Keynes' cross model. The only significant difference between the two is that while the IS-LM regards investment as sensitive to the interest rate, the cross model ignores this. This renders the product and money markets interdependent, fiscal policy less effective and the monetary policy turning effective in the IS-LM model in comparison to the cross model. Recall that in the cross model, income is determined in the product market and at the so determined income level, the money market determines the interest rate, and the factor market the level of employment/unemployment. In contrast, in the IS-LM model, the income and the interest rate are determined simultaneously in the product and money market, and at the so determined income level, the factor market (vide Chapter 9), not shown here, determines the level of employment/ unemployment. A common point in the two models is that the output and, hence, the employment is determined exclusively by the demand, supply has no role whatsoever. Further, in cross model, demand is governed by all the autonomous expenditure, including government expenditure, with no influence of the money supply. In contrast, in the IS-LM model, the demand is influenced not only by all autonomous expenditures, including government expenditure, but also by the money supply. Remember, in the classical model, output is purely supply determined and demand, which governs the price of a given full employment output, is governed merely by the supply of money. The relative effectiveness of the fiscal and monetary policies is analysed in the following section.

What is new in the Keynesian model vis-à-vis classical model? Three important postulates of Keynes are

(a) Nominal wage rigidity and money illusion on the part of workers, which contradicts the classical assumption of flexible wage rate and no money illusion.

(b) Consumption/saving function, which state spending on consumption (and saving) depends on income in contrast to the classical model's claims that it depends on interest rate only.

(c) Money demand function, which argues that people and business hold money not just for carrying out transactions, as the classical model recognized, but also for speculative purpose, which the classicalists could not foresee.

Economic Fluctuations and Stabilisation Policies

The factors that cause fluctuations in income and interest rate in the IS-LM model are the same that determine the shape (position and slope) of the IS and LM curves. As will be apparent in the IS function (equation 11.8), the position (intercept) of the IS curve depends positively on the following:

(i) Parameter *k,* which varies directly with the marginal propensity to consume (and, as seen earlier in the Keynesian cross model, negatively on the tax rate; and as would be shown later, positively on the marginal propensity to invest and negatively on the marginal propensity to import) .

(ii) Level of the autonomous expenditure A_0, which is composed of autonomous consumption, autonomous investment, and autonomous government expenditure (and autonomous net exports in an open economy), less the autonomous tax multiplied by the marginal propensity to consume.

Accordingly, the IS curve shifts upwards when either the parameter k increases or any component of the autonomous expenditure increases. The said curve shifts downwards in the event of a decrease in the said parameter or a decrease in autonomous spending. The slope of the IS curve depends on the parameter k and the sensitiveness of investment to changes in the interest rate (vide equation 11.8). The IS curve is steeper (i.e, dY/di is smaller when the angle of the IS curve on interest rate axis is small).

(iii) The lower the value of the parameter *k,* and lower the interest sensitiveness of investment *d*

A similar examination of the *LM* curve equation **(11.11)** would reveal that the position of the *LM* curve depends:

(iv) positively on the nominal quantity of money M_0, and

(v) negatively on the price level *P* and the sensitiveness of the money demand to the changes in income (parameter *e*).

And the said curve is flatter (i.e., dY/di is larger when the angle of the *LM* curve on income axis is small), that is:

(vi) larger the interest sensitiveness of the money demand (parameter *f*), the lower the income sensitiveness of the money demand (parameter *e*).

Accordingly, the *LM* curve shifts downwards if either the money supply increases or the price falls, or the responsiveness of the money demand to changes in income falls. In the opposite case, the *LM* curve shifts upwards. The said curve rotates clockwise if either the interest sensitiveness of the money demand increases or the income sensitiveness of the money demand decreases.

Under the IS-LM model, the income (and, hence, the levels of employment and unemployment) is determined solely in the product market and, hence, business cycles could be caused only by changes in the *IS* and/or *LM* curves. Therefore, the causes for economic fluctuations are found in factors that could cause changes in the IS-LM curves. Thus, the factors listed under points (i) through (vi) above are the potential causes of all business cycles. In particular, recessions could be caused by the paucity of the autonomous expenditure and/or that of the money supply, even if the various parameters were stable. Similarly, upswings in business cycles could come through excessive doses of autonomous spending and/or the money supply. The Keynesians, thus, blame government failures, and the business and consumers' expectations for the persistence of business cycles.

Role of the Stabilisation Policies in the IS-LM Model To some extent, the role of the fiscal policy is obvious from the point (ii) above, and that of the monetary policy from the point (iv) above. However, their exact effectiveness with respect to the real income (and, hence, with respect to employment/unemployment) hinges on the values of the two parameters, which are *d* and *f*, which represent the interest sensitiveness of investment and money demand, respectively. In particular, the following observation summarises their positions:

The fiscal policy is the most effective and the monetary policy the least effective, the higher the interest sensitiveness of the money demand (parameter *f*) and the lower the interest sensitiveness of the investment demand (parameter *d*), and vice versa.

In the event of either $f =$ infinity or $d = 0$, the fiscal policy is the most powerful in arresting business cycles, and the monetary policy has no role whatsoever. Under the other extreme condition, which is, $f = 0$ or $d =$ infinity, the fiscal policy has no role and the monetary policy is the most powerful in dealing with economic fluctuations. In all intermediary cases, that is, when neither of the two parameters takes extreme values, both the fiscal and monetary policies have roles in controlling business cycles.[8] Since in the real world, the extreme cases are rarely found, both the policies assume the stabilisation role. The above conclusion would be easy to understand through the graphs in Fig. **(11.7)**.

[8] The mathematically inclined readers could see these factors easily through the equilibrium value of the real income in equation **(11.12)**. The partial derivative of *Y* with respect to *G* would give $\frac{1}{1/k + de/f}$ and of *Y* with respect to *M* would give $\frac{d/fp}{1/k + de/f}$, which represents the effects of the fiscal and monetary policies on the real income, respectively.

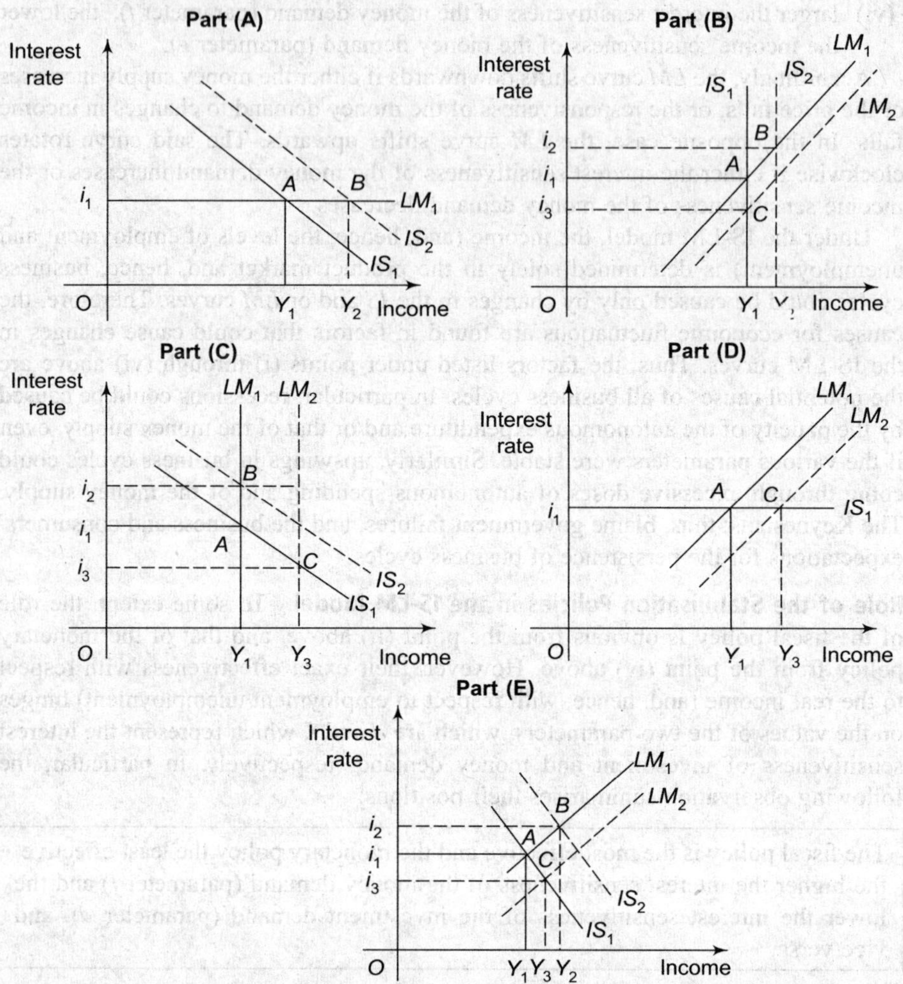

Fig. 11.7 Roles of Stabilisation Policies

Figure 11.7 has five parts. Part (A) assumes $f = \infty$ part (B) takes $d = 0$, part (C) is based on $f = 0$, part (D) is drawn on the assumption that d = infinity and part (E) on the intermediate values of both these crucial parameters. The solid lines indicate the original *IS* and *LM* curves, and the dotted ones the corresponding curves when the government expenditure and the money supply increases, respectively. Corresponding to these, Y_1 and i_1 give the equilibrium values of the real income and the interest rate under the original situation, and Y_2 and i_2 those under the new situation when either the government expenditure is up or taxes down, and Y_3 and i_3 those under the new situation when the money supply is up.

Incidentally, note that when the *LM* curve is horizontal (vide Fig. 11.5, part A), a change in the money supply leaves this curve unchanged. This is due to the **liquidity trap**, which arises when the rate of interest is so low that people hold all their assets in money (nothing in bonds), making the speculative demand for money perfectly interest elastic. In such a situation, all increase in the supply of money goes into an equivalent increase in the demand for money, and vice versa, and thus, changes in the money supply do not cause any change in the interest rate and, therefore, no change in investment or real income. Note that in the Keynesian model, money supply affects the economy through interest rate since money serves as a store of value, and not just as a medium of exchange, as visualised by the classicalists. Similarly, when the *IS* curve is horizontal (vide Fig. 11.5, part *D*), i.e., when investment does not respond at all to changes in the interest rate, a change in government expenditure or taxes leaves the *IS* curve unchanged. This happens because all the changes in government expenditure are exactly balanced by an equivalent change in the sum total of investment and consumption spending in the opposite direction (as in the Keynesian cross model).

In the IS-LM model there are two instruments of fiscal policy, which are government expenditure and taxes, and one instrument of monetary policy, which is money supply. If either government expenditure increases or taxes decline, the *IS* curve shifts rightwards, and vice versa, without causing any change in the *LM* curve. Similarly, increases in the money supply leads to a downward shift in the *LM* curve, and vice versa, leaving the IS curve unaltered. The various parts of Fig. 11.5 indicate the original equilibrium position (point A), the new equilibrium position (point B) triggered by increased government expenditure or decreased taxes, and another equilibrium position (point C), which arises when the money supply is increased, *ceteris paribus*. Parts A and B indicate that while the fiscal policy is effective with regard to the real income, the monetary policy is totally ineffective in this respect. Parts C and D reveal the opposite, that is, the monetary policy is highly effective and the fiscal policy has no influence on the level of the real income. Part E, the intermediate case, suggests the effectiveness (though less) of both the policies. The effects of these policies, with regard to the interest rate, are different, but they are better understood through the perusal of Fig. 11.7. While an increase in the government expenditure, *ceteris paribus*, causes the interest rate to rise, an increase in the money supply, *ceteris paribus*, triggers a fall in the interest rate, and vice versa.

To understand why this happens, we need to explain a rather popular concept, which is, the **crowding out effect**. This tells that when a pure expansionary fiscal policy is applied, government expenditure goes up and it is neither financed through taxes (for otherwise, the policy would not be expansionary) nor through monetisation (for otherwise it would be a mix of the expansionary fiscal and expansionary moneteary policy), and hence only through borrowing in the domestic or foreign market. Further, for the government to be able to borrow, it must make its bonds attractive by offering a higher interest rate. But as the interest rate goes up, private expenditure (consumption and investment spending) goes down.[9] Thus, a part of the increase in government expenditure is nullified (crowded out) through a decrease in private expenditure.

[9]If the economy is open and it is on the freely floating exchange rate system, an increase in the domestic interest rate will lead to a crowding out of net exports as well (see Chapter 12).

The crowding out is zero when:
(a) There is liquidity trap (*LM* curve is horizontal), or
(b) Investment is perfectly interest inelastic (*IS* curve is vertical)
The crowding out is full (= increase in government expenditure) when:
(c) Money demand is perfectly interest inelastic (*LM* curve is vertical), or
(d) Investment is perfectly interest elastic (*IS* curve is horizontal)
The crowding out is only partial under:
(e) Intermediate situations (when the *IS* curve is falling and the *LM* curve is rising).

The situation **(c)** represents the classical case, situation **(b)** the Keynesian cross and situation **(e)** the Keynesian *IS-LM* model. This is why fiscal policy was found to be of no significance in the classical model, very effective in the cross model and only partially effective in the *IS-LM* model. The results on the monetary policy follow similarly from the various models' assumptions with regard to the interest sensitiveness of the investment and money demand functions. The controversy between the monetarists and the non-monetarists (Keynesians), discussed in detail in Chapter 13, rested basically on their different beliefs about the values of the parameters *d* and *f*. While the former thought that *d* was relatively large and *f* relatively small, the latter thought quite the opposite; and accordingly, while the former argued that the monetary policy was relatively stronger, the latter suggested that the fiscal policy was relatively stronger.

The *IS-LM* model (output-interest rate axes) could easily be transformed into the *AD-AS* framework (output-price axes). The *AD* curve would be vertical at the output level where the IS curve intersects the *LM* curve. The *AS* curve would be horizontal at the exogenously given fixed price level. Thus, the situation would be similar to Fig. 11.3 above.

The above analysis concludes that the **two policies never fail simultaneously in stabilising the economy**. If the monetary policy is not effective, the fiscal policy would be highly effective, and vice versa.[10] In the intermediate case, when both the policies are partly effective, each policy supports the other. Increased government expenditure financed through increased money supply (i.e., a mix of both expansionary policies) will surely lead to an increase in the real income, with uncertain effects on the interest rate (vide Fig. 11.7, parts A to E), and vice versa. Furthermore, AC Pigou has argued that the monetary policy would be effective even under the extreme case of the liquidity trap and/or the perfectly interest insensitive investment spending, if we recognise the effect of the real balances on consumption and investment spending (vide Chapters 5 and 6). This is called the **Pigou effect** or the **real balance effect** and it works as follows: when the money supply is increased, all the additional money goes into the liquid assets with households and firms (under the liquidity trap) and, thus, the real balances go up (remember, the price is fixed in the

[10] By emphasising the liquidity trap and the interest insensitiveness of the investment spending, particularly when the interest rate was very low, Keynes criticised the classical belief in the effectiveness of the monetary policy. In contrast, the classicists criticised the Keynes' argument in favour of effective fiscal policy, by focusing on the interest insensitiveness of the money demand and interest sensitiveness of investment.

IS-LM model). Consequently the consumption and investment increase, which, in turn, cause the IS curve to shift rightward (with no change in the *LM* curve), which leads to an increase in the real income. Quite the opposite is true when the money supply decreases. Thereby, Figures 11.4, 11.5 and 11.7 ignore the Pigou effect.

The Pigou effect restores the effectiveness of the monetary policy under the liquidity trap.

From the above analysis it is clear that either the fiscal or the monetary policy is always available to stimulate the economy when it is in recession and to restrain it when it is overheated. This, in turn, implies that the Great Depression could have been avoided if an appropriate stabilisation policy had been enforced. Also, an appropriate mix of the two policies could well be used for the purpose. If the two policies are used simultaneously, their total effects would always equal the sum of their independent effects. If both the policies are either easy or tight, their total effects on the real income will be unidirectional while that on the interest rate will be bidirectional and, hence, ambiguous. Thus, for example, an easy policy mix of increase in government expenditure and increase in money supply will result in an unambiguous increase in the real income but its effect on the interest rate will be ambiguous. This is so because while each expansionary policy leads to an increase in real income; an expansionary fiscal policy tends to raise the interest rate and an expansionary monetary policy causes the interest rate to fall. Depending on the policy objective, an appropriate policy mix could be designed and implemented. Thus, if the government is pro-consumer, it must use an expansionary fiscal policy to achieve higher income with higher interest rate; if it were pro-business, it must employ expansionary monetary policy to secure higher income with lower interest rate; and if neither, it must practice an appropriate mix (both expansionary, i.e., increased government expenditure financed through increase in money supply, called **pump priming policy**) of the two policies to attain higher income with little or no change in interest rate. However, if policies were really effective there would be no business cycles. Business cycles persist due to limitations of the stabilisation policies which will be explained in subsequent chapters. Nevertheless, the Keynesians argued towards an interventionist policy. Note that while the **classicalists advocate a balanced budget, the Keynesians recommend a deficit budget during recessions and a surplus budget during prosperity**.

It is instructive to note here that any increase in government expenditure has to be financed—a fact that has been ignored above in the analysis of fiscal policy effectiveness. If such financing has any bearing on the real income/employment, it has to be subtracted from the positive effect of government expenditure, as shown above in the balanced budget multiplier case. Nevertheless, as mentioned in Chapters 4 and 10, the government need not bother to balance its budget every year and even forever, and surely it may be prudent to resort to deficit financing during recessions. To this extent, the above analysis is fine. Also, recall that as noted in Chapter 8, monetary policy could be conducted through regulating money supply or interest rate. In our analysis above, we explained it through money supply only, which is generally the case in most macroeconomics texts. Until recently, most Central Banks were operating through the quantity of money, though lately they (including the RBI) are concentrating on the interest rate. Further, in the *IS-LM* analysis, we have assumed a closed economy throughout and, thus, the above analysis holds good basically for a closed economy. The openness of the economy and its foreign exchange rate system has implications for the effectiveness of both the fiscal and monetary policies, and these are dealt with in the next chapter.

Keynesian IS-LM Model—An Illustration

To illustrate the working of the IS-LM model, we simply change the investment function, as discussed in an earlier section, to the following, keeping all other relations as before:

$$I = 210 - 100\,i$$

With this change, the product market and the money market are no longer independent. They determine the income and the interest rates together. To get the equation of the *IS* curve, we substitute the relevant functions in the income identity[11]

$$Y = C + I + G$$

$$Y = [150 + 0.8(Y - 100 - 0.1Y)] + [210 - 100\,i] + 300$$

or, $\quad Y(1 - 0.8 + 0.08) = 580 - 100\,i$

or, $\quad Y = [580 - 100\,i](3.57)$

$\Rightarrow \quad Y = 2071 - 357\,i \qquad$ **(11.14)**

The LM curve equation is given by the equilibrium in the money market:

$$\frac{L}{P} = 0.4Y - 100i$$

$$\frac{L}{P} = \frac{M}{P} = \frac{800}{1}$$

Thus, $\quad 0.4\,Y - 100\,i = 800$

$\Rightarrow \quad Y = 2000 + 250\,i \qquad$ **(11.15)**

Solution of equations **(11.14)** and **(11.15)** yield:

$$Y = 2029$$

$$i = 0.117 = 11.7\%$$

Again the equilibrium income (2029) falls short of the full employment level of income (2100), and, thus, there is under-full employment equilibrium. The cause of under-full employment is the lack of effective demand. In the Keynesian cross model of the previous section, the remedy lay simply in raising the autonomous expenditure by the size of the deflationary gap, given by

$$\frac{Y_F - Y}{k}$$

In the *IS-LM* model, the remedy lies either in raising the autonomous expenditure by a certain amount (not equal to the above deflationary gap) or in raising the money supply by an appropriate amount, or a mix of the two. Thus, for example, if government expenditure increases from 300 to 325, *ceteris paribus* (pure fiscal

[11]In the calculations that follow, all the numbers have been rounded off to the closest integers for the income and to three decimals for the interest rate.

stimulus), the equilibrium level of income would be given by the intersection of the erstwhile (unchanged) *LM* curve and the new IS curve, whose new equation will be

$$Y = [150 + 0.8\ (Y - 100 - 0.1Y] + [210 - 100\ i] + 325$$

or, $$Y = \frac{1}{0.28}[605 - 100\ i]$$

⇒ $$Y = 2161 - 357\ i \qquad \textbf{(11.16)}$$

The solution of **(11.16)** and **(11.15)** yields

$$Y = 2066$$
$$i = 0.265 = 26.5\%$$

Therefore, income has increased and so has the interest rate, due to the expansionary fiscal policy. However, it must be noted that the increase in income here is less than it would have been under the Keynesian cross model. This is due to the crowding out effect. To see this clearly, in the numerical example of the Cross model, the fiscal multiplier was 3.571, while in the example here said multiplier is just 1.48, as an increase in government expenditure by 25 lead to an increase in income by just 37 (=2066 – 2029).

Further, in this IS-LM model, if the money supply increases from 800 to 825, *ceteris paribus* (pure monetary stimulus), the IS curve would remain the same as in equation **(11.14)** and the new LM curve equation would be:

$$0.4\ Y - 100\ i = 825$$

or, $$Y = 2062 + 250\ i \qquad \textbf{(11.17)}$$

The solution of equations **(11.14)** and **(11.17)** would give:

$$Y = 2066$$
$$i = 0.015 = 1.5\%$$

Thus, the expansionary monetary policy causes the income to rise and the interest rate to fall. If both the policies are used simultaneously, where in government expenditure increases from 300 to 325 and the money supply increases from 800 to 825, *ceteris paribus* (mix of fiscal and monetary stimulus), the IS curve will be given by equation **(11.16)** and the LM curve by equation **(11.17)**, and their solution would yield:

$$Y = 2103$$
$$i = 0.163 = 16.3\%$$

Thus, under the expansionary fiscal and monetary policies, income has increased more than that under either case but the effect on the interest rate is a mixed one. Only the last policy change has hit (rather crossed) the full employment level of income. Needless to point out, one can always design a policy to achieve the full employment output exactly. Also, one can determine the required change in the quantity of money supply and government expenditure so that an expansionary fiscal-monetary mix policy would raise the income by a required amount without altering the equilibrium rate of interest.

The controlled experiment of changing the value of one or more policy variable, holding all others as constants, and examining the effects on the target variables, is referred to as the **comparative static**. It is this technique which allows one to evaluate the effectiveness of various policies with respect to the target variables.

APPLICATIONS OF THE KEYNESIAN MODEL

The Keynesian idea of stabilisation policies (particularly fiscal policy) having a significant role in a capitalist economy has been very important for taming business cycles and promoting economic growth. The idea was applauded the world over. The role of economics was expanded from the mere efficient allocation of scarce resources among the alternative uses to include the countering of business cycles and promoting economic growth. This gave birth to macroeconomics. Further, the public sector was expanded in most countries, and so emerged the mixed economy. India accorded the 'commanding heights' status to the public sector, and investment in the public sector grew substantially during the late 1950s and 1960s. Public investment became the engine of growth. Also, the various tax rates were raised in almost all budgets during the said period. The United States had suffered a serious recession during August 1957 through April 1958 and once again during April 1960 to February 1961. The Kennedy-Johnson tax cuts were implemented and the money supply was increased substantially to then stabilise the economy. When a reporter asked the US President, John F. Kennedy, why he advocated a tax cut, Kennedy replied "**to stimulate the economy, do you remember your Economics 101**". More recently, another US President, George Bush implemented tax cut to move out of recession in 2001 and explained "the best way to increase demand for goods and services is to let people keep more of their own money (income) and when somebody meets that demand by additional production, somebody is more likely to find a job". Further, to counter the Great Recession 2007-09, the G-20 (newly formed group of 20 developed, emerging, and large countries) mounted a coordinated fiscal stimulus. Until recently, many countries, including India, were on the soft interest rate regime and thus they were close to the Keynes liquidity trap. In such situations, recall that the monetary policy only has a little influence on real income and employment. While the lowering of the Federal Fund Rate in several quick installments from 6.5 per cent to 1.25 in 2001 might have helped the US to check the recession to a certain extent, the further effectiveness of such a measure had approached a zero zone. Similar was the case during the Great Depression, when the interest rates were fairly low. Recently, inflation has reemerged and interest rates have moved up globally. Accordingly, the tight monetary policy is being practiced. As most governments have become conscious about sound finance, the fiscal policy has become less popular.

The Great Depression could also be explained through the IS-LM model. For the purpose, three alternative hypotheses have been advanced. These are

(a) Spending hypothesis
(b) Money hypothesis
(c) Deflation-debt hypothesis

The first hypothesis suggests that Great Depression could have happened entirely due to a downward shift in *IS* curve, caused by a fall in total spending and loss of confidence (private consumption and investment, in particular), caused, in turn, by depletion of wealth, which was triggered by stock market crash. The second hypothesis suggests that stock market fall led to bank failures, increase in currency to money and reserve to deposit ratios and consequent fall in nominal money stock triggering LM curve to shift leftward. The third and last hypothesis (advanced by

Ben Bernanke, former Governor, Federal Reserve Bank, USA) argues that the fall in price caused a transfer of income from debtors to creditors, which, due to a relatively lower marginal propensity to consume of creditors than that of debtors, led to a decrease in private consumption and thereby to a leftward shift in *IS* curve. It is easy to see that a leftward shift in either the *IS* curve or the *LM* curve alone in the IS-*LM* model can lead to a fall in income and employment, and such a shift in both the curves simultaneously can very well cause a deep recession. Thus, the *IS-LM* model offers an explanation of the Great Depression.

Case Study: Great Depression (contd.)

Using the data from the Case Study of the previous section (pp. 294), attempt the following questions:

(a) Draw the *IS-LM* curves for 1929 and for 1933 on the same graph such that the equilibrium values of income and interest rate corresponds to their actual values in those years.

(b) Analyse the magnitudes of real money supply and real government expenditure for various years. How the changes in the money supply and government expenditure would have affected the *IS* and *LM* curves? Do these changes explain the shift in these curves as required in question **(a)** above? If not, what else could have changed in the US economy during the period so as to cause the Great Depression?

(c) Examine the appropriateness of the use of the fiscal and monetary policies during the Great Depression. If the use was inappropriate, what could have been the reasons for the same?

(d) Are the data consistent with the Keynesian assumption of the fixed price? If not, discuss its consequences on the *IS-LM* model.

(e) Consider the following additional US data (in $ Billions at 1958 prices) on consumption and investment during 1929-1940, and note that the Great Depression was preceded by the stock market crash and the United States, like most other countries, was on the gold standard at that time. Based on this additional information, throw some light on the potential causes of the Great Depression and the role that fiscal and monetary policies could have played in the same.

Item	*1929*	*1930*	*1931*	*1932*	*1933*	*1934*	*1935*	*1936*	*1937*	*1938*	*1939*	*1940*
Consumption	140	130	126	115	113	118	126	138	148	140	148	156
Investment	40.4	27.4	16.8	4.7	5.3	9.4	18.0	24.0	29.9	17.0	24.7	33.0

Conclusion

The classical model postulates a full employment output all the time and, thus, accords no role to the fiscal and monetary policies in effecting the real output, employment and unemployment. However, the monetary policy plays the role in effecting the general price and, hence, all the nominal magnitudes, and the role is direct and proportional. In contrast, in the fixed price versions of the Keynesian model, under-full employment equilibrium is possible, and the real output is governed purely by the effective demand, which could be managed through the fiscal and monetary policies. The fiscal policy is powerful but its strength is reduced by its crowding out feature, and it is, of course, subject to the budget (financing) constraint. The monetary policy is effective but its effectiveness is impaired by the liquidity trap and improved by the Pigou effect. Keynes criticised the classicalists and, thereby, undermined the role of the monetary policy by emphasizing the liquidity trap and the interest insensitiveness of investment spending. Within these constraints, the fiscal and monetary policies could be used to regulate effective demand and, thereby, taming any business cycle. It is this spirit that led the Keynesians to blame governments for all business cycles. Further, just as appropriate policies can counter cycles, inappropriate policy actions can create cycles as well. For example, during the Great Depression in the United States; while the real government expenditure increased only marginally from $22 billion in 1929 to $23.3 billion in 1933, the nominal money supply declined from $26.6 in 1929 to $19.9 billion in 1933. Obviously, these actions, whatever the reason may be, only aggravated the recession. This is why some economists talk about the **political business cycle theory** as well. In support of this, we may state that, generally, government spending goes up during election periods and war periods, and that is why we often see a faster growth rate in real GDP in such years than others, *ceteris paribus*. Further, it is argued that the fiscal stimulus of World War II really served as some kind of a rescuer from the troubles of the Great Depression.

Before we conclude, it must be emphasised that Karl Marx's fear of the collapse of the capitalist system has not happened till date and it is unlikely to happen in future as well. The credit for this is surely shared by the Keynesian theory and thus some people regard John Maynard Keynes as the **saviour of capitalism**. Unfortunately, his assumption of the price-wage rigidity proved grossly wrong after the mid-1960s and this has reduced his theory's relevance thereafter.

KEYWORDS

Classical-Keynesian model; Optimisation theory; Laissez faire; Capitalism; Principle of comparative advantage; Say's law; Quantity theory of money; Price equation; Segmentable model; Fiscal-Monetary policy; Crowding out; Hyperinflation; Supply creates its own demand; Keynesian cross model; Autonomous expenditure multiplier; Balanced budget multiplier; Effective demand; Deflationary/Recessionary-Inflationary gap; Paradox of thrift; Marginal leakage rate; Economic fluctuations; Stabilisation policy; Automatic stabilisers; Keynesian IS-LM model; Closed economy; Liquidity trap; Interest sensitiveness investment–money demand; Pigou effect, Pump priming policy; Interventionist policy; Kennedy-Johnson tax cut; Political business cycle.

REFERENCES

1. Gupta GS, GS Laumas, Some Properties of Fiscal and Monetary Policy Multipliers, *Southern Economic Journal* 40, (April, 1983): 1137-40.

2. Hicks John R, Mr Keynes and the Classics: a Suggested Interpretation', *Econometrica* 5, (1937).
3. Keynes John Maynard, *General Theory of Employment, Interest and Money*, (London: Macmillan, 1936).
4. Pigou A C, 'The Classical Stationary State', *Economic Journal* 53, (1943): 343-51.
5. Samuelson Paul, Interactions in the Multiplier and the Principle of Acceleration, *Review of Economics and Statistics* 21, (May, 1939): 75–78.
6. Say J B, *A Treatise on Political Economy*, (Philadelphia: 1834).

Review Questions

1. The fiscal policy is impotent; both in causing and curing economic fluctuations, under the Walrasian (perfectly competitive markets) model but not so under the nominal stickiness (Keynesian) model. Discuss.

2. Use the IS-LM model to suggest a policy mix to reduce the interest rate with no change in income.

3. Money illusion and money neutrality are mutually exclusive. Explain.

4. Consider an economy which is represented by the following model:

$$C = 400 + 0.75\, Y^d$$
$$I = 400 - 20\, i$$
$$G = 300,\ T_0 = 400$$
$$L/P = 0.25\, Y - 10\, i$$
$$M = 1{,}000,\ P = 2$$

(Y^d = disposable income, other notations have the usual meaning)

(a) Determine the equilibrium values for Y and i

(b) If G goes up to 400, *ceteris paribus*, find the new Y and i.

5. Suppose the Hotland economy has just moved from autonomous taxes to both the autonomous as well as the induced (income based) taxes, *ceteris paribus*. Discuss the effect of this change on the

(a) slope of the *IS* curve

(b) effectiveness of the fiscal and monetary policies

(c) balanced budget multiplier

Does your answer have anything to do with the automatic stabilisers?

6. Which of the following is an automatic stabiliser? Anti-stabiliser? Why?

(a) Pensions that vary directly with income

(b) Lump sum taxes that are independent of income

(c) Imports that vary directly with income

7. Suppose the Coldland economy moves from the system of exogenous money supply to the system of some target interest rate (i_o) and adjusting the money supply to maintain $i = i_o$. What effect, if any, would this change have on the slopes of the *LM* and *AD* curves, and on the effects of the fiscal and monetary policies?

8. Suppose the government uses its expenditure as a stabiliser tool, that is, it goes up when the real income is low, and vice versa, as follows:

$$G = G_0 + g\,(Y_F - Y)$$

where, G = Government expenditure,
G_o = Autonomous component of G,
g = parameter,
Y_F = Full employment level of real income, and
Y = Real income

Incorporate this in the IS-LM model and answer the following questions:

(a) Determine the value of the autonomous expenditure multiplier.

(b) Examine the effect of changes in parameter g on the multiplier.

(c) Suggest the possible ways for financing the counter cyclical government expenditures.

(d) Does the Indian government behave this way? How?

9. In Chapter 5, consumption was argued to be affected negatively by the (real) interest rate. If this were true, would 'crowding out' be more or less than in the absence of it? Give reasons in support of your answer.

10. Suppose an economy is represented by the following system of equations:

IS Equation: $Y = k[C_0 - bT_0 + I_0 + G_0] - (k)(d)i$

LM Equation: $\dfrac{M_0}{P_0} = eY - (f)i$

Multiplier definition $= k = \dfrac{1}{1 - b(1 - t)}$

The variables have their usual meanings. The 2014 values of various variables are as follows:

$$C_0 = 100,\ I_0 = 300,\ M_0 = 920,\ P_0 = 10,\ G_0 = 100,\ T_0 = 0$$

The parameters have the following values, which could be assumed constants throughout the period:

$$b = 0.6,\ t = 1/6,\ d = 10.0,\ e = 0.2,\ f = 5.0$$

The following additional information is available:

(i) Prices are fixed so that the output is given by the IS-LM model

(ii) The output grows at the rate of 10 per cent per annum

(iii) Government expenditure grows at the rate of 20 units (in real terms) per annum due to unavoidable non-developmental expenditure.

Answer the following questions:

(a) If the government wishes consumption to grow at the rate of 8 per cent per annum in 2015, what must the tax rate be in that year? What is, consequently, the rate of growth of private investment for the year 2015?

(b) If the government invests 50 units (in real terms) in new capital every year and the private inventory stock is constant, what is the incremental capital-output ratio in the year 2015?

Chapter 12

Keynesian Fixed Price, Open Economy (Mundell-Fleming) Model

Learning Objectives

After reading the chapter you should be able to:

1. Understand the features of an open economy, in particular
   - **(a)** Its new market, i.e. foreign exchange (also called the balance of payments) market besides the earlier product and the money markets.
   - **(b)** Net export and net capital outflow, which equals the excess of national saving over domestic investment.
   - **(c)** International trinity also called the impossible trilemma, according to which an open economy must choose any two of the three systems, viz. integration, regulation and sovereignty.
2. Appreciate that the open economy IS equation has a new term in the real exchange rate and accordingly, the autonomous expenditure multiplier has a new parameter in the marginal propensity to import.
3. Know that an open country has the option of choosing the fixed or floating exchange rate system with the unconstrained integration, or even a partially restricted integration with a managed exchange rate system and monetary sovereignty.
4. Learn that the BP curve slopes upward both under the output-interest rate axes and the output-exchange rate axes, and that the open economy IS-LM-BP model is a very short run model as it takes the prices as fixed.
5. Comprehend that under the pure floating exchange rate system and full integration, the monetary policy is effective with respect to output, employment and other real magnitudes while the fiscal and trade policies are redundant in this regard. Quite the opposite holds true under the fixed exchange rate and full integration.

The IS-LM model of the previous chapter assumed closed economy and fixed prices. Accordingly, that model and its implications are valid for a closed economy and in the very short run only during which prices are fixed. In the present day world, all economies are open as they have international trade in goods and services, lend/borrow abroad, participate both ways in portfolio and direct investments, and their people and business perform tasks abroad. Thus, one needs to relax the assumption of a closed economy. Also, while the assumption of the fixed price is reasonable for the very short run, the said assumption is no longer appropriate for the medium and long runs. Accordingly, the present chapter relaxes the assumption of closed economy and the next chapter would further relax the other assumption of the fixed price. The chapter first deals with the specification of the IS-LM-BP (balance of payments) functions for an open economy and then goes to develop and analyse the IS-LM-BP models for **(a)** a well-integrated open economy under the floating exchange rate system, **(b)** a well-integrated open economy under the fixed exchange rate system, and **(c)** a partially integrated economy under partially managed exchange rate system.

Open Economy IS-LM-BP Functions

Currently all countries are characterised by international flow of goods and services, capital and people. It is said globalisation is not a choice but a fact. Mundell (1968) and Fleming (1962) contributions are credited with developing such a model, and thus the model presented here is also referred to as the Mundell-Fleming (M-F) model. The M-F model assumes **perfect capital mobility** (integration) across countries and uses the IS-LM apparatus. Accordingly, the model is also referred to as the open economy IS-LM model, to distinguish it from the previous chapter's closed economy IS-LM model. Since most countries are currently emphasising globalisation, this is the right model to understand the working of an economy and the role that various stabilisation policies play in the short run. During 1945 through 1973, under the Bretton Woods system, all member countries of IMF (International Monetary Fund) were on the fixed exchange rate system. However, after the breakdown of that system, while some countries are still on the fixed (and common) currency system, most countries are on some sort of floating rate system. This change is considered as one of the **main international events**. Accordingly, two versions of the model are developed, one applicable to countries on the floating rate and the other pertinent to countries which have opted for the fixed exchange rate system. In what follows, the general form of the IS-LM functions of both these versions is presented. Since many countries have restrictions on capital flows, an additional model for imperfect capital mobility, and the corresponding exchange rate system and their implications on the Central Bank's power of monetary sovereignty is also presented and analysed.

Open Economy IS Equation

The IS equation proceeds with the definitions of investment and saving. In an open economy, domestic investment (I) is given by:

$$\begin{aligned} I &= S + \text{Net foreign investment} \\ &= S + \text{NKI} \\ &= S + (Z - X) \end{aligned}$$

or,

$$I = S - NX \tag{12.1}$$

where, S = domestic saving, NKI = net capital inflow, Z = imports of goods and services, X = exports of goods and services, and NX = net exports of goods and services.

The first equation holds because with free movement of capital across countries, a country can invest abroad or can receive investments from abroad. As seen in

Chapter 7, the difference between foreign investments in the domestic economy and domestic investments abroad is same as net capital inflow in the domestic country, hence the second equation above. Further, if the country's balance of payments (BOP) balances exactly, the surplus in the capital account of its balance of payments (BOP) (= NKI) must equal the deficit in its current account of the BOP (= $Z - X$). For simplicity, if we ignore net transfers, which is a relatively small magnitude, then the deficit in the current account equals net imports of goods and services, which is same as the negative net exports of goods and services, hence equation **(12.1)** above.

Recall from Chapter 2 the definition of domestic saving, which states that domestic saving equals the sum total of private saving and government savings. Recalling further the definitions of private and government savings, equation **(12.1)** can be rewritten as follows:

$$I = [(Y - C - T) + (T - G)] - NX$$

Rearranging the terms and solving for Y gives

$$Y = C + I + G + NX \tag{12.2}$$

Equation **(12.2)** gives the income identity (aggregate demand) in an open economy in contrast to equation **(11.7)** in a closed economy. Incidentally note that, here Y = GDP at market price and T stands for taxes net of transfer payments. Thus, for an open economy, we need functions for exports (X) and imports (Z). Recall from Chapter 7 that exports are a function of the world income (Y^w) and the relative (world versus domestic) price $[(E)(P^w)/P^d]$ and imports are functions of the domestic income (Y) and the relative price. If, for simplicity, we assume these functions as linear, then we have

$$X = X_0 + \alpha Y^w + \beta\left[\frac{(E)(P^w)}{P^d}\right]$$

or, $$X = X_0 + \alpha Y^w + \beta E_r \tag{12.3}$$

and $$Z = Z_0 + \gamma Y + \delta\left[\frac{(E)(P^w)}{P^d}\right]$$

or, $$Z = Z_0 + \gamma Y - \delta E_r \tag{12.4}$$

where, X_0 = autonomous export

Z_0 = autonomous import

E = nominal exchange rate (₹/$)

$[(E)(P^w)/P^d]$ = real exchange rate = E_r

As above in Chapters 4 and 7, the nominal exchange rate (E) and the real exchange rate (E_r) are defined in direct quotation (i.e. number of domestic currency per unit of foreign currency, like rupees per dollar: ₹60 = $ 1). Further, while the domestic price (P^d) is in domestic currency (rupees) the world price (P^w) is in foreign currency (dollars)

Incorporation of these equations (12.2, 12.3 and 12.4) into the Keynesian IS-LM model consisting of equations **(11.1)**, **(11.4)** and **(11.6)** of Chapter 11 would give the new IS equation. Thus, substituting for C from Equation **(11.1)**, for T from equation **(11.4)**, for I from equation **(11.6)**, and for NX (= X — Z) from equations **(12.3)** and **(12.4)** above, in the income identity **(12.2)** above, and assuming $G = G_0$, we get

$$Y = [C_0 + b\,(Y - T_0 - tY)] + [I_0 - d\,i] + G_0 + [(X_0 - Z_0) + \alpha Y^w - \gamma Y + (\beta + \delta)E_r]$$

Solution of the above for Y would give

$$Y = k_1 A_1 - k_1 d(i) + k_1(\beta + \delta)(E_r) \qquad \textbf{(12.5)}$$

where, $A_1 = [C_0 + I_0 + G_0 - bT_0 + X_0 - Z_0 + \alpha Y^w]$

$$k_1 = \frac{1}{1 - b(1-t) + \gamma}$$

Equation **(12.5)** is the equation of the IS curve for an open economy. A comparison of this with the closed economy IS equation (vide equation 11.8 of Chapter 11) would suggest that the open economy autonomous expenditure parameter (k_1) has an additional parameter (γ) and its autonomous expenditure (A_1) has three additional exogenous variables, viz. X_0, Z_0 and Y^w. In the open economy, the autonomous expenditure parameter k_1 varies directly with the marginal propensity to consume (MPC = b), and inversely with the tax rate as well as the marginal propensity to import (MPI = γ). A comparison of this with that of a closed economy (vide Chapter 11) would indicate that the autonomous expenditure parameter is lower in an open economy than in the closed economy, and this is because import is a leakage from the income (export is an injection but it does not depend on domestic income). For example, if MPC (b) = 0.8, marginal tax rate (t) = 0.1 and marginal propensity to import (γ) = 0.1, then

$$k_1 = \left(\frac{1}{1 - 0.8(1-0.1) + 0.1}\right) = 2.63$$

The closed economy autonomous expenditure parameter would equal 3.57 {= 1/[1 – 0.8(1 – 0.1)]}. While the said parameter takes a value of 2.63 in an open economy, it takes a value of 3.57 in a closed economy, *ceteris paribus*. Since the autonomous expenditure multiplier varies directly with the autonomous expenditure parameter (k_1), the effect of autonomous expenditure on income is less in an open economy than in a closed economy. This renders the **fiscal policy less effective in an open economy than in a closed economy**.

A similar comparison of the open economy autonomous expenditure (A_1) with its counterpart closed economy autonomous expenditure (A_0) of Chapter 11 would suggest that the autonomous expenditure in an open economy differs from that in a closed economy, though it is uncertain as to which one is higher than the other. In particular, in the expression for A_1 the last three terms are the specific ones in an open economy which are not there in a closed economy system. Of these three terms, the two, when combined into one, viz. autonomous net export ($X_0 - Z_0$), becomes an additional item of autonomous expenditure, which provides a new source for, as well as a new measure to tame, business cycles. In addition, the fiscal policy produces an additional effect on net export or the current account of balance of payments. To see this, consider a pure expansionary fiscal policy through, say, an increase in government expenditure, *ceteris paribus*. As argued several times earlier, its effect would be an increase in real income and employment, no matter how much. Thus, internally, the economy would be in better shape than before. But, the increase in domestic income would also lead to an increase in imports as per equation **(12.4)**, with no consequence in exports (vide equation **12.3**), resulting in a fall in net export. Thus, while an expansionary fiscal policy would help improve the domestic balance (i.e. reduce unemployment), it would only harm the external balance. Quite the opposite would be the consequences of a purely restrictive fiscal policy. Further, our exports depend positively on the incomes of the rest of the world and accordingly we have the world income as a component of autonomous expenditure (A_1). In view of these twin arguments, it is said that the **prosperity abroad is good for every economy**. Macroeconomics thus suggests that various countries should cooperate rather than compete: "United we win, divided we fall".

Furthermore, the IS equation has a new variable in the real exchange rate (E_r) which was not there in the closed economy IS equation (vide equation **11.8**, Chapter 11). Accordingly, the global economy offers yet another policy tool to cause/counter business cycles, viz., the foreign exchange rate. If the economy is on the fixed exchange rate system or is willing to tamper with the freely fluctuating exchange rate, as most countries currently do, then the exchange rate is a policy tool and could be employed as and when deem appropriate. For example, if RBI devalues rupee, *ceteris paribus*, E_r would increase and thence exports would increase and imports would fall (vide equations **12.3** and **12.4**). In effect, net exports would increase, which, in turn, would boost the aggregate demand and hence income and employment. Quite the opposite would happen if the domestic currency was re-valued. Thus, the exchange rate becomes a tool of affecting the real income and through that to both cause and tame the business cycle. This conclusion is, of course, subject to the price elasticities of exports and imports, and to the Marshall-Lerner condition (vide Chapter 7). Another implication of the exchange rate tool is on the trade/current account deficit. Since the depreciation of the domestic currency causes the real income to increase, which tends to increase our import of goods and services via equation **(12.4)**, with no effect on our exports of goods and services (vide equation **(12.4)**), it tends to widen our current account deficit. Thus, devaluation has a dual effect on the current account balance. One, it increases our net exports via the price effect. Two, it lowers our net exports via the real income effect. Since the two effects work in the opposite directions, the total effect of devaluation on the current account deficit is ambiguous. For a relatively closed economy like India, the price effect would generally dominate. Hence a depreciation of the currency would only reduce the current account deficit, and an appreciation of the same would increase the said deficit.

The above analysis has ignored the reactions of foreign countries to the depreciation of the home currency. Since it inversely affects their current account balance, it is wrong to assume that they would not react. If they do, they would retaliate very soon, if not immediately, and reduce the external value of their currencies in relation to the home currency. In consequence, our gain would be wiped out or at least curtailed to an extent. This may lead to further reactions from our side and counter reactions from them, and the process could ultimately harm rather than do any good to us and all the other competing countries. Since devaluation, as well as the restrictive trade policies attempt to increase domestic aggregate demand at the cost of some other countries demand, they have been termed as the "expenditure switching" as well as the "beggar thy neighbour" policies. Further, these policies tend to restrict imports and thus deprive of their consumption and reduce the supply of goods and services in the economy, which tend to lower the standard of living and aggregate inflation, respectively.

There is an additional factor in the exchange rate policy as a stabilisation tool. This is with regard to its effect on external debt. In case of developing countries like India, external debt is denominated in foreign currency. Thus, when a country's currency depreciates in relation to the currency in which its debt is denominated, the debt, in terms of the home currency, goes up, and vice versa. Further, the interest payments on such debts go up, and that being a part of the current account of the balance of payments, the net exports of goods and services go down and real GDP falls. This, thus, nullifies a part of the positive effect of depreciation on real GDP. Quite the opposite holds in the face of an appreciation of the home currency.

Thus, on the whole, the open economy *IS* equation differs from the *IS* equation of the closed economy in the following three ways:

(a) The autonomous expenditure parameter has a new component, viz. marginal propensity to import, which reduces the magnitude of the said parameter.

(b) The *IS* equation has a new variable, viz. the real exchange rate, which exerts a positive effect on the level of income. This gives an additional reason for the falling *IS* curve. As the domestic interest rate falls, world rate remaining the same, capital tends to flow out of the economy, resulting into increased supply of the domestic currency, causing it to depreciate. The said event would trigger an increase in net exports and thereby an increase in income. For this reason, the open economy *IS* curve would be flatter than the closed economy *IS* curve.

(c) Autonomous expenditure has three new variables, autonomous export, world (or rather rest of the world) income and autonomous imports, the first two tending to increase the said expenditure and the last to decrease the same. Through this, one country's government expenditure and other autonomous expenditures affect the other countries' real income and price: As G goes up, Y goes up; increase in Y leads to increase in domestic import, that is exports of foreign countries go up, and hence, incomes of foreign countries tend to rise.

These suggest that besides the interest rate and the exogenous variables (C_0, T_0, I_0 and G_0), there are autonomous exports, autonomous imports, real exchange rate and world income as the additional determinants of domestic income in an open economy.

Before we move to the next section it is worthwhile to collect together the three sources of international linkages that exist among the open economies in the world:

(a) **Autonomous expenditure multiplier:** Under this, one country's government expenditure and autonomous expenditures affect (via imports) the other countries' real income and price.

(b) **Saving-investment gap:** The gap equals net exports, which equals net investment abroad, called also as net capital outflow (NKO).

(c) **Money supply:** Money supply in one country affects the interest rate and the exchange rate in other countries. As M goes up, *ceteris paribus*, interest rate at home falls, tending to cause capital flight, which, in turn, causes the foreign currency to appreciate and foreign interest rate to fall.

Open Economy LM Equation

The demand for and supply of money functions in the open economy would be similar to the ones in a closed economy. Recalling the LM equation of the closed economy (viz. equation 11.11) from Chapter 11 above, we have

$$Y = \frac{1}{e}\left(\frac{M_0}{P}\right) + \left(\frac{f}{e}\right)i \qquad \textbf{(12.6)}$$

Equation **(12.6)** represents the LM equation in the open (as well as in the closed) economy. The equation suggests that income depends positively on real money balances (which is exogenous, for nominal money is a monetary policy variable and price is assumed as constant in this short-run Mundell—Fleming model), and also positively on the (nominal) interest rate. The other income determinants in the said equation are the two parameters, viz. *e* and *f* which denote the sensitiveness of real money demand to changes in income and interest rate, respectively. It is important to note here that the LM equation does not have the exchange rate and thus the LM curve is independent of the exchange rate.

Open Economy Balance of Payments (BP) Equation

The equilibrium in the balance of payments (BP), which is same as that in the foreign exchange market requires that net exports (= surplus in the current account) must equal net capital outflows (NKO)(= deficit in the capital account):

$$NX = NKO$$

Or, $$NX + NKI = 0 \qquad \textbf{(12.7a)}$$

Incidentally, note that the current account of the balance of payments has three items, viz. NX, net factor income from abroad (NIA) and net transfer payments (NTP) and accordingly, the surplus in it is given by the sum of all these three items. However, NIA and NTP take relatively small magnitudes, and accordingly for simplicity, these items are ignored in equation (12.7a). The NX function is given by the difference between exports and imports equations, viz. equations 12.3 and 12.4 above. Thus,

$$NX = (X_0 - Z_0) + \alpha\, Y^w - \gamma\, Y + (\beta + \delta)\, E_r \qquad \textbf{(12.7b)}$$

Recall that net capital inflows (NKI) varies positively with the difference in the domestic interest rate (i) and the world interest rate (i^w). Hypothesising a linear relationship for simplicity, we have

$$NKI = \lambda\,(i - i^w) \qquad \textbf{(12.7c)}$$

Note that NKI also varies with the changes in the exchange rate. For example, if the domestic currency appreciates, *ceteris paribus*, the returns in dollar terms on dollar investment would increase and thus NKI will increase, and vice versa. For simplicity, this factor has been ignored in function (12.7c). The NKI function could have an intercept term as well but the same has been ignored, again for simplicity. The said term would catch the effect of autonomous capital flows which may happen due to political, social cultural and structural factors. Substitution of the expressions for NX and NKI in equilibrium condition **(12.7a)** above, gives the following:

$$(X_0 - Z_0) + \alpha\, Y^w - \gamma\, Y + (\beta + \delta)\, E_r + \lambda\,(i - i^w) = 0$$

Simplification of the above equation gives,

$$\text{BP equation } Y = \frac{1}{\gamma}\left[X_0 - Z_0 + \alpha Y^w - \lambda i^w\right] + \left(\frac{\lambda}{\gamma}\right) i + \left(\frac{\beta+\delta}{\gamma}\right) E_r \quad \textbf{(12.7)}$$

In this equation, income is a positive function of each of the interest rate and exchange rate. Defining BP curve, also known as the foreign exchange market equilibrium condition (*FE*), as the locus of all possible combinations of income and interest rate (exchange rate) that are consistent with the balance of payments (or foreign exchange market) equilibrium [equation **(12.7)**], we can draw the BP curve either in *Y-i or Y-*E_r axes, for a given value of E_r or *i*, respectively. It would be seen that the **BP curve in *Y* and *i* as well as in *Y* and E_r is upward sloping**. Why? As *Y* goes up, *ceteris paribus* (E_r no change), imports increase with no change in exports, and thus NX falls. Fall in NX must be accompanied with equal increase in NKI for BP equation (12.7a) to hold. Thus, NKI must increase, which could happen only if interest rate goes up. Thus, as *Y* goes up, *i* goes up and vice versa, and accordingly the BP curve in *Y* and *i* slopes upward. To understand the positive relationship between *Y* and E_r when *i* is constant, we must note that NKI cannot change as it depends on *i* only. Thus, when NX falls due to an increase in *Y*, for BP equation to hold good, NX fall must be reversed through a change in E_r only. This would require E_r to increase (depreciate). Accordingly, *Y* and E_r are positively related and the BP curve in *Y* and E_r slopes upward.

Note that the intercept of the BP equation depends positively on autonomous exports and world income, and negatively on autonomous imports, world interest rate and the sensitiveness of imports to world income. These factors are shifters of the BP curve. In addition, as mentioned above, the shifters of this curve would include the autonomous factors for capital flows which have been left out from equation (12.7c) for simplicity. Since the direction of relationships vary and there are no a priori reasons to support either sign for the full intercept term, the intercept term could assume either a positive or a negative value. These factors which affect the intercept are the shifters of the BP curve.

The slope of the BP curve in *Y-i* axes depend positively on the sensitiveness of net capital inflows to domestic interest rate (λ) and negatively on the sensitiveness of imports to world income (γ). In contrast, the slope of the BP equation in $Y - E_r$ axes varies positively with the sensitiveness of exports and imports to the relative price ($\beta + \delta$) and negatively with the sensitiveness of imports to world income (γ). Incidentally, note that the BP equation does not have money supply and thus the BP curve is independent of money supply.

If capital is freely mobile across countries and is homogenous, as assumed in the Mundell-Fleming model, then the arbitrage activities in the capital market would ensure that the two interest rates are equal ($i = i^w$) and consequently, $NKI = 0$. If so, equation (12.7a) reduces to $NX = 0$, i.e., BOP means no surplus or deficit in the current account of BOP. This would be true under free movement of capital and freely floating exchange rate system. Under such a situation, BOP would always balance exactly and so the equation **(12.7)** would become redundant. In other words, under perfect capital mobility, BP curve would be horizontal at $i = i^w$ in $Y - i$ axes. In contrast, if capital is perfectly immobile, BP curve in *Y-i* axes would be vertical at the income level given by the intersection of the IS-LM curves. Under the intermediate situation of imperfect capital mobility, the BP curve in *Y-i* axes would be upward sloping. Further, the greater the mobility of capital, flatter would be the BP curve. These curves are depicted in Figure 12.1.

Note that each of the above BP curves is for a given value of the real exchange rate. Accordingly, it would shift to right if E_r goes up and vice versa. Also, note that above the BP curve in Figure 12.1(a), and to the left of BP curves in Figures 12.1(b) and 12.1(c), there would be surplus in the balance of payments, while the balance of payments would have deficit below and to the right of the respective curves. This is so, for in Figure 12.1(a), above $i > i^w$, NKI would be positive, while $NX = 0$ at all points on the horizontal BP curve. Similarly, for Figures 12.1(b) and 12.1(c), to the left of the curves $Y < Y$ at which $NX = 0$ (i.e. along the BP curves). The low Y would mean less import, which, in turn means $NX > 0$ as X are independent of the domestic income. The BP curve in $Y - E_r$ axes will be horizontal at the fixed E_r under the fixed exchange rate system and it will be upward sloping under the floating exchange rate system.

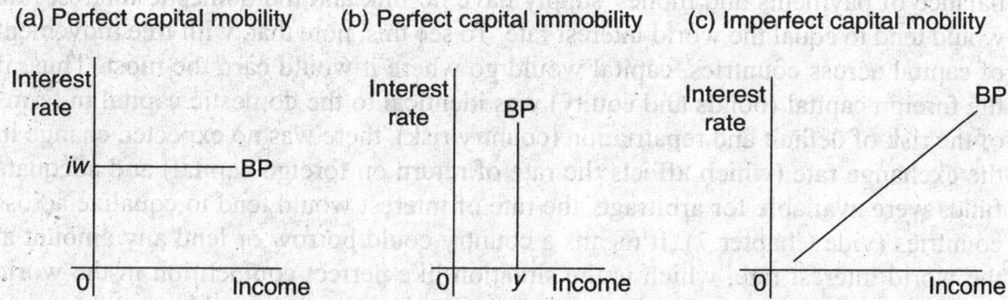

Fig. 12.1 BP curves under Varying Capital Mobility

Recall that the BOP does not have to balance every year; all that is required is that it should be consistent with the sustainability of the current account balance, i.e. it should not violate the **country's inter-temporal budget constraint** (vide Chapter 10,). Thus, the validity of equation (12.7a) is not a requirement of a macroeconomic model. Given the equilibrium values of income, exchange rate/interest rate, the extent of imbalance (deficit/surplus) can be found. However, if a country aims at BOP equilibrium, then the equilibrium requires that each of the IS, LM and BOP equation is valid exactly. This would require that the three (IS, LM and BOP) curves meet at the same point in the income and interest rate/exchange rate/money supply graph. If the interest rate differs across countries, the capital flows into or out of a country would still be finite due to capital controls, limited supply of arbitrage funds and risk aversion resulting in a risk premium that increases with the flow of funds into the home country.

Open Economy IS-LM-BP Equations Combined

The integration of the IS-LM-BP would allow us to explain the determination of income as well as the roles of various stabilisation policies in an open economy. The open economy IS equation **(12.5)**, open economy LM equation **(12.6)** and the BP equation **(12.7)**, constitutes the open economy model. The model has **two endogenous variables**, viz. Y, and (zero) balance in balance of payments (BP = 0) in **three equations**, and so is over-determined. To make it the complete model, we need to recall the **international trilemma,** also called **impossible trinity,** of Chapter 7, which states that the following three systems are incompatible:

(a) Integration
(b) Regulation
(c) Sovereignty

Any two of the above three systems alone are feasible (for explanation, see Chapter 7), and hence one of the three otherwise exogenous variables (viz. interest rate, exchange rate and money supply) becomes an endogenous variable making the IS-LM-BP model complete in three equations and three endogenous variables. The Mundell- Fleming model assumes integration (i.e. no restrictions on the movements of capital—and also goods—across nations). Under this, if a country opts for sovereignty (i.e. control on money supply), it must have the floating exchange rate system (i.e. it gives up the regulation of the exchange rate), and it could **target the money supply**. Under such a choice where a country has integration and floating exchange rate, balance of payments and money supply have no link and the domestic interest rate would tend to equal the world interest rate. To see this, note that, with free movement of capital across countries, capital would go where it would earn the most. Thus, if the foreign capital (bonds and equity) was identical to the domestic capital in terms of the risk of default and repatriation (country risk), there was no expected change in the exchange rate (which affects the rate of return on foreign capital) and adequate funds were available for arbitrage, the rate of interest would tend to equalize across countries (vide Chapter 7). It means a country could borrow or lend any amount at the world interest rate, which is the situation like perfect competition in the world capital market. Under such a scenario, domestic interest rate would equal the world interest rate (i^w):

$$i = i^w \qquad \textbf{(12.8)}$$

Further, if the domestic and foreign capital were not identical, there were restrictions on inflows and outflows of capital, or the funds available for arbitrage were limited, then the domestic interest rate would differ from the world interest rate by the risk premium and other such factors (d):

$$i = i^w + d \qquad \textbf{(12.8a)}$$

In either case, the domestic interest rate becomes an exogenous variable. Accordingly, the open economy-floating exchange rate IS-LM-BP model has exactly three endogenous variables, viz. income, exchange rate and BP (= 0), in three equations, making the model complete. Alternatively, if the integration is chosen to accompany regulation, thus sacrificing sovereignty, the **exchange rate becomes a policy or the target variable** (fixed exchange rate, and hence exogenous) variable and the IS–LM–BP model is once again reduced to three endogenous variables, viz. income, money supply and BP (= 0), in just three equations, making it again the complete model. Note that, under the fixed exchange rate, money supply and BP both are endogenous variables and thus they are related or linked. Thus, in both the floating and the fixed exchange rate systems, the model is complete. Both these scenarios are examined in what follows. Under the third alternative, a country could opt for regulation and sovereignty, and give up integration. In that case, the IS-LM-BP model would have income, interest rate and BP (need not equal zero) as the endogenous variables, and money supply (sovereignty) and exchange rate (regulation) as the exogenous variables. The model will still be complete with three equations in three endogenous variables. The last model, may suffer from the conflict between the internal and external balances/equilibrium. The **internal equilibrium** exists if IS and LM gives $Y = Y_n$ (natural level of income) and **external equilibrium** requires that NX=0 or balance of payments balances.

If we look at the current situation in the world, we can find examples of all three scenarios. For example, USA has free capital flows (integration) and independent monetary policy (sovereignty), and a floating exchange rate system (no regulation). Hong Kong has opted for free capital flows, fixed exchange rate and no independent monetary policy. China has (almost) fixed exchange rate, independent monetary policy and no free capital flows. India has opted for an intermediate situation where she enjoys independent monetary policy and some restrictions both on capital flows as well as on free floating exchange rate; while all large capital flows go through scrutiny and exchange rate is managed to some extent depending on the situation. In what follows, the next two sections will present M-F model of pure open economy under floating and fixed exchange rate system, respectively, which will be followed by the model of restricted open economy model with independent monetary policy.

Distinctions are made between large and small open economies. The former is considered as the one which exerts influence on the world interest rate and exchange rates, and the latter which do not have such implications. By this classification, USA is a large open economy while India is a small open economy.

Open Economy IS-LM-BP Model Under Perfect Capital Mobility and Floating Exchange Rate System

After the break down of the Bretton Woods system in the early 1970s, most countries in the world are operating under the floating exchange rate system. Under such a system, the exchange rate is determined, as seen in Chapter 7 above, through the market. Accordingly, income and exchange rate are the endogenous variables. Further, under the Mundell-Fleming model of perfect capital mobility, the appropriate BP equation is **(12.8)** and not equation **(12.7)**, and thus the domestic interest rate equals the world interest rate, and accordingly, the interest rate is an exogenous variable. Under such a scenario, the open economy IS-LM-BP model is contained in equations **(12.5)**, **(12.6)** and **(12.8)** above. Substitution of the value of the interest rate from equation **(12.8)** into equations **(12.5)** and **(12.6)** gives the open economy, floating exchange rate IS-LM model:

IS equation $$Y = k_1A_1 - k_1d(i^w) + k_1(\beta + \delta)(E_r) \quad \textbf{(12.9)}$$

LM equation $$Y = \frac{1}{e}\left(\frac{M_0}{P}\right) + \left(\frac{f}{e}\right)i^w \quad \textbf{(12.10)}$$

The model has two equations in as many endogenous variables and thus has a unique solution for income and exchange rate. The exogenous variables are fiscal policy G and T, monetary policy M, price level and the world interest rate. A careful look at the above equations would indicate that the LM equation has simply income as the sole endogenous variable. Accordingly, income gets determined by equation **(12.10)** itself. Substitution of the so determined value in equation **(12.9)** would give the equilibrium value for the real exchange rate. From these it would be obvious that in the open economy-floating exchange rate—Mundell–Fleming model, income depends just on two variables, viz. the nominal money supply and the world interest rate, and positively on both. Since neither of the two fiscal instruments is present in the LM equation, which is the sole determinant of income, fiscal policy exerts no influence on income.

> Accordingly, in the open economy—floating exchange rate model, while the monetary policy is fully effective with respect to income (and hence employment), fiscal policy is impotent in this regard. Also, since the exchange rate is absent from the LM equation, the exchange rate has no bearing on the equilibrium level of income and employment.

Given the value of income solely by the LM equation, the IS equation would then determine the magnitude of the exchange rate. A mathematically inclined reader could easily see that the exchange rate (units of domestic currency per unit of the foreign currency) depend negatively on all components of autonomous expenditure (including government expenditure and net autonomous exports) and positively on money supply, among several parameters.

Thus, in the open economy—floating rate model, while an expansionary fiscal policy would appreciate the domestic currency value, an expansionary monetary policy would tend to depreciate the domestic currency value, and vice versa.

The effects of the trade policy can similarly be examined. Trade policy works through tariffs and quotas. These are not present explicitly either in the export or import functions above. However, tariffs tend to raise the domestic price and so they are contained in the real exchange rate. Quotas could affect the domestic price as well as autonomous net exports ($X_0 - Z_0$). Thus, tariffs and quotas could exert influence on net exports through such variables. Since no such variable is present in the LM equation, which happens to be the sole determinate of the income level, the trade policy is impotent with respect to income. Further, since trade policy does not affect income, it would have no bearing on consumption, investment and government expenditure, and hence no effect on net exports as well. This is so because, though an increase in net autonomous exports tends to increase total net exports ($X - Z$), appreciation of the exchange rate (which is the consequence of an increase in autonomous net exports—vide IS equation) tends to reduce net exports by the same amount. It must be noted here that **while the restrictive trade policy aims at reducing the trade deficit, it does not so happen in the open economy floating exchange rate system**.

Trade policy exerts influence on the exchange rate. A tight policy restricts imports and thereby increases net exports, which, in turn, tends to increase net capital inflows, causing arbitrageurs to sell foreign currency for domestic currency, leading to appreciation of the domestic currency. Quite the opposite would happen in the face of a liberal trade policy.

For less mathematically inclined readers, the above conclusions can be drawn through the geometry. The open economy IS and LM curves are drawn in Fig. 12.2. In the figure, both the IS and LM curves are drawn at the fixed world interest rate; BP curve is not shown here but it is simply given as i-i^w, which is implicitly there

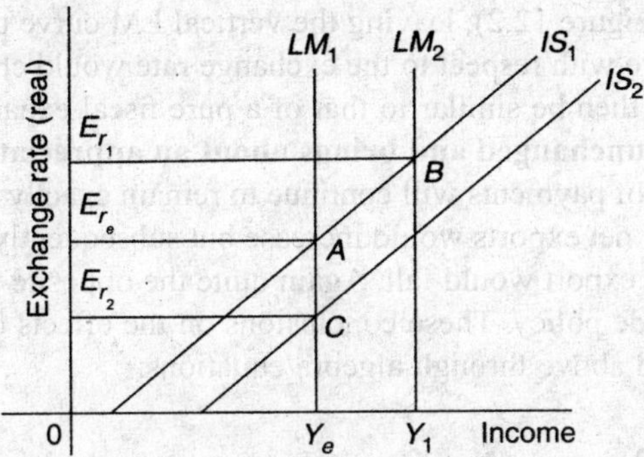

Fig. 12.2 Open Economy IS-LM Model under Floating Exchange Rate

in the model. The IS curve is upward sloping because income and exchange rate in equation **(12.9)** are positively related and the relationship could be rationalized like this. As the real exchange rate increases (depreciates), *ceteris paribus*, net exports increase, and thence income goes up, and vice versa. The LM curve is vertical because the exchange rate does not enter the LM curve. In other words, as noted above, the LM curve determines income level irrespective of the exchange rate. The intersection of these two curves gives the equilibrium levels of income (Y_e) and exchange rate [$(E_r)_e$]. At these equilibrium values, both the goods market and the money market are simultaneously in equilibrium. Now, if money supply goes up, *ceteris paribus*, the intercept of equation **(12.10)** increases and thereby the LM curve shifts to right, i.e. from LM_1 to LM_2. In consequence, the equilibrium moves from point *A* to point *B* in Fig. 12.2, resulting in an increase in income from Y_e to Y_1 and an increase (depreciation) in exchange rate from $(E_r)_e$ to $(E_r)_1$. Thus, an expansionary monetary policy causes an increase in both income and exchange rate. Quite the opposite would hold good in the face of a fall in money supply brought through a dear monetary policy. A corollary of this is that when a country being on the floating exchange rate system, wants to get rid of the twin deficits with which it is currently suffering, it must apply expansionary monetary policy. Similarly, the role of the fiscal policy can be analysed through this graph. For example, if government expenditure increases (or taxes decline or transfer payments increase), *ceteris paribus*, the autonomous variable A_1 in the intercept term of IS equation **(12.9)** would increase, causing a right ward shift in the IS curve, say from IS_1 to IS_2. Since government expenditure is not present in the LM equation, the *LM* curve would remain unchanged. Consequently, the relevant curves would be IS_2 and LM_1, intersecting at point C. In consequence, the exchange rate falls (appreciates) from $(E_r)_e$ to $(E_r)_2$ and the income remains at the earlier level of Y_e. Thus, a fiscal expansion causes the exchange rate to fall (appreciate) with no effect on the level of income. Quite the opposite would happen under a pure fiscal contraction.

The effects of trade policy can also be examined through the above graph; since exchange rate is free floating, policy-makers do not have this as a tool. If tariffs or/and quota are increased (tight trade policy), the net autonomous exports would increase due to restrictions on imports and thus the IS curve would shift to down (from IS_1 to IS_2 in Figure 12.2), leaving the vertical LM curve unchanged. Even the slope of the IS curve with respect to the exchange rate would change. The effects of trade policy would then be similar to that of a pure fiscal expansionary policy, i.e., **leaves the income unchanged and brings about an appreciation of the domestic currency**. Balance of payments will continue to remain exactly balanced as first due to tight trade policy net exports would increase but subsequently due to appreciation of the currency, net export would fall. Again quite the opposite would happen in the face of a liberal trade policy. These conclusions on the effects of policy are exactly the same as derived above through algebra/equations.

An Illustration

To illustrate the working of the fixed price open economy under the floating exchange rate model, we incorporate the open economy features in the fixed price closed economy of Chapter 11. The specific features of the open economy with the floating rate system, as seen above, include exports and imports functions, domestic interest rate equals world interest rate and real exchange rate being the new endogenous variable. The resulting IS-LM equations are equations **(12.9)** and **(12.10)** above. These were obtained using equations 11.1, 11.4 and 11.6 of Chapter 11, and equations 12.2, 12.3 and 12.4 of this chapter. We assume the following values of the various parameters and exogenous variables (we retain the same values for all those of these which were used in Chapter 11 and take values for the new parameters and exogenous variables):

$C_0 = 150$, $I_0 = 210$, $G_0 = 300$, $T_0 = 100$, $M_0 = 800$, $P = 1$, $X_0 = 50$, $Z_0 = 60$, $i^w = 0.05$, $Y^w = 50{,}000$

$b = 0.8$, $t = 0.1$, $d = 100$, $e = 0.4$, $f = 100$, $\alpha = 0.0009$, $\beta = 50$, $\gamma = 0.05$, and $\delta = 40$.

Substituting these values in LM equation **(12.10)** gives

$$Y = \frac{1}{e}\left(\frac{M_0}{P}\right) + \left(\frac{f}{e}\right)i^w$$

$$= 1/0.4\ (800) + (100/0.4)\ (0.05) = 2{,}012.5$$

To get the solution for IS equation, we first find the values of k_1 and A_1:

$$k_1 = \frac{1}{1 - b(1-t) + \gamma} = 1/\{1 - 0.8(1 - 0.1) + 0.05\} = 1/0.33 = 3.03$$

$$A_1 = [C_0 + I_0 + G_0 - bT_0 + X_0 - Z_0 + \alpha Y^w]$$

$$= 150 + 210 + 300 - 0.8(100) + 50 - 60 + 0.0009(50{,}000)$$

$$= 615$$

Substitution of these values in IS equation **(12.9)** yields

$$Y = k_1A_1 - k_1d(i^w) + k_1(\beta + \delta)(E_r)$$

$$= 3.03(615) - 3.03\ (100)(0.05) + 3.03(50 + 40)E_r$$

or, $$Y = 1848.3 + 272.7E_r$$

Putting the value of Y as obtained through LM equation gives

$$2012.5 = 1848.3 + 272.7E_r$$

or, $$E_r = 0.60$$

Thus, the equilibrium values are Y = 2,012.5 and E_r = 0.60. To examine the effects of stabilisation policies, we perform comparative statics.

(a) Suppose government expenditure increases from 300 to 325, *ceteris paribus*. In consequence, LM equation would remain the same (as government expenditure does not affect it) and since income is solely determined by LM equation, income does not change. However, IS equation would change due to change in A_1 from 735 to 760, *ceteris paribus*. The new IS equation would then become

$$Y = 3.03(640) - 3.03(100)(0.05) + 3.03(50 + 40)E_r$$

or, $$Y = 1924.05 + 272.7E_r$$

Putting the value for Y, we get

$$2012.5 = 1924.05 + 272.7E_r$$

or, $$E_r = 0.32$$

A comparison of these equilibrium values with the ones with $G = 300$ suggest that increase in government expenditure, *ceteris paribus*, results into no change in income and a decrease (appreciation) in the real exchange rate. This is consistent with the above explanation.

(b) Suppose money supply increases from 800 to 825, *ceteris paribus*. This would change LM equation to

$$Y = 1/0.4(825) + (100/0.4)(0.05) = 2075$$

IS equation would remain unaffected:

$$Y = 1848.3 + 272.7E_r$$

Putting the new value of Y gives

$$2075 = 1848.3 + 272.7E_r$$

or, $$E_r = 0.83$$

A comparison of these values with those under the initial values of G and M would suggest that a pure expansionary monetary policy leads to an increase in income as well in the real exchange rate (depreciation). This is also in line with the results shown above through algebra and geometry.

Open Economy IS-LM Model Under Perfect Capital Mobility and Fixed Exchange Rate System

As discussed in Chapter 7 above, most countries in the world were under the fixed exchange rate (Bretton Woods) system during 1945 through early 1970s, many countries (including Hong Kong and the group of European countries with common currency-euro) are still on such a system, and many economists/policy-makers are still advocating for countries to move under such a system. Thus, it is important that we analyse the role of stabilisation policies under the fixed exchange rate system as well. The same is attempted in this sub-section.

Under the fixed exchange rate system, the monetary (or any other assigned) authorities decide the exchange rate and that makes the said rate a policy variable, and hence an exogenous variable. Recall that, by virtue of the Impossible Trinity (alternatively called as the International Trilemma), when the exchange rate is regulated and the concerned country is open (integrated with the world), she loses the sovereignty in deciding the quantity of money. This so happens because under the fixed exchange rate, the Central Bank stands ready to buy or sell foreign currencies through domestic currency at a fixed exchange rate. As a foot note, one should note that for the Central Bank to be able to carry on such transactions, it would have to have adequate foreign exchange assets and be ready to add to such a stock to any level. When the Central Bank buys and sells foreign currency at a fixed exchange rate, it leaves the money supply to be determined by the market forces, rendering the money supply an endogenous variable. Thus, the IS-LM-BP model of equations **(12.5)** and **(12.6)** and **(12.8)** then reduces to two endogenous variables, viz. income and money supply, in as many equations; the BP curve is implicitly there through $i = i^w$. The variable real exchange rate (E_r) which is endogenous in equation **(12.9)** becomes exogenous (E_{r0}), and money supply which is exogenous (M_0) in equation **(12.10)** becomes endogenous (M) in this model, and i continues to remain exogenous and equal to i^w due to the assumption of perfect capital mobility. In other words, the three just mentioned equations, get reduced to two following equations:

IS equation $\quad Y = k_1A_1 - k_1d(i^w) + k_1(\beta + \delta)(E_{r0})$ **(12.9a)**

LM equation $\quad Y = \frac{1}{e}\left(\frac{M}{P}\right) + \left(\frac{f}{e}\right)i^w$ **(12.10a)**

The above equations represent the open economy, perfect capital mobility and fixed exchange rate model. Equations (12.9a) and (12.10a) have two endogenous variables, Y and M. In this model, the monetary policy variable is exchange rate (E_{r0}) and the fiscal policy variables are government expenditure (G) and net (net of transfer payments) tax revenue (T). An increase in the exchange rate (i.e. depreciation of domestic currency) would tend to increase net export and thereby the aggregate demand and income level through the IS equation. It would have no effect on income through the LM equation. Thus, on the whole, if RBI devalues the rupee, income would increase.

Also, the money supply would tend to increase through the LM equation, as income rises. Thus, depreciation of the domestic currency would lead to an increase in income and also to an increase in money supply. Quite the opposite would happen when the Central Bank decides to revalue the domestic currency. The process goes through the following sequence:

> RBI devalues the rupee ⇒ net exports go up ⇒ net capital inflows go up ⇒ arbitrageurs sell dollars to the country's Central Bank (RBI) for money at the fixed exchange rate ⇒ domestic money supply goes up.

Similarly, the effects of a pure fiscal policy could be analysed. For example,

> If G goes up, *ceteris paribus*, the intercept term of the IS equation (A_1) would increase, causing an increase in income. Due to this increase in income, the left hand side of the LM equation would increase, for that to balance with its right hand side, money supply must go up (P and i^w are exogenous).

Same results can be obtained through geometry. The geometric version of the IS- LM equations **(12.9a)** and **(12.10a)** above would be as shown in Fig. 12.3 below.

The LM curve starts with a positive value of Y, for the second term in equation **(12.10a)** is positive and it slopes upward because the coefficient of M in that equation is also positive. The IS curve is vertical, for it is independent of M. The intersection of the two curves gives the equilibrium values for money supply and income, viz., M_e and Y_e, respectively. If the Central Bank of the country raises the exchange rate (depreciation), IS curve shifts to the right, LM curve remains unchanged, and the equilibrium moves from point A to point B, resulting into a higher level of income (Y_2) and a higher level of money supply (M_2). Quite the opposite would happen if RBI decides to lower the exchange rate.

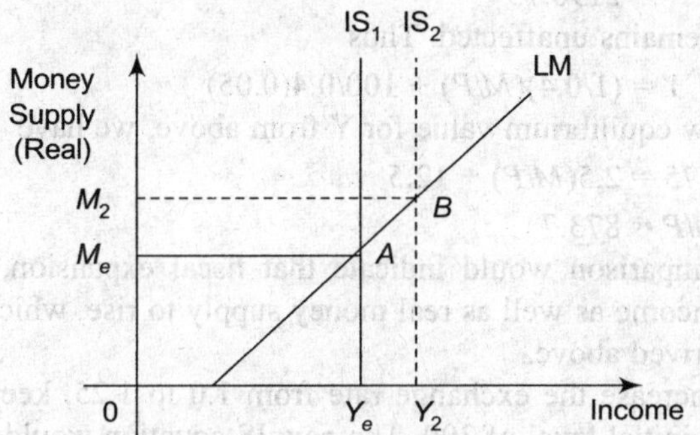

Fig. 12.3 Open Economy IS-LM Model under Fixed Exchange Rate

Similarly, if the government adopts an expansionary fiscal policy, the IS curve shifts to the right, *LM* curve remains unchanged, causing both income and money supply to increase. Under the tight fiscal policy, IS curve shifts to the left, *LM* curve not affected, and accordingly, both income and money supply fall.

If the effects of trade policy are analysed, one would see that a tight trade policy, which would restrict imports or expands net exports, would tend to shift the vertical IS curve to the right and leave the upward sloping LM curve unaffected. In consequence, both **income and money supply would increase**. Quite the opposite would happen if a liberal trade policy was exercised. Under the fixed exchange rate, policy-makers have the exchange rate also as a tool. Thus, if the Central Bank of the country devalues its currency, net export would increase, and thereby IS curve would shift to right with no change in the LM curve. In consequence, each of income and money supply will increase. Balance of payments would remain balanced, as first due to devaluation it worsens but then through increase in income it improves.

An Illustration

In this model, while money supply is an endogenous variable, exchange rate is an exogenous (policy) variable. Accordingly, we do not take M = 800 but assume E_r= 1.0. Under this situation, as suggested above, equations (12.9a) and (12.10a) constitute the model. Putting the assumed values for the various parameters and exogenous variables as before in these equations, we get

IS equation: $Y = 3.03(615) - 3.03(100)(0.05) + 3.03(50 + 40)(1.0)$

or, $Y = 2121$

LM equation: $Y = (1/0.4)(M/P) + 100/0.4(0.05)$

Putting the equilibrium value for Y from above, we have

$$2121 = 2.5(M/P) + 12.5$$

or, $M/P = 843.4$

Going for the comparative statics,

(a) We increase government expenditure from 300 to 325, *ceteris paribus*, the IS equation changes to

$$Y = 3.03(640) - 3.03(100)(0.05) + 3.03(50 + 40)(1.0)$$
$$= 2196.75$$

LM equation remains unaffected. Thus

$$Y = (1/0.4)(M/P) + 100/0.4(0.05)$$

Putting the new equilibrium value for Y from above, we have

$$2196.75 = 2.5(M/P) + 12.5$$

or, $M/P = 873.7$

The pertinent comparison would indicate that fiscal expansion, *ceteris paribus*, causes both the income as well as real money supply to rise, which is consistent to the conclusion arrived above.

(b) We next increase the exchange rate from 1.0 to 1.25, keeping government expenditure at its initial level of 300. The new IS equation would then be

$$Y = 3.03(615) - 3.03(100)(0.05) + 3.03(50 + 40)(1.25)$$

or, $Y = 2189.2$

There is no change in LM equation:

$$Y = (1/0.4)(M/P) + 100/0.4\ (0.05)$$

Putting the new equilibrium value for Y, we get

$$2189.2 = 2.5(M/P) + 12.5$$

or, $M/P = 870.68$

It shows that, due to an increase in the real exchange rate (i.e. depreciation of the domestic currency), *ceteris paribus*, both income as well as money supply increase: increase in E_r from 1.0 to 1.25, *ceteris paribus*, raises income from 2121 to 2189.2 and real money supply from 843.4 to 870.68. It is pertinent to note that the effects of a change in both G and E_r on real income and money supply would simply equal the sum total of the two individual effects.

Open Economy IS-LM-BP Model with Imperfect Capital Mobility, Managed Exchange Rate and Moneatry Sovereignty

An economy which is open but subject to restrictions on capital account, have managed floating exchange rate system and enjoys independence in monetary policy falls between the two extremes of an open economy under the floating exchange rate and a closed economy with independent monetary policy. India falls under such a group. In such economies, the roles of stabilization policies also fall between those of its two extremes. The exact roles depend on the degrees of restrictions on each of capital mobility and free floating of the exchange rate. The more the restrictions, the more the roles will be closer to those under a closed economy (vide Ch. 11); and the less the restrictions, the more close the effectiveness of policies will be to those of an open economy with perfect capital mobility and pure floating exchange rate (vide Ch. 12 above). This means, under such a system, both the fiscal as well as monetary policy would be effective with respect to output (real income) as well as interest rate, though their impacts would be smaller than otherwise. The algebra and geometry would be a mix of the two extreme systems. In particular, the model under the system consists of equations **(12.5)**, **(12.6)** and **(12.7)**. The three endogenous variables are Y, i and BP. The managed exchange rate could be closer to floating rate if the management is carried out rarely and to a small extent only (as in India currently), and it could be closer to the fixed rate if it is frequent and significant (as in China today). Under the former, the exchange rate is largely market determined and hence endogenous in the model, while in the latter case it is basically a policy variable and hence exogenous in a macro-economic model. In the above models, we considered the equilibrium condition of the balance of payments (foreign exchange market) implicitly through the assumption of $i = i^w$. Due to this identity, the interest rate was taken as exogenous and accordingly the equilibrium in the balance of payments was guaranteed, rendering the need for BP equation redundant. While equilibrium in foreign exchange market is not a requirement in short run, in long run no country would like to have persistent deficits or even surplus in its balance of payments. Thus, if capital mobility in and out of the country is imperfect (i.e. i not equal to i^w), the macroeconomic model must not only have the equilibrium conditions in the product and money markets but also in the foreign exchange market. Thus, besides the IS and LM equations/curves we must have the BP equation/curve as well. Accordingly, the geometry would be as in Figure 12.4 below.

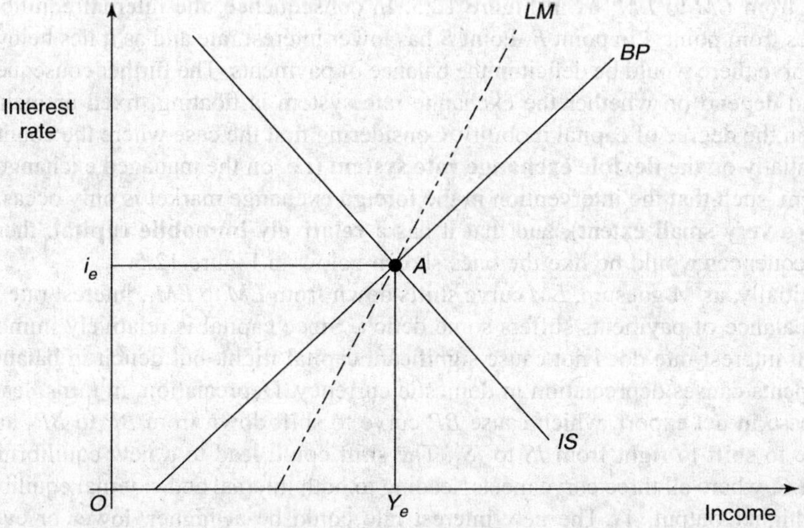

Fig. 12.4 Internal and External Equilibrium

Recall that while the BP curve will be upward sloping, its exact slope depends on the degree of capital mobility (i.e. the magnitude of λ in BP equation **(12.7)**. The greater the mobility, the flatter would be the BP curve and vice versa. The LM curve slopes upward too. The relative slope of the BP and LM curves depends on the degree of capital mobility. In Figure 12.4, BP curve is falter than LM curve, which assumes that capital is relatively mobile. Under the situation where capital is relatively less mobile, LM curve would be falter than BP curve. The economy in Figure 12.4 is at full equilibrium at point A where all the three curves meet. At this point, balance of payments balances exactly, and each of the product market and money market are in equilibrium. Since the model has not incorporated the factor market, it is not sure if the latter market is also in equilibrium (meaning giving full employment or natural rate of unemployment). If by chance, the factor market happens to be in equilibrium as well, then we have the BEST outcomes of both **internal as well as external equilibrium** at point *A*, and the policy-makers can just sit and relax until some shock happens.

Internal and External equilibrium An economy is in internal equilibrium when actual income = potential income (i.e. unemployment=0 or at its natural level) and in external equilibrium when balance of payments balances exactly. Under such a model, shocks to the economy could come from the internal or external sources. The former would include any change in policy variables like government expenditure, taxes, money supply or the exchange rate, or non-policy factors, like business expectations, weather, etc. The latter kind of shocks includes any change in the world income, autonomous part of exports or imports, and autonomous part of capital flows (like structural, political-social-technical-environmental factors).

To understand the effectiveness of the various policies, assume that the country was at both internal as well as external equilibrium at *A* in Figure 12.4. Suppose an internal event, like the Central Bank of the country increases money supply (*M*), *ceteris paribus*, happens. Since *M* affects *LM* curve only, *LM* curve alone shifts to right from *LM* to LM_1 as in Figure 12.5. In consequence, the internal equilibrium moves from point *A* to point *B*. Point *B* has lower interest rate and as it lies below the *BP* curve there would be deficit in the balance of payments. The further consequences would depend on whether the exchange rate system is floating, fixed or managed and on the degree of capital mobility. Considering first the case where the country is essentially on the **flexible exchange rate system** (i.e. on the managed exchange rate system, such that the intervention in the foreign exchange market is only occasional or to a very small extent), and that it has a **relatively immobile capital**, then the consequences would be like the ones shown below in Figure 12.5.

Initially, as M goes up, *LM* curve shifts down from *LM* to LM_1, interest rate falls, and balance of payments suffers some deficit. Since capital is relatively immobile, fall in interest rate does not cause significant capital flight, but deficit in balance of payments causes depreciation in domestic currency. Depreciation, in turns, leads to increase in net export, which cause *BP* curve to shift down from *BP* to BP_1 and *IS* curve to shift to right from *IS* to IS_1. The shift could lead to a new equilibrium at point *C*, where all three curve meets, leading to both internal and external equilibrium at a higher output, Y_1. The new interest rate could be at higher, lower or even at

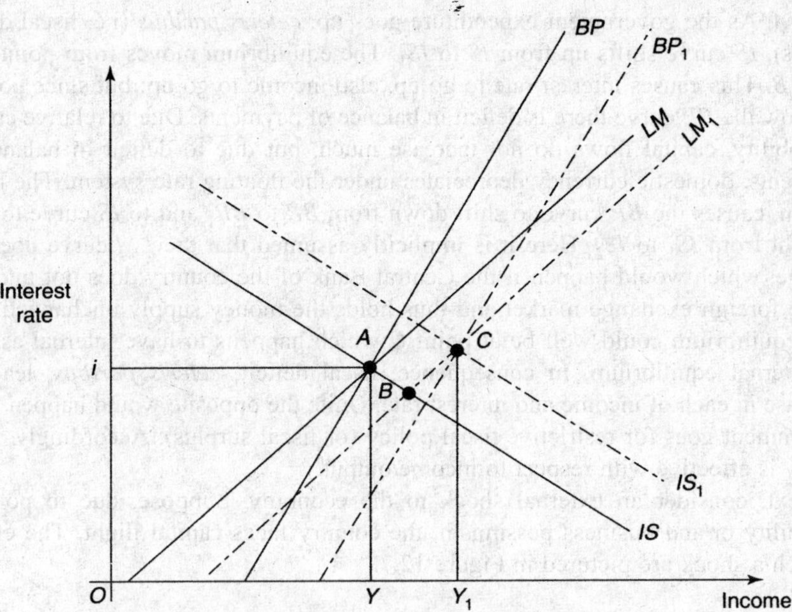

Fig. 12.5 Effects of Expansionary Monetary Policy

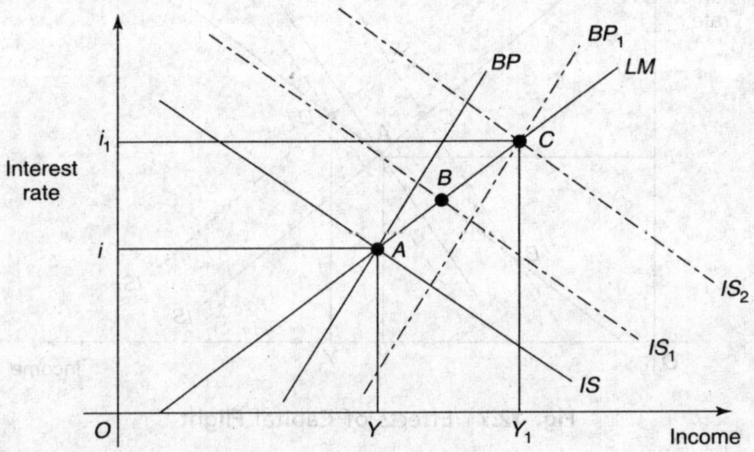

Fig. 12.6 Effects of Expansionary Fiscal Policy

equal level as before, depending on the relative slopes of three curves. In fact, it is possible that the new equilibrium may even not be at a point where all three curves meet and if so there would be disequilibrium either internal or external. In any case, increase in money supply would lead to an increase in income and vice versa. Thus, as before under floating exchange rate, money supply would be effective with respect to income.

To see the role of fiscal policy under essentially floating exchange rate and relative capital immobility, consider Figure 12.6. Let initially, the economy is at point A. As the government expenditure goes up, *ceteris paribus* (i.e. fiscal deficit occurs), IS curve shifts up from IS to IS_1. The equilibrium moves from point A to point B. This causes interest rate to go up, also income to go up; but since point B is below the BP curve there is deficit in balance of payments. Due to relative capital immobility, capital flows do not increase much, but due to deficit in balance of payments, domestic currency depreciates under the floating rate system. The latter, in turn, causes the BP curve to shift down from BP to BP_1 and to IS curve to shift to right from IS_1 to IS_2. Here it is implicitly assumed that the LM curve does not change, which would happen if the Central Bank of the country does not interfere in the foreign exchange market and thus holds the money supply unchanged. The new equilibrium could well be at point C which happens to have internal as well as external equilibrium. In consequence, fiscal deficit, *ceteris paribus*, leads to increase in each of income and interest rate. Quite the opposite would happen if the government goes for restrictive fiscal policy (or fiscal surplus). Accordingly, fiscal policy is effective with respect to income/output.

Next, consider an external shock to the economy. Suppose, due to political instability or/and business pessimism, the country faces capital flight. The effects of such a shock are pictured in Figure 12.7.

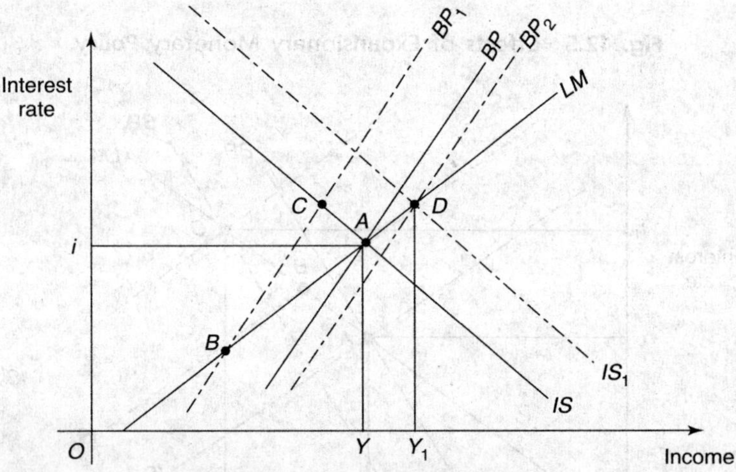

Fig. 12.7 Effects of Capital Flight

The economy begins at a triple intersection point A. The adverse capital flow shock causes a parallel shift of the BP curve to the left from BP to BP_1. In consequence, while the country has internal equilibrium at point A, her external equilibrium is at point B or C. At internal equilibrium point A, the country now has balance of payments deficit. If the exchange rate is flexible, domestic currency would tend to depreciate. This, in turn, would trigger both the IS curve and BP curve to shift to the right, from IS to IS_1 and BP_1 to BP_2, respectively. A new triple equilibrium will occur at a point such as D. At point D, both the income and interest rate are higher than their levels before the adverse capital shock. However, this may or may not be the outcome. The exact result depends on the relative sensitivity of the BP and IS

equations to changes in exchange rate and of the former even to its intercept term, later caused by the capital flight. Thus, it is possible that such an adverse external shock could result in a decrease in income, though interest rate will always tend to increase. In other words, the new triple equilibrium (point *D*) could well be at income below *Y* but at interest rate above *i* (vide Figure 12.7). In particular, if capital outflow and currency depreciation lead to disruptions in domestic financial markets, GDP could well fall during capital flights, *ceteris paribus*.

As hitherto mentioned, the new equilibriums under a change in the money supply or fiscal deficit (government expenditure) or even capital flight could well lead to inconsistency between internal and external equilibrium, i.e. new equilibrium at point *C* in Figures 12.5 and/or 12.6, may occur at some point where just two of the three curves meet instead all three curves meeting there. If so, the country would face the dilemma of a **trade-off between the internal and external equilibrium**. To eliminate such a dilemma, the policy makers would have to use two policy tools as there are dual targets of internal ($U = U_N$) and external equilibrium ($BP = 0$). The two instruments could be the fiscal and monetary policies, or the trade and monetary policy or any other such combination. Towards this, Robert Mundell has proposed an **assignment rule** under which the fiscal policy may be entrusted with the responsibility of internal equilibrium and the monetary policy with the external equilibrium.

Similarly, one could easily analyse the effects of any other internal or external shock on the economy. Also, the effects of all such shocks on the economy under relatively fixed exchange rate or/and relatively high capital mobility could be examined. We leave it to the readers to experiment this.

In concluding this section, we could highlight that the stabilization policies do have a role in taming business cycles under any situation. In general, fiscal and trade policies are more effective (with respect to output/real income) under relatively fixed exchange rate system and relatively less capital mobility, and monetary policy is more effective in opposite situations, i.e. relatively floating exchange rate system and relatively more capital mobility. Incidentally, note also that a large open country like USA possesses power to influence the world interest rate and exchange rates. In such an economy, even if capital is perfectly mobile, its interest rate may not be taken as a constant (fixed) or an exogenous variable.

A Comparative Analysis

At this point it would be useful to compare the roles of the various stabilization policies in a closed economy vis-à-vis that in an open economy. The closed economy model was discussed in Chapter 11. Remember that in a closed economy, the exchange rate is irrelevant, RBI enjoys the freedom to regulate money supply (i.e. money supply is a policy variable) and the interest rate is left to the economy to determine through the market forces (i.e. endogenous). Accordingly, in the closed economy macroeconomic model, the IS and LM curves determine the levels of income and interest rate. In contrast, in an open economy, depending upon the exchange rate regime, the IS-LM curves determine either the levels of income and exchange rate or the levels of income and money supply. The consequences of various policies under various systems are summarised in Table 12.1.

Table 12.1 Effects of Stabilisation Policies under Various Models

			Open Economy			
	Closed Economy		*Floating Foreign Exchange Rate*		*Fixed Foreign Exchange Rate*	
	Impact on					
Policy	*Income*	*Interest Rate*	*Income*	*Exchange Rate**	*Income*	*Money Supply*
Fiscal Expansion	Increase	Increase	None	Decrease	Increase	Increase
Monetary Expansion	Increase	Decrease	Increase	Increase	NA	NA
Devaluation	NA	NA	NA	NA	Increase	Increase
Import Restrictions	NA	NA	None	Decrease	Increase	Increase

NA: Not Applicable.
* Increase in exchange rate here means depreciation of the domestic currency and vice versa.

The table assumes normal values for the various parameters in the various functions giving rise to the corresponding IS-LM model. For example, the coefficients of interest rate in the investment and money demand functions are assumed to be neither zero nor infinity but somewhere in between these extreme values. When either of these two parameters takes a zero or infinite value, as seen above, the policies have significantly different effects. Similarly, the coefficients of the relative price (or the real exchange rate) in the exports and imports functions are assumed to be non-zero and finite, and so on.

Conclusion

Globalisation is the fact of life. This affects the IS equation/curve in terms of some new determinants of income, the LM equation/curve in terms of the distinction between the endogenous and exogenous variables, and gives the macroeconomic model a new equation, called the BP (or foreign exchange market equilibrium) equation with a new endogenous variable, called the imbalance in the balance of payments. Accordingly, the model gets new sources of business cycles and the policy makers get yet another set of tools for countering business cycles. The new tools consist of trade controls (like tariffs and quotas) and the choice between regulating the exchange rate or the money supply and imposing restrictions on international capital mobility (International trilemma). In consequence, depending upon the choice the open well-integrated country makes between the floating exchange rate system and the fixed exchange rate system, one of the two standard policies (viz. monetary and fiscal) become more effective while the other is rendered impotent with regard to output and employment. In particular, countries which opt for a floating rate system, have monetary policy very effective and fiscal policy redundant, while those countries which choose to operate under a fixed exchange rate regime have a rather powerful fiscal policy but an impotent monetary policy. Alternatively, an open country could restrict capital mobility, and then enjoy both the fixed exchange rate as well as the monetary sovereignty. Under such a scenario, both the fiscal and monetary policy would be partially effective, and the extent of their relative effectiveness would vary depending on the degree of capital immobility. Thus, unlike a closed economy (as also in open economy with imperfect capital mobility) where the policy makers have the option of applying either or both the said policies, they have only one of these two tools under a well-integrated open economy. Nevertheless, since trade regulation is a new tool for open economies, they are better off than the closed economy in this respect. Further, if the open economy is on the fixed exchange rate, the exchange rate is another new tool in its command. Thus, it can be concluded that tools do exist to manage business cycles even in open economies.

Hitherto we have assumed fixed prices, which is untenable in the medium and long runs. The next chapter would relax this assumption, and examine the sources and options to policy makers for managing business cycles under the new scenario.

Keywords

Open economy; Mundell-Fleming model; IS-LM-BP curve; Open economy IS equation; Open economy LM equation; Open economy BP equation; Expenditure switching policy; Beggar-thy neighbour policy; External debt; Keynesian/Autonomous expenditure multiplier; Autonomous expenditure; International trilemma; Integration; Regulation; Sovereignty; Fixed-Floating exchange rate system; Perfect capital mobility; Relatively immobile capital; Fiscal-Monetary-Trade policy; Country's inter-temporal budget constraint; Money supply target; Target-Policy variable; Depreciation-Appreciation of currency; Internal-External equilibrium; Target; Instrument; Trade-off between internal and external equilibrium; Assignment rule.

References

1. Brunner Karl, 'The Role of Money and Monetary Policy', *Federal Reserve Bank of St. Louis Review* 71, (September-October, 1989): 4–22.
2. Fleming Marcus, 'Domestic Financial Policies Under Fixed and Under Floating Exchange Rates', IMF Staff Papers 9, (November 1962): 369–379.
3. Friedman Milton, *A Program for Monetary Stability*, (New York: Fordham University Press, 1959).
4. Mundell Robert A., *International Economics*, (New York: Macmillan, 1968).

Review Questions

1. The IS curve is flatter in an open economy than in a closed economy. Explain.
2. Under what conditions the LM curve is vertical in an open economy? Upward sloping? Explain.
3. Under the floating exchange rate system, while the monetary policy is a beggar thy neighbor policy, the fiscal policy is not. Do you agree? Defend your answer.
4. While the monetary policy is stronger, the fiscal policy is weaker with regard to real income and employment in an open economy than in a closed economy. Do you agree? Why or why not?

5. Suppose an open economy is depicted by the following macroeconomic model:

$$Y = C + I + G + NX$$
$$C = 50 + 0.9(Y - T)$$
$$T = 200 + 0.2Y$$
$$I = 300 - 1000(i - p^e)$$
$$NX = 100 - 0.12\ Y - 500\ i$$
$$G = 730$$
$$L/P = 387.5 + 0.1\ Y - 1000\ i$$
$$M = 500$$
$$L = M$$
$$P = 1, p^e = 0$$

The notations have the same meanings as in the text (NX = net exports, p^e = expected inflation).

(a) What is the equation of the IS curve for the economy? Put it in terms of the specific quantitative values that describe the economy.

(b) What is the equation of the LM curve, again with specific values?

(c) Suppose this economy is initially in both the short run and long run, equilibrium in terms of the complete AD–AS model. Find the specific equilibrium values of i, Y, C, I, NX and the budget deficit.

(d) What happens to the equilibrium i, Y and budget deficit if government spending rises by 110 and if money supply rises by 100?

(e) Several economists optimistically feel that the economy could grow out and abolish the budget deficit without raising tax rates or cutting spending. Without any change in the tax rate or government spending, how high would the real output (and income) have to grow in this economy to bring about a balanced government budget?

(f) In what respects, if any, does the economy differ from the classical model, Keynesian cross model and the flexible price but nominal wage rigidity model (Chapter 9)?

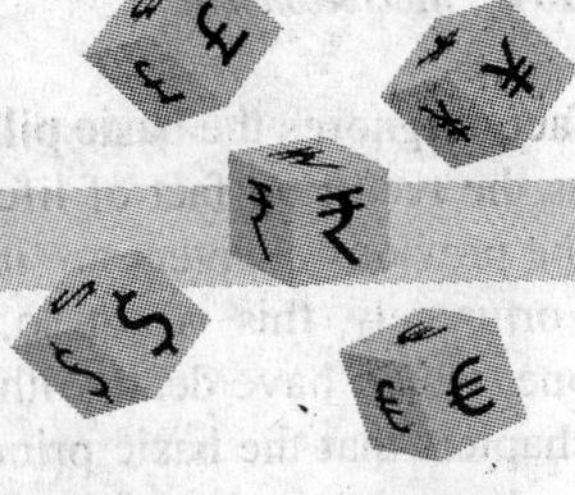

Chapter 13

Keynesian Flexible Price (AD-AS-BP) Model and Policy Debate

Learning Objectives

After reading the chapter you should be able to:

1. Learn the medium term fully fledged model incorporating all significant macroeconomic variables and all the markets, barring the bond market, which is irrelevant as per the Walras' law.
2. Appreciate how the AD curve combines the IS curve and the LM curve, and what makes the AD curve slope downward from left to right.
3. Recognise that the BP curve in output and price axes slopes downward from left to right; and that to the right of it, the balance of payments is in deficit while to the left of it the said balance is in surplus.
4. Appreciate further that the AD curve is flatter than the BP curve, for the former includes consumption and investment spending in addition to the net export, all of which vary negatively with price through the Pigou's wealth effect.
5. Comprehend that while the intersection of the AD and SAS curves give the internal equilibrium ($Y = Y_N$), the *BP* curve alone marks the external equilibrium ($BP = 0$). Understand that under this model, the business cycles can be caused by any events/shocks affecting the AD or AS curves and can be countered through an appropriate stabilisation policy.
6. Grasp the mechanisms through which the fiscal and monetary policy operates.
7. Know the Phillips curve, which describes the famous trade-off between the rate of inflation and the rate of unemployment in the short-run. Also, it gives the menu from which the policy makers could choose any suitable mix of the inflation and unemployment rates and an appropriate stabilisation policy could be designed to attain the same.
8. Get familiarized with the constraints on the effectiveness of the stabilisation policies that come when the economy suffers stagflation, and due to policy lags, fiscal and other constraints.
9. Catch on the role of the supply side economics, the debate between the active (also known as the discretionary) vs. passive (also called rule based) policies, and on the fiscal deficit ceiling rule and the Taylor rule for the fiscal policy and monetary policy, respectively if the rule based policies are implemented.

The Keynesian fixed price (closed/open economy) model assumes that firms supply any quantity of their goods at fixed prices so as to meet with the consumers' demand for them. Since production requires resources (called the factors of production), the assumption implies that the producers of goods and services have an unlimited supply of the factors of production at fixed prices. This is obviously not true and, in fact, it ignores the basic pillar of economics, viz., the **scarcity of resources**, as well as the recurring fact of life, viz. inflation/deflation. This means that the models of the previous chapters are irrelevant in the world of scarcity and inflation/deflation. Fortunately, this is not so, otherwise no text on macroeconomics, including this one, would have dealt with the fixed price models. It will be seen in this and later chapters that the basic principles of the fixed price models, the sources of business cycles and the roles of the fiscal, monetary and trade policies hold good under certain situations, and in particular in the short-run (during which the prices are rigid, even if not fixed) even in the present world characterised by the scarcity of resources. The models of this and subsequent chapters will only add to those principles and thereby provide an extension to earlier theories. Unfortunately, macroeconomic theory is still incomplete and so the policy makers only have a partial kit to regulate the economy in their desired path.

Recall from the last two chapters that the fixed price model has basically two equations in as many endogenous variables. The equations are the IS and LM equations. The endogenous variables are real income (output) and one of the three other variables, viz. interest rate if closed economy, exchange rate if well integrated open economy with floating exchange rate system and money supply if well integrated open economy with fixed exchange rate system. However, if the economy is open and imposes restrictions on capital mobility, then the model has three equations (IS, LM and BP equations) in as many variables, viz. real income, interest rate and exchange rate (if pure floating) or BP imbalance in balance of payments or money supply (if fixed exchange rate). The **IS-LM-BP model** is termed as the very **short-run model** as it is based on the assumption of fixed price. In the medium and **long-run version** model of flexible price, the corresponding model is called the **AD-AS model**. To put it differently, the fixed price model has a horizontal AS curve at the fixed price, and the shape of AD curve, as would be clear soon, depends on whether the economy is closed or open; if open, whether it is on the floating or the fixed exchange rate system; and the degree of restrictions on international capital flows if any. Accordingly, a fixed price model is subject to three significant flaws:

(a) It does not explain how the aggregate price is determined.

(b) Its assumption of fixed price is highly untenable even for the short run. While small increases in the cost of production could be absorbed through reductions in profits or even in incurring some losses, significant cost increases, caused by the factors such as the oil price hikes (of 1973-74, 1979-80, 1990-91, 1999-2000, 2003-04 and so on), all round wage increases (like the ones through the implementation of the 6th Pay Commission's report in India during 2006-07) or even the devaluation of the domestic currency (of 1966, 1991 and 2013 in India), do force upward revisions in all prices. Decreases in indirect tax rates, falls in oil price (like those in 1982-83, 1985-86,1997-98, 2001-02 and so on) and appreciation of the domestic currency (like the one during 2003-04 in India) etc., must similarly induce firms to lower the prices of their products. Further, it was observed that the increases in output through higher factor productivities were accompanied by falls in the unemployment rate and thereby increases in the wage and inflation rates.

(c) It is static, for its very assumption of the fixed price over time. The expectations about the future prices affect the aggregate supply (AS) (vide Chapter 9) and the aggregate demand (AD) through consumption of durable goods and investments (vide Chapters 5 and 6).

The price level happened to be relatively invariant over time (barring the rare cases of hyperinflation in Germany during 1922-23, Hungary during 1945-46 etc.) until around the mid-1960s, and so the fixed price (IS-LM) model was quite acceptable until then. As the price changes turned significant, the above factors turned binding and that led even the Keynesians to give up the contention of the fixed price model. Also, as noted in Chapter 9, A W Phillips came out with his **Phillips curve** in 1958, which gave the missing price equation to the IS-LM model, a version of the aggregate supply function. All these developments have impressed economists to move to the flexible price models which happen to explain the working of the economies much better than the erstwhile fixed price models.

Flexible Price IS-LM Functions

Under the flexible price model, the IS-LM model for a closed economy and IS-LM-BP model for an open economy alone does not determine the level of income. This is because they yield a model which is under-determined, for it has more dependent variables than the number of equations. To see this clearly, we have to go back to each of the IS, LM and BP equations and see how they are affected when the price no longer assumes a fixed magnitude. As would be seen in what follows, the integration of these three functions would give a new function, called the aggregate demand (AD) function, which together with the aggregate supply (AS) function (vide Chapter 9) would determine the level of real income and the general price.

When the price is not fixed, the distinction between the nominal interest rate (i) and the real interest rate ($r = i -$ expected inflation rate (p^e)), and the nominal exchange rate (E) and the real exchange rate $[EP^w/P^d]$ become relevant. The former because the relevant interest rate in the IS equation is the real rate (vide Chapters 5 and 6) and that in the LM equation is the nominal rate (vide Chapter 8). The latter because in an open economy, a change in the domestic price, *ceteris paribus*, exerts influence on net exports which happens to be a component of AD. All this would become obvious in what follows.

Flexible Price IS Function

The IS equation under flexible price would have the domestic price variable as a new determinant of real income. To see this, recall the open economy-fixed price IS equation **(12.5)** of the previous chapter:

$$Y = k_1A_1 - k_1d(i) + k_1(\beta + \delta)(E_r) \quad \textbf{(12.5)}$$

Since the relevant interest rate in the investment function is the real interest rate, we replace the interest rate variable i by its real magnitude (vide the Fisher theory, Chapter 5, where $r = i - P^e$) and insert back the value of the real exchange rate in terms of the nominal exchange rate and the relative inflation rates, and get the relevant IS equation under flexible price:

$$Y = k_1A_1 - k_1d(i - p^e) + k_1(\beta + \delta)[(E)(P^w)/P^d] \quad \textbf{(13.1)}$$

where, P^e = expected inflation rate

In equation **(13.1)**, income depends on price (i.e., the IS curve shifts as the price change) through two sources, viz, price expectations and international trade effects. The former happens via the price expectations theory (vide Chapter 9). The price expectations theory suggests that an increase in price causes the expected price to rise, which lowers the real interest rate, which, in turn, leads to an increase in consumption and investment, and thereby an increase in income. This gives a positive relationship between real income and price. The latter arises from the presence of variable P in the last term of equation **(13.1)**. In a global economy, net exports, which happens to be a component of the aggregate demand, depends negatively on the domestic price and so price is a determinant of income in the IS function. In addition, there are two more factors operating in the IS function which makes income to depend on price. These are hidden in the said function due to simplification. They are called the **Pigou (or the real balance) effect** and the **income redistribution effect**. Recall from Chapters 5 and 6 that each of the consumption and investment expenditures depends on the real money balances (*M/P*) with the consumers and firms, respectively. These have been ignored in the consumption and investment functions (and hence in the IS equation) in the models presented above merely for simplicity. Given this, a decrease in price would lead to an increase in the real balances with consumers and firms, which would result in an increase in consumption and investment expenditures and hence in aggregate demand and income. Quite the opposite would hold in the face of an increase in price. Thus, recognition of the Pigou effect makes the IS curve to have price effecting real income and in a negative way. Also, recall the consumption function of Chapter 5 once again, where we had argued that the marginal propensity to consume (MPC) is higher for the poor than for the rich. If so, a change in income distribution would affect the aggregate consumption expenditure. Also, as would be explained in detail later in Chapter 15, when price increases, creditors lose while debtors gain and since the former are usually richer than the latter, an increase in price causes income distribution to change in favour of the debtors at the expense of the rich. Given that the MPC of the poor is higher than the rich, price increase leads to an increase in consumption and vice versa. Thus, price is an argument in the consumption function and hence in the IS function. However, note that the direction of the relationship is perverse to the Pigou and international trade effects. These are discussed further later under the head, falling AD curve.

In view of the above, in the open economy–flexible price model, income is related to price through the IS function. The relationship between the two variables, though appears ambiguous, is generally negative. This is so because of the four effects noted above, the Pigou effect and international effect, both of which suggest a negative relationship, are generally much stronger than the other two effects (expectations and redistribution), which indicate a negative relationship between the related two variables. Incidentally note that the trade effect is absent in a closed economy.

Flexible Price LM Function

The LM function when the price is flexible would be the same as equation **(12.6)** of the previous chapter:

$$Y = \frac{1}{e}\left(\frac{M_0}{P}\right) + \left(\frac{f}{e}\right)i \quad \textbf{(12.6)}$$

However, there is one difference, i.e., price is now a variable, as contrast to it being a fixed variable hitherto. This renders income to vary with price through yet another source, in addition to the four sources noted above. The new fifth source is referred to as the **Keynes effect** (also known as the **interest rate effect**) in the literature. Under this, as price falls, *ceteris paribus*, real money supply (M_o/P) increases, money demand remaining the same, nominal interest rate falls. The fall in the nominal interest rate would, in general, cause the real interest rate (recall $r = i$ – expected inflation) to fall, for, though both the nominal interest rate as well as the expected inflation rate would fall but usually the fall in the former would outstrip that in the latter. Further, if the real interest rate falls, both consumption and investment would increase, leading income to go up.

Integration of the IS and LM functions give the famous AD function. However, we would derive the latter function separately as it varies across the closed economy, open economy-flexible exchange rate and open economy-fixed exchange rate system.

FLEXIBLE PRICE AD FUNCTION

The AD function/curve gives the menu of the real income (output) and the general price level at each combination of which the product and the money market are simultaneously in equilibrium. The said equation/curve is derived by solving the IS–LM equations simultaneously for income in terms of price and other variables. Recall that the set of the relevant IS–LM equations depends on as to whether the economy is closed or open, and if open, whether on the floating or the fixed exchange rate system. Accordingly, we discuss the same under these three heads.

Closed Economy AD Function

Equation **(11.12)** of Chapter 11, which was obtained as the solution of the IS–LM model (vide equations **11.8** and **11.11**, Chapter **11**) for income, denotes the AD equation for the closed economy, if we ignore the distinction between the nominal and real interest rate. However, the said distinction is relevant under flexible price. Recognition of this requires us to substitute the IS equation **(11.8)** of Chapter 11 by the following:

$$Y = kA_0 - kd(i - p^e) \quad \textbf{(13.2)}$$

where, the notations have the same meaning as above and in Chapter 11 except that the interest rate (i) is in nominal term now. The LM equation remains the same as equation **(11.11)** in Chapter 11.

$$Y = \frac{1}{e}\left(\frac{M_0}{P}\right) + \left(\frac{f}{e}\right)i \quad \textbf{(11.11)}$$

The above two equations constitute the closed economy flexible price IS–LM model. The model has two endogenous variables Y and i and can be solved uniquely. The solution for Y would give the equation of the AD function. The said function would have a negative relationship between income and price. This is partly because in equation **(11.11)**, Y and P are negatively related. The other part of the reason is silent as the Pigou (real balance) and income redistribution effects are left out from equation **(13.2)** for simplicity, as suggested above. Recall that the perverse role of expected inflation (under the adaptive or rational expectations theory) through the IS equation would be weaker than the role of price through the LM equation, Pigou effect and redistribution effect. The AD function would further indicate that income varies directly with autonomous expenditure including the government expenditure and nominal money supply. Further, the solution would suggest that the position (intercept) of the AD curve in a closed economy depends positively on (i.e., the curve shifts upward with an increase in) the:

(a) autonomous expenditure A_0
(b) autonomous expenditure parameter k
(c) interest sensitiveness of the money demand (f)

and negatively on (i.e., the curve shifts downward with an increase in) the

(d) interest sensitiveness of investment spending (d)
(e) income sensitiveness of money demand (e)

The slope of the AD curve depends on one autonomous variable (money supply: M_0) and four parameters (d, e, f and k). The larger the money supply, the interest sensitiveness of investment (d) and the autonomous expenditure parameter (k), and the smaller the income sensitiveness of the money demand (e) and the interest sensitiveness of money demand (f), the flatter the AD curve is. However, since the parameters' values change, if at all, only marginally over time, the major determinant of the position is the autonomous spending and of the slope, the money supply.

The above way of describing the AD curve should be easy for readers proficient in mathematics. For the others, the geometrical explanation may be more suitable. Incorporating the Pigou and redistribution effects, the IS curve would shift to the right as price falls and vice versa. Thus, we have a family of the IS curves, one for each price levell.[1] Similarly, the position of the LM curve varies with the price level. In particular, equation **(11.11)** above, which represents the LM curve, implies that the LM curve shifts downward as price falls, and vice versa. Thus, as there is a family of the IS curves, there is also a family of the LM curves, one for each price level. The same are plotted in Fig. 13.1.

In Figure 13.1, the upper part shows the IS curves and the LM curves for two different price levels: $P_0 > P_1$. Corresponding to two prices, there are two equilibrium positions A and B, where the product and money markets are simultaneously in equilibrium. Thus, other things remaining the same,

if $P = P_0$, $Y = Y_n$
if $P = P_1$, $Y = Y_1$, and so on

The lower part of Fig. 13.1 plots the above points on the income-price axes, and joining the resultant points gives the AD curve. It indicates the set of maximum prices the buyers of the GDP would pay for the corresponding quantities. Incidentally, note

[1] The Pigou effect, which incorporates M/P in the consumption and investment functions, is ignored here. If the Pigou effect was considered, the *IS* curve would shift up with the fall in the price and down with the rise in the price, making the *AD* curve flatter than otherwise.

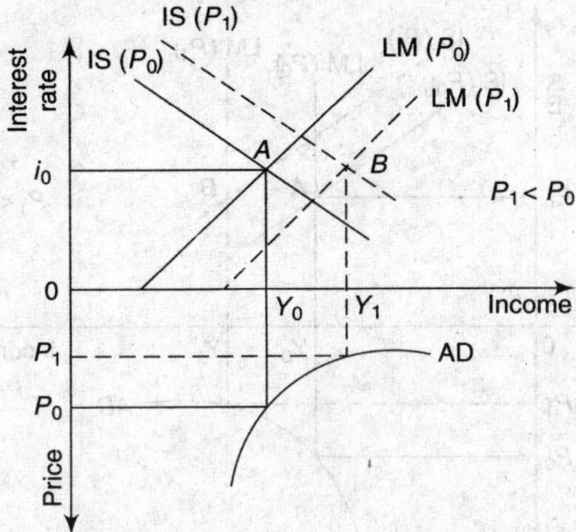

Fig. 13.1 Derivation of AD Curve for a Closed Economy

that the AD curve would be non-linear even if the IS and LM curves were linear (vide equation 11.12, Chapter 11). As expected, the AD curve is downward sloping. Why? The reasons are given later towards the end of this section.

Open Economy—Floating Exchange Rate AD Function

For an open economy, the relevant IS-LM equations vary with the exchange rate system the country has. If the concerned economy were on the floating rate, the said equations would be **(12.9)** and **(12.10)** of Chapter 12 above. Modifying these for the flexible price, we have:

IS equation $$Y = k_1A_1 - k_1d(i^w - p^e) + k_1(\beta + \delta)[(E)(P^w)/P^d] \qquad \textbf{(13.3)}$$

LM equation $$Y = \frac{1}{e}\left(\frac{M_0}{P}\right) + \left(\frac{f}{e}\right)i^w \qquad \textbf{(12.10)}$$

The two equations have three endogenous variables, viz. Y, P and E (nominal exchange rate). The three equation model could be solved to remove one endogenous variable and thus if E is removed, we would have one equation in two endogenous variables, viz. Y and P. The resulting equation would be the equation of the AD curve. Since the equations are non-linear, the algebra would be complicated and hence the solution into the AD equation is not included here. However, it must be noted that the relationship between Y and P would be negative because in both the equations Y and P are negatively related. For example, as P (domestic price) falls, net exports increase and thus Y goes up under the IS equation. Also, recall, there are real balance and redistribution effects which are silent in the above IS function, which further support the negative relationship between Y and P. In the LM equation, as P falls real money supply goes up and hence Y goes up, and vice versa.

The derivation and shape of the AD curve can be demonstrated through the geometry as in Figure 13.2:

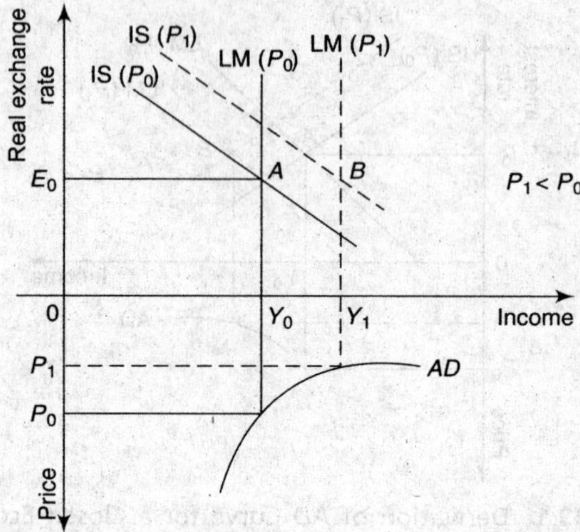

Fig. 13.2 Derivation of the AD Curve for an Open Economy under Floating Exchange Rate

As in Fig. 13.1 above, the upper portion gives the IS and LM curves, and the lower portion the AD curve. The IS equation is in *Y, i, E* and *P.* The said curve is drawn in Y and real E axes, and thus the IS curve varies with *i* and *P*. The lower the *P*, the higher is the IS curve. The figure above has two IS curves, one for each price level. The LM equation is in Y and *P*, and it has no real *E*. Thus, in *Y* and real *E* axes, it is vertical at a given *Y* and it shifts as *P* changes. The lower the *P*, the higher is *Y*, *ceteris paribus*. Accordingly, as price falls, the LM curve shifts to the right. There are two LM curves, one for each price level in the above figure. The IS and LM curves together determines *Y* and real *E* for a given *P*. Thus,

if, $P = P_0$, $Y = Y_n$,

and if, $P = P_1$, $Y = Y_1$, and so on.

Plotting the above two points on the lower part of the figure in *Y* and *P* axes, gives the AD curve, as shown in the graph. As expected, the AD curve slopes downward. Why? The reasons are discussed later in this section. Since the LM equation/curve is the key determinate of *Y*, nominal money supply has a positive impact on *Y* while government expenditure has no effect.

Open Economy—Fixed Exchange Rate AD Function

For an open economy with fixed exchange rate system, the IS-LM equations are given by equations (12.9a) and (12.10a) of Chapter 12. These when modified for the flexible price become:

IS equation $Y = k_1A_1 - k_1d(i^w - p^e) + k_1(\beta + \delta)[(E_0)(P^w)/P^d]$ **(13.4)**

LM equation $Y = 1/e(M/P) + (f/e)i^w$ **(13.5)**

In this model, endogenous variables are *Y, P* and *M* (nominal money supply). While the nominal exchange rate is now fixed at E_a exogenously, the real exchange rate depends on the domestic price level (besides the foreign price level), which is endogenous. The two-equation model in three endogenous variables can be reduced to one equation model in two endogenous variables by eliminating one of the endogenous variables. Thus, if M is eliminated, we would have an equation in Y and P, among other exogenous variables and parameters. The so obtained equation would be the AD equation for an open economy—fixed exchange rate system. In this equation, Y and P would be inversely related and accordingly the resulting AD curve would be falling. The relationship would be negative for the same reasons (viz. in both the equations Y and P are negatively related) as for the AD equation under the open economy-floating exchange rate system. As before, the two equations are non-linear, making the algebra complicated and hence the solution of the IS-LM model into AD equation is not provided here. However, geometric derivation of the AD curve is illustrated in Fig. 13.3.

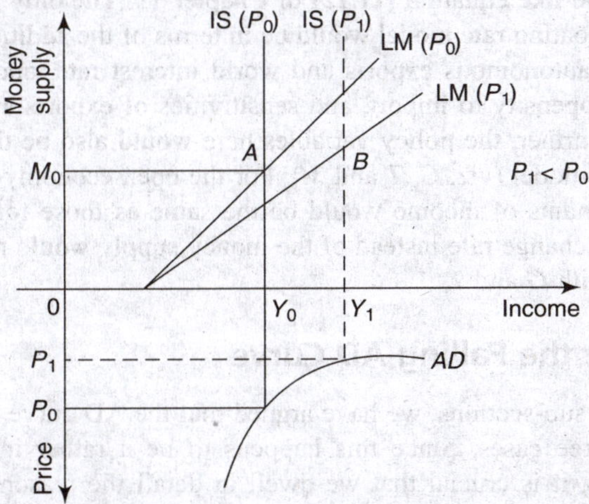

Fig. 13.3 Derivation of the AD Curve for an Open Economy under Fixed Exchange Rate

As before, the upper part of the graph shows the IS and LM curves and the lower portion the AD curve. The axes for the IS-LM curves are income and nominal money supply; and for the AD curve, as before, the income and price. Since the IS equation does not have 'money' variable, it is independent of the quantity of money supply, and hence it is a vertical line at a given level of income. However, the equation has the price as a variable and hence in the Y-M axes, the IS curve shifts as the price changes. Since P affects Y in the IS equation negatively, the IS curve shifts to the right as the price falls. The LM equation reveals a positive relationship between Y and M, and accordingly the LM curve slopes upward in Y and M axes. Further, since P affects the slope of the LM curve negatively, the LM curve gets flatter as P falls, and vice versa. The intersection of the IS and LM for a given price, gives the equilibrium level of Y and M. Thus,

if, $P = P_o$, $Y = Y_o$,

and *if*, $P = P_1$, $Y = Y_1$, and so on.

Joining the relevant points on the lower part of the graph gives the AD curve. Since the IS curve is the key factor in the determination of income, government expenditure and the nominal exchange rate (both of which are present in the IS equation but neither is present in the LM equation) play the dominant role in the size of income. As expected, the curve once again slopes downward. Why?

From the above discussion it is clear that the AD equation/curve is obtained by solving the IS and LM equations for Y in terms of P and other variables. While the IS equation differs significantly across closed and open economy, the LM equation is the same in two cases. In all cases, these two equations determine income but the other dependent variable varies across the model. In consequence, the algebraic solution of the IS-LM equations gives income, in terms of the policy variables (like G, T and M), non-policy variables and parameters. For a closed economy, the solution would be like equation **(11.12)** of Chapter 11. The only difference for the open economy-floating rate model would be in terms of the additional determinates of income, like autonomous exports and world interest rate, and new parameters like marginal propensity to import, and sensitivities of exports and imports to the exchange rate. Further, the policy variables here would also be the same as in the closed economy model (viz. G, T and M). For the open economy-fixed rate model, the new determinants of income would be the same as those for the floating rate model but the exchange rate instead of the money supply would now be the policy variable along with G and T.

Reasons for the Falling AD Curve

In the foregoing sub-sections, we have argued that the AD curve slopes downward under all the three cases. Since this happens to be a rather important curve in macroeconomics, it is crucial that we dwell in detail the reasons for it being so, even at the cost of some repetition. At the outset, let us note that there are a total of four factors that affect the shape of the AD curve in a closed economy and that there is an additional factor, viz. international trade affect, for an open economy. It is because of three of these five factors that the said curve slopes downward and the other two factors support its upward slope.

(a) Keynes (interest rate) Effect As the aggregate price falls, *ceteris paribus*, the real money supply (M/P) increases; the demand for real money (L/P) remaining the same, the nominal interest rate (i) falls. Further, a fall in price lowers the expected inflation (p^e) through the adaptive expectations theory. Since the real interest rate (r) = $i - p^e$ (vide Fisher's theory), and since a fall in price causes a fall in both i and p^e, the effect of a fall in price on the real interest rate is ambiguous. However, in general, the expectations affect is relatively weak and hence a fall in price brings about a fall in the real interest rate as well. Further, as the real interest rate falls, the investment spending (and even personal consumption of durable goods) increases, and hence the aggregate demand increases. Thus, as price falls, AD increases and vice versa. This is true in a closed economy as well as in a large open economy where the domestic interest rate is an endogenous variable.

(b) Pigou (real balance or wealth) Effect As the general price falls, *ceteris paribus*, the real money balances (M/P) with households and firms increase, which is tantamount to an increase in each group's real wealth. Further, as the wealth of the two sectors in the economy goes up, personal consumption and investment spending tend to rise. Both of these happen to be components of total spending and hence an increase in each of them leads to an increase in aggregate demand. Accordingly, the AD curve with the Pigou effect would be flatter than the one without it.

(c) International Trade (exchange rate) Effect As the domestic price falls, the world price staying constant, the real exchange rate depreciates and thereby exports rise and imports fall, resulting in an increase in net export. Since net export is a component of aggregate demand, increase in net export leads to an increase in aggregate demand. Similarly, an increase in domestic price would tend to appreciate the exchange rate and reduce net exports and thereby reduce the aggregate demand. Accordingly, the AD curve would be flatter for an open economy as compared to a closed economy.

Since all the three effects work in the same direction, a fall in the aggregate price leads to an increase in aggregate demand and vice versa. Hence, the AD curve slopes downward from left to right.

Expectation and Redistribution Effects The above analysis has ignored two other effects of the price change on the aggregate demand, viz., expectations effect and redistribution effect. Under the former, a fall in the price might cause expectations of further falls (vide the adaptive expectations theory, Chapter 9), which would induce consumers to postpone the purchase of durable goods (like furniture, vehicles, kitchen gadgets etc.) and even investments in housing. If so, the AD would fall, and given the AS, the real income would fall as well. Thus, a fall in price tends to lower real income through the expectations effect, and vice versa. For simplicity, we have ignored the expected price from the consumption and investment functions while deriving the IS function. Under the latter (redistribution effect), a price fall would change the income distribution in favour of the creditors. For example, if P falls from, say, 1 to 0.9, the real value of ₹100 of loan would increase to 100/0.9 = 111.1, which would make the creditors richer and debtors poorer. Further, in general, creditors are richer than the debtors. The theory of consumption states that the marginal propensity to consume (MPC) is lower the richer the consumer is. Thus, as the price falls, the rich gets richer and the poor gets poorer, and since the MPC is lower for the rich than for the poor, overall consumption falls. Quite the opposite happens in the face of an increase in the general price. Since consumption is a component of AD, the above implies that a fall in price leads to a fall in AD, and vice versa. It is thus seen that both the expectations as well as the redistribution effects operate counter to the above Keynes', Pigou and international trade effects. However, these two later effects are quite minor compared to the above effects and hence the AD curve is falling.

> It is interesting to note that since the Keynes, Pigou and international trade effects are dominant ones and they reinforce each other in rationalising the downward slope of the AD curve, they are referred to as the **stabilising effects of inflation**. In contrast, the expectations and redistribution effects are known as the corresponding **destabilising effects**.

It will be interesting here to compare the reasons for the falling AD curve (macro) with those of the falling industry (micro) demand curve. Recall that the AD curve is falling primarily due to the Keynes' and Pigou effects. Further, both these effects work through the changes in (real) money supply and, thus, the money supply is the vehicle for a falling macro demand curve. In contrast, microeconomic theory suggests that the law of demand holds basically due to the substitution effect. That is, when the price of, say, car falls, ceteris paribus, the car becomes relatively cheaper than its substitutes (like the two wheelers) and thus rational consumers substitute cars for scooters, and accordingly the demand for cars goes up. The opposite holds when the price of car goes up. Hence, the micro demand curve is falling. Note that there is one more reason for this law and that comes from the other component of the price effect, called the income effect. According to this, as the price of a product falls, consumers' real income goes up and if the product is a superior one, the demand goes up, and vice versa. For inferior goods, the income effect works in the opposite direction. Thus, the income effect reinforces the substitution effect in the case of superior goods and the former partly nullifies (partly because, in general, the substitution effect is much stronger than the income effect) the latter in the case of inferior goods. Thus, the reasons for the falling macro demand curve and the falling micro demand curve are totally in variance.

It is instructive to note that the AD curve would not be a falling one under certain extreme values of some parameters. For example, if the demand for money were perfectly interest elastic, i.e, liquidity trap case ($f = cc$) or if the investment were perfectly interest inelastic ($d = 0$), the closed economy AD curve would be vertical at some level of real income. This is apparent from equation **(11.12)**, Chapter 11. Substitution of either $f = \infty$ or $d = 0$ in the said equation would transform the equation to $Y = k A_0$, and both k and A_0 are constants. Similarly, the AD curve would be horizontal at some level of P if either the parameter f (interest sensitiveness of money demand) was zero or the parameter d (interest sensitiveness of investment) was infinity. Since such extreme values of the parameters are rarely true, the AD curve is taken as a falling one only. Further, even if both the IS and LM curves were linear, the AD curve would be non-linear such that it gets flatter as the price falls (or convex to the output axis).

Flexible Price AS Function

Under all the three versions of the flexible price system, the price is a variable and thus equation **(11.12)**, or its alternative, no longer remains the sole determinant of the real income; it rather gives the equation of the AD function. In other words, the IS-LM model is now incomplete as it has one more endogenous variable P and that makes the number of endogenous variables (Y and P) exceed the number of independent equations (= 1).

We need another curve in the income-price axes to determine the income (and price level). This missing link to the IS-LM model is provided by the AS function. As discussed in Chapter 9, the shape of the AS function depends upon as to whether there is the wage-price flexibility or something else. Since the fixed price assumption is unreasonable even in the short run, we have already ruled out the horizontal AS curve. The classical assumption of the flexible wage-price is also not acceptable as it fails to explain the existence of unemployment, which was witnessed in a significant way during the Great Depression and is found to exist in all countries most of the time. Thus, the only options left are the assumptions of either a mix of flexible and sticky prices, the fixed nominal wage rate or the imperfect information in the short run, each of which gives an upward sloping AS curve in the short run. Recall from Chapter 9 that the SAS curve is upward sloping because, as the general price rises, the nominal wage rate remaining fixed, the real wage rate goes down, which induces firms to hire more labour (workers do supply more labour until the full employment is hit because they are bound by nominal wage rate contracts), which leads to an increase in output, and vice versa. Because of the imperfect information, firms think that the prices of only their own products have gone up and, thus, their profit motive induces them to raise their productions. Workers are happy to supply the additional work force as they are unaware of the price increase (Friedman's fooling of workers' Model) or because their real wage has gone up through a little increase in their nominal wage (Lucas's information barrier model). The AS equation (expectations augmented) would thus be like equation **(9.11)** Chapter 9:

$$Y = Y_n + \alpha(P - P^e) \qquad \textbf{(9.11)}$$

Rearranging the terms and adding the price of raw materials (P_R), we get

$$P = P^e + \frac{1}{\alpha}(Y - Y_n) + P_R \qquad \textbf{(13.5a)}$$

which gives the upward sloping AS curve, for the given values of P^e, Y_n *and* P_R. The Keynesian model does not recognise the role of price expectations (P^e) in the AS function and, accordingly, the same would be kept silent in this chapter; but would be considered in the next one.

Flexible Price BP Function

Recall that in an open economy, every country has a balance of payments equation, which though need not balance year to year, must balance over long-run. Recalling it from the previous chapter, we have

$$\text{BP equation} \quad Y = \frac{1}{\gamma}[X_0 - Z_0 + \alpha Yw - \lambda i^w] + \frac{\lambda}{\gamma} i + \left(\frac{\beta + \delta}{\gamma}\right) E_r \qquad \textbf{(12.7)}$$

Substituting for E_r in terms of nominal exchange rate and prices, we get

$$\text{BP equation} \quad Y = \frac{1}{\gamma}[X_0 - Z_0 + aYw - \lambda i^w] + \frac{\lambda}{\gamma} i + \frac{\beta + \delta}{\gamma}\left(\frac{E\,P^w}{P^d}\right) \qquad \textbf{(13.6)}$$

Equation (13.6) contains the domestic as well as the world price, and it shows that balance of payments depends positively on the world price and negatively on the domestic price, among other variables.

Flexible Price AD-AS Model

Recall that the balance of payments must balance in the long run but need not be so in the short run. Further, business cycles and stabilization policies are generally concerned with short term fluctuations. Accordingly, concentrating first on the internal equilibrium, we ignore the external equilibrium and thus deal with the AD-AS model and leave the foreign exchange equilibrium BP equation. Figure 13.4 provides the AD and AS curves in their normal shapes.[2]

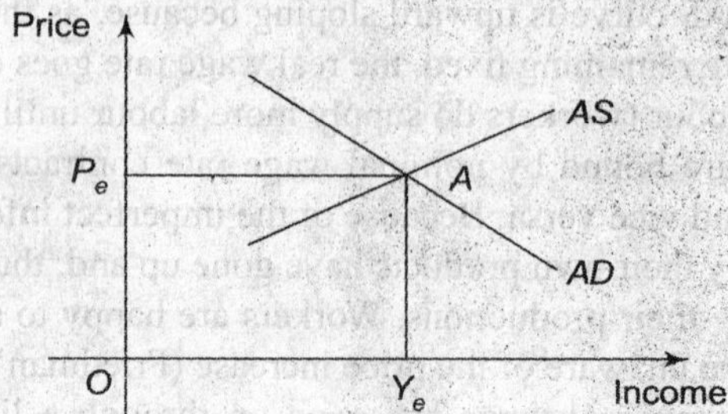

Fig. 13.4 AD-AS Curves Under Flexible Price

The point of intersection of the AD and AS curves (A) denotes the equilibrium both in the product and money markets and, therefore, the corresponding levels of income and price constitute the solution of the model. Accordingly, Y_e is the equilibrium real income and P_e, the equilibrium price. However, one is not sure if Y_e happens to be at full or natural employment level or whether or not the factor market is in equilibrium. If Y_e coincides with the full or natural level of employment, then the economy is at internal equilibrium and we have the classical result. However, the above model could well yield an income level that is below the full employment output. If so, we get an under-full employment level of income, which could explain the Great Depression. In the event of $Y_n > Y_F$, we have an overheated economy, where the demand for goods and services (Y_n) exceed the capacity to produce (Y_F) them. Under such a situation, the factors' supplies are beyond their full employment levels and that could happen due to over exploitation of the fixed capital (plant, structure and equipments) and/or overtime working of workers (substitution of labour for leisure), both of which are feasible in the short run only and would result in an increase in the cost of production. Thus, the AD-AS price flexibility model provides an explanation of all such possibilities without the unreasonable assumption of price rigidity. Further, note that in this model, income and price are determined simultaneously by the AD, and AS functions; unlike the classical model where the income is determined by the supply side and the price by the demand side; and also unlike the fixed price model, where the income is set by the demand side and the price by the prior contract between firms and workers.

Economic Fluctuations and Stabilisation Policies

In the flexible price AD-AS model, economic fluctuations could arise from either the demand or the supply side. Thus, any factor that exerts an influence on the shape of the AD curve or the AS curve could cause instability in the economy. The factors

[2] The *AD* and *AS* curves are non-linear; for simplicity, they are assumed linear in the graphs illustrated in this chapter.

governing the AD curve are discussed in the previous section and those governing the AS curve in Chapter 9. To highlight a few, the significant factors for both curves are analysed below.

What effects AD curve depend on whether the economy is closed or open and if open whether on the floating or the fixed exchange rate system. Recall that in the closed economy, autonomous expenditure happens to be the major determinant of the intercept and the nominal money supply of the slope of the AD curve (vide Equation **11.12**, Chapter 11). The former consists of the autonomous consumption, autonomous investment, autonomous government expenditure and (minus) autonomous taxes. An increase in any one of them (barring autonomous taxes, which must decrease), *ceteris paribus*, shifts the AD curve parallel to the right (outward) and a fall in any of them to the left (inward). In consequence, the real income and price change are illustrated below in parts A and B, Fig. 13.5.

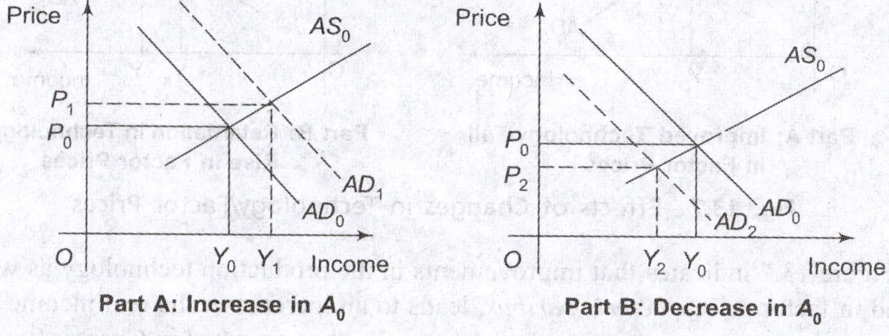

Fig. 13.5 Effects of Changes in Autonomous Expenditure (A_0)

AD_o and AS_o represent the initial AD and AS curves; AD_1, the AD curve after the autonomous expenditure has increased; and AD_2, the AD curve after the autonomous expenditure has decreased, *ceteris paribus*. In this chapter, various supply curves are drawn upward sloping, which, as explained in Chapter 9, represents **short run supply curves,** for in the long-run, supply curve is vertical at the full employment (or natural level of employment) level of output. The graphs clearly show that an increase in the autonomous expenditure, *ceteris paribus*, leads to an increase in both real income and price, and vice versa.

A change in the money supply under the closed economy causes a parallel shift in the LM curve and a non-parallel shift in the AD curve (recall that the money supply affects the slope and not the intercept of the AD curve; vide equation **(11.12)**, Chapter 11) as shown in Fig. 13.6.

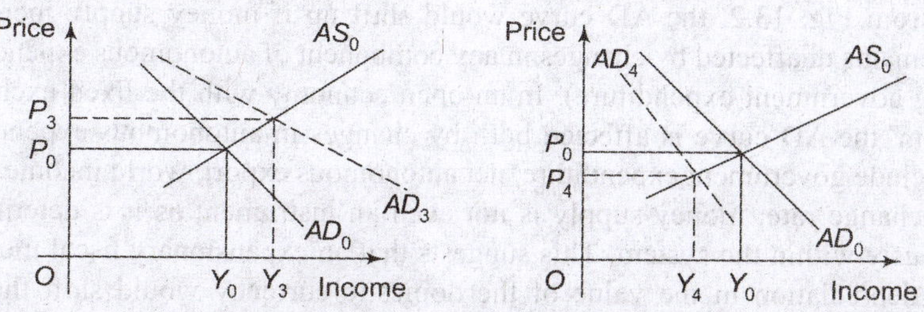

Fig. 13.6 Effects of Changes in Money Supply (*M*)

The AD_3 corresponds to the AD curve after the money supply increases, *ceteris paribus*, and AD_4 to that after the money supply decreases. While the former event causes both the real income and price to rise, the latter events bring both these endogenous variables down.

Recall from Chapter 9 that the shape of the AS curves follows from the production function and the behaviour of factor prices. If factor productivity increases, caused by improved technology or the factor (and raw materials) prices go down, ceteris paribus, the AS curve shifts to the right (downward) and vice versa. Such changes trigger changes in the real income and price as illustrated in Fig. 13.7.

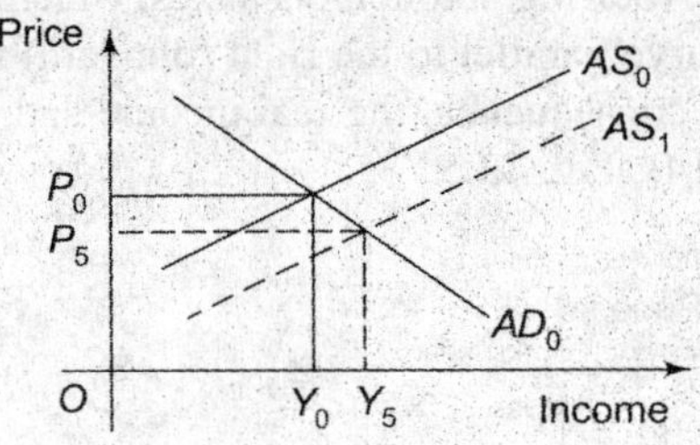

Part A: Improved Technology/Fall in Factor Prices

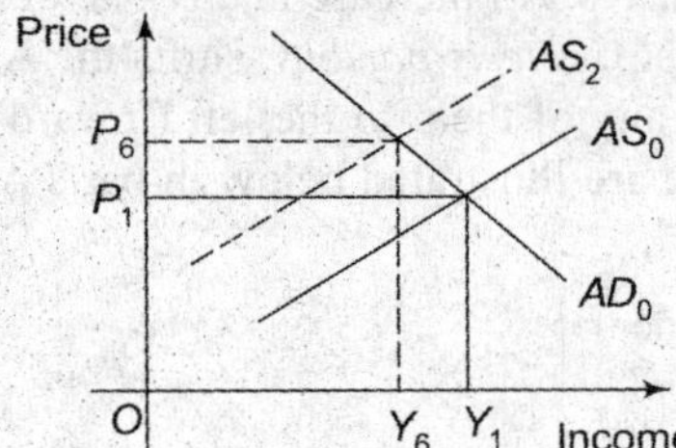

Part B: Retardation in Technology/ Rise in Factor Prices

Fig. 13.7 Effects of Changes in Technology/Factor Prices

Figure 13.7 indicates that improvements in the production technology as well as a fall in factor prices, *ceteris paribus*, leads to an increase in the real income and a decrease in the general price, and vice versa. Further, as noted in Chapter 9, supply shocks, favourable or otherwise, could emanate even through changes in the work force size (i.e, population, work participation rate, leisure-work preference, minimum wage regulations, working hours, unemployment benefits, immigration laws, retirement age etc.), climate/weather/rainfall and stock of capital (propensity to save, tax and other incentives for investments, attitude to risk, discovery of new resources like oil/mines etc.). Obviously, if any of such resources increase or if the weather becomes more production friendly, the AS curve would shift down and income would increase while price would fall, and vice versa.

In an open economy, while the effects of changes in the supply factors (supply shocks, like weather, oil price, discovery of minerals) would be similar to those in a closed economy, the effects of demand management policies (fiscal and monetary) would be quite different. Money supply remains the only effective policy instrument if the open economy had the floating exchange rate system. This is because, as would be clear from Fig. 13.2, the AD curve would shift up if money supply increases while it remains unaffected by changes in any component of autonomous expenditure (including government expenditure). In an open economy with the fixed exchange rate system, the AD curve is affected both by changes in autonomous expenditure (which include government expenditure, net autonomous export, world income, etc.) and in exchange rate; money supply is not even an instrument as it is determined endogenously within the system. This suggests that an expansionary fiscal measure and or a depreciation in the value of the domestic currency would shift the AD curve to the right and vice versa, and accordingly, given the AS curve, would lead to an increase in both income and price. In general, supply shocks dominated the fluctuations during 1973 through 1986 (triggered through significant oil price increases during 1973 to 1980, and oil price decreases during 1981 to 1986), and demand shocks played the dominant role during most other periods' fluctuations (like fiscal policy activism until around 1970, internet invention induced favourable demand increases during 1996-2000, asset price bubble induced demand pull during 2002-2006 and global recession period adverse demand shocks during 2007-09). The effect of various policies is summarised in Table 13.1.

Table 13.1 Effects of Stabilisation Policies under Flexible Price (AD-AS) Models

Policy Instrument	*Closed Economy*			*Open Economy Floating Exchange Rate*			*Open Economy Fixed Exchange Rate*		
	Income	*Price*	*Int. Rate*	*Income*	*Price*	*Exch. Rate*	*Income*	*Price*	*Money Supply*
Fiscal Expansion	+	+	+	0	0	+	+	+	+
Monetary Expansion	+	+	–	+	+	–	NA	NA	NA
Devaluation	NA	NA	NA	NA	NA	NA	+	+	+

Notes: + means increase; – means decrease; 0 means no change; and NA means not applicable.

The table gives the effects of only the expansionary policies. Needles to point out that the consequences of the tight policies would exactly be the opposite of those of the expansionary ones. The above results if compared with those of the fixed price (IS-LM) models (vide Chapter 12) would indicate that the directions of the various effects are exactly the same under the two scenarios. Since price is an additional endogenous variable here, the effects of various policies here are split between income and price.

Also, note that the various policies affect both income and price always in the same direction. This is primarily because the AS curve is assumed to be upward sloping monotonously. The latter assumption is reasonable up to the point of full employment, as beyond that point more output is just not possible. In other words, we are assuming that the AD meets AS within the full employment constraint.

The above analysis clearly indicates that the ups and downs in economic activities (as measured by the real income), and hence the business cycles, could be caused by changes in any one of the following factors: **(a)** Autonomous expenditure; **(b)** Money supply (nominal) or Exchange rate (nominal); **(c)** Technology; **(d)** Factor prices, including raw materials' prices; **(e)** Work force; **(f)** Capital stock; and **(g)** Weather.

In view of the above, recessions could arise if the consumers and/or firms have pessimistic outlooks, governments suddenly decide to cut on their expenditure or the rest of the world is in the grip of recession (causing net export to fall). Reverse situations would bring prosperity. Similarly, firms' forgetfulness (absent mindedness or carelessness) of erstwhile good techniques of production, increase in the wage and capital rentals and increase in the prices of raw materials and energy could lead an economy into a slump. Discovery of new technology and fall in factor, raw materials and energy prices could well lead to boom in the economy. A tight monetary policy could also trigger recession, and an easy one prosperity. Increases in the female participation in the work force and the retirement age, which is currently happening in most parts of the world, among other reasons, would accelerate the prosperity phase; while increases in social security benefits and minimum wage regulations, among others, would accentuate recession. Also, the globalisation wave is enhancing competition and thereby reducing the cost of production and, hence, is triggering the prosperity.

Thus, the AD-AS model offers various possible explanations for the occurrences of business cycles. For the sake of comparison, while the real factors (availability of labour and capital, technology, weather etc.) alone could cause business cycles in the classical model (barring the money supply when the adjustments to changes were slow) and the monetary factors (money supply, exchange rate, government expenditure, net exports, other autonomous demands etc.) alone in the Keynesian fixed price model, business cycles under the flexible price model could be either real or/and a monetary phenomenon.

Do the Stabilisation Policies in the AD-AS Model have any Role? The answer is obviously affirmative. Since changes in government spending and autonomous (and even induced) taxes enjoy a significant impact on the real income (and also on the general price), the appropriate changes in these fiscal policy instruments could bring any desired change in the real income, and accordingly stabilise the economy in the face of economic disturbances. For example, recessions could be countered through an increase in government expenditure and/or a cut in taxes.

The exact amount of increase/cut depends on the values of the various parameters (shapes) of the AD-AS functions (curves). Similarly, the booms could be tampered through appropriate decreases in government spending and/or increase in taxes. However, any increase in government expenditure under the pure (not accompanied by any other policy measure) expansionary fiscal policy, as noted in Chapter 10, has to be financed through internal or/and external borrowings, and would thus lead to an increase in the fiscal deficit and thereby in public debt. Consequences of the latter are often not prohibitive and in any case far less harmful than those due to the recession. A purely restrictive fiscal policy only helps reduce the public debt, and, hence, it poses no problem in terms of budget constraint, though it does suffer from political compulsions (Chapter 10). In view of this, one can suggest that the fiscal policy is available to counter business cycles under the AD-AS model. The said conclusion ignores the international interdependence and the policy lags, which are discussed later in this chapter.

Case Study: The fiscal tool was well used during the 1960s to boost growth. The Kennedy-Johnson tax cuts and 'great society' spending programmes of 1964–66 as well as the Vietnam War expenditure, are suggested to be among the factors for relatively faster growth in the United States during that period. During the

1960s many developing countries, including India, had embarked on state led industrialisation and public investment programmes through external borrowings to promote their growth. Public investment was seen as an engine of growth.

The monetary policy also enjoys an adequate role in taming the business cycles in the AD-AS model. For example, appropriate increases in the money supply/exchange rate, ceteris paribus, would bring desired increases in the real output, to hold the economy up in the face of recessions. Similarly, unwarranted upswings in the economy could be checked through an appropriate decrease in the money supply/exchange rate. Again, the exact change needed in the money supply for controlling such events depends on the values of the various parameters of the AD-AS functions. This conclusion also ignores the international interdependence and policy lags that are discussed below.

It is instructive to note that under the AD-AS model, both fiscal and monetary/exchange rate policies affect output and price in the same direction. Thus, an expansionary policy of either kind (and devaluation of domestic currency) tends to raise the output (lower the unemployment through the Okun's Law) and raise the price, while a restrictive policy of either type (and revaluation of domestic currency) leads to a fall in output, fall in price and an increase in unemployment. This implies that such policies could counter recessions but at the cost of inflation or counter recovery at the cost of unemployment. This means they are subject to the **Phillips' trade-off** between inflation and the rate of unemployment. During the 1950s and until almost the late 1960s, the world experienced neither a serious inflation nor a significant unemployment rate and accordingly Keynes' theory was well applauded. Economists thought the macroeconomic theory was complete and they could give a menu to the policy makers in the form of a simple downward sloping Phillips' Curve, relating the rate of inflation to the rate of unemployment, as in the Fig. 13.8.

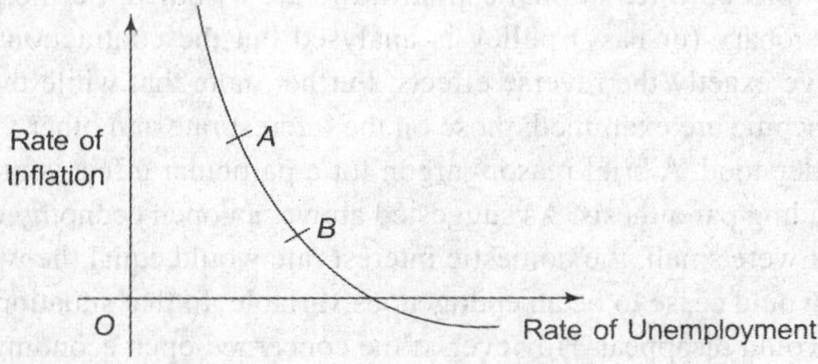

Fig. 13.8 Phillips' Curve

As discussed in Chapter 9, the Phillips' Curve is downward slopping and convex from below.[3] It provides the menu of the rates of inflation and the corresponding rates of unemployment. Policy makers have the option to choose any point on this curve, and economists would be able to design an appropriate stabilisation policy (either a pure monetary or a pure fiscal policy or a mix of the two) to induce the economy to reach

[3] Subsequently this curve was named as the short run Phillips' curve to distinguish it from the long run Phillips curve, which is vertical. This is discussed in Chapter 14.

the so chosen point on the curve through an appropriate shift in AD curve, given the AS curve in the AD-AS framework. For example, if the economy was on point A and the policy makers desired point B, then the stabilisation policy was expected to reduce the inflation rate, even though this would mean higher unemployment rate. The said policy would call for a cut in the aggregate demand, which could be achieved through appropriate cuts (tight policy) in the government expenditure and/or in the money supply and/or an increase in the taxes. The opposite (easy policy) would be the policy if the economy was to be moved from point B to point A.

The neat Phillips' Curve was so popular that it led some economists to go to the extent of saying that we could say **good bye to business cycles**! Alas, this belief was not to last long. The factors (events) that caused trouble to this belief and the suggested solutions for the same are discussed later in this chapter.

THE AD-AS MODEL: POLICY MECHANISMS/CHANNELS

Hitherto we have analysed the effects of various policies on significant macroeconomic variables. In this section, we discuss the mechanisms or channels through which these effects take place. Recall that the roles of the fiscal and monetary policies undergo a significant change when an erstwhile closed economy is opened up, and the exchange rate policy emerges as an additional tool for stabilisation. Accordingly, we will explicitly demark the discussion between the closed and the open economy. It must be noted that only one instrument is changed at a time and thus the *ceteris paribus* rule applies. Also, note that each of the fiscal and monetary policies exert two influences in a closed economy (1 and 2) and an additional influence in an open economy, which is number 3 or number 4 below, depending on whether it is on a floating or a fixed exchange rate system, respectively. For an open economy, no restrictions on international capital flows are assumed. Further, for each policy, an expansionary (or easy) policy is analysed but the contractionary (dear) policy would have exactly the reverse effects. Further, note that while the effects only on the real income are examined, those on the interest rate and other variables could be easily understood. A brief reason/jargon for a particular effect is provided under the corresponding parenthesis. As suggested above, an open economy could be small or large. If it were small, the domestic interest rate would equal the world interest rate, and thus would cease to be an endogenous variable. In that situation, the interest rate channel would disappear. However, if the concerned open economy were large, like the USA, she would exert influence even on the world interest rate. Accordingly, the interest rate channel would work in such an economy. Thus, in a large open economy, a mix of the closed and open economy results would happen. In what we discuss below, we are assuming that the open economy is a large one. For small open economy, one has to just ignore the interest rate channel. For convenience, we will use the following symbols:

$\uparrow$ = increase
$\downarrow$ = decrease
$\Rightarrow$ = implies

Fiscal Policy Mechanism /Channels

Closed economy

1. $G^{\uparrow} \Rightarrow \text{AD}^{\uparrow} \Rightarrow Y^{\uparrow}$ (G is a component of AD)
2. $G^{\uparrow} \Rightarrow i^{\uparrow} \Rightarrow I^{\downarrow} \Rightarrow \text{AD}^{\downarrow} \Rightarrow Y^{\downarrow}$ (domestic crowding out)

Additional for open economy

3. If on the floating exchange rate system:
   $G^{\uparrow} \Rightarrow i^{\uparrow} \Rightarrow$ net foreign capital inflow$^{\uparrow} \Rightarrow$ domestic currency value$^{\uparrow} \Rightarrow$ $NX^{\downarrow} \Rightarrow \text{AD}^{\downarrow} \Rightarrow Y^{\downarrow}$ (NX is a component of AD/international crowding out)
4. If on the fixed exchange rate system
   $G^{\uparrow} \Rightarrow i^{\uparrow} \Rightarrow$ net foreign capital inflow$^{\uparrow} \Rightarrow$ central bank buying of foreign exchange$^{\uparrow} \Rightarrow$ foreign exchange assets$^{\uparrow} \Rightarrow M^{\uparrow} \Rightarrow i^{\downarrow} \Rightarrow I^{\uparrow} \Rightarrow \text{AD}^{\uparrow} \Rightarrow Y^{\uparrow}$ (I is a component of AD/fiscal policy gains control over money supply)

The above mechanism was partly explained in the previous chapter and earlier in this chapter. Nevertheless, due to its importance, we will briefly review it again. The first channel happens simply because government expenditure is a component of AD. Further, if AD goes up, given the AS, real income goes up. In the second channel, under a pure easy fiscal policy, all increases in G have to be financed through borrowing, which means selling of government bonds in the open market. To sell government bonds in an erstwhile equilibrium system, bonds price has to be reduced, which results in an increase the interest rate on those bonds. In consequence, other interest rates would tend to increase. Alternatively, this part of the second channel could be explained like this–as G goes up, income goes up, which triggers an increase in demand for money, which with given money supply, leads to increase in the interest rate. To move to the channel further, increase in interest rate would tend to reduce private investment. As investment is a component of AD, AD would decrease and so real income would fall. Under channel 3, increase in domestic interest rate (caused by an easy fiscal policy as just explained), foreign interest rate remaining the same as before, would attract foreign capital at home until the two rates are equalised again. This, in turn, would require the conversion of foreign currency into domestic currency, leading to an increase in the demand for domestic currency in relation to foreign currency, which, in turn, would lead to an appreciation of the domestic currency under the freely floating rate system. In consequence, net exports would suffer, which is a part of AD, and so AD would fall and, given the AS, real income would fall. Under the last channel, which is an alternative to channel 3, the first two steps are identical to channel 3. In its third step, since the Central Bank is mandated to hold the fixed exchange rate, all increases in net foreign capital flows would be purchased by the latter which, in turn, would increase its foreign exchange holdings, leading to an increase in its assets in the currency issue department, forcing/enabling it to issue new money; thus raising its liabilities to balance the balance sheet of the issue department. Money supply would thus increase (unless it is sterilized-recall from Chapter 8 that the RBI has been using the sterilisation tool to partly counter such increases). Increased money supply, demand for money remaining the same, would lower the interest rate; investment would increase consequently and so would the AD, and through that the real income. Under the last scenario, expansionary fiscal policy effect is reinforced by impending increase in money supply, and accordingly, the policy is highly effective with respect to income.

If the open economy is small and is on the floating exchange rate system (vide Chapter 7), the domestic interest rate would equal the world interest rate. If so, channel 2 would not operate. However, channel 3 would become stronger. As G goes up, there is a pressure on the domestic interest rate to go up, which would be eased /cancelled through inflow of foreign capital, causing the domestic currency to appreciate. This, in turn, would affect net exports adversely. The crowding out of net exports (channel 3) would nullify the expansionary effect on income (channel 1), and the fiscal policy would be rendered impotent. However, if such an economy was large, like that of the United States, both channels 2 and 3 would operate and the crowding out of investment and net export would occur and, thus, the fiscal policy would be rendered ineffective. If the open economy is on the fixed exchange rate system, the fiscal policy would be more effective in it rather than in a closed economy, due to the channel 4 above; but, as explained below, it is no more a pure fiscal expansion. Again, the smaller the open economy is, the stronger would be its impact under channel 4 above, and the more effective the fiscal policy would be. We must recall here from Chapter 7 (vide the international trilemma) that under the fixed exchange rate system (with free movement of capital across countries), the Central Bank of the country (RBI) ceases to enjoy sovereignty with regard to the regulation of money supply. Thus, as seen under channel 4, all increases in government expenditure, *ceteris paribus*, must accompany similar increases in money supply. Accordingly, the fiscal policy is no longer a pure one; instead, the policy is a mix of the expansionary fiscal and expansionary monetary policies.

Monetary Policy Mechanism/Channels

Closed Economy

1. $M^{\uparrow} \Rightarrow i^{\downarrow} \Rightarrow I^{\uparrow} \Rightarrow AD^{\uparrow} \Rightarrow Y^{\uparrow}$ (*I* is a component of *AD*/Keynes effect)
2. $M^{\uparrow} \Rightarrow (M/P)^{\uparrow} \Rightarrow C^{\uparrow}, I^{\uparrow} \Rightarrow AD^{\uparrow} \Rightarrow Y^{\uparrow}$ (both *C* and *I* are components of *AD*/ real balance (Pigou) effect)

Additional for Open Economy

3. If on the floating exchange rate system
$M^{\uparrow} \Rightarrow i^{\downarrow} \Rightarrow$ net capital inflow$^{\downarrow} \Rightarrow$ domestic currency value$^{\downarrow} \Rightarrow NX^{\uparrow} \Rightarrow AD^{\uparrow}$ $\Rightarrow Y^{\uparrow}$ (*NX* is a component of *AD*)
4. If on the fixed exchange rate system
$M^{\uparrow} \Rightarrow i^{\downarrow} \Rightarrow$ net capital outflow$^{\uparrow} \Rightarrow$ central bank selling of foreign exchange$^{\uparrow}$ $\Rightarrow$ foreign exchange assets$^{\downarrow} \Rightarrow M^{\downarrow}$ (policy is forced to reverse)

The working of the above channels must be fairly clear, particularly after having grasped the fiscal policy channels' working. Only channel 2 is different, which through the Pigou or the real balance effect, may need some explanation. As money supply increases, ceteris paribus, the real balances with households as well as the business goes up; their wealth, in turn, goes up and so private consumption and investment go up (vide Chapters 5 and 6), AD goes up and real income increases. The effects on real balances on consumption and investment are not incorporated in the IS function above for simplicity.

If the open economy is on the floating exchange rate system, all the three channels above would work in the same direction. The additional channel for the open economy (number 3) reinforces the other two. Thus, the effectiveness of the monetary policy is more in such an open economy than in a closed economy. However, channel 4 forces the expansionary monetary policy to roll back the expansion. Thus, as noted above, the monetary policy is rendered impotent in an open economy with the fixed exchange rate system and free movement of capital across international borders (international trilemma). At the cost of repetition, the important trilemma/result may be recalled here. It states that a country can choose only two out of the three possible systems, viz, **(a)** integration (free movement of goods, services and capital across the globe), **(b)** regulation (fixed exchange rate system) and **(c)** sovereignty (independent monetary policy). The said trilemma was proved in Chapter 8. Mundell and Fleming were the first to draw our attention to this result and accordingly in their honour, it is known as the Mundell–Fleming model.

The above analysis asserts that both the policies are effective in a closed economy. However, the potency of the pure fiscal policy is restrictive/insignificant in an open - floating exchange rate economy, while that of the pure monetary policy in an open-fixed exchange rate economy. Further, while either expansionary policy would tend to increase the real income and lower unemployment, it must be emphasised that since the real income is increased, in an open economy, imports would go up [vide equation **(12.4)**] without a corresponding change in exports [vide equation **(12.3)**] and, thus, the current account deficit would increase as well. This, together with the effect of the easy fiscal policy on fiscal deficit, suggests that a pure easy fiscal policy tends to raise the real income and lower unemployment, but also tends to raise both the fiscal deficit as well as the current account deficit. The monetary policy is free from fiscal consequences, but nonetheless it is subject to the trade effect. Accordingly, an easy pure monetary policy tends to raise the real income and lower unemployment, but it also adversely affects the current account balance of the balance of payments. Thus, the economists' adage that "there is nothing like free lunch" holds here as well. This result must qualify the analysis of Chapter 11 and of this Chapter by the end of this section. Nevertheless, the above analysis maintains the earlier conclusion that at least one of these two policies is always effective to counter business cycles. The puzzle then is "why do business cycles still occur and reoccur?" The reason is that these policies are subject to certain constraints, which were addressed in Chapter 10, and some limitations, which would follow soon. The new measures to take care of such limitations are also discussed alongside.

The AD-AS Model—Illustrations

The illustrations are done separately for the closed economy and both the types of the open economy.

(a) Closed Economy Considering the closed economy first, we take the IS-LM model of the previous chapter. Under the flexible price model, the price level is no more a constant. Thus, the IS-LM equations under the flexible price system [and on the assumption that expected inflation (p^e) = 0] would be as follows:

IS equation: $Y = 2071 - 357\,i$ **(11.14)**

LM equation: $800/P = 0.4Y - 100\,i$ **(13.7)**

These are two equations in three variables (*Y, P and i*) and thus the model is incomplete. However, these could be solved into one equation in two variables.

Since the AD curve is in income and price, we solve these into Y and P, and thus eliminate the interest rate.

Solving equation **(11.14)** for the variable *i*, we get

$$i = 5.80 - 0.0028Y$$

Substituting the above value of *i* in equation **(13.7)**, we get

$$800/\text{P} = 0.4\,Y - 100(5.80 - 0.0028Y)$$
$$= -580 + 0.68Y$$

or, $$Y = 853 + 1176\,(1/P) \qquad \textbf{(13.8)}$$

Equation **(13.8)** represents the equation of the AD curve in a closed economy. This is non-linear in *Y* and *P*, even though both the IS and LM equations, on which it is based, are linear in *Y* and *i*. It reveals, as expected, a negative relationship between *Y* and *P*.

Suppose the economy has the following AS equation (vide Chapter 9):

$$P = P^e + (1/\alpha)\,(Y - Y_n) + P_R \qquad \textbf{(13.9)}$$

and we assume

$$Y_n = 2100, \quad \alpha = 1.5 \quad \text{and} \quad (P^e + P_R) = 1.2$$

Substitution of the values of the exogenous variables and parameters in the AS equation, and solution of the same for *Y* gives

$$Y = 2100 + 1.5(P\text{–}1.2)$$

or,

$$Y = 2098.2 + 1.5P \qquad \textbf{(13.10)}$$

Solution of equations **(13.8)** and **(13.10)** yields

$$Y = 2099.61 \quad \text{and} \quad P = 0.9433$$

The equilibrium income is close to the natural rate of output, Y_n, which is incidental. The equilibrium price is less than unity, which is so because here the price is denoted by the index number with a base period value of 1.00.

Comparative Statics To analyse the role of the fiscal and monetary policies in the closed economy AD-AS model, we now change the values of government expenditure and money supply, one by one. In the above example, government expenditure was 300 and money supply was 800. Now, if government expenditure increases to 325, *ceteris paribus*, the IS equation changes to equation (11.16 and the LM equation remains the same as above. Thus, we have

IS equation: $Y = 2161 - 357\,i$

LM equation: $800/P = 0.4Y - 100\,i$

The solution of the first equation for *i* and substitution of the result into the second equation yields

$$800/P = 0.4Y - 100\,(6.05 - 0.0028Y)$$

or,
$$Y = 890 + 1176\,(1/P) \tag{13.11}$$

This is the equation of the AD curve under the new situation. A comparison of equations **(13.8)** and **(13.11)** would indicate that a change in government expenditure merely changes the intercept of the AD curve. Solving the erstwhile AS equation **(13.10)** and the new AD equation **(13.11)** gives

$$Y = 2099.65 \quad \text{and} \quad P = 0.967$$

A comparison of the equilibrium values under G = 300 and G = 325, *ceteris paribus* would suggest that fiscal expansion leads to an increase in income as well as in price.

Next, suppose the money supply changes from 800 to 825, *ceteris paribus*, then the IS equation remains unaltered as equation **(11.14)** of Chapter 11 and the LM equation changes as follows:

IS equation: $Y = 2071 - 357i$

LM equation: $825/P = 0.4Y - 100i$

Solving the first equation for *i* and substituting the result in the second equation gives

$$825/P = 0.4Y - 100i\,(5.80 - 0.0028Y)$$
$$= -580 + 0.68Y$$

or,
$$Y = 853 + 1213(1/P) \tag{13.12}$$

This is the equation of the AD curve under the new situation. A comparison of equations **(13.8)** and **(13.12)** would suggest that a change in the money supply, *ceteris paribus*, merely changes the slope of the AD curve. Solution of the erstwhile AS equation **(13.10)** and the new AD equation **(13.12)** would yield

$$Y = 2099.66 \quad \text{and} \quad P = 0.973$$

A comparison of these values with the corresponding values under M = 800, ceteris paribus, would indicate that monetary expansion leads to increase in both income and price. Thus, it can be concluded that in the model under reference, both fiscal and monetary policies have positive impact both on income and price.

(b) Open Economy-Floating Rate Model We recall the open economy-floating exchange rate model illustration of the previous chapter and note the IS equation, and adjust the same for the flexible price as

$$Y = k_1A_1 - k_1d(i^w - p^e) + k_1(\beta + \delta)[(E)(P^w)/P^d]$$

Substitution of the values of the various parameters (as assumed in Chapter 12 and assuming further $p^e = 0$) gives

$$Y = 1{,}848.3 + 272.7[(E)(P^w)/P^d]$$

Further inserting the assumed value for $P^w = 0.025$, gives

$$Y = 1{,}848.3 + 6.8178\,(E/P^d) \tag{13.13}$$

This is the equation of the IS curve for the model under discussion. Let us now recall the LM equation of the example of Chapter 12:,

$$Y = \frac{1}{e}\left(\frac{M_0}{P}\right) + \left(\frac{f}{e}\right)i^w$$

Substituting the values of the various parameters and exogenous variables, we get

$$Y = 1/0.4(800/P) + (100/0.4)(0.05)$$

or, $$Y = 2{,}000/P + 12.5 \quad \textbf{(13.14)}$$

This is the equation of the LM curve. Add to these the AS equation **(13.10)**, which would complete the IS-LM-AS model in three equations **(13.13)**, **(13.14)** and **(13.10)**, respectively. Solution of these three equations in three endogenous variables would give the equilibrium values for Y, P and E. To analyse the role of stabilisation policies, one needs to change the values of G and M, and compare the results. This is left for the readers to work. Nevertheless, it must be noted that the fiscal policy would have no effect on income (real), for Y is given simply by solving the LM and AS equations, each of which is independent of the size of government expenditure.

(c) Open Economy Fixed Exchange Rate Model The IS equation under this model is

$$Y = k_1A_1 - k_1d(i^w - p^e) + k_1(\beta + \delta)[(E)(P^w)/P^d]$$

Putting the values of the exogenous variables (E = 60, $P^w = 0.025$) and parameters as in Chapter 12 (and $P^e = 0$), we get

$$Y = 1848.3 + 272.7[(60)(0.025)/P]$$

or, $$Y = 1848.3 + 409\ (1/P) \quad \textbf{(13.15)}$$

This is the equation of the IS curve. The LM equation in the model would be

$$Y = 1/0.4\ (M/P) + (100/0.4)\ (0.05)$$

or, $$Y = 2.5(M/P) + 12.5 \quad \textbf{(13.16)}$$

The above two equations together with the AS equation **(13.10)** constitute the model here, which can be solved for the equilibrium values of the three endogenous variables, viz. Y, P and M. Since both the IS as well as LM equations are non-linear (AS equation is linear), one has to resort to a little advanced mathematics to solve this three equations model. In particular, the method would involve differentiation and then solving for the derivatives (change) at initial values of some variables. We leave it here and the interested readers with competence in mathematics could attempt to solve the model. Similarly, exercise on comparative statics to evaluate the roles of stabilization policies is also left for such readers. Suffice to mention here, note that since money supply itself is an endogenous variable in this model, it ceases to be a policy instrument in the hands of the Central Bank of the country (RBI). Instead, the RBI has the nominal exchange rate at its command to tame business cycles.

The AD-SAS-BP Model and Internal and External Equilibrium

The aggregate demand-aggregate supply model presented above has ignored the balance of payments considerations. To incorporate this issue, we need to have the AD-AS-BP model, which is given below in Figure 13.9.

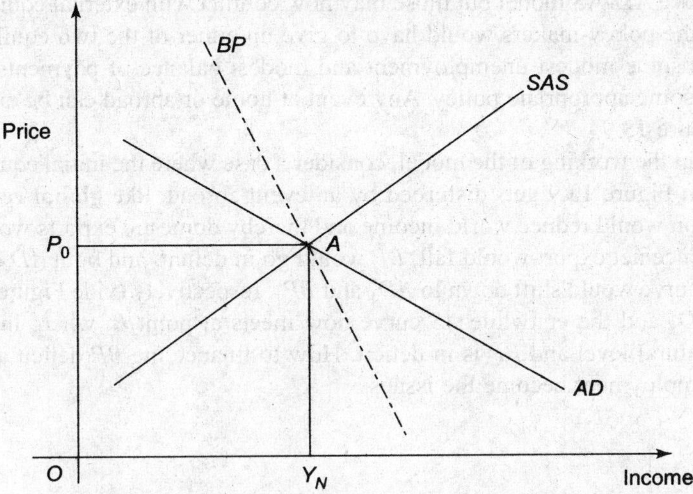

Fig. 13.9 AD-AS-BP Curves under Flexible Price

Recalling the BP equation **(13.6)**, we note that under this, real income/output is a positive function of domestic interest rate and exchange rate, and negative function of domestic price. The BP curve in income and price (holding i and E as constants) is a downward sloping curve, and it shifts up (to the right) with any increase in either interest rate or exchange rate, or with exogenous factors leading to capital inflows (like the country's improved credit rating). The curve slopes downward because if income goes up, *ceteris paribus*, imports increase and thereby net exports falls which leads to deficit in balance of payments. Capital flows remain unaltered, and thus to bring back the BP to equilibrium, fall in net exports must be reversed, which can happen only if domestic price falls. Quite the opposite happens when income falls. Thus, the BP curve slopes downward in income-price axes. The slope of BP curve varies with changes in exchange rate, world price, interest rate and several domestic and foreign parameters. The AD curve slopes downward as well. While the AD curve is likely to be flatter than the BP curve, it could well be otherwise. In the figure above, the AD curve is assumed to be flatter than the BP curve. It is easy to see that to the left of the BP curve, the balance of payments is in surplus and to the right of it is in deficit. Since the discussion here is about business cycles and stabilization policies, the relevant aggregate supply curve is the short-run AS curve (denoted as SAS), which slopes upward as discussed in Chapter 9. The long-run AS (LAS) curve is vertical at $Y = Y_N =$ potential output.

The AD-SAS-BP curves intersect at point A, which marks the equilibrium in all the three corresponding markets, giving income equals Y_N and Price $= P_0$. At this point the country is at external equilibrium, and also at internal equilibrium if Y_N happens to equal full employment or natural level of output. If so, we have an ideal situation and the policy-makers could just relax and take the credit for the GREAT outcome! However, if Y_N falls short of the full employment output, then one needs to examine the alternatives the policy-makers have to take the economy to its full potential. The alternatives for attaining the internal equilibrium would be the same as in the above AD-AS model but those may now conflict with external equilibrium. If conflict, the policy-makers would have to give up either of the two equilibriums or live with some modest unemployment and modest balance of payments deficit, or to apply some appropriate policy. Any event at home or abroad can be examined through Figure 13.9.

To explain the working of the model, consider a case where the initial equilibrium at point *A* in Figure 13.9 gets disturbed by an event abroad, like **global recession**. The recession would reduce world income and thereby domestic exports would fall. In consequence net export would fall, *BP* would go in deficit, and both *AD* curve as well as *BP* curve would shift down to AD_1 and BP_1, respectively (vide Figure 13.10). The new AD_1 and the erstwhile *AS* curve now meets at point *B*, where income is below its natural level and *BP* is in deficit. How to finance the *BP* deficit and how to cure unemployment become the issues.

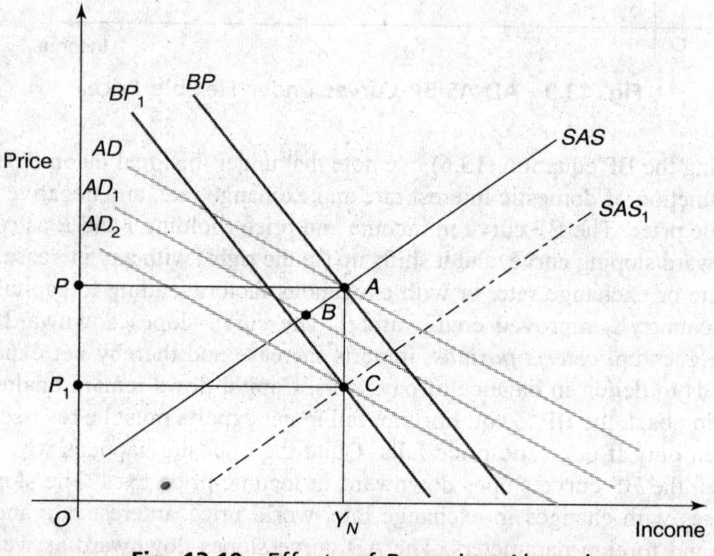

Fig. 13.10 Effects of Recession Abroad

One way to resolve the issues is for RBI to sell the foreign currency (i.e. buy domestic currency), which would cause money supply to fall, which would lead to a fall in AD (AD curve shifts to AD_2); and thereby price and wage rate would fall and SAS curve will shift to right to SAS_1. The new equilibrium would be hit at a point like *C*, where all three curve meets once again, leading to both internal and external equilibrium. However, the said process could take long time! Alternatively, the active policy may be applied. Since we **have two target variables** (viz. $Y = Y_n$ and BP = 0), we **need two policy tools**. Letting the latter be the exchange rate (assuming fixed exchange rate system) and government expenditure, devalue the domestic currency and reduce government expenditure simultaneously. The former tool would switch expenditure from domestic demand to export, and the latter tool would reduce the overall AD. In consequence, AD curve would shift down and equilibrium would hit at point *C* in Figure 13.10. If the economy were at floating exchange rate (fiscal policy is then ineffective), then BP will balance automatically and an appropriate increase in money supply will take the economy back to point *A*.

Let us now consider an example of international capital flow shock. Suppose the foreign investors and speculators believe that the country is likely to go for devaluation of its currency or/and fear that the government is likely to fall prematurely. This belief would cause **capital flight**, triggering a leftward shift in the *BP* curve, from curve *BP* to BP_1, resulting in to deficit in the balance of payments (vide Figure 13.11).

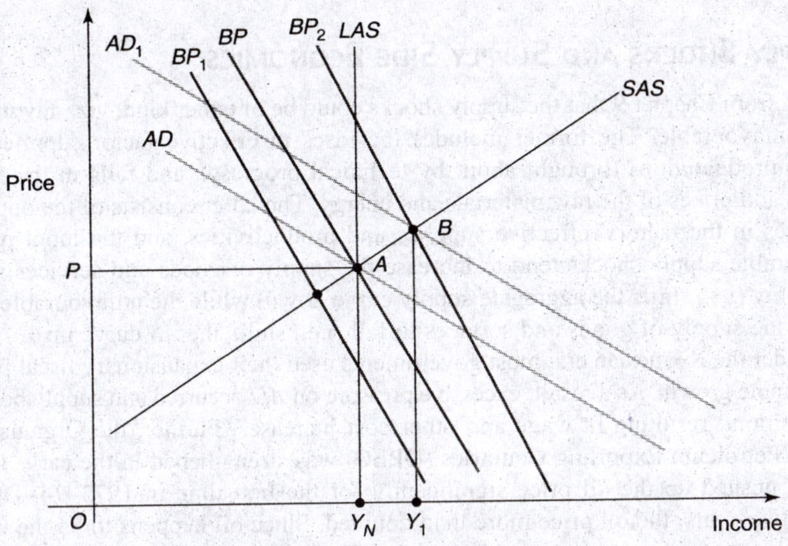

Fig. 13.11 Effects of Capital Flight

Capital flight would tend to put downward pressure on the exchange rate to devalue if the country were on the floating rate. Devaluation, in turn, would tend to increase net export, leading to rightward shift both in *BP* and *AD* curves, to curves BP_2 and AD_1, respectively, leading to another short run triple equilibrium at point *B*, where the income level and the price are higher than their erstwhile levels. However, in case the country were on the fixed exchange rate system, capital flight would put a pressure on the domestic currency to fall, which will be neutralised through the selling of the foreign currency by the country's Central Bank, which, in turn, would reduce the money supply, causing the *AD* curve to shift down. In consequence, the new short run triple equilibrium will occur at a lower income level and lower price than the one before the capital flight occurred. The long run adjustments will take place and there may be conflict between the internal and external equilibrium, solution of which will call for two policy interventions, as detailed in the previous paragraph.

The effects of fiscal and monetary policy on income, price and balance of payments could similarly be analysed. Suffice to mention here that while fiscal policy would affect the *AD* and *BP* curves, monetary policy would affect only the *AD* curve. Easy stance by either policy would tend to raise output and price in the short run, and raise only price in the long run. Under floating rate, exchange rate would tend to depreciate. Since price adjustments are sluggish while exchange rate adjusts rapidly, exchange rate adjustments may even **overshoots**. Incidentally note that according to the natural rate hypothesis, levels of output and employment depend on *AD* in the short run but not in the long run. In other words, the demand management policies are effective in the short run but in the long run they are neutral (non-effective) to real GDP and employment/unemployment. This will be elaborated in detail in Chapter 14. Below, we consider some significant factors which tend to limit the effectiveness of stabilization policies.

Supply Shocks and Supply Side Economics

Recall from Chapter 9 that the supply shocks could be of either kind, viz., favourable and unfavourable. The former includes increases in effective factor supplies and factor productivities (brought about by technical progress), and falls in the factor prices and prices of the raw materials and energy. The latter consists of the opposite changes in the factors' effective supplies and productivities, and the input prices. Favourable supply shocks tend to increase the supply of goods and services in the economy (i.e., shifts the aggregate supply curve down) while the unfavourable ones cause the supply of goods and services to fall (i.e., shifts the *AS* curve up).

Under the Keynesian era, most governments used their expansionary fiscal policy to promote growth. As a result, excessive pressure on *AD* occurred and supply became a constraint, resulting in wage and other cost increases. Further, the Organisation of the Petroleum Exporting Countries (OPEC) was strengthened in the early 1970s and it pushed up the oil price significantly for the first time in 1973–74. During those two years, the oil price more than doubled. Since oil happens to be the major source of the energy (directly or indirectly) for the production of almost all goods and services all over the world, the oil price hike triggered the adverse supply shock, leading to a significant upward shift in the *AS* curve. Vietnam War further aggravated the situation. Consequently, the world as a whole faced, what is now known as **stagflation** or slumpflation, which means stagnation (or unemployment) and inflation, i.e., the simultaneous occurrence of both the evils. After the Great Depression (1929-33) and before this event, subject to some exceptions, the world was getting economically stronger with time, and, if at all there was an economic issue, it was either a serious inflation or a significant unemployment, but not both the evils together. The Keynesian theory was then well vindicated and applied successfully to counter the booms and busts of the business cycles. In 1966, Milton Friedman, a staunch critic of the Keynesian theory, said, **"we are all Keynesians now"** [vide Raphael, et. al (1997), page 344].

Doubts regarding the relevance of the Keynesian theory were raised during the second half of the 1960s, when inflation started raising its head in several parts of the country. The situation turned worse post-1973. For example, in the Paris based rich countries' forum, called the Organisation of Economic Cooperation and Development (OECD), where consumer prices rose by 3.1 per cent a year on average during 1960-68, the prices rose by 10.5 per cent a year on average during 1973-79. In India, the inflation had crossed 28 per cent in 1974 and remained in double digit during the early 1980s. The inflation rate in the world as a whole remained in two digits in almost all years during 1973-1995. Inflation, and not the unemployment rate became the overriding objective of all economic policies. During the 1970s, even the unemployment problem became more serious. The rate of unemployment, which was at an average rate of 3.1 per cent in OECD countries during 1960-68 increased to 5.1 per cent during 1973-79; and the growth rate in real GDP fell from 3.9 per cent to 1.9 per cent in those countries within the same period. The US data suggested that the negative relationship that existed between the rate of inflation and the rate of unemployment in United States during 1953-69 was much less clear during the post-1970 period (vide Chapter 9). It was the happening of the stagflation, during the post 1973, which converted the doubts to the rejection of the Keynesian theory of income determination. The Bretton Woods system of exchange rate also broke in 1971 and the Keynesian theory is blamed even for this. In 1976, the then Prime Minister of the United Kingdom, James Callaghan, announced at the Labour Party Conference that the option of **"spending our way out of recession no longer existed"**; it had worked in the past only by "injecting bigger and bigger doses of inflation into the economy". Some even thought that **"the Keynesian was dead and buried"** [vide Raphael, Winch and Skidelsky (1997)]. This is illustrated in Fig. 13.12.

AD_0 and AS_0 represent the original *AD* and *AS* curves, and Y_n and P_0 the equilibrium income and prices, respectively. The adverse supply shock shifts the *AS* curve to AS_1, taking the economy to point *B* with income of Y_1 and price of P_1. A comparison of the new equilibrium values with the old equilibrium values would indicate that supply shock has led to a fall in the real income (which means increase in unemployment) and an increase in the general price (i.e, inflation). The twin evils are the outcome of adverse supply shock. Could the Keynes' stabilisation policies help remove these twin evils simultaneously?

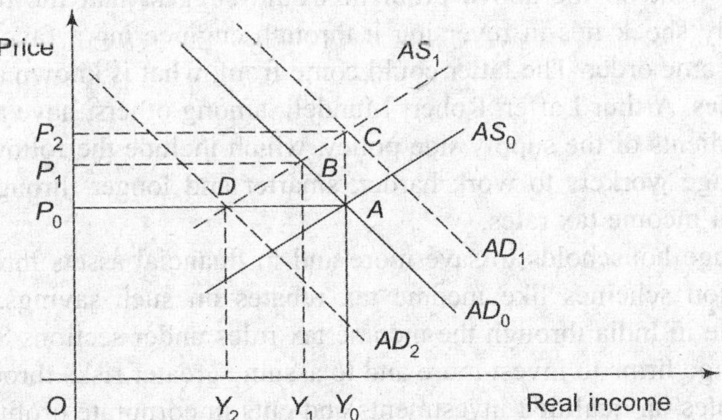

Fig. 13.12 Supply Shock and ***AD-AS*** Curves

The answer is a clear "no". For, the stabilisation policies, which constitute the fiscal, monetary and trade and exchange rate policies, operate through the *AD* curve (hence also called demand management policies) only. Thus, when the economy moves from point *A* to point *B* in Fig. 13.12 due to an adverse supply shock, demand management policies have three alternatives:

(i) Increase government expenditure, reduce taxes, increase money supply, or/ and restrict import and devalue domestic currency so as to shift the *AD* curve from AD_0 to AD_1

(ii) Decrease government expenditure, increase taxes, reduce money supply and/ or liberalise import and revalue domestic currency such that the *AD* curve shifts from AD_0 to AD_2

(iii) Do nothing or act in part so as to shift the *AD* curve somewhere in the middle of AD_1 and AD_2

If the alternative **(i)** is adopted it implies a demand management policy, called the **accommodating policy**. Under this the economy is moved from point *B* to point *C*, where the income (and employment and unemployment) just equals the level Y_0, which equals its level that was before the supply shock, and thus newly created unemployment is removed. However, at point *C*, the price level P_2 is higher even as compared to the one after the supply shock P_1. Thus, the accommodating stabilisation policy removes the additional unemployment generated by the adverse supply shock but aggravates the inflation problem. As against this, if the policy alternative **(ii)** is implemented, which is called the **extinguishing policy**, the economy moves from point *B* to point *D*, where the price level P_0 is exactly equal to that before the supply shock but the real income is lower at Y_2, even as compared to the post-supply shock position. Thus, the extinguishing stabilisation policy helps avoid inflation but aggravates the problem of unemployment. Under the policy alternative **(iii)**, which is called the **neutral policy**, the economy would be somewhere on the cord *CD*, which is plagued by some level of the twin evils, viz. inflation and unemployment. This clearly shows the limitations of the stabilisation policies in dealing with the twin evils of unemployment and inflation simultaneously and thereby demonstrates that stabilisation policies are no panacea for the troubles caused by an adverse supply shock.

A little thought on the above problem would suggest that the remedy for an adverse supply shock lies in reversing it through engineering a favourable supply shock of the same order. The latter could come from, what is known as, the **supply side economics**. Arthur Laffer, Robert Mundell, among others, have articulated the various ingredients of the supply side policy, which include the following:[4]

(a) Encourage workers to work harder, smarter and longer through cuts in the personal income tax rates.

(b) Encourage households to save more and in financial assets through savings' promotion schemes like income tax rebates on such savings, as currently available in India through the income tax rules under sections 88C.

(c) Encourage firms to invest more and to assume greater risks through corporate tax rebates on qualified investments and cuts in corporate profit tax rate.

If a policy like **(a)** above were implemented, the effective supply of labour would increase, *ceteris paribus*, the potential output would go up, and the *AS* curve would shift downwards. Similarly, if the policy like **(b)** above were followed, savings in financial assets would increase, leading to an increase in the supply of funds for

---

[4] Aurthur Laffer has advanced a hypothesis, called the Laffer Curve, which suggests that the relationship between the tax revenue and the tax rate is like an inverted *u*-shaped curve (vide Chapter 7).

investments and thereby the stock of capital and, hence, the output would expand. Consequently, the *AS* curve would shift downwards. A policy like **(c)** above would encourage firms to undertake more investment, other things remaining the same, this would boost up capital formation; which, in turn, would trigger a downward shift in the *AS* curve. If the shift in the *AS* curve is sufficient, which could be ensured through the appropriate levels of the policies **(a)**, **(b)** and **(c)** above, the post-adverse supply shock *AS* curve (viz., AS_1) would shift back to its pre-adverse supply shock, AS_0, position, and accordingly, the said policy would have ensured return to the original equilibrium point A, curing both inflation and unemployment simultaneously. It is because of this feature of the supply side policy that, it alone could attack stagflation, made supply side economics so popular in the 1970s and for some time thereafter. The policy supports the classical theory and was called **ultra classicism**. Keynes had ignored the supply side effects of an expansionary fiscal policy. The tax rates were quite low until the 1940s (in Unites States, the average marginal tax rate across all tax brackets was at 1.2 per cent in 1916, 4.6 per cent in 1920, 3.5 per cent in 1929, and at 19.6 per cent in 1950), started the upward move thereafter, rising at perhaps the fastest rate during the 1970s. Impressed by the supply side economics, Ronald Reagan implemented the tax cut policies during his Presidency of the United States (1981-1989), Margaret Thatcher in her Prime Ministership in the United Kingdom (1980s), Rajiv Gandhi in his Prime Ministership in India (1984-1989), and heads of many other governments, and their followers. It is instructive to note that the adverse supply shock of the 1973-74 type was repeated in 1979-81,1999-2000, 2002-2004 and occasionally, though somewhat lighter, even thereafter; and reversed during 1982-86,1997-98, 2001 and occasionally even in later periods.

The prescription of the supply side economics did not survive for long. While most countries went into low tax rate regimes; the growth rate in real GDP slowed down, saving rate did not increase much, tax proceeds increased at below the trend rate, and only inflation and unemployment rates went up. To cite some data, the growth rate in the world real GDP, during the first four years of the 1980s, fell to about half of its previous four years' record; the United States faced its worst ever recession in 1982 after the Great Depression; the unemployment rate hit the two digit level in the United States, the United Kingdom, etc. in 1982-83; and the world inflation rate remained in two-digits almost throughout the post 1973 until 1995. The then President of the United States, George Bush, Senior, during the late 1980s, labeled supply side as **'voodoo economics'**.

It was noted that the supply side initiatives affect not only the *AS* but also the *AD*. For example, when income tax rates fall, people supply more labour (*AS* goes up) and their income goes up; and therefore consumption and *AD* go up. Further, if the lump-sum or autonomous (rather than the income/profit tax) taxes fall, the *AS* is left unaltered and only the *AD* is favourably affected. Since the *AS* and *AD* both increase as the tax rate falls, the real income increases but the effect on price is ambiguous. Also, if these effects are inadequate to cure the unemployment problem, policy makers might supplement the supply side actions with further doses of the easy fiscal/monetary policy, and, if so, the increase in *AD* could well outstrip the increase in *AS*, resulting in more output as well as higher price. This explains why the supply side policy led to the cure of the unemployment problem but left the inflation issue unresolved. During the 1980s, the price stability rather than the full employment became the stated objective of all macroeconomic policies throughout the world. The dual goals of growth and price stability continue to cause problems to decision-makers.

Policy Lags and Discretionary Versus Rule Based Policy

Milton Friedman (1959) discovered yet another problem faced by the demand management policies in stabilising the economy. He pointed out that the fiscal and monetary policies are subject to the following policy lags:

(a) Inside lag; these could be further classified into
- **(i)** Information/recognition lag
- **(ii)** Decision lag and
- **(iii)** Implementation lag

(b) Outside lag

The **inside lag** is the time between a shock to the economy and the policy action responding to that shock. It has three components. First, the data about the real state of the economy (real GDP, unemployment, inflation) are not available instantly (vide Chapters 2 and 3) and thus it takes some time before policy makers learn of any trouble in the economy. Accordingly, the first lag is called the **information** or the **recognition lag**. Second, no economic policy is made by a single person but rather by one or several committees. It takes time to convene the meetings, deliberate and to arrive at decisions. Since all policies have pros and cons, and as seen above, they affect the economy in various ways. Further, policy makers get carried away by their earlier policy prescriptions. Accordingly, they differ in their opinions/recommendations. In view of all this, all policies take time to formulate and accordingly there is **decision lag**. Once decision is made, the execution goes through various levels in the government, which again consumes time. This is called the **implementation lag**, i.e. time lapsed in implementation of decisions. The last lag, viz., the **outside lag**, is the time between a policy action and its influence on the economy. This lag arises because policies do not influence spending, employment, income and prices directly and instantly, but rather indirectly. We have seen above that such policies operate through various processes/mechanisms, which involve a series of intermediate variables in between the instruments and target variables.

The length of the various policy lags varies across policies, time and countries. It is argued that, in general, the fiscal policy has a longer inside lag than the monetary policy but the opposite is true with regard to the outside lag. This appears to hold good in India, for the fiscal policy design and implementation goes through the cabinet (politicians) and a series of secretaries (professionals), while the monetary policy is conceived and implemented basically by the governor, deputy governors and senior bankers, all of whom are supposedly professionals. In terms of the outside lag, the fiscal policy has a shorter one because government expenditure and taxes affect the income directly while the money supply exerts influence on the real income only through the interest rate. It is argued that the inside lag is shorter under the Parliament form of the government than under the Presidential form of the government, for the former could design and implement policies faster, particularly if the party in the power has the majority, while the latter takes time as each policy requires the approval of the President and both houses of the Congress. The President and the Congress must agree to a policy action, pass the action and then implement it. There is now almost a consensus among economists that normal business cycles are best managed by the monetary policy.

Milton Friedman and others have argued that these **policy lags are long and variable**. The exact length of these lags is an empirical matter. Since they are long, a policy may just turn out to be too late or even less or more aggressive. In other words, a policy may end up stimulating the economy when it is overheated or depressing her when it is cooling off. Such a position occurs if the economy's condition undergoes a change between the recognition of a shock and the impact of the policy on the economy. This suggests that policy makers need to be vigilant to avoid such possibilities.

The variability of the policy lag is worse than the length of the lag. If the longevity of the lag is known in advance, policy makers are at least aware of the time when the impact would take place. Further, if the effects were distributed over time (i.e., followed the **distributed lag pattern**), as they do, they would know the degree of the effect by time as well. Unfortunately, the length of the lag varies from instrument to instrument, and over the time and space. This renders policies still less meaningful.

There are two additional factors that aggravate policy making:

(a) There is no unanimity among economists about the source of business cycles. While some economists like Milton Friedman argue that the economy is stable without policies and it is the policies which cause economic fluctuations, other economists attribute business cycles to the inherent instability of all economies, arising from the supply and non-policy demand shocks. Accordingly, while Milton Friedman argues that the less government is better, Keynes recommends for more government.

(b) Forecasting of future economic events is erroneous. This was true during the Great Depression and is true even currently with all the sophisticated tools of forecasting.

The presence of policy lags and these two factors have raised another question, viz.,

- Should stabilisation policies be active or passive? Or put differently
- Should policy be based on discretion or on rules?

There has been a lively debate among economists on both these concerns. There are economists called **non-monetarists** (e.g., Karl Brunner 1989), who argue that the large adverse shock to private spending caused the Great Depression, which could have been avoided through an expansionary demand management policy (in the United States, government expenditure was $22.0, 24.3, 25.4, 24.2 and 23.2 billion in 1929, 1930, 1931, 1932 and 1933, respectively). The other group of economists, called the **monetarists** (e.g., Milton Friedman), believe that the large fall in the money supply was responsible for the Great Depression (in the United States, the nominal money supply was $26.6, 25.8, 24.1, 21.1 and 19.9 billion in 1929, 1930, 1931, 1932 and 1933, respectively). Accordingly, the non-monetarists advocate an **active policy** while the monetarists, a **passive policy**.

There are pros and cons of both **discretionary (active/fine-tuning)** and **rule based (passive) policies**. There is a trade-off between the flexibility of the policy makers in responding to shocks that is available under discretion and the certainty about future policy that comes from rules. In particular, the advantage of the former is that these could be designed as per the need of the hour and thus be **fine-tuned** or tailor made to face specific issues. The difficulty of this system lies in the identification of the specific issues and the politics of discretion, besides the existence of the long and variable policy lags. The advantage of the policy through a rule is that it is free of the problems of the discretionary policy but its problem is that it misses the benefits of the fine-tuning. It thus faced with twin problems. One, political, if doing nothing to counter business cycles, then the activists blame the government. Two, economic, if governs business cycles through rules, then how the rules for the various policies are to be designed. While some suggestions for the latter issue have been forwarded, which are discussed below, the debate has remained unresolved and we need a good mix of the two extremes. To add to this are issues—whether the rule based policy should be **publicly announced or not**, and whether it should be **subject to revision**, if deemed appropriate.

Milton Friedman, the most famous monetarist, suggests that the monetary policy be conducted through a rule. To him, the quantity of money was more important than anything else in the economy and no one, including the Central Bank of the country, could get it right. The rule could be in terms of the growth rate in the nominal money supply, which could be determined on the basis of the demand for money function. The Chakravarty Committee Report (1985), to which the author of this book was a consultant, suggests such a formula. For example, if the income elasticity of the demand for, say, broad money (M_3) = 1.5, expected growth rate in real income = 8 per cent, and the desired inflation rate = 5 per cent, the nominal money supply (M_3) may be increased by 17 per cent (= 1.5 × 8 + 5). If the velocity of money is unstable, an appropriate adjustment for that may be made in the money supply growth rate. The Committee further recommended that the rule should be announced but may be subject to periodic revision, particularly if the weather and consequently the growth rate changes significantly. Lately, most Central Banks are using the nominal interest rate policy tool rather than the money supply. The rule for setting the nominal interest rate is suggested by John B Taylor, and is known as the **Taylor's Rule**. This is expressed as below.

$$i_t = 2 + \pi_t + 0.5(\pi_t - \pi_t^*) - 0.5\left[100\left(\frac{Y_t^* - Y_t}{Y_t^*}\right)\right] \tag{13.17}$$

Where, i = nominal interest rate, π = current inflation rate, Y = real income, π^* = target inflation rate, Y^* = potential (full employment) level of income, and subscript t stands for time period. To take an example, if $\pi = 8$, $\pi^* = 5$, and output gap = 4 percent, then the nominal interest rate must be set equal to

$$2 + 8 + 0.5(8-5) - 0.5[100(0.04)] = 9.5\%$$

As the formula indicates, the nominal interest rate varies positively with the current inflation rate and the deviations of the current inflation rate from its target level, and negatively with the output gap. Further, the Rule suggests that

(a) If the target inflation rate were zero (as in countries like New Zealand and Canada) and the actual inflation rate and the output gap were also zero, then the nominal interest rate must be set at 2 per cent, which would also equal the real interest rate.

(b) Since the real interest rate denotes the reward for waiting, the Rule takes it as 2 per cent. This is the rate which even the Chakravarthy Committee report on the monetary system had recommended for India.

(c) For every one per cent increase in inflation rate, *ceteris paribus*, the Central Bank must raise the nominal interest rate by 1.5 per cent.

(d) For every one per cent output gap, ceteris paribus, the nominal interest rate must be set at 0.5 higher levels than otherwise.

The suggested rules for the fiscal policy are in terms of the extent of the fiscal/primary deficit. While some (like the **Gramm-Rudman-Hollings Act** of the United States) suggest a balanced budget operation, others, including the International Monetary Fund (IMF), the European Monetary System (EMS) and our **Fiscal Responsibility and Budget Management** (FRBM) Act 2003, argue for the fiscal deficit to be around 3 per cent of the GDP. Fiscal deficits are inflows to the public debt and hence the appropriate size of the latter is a concern. Recall from our discussion in Chapter 10 that though public debt of any likely magnitude may not always be a real worry; if it is not allowed to rise in relation to the GDP, it may not be a concern at all. Further, we have seen that to hold the public debt to GDP ratio at or below its previous level, all that we need is to ascertain that the primary deficit to GDP ratio is no more than the difference between the growth rate in nominal GDP and the effective nominal interest rate on the debt [vide equation **(10.5)**, Chapter 10]. Also, lately, Reinhart and Rogoff (2012) of Harvard University have argued that growth slows sharply when the ratio of public debt to GDP exceeds 90 per cent. Thus, though there is no hard rule, the fiscal policy rule could be designed according to one or more of such considerations.

Fiscal Policy vis-à-vis Monetary Policy

In the frameworks of the classical model and the different versions of the Keynesian model, we have examined the effects of the fiscal policy on the economy. To recall, in the classical version, the said policy has no effect either on the real output/unemployment or the price level. In the Keynesian cross model, it has the maximum effect on output/unemployment (as the crowding out of the private expenditure is zero) and no effect on price. In the *IS-LM* version, the said crowding out exists, and so the effect on output/unemployment is less than otherwise, with, of course, no effect on the price. Under the *AD-AS* model, the policy affects both, the output/unemployment and price, through both the *AD* as well as *AS*. Since both the *AD* and *AS* sources affect the output/unemployment in the same direction, the fiscal policy is more effective with respect to output under the *AD-AS* model than under the IS-LM model. As the said two sources have opposite effects on the price level, the effect of fiscal policy on price/inflation is ambiguous. In an open economy, the fiscal policy ceases to have any effect on the output, unemployment and price if the country is on the floating exchange rate system; under such a situation the monetary policy enjoys the most powerful status. However, if the economy is open and is on the fixed exchange rate system, then the fiscal policy enjoys significant impact on output, employment, interest rate, etc., and the monetary policy is totally impotent with respect to real magnitudes. Further, in Chapter 10, we have examined the constraints on the fiscal policy that arise particularly when its easy version is applied, viz., consequences on public debt and the country's sovereignty. The said constraints are practically non-binding (government can always violate/seek exception to its own rules) and thus the fiscal policy does have counter cyclical power. In contrast, we have seen in Chapter 10 that if the **Barro-Ricardo equivalence theorem** holds, the fiscal policy would have no bearing on the national saving, interest rate and *AD*, and hence on the economy as a whole. The above are mixed results and, thus, the exact role of fiscal policy depends on the conditions in the economy. Further, the above are mostly short run effects, which alone are important in the discussion of business cycle theories and stabilisation policies. However, the long run consequences are significant from the point of view of growth, and so the same are discussed below together with some caveats to the above discussion and other observations on the said policy.

(a) Expansionary fiscal policy affects national saving adversely through reduction in government saving (unless the Barro-Ricardo theorem holds, under which private saving increases by the amount of increase in government bonds). Fall in national saving, in turn, tends to reduce investment and, thereby, the capital stock, and hence the output in the long run.

(b) Expansionary fiscal policy (increase in government consumption expenditure and not in public investment) crowds out private investment through an increase in the rate of interest. A fall in investment, in turn, retards economic growth.

(c) Fiscal deficit leads to a vicious cycle. As deficit grows, public debt grows, debt servicing grows, government expenditure increases, fiscal deficit increases, debt grows, and so on.

(d) Fiscal deficit may encourage an expansionary monetary policy, which may endanger inflation. All hyperinflations have been associated with increased government expenditure financed through monetisations, called the **pump priming policy**.

(e) Fiscal deficit causes government debt to increase, which may lead to capital flight. Further, if the debt is external and heavy, it has the potential of default and lead to a world debt crisis. These events would reduce the country's credit rating, leading to serious repercussions on many fronts.

(f) Effects of fiscal policy depend, among others factors, on how the fiscal deficit/surplus caused by it is financed/used. Excessive use of any means results in macroeconomic imbalances. For example, financing deficits through monetisation leads to inflation. Financing deficits via internal debt causes credit squeeze, high interest rate and significant crowding out of private expenditure. External debt financed deficits tend to result in current account deficits, domestic currency appreciation, and balance of payments and external debt crises.

(g) Two kinds of fiscal deficits are distinguished: cyclical and structural. Cyclical deficit arises when the output falls short of the full employment level. Because the real income is low, the tax proceeds and other revenues are less and transfer payments (by way of social security etc.) are more, and accordingly the government runs a fiscal deficit. In contrast, the structural deficit results when the real income is at its full employment level. Thus, the structural deficit equals the actual deficit minus the cyclical deficit. The distinction is significant for the use of an expansionary fiscal policy. Keynesians recommend its use, particularly when the economy is facing recession, so that the additional government expenditure would be negligibly inflationary. Thus, the Great Depression was a good time for its use; while in the 1980s when the world was facing inflation more than the unemployment, its use was inappropriate. Currently also, most of the unemployment is structural, caused by a mismatch between job vacancies and the skills of unemployed people, and not cyclical (due to the lack of effective demand), and thus fiscal expansion may not be an ideal policy.

(h) During the Great Depression and even for a few decades thereafter, government expenditure happened to be a small fraction of the total demand, and so the fiscal policy had a limited role. However, under the Keynes' impact during the 1950s and 1960s, public sector expanded a great deal in most countries and, though the privatisation move of the 1980s and thereafter has curtailed its size to a certain extent, it still remains a fairly large part of any economy's total expenditure (the world average government consumption expenditure stands at above 15 per cent of the GDP currently). In view of this, the fiscal policy has gained significance.

(i) The fiscal policy in relation to the monetary policy has two good features, viz.,

- It is a direct policy and thus has a lower outside lag
- It could be a discriminatory policy

Changes in the money supply affect the aggregate demand only indirectly through the changes in the interest rate and the real (cash) balances and, thereby, the changes in investment and consumption expenditures. Thus, to illustrate this limitation of monetary policy, it is said that **"one can lead a horse to water but cannot make it drink"**, also that monetary policy is like "pushing on a string". In contrast, changes in government expenditure and taxes directly and almost immediately affect the aggregate demand, as the former happens to be the components of the latter. Also, while changes in the money supply affect the various sectors uniformly (barring those induced through selective credit controls), those in government expenditure and taxes could very well be **discriminatory**. For example, new (planned) government expenditure may be biased in favour of the projects in developed areas or in favour of certain industries (e.g. knowledge based instead of the traditional industries). Similarly, tax burdens may be reduced for firms locating themselves in erstwhile backward areas and increased for the other firms, or they may be reduced on the manufacturing industries and increased on service industries, and vice versa. The use of progressive taxation on income and wealth, and the awards of social security benefits are designed to move towards social goals through the use of fiscal instruments.

(j) The fiscal policy suffers from some limitations as well:

- Asymmetric/Ambiguous
- Longer inside lag

Recall from Chapter 10 that fiscal policy is **asymmetric**, for while it is easy to increase government expenditure and reduce taxes, the reversal of these is hard to implement. There are many social and political programmes, and the expenditure on them is rigid in the downward direction. Any reduction in the expenditure on education, health services, pensions and other social security measures will be very strongly resisted. Even investment on projects like road, rail, airport and port constructions, school, college and hospital buildings etc. is hard to reduce. The application of indirect tax instruments on the higher side is constrained by their cost of living effects, which provokes reactions from trade unions. If the indirect tax rate increases, the prices of goods and services go up and therefore the cost of living. This prompts trade unions to ask for dearness allowances, which, if allowed, aggravate the price increase, and set the wage-price spiral in motion. This reduces the role of indirect taxes in restricting aggregate demand. The effects of direct taxes on consumption expenditure are unambiguous, but their effects on the investment expenditure are uncertain. Also, as seen above changes in direct taxes affect the aggregate supply as well. Thus, the effect of taxes on the aggregate demand, income and price are somewhat uncertain. These factors do limit the role of the fiscal policy in countering business cycles.

As mentioned above the fiscal policy has a **longer inside lag** than the monetary policy. It is not just that decision-making is very time consuming, the implementation of fiscal policy decisions are so as well. For example, decisions on large scale government expenditure can be implemented only after ensuring the availability of funds as well as equipment and the construction material, etc. There are plenty of examples where significant decisions on public investments had significant time over runs.

Case Study: Oil price hike and the resulting leftward shift in the *AS* curve caused the stagflation during 1970s. Similarly, the invention of the internet raised the productivity and triggered stock market bubble during the second half of the 1990s, leading to increase in both *AD* and *AS*, bringing prosperity with near price stability. The bust of the bubble triggered a fall in *AD*, causing world-wide recession in 2001. Once again, housing price bubble and low interest rate, leading to subprime mortgage lending under high financial leverage, gave an upward push to *AD* and brought world–wide prosperity during 2002-06. Subsequent securitization of bad debts during 2006-07, resulted into bank and corporate failures and collapse of the asset prices, and fall in *AD*, resulting into the Great Recession during 2007-09.

Conclusion

In the open economy models, there is interdependence among countries and there are new tools for stabilising the economy. The former comes through imports and exports of goods and services, and movement of capital across countries. The latter includes the trade policy and the choice of the exchange rate regime. In addition, countries face a trilemma, called impossible trinity. Depending on the option chosen, a well-integrated open economy can regulate/target either the money supply or the exchange rate but not both. Stabilisation policy remains effective both in the fixed price as well as in flexible price models. In the Keynesian open economy flexible price model, income and price are simultaneously determined by aggregate demand and aggregate supply. Further, aggregate demand is influenced not just by the money supply, as in the classical model, but by several other exogenous variables, including government expenditure, autonomous taxes, autonomous consumption, autonomous investment, autonomous net exports, world income, world interest rate and the exchange rate. Unlike the classical model where the *AS* is fixed, in the *AD-AS* model, *AS* is subject to supply shocks (favourable or/ and adverse), which could come from work force, raw material prices, weather, etc. The business cycles in this model could thus be caused by any demand and supply shock. At least one of the stabilising policies (fiscal, monetary, trade or exchange rate) is always (barring during stagflation) effective in stabilising the economy, though their influence is limited by the policy lags and problems associated with fiscal and balance of payments' deficits and public debts. The presence of international transactions has repercussions on the potencies of both policies. Under the floating exchange rate system, the fiscal policy becomes impotent (with regard to income and price), while the monetary policy gains strength and quite the opposite is true under the fixed exchange rate system. An open economy could face a dilemma of conflict between the internal and external equilibrium. Favourable supply shocks provide the only solution to attack stagflation caused by adverse supply shocks. The various stabilisation polices affect the economy through a variety of sources, which at times are conflicting as well. The Keynesian model and even the supply side economics could not explain the persisting inflation during and after the late 1970s thus, indicating the need for a better macroeconomic theory. This is the subject matter for the next chapter.

KEYWORDS

Flexible price model; Closed/Open economy; Flexible/Fixed exchange rate; AD function; Keynes' interest rate effect; Pigou's real balance/wealth effect; International trade's exchange rate effect; ; Price expectations effect; Income redistribution effect; Stabilising-Destabilising effect of inflation; Substitution-Income effect; SAS- LAS Curve; AD-SAS-LAS-BP model; IS-LM-SAS-LAS-BP model; Phillips curve; Fiscal-Monetary policy operating mechanism; Internal-External equilibrium; Target; Instrument; Recession; Capital flight; Kennedy-Johnson tax cuts; Vietnam War; OECD group of countries; Stagflation/Slumpflation; Accommodating-Extinguishing-Neutral policy; Supply side economics; Ultra classicism; Voodoo economics; Inside-Outside lag; Information/recognition-Decision-Implementation lag; Long and variable lag; Active/discretionary–Passive/rule based policy; Monetarists-Non-monetarists controversy; Asymmetric-Discriminatory policy; Gramm-Rudman-Hollings Act; FRBM Act, Taylor rule.

REFERENCES

1. Brunner Karl, 'The Role of Money and Monetary Policy', Federal Reserve Bank of St. Louis Review, 71, (September–October, 1989): 4-22.
2. Fischer Stanley, 'Rules Versus Discretion in Monetary Policy', in Benjamin Friedman, Frank Hahn, (eds.) *Handbook of Monetary Economics*, Vol.2, (Amsterdam: Elsevier Science Publishers, 1990), pp. 1156-84.

3. Friedman Milton, *A Program for Monetary Stability*, (New York: Fordham University Press, 1959).
4. Friedman Milton, The Lags in the Effect of Monetary Policy, in Milton Friedman, The Optimum Quantity of Money and Other Essays, (Chicago: Aldine, 1969).
5. Laffer Arthur, *The ellipse: An Explication of the Laffer Curve in a Two factor Model,* (Sydney: Grenwood Press, 1986).
6. Raphael D D, Donald Winch, Lord Skidelsky, *Three Great Economists: Smith, Malthus and Keynes*, (Oxford and New York: Oxford University Press, 1997).
7. Reinhart, Carmen and Kenneth Rogoff, Growth in a Time of Debt, *American Economic Review*, 100, 2 (January 2010), 573-8.
8. Reserve Bank of India, Chakravarty Committee Report, (Mumbai, 1985).
9. Taylor, John B, Discretion versus Rule in Practice, Carnegie-Rochester Conference Series on Public Policy, 1993.

Review Questions

1. Describe in words each of the following curves:
IS curve
LM curve
BP curve
AD curve
AS curve

2. Explain whether each of the following events shift the *AD* curve, *AS* curve or both, or neither. For each event that shifts the curve(s), draw a diagram to illustrate the effect on the economy.

(a) Due to stock market boom, households wealth increases
(b) Government cuts tax rate
(c) Crude oil price goes up
(d) Technical improvements raise labour productivity
(e) A recession abroad reduces domestic exports

3. List and explain at least three factors that cause the short-run aggregate supply curve to slope upward. For Aggregate demand curve to slope downward.

4. Suppose the Woodland economy is subject to the AD-AS-BP model described in this chapter. Discuss the factors that could cause fluctuations in output, unemployment and the price level in this economy. Describe the mechanisms through which such consequences would proceed.

5. The Keynesian multiplier is lower in an open economy than in a closed economy. Explain.

6. The Pigou effect restores the effectiveness of monetary policy in the presence of liquidity trap. Discuss.

7. The fiscal policy is ineffective in an open economy having the freely floating exchange rate system. Why?

8. The monetary policy has no role in the determination of real income and price in an open economy with the fixed exchange rate system. Is this true? Why?

9. Demand management policies are inadequate to deal with stagflation. Explain.
10. Both the fiscal and monetary policies are subject to the similar lags, and hence both are useless tools in the hands of the policy makers. Do you agree? Why or why not?
11. Imperfect information and policy lags render a discretion based approach less effective than would have been the case otherwise.
12. The governments, including the Central Bank of the country, enjoys the unlimited power of taxation and printing of money, and the balanced budget multiplier is positive, hence business fluctuations are due to ineffective governments. Do you agree? Why or why not?
13. Suppose an economy was characterized by the following system of the IS-LM-AS model:

IS equation $Y = k_1A_1 - k_1d(i - p^e) + k_1(\beta + \delta)[(E)(P^w)/P^d]$

LM equation $Y = 1/e(M/P) + (f/e)i^w$

AS equation $P = P^e + (1/\alpha)(Y - Y_n) + P_R$

where, $k_1 = 3$, $A_1 = 750$, $d = 100$, $p^e = 0$, $(\beta + \delta) = 1.6$, $P^w = 0.03$, $e = 0.4$, $f = 1680$, $i^w = 0.07$, $P^e = 1$, $\alpha = 50$, $P_R = 0.5$ and $Y_n = 2{,}250$. Notations have the same meaning as in the text (Chapters 12 and 13), interest rates are in basis points, prices are in index numbers with a base value = 1 and exchange rate is in direct quotation. Answer the following questions:

(a) Transform the above model into a closed economy model. Solve the resultant model for income, price and the interest rate (assume $M = M_0 = 750$ and G = 350). Examine the effects of each of the following demand management policies on Y, P and i:

(i) Government expenditure increases by 100

(ii) Money supply falls by 100

(iii) Both **(i)** and **(ii)** above

(b) Treat the above model as for an open economy with the floating exchange rate system. Solve the system for Y, P and E (assume $M - M_0 - 750$ and $G = 350$). Examine the effects of each the above three policy initiatives [as in **(a)** above] on each of the model's three endogenous variables (if you think there is some missing information on any variable/parameter, please assume some reasonable values and proceed).

(c) Consider the above model as that of an open economy with the fixed exchange rate system. Solve the system for Y, P and M (assume $E = E_0 = 40$ and G = 350). Evaluate the effects of each the above three policy initiatives [as in **(a)** above] on each of the model's three endogenous variables (if you think there is some missing information on any variable/parameter, please assume some reasonable values and proceed).

(d) Compare the results in **(a)**, **(b)** and **(c)** above and comment. (Hint: For an open economy $i = i^w$)

Chapter 14

New Classical and New Keynesian Models

Learning Objectives

After reading the chapter you should be able to:

1. Learn the difference between the old and new for each of the classical and the Keynesian models.
2. Comprehend the role of price expectations which demonstrates that while in the medium term the output fluctuates around its natural level, it always returns to its natural level in the long run—the natural rate hypothesis.
3. Appreciate that, the business cycles are the short run phenomenon, which can be triggered by the ill found stabilisation policies and/or the actions of the private sector and can be countered by the appropriate fiscal, monetary, trade, exchange rate, and income policies.
4. Understand that the so-called trade-off between the rate of inflation and the rate of unemployment is valid in the short-run but not in the long-run, and that too if and only if there are policy or non-policy surprises.
5. Grasp the theory of policy irrelevance which states that the stabilisation policies are ineffective with respect to real variables, like real GDP and unemployment, unless there are policy surprises.
6. Acquire the knowledge that while the short business cycles can be rationalised through the Friedman-Lucas kind of (misperceptions) models, the multi-year business cycles, such as the Great Depression of the 1930s, the stagflation of the 1970s and the Global recession of the 2007-09 are best explained through the real business cycle theory.
7. Know the rationale that the new Keynesian theory has advanced to explain its belief that the prices and wages are rigid in the medium term.

Developments in macroeconomic theory have evolved in response to economic events in the real world. Before the Great Depression, the world did not face any serious problem of unemployment, and accordingly, the classical theory of macroeconomics dominated the scene. The Great Depression defied classicalists belief of full employment and so emerged the Keynesian theory of (possible) under-employment equilibrium. The latter theory culminated in the downward sloping Phillips Curve, implying a permanent trade-off between the rate of unemployment and the rate of inflation. The threat of inflation and the emergence of stagflation during the late 1960s and 1970s provided proof against the said trade-off, and established the inability of the Keynesian demand management policies to cure the twin economic ills occurring simultaneously. The revival of the supply side economics provided temporary solace but it failed to explain the continuing inflation. The new classical model, to distinguish it from the erstwhile (orthodox) classical model, was then advanced to account for the emerging world scenario. The latter, also known as the Friedman-Lucas-Sargent-Wallace model of the imperfect information and rational expectations theory, could not explain the multi-year business cycles that plagued the world in the late 1920s and 1930s; thus, an another version of the new classical school—the real business cycle theory—emerged during the 1980s. This led to some academic debate among the classicists and the Keynesians, and the latter took recourse to microeconomic principles to justify the Keynesian assumption of the wage-price rigidity, and that has now come to be known as the new Keynesian model, again to distinguish this from the erstwhile (orthodox) Keynesian model. Further developments have taken place with regard to the direction of the causation between the money supply and nominal GDP, and towards the variability of the natural rate of unemployment over time. All these developments have marked significant improvements in understanding the existence of business cycles, and the roles of the fiscal and monetary policies in taming them. The chapter covers such developments from the point they were left off by the previous chapter.

New Classical Model

The new classical model, like its cousin (old classical model), proclaims wage-price flexibility and, hence, the market clearance; appeals to the optimum behaviour of all the agents; and postulates the full employment equilibrium in the long run and the possibility of the under/over full employment equilibrium in the short run. Thus, the model provides a source for business cycles on the classical postulates of market clearance, and it therefore marks an alternative to the Keynesian theory of under employment equilibrium. Initially, the model was regarded as a variant of the **monetarism**. However, it was subsequently seen to be based on a new methodology and more so in its real business cycle version and, accordingly, the model is now treated as a separate body of thought under the name, 'New Classical Model'. The model offers two independent explanations of business cycles, and accordingly it is split into two independent parts: **(a)** Friedman-Lucas model, **(b)** Real business cycle model.

The former explains business cycles through the monetary impulses and the latter via the real factors of the supply side. Further, the first part has two slightly varying assumptions about market imperfections as well as expectations; hence, this is dealt below under two sub-parts to highlight the differences between them.

Friedman's Workers' Fooling Model

Milton Friedman (1968) and Edmund Phelps (1967) were the first to suggest that the expectations about the future price level play a role in setting the nominal wage rate and the product price. Labour supply was postulated to be governed by the expected real wage rate, like the Keynesian model, and so the aggregate supply varies inversely with the expected price in this model (vide Chapter 9). The introduction of the expected price in the aggregate supply function created a significant impact on macroeconomics and thus it could be called as a revolution in macroeconomics. In his 1968 article, which is considered the most influential publication in macroeconomics after the Keynes General Theory, Friedman also provided a new theory, called the **theory of natural rate of unemployment**. The said theory states that if the rate of unemployment fell below its natural level, the rate of inflation will accelerate (i.e., the rate of inflation, not just the price, will increase); and if it exceeded the natural level, inflation will decelerate. Due to this meaning, the natural rate of unemployment is also referred to as the non-accelerating inflation rate of unemployment (NAIRU) (Chapter 9). Recall that under the Keynesian flexible price model (vide Chapter 13), either both or at least one of the fiscal and monetary policies (called the demand management policies) are generally effective in countering business cycles. Therefore, knowing well the trade-off between the unemployment rate and the inflation rate, if these demand management policies were pressed so much that they reduce the unemployment rate (u) below its natural level (u_n), inflation will accelerate. What would make this happen and what will be the further consequences?

Milton Friedman advanced the **"fooling of workers"/"asymmetric information"** theory. Also, as explained in Chapter 9, Friedman had proposed the **adaptive expectations theory** (AET) for formulating the expectations about the future inflation rate. Thus, when the expansionary demand management policies are implemented, the AD curve would shift upwards/flatten (shift upwards due to an increase in government expenditure and flatten if the money supply increases, *ceteris paribus*), the AS curve (which is upwards sloping under the Friedman's model, vide Chapter 9) remaining constant, the price and also the output and employment would go up. The output and hence employment would increase because the increase in price would not be noticed by workers but firms would learn of that under the Friedman's fooling model. This is so because the workers buy a number of items and while some prices might have even fallen, the others may have increased at various rates. In contrast, firms monitor the general price trend rather carefully. As product price increases, firms are happy to grant some increase in the money wage rate but ensure a reduction in the real wage rate. Therefore, since the real wage is reduced, firms would find it profitable to hire additional labour. Since the money wage is somewhat higher now than before, and the workers do not know about the increase in the product price, they think their real wage rate is up and, accordingly, they will be happy to supply the additional labour. In consequence, the increased demand caused by the expansionary demand management policy would be matched by increased supply, and in consequence, the output and employment would increase, and so would the product price. This is illustrated below in Fig. 14.1.

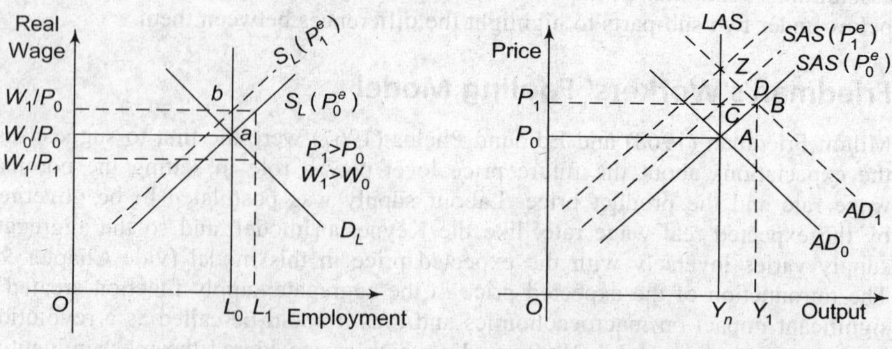

Fig. 14.1 Workers' Fooling Model

The basic philosophy behind the above diagrams is that Friedman has introduced a new theory for labour supply, and accordingly for the AS function and the Phillips curve. He hypothesised that the supply of labour depends on the workers' expected real wage rate rather than on the true real wage rate. Thereby, if the workers' expected price increases, *ceteris paribus*, their expected real wage falls, and so the labour supply falls and thus the labour supply curve shifts up, and vice versa. This renders the labour supply curve a negative function of the workers' expected price. Thus, if the expected price increases, *ceteris paribus*, the supply of labour goes down; the demand for labour remaining the same, the employment of workers would fall. The latter, other resources (inputs) remaining the same, results in a fall in short run aggregate supply (SAS). Putting all these sequential effects together, an increase in the expected price causes a decrease in SAS. Quite the opposite would happen in the event of a fall in the expected price. Consequently, the SAS curve is a negative function of the expected price. Since the Phillips curve is a mirror image of the AS curve (vide Chapter 9), the Phillips curve would be a positive function of the workers' expected price, i.e., as the expected price increases, the Phillips curve shifts to the right, and vice versa. However, the demand for labour still remains a negative function of the actual real wage rate.

The curves marked D_L and S_L in part A, Fig. 14.1 denotes the labour demand and labour supply curves, respectively. S_L is drawn on the workers' expected product price = P_0^e. The market clearing employment and the real wage rate are L_o and W_o/P_o, respectively. AD_0 and $SAS\ (P_0^e)$ in part B, Fig. 14.1, denote the *AD* curve and SAS curve (for $P^e = P_0^e$), and the market clearing output and price are Y_n and P_o, respectively. Both the labour market and the product market are in equilibrium at the above values. This is now disturbed by an expansionary demand management policy, which shifts the *AD* curve to AD_1. Consequently, the equilibrium in the product market moves from point *A* to point *B*. The new price is higher than the old price. Firms learn of it, but the workers do not under the Friedman model. The labour market accordingly responds through an increase in the money wage from W_o *to* W_1, an increase in employment from L_o to L_1, and a decrease in the real wage rate from W_o/P_0 *to* W_1/P_1 and yet, demand for labour equals the supply of labour at L_1, thus, ensuring the labour market clearance. The labour market position is calculated on the basis of the workers' fooling model, as described above. To repeat for convenience, since firms know about the price increase, they offer a little (less than the proportionate) raise in the money wage rate (from W_o to W_1 but W_1/P_1 less than W_o/P_0), which induces workers to supply more labour at L_1 as they do not know of the price increase and they retain their expected price at P_o thinking their expected real wage rate is up (W_1/P_0 is more than W_o/P_0). As the increase in the nominal wage rate is less than the increase in the price, the actual real wage rate is now lower than before (W_1/P_1 is less than W_o/P_0), firms hire more labour equal to L_1.

Thereby, the new equilibrium at point *B* in part B, Fig. 14.1, is consistent with the equilibrium in the labour market. A comparison of the equilibrium values at points *B* (Y_1 and P_1) and *A* (Y_n and P_0) would indicate that the expansionary demand management policy has resulted in an increase in output and also an increase in price level. Thus, an upturn in the economy could be triggered through an expansionary fiscal/monetary policy, and vice versa. Hence, the fiscal/monetary policies, which constitute the monetary impulses, could cause business cycles. The cycles are the short-run phenomena, and so is the equilibrium at point B in part B, Fig. 14.1. This is because the actual price P_1 is not equal to the expected price (P_0^e). In terms of the Phillips curve, the situation would be as follows:

In Fig. 14.2, the *SP* (called the short term Phillips curve) is a positive function of the expected price. The curve shifts up as the expected price goes up, and vice versa. The initial equilibrium is at point P with the unemployment rate = u_n and the actual inflation rate = $\dot{P}_0$. The expected price equals the true price and so the equilibrium is a long run one. An expansionary fiscal or/and monetary policy moves the equilibrium point from P to Q. The equilibrium at point Q is only a short run one, as the actual inflation rate ($\dot{P}_1$) is not equal to the expected inflation rate ($\dot{P}_0^e$).

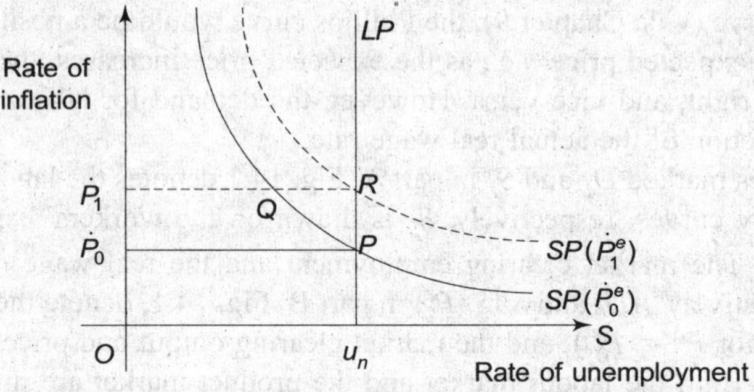

Fig. 14.2 Phillip's Curve under the "Fooling Model"

What will happen in the long run? The workers would be surprised to find that the actual price/inflation rate is higher than their expected one. Basing their expectations on the Friedman's adaptive expectations model, they would revise their price expectations upward, which would tend to shift each of the labour supply curves, SAS curve as well as *SP*, upward, as shown by the dotted lines in the three figures above. The new labour supply curve would be the one marked as S_L (P_1^e) in part A, Fig. 14.1, and the *SAS* curve as marked *SAS* (P_1^e) in part B, Fig. 14.1 (the resulting- intermediate-Phillips curve is not shown in Fig. 14.2 for simplicity). The new equilibrium in the labour market would be given by point b in part A, Fig. 14.1, and in the product market by point D in part B, Fig. 14.1. These equilibrium at points b and D are also short term, for the new price at point D in part B, Fig. 14.1, is higher than the workers' expected price (P^e). In consequence, workers would find that they have been fooled once again. This would trigger another adjustment on the lines similar to the earlier one and the process would continue until the long run equilibrium is re-established at point Z in part B, Fig. 14.1, where the expected price is identical to the true price.

In terms of the Phillips curve, the new equilibrium would be at point R in Fig. 14.2. Exactly the opposite will happen if and when the money supply and/or government expenditure decreases: the *AD* curve would shift downward, output and price would fall, the real wage rate would increase and the firms would hire less labour in the short run, in the long run, the expected price/inflation rate will fall, the AS curve would shift down, output would increase and the price would fall and the process would continue until the output level returns to the pre-contraction of the money supply/government expenditure level and a proportionate fall in the price level/ inflation rate. Thus, the short run and long run effects are different. It is seen that an expansionary demand management policy would lead to an increase, both, in output (and employment) and price in the short run but only to an increase in the price in the long run, and a restrictive said policy to a fall in both output and price in the short run and to only a fall in price in the long run. In terms of graphs, the curves marked *SAS* in part B Fig. 14.1 and *SP* in Fig. 14.2 are the short run curves, and those marked *LAS* and *LP* in the two graphs, respectively, are their long run counterparts. In consequence, while the short run Phillips curve is a downward sloping one, the long run Phillips curve is vertical. Accordingly, Friedman suggests that the hitherto **Phillips' curve trade-off between inflation rate and unemployment rate is merely a short run (temporary) phenomenon and not a long run (permanent) one**. This marks a significant result in macroeconomics. The new Phillips' curves incorporate price expectations and accordingly they are referred to as **Inflation Augmented Phillips' Curves**.

Milton Friedman suggests that when expectations are accurate, output equals its natural level, i.e., the one associated with the natural rate of unemployment. Thus, the fooling model suggests that the long run *AS* curve (*LAS*) is vertical at the natural output level and the long run Phillips curve (*LP*) is vertical at the corresponding natural rate of unemployment. Along the long run *AS* curve (*LAS* in part B, Fig. 14.1) and the long run Phillips curve (*LP* in Fig. 14.2), the expected price/inflation equals actual price/inflation; hence, these curves are also called the **accurate expectations curves**. This is how Friedman's model explains the occurrences of business cycles with the classical assumption of market clearing or flexible wage-price assumption. His model is also called as the **natural rate model of the business cycle,** under which the stabilization policies are effective with respect to the real magnitudes (like output, employment etc.) in the short run but neutral in the long run. This is known as the **natural rate hypothesis**. Stated briefly, it says that changes in the aggregate demand, which could be caused by the demand management policies and/or by non-policy variables, influence output, employment, unemployment only in the short run and that in the long run these real variables always return to their respective natural levels. Thus, while the long-run GDP is given by the factor market (supply side), the short run GDP is governed by both the supply and demand side factors. Accordingly, the natural rate hypothesis rationalizes the classical theory as well as explains the historical fact of persisting inflation (or even deflation) with a stable unemployment rate, a phenomenon the Keynesian model of the previous chapters could not predict.

Money is neutral in the old classical model. However, in the natural rate model it is not so in the short run, whereas it is neutral in the long run. As seen above, an increase in the supply of money (or an increase in government expenditure) would shift the AD curve to the right in Figure 14.1, Part B (and the equilibrium from point *P* to point *Q* in the Phillips curve in Fig. 14.2), which, in turn, would lead to an increase in real income as well as in the price level in the short run. However, this event would cause an upward revision in the expected price, which would push up the *SAS* (SP) curve until the equilibrium returns to the point *Z* (point *R* in Fig. 14.2) on the *AD-AS* diagram (vide Part *B*, Fig. 14.1), where the output exactly equals that before the change in the money supply and the price is higher than before. Quite the reverse would happen when the money supply decreases. Thereby, the money supply is neutral in the long run but not in short run in the Friedman's fooling model. Incidentally, note that the shift in *AD* need not arise through a monetary or/ and a fiscal policy initiative, it can as well be triggered by any other factor that has a bearing on aggregate demand, like a change in foreign demand for a firm's product (net export), consumers' and/or business expectations about the future (which affect autonomous consumption and autonomous investment, respectively) etc. In view of this, business cycles could be caused by the demand management policies as well as by such other events.

Critics of the fooling model argue that even workers cannot be fooled consistently for long: "You cannot fool all the people all the time". Media informs people about price trends on a regular basis; and if the high output and high general price always occur simultaneously, workers would suspect this in future and would forbid any systematic changing. If so, even if the nominal wage rate increase is proportional to the price increase, workers would supply no extra labour and, thus, there would be no increase in output in the face of an expansionary fiscal/monetary policy, and hence no business cycle. Quite the opposite logic would apply in the face of a simultaneous fall in output and price due to some dear demand management policy. Nevertheless, though the Friedman's asymmetry of information may not hold much water, its cousin, the **information barrier**, which is the contention of the Lucas model (explained in the next section), would justify business cycles.

Milton Friedman's name is also associated with a school of thought, called **monetarism**, and thus it is pertinent to understand it in relation to other thoughts. Though there is no unambiguous definition of it, monetarism is usually characterised by the following:

(a) The money demand function is stable in the long run. This means that the money demand is a stable function of known variables with stable parameters/ elasticities. It implies that the velocity of money is stable over time.

(b) Monetary authorities enjoy full powers to control the money supply.

(c) The trade-off between unemployment and inflation rates exists in the short run and not in long run. This implies that fiscal and monetary policies enjoy the role of causing and taming business cycles.

(d) The monetary policy is more powerful than the fiscal policy in managing the economy, and fluctuations in money supply are the primary cause of fluctuations in *AD* and real income.

(e) Rule based policies are preferred to fine-tuned ones.

While the demand for money function worked well until about the mid-1970s, it first over predicted the money demand during the second half of the 1970s and then under predicted the said demand during the 1980s. This being its major constituent, monetarism has lost its significance ever since. Robert Lucas has even argued that if the rule-based approach were followed, the velocity of money would become unstable. Keynesianism, also known as **non-monetarism**, is understood as the opposite of monetarism. As explained here and below, the new classicalism stands only for point **(c)** above, and that too with a modification that the short run tradeoff is also subject to 'surprises' only. New classical economics is also considered as another name for the flexible price Walrasian general equilibrium analysis, normally applied to macroeconomic issues.

Lucas Information Barriers Model

Robert Lucas' (1987) theory retains Friedman's assumption of market clearance, and substitutes the (symmetric) **imperfect information** for the asymmetric information used in the workers' fooling model and the **rational expectations hypothesis** (REH) for the adaptive expectations theory (AET) of the Friedman's model (vide Chapter 9). The new theory purports that it is not that workers do not know, while firms know the true price (vide the Friedman model) but rather that there are 'information barriers' that hinder the perfect information from passing to both firms and workers alike. The information about the real economy is often inaccurate (vide Chapters 2, 3 and 4) and quite delayed; besides it is very expensive to collect, maintain and understand information. The AET was acceptable during the 1950s and 1960s when the price change was usually low and bi-directional, but it proved highly inappropriate during the 1970s when the inflation rate was usually positive and high (vide Chapter 9).

Under the Lucas model, firms are small entities operating in a perfectly competitive market. When the demand conditions for their products improve, could be due to an expansionary monetary/fiscal policy or any other factor, the prices of their products rise, which they know too well. However, due to **information barriers**, firms do not learn of increases in prices of other products, their raw materials and supplies. In consequence, firms think that the relative prices of their products have increased, and thereby they think their business have become more profitable than before. Accordingly, firms react to such developments by hiring more labour and even offering them a slightly higher nominal wage rate and thereby tend to increase their outputs. Workers are happy to supply the extra labour at a little higher money wage rate, which means a higher expected real wage rate than before. In consequence, the output expands and the price increases in the short run. Once the information about the prices of other goods (raw materials and supplies included) become public, the price expectations will be revised upward and the supply curve would shift up (to left) so as to bring back the output to the original level (pre-expansionary policy) and the price proportionately so as to lie on the vertical long run *AS* curve. Quite the opposite will happen when the aggregate demand falls due to a tight monetary/fiscal policy or any other demand-influencing factor.

Firms and workers form price expectations on the basis of rational expectations. Thereby, if the changes in the demand conditions were systematic, firms and workers would predict them well, have no handicap of the information barrier, and would refuse to change their productions. For example, if past movements in the prices of their products have always been accompanied by similar movements in the prices of their raw materials and supplies, firms should expect that this will happen. In that case, when they see a rise in their products' prices, they would revise their expected price upward and the *AS* curve would shift up so as to leave the real output unaltered and the general price to rise proportionately in response to an upward shift in the *AD* curve. However, if the price of the firm's product had often exhibited unique movements in response to local conditions, then the product price may rise without any increase in the prices of raw materials, and firms may not revise their expected price, and instead, accordingly raise their productions. Thus, if **changes in the demand and prices** (caused by expansionary fiscal/monetary policy) were **systematic, they would be predicted** and result in no change in output and a proportionate change in the price and, accordingly, the fiscal/monetary policy will be neutral to real magnitudes. However, if the changes in demand and prices were random, they would not be expected even under rational expectations, and firms would change their productions, making the fiscal/monetary policy non-neutral with respect to the real magnitudes in the short run. In the long run, by definition, price expectations have to be consistent with the actual price and, hence, the said policies would be neutral to real magnitudes and they would cause proportionate changes in nominal magnitudes. As the Lucas theory leads to results similar to the Friedman theory, the two are generally combined into one.

Recall from Chapter 9 (equation 9.9) that the above logic results into the *AS* function, the so-called Friedman-Lucas' equation, which is as follows:

$$Y = Y_n + \alpha (P - P^e)$$

Where α denotes the response of output to the price surprises $(P - P^e)$.

This is the short run *AS* equation, and its long-run (when $P = P^e$) counterpart is

$$Y = Y_n$$

The Lucas theory postulates that the supply is fixed at Y_n in the long run. In the short run, the supply response will be:

(a) High for firms that have previously experienced unique price movements and low for firms that have experienced price movements mimicking them in the aggregate economy. This is so because the former group of firms could think that the price of their products alone has gone up, and so they would try to take advantage of their expected enhanced profitability. In contrast, the latter group of firms would take the price increase as a general phenomenon and so would not react much.

(b) High in countries where the inflation rate has been relatively stable and low in countries where the inflation rate has varied significantly over time. The rationale for this lies in the fact that in the midst of stable prices, firms would think that the increase in price is a new opportunity, while in case of fluctuating price they would think that the price increase may be reversed in future.

It would be obvious from the *AD-AS* diagrams that the lower the supply response, the steeper the short run *AS* curve; and the lesser the (short run) fluctuations in output due to demand shocks. Given this and the point **(b)** above, it is clear that countries with a relatively fluctuating inflation rate should have had smaller fluctuations in their real incomes than the ones with a relatively stable inflation rate. History does provide some support to this implication. For example, for the period 1964 to 2000, the coefficient of variations (standard deviation divided by mean) of the growth rate in real GDP and inflation rate for the select countries were as follows:

Table 14.1 Coefficient of Variations in Growth and Inflation Rates in Select Countries

Country	*Coefficient of variation of growth rate in real GDP (%)*	*Coefficient of variation of inflation rate (CPI) (%)*
India	82	31
USA	79	62
China	73	97
Japan	69	128
UK	96	74

Source: IMF. International Financial Statistics, various issues.

India has had the most stable inflation rate and Japan the most unstable one; but the fluctuations in real GDP were more in India than Japan. Further, the United Kingdom has experienced the most fluctuating real GDP and Japan the least; but the inflation rate was more stable in the former than the latter. Of course, the relationship may not have been be so uniform in case of some other countries.

Like in the Friedman's model, in the Lucas-Sargent-Wallace model (1975), the labour supply curve as well as the aggregate supply curve depends negatively on the expected price. Further, in the latter model, price expectations are formed on the basis of the REH, and thus, they incorporate all the expected/systematic changes in money supply, government fiscal operations, private sector behaviour with regard to autonomous expenditures, and so on. Accordingly, all the systematic, expected or announced policy changes have no effect on the economy's output, and as such, the said policies are ineffective (neutral) with respect to the real magnitudes. This is the **policy irrelevance (ineffectiveness) proposition of the Lucas theory**. However, the surprise or random changes in the demand management policies cannot be predicted and, hence, they affect the real income and unemployment, and so are effective. This implies that the **Phillips curve is not** only, not a downward sloping curve in the long run (as per Friedman's theory), but that it is not **a downward sloping curve even in the short run unless the policy changes are random/ surprises**. In other words, the trade-off between the inflation and unemployment rate (or between the inflation and economic growth rate, vide Chapter 9), which was considered as the permanent one under the Keynesian model and the temporary one under the Friedman model, does not exist at all unless there are policy or non-policy surprises in the economy, in the Lucas model. Accordingly, the quantity theory of money results (i.e. any change in money supply results in the direct and proportionate change in the price level) holds in the absence of any surprise. Further, if surprise, any change in money supply is split into changes in price and output, and the less is the surprise, the more is the change in price and the less in output, and vice versa. The conclusion is close to the classical theory based on the assumption of the wage-price flexibility (market clearance) and perfect information, hence, the Lucas model is a new classical one. A point of difference between the new classical result and the old classical one is that the former is more skeptical than the latter about the roles of fiscal and monetary policies in affecting real magnitudes. Both the versions support the **classicist's noninterventionist policy**.

At the cost of some repetition, let us recall that all the classical models assume wage-price flexibility, the difference among them lies only with regard to their assumption about the information. While the old classical model assumes perfect information and thereby preempts the need for any expectation formulation model; Friedman takes the information as asymmetric and thereby imperfect, and suggests the adaptive expectations model. The Lucas model is based on symmetric but imperfect information and rational expectations. Robert Lucas' rational expectations theory criticises the Milton Friedman adaptive expectations theory (known as the **Lucas critique**) on the ground that the latter ignores the impact of policy stance on expectations, which play a crucial role in economic behaviour. In other words, the said criticism arises because while the Lucas theory incorporates the effects of the expected/systematic policy changes in forming the price and other expectations, the same are ignored by Friedman's adaptive expectations theory. In the Lucas' Model, people read the "lips and faces" of the policy makers in predicting the future while in the Friedman Model they just ignore such factors. Under rational expectations, there is no reason for markets to fail and so they always clear. It may also be noted here that the old classical model is alternatively called the **monetarist model**, which is synonymous with any model in which money (and other monetary variables, like government expenditure) is neutral with regard to real variables (real income, employment/unemployment, real interest rate etc.); in contrast to the **Keynesian** (or the non-monetarist) **model** in which the money is non-neutral.

The Lucas model may be considered as a revolution in macroeconomics. It implies that business cycles could be eliminated if we could ensure accurate (perfect) information about the general price level and have systematic policies. Critics argue that the information on the price trend is now available with short lags (though it varies from country to country); and if so, firms and workers may wait for such periods rather than revising their production and efforts' plans, thereby avoiding business cycles. However, business cycles are a fact of life and accordingly the new classical theory fails to provide the much needed explanation. Further, the short lags can only cause short cycles of a few weeks or months, and not the multi-year cycles, which have plagued the world. Historical data reveals that the unemployment rate stood at a two-digit number in the United States, the United Kingdom and many other countries for over ten consecutive years, during the 1920s and the 1930s, and the growth rate in real GDP remained negative during the Great Depression in almost all countries across the world. Further, the golden period of the 1950s and 1960s, the worldwide stagflation of the second half of the 1970s and early 1980s, relative prosperity of the 1990s, and the great recession of 2007-09, among other such events, provide enough evidence of the existence of multi-year cycles. Also, the Lucas-Sargent theory has been attacked on the grounds that the information is costly, both in terms of collecting and processing; that the knowledge needed to process the information is scarce and that there exists labour contracts which prohibit the wage flexibility, at least in the short run. All these factors render the Lucas theory inappropriate to explain business cycles, just as the stagflation of the 1970s ruled out the policy menu represented by the then downward sloping Phillips Curve.

Real Business Cycle Theory

The failure of the Friedman-Lucas theory to explain the multi-year business cycles and the supply shocks of the 1970s (oil price hikes of 1973-75 and 1978-80) led Finn Kydland and Edward Prescott (1982), among others, to offer an alternative explanation to business cycles through a new theory, called the real business cycle (RBC) theory. The RBC theory retains the classical assumption of the wage-price flexibility and suggests that the origins of the business cycles lie in the real (or supply) shocks rather than the monetary/fiscal/other (demand) shocks (price surprises) of the Friedman-Lucas model. Recall that supply shocks refer to the events that cause changes in factor supplies, factor productivities and the prices of inputs (factors of production, raw materials and supplies), which affect the production cost, and these could be both favourable (cost reducing) and adverse (cost raising). They affect the production and, hence, the real income directly. The RBC theory, in particular, stresses on technological shocks but includes other supply shocks such as environmental, prices of imported raw materials (like oil price) and workers preference between leisure and income. The old classicists took such factors as constants in the short run and accordingly they considered them to affect growth and not business cycles. In contrast, RBC theorists argue that these factors do change, albeit a little, even in the short run, and thus cause cycles as well affect the long run growth. This is illustrated for an adverse supply shock in Fig. 14.3.[1]

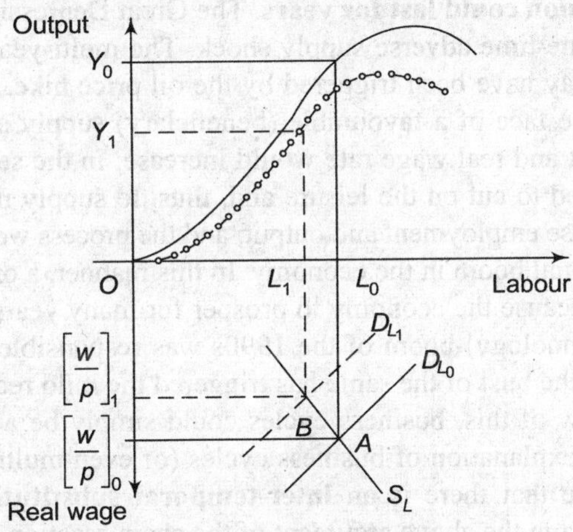

Fig. 14.3 Adverse Supply Shock

The upper part of the diagram plots the production function and the lower part the corresponding labour market, that is, labour demand (D_L) and labour supply (SL) curves. The solid curves/lines indicate the original graphs and the dotted lines the curves after the adverse supply shock. Recall that the labour demand curve follows from the production function, and therefore, when the production curve shifts downward due to the adverse supply shock, the labour demand curve shifts down (towards the labour axis) as well. Thus, the adverse supply shock lowers the production and labour demand curves; leaves the labour supply curve unaltered, and accordingly, reduces the labour input from L_0 to L_1, the output from Y_0 to Y_1 and the real wage rate from $(W/P)_0$ to $(W/P)_1$. Exactly the opposite would happen in the face of a favourable supply shock. In consequence, note that the **real wage is pro-cyclical**: real wage rate goes down when output falls and it goes up when output increases. In the *AD-AS* curves framework, an adverse supply shock would shift the AS curve upward (to the left), the *AD* curve remaining unaffected, output would fall and the

[1]For simplicity, the labour demand and supply curves are drawn as linear.

aggregate price would increase. Quite the opposite would happen in the midst of a favourable supply shock. Note here that the **price level is anti-cyclical**: price goes up when output falls and it goes down when output expands.

The adjustment process does not stop after the first change. Thus, the initial adverse supply shock only initiates the downswing, which continues in the same direction subsequently. To see this, consider the sequence, viz., when the real wage rate has fallen due to the initial adverse supply shock, as noted above, workers would be encouraged to enjoy more leisure now than before. They would thus substitute leisure for work. This would reduce the supply of labour, and given the labour demand, the labour employment and output would fall. This is the second fall in labour input and output due to suffering only a one-time adverse supply shock. Like the Keynesian/investment multiplier of Chapter 11, the downward process would continue for long, resulting in a series of falls in real income. The downswing will thus be aggravated and the economy may go into a deep recession. The resulting **recession could last for years**. The Great Depression could thus have been caused by a one-time adverse supply shock. The multi-year stagflation of the 1970s and 1980s may have been triggered by the oil price hike. Quite the opposite would happen in the face of a favourable (beneficiary) supply shock. Initially, the employment, output and real wage rate would increase; in the second round labour would be encouraged to cut on the leisure and, thus, to supply more labour, which would further increase employment and output; and the process would continue, thus, producing a substantial boom in the economy. In this manner, a one-time favourable supply shock could cause the economy to prosper for many years. It is said that the IT (information technology) boom of the 1990s was responsible for the prosperity of that decade, and the bust of the same has triggered the mild recession of the early 21st century. In view of this, business cycles could simply be a real phenomenon. This is yet another explanation of business cycles (of even multi-year ones).

Incidentally, note that there is an **inter-temporal substitution of labour for leisure**, or vice versa in the above argument of the chain reaction to an initial supply shock. When the wage rate is low during recessions, workers substitute leisure for work; and when the wage rate is high during prosperity periods, workers substitute work for leisure. In other words, people work harder and longer during boom periods and they take time off during recessions. This is known as the **propagation effect**. This is quite a rational behaviour because there is always a trade-off between leisure and work, and the trade-off is determined by the reward for work or the opportunity cost of leisure, which is the wage rate.[2] Evidences for the inter-temporal substitution of leisure are found in plenty in real life. In start-up companies, executives work for long hours as they expect to make big money, which would enable them to avail long holidays later. Share brokers and dealers work longer hours when the stock market is rising, and vice versa. Companies ask their employees to work overtime when their business is booming and encourage them to avail their accumulated leave/compensatory offs during lean periods. Tourists make efforts to enjoy their holidays/leave during lean periods.

[2]Recall from Chapter 9 that the theoretical labour supply curve is backward bending. Thus, while hypothesising the inter-temporal substitution of labour, the RBC theory is assuming that the substitution effect dominates the income effect.

As seen in the last couple of paragraphs, the chain events of falling output triggered by a one time adverse supply shock and that of a rising output brought about by a one time favourable supply shock are effected through inter-temporal labour substitution. Accordingly, the **inter-temporal substitution of labour for leisure, and vice versa, is the basis on which the RBC theory rests**. Further, in the RBC theory, the economy is postulated to respond to supply shocks according to the new classical assumption of continuous market clearing. Firms always produce the amount they desire, at prices and wages that respond flexibly to changing economic conditions, and hire the number of workers they want. Workers work for the hours they desire at the market determined real wage rate. Accordingly, output always equals its natural level. Also, money is neutral even in the short run. Further, by this theory, economic fluctuations are caused by supply shocks, which, as would be seen in Chapter 16, also cause economic growth. Thus, the RBC model of business cycles falls within the realm of the classical framework. To distinguish it from the old classical school (under which there are no business cycles, or if they exist they could arise from one of the two sources: one, from a change in the real factors' supply, productivities and/ or input prices, making a one-time impact on the economy—real business cycles—which are normally restricted to the long run and hence cause growth rather than cycles; two, from the economy's inertia in adjustment when the quantity of money supply undergoes a change—quantity theory of money), the new theory is called the new classical school's real business cycle theory. The RBC theory is also not free from criticism. The main ones are the following:

(a) Technological changes are usually gradual and unidirectional. While there are plenty of examples for technical advances, technical retreats (forgetfulness/ careless) are hard to find. Defenders of the RBC model suggest that adverse technology includes bad harvests, oil price shocks, and government regulations requiring heavy investments and extra workers to reduce air and water pollution. The latter do occur and reoccur, and they lead to increases in the cost of production, which trigger recessions. The economic performance of developing countries, particularly of those where the agricultural sector commands a significant share of GDP, is heavily governed by the rain god (monsoon). For example, almost all significant economic performances, good as well as bad, in India could be attributed to a fairly large extent to the mercy or otherwise of the monsoon. The country experienced serious drought conditions in 1965 and 1979 and had negative growth rates in 1965-66 and 1979- 80; it had a good monsoon in 1988 and again in 2003, and enjoyed/enjoying good growth rates in 1988-89 and 2003-04. Significant changes in industrial relations (strikes, lockouts etc.), wars, natural calamities (earthquakes, diseases etc.), immigration laws, foreign sector policy (foreign exchange rate system, trade, foreign capital, technology transfer etc.) and the privatisation programme (disinvesting in public sector enterprises), among others, could well trigger up and down swings in any economy.

(b) If recessions are caused by adverse supply shocks and booms by beneficiary supply shocks, then, as seen above, the general price should move counter-cyclical. In other words, if the RBC theory were true, the price must rise in recessions and fall in booms, producing a negative relationship between the price and output. Critics point out that the relationship between the output and general price has, however, been positive sometimes (as during the Great Depression) and negative at others (as during the oil price shocks of the 1970s). While this bi-directional relationship refutes the RBC theory, it supports the theory that business cycles could be caused by both demand as well as supply shocks, and not just by either. Defenders of the RBC theory suggest that the positive relationship between the output and price could come through induced changes in money supply. They argue that when the output rises due to a favourable supply shock, demand for money goes up; which, in turn, may lead the Central Bank to increase the money supply, which, in turn, may cause the price to increase. Note that in this argument money supply is treated as an endogenous variable. This has led to another debate regarding to whether **income causes money** (RBC theory) or **money causes income** (Keynesian theory). The matter is thus empirical. However, research findings are inconclusive.

(c) Recall our earlier observation that the RBC theory suggests that adverse supply shocks cause both the output and the real wage rate to fall, and favourable supply shocks cause both of them to rise. This means the real wage rate moves pro-cyclically. This has been attacked by the critics on two counts: One, it contradicts the relationship between output and real wage rate (counter-cyclical), as predicted by the Friedman's fooling model, (Chapter 9). Two, though we do not have hard time series data on the real wage rate, news reports do suggest that real wages have moved both ways during the prosperity/recession phases.

(d) Desired employment is not very sensitive to the real wage rate. History suggests that the (involuntary) unemployment rate has been relatively high during the recessions and low during booms. This would not be so if people voluntarily withdraw from the job market in recessions, for then they would not even be a part of the labour force. Defenders of the RBC theory argue that individuals who voluntarily choose not to work may call themselves unemployed so that they could collect unemployment benefits or because they would be willing to work if they were offered the wage rate of the prosperity periods. Since the data on such items are highly ambiguous/not available, there is no way of accepting or rejecting the said arguments. A relevant point to note here is that the Keynesian distinction between voluntary and involuntary unemployment is also equally ambiguous—if a person with an MBA refuses to accept the offer of ₹5,000/month in Godhra (Gujarat), and he has no other offer, would you call him voluntarily or involuntarily unemployed (vide Chapter 15). To classicists, all unemployment is voluntary; and to Keynesians, it is entirely involuntary!

In view of the above controversy, the RBC model provides only a partial explanation of business cycles. Its major strength over the Friedman-Lucas explanation of the business cycles lies in explaining the length (multi-year) of these cycles. While the early version of the RBC model emphasised technological change as the main source of business cycles, its recent version recognises other supply shocks (like labour supply and investment) and even demand shocks as the possible causes of business cycles. Changes in consumers' tastes and preferences and in business outlooks are deemed as the real demand shocks. If these change significantly, autonomous consumption and autonomous investment would change, and these, through the Keynesian multiplier effect, could well trigger ups and downs in the economy. Recall our earlier assertion that during the Great Depression, low business and consumers' confidence did add fuel to the fire. Similarly, the prosperity of the 1990s is attributed partly to improved business confidence. The RBC theory recognises that cycles can even be caused by changes in money supply and government expenditure, but the theory attaches a secondary role to such factors. Inclusion of business/consumer confidence and demand management policies in the RBC theory surely improves the theory's acceptance and validity. If output fluctuations are permanent, business cycles are caused by the real factors; and if they are transitory, business cycles are caused by demand shocks. Further, since productivity shocks are rate, though permanent, changes in aggregate demand are deemed to be the primary source of business cycles.

There is yet another theory of output, called the **random walk theory**, under which the current output equals the previous period output plus a random term, which could take a positive, negative or a zero value, and which is unpredictable. By this, **business cycles would be purely random**. The theory further suggests that the supply shocks are more powerful than the demand shocks, and that most shifts in output are permanent rather than temporary, resulting in long cycles.

NEW KEYNESIAN MODEL

Keynesians do not accept the classical or new classical assumption of continuous market clearing. They argue that workers and firms do not appear to be making a voluntary choice to cut hours of work and production, respectively, during the recessions. It is a well-known fact that all firms are not able to sell all their outputs at the going prices and all workers are not able to find jobs at the going wage rate during bad times. This observation clearly contradicts the classical postulates of the wage-price flexibility and continuous market clearing. All Keynesians assume that the wage-price adjustments are slow and not instantaneous, hence, market disequilibrium exists. Due to this, **Keynesian models are dubbed as non-market-clearing models**.

The old Keynesian model assumes either the fixed price or/and the fixed nominal wage rate. Further, they take this as a granted fact of life rather than bother to explain this fact. The new Keynesian model retains this assumption and explains the same on the principles of economics, including the new classicists' rational expectation theory. Further, the said model reinforces the old Keynesians' conclusion that the under-full employment equilibrium is possible and fiscal and monetary policies have a role in taming business cycles. This is so because under the price rigidity, the aggregate supply curve is horizontal at the fixed price; firms supply any quantity that consumers and investors wish to buy at the fixed price, and they hire any quantity of labour they need to produce that quantity rather than operate on their labour demand curve; buyers of their products operate on their demand curve; and workers operate on their labour supply curve (Chapter 9). Since firms do not operate along their labour demand curve, the labour market may not be cleared and there could be under/over-full employment equilibrium. In such a scenario, unemployment could occur and if it does, it would be due to the shortage of effective aggregate demand (AD). The results of the IS-LM, of Chapter 11, and other models of Chapters 12–13 would hold for the sources of business cycles as well as for the roles of fiscal and monetary policies.

In contrast, under the nominal wage rigidity, the AS curve is upward sloping; firms operate on their labour demand curve; workers supply any quantity of labour that firms wish to hire to be able to operate along their upward sloping AS curve rather than operating along their labour supply curve; and buyers of the product operate along their AD curve (Chapter 9). Since workers do not operate along their labour supply curve, there is a possibility of non-clearance of the labour market and thereby of the under/over full employment equilibrium. In such a scenario, unemployment could occur and if it does, it would be merely due to the **mistaken expectations** about prices. The results of the AD-AS model of Chapter 13 would apply for the sources of business cycles as well as the roles of fiscal and monetary policies.

Let us now go to the new Keynesian's rationale for the wage-price rigidity. According to them, the money wage rate and price are sticky for the following reasons:

(a) **Menu Cost**: Menu cost refers to the cost a firm has to incur in printing the menu, price list and/or catalogue, and forwarding the same to its dealers/customers whenever it decides to change the price of its products. These are unavoidable and thus serve as a disincentive to change the price. Sometimes they may even exceed the benefits of price increases. Thus, when the benefits of price change falls short of the said menu cost, it is economically prudent to not go for a price change. Such a situation would arise when the change in the cost of production was a relatively small one. Such minor cost changes are then absorbed through a fall in the profit, which would fall more if the price change was implemented. Examples for this would be like the times when firms face increases in postal, telephone or electricity tariffs. If a firm is running largely on equity, with little debt funding, even changes in the interest rate may not justify price changes. Similarly, if the particular entity is mainly concentrating on the domestic market, even changes in the foreign exchange rate may be worth ignoring. The rationale is similar to the microeconomic oligopoly market situation, where the marginal revenue curve is discontinuous (demand curve is kinky), thereby, small changes in the marginal cost do not warrant changes in the optimum price. Since the menu cost is incurred both in the price increases as well as price decreases, it is symmetric with respect to either change. Accordingly, the menu cost tends to support price rigidity on both the sides—increase and decrease. Nevertheless, since the menu cost is a relatively small component of the total production cost, it can explain only mild recessions and mild recoveries.

There are critics of the above rationale. To understand them, it is pertinent to look into the difference between the private and social costs of the price stickiness. In the previous paragraph, we merely considered the private cost in decision-making. The social cost is the cost that the society/country, at large, incurs due to a decision. Thus, the social cost is much broader; it includes the private cost plus **externalities**—costs/benefits to the third party not related to the decision. Consider the case when there is a small fall in the cost of production and economics suggests that the firm not change/lower its product price due to this small change. The private cost is the loss of additional profit that the firm would have made if it had entertained price reduction, versus the menu cost that the firm has saved by not going for the change. Obviously, this loss must have been less than the saving in cost, for only then would the firm's decision be justified on economic grounds. Now, moving to the social cost of the fall in production cost, not accompanied by the fall in product price, we see the following chain of losses/costs. When the price of even one product falls, the general (average) price level falls as well, may be just a little. When the general price level falls, the real money balances increase; which, in turn, tend to shift the *LM* curve to the right (and also the *IS* curve to the right through the real balance effect), thus, raising the real GDP. An increase in national income would increase the demand for all (superior) goods in the economy, which would trigger an expansion in the economy. The loss of this expansion is the social cost of the individual price rigidity (not implementing the price cut in the face of a fall in production cost), and it is called the **aggregate demand externality** or the **macroeconomic externality**. If the social cost is prohibitive, even if the private cost is not (thereby an optimal decision of the firm not to change the price of its product due to the menu cost), the said decision would be socially undesirable. Accordingly, critics of the Keynesian menu cost logic argue that if the firms have society's welfare in mind or are forced by society to be so, they would not hold prices fixed in the face of a change in the menu cost. In other words, the trivial menu cost may be optimal for the individual firm to ignore but it cannot justify price rigidity.

(b) Information Cost/Imperfect Competition: The information barrier hypothesis of the new classical school itself suggests that information is both inaccurate and late, and costly to collect and analyse. Thus, when the production cost undergoes a change, all firms may not believe it or may not agree to a common rate by which the same has changed. It is a well-known fact in economics that costs are not uniform for any product across firms. Firms that have better factors of production (FOP), including management, produce an identical item at a lesser cost than the others who have inefficient FOP. Thus, even when some costs go up for all the firms (like a little increase in the crude oil price), while the average production cost of some may not increase at all (energy conservative firms), for others (energy wasteful firms) it may increase quite a bit. Further, the change in cost may still be uncertain and therefore it may be hard to decide the rate of price hike. Similarly, firms may not be sure about the change in the cost of living, trade union pressures etc. and thus may wait for a while before they grant wage increases. These are the facts that make markets imperfect, where firms are price makers and not takers. Price changes can cost fortunes in such markets. In view of such factors, firms may hold wage-price at their earlier levels, at least for the time being. If so, we have the Keynesian wage-price rigidity on both the up and down sides, and its conclusions for business cycles.

(c) Staggered Contracts: Keynesians suggest that due to the presence of labour unions, and even otherwise, nominal wage contracts are made for good economic reasons between workers and employers, lasting for a year or even longer. During the contract period, the nominal wage is fixed or may simply be subject to full or partial price indexing.[3] Further, such wage contracts are staggered as they are often signed at different points of time and have varying periods of validity across firms. This tends to render the nominal wage rate rigid, not only during a certain period but over a fairly long period. Similarly, buyers and sellers of durable goods, in particular, also enter into contracts of transacting products during the pre-specified future period at pre-decided fixed prices. We have plenty of examples of business selling forward of heavy plants/machines/vehicles at a pre-negotiated price at predetermined future dates, contracting out the transportation job to travel agencies and outsourcing sanitation, security, canteens etc. to outsiders at fixed rates to remain valid for fixed periods. Such practices obviously support fixed wage-price models. Nevertheless, such contracts are more often against cost/price increases than their falls and, if so, they merely explain downward rigidity. In consequence, the Keynesian theory would explain recessions and not recoveries. Incidentally, note that wage-price contracts render the market imperfect, and to this extent the rationale for rigidity overlaps the previous point.

(d) **Coordination Failures**: Firms setting prices (wages) are mindful of the prices (wages) other firms charge (pay). This is so partly because of the input-output relationship among firms. A garment firm cannot set the price of its garments until it is sure of the price the textile firm would charge on its textiles, as textiles are inputs of the garment firm. These are also the features of an imperfect market. If the market structure were an oligopoly one, there would be a problem as to who should lead the price change. The kinky demand curve theory of such a market states that the one who leads the price increase suffers and the one who leads the price fall does not gain; for while the price increases are not followed by rivals, price decreases are followed by them. Accordingly, no firm would like to bell the cat. In such a situation, a price change could be optimal socially, but not privately. Thus, in the absence of any policy regulation, no one would like to change the price and there would be the price rigidity. However, while the above logic holds good against all price cuts, it merely applies only against those price raises that are prompted through small increases in production costs. For, while small increases in costs can be absorbed in small reductions in profit, such large increases would threaten the profit to turn into losses. Thus, if the increase in cost were prohibitive, threatening profit to turn to zero or negative, rational behaviour would persuade all firms to raise the price and it hardly matters as to who makes the first move. Also, if there are no strict rules against cartels, competing firms would form cartels and avoid the issue. In view of this, the point under discussion only supports the downward wage-price rigidity and a little of the upward rigidity. Accordingly, the Keynesian theory is good to explain the recessions and mild recoveries only, and not all business cycles that the world has experienced.

(e) **Efficiency Wage Model**: Firms are reluctant to reduce the nominal wage rate even during recessions due to the fear of either losing efficient employees or

[3] Under the price indexing, the nominal wage rate moves up and down directly with the general (specified) price index, either proportionately (if full indexing) or less than proportionately (if partial indexing) as per the system of indexation.

reducing their efficiencies, and they often prefer to pay high wage to reduce the employees' monitoring cost. Such a hypothesis has been advanced by Edmund Phelps, Shapiro and Joseph Stiglitz, among others, who argue that high wages leads to higher productivity. This is so because a high wage rate enables workers to enjoy good nutritional diets, be healthy and happy, motivates them not to shirk from work and have good morals, stimulates employees to work effectively and discourages workers from quitting the job. In addition, happy employees serve as a good magnate to attract other good workers to the firm, and the high wage enables the firm to recruit good workers. In 1914, the Ford Motor Company was paying \$5 per hour to its workers when the going wage rate was under \$3. The policy was subsequently declared to have resulted in 'good business'.

Unlike the above four factors, which explain the absolute nominal wage (price) rigidity, this factor explains the real or relative wage and the relative wage-price rigidity. By this factor, a particular firm does not reduce the nominal wages of its employees even when the general wage trend is downward, or even when the price of its product is falling. Also, the theory rationalises why the unemployed workers are unable to find jobs even if they offer their services at the wage rate below the going market rate. The firm knows that it can hire workers at a relatively low wage rate, and yet, it refuses to do so because it fears that new workers (currently unemployed) may be less efficient than the existing ones. Further, the theory could rationalise even the rising wage rate in the midst of involuntary unemployment as well as the coexistence of vacancies and involuntary unemployment. The former because the firms would like to retain efficient employees and it feels that unless it pays them well they would quit, and the unemployed lot is doubted for its efficiency/faithfulness. The latter, for the firms may have their own doubts regarding the suitability/ efficiency/ faithfulness of the unemployed people. It is sometimes observed that workers quit their jobs or accept retrenchment when their wages are threatened to be lowered due to recession and/or the eroding profitability of such firms. The efficiency model offers a rationale even for this, for such workers may think that their work/efficiency was not valued well by their bosses, particularly in relation to other colleagues whose wages were not being reduced or who were relatively less efficient. It is clear to see that the efficiency theory only supports downward wage rigidity, thus making it useful only in accounting for the recession phase of business cycles.

The efficiency wage theory thus provides an alternative (to Friedman's mistaken expectations hypothesis) explanation for the existence of the under-fullemployment equilibrium.

(f) Insiders-Outsiders Model: The model is based on the premise that the recruitment of workers is a costly affair, both in terms of money and time, which creates rent and market power to the incumbent workers in the existing firms. Recruitments involve advertisement, evaluation of a good number of applications, short listing of candidates, interviewing them and debating the final selections. This would take the firms to the decision stage and offers would be issued. Some prospective employees may prefer to negotiate the wage and other terms, yet, some offers may go 'unaccepted'. To avoid all these costs and hustles, firms may prefer to retain highly paid employees, even though 'outsiders' are apparently available at a relatively lower wage. This leads to downward wage rigidity, though not to upward wage sluggishness. The model is clearly consistent with the existence of involuntary unemployment, even with the presence of rising wage rate in the midst of involuntary unemployed people as well as with the situation of workers preferring retrenchment over a wage cut. Further, the model explains both the nominal as well as the real (relative) wage rigidity.

The above provides the rational reasons for the wage-price rigidity. However, such rigidities are merely a short run phenomenon, and thus they still leave the long run position unaltered. Further, while some factors explain both the price as well as the wage rigidity (like menu cost, information cost, staggered contracts and coordination problems), the others (efficiency wage and insider-outsider models) merely justify the wage rigidity. Also, they usually justify only downward rigidity as well as a mild upward one. Recall from Chapter 9 that if there were price rigidity both ways, the short run *AS* curve would be horizontal at the fixed price level and the conclusions of the IS-LM model of Chapter 11 would hold good for business cycles as well as the effectiveness of demand management policies for countering business cycles. In contrast, if only the money wages were rigid both ways, the short run *AS* curve would be upward sloping and the conclusions of Chapter 13 would prevail.

There are other strands of the new Keynesian thought besides those focused on the wage-price rigidities. These include the implications of the incomplete contracts (like important **Inflation indexation**) and the **role of risk in pricing**. It is argued that even if the wage-price rigidity did not exist, output and employment would be highly volatile due to the incomplete contracts and risk. Economists have even gone to the extent of arguing that the real income is a random variable (vide page 411 above).

In conclusion, it may be noted that the basic new thing in the 'new' Keynesian model over its 'old' counterpart is the rationale for the price-wage rigidity. It is, thus, considered mainly an intellectual contribution, which, unlike the 'old' Keynesian and 'new' classical models, was not inspired by some unexplainable event like the Great Depression or stagflation.

CONCLUSION

The chapter may be concluded by summarising the principal tenets of the various theories of business cycles. These could be grouped into three heads, which are assumptions, sources of business cycles and the role of fiscal and monetary policies in taming the cycles.

Assumptions The old classical theory assumes the perfect price-wage flexibility and perfect information on the part of firms, workers and consumers. The real business cycle (RBC) theory, a part of the new classical theory, assumes the continuous labour market equilibrium and it implies pro-cyclical real wage movement. The Friedman natural rate (fooling) theory retains the assumption of price-wage flexibility but substitutes the asymmetric information (fooling of workers) for perfect information. The Lucas theory also retains the price-wage flexibility assumption and substitutes the symmetric information barrier for perfect information. In contrast, both the old and new Keynesian models assume the non-market clearance based on the wage-price rigidity of some kind, the former without rationalising it and the latter through an explanation on the basis of optimum behaviour.

Sources of Business Cycles For the old classicists, output and employment are determined solely by the aggregate supply. There is never (barring the rare one possibility caused by slow adjustment of price to change in the quantity of money) any involuntary unemployment and fluctuations in the real output could be caused by the supply shocks only. The price flexibility ensures the aggregate demand, which is effected by the money supply alone, to equal the fixed aggregate supply. In the Friedman and Lucas models, the output and employment are determined by the *AD* and *AS* functions, and while they could deviate from their natural levels in the short-run, they would always return to their respective natural levels in the long run. In these models, price expectations affect the labour supply and thereby the aggregate supply. The inaccurate price expectations cause output to deviate from the natural level in the short run. The said mistakes could be caused by the drastic changes in the policies in the Friedman model and by the 'policy surprises' in the Lucas model. Accordingly, the business cycles in these two models could be caused basically by the unexpected fluctuations in money supply and government's fiscal operations in the short run and by the supply shocks in the long run. In other words, they believe that mis-perceptions about the wage and price movements lead people to supply too much or too little labour, which leads to cycles of unemployment and output. In the RBC theory, the output and employment are determined simultaneously by the *AD* and *AS* curves, and there would be no involuntary unemployment in both the short and long runs. Shocks in the technology are the main cause of business cycles, though, in its later version, they could also be caused by the other supply shocks and even the demand shocks. In both the old and new Keynesian models, the *AD* and *AS* curves simultaneously determine the output and aggregate price. The *AD* is affected not just by the money supply but also by the other exogenous variables including the government expenditure, taxes, autonomous consumption, autonomous investment, autonomous net export and autonomous world (rest of the world) income. The Mundell-Fleming version of the Keynesian model suggests that in a globalised world, a country could choose either the floating exchange rate system or the fixed rate one; and if the latter is the choice, money supply ceases to be a policy tool. Involuntary unemployment could exist in both the short and long run, and business cycles could be caused equally by both the demand and supply shocks.

Role of Stabilisation Policies In the old classical model, the fiscal policy has no role and the only role of the monetary policy lies in proportionately influencing the nominal magnitudes. Money is neutral in the system. In the Friedman model, money is neutral in the long run but it exerts influence on the real income in the short run if there are errors in price expectations. In the Lucas model, money is neutral in the long run, and also in the short run, unless the changes in the money supply are 'surprises'. The same is true for the fiscal policy. The Friedman-Lucas models thus agree with the old classical (monetarist) model that the macroeconomic policies affect the nominal but not the real variables and that the unemployment will gravitate to its natural level. In the milder version of the RBC model, the money and fiscal instruments can cause demand shocks and, thereby, business cycles. In the Keynesian models, both the 'old' and 'new' versions, both the fiscal and monetary policies are effective in causing as well as in taming business cycles. They believe that the aggregate demand matters and there is a significant role for purposeful government policy in reducing unemployment. However, the Mundell-Fleming model suggests that in a globalised world; in countries which have opted for a floating exchange rate system, the fiscal policy has no role but the monetary policy is very powerful, and quite the opposite is true in countries having the fixed exchange rate system. In such countries, even the trade policy serves as an additional tool, and of course, the exchange rate is yet another tool but only in countries having the fixed rate system. In short, in the Keynesian systems, at least one of the stabilisation tools is always effective in regulating business cycles; and note that when only one tool is available, it is very strong. Thus, the **macroeconomic policy has been considered as an insurance against the recessions**. The public sector expanded on such beliefs during the 1950s and 1960s. Unfortunately, the large fiscal deficits and the growing public debt-GDP ratio have put some constraints on this belief. European countries have been experiencing significant unemployment for over two decades now and even USA has experienced this during and after the great recession of 2007-09. This, among others, bears out the Keynesian contention that demand shocks—emanating from the private or/and the public sector—can lead to persisting unemployment. Friedman, of course, believes that the private sector is quite stable and that the most dramatic shocks come from governments. In the United States, the unemployment rate trended upward in the 1970s and 1980s, came down during the late 1990s and went up again during the early 21st century. The theory of the natural rate of unemployment limits the trade-off between inflation and unemployment rates as well as the role of the demand management policies in reducing unemployment below its natural level without ever accelerating inflation. However, large variations in the unemployment rate across countries have left doubts among economists about the usefulness of the natural rate of unemployment concept as well as the role of demand management policies in tampering it.

In short, while the **classical theory emphasizes market clearance, aggregate supply and policy irrelevance; the Keynesian theory has stressed on the wage-price rigidity, aggregate demand and monetary-fiscal-trade-exchange rate interventions**. While the classicists argue for the rules and a non-discriminatory approach to policy making so that the problems of information barrier and uncertainty are minimised, the Keynesians suggest for some type of the discretionary policy to cope with rigidities. Further, the recent emphasis on globalisation and the floating exchange rate system have undermined the role of the fiscal policy and elevated that of the monetary policy in dampening business cycles.

Thus, we have several models to explain the recurrence of business cycles that last for several years. While no model is worthless, none of them provide a perfect theory for economic fluctuations. Thus, unlike the period of the 1950s and 1960s when economists thought that macroeconomics was contained in the then downward sloping Phillips curve, giving a menu of the alternative combinations of the inflation and unemployment rates to policy makers, today there is no such unique theory. However, the developments have been beneficial and they do offer good insights into understanding the complicated economic system. Economics is a live discipline and an **inexact science**. Surely new developments would be forthcoming and they would further our understanding of business cycles and the power of stabilisation policies.

What is the concluding remark on business cycles and stabilization policies? Neither the classical assumption of the fixed output, nor the IS-LM model's assumption of the fixed price is valid in the real world. Accordingly, the *AS* curve slopes upward and the *AD* curve slopes downward. The AD-AS model determines the real income and average (macro) price. Either the demand shocks, supply shocks or both could cause business cycles and inflation/deflation. In short run, the real and monetary variables are highly intertwined, and changes in money supply and government spending can temporarily push the real GDP away from its long run trend. In the long run, policy interventions have little effects on output and their effects concentrate on price alone.

Keywords

New classical model; Friedman-Lucas-Sargent-Wallace model of imperfect information and rational expectations; Theory of natural rate of unemployment/ output; NAIRU; Adaptive-rational expectations theory; Workers' fooling model; Inflation augmented Phillips curve; Policy irrelevance proposition; Lucas critique; Real business cycle theory; Pro-anti-cyclical; Inter-temporal substitution between labour and leisure; Random walk theory; New Keynesian model; Non-market clearing model; Menu cost; Aggregate demand/ Macroeconomic externality; Information cost; Staggered contracts; Coordination failure; Kinky demand curve theory; Efficiency wage model; Insiders-outsiders model, Keynesian wage-price rigidity model.

References

1. Friedman Milton, 'The Role of Monetary Policy', *American Economic Review* 58, (March, 1968): 1-17.
2. Greenwald Bruce, Joseph Stiglitz, 'New and Old Keynesians', *Journal of Economic Perspectives* 7, (Winter, 1993): 23-44.
3. Kydland Finn E, Edward Prescott, 'Time to Build and Aggregate Fluctuations', *Econometrica* 50, (November, 1982): 1345-70.
4. Lucas Robert E, *Models of Business Cycles*, (Oxford: Basil Blackwell, 1987).
5. Mankiw N Gregory, 'Real Business Cycles: A New Keynesian Perspectives', *Journal of Economic Perspectives* 3, (Summer, 1989): 79-90.
6. Mankiw N Gregory, 'A Quick Refresher Course in Macroeconomics', *Journal of Economic Literature* 28, (December, 1990): 1645-60.

7. McCallum Bennett T, 'Real Business Cycle Models', in Robert J, Barro ed. *Modern Business Cycles Theory*, (Cambridge: Harvard University Press, 1989), 16-50.
8. Phelps Edmund S, 'Phillips Curves, Expectations of Inflation and Optimal Unemployment Over Time, *Economica* 34, (August, 1967): 254-81.
9. Sargent Thomas J, Neil Wallace, 'Rational Expectations, the Optimal Monetary Instrument and the Optimal Money Supply Side Rule', *Journal of Political Economy* 83, (April, 1975), 241-254.
10. Tobin J, 'The Natural Rate as New Classical Economics', in R. Ross ed., The *Natural Rate of Unemployment: Reflections on 25 Years of the Hypothesis*, (Cambridge: Cambridge University Press, 1995).

REVIEW QUESTIONS

1. The data on some important macroeconomic variables of the United States and India are provided in the table below:

(Percentages)

	USA			*India*	
*Year**	*Growth rate in GDP*	*Unemployment rate*	*Inflation rate*	*Growth rate in GDP*	*Inflation rate*
1953	4.0	2.9	0.6	6.1	3.1
1954	−1.3	5.5	−0.5	4.2	−11.9
1955	5.5	4.4	−0.3	2.6	11.7
1956	2.1	4.1	2.9	5.7	7.8
1957	1.7	4.3	3.0	−1.2	−2.9
1958	−0.8	6.8	1.8	7.6	5.7
1959	5.5	5.5	1.5	2.2	5.8
1960	2.2	5.5	1.6	7.1	6.4
1961	2.1	6.7	0.7	3.1	−2.6
1962	6.0	5.5	1.2	2.1	3.6
1963	4.3	5.7	1.6	5.1	8.0
1964	5.7	5.0	1.3	7.6	7.9
1965	5.6	4.4	1.7	−3.7	12.4
1966	5.9	3.6	3.0	1.0	15.6
1967	2.6	3.7	2.8	8.1	0.9
1968	4.1	3.5	4.2	2.6	3.0
1969	2.7	3.4	5.4	6.5	6.4
1970	−0.1	4.8	5.9	5.0	2.8
1971	3.2	5.8	4.3	1.0	5.6
1972	4.8	5.5	3.3	−0.3	10.0
1973	5.4	4.8	6.2	4.6	20.2
1974	−0.5	5.5	11.0	1.2	25.2
1975	−1.1	8.3	9.1	9.0	−1.1
1976	5.1	7.6	5.7	1.2	2.1
1977	4.6	6.9	6.5	7.5	5.2
1978	4.8	6.0	7.6	5.5	0.0

(Contd.)

(Contd.)

1979	2.8	5.8	11.3	–5.2	17.1
1980	–0.6	7.0	13.5	7.2	18.2
1981	1.6	7.5	10.3	6.0	9.3
1982	–2.3	9.5	6.2	3.1	4.9
1983	3.8	9.5	3.2	7.7	7.5
1984	6.0	7.4	4.3	4.3	6.0
1985	2.9	7.1	3.6	4.5	4.4
1986	2.8	6.9	1.9	4.3	5.8
1987	3.0	6.1	3.7	3.8	8.2
1988	4.0	5.4	4.0	10.5	7.5
1989	2.4	5.2	4.8	6.7	7.4
1990	1.1	5.4	5.4	5.6	10.3
1991	–1.2	6.6	4.2	1.3	13.7
1992	2.0	7.3	3.0	5.1	10.1
1993	23.0	6.8	3.0	5.9	8.4
1994	3.5	6.1	2.6	7.3	10.9
1995	2.3	5.6	2.8	7.3	7.7
1996	3.4	5.4	2.9	7.8	6.4
1997	3.9	5.0	2.3	4.8	4.8
1998	3.9	4.6	1.6	6.6	13.1
1999	4.1	4.2	2.2	6.4	5.6
2000	3.1	4.0	3.4	4.1	4.9
2001	1–0.15	4.7	2.8	5.54	34.73
2002	1.81	5.8	1.6	4.0	4.41
2003	23.51	6.0	2.3	8.15	3.89
2004	34.53	5.5	2.7	7.05	3.8
2005	3.15	5.1	3.4	9.50	4.25
2006	2.7	4.6	3.2	9.6	6.1
2007	1.9	4.6	2.9	9.3	6.4
2008	–0.3	5.8	3.8	6.7	8.4
2009	–3.1	9.3	–0.4	8.6	10.9
2010	2.4	9.6	1.6	9.3	12.0
2011	1.8	9.0	3.2	6.2	8.9
2012	2.2	8.1	2.1	5.0	9.3

Note: * For the United States, these are calendar years and for India, the fiscal years. Thus, 1953 means 1953 calendar year for the United States and 1953–54 financial year for India.

Sources: (a) *International Financial Statistics,* IMF 2013
(b) *National Accounts Statistics of India,* 2013

(a) Identify the business cycles in each country and analyse the likely causes of the same. You may look up the relevant information elsewhere in this text, in the library or from any other source.

(b) Examine the roles the fiscal, monetary and exchange rate policies had played in each of the two countries, and comment on whether each of these policies played a pro-cyclical or counter-cyclical role. You may seek the additional information from any source.

2. Suppose the Snowwhite economy is characterised by the following IS-LM-AS macroeconomic model:

IS equation: $Y = k\,[C_0 + I_0 + G_0 - bT_0] - k\,d\,i$

LM equation: $\dfrac{M_0}{P} = e \cdot Y - f\,i$

AS equation: $P = P_{-1}\left[1 + \epsilon\left(\dfrac{Y}{Y_n} - 1\right)\right]$

Production function: $Y = a\,N$

Autonomous expenditure parameter: $k = \dfrac{1}{1 - b(1-t)}$

All the notations have their usual meanings. The values for the various exogenous variables are

$$C_0 = 10,\ I_0 = 30,\ G_0 = 15,\ T_0 = 6.25,\ M_0 = 350,$$

$$P_{-1} = 100/9,\ Y_n = 120,\ U_n = 0.1,\ \dot{p}^e = 0.05$$

The parameters take the following values

$$b = 0.8,\ t = 0.25,\ d = 2.0,\ e = 0.4,\ f = 1.0,\ a = 1.25,\ \varepsilon = 0.6$$

(a) Determine the equation of the *AD* curve.

(b) Solve the AD-AS model for the equilibrium income, interest rate and price in the short run.

(c) Solve the model for the equilibrium income, interest rate and price in the long run (hint: the long run *AS* curve is vertical at $Y = Y_n$).

(d) Write down the short run Phillips curve equation and determine the short run inflation rate.

3. While the old classical economists emphasised the supply side and the non-interventionist policy and the old Keynesian economists laid stress on the demand side and the interventionist policy, modern economists give credit to both thoughts in understanding business cycles and the stabilisation policies in the real world. Discuss.

4. During the Great Depression, both the output and price fell; output growth fell and price rose during the stagnation; and currently while the output growth is somewhat down, inflation is low and stable. What could have caused such varying scenarios in most economies and why have the stabilisation policies failed to avoid the economic ills?

5. Answer the following short questions:

(a) When the involuntary unemployment exists and the money wage rate is rigid, are the demand management policies effective? Why?

(b) Under what conditions, if any, do the demand management policies fail to cure recession and counter inflation? Explain.

(c) Historical data witness the co-existence of involuntary unemployment and job vacancies. Reconcile the apparent paradox.

(d) Historical facts suggest that the wage rate may not only not fall but it could even increase when there is involuntary unemployment. Which theory/theories would support such a possibility? Why?

(e) Many workers accept retrenchment over wage cut. Why?
(f) What is 'new' in each of the New Classical model and New Keynesian model?
(g) Distinguish the monetarism from, each of the New Classicalism and Non-Monetarism (Keynesianism).

Chapter 15

Unemployment and Inflation: Causes, Consequences and Cures

Learning Objectives

After reading the chapter you should be able to:

1. Learn the distinctions among the various kinds of unemployment and inflation, like the natural and cyclical unemployment, frictional and structural unemployment, headline and core inflation, demand-pull and cost-push inflation.
2. Understand the causes, consequences and possible cures for the two worst economic maladies (viz. unemployment and inflation), the sum of which two known as the index of misery, and the cost of one in term of the other known as the sacrifice ratio.
3. Become aware that if the inflation is coupled with economic growth, the inflation is of the demand-pull variety; while if it is accompanied with recession, it is the cost-push one.
4. Know that while the main cost of unemployment is the loss of output, the main cost of inflation is in redistribution of resources and uncertainty. In general, both the country and the unemployed people suffer due to unemployment; fixed income people and creditors lose while the government, business and debtors gain during inflation.
5. Comprehend that while the high inflation is generally bad, the low inflation may be good and surely the deflation is worse than inflation for any given rate.
6. The government could be held responsible for the core inflation but not for the headline inflation.

Unemployment and inflation are two of the greatest economic ills. Business cycle discussions and analysis of the last five chapters suggest that business cycles are a fact of life and they do cause unemployment and/or inflation from time to time. While the gravity of these cycles, in terms of the periodicity, length and the depth, has gone down over time, they remain a universal phenomenon throughout the world. While the increasing integration of the world has helped soften these cycles, it is equally responsible for spreading economic fluctuations across countries. Still all countries have not suffered equally from such worries. The secret of a high standard of living and sustained growth in the developed world is the outcome of insignificant rates of unemployment and inflation in these countries. Low per capita income countries, called the developing economies, have usually been plagued with high rates of these maladies; and even developed countries have often been caught up by at least one of these diseases. Though the growth rate was low, the world did not face serious unemployment or inflation troubles until the Great Depression of

1929-33, when unemployment was rather high and there was deflation instead of inflation; **deflation is worse than inflation**.

The Keynesian revolution of the post mid-1930s and its adoption, particularly after the World War II, brought about prosperity during the 1950s and 1960s. During the late 1960s, many countries experienced high rates of inflation but mild unemployment. However, during the 1970s most countries suffered the twin problems simultaneously. During the 1980s, though the unemployment issue softened, inflation continued to cause worries. In general, the 1990s were the good period but the beginning of the 21st century was associated with an increasing unemployment rate and the threat of deflation, particularly in large countries like Japan and China. Subsequently, most economies witnessed prosperity and low inflation during 2002-07, which was followed by the great recession during 2008-09 together with the threat of deflation. Currently, recession is behind and prosperity is seen all around. In nutshell, there is no country in the world that has never suffered from at least one of these two evils. General polls have invariably rated these as number one or two of the most burning economic issues, the other issue being poverty, corruption and policy paralysis. Even poverty, in either the absolute or the relative version, is due to unemployment and inflation. As employment is the only ultimate source of income/consumption expenditure, absolute poverty is due to unemployment. As we shall see later in this chapter, inflation usually worsens income inequalities; thus relative poverty is accentuated by inflation. Even the performance of the incumbent government is judged on the basis of unemployment, inflation, poverty and growth rate. While some degrees of unemployment and inflation may be inevitable in free economies; large sizes of these represent the failures on the part of the market and/or the government. All the inhabitants of the country, that is, workers, firms and the government are responsible for this failure. To understand the dynamics of unemployment and inflation, it is imperative to understand the causes, consequences and cures behind these.

Unemployment–Definition

Recall from Chapter 3 that unemployment actually refers to all persons who are not fully engaged in any productive activity.[1] The said definition is quite ambiguous as it is hard to define the terms fully engaged and productive activity. While there are persons who are too old or sick, children who are too young to perform any work, and students who are studying full-time; there are others who have none of these attributes and are yet not engaged in any worthwhile activity most of the time, either because they do not want to or they do not find one. Obviously, to include all such persons in the common group unemployed is not a correct approach. Accordingly, economists make a distinction between the population and work force, divide the work force into employed and unemployed, further categorise unemployment into voluntary and involuntary, and define the **unemployment rate as the involuntarily unemployed people as a percentage of the total work force** (vide Chapter 3). While both kinds of unemployment are bad for the economy (loss of GDP), involuntary unemployment is associated with social and psychological issues as well.

---

[1]In economics, unemployment includes both of human beings and capital (structures and equipment), and both lead to the loss of GDP. However, since unemployment of people causes social and psychological problems besides economic ones, it is this one alone which is usually analysed in detail.

Causes of Unemployment

To understand the sources/causes of unemployment, it is better to go by its categories: **(a)** Voluntary and **(b)** Involuntary.

The latter is further classified into: **(a)** Structural or mismatch; **(b)** Frictional or turnover; **(c)** Seasonal; and **(d)** Cyclical.

Further, if the wage rate is not flexible, there is another category of involuntary unemployment, called 'wait'.

The reasons for each of the above kinds of unemployment are somewhat unique. **Voluntary unemployment** could be caused by:

(a) Frustration: When a person fails to find a job for long, he/she may decide to opt out of the work force to save embarrassment and mental tension. If so, the said person is unemployed due to frustration.

(b) Income effect: Recall from Chapter 9 that every potential worker faces the trade-off between work (which brings income) and leisure, and that the labour supply curve is **backward bending**. This implies that when people are rich, the income effect of an increase in the wage rate on the supply of labour (which is adverse) outstrips its substitution effect (which is favourable), and accordingly, such people opt for more leisure than work, leisure happens to be a desirable (normal) good. The same logic would apply even for the zero versus non-zero supply of labour. People who are rich, may just like to enjoy full time leisure (for them the marginal utility of leisure would exceed the marginal dis-utility of leisure—the latter also means the marginal utility of work/income) and, thus, supply no labour at all. This is primarily because they are rich and can afford and prefer leisure to work. In proof of this, we do have people, particularly ladies in the rich families in developing countries, who spend most of their time in recreational activities or idleness. Fortunately, improving education, job opportunities, vast avenues for pleasure, preference for economic independence, among others, are helping in minimising such practices.

(c) Attitude to work: Some people do not enjoy work or are frustrated in their employment, and therefore quit their job when they can afford it. Premature retirement from work is one such example. Also, there are those who are just too lazy to work and thus refuse to take up any job.

Structural unemployment is caused by the changing structure of the economy (i.e., primarily agriculture based economy to an industrial economy, and subsequently to an overwhelming service sector; traditional industries to knowledge based industries; a predominately rural to an urban economy; public to private sector; small to large sector; monopoly to competition etc.) as human beings (skills, location etc.) may change slowly compared to the economy. It arises because of the capital structure and the relative wage across various sectors of the economy, which is at variance with the skills and location of the existing work force. Its sources may be described as[2]:

(d) Mismatch of skills: Economic models often assume that all labour is homogenous. Also, to some it is a puzzle that unemployment and vacancies co-exist.

---

[2]The various points are in continuation of those that preceded so that all the sources of unemployment are recorded on a continuous basis.

However, labour is highly heterogeneous and different jobs require different skills. On the one hand, we have the great businessmen like Bill Gates and the Late Dhirubhai Ambani, among so many others, and Nobel laureates in all sciences; while on the other hand, we have a lot more people who are not even sincere unskilled workers. Obviously, the two kinds of people are very different and one may not be able to do the job of the other. In other words, a shortage of skilled persons cannot be filled up by unskilled persons. Further, a psychology expert cannot teach economics or accounting, and a secretary or nurse can teach nothing. Also, an economics professor may be an inefficient secretary or a farmer or even a businessman. With the growth in information technology (IT) and the knowledge-based industries, there are plenty of opportunities in the IT industry and people with no background in computers are becoming redundant. Similarly, earlier emphasis on industrialisation had left some peasants and farm workers unemployed, and industries craving for workers. Globalisation has infused competition, and privatisation demands efficiency. Competition has led to cost cutting, out-sourcing, mergers and large-scale productions. If a person is not dynamic to these trends, he/she would surely lose the job. Currently, a significant part of the unemployment in the world is deemed to fall in this category.

(e) Mismatch of locations: Jobs and workers are not perfectly mobile geographically. Immigration laws forbid the mobility of labour across countries, besides, transport cost, language and other factors. Transport cost, hassles of finding accommodation, higher costs of living, family and land attachments, lack of knowledge about job openings elsewhere and such other factors inhibit labour mobility within the country of residence. There may be a shortage of labour in the developed world, but the unemployed in developing countries are unable to offer their services to them. Similarly, there may be opening in metropolitan cities but the unemployed in rural areas cannot take those jobs. Metropolitan cities are often overcrowded and it is said, "you can get a job, spouse and what not, but not a roof to cover your head". Unfortunately, such a mismatch is more profound in developing countries than in the developed ones.

Frictional unemployment, that is unemployment in between jobs—turnover unemployment—is the outcome of several forces, like:

(f) Job separation: Employed persons do change jobs due to frustration in jobs and changes in career and location preferences, and also if and when they are fired from their jobs. Workers' preferences about the kind of job and the sector where they would like to work undergo a change partly because they are dynamic and the world is changing fast. Job satisfaction, salaries and career opportunities move over time from job to job, and rational people always look for the best combination. Their location preference change due to climate, cost of living, marriage, children's education and so on. Senior executives are paid highly and if they do not perform, they are asked to quit. Currently, the average term of CEOs has fallen significantly and while some may be leaving for greener pastures, others are thrown out of jobs. Lately, many CEOs are moving towards entrepreneurship, and we have examples of Anupam Kher and Manisha Koirala, who retired prematurely from anchoring the television serial *Sawal Dus Crore*

Ka, and Shah Rukh Khan, who anchored *Kaun Banega Crorepati* rather briefly. Also, downsizing, recessions and outsourcing cause retrenchments and layoffs. Thus, workers do leave their jobs, either voluntarily or involuntarily, and due to imperfect information regarding job/business opportunities, an unemployed person may just take time off to concentrate on finding the most appropriate activity for him/her. Until the separated worker is absorbed in the new activity, he/she remains unemployed. In India, job separation is not a serious issue, for the job market is not that rosy and there is hardly any exit policy. However, the most skilled executives (e.g., MBAs, IT professionals, Chartered Accountants) do suffer from job hopping activity.

(g) Job search: The labour market is far from perfect. There are no set standards/ qualifications for most jobs, and people with similar background do get different salaries, perks and career prospects. Detailed information on existing vacancies and the available work force is highly inadequate. This renders the finding of a job a difficult task. This, in turn, makes it a time consuming process, and there by renders job quitting and job searching an ongoing activity. In India, most government jobs have lengthy recruitment procedures and insist on graduation even before applying. Only graduates from centres of academic excellence have campus recruitment facilities. This renders graduates unemployed from the time they graduate till the time they join jobs. Such unemployment is relatively higher in developing countries and during recessions than otherwise.

Seasonal unemployment is caused by:

(h) *Fluctuations in seasons*: In agriculture-based economies like India, farmers and agricultural labourers have little work during off-seasons (post-Rabi, pre-Kharif periods etc.). Also, people like college students and construction workers for example, may not be able to find adequate work during their respective off seasons (i.e., summer vacations and monsoon season). In the developed world, too, there are seasonal jobs, like hotels and resorts that remain partly idle during off tourist periods and travel agents, who have very little business during such periods. People who have jobs only in busy seasons are deemed seasonally unemployed.

Cyclical unemployment: It occurs due to:

(i) Adverse supply and demand shocks: Recall from Chapters 9-14 that adverse supply shocks come in the form of falls in the work force and capital inputs; increases in the costs of labour, raw material, energy and supplies, tax rates and firms' expected inflation; poor weather; technological retardation (forget fullness); natural calamities like earthquakes and epidemics; trade unions and cartelization formations; and government stipulations regarding pollution and safety regulations, etc. Some of these tend to increase the cost of production, which, *ceteris paribus*, induces firms to cut their production; the others adversely affect the aggregate supply directly. Given the aggregate demand, the real income and employment falls. This, in turn, renders some workers redundant and leads to lay-offs and retrenchments. Similarly, adverse demand shocks like a decline in consumers' and firms' confidence, increased thriftiness (i.e., decrease in marginal propensity to consume and/or in the autonomous consumption), increased risk averseness of investors, fall in net exports and decrease in government expenditure or increased tax rates, leave firms in the buyers' market. If AD falls short of AS, inventories get accumulated, which induces firms to cut their productions and to lay-off some of their workers. This kind of unemployment is hopefully temporary, and hence, is referred to as cyclical unemployment. Once the recession is over and the bottom is hit, recovery begins and job opportunities re-emerge to absorb the hitherto laid- off workers.

Wait unemployment is the labour force that is waiting for a fall in the wage rate to open up employment opportunities for them. This arises basically due to the:

(j) *High or non-equilibrium wage rate:* Classical economists advocate wage flexibility and full employment equilibrium. However, the real world is far from such an ideal situation (vide Chapter 14). The nominal and even the real wage are rigid and inflexible downward for various reasons, including the minimum wage laws, and the efficiency wage and insider-outsider models (vide Chapter 14). Firms may find the wage rate too high to enlarge their work force. They are guided by the marginal productivity of labour, which suggests that they could hire more workers only at the lower wage rate. Though unemployed workers are willing to work at a lower wage, wage rigidity/efficiency wage theory/insider-outsider theory forbids firms offering lower wage. This leaves some people unemployed even when they are willing to work at the ruling wage rate. These unemployed people are eagerly waiting for the wage rate to fall, hence, wait unemployment. If the wage rate were fixed only in certain industries, say, due to strong trade unions there, then wait unemployment would be lesser than otherwise. For, if the textile sector had wage rigidity but not the automobiles sector, then during recession, some workers from the former sector could move to the latter sector, thereby salvaging the unemployment issue to some extent. The unemployment caused by the wage rate being higher than the market-clearing wage, is called the classical unemployment.

In addition to these specific sources, classified according to the type of unemployment, there are some universal factors that are responsible for all kinds of unemployment. These include:

(k) *Unemployment benefits:* Most developed countries have provisions to pay compensations to unemployed people. For example, in the United States, an unemployed person currently gets this compensation at the rate of 50 per cent of his erstwhile income up to six months of his/her unemployment, and nothing beyond that. In many countries in Europe, the compensation is more generous and can be collected indefinitely. The availability of unemployment benefits renders employment less attractive and, accordingly, encourages people to refuse jobs and to consume leisure instead. This causes all kinds of unemployment to rise. One of the reasons economists attribute to a relatively higher unemployment rate in Europe, compared to the United States, is its better unemployment compensation package.

(l) Discrimination: Statistics on the work force, employment and unemployment all over the world suggest that the rate of unemployment is more among teenagers/youth, women and minority classes (blacks) groups. This speaks of some in-built discrimination against these groups of people. While this may be rational as teenagers and women are perhaps more unstable (have higher turnovers) and the minority perhaps less trustworthy or committed to work, such a discrimination becomes a source of all kinds of unemployment among these groups. Due to this, some firms just refuse to expand their otherwise high prospect business when they are not able to find workers from preferred groups. This leads to the uncalled for unemployment caused by sheer discrimination.

(m) Hysteresis Theory: According to this theory, the natural rate of unemployment (= sum of the structural, frictional, seasonal and wait unemployment) automatically follows the path of actual unemployment, and accordingly it changes regularly. The natural rate of unemployment fell in most countries during the 1990s and it rose during the great recession of 2007-09. The theory partly explains the falling rate of unemployment in developed countries like the United States and in over-heated economies like Singapore, Hong Kong, Taiwan, South Korea and Malaysia, particularly before the July 1997 Asian economic crisis. Also, it explains why the increase in unemployment during the great recession of 2007-09 is falling so slowly even after the recession has already been succeeded by prosperity. According to this theory, when the unemployment is large, the unemployed people lose skills, get accustomed to laziness and feel too disheartened to even look for jobs. Also, during recessions, wait unemployment often goes up as the wage rate is maintained at a relatively higher rate by workers who care more about the wage rate rather than employment. Thus, because the unemployment rate was high yesteryears, it is high even today. Under the opposite situation when unemployment is low and most people are working, workers improve their job skills through the job and put in their best efforts to find new jobs quickly if they lose their old ones. Accordingly, the unemployment rate becomes low if it was low in the past. Many economists suggest that the natural rate of unemployment has fallen in the United States due to this hysteresis theory. By this theory, one is unemployed because he/ she is unemployed.

The above factors may not provide an exhaustive list of the sources of all unemployment, as no list can ever be complete. Also, the different sources listed above may not be totally independent of others, for they often get mixed. Nevertheless, we leave it here and the readers are encouraged to ponder on the issue.

The **natural rate of unemployment**, which stands for the non-cyclical unemployment, is the sum total of the frictional, structural and seasonal (and wait, if there is wage rigidity) unemployment is caused by all those factors that trigger any of its components. Thus, the theory of the natural rate of unemployment hypothesises all such factors as the determinants of the natural rate of unemployment. To recall, these include trade unions, minimum wage rules, hysteresis, unemployment benefits, discrimination, firing cost and so on. Since many of these determinants are subject to public policy (for example, the minimum wage legislation affects wait unemployment and unemployment benefits exert influence on frictional unemployment), the government has a role in the magnitude of the natural rate of unemployment. Due to the changing magnitudes of its determinants, the natural rate of unemployment is also not a fixed number. Nevertheless, it is believed to fluctuate around 4 per cent in developed countries.

Consequences of Unemployment

Unemployment is considered universally bad, both for the economy (including the world) as well as for the individuals concerned. While some costs of unemployment are economic, others are social and psychological. There are some benefits of unemployment as well. Considering the economy wide economic costs first, unemployment leads to:

(a) GDP loss: By definition, an employed person is engaged in some productive activity.[3] Accordingly, unemployment leads to the loss of production directly. Since the contribution to production (i.e., the marginal product of the labour) varies with the person employed as well as the job in which the person works, the true extent of this loss depends on who is unemployed and where he/she could have been working. This is a hypothetical situation if the unemployed person never had a job. Further, even if the said person had a job, in the present day highly specialised production, the marginal production of any particular worker can hardly be estimated with any fair degree of accuracy. Thus, the exact determination of the production loss due to unemployment is just not possible. Nevertheless, empirical research has been carried out in several countries on the corresponding macroeconomic data to come out with certain estimates for the average (overall) loss in output due to unemployment. In this respect, Arthur Okun's research (1962) on the United States data is the most significant one. He was the first to estimate this negative relationship between the rate of change in the GDP and the rate of change in the unemployment rate, and in his honour, the said relationship is known as the **Okun's Law**. For the most recent United States data of 1930 to 1980, the results on the Okun's law are the following:

$$g = 3.0 - 2\,\Delta u \qquad \textbf{(15.1)}$$

where

g = rate of change in real GDP (in per cent)

Δu = rate of change in unemployment rate (in per cent)

Equation **(15.1)** indicates that the growth rate in real GDP would be 3 per cent if the unemployment rate remains the same, and it would fall to nil if the unemployment rate increases by 1.5 per cent. Thus, the output loss would be equal to 2 per cent for every 1 per cent increase in the unemployment rate. In USA in 2012, the unemployment rate was 8.1 per cent, the nominal GDP $15.7 trillion and the natural rate of unemployment is estimated at about 5 per cent. Thus, the unemployment rate happened to be above its natural rate by 3.1 per cent. Given the Okun's law result, this means that the output loss in the United States in 2012 comes to 6.2 per cent of her GDP, which gives a figure of $950 billion for the GDP loss. The said amount comes to over 50 per cent of India's GDP. This loss by any standard is very high and this speaks for the economic cost of unemployment.

Obviously, equation **(15.1)** constitutes no iron law, for, as stated above, this is an average result; and that too for the United States economy for the period

[3] A person who does not contribute to production but just gives the impression of being employed deemed unemployed in economics.

of the study only. The estimates could/and do vary over space as well as time. The 1962 study of Okun himself had slightly different estimates: the intercept was 2.5 and the slope at 2.5. For India, we do not have such results, for we do not even have the proper time series data on the rate of unemployment in the country. However, some rough estimates are still available. Planning Commission (1992, Page 56) has provided the estimate for the elasticity of real GDP with respect to the employment of labour. This is close to plus 0.5. This implies that if the employment rate decreases by 1 per cent, *ceteris paribus*, the real GDP falls by 0.5 per cent, and vice versa. This, though smaller than the loss of GDP in United States, is no small a figure particularly for a poor economy like India. Incidentally, note that a decrease in employment does not necessarily mean an increase in unemployment, for the former could come through a decrease in population, decrease in the proportion of labour force in a population or a decrease in the average number of working hours. However, the said elasticity does throw some light on the GDP loss due to an increase in the unemployment rate.

(b) *Income redistribution*: Since unemployed people do not work, they have no income. In contrast, employed people continue earning their respective incomes. This widens income inequalities between those having employment and those not having employment. Income inequalities have economic effects in terms of the poverty ratio (more the inequality, the larger is the poverty rate), saving rate (more the inequality, the larger is the saving rate) etc., and through these on the economic performance of the economy. For example, saving is a source of funds for investment and thus if the saving rate goes up, *ceteris paribus*, investment tends to go up, and as the investment rate goes up, *ceteris paribus*, the growth rate in the economy goes up. Further, income inequality has non-economic consequences as well. For example, it causes the poor to envy the rich, which leads to social unrest, including thefts, terrorism, murder and suicide. It is because of such economic and non-economic costs that unemployment benefits have been designed to cope with the hardships of unemployment.

(c) *Control on wage-price*: In the flexible labour market (and even in others to a large extent), the wage rate is determined by the demand for and supply of labour. Thus, if there is a reserve army (the term due to Karl Marx) of unemployed people, wages would be lower than otherwise. Further, the mere presence of unemployed people would motivate workers to work hard and sincerely, and prevent the employees from demanding higher wages, lest they are replaced. In view of this, unemployed persons help maintain a downward pressure on the wage rate, and thereby on product prices. This helps the economy to hold the inflation rate down, which happens to be a macroeconomic objective. On this criterion, unemployment is deemed good for the economy. Incidentally note that the unemployment, which is needed to motivate workers to perform well and to keep the wage rate down, is referred to as the Marxian unemployment.

Unemployment affects individuals who are unemployed adversely due to the:

(a) *Loss of income:* When people do not work, they earn nothing. If they were employed, they would have earned some income. Thus, unemployment causes the loss of income, which would have been earned if he/she had the job.

(b) *Psychological cost:* Unemployed people are looked down upon by everyone and they are considered a burden on the nation and on the employed persons in the respective families. This leads to frustration even among those who are capable and sincerely looking for openings, and other members of their families who have to support them. People lose their human capital if they remain unemployed for long; they cannot even get up in the morning. Being fired from a job is like getting an 'F' grade in the exam. We do read in newspapers about cases of suicides and heart ailments among unemployed/failed people. As said above, due to such fears many unemployed people (particularly ladies) even tend to withdraw themselves from the work force.

At the individuals' level, unemployment has some favourable effects as well. These include:

(a) Leisure: Leisure is a desirable product and we know that busy executives envy people having plenty of free times. Some foreigners have been heard commenting that Indians spend a lot of time on gossip and lazing around. Americans make such comments even regarding Europeans whose average working hours are relatively less. However, note that leisure is welcome for those who have a scarcity of this, and may not be for those who have a lot of it. The law of diminishing marginal utility must apply to leisure as well, and if it does, an unemployed person may already have crossed the saturation point with respect to the quantity of leisure in his/her possession. Nevertheless, to the extent unemployment gives the time to search for a most appropriate job, to relax and to have valuable time with the family, it is a sought after product, and, if so, leisure is a benefit flowing from unemployment.

Of the above, the heaviest cost of unemployment is the loss of GDP to the economy (world) and the loss of income to the individual. These are both prohibitive and, accordingly, all countries make their best efforts to alleviate or remove unemployment. Needless to say, both voluntary as well as involuntary unemployment are associated with loss of GDP and loss of personal income, and accordingly both have to be checked. Of course, involuntary causes less social and psychological tensions than do the voluntary, and short term unemployment (like frictional and structural to some extent) is a less serious issue than long run one. The possible cures for all these are analysed next.

CURES FOR UNEMPLOYMENT

The cures for unemployment lie basically in attacking the sources of unemployment. The foremost cures would be:

(a) Education: An analysis of the data would suggest that unemployment is more prominent among illiterates and less educated persons than among well-educated persons. Education inculcates a sense of duty and dignity of labour, and imparts knowledge about the labour market and other related matters. It, thus, impresses the person about the fruits of employment and the opportunity costs of his/her idleness. Relevant education not only eliminates the skill matching issue but also reduces the barriers to mobility. Even the adult education is highly recommended for alleviating unemployment. Education would thus help reduce all kinds of unemployment, natural as well as others.

(b) Retraining: As the structure of the economy undergoes a change, some jobs become redundant and others emerge. Thus, computerisation has adversely affected clerical and manual computational jobs but has created the need for software professionals. It has also reduced the demand for typewriters and increased the demand for computers. This has thrown out of jobs some workers in typewriter manufacturing firms and those performing clerical and accounting jobs. If this surplus labour is retrained to perform the emerging jobs of computer making and software development, those rendered unemployed due to the changed structure would be reabsorbed in the labour market. Similarly, erstwhile agricultural workers become redundant under the impact of industrialisation, but if they are provided the necessary training towards new skills needed for industries, they could be re-employed. Human beings are intelligent, and new skills are not impossible to acquire even at a relatively old age. Of course, training requires funds and trainers, but there is never a 'free lunch'. Governments of all countries are earmarking funds for this activity and encouraging firms to provide such training through tax shields. This is a worthwhile activity, and more and more needs to be done in this direction to alleviate unemployment. Retraining would particularly help eradicate structural unemployment, which is on the rise due to increasing specialisation and globalisation.

(c) Dissemination of information: Imperfect information about job opportunities and the wage structure is a cause of unemployment. Collection and dissemination of such information would help reduce the time between job separation and job finding, thereby, reducing frictional unemployment. Also, if people in rural areas and the unorganised sector have such information, they would be encouraged to move to urban centres and the organised sector, which would reduce unemployment due to mismatch of location. People, who have quit the workforce out of frustration, may return to the labour market when they get reliable and prompt information on job openings. Even some housewives, who are currently not seeking jobs, and therefore, technically 'not unemployed', may offer their services, which would only add to the gross domestic product.

(d) Infrastructure development: Development of infrastructure, that is, transport and communication networks, power and water resources, education, health and such other facilities, etc. in rural/less-developed areas would reduce the location barrier and provide a boost to industrialisation. This would directly cut the mismatch unemployment due to location and create new job opportunities, which would absorb some erstwhile unemployed persons. Under this avenue, you take the job to the worker rather than otherwise and thereby also help curb regional inequalities.

(e) Improvement in industrial relations: Trade unionism is an inevitable outcome of the corporate world. Such unions are not necessarily bad but when their leadership goes in wrong hands, they do more harm than good. If a wage rate hike is unjustified on the basis of economic considerations, it only affects employment adversely. While those who are able to retain their jobs get the benefits, those who are retrenched and denied employment suffer. A healthy relationship between the management and the workers goes a long way not only in terms of a regular flow of production but also in maximising the employment opportunities and output. The tool of trade unionism could also be used to curb discrimination against young, females, and minority classes, and thereby check unemployment.

(f) Expansionary demand management policies: Easy fiscal and monetary policies lead to increase in aggregate demand and, thereby, help raise the real income and employment. We know from the earlier chapters that if an economy is facing recession, it would have the situation where AD falls short of AS. Demand is the engine of growth and if that engine has no steam, the economy would stop growing; and if the engine is refuelled, growth would sustain. During recession, private sector lacks the purchasing power but the government has unlimited such powers; it can print money and spend the same to create new demand-deficit financing. Such deficits do not even cause inflation and even the non-Keynesians are not uncomfortable with cyclical fiscal deficits; they merely oppose structural deficits. Thus, expansionary demand management policies may be applied during recessions and these would help remove cyclical unemployment. However, expansionary demand management policies may not be the appropriate tool to counter structural unemployment, which is rampant today.

The above are just a few suggestions to suppress unemployment. Surely there are more possibilities to attack this menace and the readers are encouraged to think aloud regarding this.

INFLATION—DEFINITION

Recall from Chapter 3 that inflation refers to a continuous increase in the aggregate (general or macro) price level rather than just a one-time increase in it. Thus, if a general price index stood at 150 in the year 2003, at 165 in 2004, 165 in 2005 and 160 in 2006, then:

(a) there is an inflation at the rate of 10 per cent [= (165 – 150) (100)/150] in 2004 as compared to 2003.

(b) there is no inflation in 2005 as compared to 2004.

(c) price is higher in 2004 than in 2003, and in 2005 than in 2003.

(d) there is deflation at the rate of 3.03 per cent [= (160 – 165) (100)/165] in 2006 as compared to 2005.

(e) there is inflation in 2005 as compared to 2003, and in 2006 as compared to 2003, whose annual rates have to be determined using the appropriate compound factor (vide equation (3.8), Chapter 3).

(f) price is lower in 2006 than 2005.

An examination of the time series data across countries would suggest that all countries have experienced some, though varying degrees of inflation over time (vide Table 3.4, Chapter 3). By the degree of inflation and the trend in the inflation rate, five kinds of inflation are distinguished, which are: **(a)** Hyperinflation/Runaway inflation; **(b)** High inflation; **(c)** Galloping inflation; **(d)** Low inflation; **(e)** Crawling inflation.

Though there is no precise criterion for some of these, attempts are made here to offer as close definitions as possible. The hyperinflation is understood to be the phenomena where the rate of inflation is around 1000 per cent per year (= 22 per cent per month, compounded monthly) and more. This appears to be too high an inflation rate to prevail anywhere but it has happened in a few countries in the past. The most famous case of hyperinflation occurred in Germany during January 1922 through November 1923 with an average rate of 322 per cent per month. The most rapid hyperinflation was in Hungary during August 1945 through July 1946, with an average rate of 19,800 per cent per month. Several Latin American countries have also experienced such inflation and that too during the 1980s and 1990s. For example, Bolivia had inflation at the rate of 11,750 per cent per year during 1985, Brazil at the rates above 1000 (ranging between 1009 and 2948) per cent per year in each of the four years during 1989, 1990, 1993 and 1994, Nicaragua at the rates of over 2900 (ranging between 2945 and 10205) per cent per year in each of the four years during 1988 through 1991, Peru at the rates of above 3000 per cent per year in both 1989 (3399%) and 1990 (7482%), Argentina at the rates of above 2000 per cent per year during both of 1989 (3080%) and 1990 (2314%) and Ukraine at the rate of 4735 per cent per year in 1993.[4] Nevertheless, hyperinflation is a rare worldwide event and it has hardly lasted anywhere beyond a couple of years. Further, such run away inflations have taken place in the aftermath of wars or the breakup of empires. It is well known that Latin American countries were moving from the authoritarian system to the democracy during the 1980s and early 1990s.

The other rare kind of inflation is high inflation. High inflation refers to inflation at the high two digit rate to the top of the three digit rate per year (remember inflation at 1000 per cent and over per year is hyperinflation). Such inflation was witnessed in the Russian Federation and in Nigeria during the 1990s (vide Table 1.1, Chapter 1) and, if we go through data, surely in some other countries as well. Galloping inflation refers to the inflation where the inflation rate is increasing over time. Examples for this are available within hyperinflation and high inflation countries, and would surely be found in some countries at least for a few years. Most countries in the world experienced fairly high inflation during 1974 through 1982 or so and a detailed analysis of that period could well identify such inflations. Low inflation refers to the inflation whose rate falls within one digit to the low two digits per year. This is the most common kind of inflation and it has been experienced by most countries in the last 50 years or so. The last, crawling inflation, is the one which is low and which moves up and down slowly. This is the common form currently (vide Table 3.4, Chapter 3).

There is another basis on which inflation is distinguished. In many countries, including India, a few prices are fixed by the government, a few others are subject to the minimum/maximum price regulations, a few are subject to dual pricing, where a

---

[4]Source: *International Financial Statistics*, IMF, 1999.

part of the output is sold at a fixed (ration) price and the rest at a free market price, and other prices are subject to the free interplay of demand and supply. Thus, on the basis of the source of inflation, three types of inflation are found, which are: **(a)** Administered inflation; **(b)** Demand-pull inflation; and **(c)** Cost-push (supply side) inflation. If inflation is caused by the revision of prices by the government, it is called administered inflation. If the inflation is triggered by an increase in aggregate demand, it is called demand-pull inflation; and if the cause for it lies in the cost increases, it is called the cost-push inflation.

There is one more kind of distinction, which is between **headline and core inflations**. The former refers to the usual inflation rate while the latter refers to the one for which the country or the government is responsible. Thus, the core inflation excludes the inflation in volatile items, such as agricultural goods and energy goods, for the former happen due to weather/rainfall and the latter due to inflation abroad. In what follows, we shall look into the causes of inflation, its effects on the economy and the methods to cure it.

Causes of Inflation

In a command economy, all prices are set by the commanding authority. In contrast, in a capitalist/free enterprise economy, aggregate price is determined by aggregate demand and aggregate supply. Thus, in a mixed economy, while some prices are set by the government, the others are determined by the market forces of demand and supply. Accordingly, inflation could be caused by price revisions by government; demand-pull factors and the cost push (adverse supply) factors. Once inflation is initiated, it can be accentuated by other factors, and the process may well lead to an inflation spiral. Accordingly, various inflation theories become complementary and it becomes hard to separate the role of each. Inflation theories will now be discussed.

(a) Increase in Administered Prices: To an extent some prices are administered by the government, an increase in them by the tight price policy can cause an increase in the aggregate price, which is a weighted average of the administered and the market determined (free) prices. Besides, when administered prices go up, a series of change/adjustment take place: non-price administered (free market) goods become relatively cheap, rational people substitute the latter goods for goods whose prices have increased, demand for the goods whose prices have not gone up increase and prices of free market goods also tend to increase. In addition, the prices of various goods are positively connected through the input-output system, thus, an increase in the administered prices triggers an increase in all prices, which further aggravates the increase in the general price. Increase in the general price in one period is followed in the subsequent periods through an increase in the cost of production, and the expectations of price rise built on the past price behaviour, leading to the self- fulfilling prophesy. This, in turn, leads to sustained inflation.

In the classical model of fully flexible prices, where there are no administered prices, the above source of inflation is not there. However, in such a system, inflation could be caused by an increase in the aggregate demand (that is, favourable demand shocks—demand pull) or/and a decrease in the aggregate supply (that is adverse supply shocks—cost-push). These are examined below.

(b) Favourable demand shocks: Favourable demand shocks could be triggered through the optimistic attitudes of consumers and firms, leading to an increase in consumption and investment expenditure; economic prosperity abroad, leading to an increase in net exports; and/or liberal fiscal and monetary policies leading to an increase in government expenditure and/or money supply. Such situations would lead to increase in aggregate demand (AD), aggregate supply (AS) remaining the same, real output and price would go up. Increase in general price, in turn, would tend to increase the nominal wage rate (may be when the new wage contract is signed, if there is price rigidity), which would increase the cost of production and, thus, shift the AS curve upward, which would further increase the price and reduce the real income. The AD will be pushed up again through the expansionary fiscal/monetary policy to restore the real income level (to neutralise the fall in employment), which would lead to further increase in price. Thus, one shot causing an increase in price would lead to more and more such shots (like the sequence: increase in a demand component—increase in AD—increase in price-increase in wage rate—increase in cost of production—decrease in AS—increase in unemployment— increase in government expenditure—increase in AD and so on) causing higher and higher prices, and in effect there would be inflation. The process is illustrated in Fig. 15.1 below.

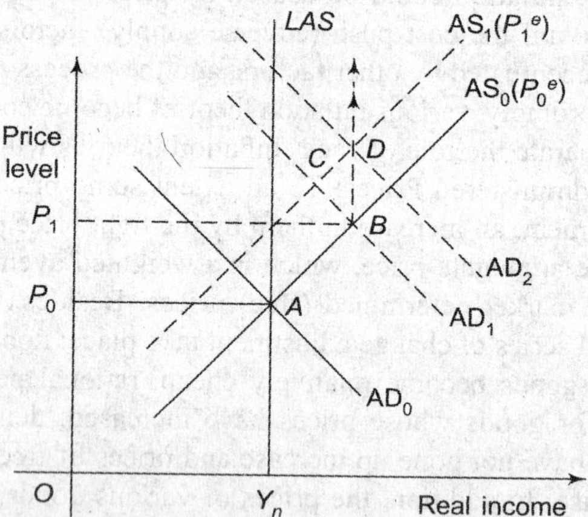

Fig. 15.1 Demand-Pull Inflation

In Fig. 15.1, AD_o and AS_o represent the original AD and AS curves and Y_n and P_o the original equilibrium output and price levels, respectively. Increase in AD shifts the AD curve to AD_1, the new equilibrium to point B, associated with higher output (lower unemployment) and higher price. The latter would cause upward revisions in the wage rate and expected inflation, which would cause a shift in AS curve to AS_1, and the new equilibrium would be reached at Point C. At point C, the output is below and unemployment is above those at the erstwhile equilibrium at point B, which would encourage a further increase in AD through another dose of expansionary fiscal/monetary policy, shifting the AD curve to AD_2, equilibrium to point D and so on. The economy may not return to a new long run equilibrium on the long run AS curve (vertical) and, thus, the price may continue increasing year after year, leading to inflation, as shown by the arrow above point D. Thus, the policy makers desire to reduce the unemployment below its natural level may cause inflation in the economy. Deflation could similarly be triggered through the chain of adverse demand shocks.

(c) Adverse supply shocks: Adverse supply shocks take the forms of bad weather, technological retardation, government stipulation about pollution and safety requirements and increases in indirect tax rates, wage-capital rental and the prices of raw materials, energy and supplies.[5] Any one or more of these, other things remaining the same, causes the cost of production to go up, which shifts the AS curve upward. In India, the implementation of the 6th Pay Commission report for the government employees, effective January 2006, and the failure of monsoon had brought adverse supply shocks. The AD curve remaining unaltered, an upward shift in the AS curve causes the price to rise and output to fall (unemployment to rise). If the stabilisation policy chooses to accommodate the supply shock, the AD curve shifts upward, which further aggravates price increase? The wage-price spiral through the **cost of living adjustments** (COLA) accentuates the price trend. Further, if the supply shock is permanent, increase in the AD will have to be on a continuation basis so as to avoid pressure on unemployment. This will give rise to inflation. This is explained below in Fig. 15.2.

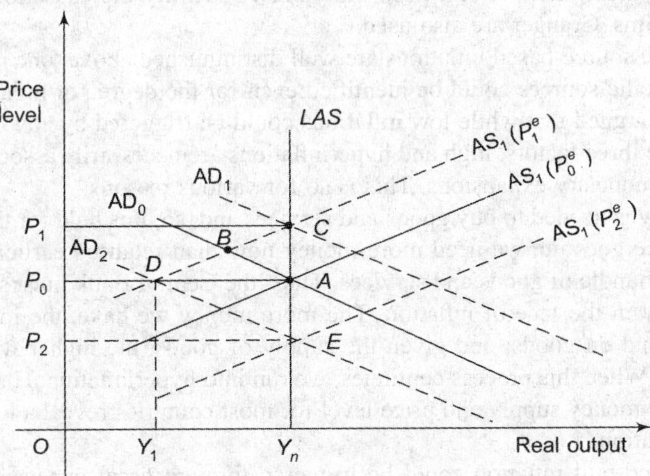

Fig. 15.2 Cost-Push Inflation

[5]Two types of supply side inflation are often distinguished; wage-inflation and cost-push inflation. If the inflation is triggered by wage increases, it is wage inflation and if it is caused by the non-wage cost factors, it is called cost-push inflation.

Original equilibrium is at point A in Fig. 15.2. The adverse supply shock moves the AS curve to AS_1 which, if accommodated by liberal fiscal/monetary policy to avoid new unemployment, shifts the AD curve to AD_1, taking the equilibrium to point C, where the price is even higher than that at point B. The rise in general price induces the nominal wage rate to rise, and inflationary expectations to be revised upward, which tend to further shift the AS curve upward, fuelling the price rise further. This **wage-price spiral**, with or without the accommodating policy ultimately lead to inflation. Thus, an adverse supply shock could lead to an inflationary situation. Incidentally, adverse supply shock could also be caused by the devaluation of the domestic currency (which makes foreign goods dearer and, thereby, imports expensive); inflation abroad (making imports expensive); increase in the indirect tax rates or by a decrease in subsidies.

Since demand-pulls are followed up by cost-push and vice versa, both the causes reinforce each other. The two kinds of inflation are, however, identified on the basis of 'which first'. If the demand-pull precedes the cost-push, we have demand-pull inflation, and if cost-push precedes demand-pull, there is cost-push inflation. When it is not possible to see which happened first, there is confusion as to what has caused the inflation. However, there is an additional test. If inflation is accompanied by a fall in unemployment, it is demand-pull and if it is accompanied by an increase in unemployment, it is cost-push. The rationale for the latter criterion is obvious: Under the AD-AS model, if AD goes up, AS remaining the same, both output and price go up and unemployment goes down. Thus, if the price increase is accompanied by unemployment increase, the increase in demand is the cause of inflation. In contrast, when cost goes, the AS curve shifts up, AD remaining the same, price goes up, output falls and unemployment goes up. Thus, if increase in cost is associated with increase in unemployment, there is cost-push inflation. To identify the causation, statistical tests, like Sims–Granger are also used.

While the source-based inflations are well distinguished above, one may wonder if some specific sources could be identified even for the degree of inflation. In this regard, it is argued that while low inflations could be triggered by any one or more of the above three factors, high and hyperinflations are necessarily associated, if not caused, by monetary expansions. This is so for various reasons:

(i) Money is needed to buy goods and services and, so, it is held for this purpose. If price goes up, we need more money now than required earlier to buy the same bundle of goods and services. Thus, the Central Bank must supply more money in the face of inflation. The more money we have, the more we like to spend on goods; and given the supply of goods, the higher would be the price. When this process continues, we run into hyperinflation. Historical data on the money supply and price level for most countries reveal a high positive correlation.

(ii) Demand-pull inflation could be triggered through fiscal expansions, that is, increases in government expenditure and/or decreases in taxes. However, such expansions *per se* have upper limits set by the availability of funds for them. All fiscal expansions (fiscal deficits) have to be funded through external debt, internal debt and monetisation (money printing). External debts have limits as when some other country or international financial institutions agree to lend, they would require servicing on a preset time schedule. If unable to honour the debt servicing, there is an external debt crisis and country's sovereignty is impinged. Internal debt does not have a servicing problem but it crowds out private expenditure, thereby reducing AD and checking inflation. Besides, of course, all debts cause the public debt-GDP ratio to rise, which again is subject to some upper bound (Chapter 10). This leaves monetisation as the only lasting means to finance fiscal deficits. However, monetisation means increase in the money supply. Thus, fiscal expansions not accompanied by monetary expansion could cause only modest inflation and not hyperinflation.

(iii) Demand-pull inflation could alternatively be initiated through increases in non-government expenditure, viz., private consumption, investment and net exports. The question then is, can any one or all of them increase without limits so as to cause a high degree of inflation? The answer is clearly no. For, private consumption is governed by disposable personal income, and the latter's purchasing power is seriously eroded by hyperinflation. Investment is dictated by profits and the real interest rate, which go haywire during hyperinflation. Inflation triggers inflation expectations, which triggers AS to fall, AD to rise, both of which cause acceleration in inflation. Further falls in AS lead to the accumulation of inventories, which discourages investment. In view of this, increase in investment cannot give the needed pull for AD to cause hyperinflation, export faces competition from the rest of the world and hence it also cannot be expanded to bring the needed push in aggregate demand to cause hyperinflation.

(iv) Adverse supply shocks could also cause inflation but not hyperinflation, for they are neutralized by the on-going technical progress.

(v) Money supply can increase unbounded under the existing flexible system of currency printing, and when all the other sources of revenue dry up. The government finances its expenditure through its last resort of seigniorage, that is, profit which the Central Bank of the country (and the governments) makes through printing/coining money is tapped liberally, causing hyperinflation. Most **hyperinflation** trends have begun when governments had inadequate tax money to pay for its spending. The government is unable to borrow under such situations as investors have little trust in the government honouring bonds when they become due and the only recourse is to print additional money, on which the government and the Central Bank of the country together have unlimited power. Once the inflationary spiral picks up, the fiscal problem becomes worse and worse. Because of the problem/delay in collecting taxes, real tax revenue falls as inflation rises. Rapid money creation leads to hyperinflation, which leads to a larger fiscal deficit, which, in turn, leads to larger debt and debt servicing, leading to further money creation and so on. As stated above, all hyperinflations have occurred due to war and break-up of empires, resulting in heavy government expenditure, financed overwhelmingly through monetisation, causing inflation and currency depreciation, capital flight, heavy public debt, external debt crisis, further conditional external finance, devaluation, monetary expansion and so on. Germany's hyperinflation during 1922-23, for example, was initiated by her requirements to pay large repatriations to victorious allies after the World War I. Rather than taxing its people to pay for those amounts;

the German government merely printed additional currency. Spending shot up and so did the price, and the process went on resulting in hyperinflation. Germany learnt the evils of such inflation the hard way and, accordingly, it is quite sensitive to inflation ever since.

For all these reasons, **all hyper inflations, and even high inflations, are monetary phenomenon**. Monetarists even go a step further and suggest that all inflation is, always and everywhere, a monetary phenomenon. Fischer and Easterly, in their article in the World Bank Research Observer, 5, 1990, while accepting the monetarists view, note that a rapid monetary growth without an undue fiscal imbalance is unlikely and, hence, they suggest that **rapid inflation is almost always a fiscal phenomenon**. If one looks up the history of rapid inflations, one would discover governments resorting to seigniorage at times of fiscal distresses. Even if one goes into the histories of inflation in developing countries, including India, one would find that fiscal imbalances and their monetisation have usually been associated with such periods. Thus, hyperinflation is both a monetary as well as a fiscal phenomenon.

CONSEQUENCES OF INFLATION

Unlike unemployment, the cost of inflation is indirect and less subject to quantification. While unemployment directly hampers output unambiguously, inflation does so only indirectly and ambiguously. Further, inflation has some significant benefits as well. Due to this, there is no consensus among economists as to whether inflation, no matter how little or serious it is, is necessarily bad. Some economists like James Tobin, consider some inflation as good for the economy as it keeps the real wage rate low and, thereby, the employment and output level higher than otherwise. However, others, like Arthur Okun, consider it as bad as unemployment. In fact, Okun (1978) has provided a new concept, called the **index of misery**, which equals the sum of the rates of unemployment and inflation. Thus, to him, both are equally bad.

The lack of consensus among economists on the virtues of inflation would be clear if we look at the possible effects (costs) of inflation. These could be analysed under two broad heads:

- Costs of fully expected or fully indexed inflation
- Costs of partly expected or partly indexed inflation

When the inflation is exactly as per the expectations, there are no surprises. This, in general, is less costly to the society as all future receipts and payments could then be fully adjusted in advance for inflation. Similarly, if the inflation is fully indexed, then even though there may be surprises, receipts and payments adjust through indexation (i.e., automatic adjustment of all the nominal transactions to the extent of actual inflation) and so no gain or loss in them due to inflation. Even under either of these situations, there are some **real costs** to the society, which could be enumerated as follows:

(a) Menu costs: Menu cards of restaurants, business catalogues of firms and bus/cinema tickets, among others, are printed; and vending machines/computers are periodically fed prices for the benefit of customers and prospective clients. If inflation/deflation occurs, the prices have to be changed, which costs the economy. This cost is independent of the rate of inflation and it is symmetric with regard to increase or decrease in price. Further, it occurs irrespective of whether the inflation is as per expectations or not as well as whether it is indexed, or otherwise. However, it is viewed as a small cost to society.

(b) Shoe-leather cost: Recall from Chapter 8 that people hold certain amount of real cash balances to meet their transactions, precautionary and asset demands for money, and that this demand varies inversely with the nominal rate of interest. When inflation occurs, by the Fisher's theory (nominal interest rate = real interest rate + expected inflation), the nominal interest rate goes up, which, in turn, induces people to hold less real cash balances. Reduced cash balances cause people to make more frequent visits to ATMs and banks than otherwise, which consumes time and reduces the life of shoes due to their increased wear and tear. This cost is referred to as the shoe-leather cost of inflation. Like the menu cost, this occurs irrespective of whether the inflation is fully expected, or partly or wholly surprised, or whether it is indexed or not. However, unlike the menu cost, it becomes the net benefit when there is deflation. Also, unlike the menu cost, shoe-leather cost varies directly with the rate of inflation. Besides the shoe-leather cost, there is also a side effect of the high nominal interest rate. As inflation crops up, the nominal interest rate goes up, people hold less real money balances and, thereby, divert funds to non-money assets like bonds, stocks and real capital (physical) goods. The latter tends to increase investment and the demand for durable goods.

(c) Money illusion: Some, particularly the less educated, act on the basis of the nominal values rather than the real values of their incomes and wealth. Economists call such persons the ones who suffer from the money illusion. Inflation/deflation can cause wrong decisions by otherwise rational people. For example, if someone's salary goes up, say, by 25 per cent when the inflation rate was 25 per cent, a person, not subject to the money illusion, would then consider this as no change in his/her purchasing power and, hence, would make no change in his purchases. However, persons subject to money illusion might take the above as an increase in their incomes and enhance their consumption spending, which is, obviously, a wrong thing for them as well as for society. Society, therefore, is worse-off now than before inflation and, accordingly, inflation is associated with a cost called the money illusion cost. This cost varies with the rate of inflation and it is symmetric to inflation as well as deflation.

(d) Inflation tax: Recall from Chapter 8 that there is high-powered money, which consists of the currency with the public and the reserves of banks held partly as deposits with the Central Bank of the country and partly in their own vaults as currency. Further, all currency (barring coins and one rupee notes issued by the Finance Ministry) is issued by the Central Bank at negligible cost and the banks' reserves are also liability of the central bank and, accordingly, the high powered money is considered government money. Thus, the government makes profit from the public (including banks) through its high-powered money, this is called **seigniorage**. People and banks hold the high-powered money to carry on their transactions smoothly and to serve as a store of value. It is argued that the demand for the high-powered money varies directly with the rate of inflation, for the demand for money as well as reserves is in terms of their real magnitudes or purchasing power. To keep constant the purchasing power of holdings of money in the face of inflation, a person/firm/bank has to add to the nominal balances which the central bank prints/issues at a negligible cost and without the need for any fresh legislation. In this process, resources are transferred from the money holders to money issuers; the latter can use them for financing its expenditures. Under this source, the government collects money from the public and banks without passing a new tax bill; hence, it is called the inflation tax, or seigniorage. It is a tax on real balances. In real terms (purchasing power terms), it is given by the product of the inflation rate and the real quantity of the high powered money (H/P),

$$\text{Inflation tax revenue} = \dot{P}\left(\frac{H}{P}\right) \tag{15.2}$$

Thus, suppose initially P = 1, H = 100. Now, if the inflation rate is 10 per cent, H could go up to, say, 110 to leave H/P at the initial level of 100. Thus, the inflation tax equals 10 (= 110 – 100), which is given by the above equation as 0.10(100/1) = 10. Under deflation, government revenue falls by the same amount and so it takes the form of **deflation subsidy**.

Inflation tax is one of the rare taxes which even the people in the underground economy cannot evade. Thus, a real estate dealer holding ₹500,000 in cash pays ₹20,000 in inflation tax if the inflation rate were 4 per cent. The moot question is that if inflation tax is available and that, too, without a new tax law, do various governments collect lots of money through this source and if not, why not. The answer to the first part of the question is negative and the reason for the same would follow soon. To see the size of this inflation tax revenue, let us look at the Indian data first. India's relevant data for the calendar year 2012-13 are as follows:

H = ₹15,149 billion; Inflation rate (CPI-all India) = 10.2 per cent;
Nominal GDP = ₹94,610 billion

Multiplying both the sides of equation **(15.2)** by P, would give us,

Nominal inflation tax revenue = Inflation rate × H
= 0.102 × ₹15,149 billion
= ₹1545 billion (= 1.63 per cent of GDP)

Thus, the size of this tax is trivial. Let us now look at the United States data, for the calendar year 2012:

H = $2674 billion; Inflation rate = 2.1 per cent;
Nominal GDP = $15, 685 billion

The above data give the nominal inflation tax revenue for the United States at $56.154 billion, which comes to a meager 0.358 per cent of its GDP. We know from Chapter 8 that the developed countries, which have a more developed banking system and habit than the developing ones, have a relatively low level of high-powered money than developing ones. This, given the inflation rate, means the size of the inflation tax revenue is lower in the developed world than in the less developed world. This proves our observation that the **inflation tax revenue is not at all substantial**, and further that it is smaller in the developed countries than in the rest. Accordingly, the government has to rely basically on tax revenues generated through tax legislations and public debt to finance its expenditures.

The reason for the inflation tax revenue to be meager is easy to see. Note that equation **(15.2)** is like the Laffer equation (vide equation (7.1), Chapter 7), where the two variables on the right hand side are not independent and, hence, the effect of a change in one of those on the left hand side variable is ambiguous. In other words, as the inflation rate goes up, the real high-powered money goes down, and vice versa. This is because, when the rate of inflation goes up, the nominal interest rate goes up (vide the Fisher equation, Chapter 6), and thereby, both the money demand (in real magnitude) by households and excess reserves (in real term) held by banks go down (vide Chapter 8). Decrease in the latter two tends to decrease the quantity of the real high-powered money. Integrating the last two sentences, we come to the conclusion that inflation tends to reduce H/P. Quite the opposite would happen in the face of deflation. Further, if the inflation rate and i move in the opposite directions, their product (which equals inflation tax proceeds, vide equation **(15.2)**) may go up, remain invariant or go down as the rate of inflation goes up. Thus, the relationship between the rate of inflation and inflation tax proceeds (in real term) is ambiguous. In fact, equation **(15.2)** indicates that the inflation tax proceeds are zero both at the zero inflation rate as well as at the infinite rate of inflation (as inflation rate tends to infinity, P tends to infinity and H/P tends to zero; also as inflation increases, money loses its purchasing power and, thereby, credibility; people reduce their holdings of H, which tends to zero as P tends to infinity). Accordingly, as the rate of inflation moves up from zero onward, the inflation tax proceeds first increases, reaches the plateau and then starts descending, hitting zero at the infinite rate of inflation. Thus, the inflation tax curve (with tax proceeds on the Y-axis and the inflation rate on the X-axis) would be an inverted U-shaped curve, like the Laffer curve (vide Fig. 7.1, Chapter 7).

This explains why governments, even if they wish, cannot depend on this source of revenue. Further, if the inflation tax were used on a large scale, inflation would invariably become extreme (for high H means high money, which means, *ceteris paribus*, high inflation), causing the said tax revenue to fall by its own doing. For this reason, **inflation tax is considered a destructive way of revenue collection** by any government. Even Keynes had warned us against this, to quote him, "A government can live by this means when it can live by no other. It is the form of taxation which the public finds hardest to evade and even weakest government can enforce, when it can enforce nothing else".

(e) Foreign exchange rate: Recall from Chapter 7 that inflation at home causes the home currency to appreciate (in real term) in relation to the foreign currency unless there is equal inflation rate abroad or the nominal exchange rate is adjusted by the inflation differential. The appreciation in the real exchange rate adversely affects our net exports and, thereby, the aggregated demand and output and price levels, among other consequences.

If inflation is not fully indexed, it causes two additional costs, called the bracket creep and capital gain tax:

(f) Bracket creep: Most countries in the world have a progressive system of personal income taxation. Under this system, the tax rate varies directly with the income bracket, where the brackets are progressing in certain income ranges. For instance, the current brackets and tax rates in India (excluding the surcharge) are as follows:

Income bracket (₹/year)	*Income tax rate (%)*
Below 200,000	0
200,000-500,000	10
500,000-1000,000	20
Over 1000,000	30

Suppose a person's current taxable annual income was ₹2000,000. Excluding exemptions and surcharge, his/her tax liability would equal:

0	on the first 200,000
30,000	on the next 300,000
100,000	on the next 500,000
300,000	on the remaining 1000,000
430,000	on the total taxable income of ₹2000,000

Now, suppose there is 20 per cent inflation and a corresponding 20 per cent increase in his/her taxable annual income, with no change in the tax laws. Under the new situation, the person's tax liability would go up to ₹550,000 as follows:

0	on the first 200,000
30,000	on the next 300,000
100,000	on the next 500,000
420,000	on the next 1400,000
₹550,000	on the total taxable income of ₹2400,000

The person's tax liability, thus, increases from ₹430,000 to ₹550,000, which marks an increase of about 28 per cent, which exceeds the inflation rate of 20 per cent. This is so because the taxpayer pays tax at the marginal tax rate on all the increase in his nominal income, and this raises his/her average tax rate. If the income of the taxpayer was a little lower than ₹1000,000, he/she would even moved to a higher tax bracket. This is an extra cost to income earners, and extra tax revenue to the government. This is a transfer of income and yet a social cost or benefit as there is a redistribution of income from taxpayers to government. If tax revenues are used to provide benefits to poor people, then it means the transfer of income from the rich to the poor, which would result in a net social gain. Nevertheless, the government benefits and taxpayers lose due to inflation through this system. This cost/benefit is independent of whether the inflation is expected or it is a surprise, but it is not there if the tax brackets are fully indexed. Under the fully indexed system, tax brackets change directly with the rate of inflation. For example, if the brackets were fully indexed, then the 20 per cent inflation will change the tax brackets to:

Income Bracket (₹/annual)	*Tax rate (%)*
Below 240,000	0
240,000-600,000	10
600,000-1200,000	20
Over 1200,000	30

The tax liability on an annual income of ₹2400,000 on the new tax laws would be ₹516,000 which would be exactly 20 per cent more than the earlier tax liability of ₹430,000 and hence no change in real magnitudes or welfare. Under deflation, while taxpayers would benefit, the government would lose. It is for this reason that many countries, including the United States have **inflation indexed tax brackets,** under which the tax brackets adjusts automatically and exactly by the inflation rate. In India, we do not have indexed tax brackets but the governments keep revising the tax brackets year after year to compensate the taxpayers for inflation. Needless to say, the extent of the cost through the bracket creep varies with the rate of inflation.

Why India and most other countries do not have indexation? Three reasons could be offered: **(a)** It would add another complication to calculations to most contracts, **(b)** Indexation will make it easier to live with inflation, which could weaken the governments fight against it, and **(c)** It would render relative prices inflexible, which would make it harder for the stabilization policy to tame business cycles.

(g) Capital gain tax: If financial assets, like bonds and stocks, are not fully indexed to inflation, then inflation leads to increase in their nominal values and, hence, to increased capital gain tax. For example, suppose a stock was purchased at, say, ₹500, and after one year its nominal value increased to ₹750 and the inflation rate during the year was 10 per cent. If the capital gain tax rate was 20 per cent and the asset was sold, the capital gain tax would equal ₹50 [(750 – 500) (0.20)]. In contrast, if the stock was fully inflation indexed, the tax would be only ₹30 [(750) – (500 × 1.20) (0.20)]. Thus, inflation causes burden through capital gain tax unless the assets denominated in nominal terms were fully indexed. This is another source of gain to the government through inflation. In many countries, including India, the option of full indexation of inflation of most assets for the purpose of capital gain tax is currently available. Incidentally, note that the capital gain tax is due on realisation only and the capital losses are permitted to be carried forward for a certain number of years, thereby providing some possible relief from the capital gain taxation.

The above costs are due to the steady/anticipated inflation. Variable or surprise inflation leads to some new costs as well. These include:

(h) Redistribution of wealth: According to the Fisher's equation, the nominal interest rate equals the real interest rate plus the expected inflation rate. Thus, 'surprise' inflation is not incorporated in the nominal interest rate. Since debts are denominated in the nominal terms, this causes inflation to affect debtors and creditors differently. During unexpected inflation, while the debtors gain, creditors lose. To illustrate this, assume expected inflation = 0, nominal interest rate = real interest rate = 4 per cent and actual inflation = 6 per cent. The person, who had borrowed ₹10,000 for one year, would return ₹10,400 in the following year. The purchasing power of ₹10,400 after one year would be ₹10,400/1.06 = ₹9,811, which is below the purchasing power of the ₹10,000 that he had borrowed. Besides, the lender is losing 4 per cent on his time preference (real interest rate). Thus, while the borrower benefits; the monetary creditor loses the equivalent amount due to the unexpected inflation. There is a possibility of another gain for the borrower. If the amount borrowed were for investment in housing or any other form of investment (like plant, machinery and inventories), the income/corporate tax rules permit such interest payments as deductible expenses for the purpose of computing the taxable income/profit. This, thus, provides another benefit of the unexpected inflation through tax shield. These gains encourage consumption spending/investing rather than lending, hence, reducing saving; and to the extent consumption is increased, funds for investment falls. It may also lead to higher interest rate to compensate for the falling value of money. Both these factors would affect investment adversely.

The amount of gain/loss due to the **surprise inflation** is proportional to the degree of that inflation. Since the government is normally the net debtor to the private sector, this is another source of gain to the government through inflation. The effect of the unexpected deflation is exactly the opposite of the unexpected inflation.

(i) Uncertainty: Unexpected inflation distorts income distribution and, therefore, rational people try to hedge against inflation. This calls for managing the uncertainty, which leads to speculations and unproductive investments. Also, there is the theory of **self-fulfilling prophecy**, which by itself becomes a source of inflation.

(j) Unemployment and sacrifice ratio: One possible method to check inflation, as will be detailed in the next sub-section, is to reduce the aggregate demand, which leads to a loss of output and increase in unemployment. This is a serious cost of avoiding inflation (i.e. to engineer disinflation) if such a method is resorted to deal with it and it is called the **sacrifice ratio**. It is defined as the ratio of the cumulative percentage fall in output and the fall in inflation rate (vide Okun 1978). This is the mirror image of the Okun's law referred to earlier in this chapter. For example, if a policy led to a reduction in inflation rate from 10 to 4 per cent over a three year period at the cost of falls in output such that the latter was 10 per cent below potential in the first year, 8 per cent below potential in the second year and 6 per cent below potential in the third year, then the total loss of GDP equals 24 per cent for achieving a 6 per cent fall in the inflation rate and, hence, the sacrifice ratio equals 4 (= 24/6). This loss is quite substantial and therefore, more often than not, policy makers try to live with inflation rather than to cure it through higher unemployment. The size of this loss, as will be seen later in this chapter, varies inversely with the degree of the credibility of the disinflation policy.

> **Case Study**: The Reagan-Volcker administration in the early 1980s in the United States applied this wrong measure (e.g., interest rates were allowed to go up to around 20 per cent) to contain inflation and created high doses of unemployment, resulting in the worst recession in the economy in 1982, since the Great Depression and until the great recession of 2007-09. The over a decade old coexistence of near zero growth rate and falling prices in Japan, until recently, had raised the specter of deflation over the global economy.

Incidentally, note that while the costs numbering **(a)** through **(i)** above are the costs which the economy bears when it faces inflation, the cost numbering **(j)**, namely, the sacrifice ratio, is the cost of stopping the inflation. Accordingly, the two sets are not additive and the society needs to compare the two sets to decide as to whether to live with the inflation or to stop it. Further, recall the natural rate hypothesis which suggests that the sacrifice ratio is zero in the long run. The decision issue here is "should inflation be tamed'? The answer is not easy as several costs of inflation are not quantifiable. However, one could through some inputs here. In general, if the inflation is hyperinflation, then it must be countered; and if it is mild, one may live with it. For medium inflation, the answer is debatable!

As would have been obvious from the above analysis, inflation costs/benefits vary from people to people. While some groups of people gain, others lose, the net benefit/cost to the society is not measurable. All that can be inferred about the effects of inflation are as following:

- Debtors gain while creditors lose
- Holders of real assets (like real estate and precious metals) gain while the holders of assets denominated in nominal terms (like currency, bonds, stock and bank deposits) lose
- Fixed nominal income earners (like widows and pensioners) lose
- Governments gain through inflation tax, bracket creep, capital gain tax and the fall in the real value of its debts.

In general, business gains as their assets are mostly in the form of real assets like structures, equipment and inventories, and their liabilities are mostly in nominal assets like equity and debt. Wage and salary earners lose, as their income usually rises lesser than the inflation rate. The government gains from inflation through inflation tax (which could be negative if inflation is high), bracket creep, capital gain tax and the government status as the net debtor. However, there are losses as well to the government, through the shoe-leather cost (people hold less government money) and increase in unemployment compensation etc. Besides, there are hidden losses to the government due to inflation. The latter come from an increase in debt servicing (as per the Fisher equation, nominal interest rate goes up during inflation) and decrease in tax collection due to the time lag between the increase in the tax base and the payment of taxes (while the tax base keeps increasing every day, taxes are paid on the realised tax base, as calculated at the end of the year). Due to such mixed effects, some even argue that fiscal deficit tends to increase during inflation. History does tell us that all hyperinflation countries have suffered large fiscal deficits.

Since interpersonal comparisons cannot be made, economists differ about the virtues/demerits of inflation. The social cost of inflation is basically the sum of the menu cost, shoe-leather cost, money illusion cost and the cost of managing the uncertainty, which is small unless the inflation rate is high or there is hyperinflation. Thus, while the unemployment is considered bad by all, a mild inflation is not considered so universally. However, the costs of hyperinflation are prohibitive and no economist would welcome it.

Inflation brings some **social benefits** as well. Tobin (1972) argues that firms find it difficult to reduce the nominal wage rate during the impending recessions (vide efficiency theory, insider-outsider model etc.—Chapter 14) and on such occasions inflation comes handy in reducing the real wage. Further, a fall in the real wage leads to an increase in employment, which is good for the economy. Another benefit of inflation comes from the improved efficiency of the monetary policy in augmenting the aggregate demand. Since the nominal interest rate cannot be negative, inflation, which keeps the nominal interest rate high, enables the use of an easy monetary policy to counter adverse shocks. Thus, inflation helps to remove the limitations of an expansionary monetary policy, arising from the negative nominal interest rate argument. Recall that the Pigou effect renders help to mitigate the liquidity trap argument against the effectiveness of the monetary policy.

A careful look at historical data would suggest that since the mid-1990s the inflation rate has been low in most countries in the world. Thus, it is no longer a serious worry. It could have been achieved through a combination of factors, like, globalisation (which took production from high cost regions to low cost ones, besides promoting foreign trade), improvements in technology (and thereby in factor productivity), change in the production structure (from agriculture to industry and services–agricultural prices are subject to wider fluctuations than others) and more meaningful applications of stabilisation policies. During the current century, some countries had, in fact, faced the opposite threat—deflation. It must be impressed that deflation is really worse than inflation. This is explained through the **costs of deflation**—some of which are obvious from the above discussion, the others are highlighted below.

(a) Deflation causes the real wage to rise, which tends to raise unemployment and reduce profit, which, in turn, triggers investment fall and thereby a fall in AD and income and increase in unemployment.

(b) Deflation leads to an increase in the real interest rate, which tends to raise the cost of debt and thereby discourages investment, causing income to fall and unemployment to rise.

(c) Deflation causes the expected price to fall, which, in turn, causes consumption and investment to fall and aggregate supply to rise. The latter two events reinforce each other to cause price to fall further.

(d) Deflation tends to redistribute income in favour of creditors and fixed income groups (like pensioners, widows and salary earners to some extent) who's marginal propensity to consume is relatively lower, thus, it tends to lower consumption, AD and real income.

The above factors are obviously very harmful to any economy and therefore all governments, including the United States and Japan, tried their best to overcome the deflationary threat. Interest rates have been reduced considerably throughout the world during the current century (vide Table 4.4, Chapter 4 and table in review question 1, Chapter 8) and the federal fund rate in the United States went down to a 45-year low of 1 per cent in 2002, which has remained low ever so. In fact, the low interest rate happened to be the single most important factor behind the great recession of 2007-09 triggered through the sub-prime lending. In the last couple of years, inflation has picked up again and so has the interest rate. Currently, some countries, including India, are facing inflationary threats.

CURES FOR INFLATION

There is consensus among economists that high and variable inflation is bad. High inflation impedes economic growth and harm social justice, and variable inflation give rise to heavy costs of managing uncertainty. However, no such agreement exists about mild and stable inflation. This is because, as seen above, a 'little' inflation is more good than bad. Again, the term 'little' is not clearly defined and it is interpreted to assume some value within one integer (1-9), and varying from country to country. For the developed world, it could be around 2 to 3 per cent and for developing countries, around 5 to 6 per cent. Further, when it comes to the management of inflation, economists generally worry about **'core' inflation** and not the **general (headline) inflation**. Core inflation excludes prices of volatile items, such as energy and agricultural prices. This is done because the latter prices are highly volatile and changes in them are triggered mostly by supply shocks (like OPEC cartel and weather conditions), which are quickly reversed. For example, energy prices are subject to cutbacks/expansions in oil exports by the OPEC cartel and agricultural prices fluctuate due to weather affecting harvests. Such prices merely create 'outliers' in the general price index and as such do not affect the long run price trend. Since economic policies must concentrate mainly on the long run trend, the proponents of core inflation suggest that the monetary policy's objective must be to control the core inflation only. However, critics of the above arguments would like the stabilisation policies to even counter such outliers, for they do disturb the smooth functioning of the economy. Thus, there is nothing like an **optimal rate of inflation**. Accordingly, policy makers must rely on their judgment in weighing different considerations.

Barring a few cases of hyperinflation and not so few cases of high inflation, most countries have experienced one-digit inflation rates most of the times (vide Chapters 1 and 3). During the mid-1970s to early 1980s, of course, the world as a whole suffered the two-digit inflation, though restricted mostly to the lower end. Currently, as hitherto stated, the world, in general, is in a happy situation of low inflation. The alternatives policy makers have to counter inflation, if and when it crosses into the red zone are dwelt upon below. In brief, all we need to do is to turn the causes of inflation on their head. In addition, the government could take recourse to the income policy. The details on these possible measures are prescribed below:

(a) Relaxation in administered prices: The government must begin from products whose prices are under its direct control. It must see to it that the administered prices are not raised and, in fact, even be reduced if possible. In general, such prices are for essential consumption goods and raw materials.

Thus, if these prices are checked from rising, the cost of living adjustments will become less mandatory and cost-based prices will be checked from rising. Creative tax and subsidy schemes could be designed to check other prices from rising.

(b) Adverse demand shocks: The government could use its fiscal and monetary policies to curb the aggregate demand and, thereby, create recession in the economy. This can be done through decrease in the quantity of money supply or increase in interest rate, decrease in government expenditure and/or raising tax rates. These restrictive fiscal and monetary policies would reduce the aggregate demand, thereby, directly attacking one of the fundamental causes of inflation. Two approaches suggested in this respect are: **(a)** Gradualism and **(b)** Cold turkey.

> Under gradualism, small changes in the money supply, government expenditure and tax rates are introduced in gradually phases. Under cold turkey, large changes in these instruments are implemented suddenly. Gradualism would take time but would work to check inflation if people have trust in these policies. The cold turkey method would move fast and stop the inflation faster, without causing extra unemployment. Cold turkey policies try hard to hit the target as quickly as possible, while gradualism does this slowly. More of cold turkey rather than gradualism were applied in the United States during 1981-82 to tame inflation.

If the inflation is a demand-pull one, then the remedy is easy. Increased demand must be reversed through a similar decrease in demand. Thus, in Fig. 15.1 above, the inflation was triggered through a shift in AD curve from AD_o to AD_1. The remedy is to reverse this shift from AD_1 to AD_o. For example, if the increase in AD was caused by, say, increase in autonomous consumption, investment and/or net exports, then the government could bring about the equivalent decrease in AD through a similar decrease in government expenditure and/or an appropriate decrease in money supply. In this case, the cause is reversed immediately and there would be no shift in the AD curve and, accordingly, the equilibrium would stay at point A, having income = Y_n and price = P_o, and no inflation.

If the inflation is caused by an adverse supply shock, then, in the short run, the new situation would be like the equilibrium at point B in Fig. 15.2. The consequence is low output and high price compared to the period before the supply shock (i.e., point A in Fig. 15.2). To check this price rise, the fiscal-monetary policy mix must follow an extinguishing policy. Therefore, government expenditure and/or money supply must be decreased such that AD curve shifts from AD_o to AD_2 (vide Fig. 15.2). If so, price would return to its original level at P_o and, of course, output would fall further to the new level at Y_1. The equilibrium at point D is the short run equilibrium, for the price (P_0) is now less than the expected price, P_1. In this way, demand management policies do help to extinguish supply-triggered inflation, but it results in recession in the short run. In the long run, the AS curve would shift down and the process would go on until equilibrium is reached at point E. Thus, in the long run, output returns to its original level, Y_n, and price falls to P_2. However, since the public may not easily believe that inflation would really slow down, the cold turkey cure for inflation is likely to be a long drawn out process. The credibility of the policy is important here. If it is credible, price could be reduced by lowering the expected price, while suffering less through low output. In the absence of credibility, people's expectations would not change and output-inflation trade-off will be more severe. In theory, this is a method to check cost-push inflation but policy makers must weigh the relative costs of inflation versus recession before acting on this strategy. Nevertheless, hyperinflation can be controlled only through a sharp reduction in money supply, which would inevitably cause recession.

(c) Incomes policy: Income policy, also known as the **wage-price control policy** or the **stick-carrot policy** attempts to check both inflation and unemployment directly and simultaneously (in contrast to demand management policies which check such maladies indirectly and one while aggravating the other) by intervening in the wage-price setting process. The intervention could take one or more of the following forms: **(a)** Wage-price guidelines; **(b)** Mandatory wage-price controls; **(c)** Tax-based incomes policies; and **(d)** Public distribution system.

Under the wage-price guidelines, the government issues the requisite guidelines on setting the wage rate and the price such that inflation is extinguished and unemployment is curtailed. For example, companies making profits could be asked to absorb cost increases in profits rather than in the prices of their products. Companies having excess capacities could be pursued to expand their production and so on. Under the mandatory wage- price controls, the government just raises the legislations so as to check price increases. For example, the prices of government regulated public utilities (like electricity, water, gas, phones, post and telegraph and railways) could be lowered, inflation indexation may be suspended temporarily; wage-price increases may be disallowed in all cases, barring select inevitable cases; banks may be asked to expand credit and be liberal in loan recoveries so as to boost production; select foreign goods may be banned for imports and so on.

Under the tax based incomes policy, government uses the 'stick-carrot approach' in taxation. The people who appear responsible for inflation are shown sticks and the ones who help check inflation are offered carrots or goodies. For instance, companies who grant wage increases could be subjected to a proportionately higher corporate tax rate, while for the rest the normal rate may be enforced. Similarly, workers who agree to settle at the original wage rate may be offered some income tax rebates, which are denied to the others. Under the public distribution system, more supplies are made available and/or the prices are lowered to counter inflation.

The proponents of the incomes policy argue that such a policy will take away the expectations out of the inflationary process and thereby put a check on inflation acceleration. The most frequent criticism of such policies is that they interfere with the operation of the free market and thus lead to misallocation of resources and dead weight loss. Further, critics argue that these policies affect different sectors differently and thus are associated with political biases. For example, controls on food prices alone would harm farmers and those on the wage rate only the workers. In addition, these policies cause bubble effects (explosions in prices) at the introduction and termination of policies, and they lead to additional administrative costs.

Case Study: Income policies of the above varieties have been used to deal with inflation in many countries. The Kennedy and Johnson's administration had made use of this strategy in the United States during their presidencies in 1960s and President Nixon had imposed controls on wages and prices during 1971-72. Malaysia used this policy to deal with the East-Asian crisis during the late 1990s. In Malaysia, firms were asked to absorb cost increases in profits, import of foreign goods were seriously monitored, allowances of government employees were reduced, the hitherto promised increases in the salaries of staff in corporatised universities and other organisations were deferred, and so on. In India, several administered prices (including those of the public utilities', petrol/diesel, and support/ minimum prices of agricultural products) and the administered interest rates are often revised in line with the need to restore price stability, and sops are offered to corporations/states for good behaviour.

In conclusion, it must be pointed out that the various approaches to control inflation are complementary rather than competitive. Thus, a restrictive demand management policy could be combined with relaxations in the administered prices and the appropriate stick-carrot policy. The heterodox approach, which would combine all complementary tools, is thus recommended to deal with inflation and even unemployment. The appropriate mix would help minimise the recession that often arises when inflation is attacked. The said approach was applied in Argentina and Israel in 1985 and in Brazil in 1986, when the government froze wages and prices that stopped inflation with a single blow. Israeli stabilisation succeeded while Argentina and Brazil did not; the difference was due to the fiscal policy—while the former carried its fiscal deficit the latter two did not. Malaysia also used such policies to cope with the South East Asian crisis of 1997-98.

Conclusion

Unemployment and high inflation are deemed evils by all and all efforts must be made to bid them goodbye. However, these are subject to a trade-off, at least in the short run and surprised policy changes (rational expectations hypothesis); in the sense that if inflation is attacked, unemployment (recession) emerges and if unemployment is checked, inflation occurs. Thus, an appropriate policy option has to be designed and implemented for the purpose. However, since the costs of unemployment are borne largely by those who are unemployed, while the costs of inflation by almost all households (though may be at different rates), no policy will be ever appreciated by all people. Controlling unemployment and inflation is, thus, an unpleasant task for all governments. From the point of the overall economy, unemployment is perhaps worse than inflation, for the former results in a significant loss of output directly and the latter to a relatively smaller amount and only indirectly. Nevertheless, as mentioned before, Arthur Okun considers both evils equally bad and he defines an index of misery for the economy as equal to the sum of the unemployment and inflation rates. However, note that the cost of these events depends positively on the degrees of these evils and the relationship is non-linear. Therefore, a little unemployment may be preferred to high inflation and the tradeoff is not one to one. Further, zero unemployment in not even a plausible goal for any economy, for none of the forms of some unemployment, (viz. frictional, structural, seasonal and wait) can be reduced to zero. This is so because no government can make the job search instantaneous, eliminate skill and location mis-matches altogether, create job opportunities to all off-seasonal unemployed, or even bring the wage rate equal to its market clearing level. Some countries like Canada and New Zealand have opted for a zero rate of inflation, which is not considered as an ideal situation by most economists (including James Tobin).

KEYWORDS

Mismatch of skills-location, Downsizing; Outsourcing; Retrenchments; Lay-offs; Job search; Wait unemployment; Classical unemployment; Discrimination; Hysteresis theory; Trade unions; Minimum wage regulations; Firing cost; GDP loss; Psychological cost; Leisure; Retraining; Inflation; Hyperinflation; Galloping-Crawling-Administered-Demand pull-Cost push inflation; Self-fulfilling prophesy; Wage-price spiral; Cost of living adjustment; Seigniorage; Index of misery; Manu cost; Shoe leather cost; Money illusion; Inflation tax; Deflation subsidy; Bracket creep; Sacrifice ratio; Social benefits; Costs of deflation; Headline-Core inflation; Optimal rate of inflation; Gradualism; Cold turkey; Incomes policy; Carrot-stick policy; Dead-weight loss; Hyper inflation; Core inflation; Headline inflation; Kennedy-Johnson administration; East-Asian crisis; Public utilities; Support/Minimum price; Heterodox approach; Rational expectations hypothesis; Index of misery.

REFERENCES

1. Fisher Irving, *The Purchasing Power of Money*, (New York, 1913).
2. Friedman Milton, 'Nobel Lecture: Inflation and Unemployment, *Journal of Political Economy* 85, (June, 1977): 451-72.
3. Government of India, *Eighth Five Year Plan: 1992-97*, Vol. 1, (New Delhi, Planning Commissions, 1992).
4. Gupta G.S, 'Jobs without Inflation', *Akashwani,* (April 4, 1982): 5-6.
5. Okun Arthur M, 'Potential GNP: Its Measurement and Significance', in Proceedings of the Business and Economics Statistics Section, American Statistical Association, (Washington D.C: American Statistical Association, 1962).
6. Okun Arthur M, 'Efficient Dis-inflationary Policies', *American Economic Review* 68, (May, 1978).
7. Tobin James, 'Inflation and Unemployment', *American Economic Review* 62, (March 1972): 1-18.

REVIEW QUESTIONS

1. The natural rate of unemployment is independent of economic policies. Comment.
2. Unemployment is worse than inflation. Analyse.
3. Hyperinflation is both a monetary as well as a fiscal phenomenon. Explain.
4. While inflation is a monetary phenomenon, unemployment is caused by supply bottlenecks. Comment.
5. Inflation is a mixed blessing. Discuss.
6. Controlling inflation through demand management policies is like breaking a thermometer to control the heat. Do you agree? Why or why not?
7. Examine the relative significance of fiscal and monetary policies in achieving full employment without inflation.
8. Distinguish between the stabilisation policies and income policies as a means of shifting the Phillips curve to a targeted position.
9. While the inflation of the late 1960s was not associated with the rising unemployment, that of the 1970s was. Why?
10. All Finance Ministers love inflation. Comment.
11. Demand for and supply of all goods and services determine the national income and general price level. Under such a system, how will the government influence the levels of unemployment and inflation in the economy? Explain.
12. While the RBI should concentrate on core inflation, the Finance Ministry should worry about the rate of involuntary unemployment. Analyse.
13. Consider the following data for a few selected countries in 2012 (or latest year available):

Country	*Real GDP growth rate (%)*	*CPI Inflation rate (%)*	*Unemployment rate (%)*	*Nominal GDP ($ billion)*	*Reserve money ($ billion)*
India	5.0	9.3	NA	1770	273
USA	2.2	2.1	8.1	15,685	2680
China	7.8	2.7	4.1	8,227	3998
Argentina	1.9	10.0	7.2	477	77
Brazil	2.7*	5.4	5.5	2255	260
Japan	2.0	–0.3*	4.4	5,964	1,735
Russian Fed.	4.3*	5.1	5.5	2052	319

Source: International Financial Statistics, IMF, 2006. *2011 data

On the basis of the above data, attempt the following questions for each country:

(a) If the natural rate of unemployment were 4 per cent in all countries, compute the GDP loss due to unemployment.
(b) Compute the misery index.
(c) Compute the inflation tax (Assume price = 1 for all countries).
(d) Compare all the above results across countries and comment.

PART 4

ECONOMIC GROWTH AND THE STATE OF MACROECONOMICS

Macroeconomics has a role both in the short as well as in the long run. In the short run, the resources (quantity and quality of the factors of production) and the production technology are practically given, and hence the potential output is almost a fixed number. However, the use of those resources would determine the actual output. The most efficiently and more fully they are employed, the more would be the actual output, and *vice versa*. Both, the efficient as well as the extent of utilisation of resources are subject to management and therefore the actual output is a variable even in the short run. What is the role of economics under such a scenario?

We may recall from Chapter 1 that the economy decides its production basket (what to produce and what to import and export, given the consumption), and as to who would produce what and how much. If the economy happens to be a free enterprise, the market forces of demand and supply would give the said decisions. In a mixed economy, which prevails everywhere currently, the market and the government together dictate such decisions. Resource allocation is the concern of microeconomics and so we leave the matter here. Moving to the extent of the utilisation of resources, efforts have to be made to use them as fully as possible so that the output is maximised. Here we are concerned with employment not only of the work force (labour) but also of the physical resources, called the capital input. This is the subject area of macroeconomics in the short run, where the unemployment of resources is minimised and price stability is emphasised. Business cycles are the fact of life and economic policies have to counter them. The last six chapters have fully dealt with this area.

The next chapter in this book deals with the long-run issue. Under this, the concern is to attain as high a growth rate as possible, and not just today but over a very long period (may be forever, as the economy has infinite life), meaning a sustainable growth. The question is what determines this growth rate. Of course, the growth would have to come through augmentation of resources as well as increase in factor productivity. The moot question is what is the best way to augment resources [which are partly natural (natural capital: land) and partly human-made (human-made capital and labour, including entrepreneurship)] and to secure their maximum sustainable productivity. History provides a good number of examples of over two hundred countries growth experiences. A good number of studies have been attempted on these case studies and yet there is no set answer to these questions. Accordingly, there are theories of growth, as of business cycles, and these have evolved over time. While these theories explain a good degree of growth over time and space, none provides a perfect explanation, for economics itself is an imperfect science. Understanding the determinants of growth remains a basic and important challenge for macroeconomists. Chapter 16 deals with all the basic growth theories and attempts to rope up the missing factors so as to appreciate varying growth experiences over space and time. Towards the end, some relevant developmental issues ignored by the traditional growth theory are also brought by for providing a social dimension.

It is argued that the real GDP grows because labour force grows; people, firm and governments save, and convert those savings into structures, capital equipment and inventories, skills and knowledge. New skills enhance productive capacity and promotes technology, and leads to higher and higher production and income, which tends to increase saving and this **virtuous circle** keeps going on continuously. It is hampered when the transformation of saving into investment is not smooth or steady. Sometimes a part of saving is hoarded (households hoard money in jewellery, cash or other unproductive assets, banks hoard it as excess idle cash, firms hold it in current assets) and that retards the growth process. Also, the quality of all investments is not the same; while sometimes a country gets good projects; some other times it gets not so good ones. This is partly due to the availability of investment opportunities and partly due to the good or poor screening and uncertainty. This makes investments volatile and as a consequence, we have business cycles.

The significance of economic growth is obvious. The newspapers regularly report the latest statistics on the growth rate, besides those on the unemployment rate and the rate of inflation. Firms and workers watch these statistics to get a feel of what is in store for them in future. High economic growth implies increased purchasing power in the hands of consumers and that encourages firms to expand their productions through additional employment of labour and capital. Employment opportunities expand, which further triggers the boom period. Quite the reverse holds good when the growth rate falls or turns negative. Due to a fall in the purchasing power, business is not able to sell all their produce, inventories get accumulated, productions are cut, labour is retrenched, machines and structures remain under-utilized, and the downswing gets aggravated.

Recent data on the unemployment rate conveys the message about the stability of workers' employment, and the prospects for employment and the expected wage rate to those who are unemployed. When the economy is overheated (i.e., unemployment falls below its natural level), the workers and their trade unions become more demanding and firms compete in recruiting new staff. Under the opposite situation, workers are left with a little bargaining power, and they are ready to behave and work well without any new expectations. Statistics on the inflation rate alert workers about their demand for dearness allowances, and the firms about the increasing production cost and, hence, the extent to which they may revise their products' prices upward.

The popularity and the actions needed by the government are dictated by the economy's performance on growth, unemployment and inflation fronts. A favourable outcome on these makes the government efficient, effective and re-elected, and *vice versa*. It is heartening to note that the 'economy's performance' has become the overriding slogan in recent elections for the incumbent government in India and of course in the United States of America. It may however be noted that a complacent government may not produce good economic policies and, if so, it would surely endanger the future of the economy. International organizations, including credit rating agencies, always have eves on country's growth rate, besides other parameters, to decide on asking for contributions, advances of loans and aids, country rating, etc. Thus, ups and downs on the growth rate are watched by everyone around the globe for many economic and non-economic decisions.

As this happens to be the last part of the book, and economic theory and policy is a dynamic field, the last chapter makes an effort to summarise the present state of macroeconomics.

Chapter 16

Economic Growth

Learning Objectives

After reading the chapter you should be able to:

1. Appreciate the stylised facts on the historical experiences on economic growth.
2. Understand that the growth rate is a long-run concept and it is basically governed by the availability of the factors of production, which includes natural resources (called land), human resources (includes labour and entrepreneurship), human made physical capital and technology (quality of factors of production).
3. Learn the Solow's model of economic growth based on some critical assumptions, subsequent challenges to these assumptions and emergence of an alternative model, the so-called endogenous growth theory.
4. Grasp that the Solow's model's assumptions have not been found valid in the real world and that each of these has been challenged through valid reasons.
5. Comprehend that the economics basic principle that "there is no free lunch", applies equally well to the theory of economic growth, for there are costs of economic growth and accordingly, there is a limit to growth.

It may be recalled from Chapter 2 that the level of real national income (or GDP) measures the state of the economic well-being (prosperity) of the people of the country and the rate of economic growth in the country. Basis this criterion, the United States with an income of about US dollars 15.1 trillion in 2011, is the richest country in the world and China with a national income (purchasing power parity—PPP) of about US dollars 11.3 trillion in that year takes the second position. In terms of the annual growth rate, China enjoys the distinction of attaining a double-digit growth rate (10.8 %) during 2000-11, with India and the United States hovering around 7.8 and 1.6 percentages, respectively during that period.

The above measures, however, ignore the size of population, which affects the income per head. The standard of living in a country is thus measured by the per capita income, which equals national income divided by the population. The United States with a per capita income of US $48,820 in 2011 belongs to the group of the countries enjoying the highest standard of living in the world. In contrast, China and India, with the PPP per capita incomes of US $8,390 and US $3,640, respectively in 2011 belong to the group of the developing economies.

While the level of income is important, the rate of growth is perhaps even more significant. This is due to the **arithmetic of compounding**. For example, consider two countries A and B. Country A has an initial per capita income of \$10,000 and an annual growth rate of 2 per cent, and country B has a per capita income of \$2,500 and a growth rate of 8 per cent. In 25 years, the per capita income of the two countries would rise to:[1]

$\$10,000\ (1.02)^{25} = \$16,406$ in country A, and

$\$2,500\ (1.08)^{25} = \$17,121$ in country B

Thus, country B, whose current income is just one-fourth of that of country A, will overtake country A in 25 years due to its four-fold higher growth rate. There are many examples in the history of the real world where poor countries with relatively high growth rates have been able to catch up (converge) or at least bridge the gap in the per capita income with the hitherto rich countries. Japan, Germany, China and S. Korea, among others, provide good proof of this fact. In 1870, the United Sates' per capita PPP national income (\$2,445) was about three times that of Japan (\$737) and by 2005, the difference was reduced to about 33 per cent (US \$41,950; Japan \$31,410). Some more striking data are given in Table 16.1:

Table 16.1 Per Capita GDP (PPP) at 1990 Prices in Select Years

(In US Dollars)

Country	*1820*	*1870*	*1950*	*1998*	*2005*	*2011@*
Australia	**1,528**	**3,801**	**7,493**	**20,390**	**30,610**	**38,610**
Brazil	**670**	**740**	**1,672**	**5,459**	**8,230**	**11,420**
China	**600**	**530**	**439**	**3,117**	**6,800**	**8,390**
Former USSR	**689**	**943**	**2,834**	**3,893***	**10,640***	**20,410***
Germany	**1,058**	**1,821**	**3,881**	**17,799**	**29,210**	**40,190**
India	**533**	**533**	**619**	**1,746**	**3,460**	**4,525**
Republic of Korea	**NA**	**NA**	**770**	**12,152**	**21,850**	**30,370**
USA	**1,257**	**2,445**	**9,561**	**27,331**	**41,950**	**48,820**
Japan	**669**	**737**	**1,926**	**20,413**	**31,410**	**35,330**

Notes: NA: Not available * Data for Russian Federation @ Data at current prices

Look at the data for India versus China: While China was richer than India in 1820, opposite was true in 1870 and 1950, and the position reversed again thereafter. Also, Republic of Korea was only a little ahead of India in 1950, the difference has widened significantly thereafter. Similar comparison of Australia and USA would suggest that while the former was richer than the latter in early years, the opposite was true in later years. The high performing South East Asian nations (named the 'tiger' and 'baby tiger' economies) have also been quite successful in bridging at least a part of their income gaps with rich nations. This is due

---

[1]The rule of 72 is relevant here. It says, the number of years it takes for a variable to double is approximately given by 72 divided by the annual growth rate in the variable. Thus, if the growth rate in per capita income equals 2 per cent, it doubles in 36 years, and if the growth rate is 8 per cent, it doubles just in 9 years.

to the differences in the growth rates and the miracle of the compounding factor, the latter is said to have been called by Albert Einstein as one of the greatest inventions of all time. The other reason for the high significance of the growth rate vis-à-vis the level of income is that while the latter is more or less a past legacy, the former is manageable through the current and future efforts/strategies.

Economic growth is the key to a higher standard of living. The redistribution of income will improve the welfare of the poor at the expense of those better off and it will be a gain only until the inequality is wiped out. Economic growth, in contrast, enables all to gain and gain continuously. Due to the significance of this growth rate, every country is making its best efforts to maximise its growth rate. In this chapter, we analyse the sources of growth and through them try to explain as to why the income levels and growth rates vary across countries during a given period, and over time in a particular country. The concept of growth may be illustrated through the economists' tool of the production possibility curve as in Figure 16.1.

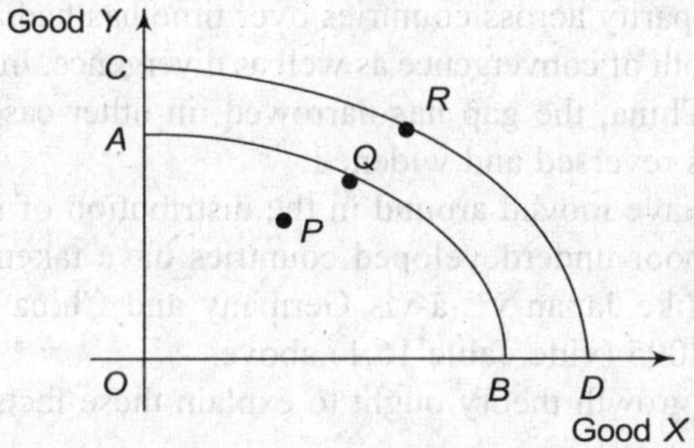

Fig. 16.1 Production Possibility Curves

With the given resources, the economy could produce any combination of the two goods on the corresponding production possibility curve (PPC). Thus, if the resources were, say, R_0, the economy could produce any output mix along the *AB* curve with full and efficient employment, or inside it (say, at point *P*) if the resources were not fully/efficiently employed. In the short run, the resources are given and accordingly the economy could not go beyond the *AB* curve. However, in the long run, the resources could be expanded and the PPC, accordingly, shifted right-ward to, say, *CD*. Shift of the PPC from *AB* to *CD* denotes economic growth. Growth could come either through the augmentation of the quantity of the resources or through improvements in the quality of the resources, the latter is called the total factor productivity or the technical progress. The choice of the output mix, along the corresponding PPC, would be dictated by the relative price/benefits of the two goods *X* and *Y*. Of course, all economies produce more than just two goods. Since the PPC approach is restricted to just two axes, we took just two goods for the purpose of illustration. The two goods case could be taken as the two sets of goods, like commodities and services, agricultural and industrial goods, civilian and defence goods, consumption and investment (capital) goods, goods for domestic consumption versus export goods, GDP versus good environment etc. Alternatively, one could use any other approach to explain the concept. Nevertheless, the message would be the same.

Before we move on to the growth theory, it would be pertinent to review the history of economic growth across countries. The **key facts on economic growth** that emerge from such a review may be summarized as follows:

(a) Economic growth has been experienced by almost all countries at almost all the time. However, the growth rates have varied significantly both over time and space. Among the 10 most populated countries, the (annual) growth rate during 2000-12 has varied between the highest at 10.6 per cent in China and the lowest at 0.7 per cent in Japan. If one were to look at the growth rate during the decade of 1960s, the picture would be quite opposite.

(b) Income disparity across countries has been a fact of life. The latest data (2011) endorse this. Among the top 10 most populated countries, the per capita income-PPP was at the highest in USA at $ 48,820 and the lowest in Bangladesh at $ 1,920, giving a difference of about 25 times.

(c) Income disparity across countries over time has had a mixed direction. There are cases both of convergence as well as divergence. In some cases like between USA and China, the gap has narrowed; in other cases like India and China, the gap has reversed and widened.

(d) Countries have moved around in the distribution of income over time. Some relatively poor underdeveloped countries have taken over the erstwhile rich countries, like Japan vis-à-vis Germany and China vis-a vis India between 1950 and 2005 (vide Table 16.1) above.

Any meaningful growth theory ought to explain these facts.

Determinants of Income and Growth

Adam Smith, the father of economics, did talk about growth and to him it was governed basically by capital accumulation and division of labour, though free trade and the government providing suitable laws and regulations, security and public institutions (like education and health) facilitated it. To Thomas Malthus, land (natural resources) was the major factor of production and he was worried about a faster growth rate in population than that in food supply. Thus, for the classical economists, the factor endowment happened to be the almost sole source of growth. The neo-classical economists attributed growth to the capital-output ratio and the technology. The institutional economists have advocated the role of institutions in promoting growth. In addition, globalisation of the economy is deemed to accelerate growth process through trade, capital flows, immigration and spillover technology. Later economists have added social dimensions to pure growth and accordingly they talk of economic development and inclusive growth.

Traditionally, the new classical model is used to explain the sources of economic growth. It assumes the full employment of all resources (factors of production) and wage-price flexibility, and thus the output is governed basically by the supply side. However, the growth rate in output, as we shall see later in this chapter, depends, at least temporarily, on the allocation of output into consumption and saving, among other factors, thus, the demand side enjoys an influence on the growth rate.

Using the new classical framework, the production function may be expressed as follows:

$$Y = f(L, K, A) \quad \textbf{(16.1)}$$

$$f_1, f_2, f_3 > 0$$

where Y = output (value added) in physical units (real income)

L = labour input in physical units (e.g, hours)

K = capital input (net of depreciation) in physical units (valued at constant prices)

A = level of technology or total factor productivity

In function **(16.1)**, the labour input includes all the unskilled and skilled (including entrepreneurship) labour, and so the difference between them is ignored. Similarly, capital consists of all the fixed physical capital, including all structures, business equipment and inventories, and, like labour, all capital is assumed homogeneous. Material resources (raw materials and intermediate goods) do aid production, but they are netted out both from the output as well as the resources—they are consumed fully in the production and, therefore, only the net production (= value added) is considered, which is gross output minus the consumed materials.

Under function **(16.1)**, the level of real national income just depends on three factors, viz., labour, capital and technology. The dependence relationships are all positive in the sense, the more of any input, *ceteris paribus*, the more the output, and vice versa. Under this theory, income differences among countries are caused simply by differences in the quantities of labour and capital inputs, and the level of technologies, as possessed by these countries. To see if there is any other determinant of output, we have to apply the above model to the real world and see if this adequately explains the income differentials among countries and over time. If it does not, as is really true, then this would mean there are other determinants as well. We shall return to this issue later.

To identify the sources of economic growth in output over time, we need to differentiate function **(16.1)**. The first difference of the function would yield

$$dY = f_L dL + f_k dK + f_A dA$$

where; f_L, f_K and f_A denote the marginal productivities of labour, capital and technology, respectively, and d the first (time) total derivative operator. Dividing both the sides by Y and carrying out some algebraic manipulations, we obtain

$$\frac{dY}{Y} = f_L \frac{L}{Y}\left(\frac{dL}{L}\right) + f_K \frac{K}{Y}\left(\frac{dK}{K}\right) + f_A \frac{A}{Y}\left(\frac{dA}{A}\right)$$

$$\dot{Y} = e_L \dot{L} + e_K \dot{K} + e_A \dot{A} \quad \textbf{(16.2)}$$

where, $\dot{Y}$, $\dot{L}$, $\dot{K}$ and $\dot{A}$ denote the rates of change in Y, L, K and A, respectively, and e_L, e_K and e_A denote the elasticities of output with respect to L, K and A respectively. Note that elasticity is simply the ratio of the corresponding marginal and average values. Thus, the elasticity of output, with respect to labour, is simply the ratio of the marginal product of labour (f_L) and the average product of labour (Y/L) and so on. Further, if the factors of production are assumed to be paid equal to their respective marginal products, then the factor elasticities become equivalent to the respective factor shares in national income (Euler's theorem). Thus, if f_L = real wage, f_L (L) is the total wage bill and f_L (L/Y) is the share of labour in total national income and so on.

Equation (16.2) represents the **fundamental equation of growth accounting**. It identifies the two sources of economic growth, viz.,

(a) Increase in the quantity of resources (labour and capital)

(b) Improvement in factor productivity (technology)

Further, the equation suggests that growth depends positively on the three output elasticities (or factor shares). However, the said elasticities hardly change from year to year and thus are usually assumed to remain constant over space and time, and hence play no role in growth. While output, labour and capital are measurable variables, technology is not amenable to direct measurement. Using the data on the growth rates in output, labour and capital, and the shares of labour and capital in output, the contribution of technology is derived as a residual using equation (16.2). This method is due to the Nobel laureate Robert Solow and is thus referred to as the **Solow residual**.

Do the above sources of growth explain the real world differences in the growth rates in different countries and over time? If yes, the model is adequate and if not, we need another model. As we shall see later, the model does not account for most of the differences in the growth rates and, thus, there are other factors causing growth variations. These, 'other factors' are analysed later in this chapter. We start with a simple yet important model of growth and then introduce the missing elements slowly.

HARROD-DOMAR MODEL

Harrod (1939) and Domar (1946) have provided a simple one-sector model of economic growth, which is very neat and, which, in spite of its limitations, is still quite popular to quickly appreciate the sources of economic growth across countries and over years. The model is based on the assumption of capital as the only factor of production and the constant return to capital.[2] Thus, the model is:

$$Y = A\,K \qquad \textbf{(16.3)}$$

Where A is the capital productivity parameter and is equal to the output-capital ratio (Y/K). The first difference of equation (16.3) would give

$$dY = A\,dK$$

where, d is the first (time) derivative operator.

Investment spending I denotes the increment to the stock of capital and thus

$$dK = I$$

Under equilibrium, investment equals savings S, substitution of these relations in the first difference function above yields:

$$dY = AS$$

---

[2] Since there is only one factor of production, constant return to capital is same as the constant returns to scale in the above model.

Dividing both the sides by real national income Y, gives

$$\frac{dY}{Y} = A\left(\frac{S}{Y}\right)$$

or, $$g = As \qquad \textbf{(16.4)}$$

where g = growth rate in real income

s = saving-income ratio

Equation **(16.4)** represents the fundamental equation of economic growth in the Harrod–Domar model. It states that the rate of economic growth is governed by just two parameters and positively by both, viz.,

- output-capital ratio
- saving rate

Thus, if the output-capital ratio (reciprocal of the incremental capital-output ratio) is 0.2, and the saving rate is 0.31, the growth rate would be

$$g = (0.2)(0.31)$$
$$= 0.062$$
$$= 6.2 \text{ per cent}$$

India has roughly the above values of the two parameters currently and also the same economic growth rate. During the 1960s and 1970s, our capital-output ratio was relatively high and the saving rate was low, and hence the growth rate was low. During the 1980s and early 1990s, though our saving rate did not go up much, the capital-output ratio fell, and accordingly, we experienced a relatively higher growth path. During the first decade of the 21th century, the saving rate picked up, and so we experienced still higher growth rates but lately the saving rate has fallen and so has the growth rate.

The model suggests that the only alternatives available for attaining high growth rates lie in reducing the capital-output ratio and raising the saving rate. However, the model is only an approximation of the growth theory, particularly because it ignores all the non-capital determinants of output and it assumes a constant capital-output ratio. The model, in particular, ignores the technology and labour input. This would have been all right during the1930s and 1940s when the model was advanced, for in those years technology was hardly moving and labour was hardly a constraint to output growth. However, technology has been making significant advances during the last few decades and labour (particularly skilled labour) has become a binding constraint in most countries in spite of the increasing labour participation rate. Efforts are now being made to increase the supply of labour by improving the incentives to work and making work enjoyable. Subsequent models have considered these limitations of this model and have attempted to avoid them to some extent.

Solow (Exogenous Growth) Model

Robert Solow (1956) has provided a simple model of economic growth by assuming that the production function takes the Cobb-Douglas (double log) form, that there are constant returns to scale and that technology is factor neutral. On these assumptions, the production function **(16.1)** reduces to

$$Y = AL^{1-\alpha}K^{\alpha} \qquad \textbf{(16.5)}$$
$$0 < \alpha < 1$$

where

α represents the elasticity of output with respect to capital; and

the parameter $(1 - \alpha)$ elasticity of output with respect to labour.

The technology (A) elasticity of output is unity in the above function. The role of capital here lies not in filling up the deflationary gap (as in the Keynesian model) but in creating the productive capacity.

Dividing both sides by L, the function **(16.5)** yields the per capita output function as follows.[3]

$$\frac{Y}{L} = A\left(\frac{K}{L}\right)^{\alpha} \quad \textbf{(16.6)}$$

Function **(16.6)** states that the per capita output depends positively on, both, the level of technology and the per capita capital (called capital deepening). Further, the relationship between the per capita output and technology is proportionate, meaning that if technology progresses by 10 per cent, per capita production will increase by 10 per cent, and vice versa. Since α is positive and less than unity, the increase in per capita output is less than the proportionate increase in the per capita capital. Implicit in this is the microeconomics assumption of the law of diminishing marginal returns, which states that as the capital input increases, the labour input remaining constant, the output increases, but at a diminishing rate.

The relationships between the per capita output and both technology and the per capita capital can be illustrated graphically (Figure 16.2) as follows:

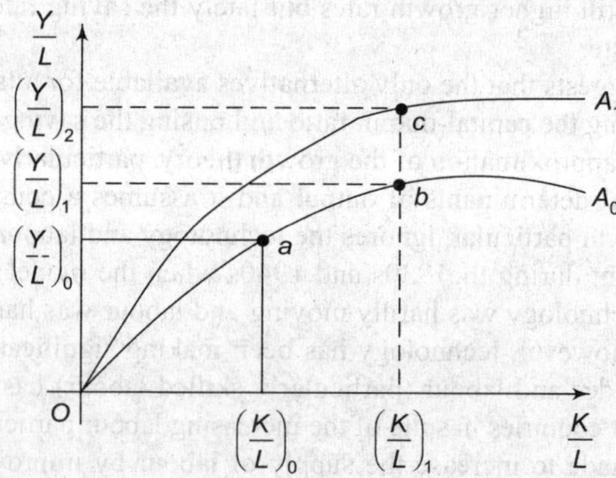

Fig. 16.2 Growth in Per Capita Output

Initially when the per capita capital = $\left(\frac{K}{L}\right)_0$ and the technology = A_0, the per capita output = $\left(\frac{Y}{L}\right)_0$. As the per capita capital increases to $\left(\frac{K}{L}\right)_1$, *ceteris paribus*, the per capita output expands to $\left(\frac{Y}{L}\right)_1$. Further as the technology improves to A_1

[3] For simplicity, we are assuming the labour input to be synonymous with the population.

ceteris paribus the output per worker goes up to $\left(\frac{Y}{L}\right)_2$. Thus the per capita output is a positive function of both the per capita capital and the technology.

What determines the level of technology and the per capita capital? Solow takes technology as an exogenous variable, and thus his model makes no attempt to explain this. The capital-labour ratio is endogenous and is given by the growth rates in capital and labour. For capital (net), investment is an inflow and depreciation (wear and tear and obsolescence of capital assets) is an outflow. Saving is the only source of investment and because saving is invested in capital equipment (productive capacity), we have economic growth. It is assumed that all savings are invested (that is there is no hoarding of savings), and so the equilibrium in the product market requires investment spending to equal saving, which is given by the income multiplied by the saving rate:

$$I = S = sY \tag{16.7}$$

where I = investment
S = saving
s = rate of saving

Depreciation is given by

$$D = dK \tag{16.8}$$

where D = total depreciation
d = depreciation rate.

Thus, the net increase in the capital stock (ΔK) is given by

$$\Delta K = sY - dK \tag{16.9}$$

Equation **(16.9)** implies that the larger the stock of capital, *ceteris paribus*, the lower the increase in the net capital, which hampers the growth rate through equation **(16.6)**. It is precisely for this reason that the destruction of capital promotes the growth rate. After the World War II, **Japan and Germany experienced high growth rates due to the wartime destruction of their capitals**.

Function **(16.6)** is in terms of the capital per worker and technology is neutral, i.e., both labour and capital augmenting. To move from the change in the stock of capital in equation **(16.9)** to the change in the capital per worker, we need to note that growth in the labour force causes the capital per worker to fall. Thus, the change in the capital per worker would be given by

$$\Delta\left(\frac{K}{L}\right) = s\left(\frac{Y}{L}\right) - (d + n)\left(\frac{K}{L}\right) \tag{16.10}$$

where, n equals the rate of growth in population/labour force. The model assumes labour force as a fixed proportion of population.

Equation **(16.10)** indicates that the change in per worker capital stock is influenced directly by the investment (= saving) rate and inversely by the rates of depreciation and population growth. Combining this result with those of function (16.6) above suggests that the:

(a) Saving rate directly affects the per capita output[4]
(b) Population growth rate inversely affects the per capita output
(c) Depreciation rate inversely affects the per capita output

[4] This is true until the economy reaches the steady state position. This would be clarified later in this section itself.

However, the above conclusions are true if the change in the capital per worker were non-zero. There is a relationship between the stock of capital and the size of depreciation, given the depreciation rate. As the stock of capital goes up, total depreciation increases, and vice versa. Thus, as new investment takes place, the capital stock increases, and the latter leads to an increase in depreciation. Similarly, as the population expands, *ceteris paribus*, the capital per worker decreases. Since these factors work in the opposite direction, increase in investment may not lead to increase in capital per worker. It is clear from equation (16.10) that the change in the capital per worker would be zero if

$$s\left(\frac{Y}{L}\right) - (d+n)\left(\frac{K}{L}\right) = 0$$

or,
$$s\left(\frac{Y}{L}\right) = (d+n)\frac{K}{L} \tag{16.11}$$

The rate of investment(s) given by equation (16.11) is accordingly called the **break-even rate of investment**. The equation, thus, gives the equilibrium condition for a steady state. This is the **key equation of the Solow model**. Incidentally note that the diminishing marginal returns to capital forces the economy to hit the steady state, for since $s > (d + n)$; even under constant returns, the equation would not hold. Equations (16.6) and (16.11), the production function (supply of goods and services) and the saving function (demand for goods and services), respectively, are the two ingredients of the Solow model.

Thus, when the relationship (16.11) holds good, an increase in saving does not lead to an increase in the capital per worker, and therefore cause no change in the per capita output. This is a significant implication of the Solow model. Under this, the **saving rate** is a determinant of the level of the per capita income, but it **is only a temporary determinant of the growth rate in per capita income**. The term 'temporary' here means, the saving rate positively affects the growth rate in per capita income so long as it tends to increase the capital per worker and not at all thereafter. This implication of the Solow model is different from that of the Harrod-Domar model, where the saving rate is a positive determinant of the per capita output for all its values. Also, it appears as a paradox; for the saving rate has been thought to always contribute to growth.

The stage at which the capital per worker reaches the saturation point (maximum value) is called the **steady state of the economy**. At such a point, even the per capita income takes its maximum value. Thus, the steady state is defined as the situation where the capital-labour ratio, the per capita output and other per capita economic variables are constant (or steady). The said capital-labour ratio is referred to as the steady state level of the capital-labour ratio. At this level, the rates of growth of output, labour and capital are all equal to the rate of growth in effective labour, i.e., $(n + t)$, where t = rate of technical progress. This implication would be easier to understand through Fig. 16.3.

The curve marked *Y/L* describes the production function (16.6). It is concave to the horizontal axis due to the law of diminishing marginal returns, by which the increase in output is less than the proportionate increase in the capital input, *ceteris paribus*. Since the saving rate is a constant fraction of the output, the curves marked

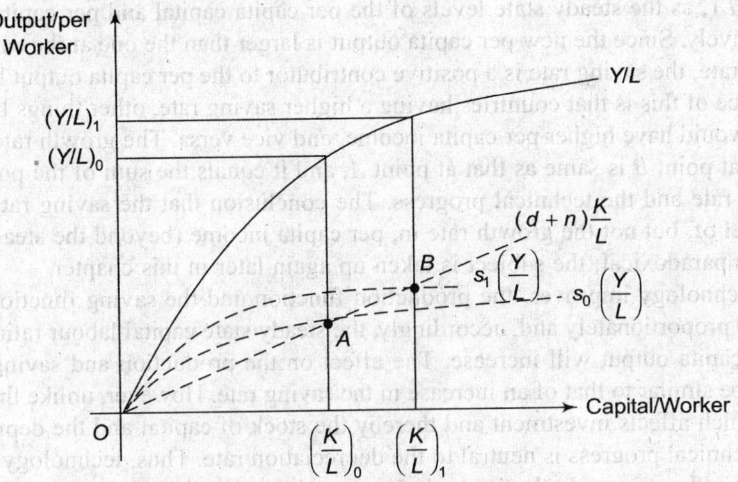

Fig. 16.3 Steady State Position

$s_o(Y/L)$ and $s_1(Y/L)$ [where, $s_1 > s_0$], the savings' functions, have a shape similar to the output curve. The $(d + n)$ (K/L) line is a straight line as the depreciation (d) and population growth (n) rates are constant fractions of capital and labour, respectively, and the technical progress (t) is assumed to be factor neutral.

If the saving rate is s_0, the relevant saving curve is $s_0(Y/L)$. This curve crosses the capital-labour ratio reduction curve $[(d + n)\ (K/L)]$ at point A, which means at this point the increase in the capital-labour ratio through investment just equals the decrease in the capital-labour through depreciation, labour growth and technical progress. Beyond this point (right of point A), the decrease in the capital-labour ratio exceeds the increase in the said ratio, and quite the opposite is true to the left of this point. Thus, the capital labour ratio corresponding to this point, viz., $(K/L)_0$ happens to be the maximum value of this ratio, and is thus its steady state level. At this steady state level, the output per worker is $(Y/L)_0$, which is the maximum the economy can achieve under the situation. Thus, as the capital per worker increases, the output per worker increases, and when the former hits its maximum value, the latter stops rising. This implies that, the saving rate, whose impact is nullified by depreciation and population growth beyond point A, has no role in the per capita output growth beyond the steady state. Hence, Solow concluded that the saving rate influences the per capita output only temporarily (up to the steady state level) and not permanently. The output per head, beyond the steady state, would grow only by technical progress, if any, and the total output would grow by the sum of the population growth rate and the technical progress. This means that if technical progress is a public good and is freely available to all countries, rich or poor, there would be no cross-country diversion of growth rate in per capita income.

Does the saving rate exert an influence on the steady state level of the per capita income? The answer is yes. This would be apparent again from Fig. 16.3. As the saving rate increases from s_0 *to* s_1, the saving function shifts up from $s_0(Y/L)$ curve *to* $s_i(Y/L)$ curve. The new curve intersects the output curve at point B, giving $(K/L)_i$

and $(Y/L)_1$, as the steady state levels of the per capita capital and per capita output, respectively. Since the new per capita output is larger than the one at the earlier low saving rate, the saving rate is a positive contributor to the per capita output level. An inference of this is that countries having a higher saving rate, other things being the same, would have higher per capita income, and vice versa. The growth rate in total output at point B is same as that at point A, and it equals the sum of the population growth rate and the technical progress. The conclusion that the saving rate affects the level of, but not the growth rate in, per capita income (beyond the steady state) appears paradoxical; the subject is taken up again later in this chapter.

If technology improves, the production function and the saving function would shift up proportionately and, accordingly, the steady state capital labour ratio as well as per capita output will increase. The effect on the production and saving curves would be similar to that of an increase in the saving rate. However, unlike the saving rate, which affects investment and thereby the stock of capital and the depreciation rate, technical progress is neutral to the depreciation rate. Thus, technology exerts a positive influence on, both, the capital per worker as well as the per capita output, and the effect is permanent.

Does the growth rate in population exert any influence on the per capita income? The answer is yes and the relationship is negative. This can be seen in Fig. 16.3 or even through the steady state equilibrium condition, equation (16.11). Using the latter approach, equation (16.11) reveals that if the population growth rate n increases, *ceteris paribus*, the steady state capital-labour ratio declines and, thereby, through the production function (16.5), the per capita income falls.

To illustrate the above conclusions, let us consider a hypothetical example. Suppose the production function of an economy was as follows:

$$\frac{Y}{L} = A\left(\frac{K}{L}\right)^{0.3} \quad \textbf{(16.12)}$$

And the values of the various parameters and the initial capital-labour ratio were

$$A = 1,\ s = 0.4,\ d = 0.1,\ n = 0.02 \text{ and } K/L_1 = 3$$

It can now be easily seen as to what happens to the economy over time. The first year per capita output will equal

$$\left(\frac{Y}{L}\right)_1 = 1[3]^{0.3}$$

$$= 1.39$$

The first year per capita consumption will be given by:

$$\left(\frac{C}{L}\right)_1 = 0.6\left(\frac{Y}{L}\right)_1 = 0.6(1.39) = 0.834$$

The first year per capita saving (investment) will be given by:

$$\left(\frac{I}{L}\right)_1 = 0.4\left(\frac{Y}{L}\right)_1 = 0.4(1.39) = 0.556$$

The first year depreciation will be given by:

$$d\left(\frac{K}{L}\right)_1 = 0.1\left(\frac{K}{L}\right)_1 = 0.1(3) = 0.3$$

The first year reduction in the capital-labour ratio due to population growth will be given by:

$$n\left(\frac{K}{L}\right)_1 = 0.02\left(\frac{K}{L}\right)_1 = 0.02(3) = 0.06$$

The corresponding figures for the second year would be as follows:

$$\left(\frac{K}{L}\right)_2 = \left(\frac{K}{L}\right)_1 + \text{(new investment)} - \text{(depreciation)}_1$$

$$- \text{(reduction due to population growth)}$$

$$= 3.0 + 0.556 - 0.3 - 0.06 = 3.196$$

$$\left(\frac{Y}{L}\right)_2 = 1(3.196)^{0.3} = 1.417$$

$$\left(\frac{C}{L}\right)_2 = 0.6[1.417] = 0.8502$$

$$\left(\frac{I}{L}\right)_2 = 0.4[1.417] = 0.5668$$

$$d\left(\frac{K}{L}\right)_2 = 0.1[3.196] = 0.3196$$

$$n\left(\frac{K}{L}\right)_2 = 0.02[3.196] = 0.0639$$

And the capital-labour ratio in the third year would be given by:

$$\left(\frac{K}{L}\right)_3 = 3.1960 + 0.5668 - 0.3196 - 0.0639$$

$$= 3.3793$$

$$\left(\frac{Y}{L}\right)_3 = 1(3.3793)^{0.3} - 1.441$$

and so on.

The steady state capital per worker is reached when equation (16.11) holds good. Thus,

$$s\left(\frac{Y}{L}\right) = (d+n)\left(\frac{K}{L}\right)$$

Substituting the value of YIL from the hypothetical production function into the above equation, we have:

$$s\left[A\left(\frac{K}{L}\right)^{0.3}\right] = (d+n)\left(\frac{K}{L}\right)$$

Substitution of the values of the parameters in the above equation yields:

$$0.4\left[1.0\left(\frac{K}{L}\right)^{0.3}\right] = (0.1+0.02)\left(\frac{K}{L}\right)$$

which on being solved gives:

$$\left(\frac{K}{L}\right)^{0.7} = \frac{0.4}{0.12} = 3.33$$

or $$\frac{K}{L} = 5.59$$

and the corresponding per capita output will be given by:

$$\frac{Y}{L} = A\left(\frac{K}{L}\right)^{0.3}$$
$$= 1.0[5.59]^{0.3}$$
$$= 1.68$$

Thus, for the above hypothetical example, the steady state capital per worker equals 5.59 and the steady state output per worker equals 1.68. Incidentally, note that these numbers are the corresponding magnitudes in dollars or rupees (could be in terms of thousands of dollars or rupees) at a constant price. Thus, if the real magnitudes were in thousands of rupees, then $(K/L) = 5.59$ means the capital of ₹5590 per worker and $Y/L = 1.68$, means the per capita real income of ₹1680.

If the saving rate goes up from 40 per cent to 50 per cent, other parameters remaining constant, the steady state per capita capital would be given by:

$$\left(\frac{K}{L}\right)^{0.7} = \frac{0.5}{0.12} = 4.17$$

or, $$\frac{K}{L} = 7.71$$

and the corresponding per capita output would be given by:

$$\frac{Y}{L} = [7.71]^{0.3}$$
$$= 1.846$$

These numbers are higher than their respective values at the low saving rate of 40 per cent. Thus, it is clear that the higher the rate of saving, the higher the steady state levels of per capita capital and per capita output. In fact, the saving rate is a key determinant of the steady state levels of capital and output in the Solow model. However, a higher savings rate boosts up the growth rate of the economy only until the economy reaches a new steady state.

If the value of the technology factor (A) changes the steady state position will change in the same direction. Thus, if A increases from its earlier value of unity to 1.5, *ceteris paribus*, the steady state level of K/L will be given by:

$$(0.4))(0.5)\left[\frac{K}{L}\right]^{0.3} = 0.12\frac{K}{L}$$

or, $$\frac{K}{L} = \left[\frac{0.6}{0.12}\right]^{0.7} = 9.99$$

And the corresponding per capital output will be given by

$$\frac{Y}{L} = 1.5\,[9.99]^{0.3}$$
$$= 2.99$$

These numbers are greater than their corresponding figures under $A = 1.0$, i.e., 5.59 and 1.68, respectively, thus, as expected, improvements in technology cause, both, the steady state levels of capital per worker and output per worker to rise. Therefore, the level of technology is also a key determinant of the steady state levels of capital and output. Unlike the saving rate, the effects of technology continues even beyond the steady state, when the growth rate in the per capita output exactly equals the growth rate in technology, for:

$$\frac{Y}{L} = A\left(\frac{K}{L}\right)^{\alpha}$$

While K/L is a fixed value equal to its steady state level, beyond the steady state, the value of A increases as technology improves, thereby proportionately increasing the per capita income as per the above relationship. Since labour is assumed to grow at the population growth rate, the growth rate in total real income beyond the steady state equals the sum of the growth rates in technology and population.

If the population growth rate increases from 2 per cent to 3 per cent, *ceteris paribus*, the steady state capital-labour ratio would be given by:

$$\left(\frac{K}{L}\right)^{0.7} = \frac{0.4}{0.13} = 3.1 \qquad \text{(vide equation \textbf{16.11})}$$
$$\Rightarrow \qquad = 5.04$$

and the corresponding per capita output would be given by:

$$\frac{Y}{L} = A\,[5.04]^{0.3}$$
$$= 1[5.04]^{0.3}$$
$$\Rightarrow \qquad \frac{Y}{L} = 1.62$$

Both the above numbers are less than their corresponding figures of the population growth rate of 2 per cent (i.e., 5.59 and 1.68, respectively) and, thus, as expected, the growth rate in population affects the steady state level of the standard of living adversely in the Solow model. However, note that the effect is only indirect and as with the rate of saving, it is through the steady state level of the capital-labour ratio. Similarly, it will be easy to see that the rate of depreciation also affects the steady state per capita income adversely and the effect comes indirectly through the steady state capital level ratio.

Incidentally, note that, unlike the Harrod-Domar model, the **capital-output ratio is a variable in the Solow model**. It will be seen through the production function **(16.6)** and Fig. (16.1), that as the capital per worker increases, the output per worker increases, but less than proportionately (due to the implicit assumption of the law of diminishing marginal returns); thus, the output-capital ratio declines or the capital-output ratio increases. Further, due to this, the rate of growth in real income or even in per capita real income is a negative function of the capital-output ratio, as in the Harrod–Domar model.

According to the Solow model, **technology and the capital labour ratio are the sole determinants of per capita income** and, thus, of the standard of living. The capital-labour ratio depends positively on the saving rate and negatively on the depreciation and population growth rates. The depreciation rate and the population growth rate have hardly witnessed any change over time, and the differences in them across countries are hardly significant. It is hard to keep technology secrets for long and high-speed communication networks have facilitated its adoption fairly uniformly. This leaves the relationship between the per capita income and the saving (investment) rate quite strong. However, this is true only until the steady state, beyond which the saving rate has no bearing on the capital-labour ratio. Thus, the validity of the Solow model hinges on the strength of the relationship between the rate of saving and the per capita income across countries and over time.

Case Study: Historical data the world around cast doubts on the strong positive relationship between the per capita income and the saving rate. As per the 2011 data, the United States happens to be a country with a rather high per capita income (US $48,820) but low saving rate (about 12 per cent), as compared to Korea's medium per capita income ($30,370 at purchasing power parity level) and medium-high saving rate (31 per cent), and India's rather low per capita income (about US $3,640 at PPP) and medium-high saving rate (31 per cent). In addition, there are intermediate examples of countries like China, which has relatively low per capita income (US $8,390 at PPP) and rather high saving rate (49 per cent). While these data contradict Solow's model, there are counter examples that support Solow's thesis. For example, Japan happens to enjoy a relatively medium-high per capita income (US $35,330 at PPP) and a medium saving rate (about 22 per cent), and Pakistan a low per capita income ($2,870 at PPP) and a low saving rate (17 per cent). An examination of the per capita income levels and the saving rates over a period of time for any one or more countries would only corroborate the above observation. Accordingly, historical data neither supports nor rejects Solow's contention. Nevertheless, data do imply that there must be some other determinants of the standard of living beyond the saving-investment rate. This will be pursued later in this chapter.

To conclude, in the Solow model, the growth rate in per capita income depends positively on the saving rate and technical progress, and negatively on the growth rate in population until the steady state position and the growth rate in the per capita income equals the rate of technical progress at (and beyond) the steady state. As the technology alone is significant both before and after the economy hits the steady state, it is accorded **utmost significance** in the Solow's model of economic growth. Further, as we shall see later, the Solow model treats the technology as an exogenous variable, and hence the growth rate in the per capita income beyond the steady state is exogenous and accordingly, the model is referred to as the **exogenous growth theory**. Still further, if the growth rate in the per capita income, beyond the steady state, is governed merely by the technical progress (which is exogenous), and if the technology is uniform across countries (as it cannot be held secret), the per capita income grows at the same rate in all countries once they have hit the steady state. This leads to the Solow's main contention, viz. the **theory of convergence**, which states that the growth rate in the per capita income across countries converges (catch ups) to the same level over time. The poor countries with the low capita capital per worker grows faster than the rich countries with the high capital per worker initially, but as the capital per head reaches the steady state level in the two set of countries, the poor countries growth rate catch up that of the rich countries, and thence the growth rates converge.

> **Case Study**: A look at the growth rate in the per capita income across countries would indicate that it is far from uniform. Further, the growth rate does not fall uniformly as one moves from the poor to the rich country. Moreover, the variations in the growth rate across countries have not fallen over decades. Accordingly, the Solow model's prediction about the **theory of convergence** has not perhaps been validated by our experience! Or, may be that the steady state has not yet arrived. Collect historical data on the per capita income and the growth rate in the per capita income over time (years) and space (across all countries), and
>
> (a) Compute the correlation coefficient on the cross section data for some select period(s) and check if it is negative and statistically significant, and
>
> (b) Compute a measure of the variation (like the standard deviation) for the per capita income across countries in selected years with significant time gaps (like every decade) and check if it has fallen over time (decade).

Lest the readers get confused, one needs to mention that there are two versions of the theory of convergence, viz. absolute and conditional. Under the **absolute convergence theory**, the high growth rate in poor countries and the low growth rate in rich countries ensure that the per capita incomes in all countries equalize (converge) to the same level at some point or in the long run, irrespective to any condition. The data suggest that such a convergence has not happened in the real world. Also, the Solow model (or the new classical model) does not mean such a convergence either. Under the **conditional convergence**, the per capita incomes in different countries converge to the same level if they have the same saving rate, same population growth rate and the same level of technical progress. It is this conditional convergence theory to which the Solow model implies. If two countries have the same population growth rate and same technical progress, but not the same saving rate, then their growth rate in the per capita income will equalize (converge) and not the level of the per capita income; the per capita income will be higher in the country having the higher saving rate.

A related question is, since saving promotes growth, should people save more? The answer is debatable. Saving involves sacrifice by present generation for posterity, does it need it? The technical progress will ensure a better standard of living for the posterity than the present generation, then why more through saving? We leave it for the readers to ponder on the issue.

GOLDEN RULE

The Golden Rule is concerned with the consumption level. It is argued that it is the consumption that determines the economic well-being and not the income per se. If so, we have another reason for why high saving may not be a big virtue. For example, if the saving rate equals 100 per cent, consumption is zero and economic welfare is the least. In contrast, if the saving rate equals zero, present consumption and, thus, the standard of living is the highest, and future welfare is adversely affected. Accordingly, the Golden Rule looks for the saving rate that gives the **maximum per capita consumption at the steady state**.

In Fig. 16.3, the gap between the production curve (Y/L) and the saving curve gives the per capita consumption. This gap would be the maximum at a point where the slope of the production curve (which equals that of the saving curve, for saving is taken as a fixed proportion of income in the Solow model) equals the slope of the depreciation and the population growth line. The slope of the former equals the marginal physical product of capital (MPP_k) and that of the latter equals the sum of the depreciation rate and the growth rate in population. Thus,

$$MPP_k = d + n \tag{16.13}$$

If there is technological progress, say, at the rate of t, the production curve would shift up parallelly by that rate, leaving the MPP_k unaltered. Thus, equation (16.13) would still be applicable to determine the Golden Rule level and equation (16.11) the steady state level. However, if the technical progress happens to be of labour augmenting type at the rate, say, t_1, the effective labour would increase not just at the rate of n but by the $(n + t_1)$ rate. Accordingly, the Golden Rule equation for the labour augmenting technology case would be

$$MPP_k = d + n + t_1 \tag{16.14}$$

The corresponding production function would be

$$Y/L = A\,(K/EL)^{\alpha} \tag{16.6a}$$

Where, E = measure of labour quality (e.g. education) which grows at the rate of t_1 over time. For the labour augmenting technology, the steady state condition would be

$$s(Y/L) = (d + n + t_1)(K/L) \tag{16.11a}$$

Equation (16.14) gives the condition for the Golden Rule value of the capital-labour ratio. Given that, the corresponding per capita income could be determined using the production function (16.6), and there after the Golden Rule saving rate is obtained using the steady state condition (16.11).

Thus, there are three steps, which are applied below to determine the Golden Rule saving rate for our hypothetical production function (16.12) and the then assumed values of the various parameters involved.

Step 1: Computing MPP_k for the hypothetical production function **(16.12)** and inserting the values of the relevant parameters (and assuming additionally, $t = 0$) in the Golden Rule condition **(16.14)**, we have:

$$0.3\left[\frac{K}{L}\right]^{-0.7} = 0.10 + 0.02 + 0$$

The solution of which yields:

$$\frac{K}{L} = 3.71$$

Step 2: Inserting the computed value of the per capita capital in the hypothetical production function **(16.12)** above, we get (Note A =1)

$$\frac{Y}{L} = A\left(\frac{K}{L}\right)^{0.3}$$

$$= 1\ [3.71]^{0.3} = 1.48$$

Thus, the Golden Rule values for the capital-labour ratio and the per capita income are 3.71 and 1.48, respectively. A comparison of these values with the corresponding steady state values on the erstwhile assumed values of the parameters (5.59 and 1.68, respectively) would indicate that the Golden Rule values are relatively small ones. This means the saving rate of 40 per cent (as hitherto assumed) is higher than the Golden Rule saving rate, given the values of the other parameters. To derive the requisite saving rate to ensure the steady state capital-labour ratio of 3.71, we go to the third and the final step:

Step 3: Recall the steady state equilibrium condition, viz., equation (16.11) above. Thus

$$s\left(\frac{Y}{L}\right) = (d+n)\frac{K}{L}$$

Substituting the values of the steady state levels of per capita income and per capita capital, and parameters, we get:

$$(s)\ (1.48) = (0.10 + 0.02)\ (3.71)$$

The solution of which yield:

$$s = 0.3008$$

Thus, the saving rate of 30.08 per cent is the Golden Rule rate for the hypothetical example. This is the only saving rate that would generate the Golden Rule level of K/L, given the values of the relevant parameters. Any change in the saving rate would shift the saving rate [$(s)\ (Y/L)$] curve (vide Figure 16.3) and would move the economy to a steady state with a lower level of consumption. As illustrated here, the Golden Rule saving rate can easily be obtained for any country given the knowledge of its production function, and the rates of depreciation and population growth. To obtain the corresponding maximum per capita consumption, we use the definition of the per capita consumption, that is

$$C/L = (1 - s)\ (Y/L)$$

Inserting the values of s and Y/L that corresponds to the Golden Rule per capita consumption level, we get

$$\text{Max } C/L = (1 - 0.3008)\ (1.48) = 1.035$$

The Golden Rule per capita saving is given by

$$S/L = (0.3008)\ (1.48) = 0.445$$

It may be verified that the sum of the per capita consumption and the per capita saving equals the per capita income at the Golden Rule, as always. Further, note that the C/L at 1.035 is the maximum possible for our hypothetical example. Thus, for example, at the saving rate of s = 0.4, the steady state levels, as shown above, are K/L = 5.59 and Y/L = 1.68, which give C/L = 1.008 [(1 – 0.4) (1.68)], which is less than the C/L at the Golden Rule level (= 1.035) of the saving rate (0.3008).

In terms of our Figure 16.3, the saving rate s_0 would equal the Golden Rule rate if the height between point A on the saving curve and the production curve Y/L were the maximum among all the heights between these two curves. From the above explanation and the computations it would be clear that the Golden Rule saving rate is the one which if achieved would ensure that the per capita capital and the per capita income levels are also at their steady state values. In other words, the Golden Rule saving rate guarantees the steady state K/L and Y/L, but not vice versa.

The significance of the Golden Rule saving rate lies in the fact that if the policy-makers are aware of its magnitude, and if they are able to manage its value, they know what rate to target! Recall from Chapter 5 that the government does have a role in influencing the saving rate, and if so, the knowledge of the Golden Rule rate is highly useful.

Limitations of The Solow Model

Limitations in the Solow model have been observed in terms of its (a) failure to confirm with historical (factual) data and (b) its assumptions. Each of these aspects is elaborated in the next two sub-sections.

Conflict between the Solow Model's Predictions and Historical Facts

Predictions of the Solow model conflict with important facts about the real world. To explain this let us consider a couple of illustrations.

(i) Saving and Population Growth Rates According to the Solow model, the steady state condition is

$$s\left(\frac{Y}{L}\right) = (d+n)\frac{K}{L} \qquad \text{(vide equation \textbf{16.11})}$$

$$\text{or,} \quad \frac{Y}{L} = \frac{(n+d)}{s}\left[\left(\frac{Y}{AL}\right)^{\frac{1}{\alpha}}\right], \quad \text{on substitution from the production function}$$

$$\text{or,} \quad \frac{Y}{L} = A^{\frac{1}{1-\alpha}}\left[\frac{s}{n+d}\right]^{\frac{\alpha}{1-\alpha}} \qquad \textbf{(16.15)}$$

The equation suggests that the steady state per capita income varies directly with the

- Level of technology (A)
- Rate of saving (s)
- Elasticity of output with respect to capital (α)

and inversely with the

- Growth rate in population (n)
- Depreciation rate (d)

Equation **(16.15)** indicates that the elasticity of the per capita output, with respect to the rate of the saving = $[\alpha/(1-\alpha)]$ is less than unity (since $\alpha < 0.5$ usually), and that with respect to the growth rate in population = $-[\alpha/(1-\alpha)]\,[n/(n+d)]$, is also less than (absolute value) unity. These values suggest that large differences in the saving rate and population growth rate will imply a smaller difference in the per capita income than those seen in the real world. To explain this, let us take a hypothetical example with some reasonable values of the parameters:

$$A = 1,\ s = 0.1,\ n = 0.01,\ d = 0.10 \text{ and } \alpha = 0.3$$

Given these values, equation **(16.15)** reduces to:

$$\frac{Y}{L} = \left[\frac{(0.1)}{0.01+0.10}\right]^{\frac{0.3}{0.7}}$$

$$= 0.96$$

In the real world, the saving rate difference across countries is usually within 20 per cent and the population growth rate within about one per cent. Thus, if the saving rate increases from 10 to 30 per cent, *ceteris paribus*, the per capita income would be:

$$\frac{Y}{L} = \left[\frac{1(0.3)}{0.01+0.10}\right]^{\frac{0.3}{0.7}}$$

$$= 1.54$$

and if the population growth rate changes from 1 to 2 per cent, *ceteris paribus*, the said income would equal:

$$\frac{Y}{L} = \left[\frac{1(0.1)}{0.02+0.10}\right]^{\frac{0.3}{0.7}}$$

$$= .92$$

Thus, the saving rate difference of 20 per cent accounts for about 60 (1.54/0.96) per cent difference in the per capita income, and the one per cent difference in the population growth rate explains about four (0.96/0.92) per cent difference in the said income. The existing differences in the per capita incomes of countries in the world are more than 15 times (e.g., the United States $48,820 versus Pakistan's $2,870 in 2011), which remain unexplained by the Solow model.[5] Thus, while several countries may have hit the steady state positions, all of them do not appear to be converging as predicted by the model. The poor countries may be growing at a faster rate than the rich countries, as predicted by the Solow model; but contrary to the model, they do not appear to hit their respective steady state per capita incomes. Some countries like Japan, Republic of Korea, Germany, Canada and Singapore have

[5] Technology is not measurable and it is hard to keep secret. The other two determinants of per capita income (α and d) are parameters that move only marginally across countries.

been successful in bridging a large part of the gaps in the per capita incomes, but countries like Malaysia, Thailand and China have not achieved that much of success in this direction in spite of having relatively high saving-investment rates over a fairly long time. Thus, the historical data on the population growth and saving rates across countries do not support the Solow model. In other words, the convergence theory (the property of catch up) of the Solow model is far from having validated. The reason is not difficult to hunt. To cite an analogy, students in any given college come from varying backgrounds and their performances often vary widely in their first tests. Even towards the end of their degree programme, their grades rarely converge. This so happens because not only that they come with varying stock of knowledge and skills (capital per head), but also because they put in varying amount of efforts (saving rate) during the programme.

(ii) Capital Flight The profit maximising condition for the application of capital input suggests that firms would employ capital up to the point where the marginal physical product of capital (MPP_k) equals the real capital rental (r). Poor countries have low capital-labour ratios in comparison to rich countries, and capital, like any other factor of production, is subject to the law of diminishing marginal return. These two factors imply that the poor countries should have the higher marginal physical productivity of capital and the higher real capital rental rate as compared to the rich countries. This, in turn, implies that if there are free movements of capital across countries, which currently exist in a good part of the world, the capital must fly from the rich to the poor countries. In the real world, while it is true that the marginal physical productivity of capital is higher in the poor countries than in the rich countries; the difference is not as large as predicted by the Solow model; and there are evidences of both ways of capital flights. To see the required difference in the productivities by the Solow model, consider the marginal physical productivity as implied by the Solow model, viz. equation **(16.5)** above:

$$MPP_k = \alpha A\left(\frac{K}{L}\right)^{\alpha-1}$$

Substituting for (K/L) from the function **(16.6)**, we get

$$MPP_k = \alpha A\left(\frac{Y}{AL}\right)^{\frac{\alpha-1}{\alpha}} \qquad \textbf{(16.16)}$$

To simplify, assume reasonable values for the parameters, viz. $\alpha = 0.3$ and $A = 1$, then

$$MPP_k = 0.3\left(\frac{Y}{L}\right)^{-2.33}$$

The difference in the per capita income between rich and poor countries is more than 15 times. Using the index numbers, thus, if the poor country's per capita income is 1.0, the rich country's said income would be 15.0. Under such a situation, the MPP_k in the poor country would be:

$$0.3\,(1)^{-2.33} = 0.30$$

and the MPP_k in the rich country would be:

$$0.3\ (15)^{-2.33} = 0.00055$$

The difference in the two productivities is 545 (0.30/0.00055) times. The existing difference in the respective productivities is much smaller than this number. This implies that the actual data on capital flight does not support the Solow model's contention about it.

Solow Model's Invalid Basic Assumptions

Solow's growth model has three basic assumptions, all of which have been questioned. These pertain to technology, factor homogeneity and the law of diminishing marginal returns. We examine each of these below:

(i) Technology In the Solow model, technology plays the most dominant role in economic growth. However, the model treats it as an exogenous variable and thus makes no attempt to explain it. While his contention that technology is an important source of growth is well received, his assumption about it is ill found. Expenditure on research and development (R&D), attainments on education and health, investment in information and communication technologies (ICT), trade volumes with countries having high levels of R&D etc. have been advanced to measure the state of technical progress. Calderon (2001) has shown that rapid accumulation of ICT capital over the last decades has played a significant role in explaining the impressive acceleration in productivity in Australia since 1995.

(ii) Factor Heterogenity The Solow model is too naive as it assumes all labour as homogeneous and also all capital. In other words, it makes no allowances for differences in skilled and non-skilled labour and the capital in agriculture, factories, infrastructure etc., which have made significant differences in economic growth.

(ii) Law of Diminishing Marginal Returns Solow's assumption of the operation of the law of diminishing marginal returns to capital has been questioned, particularly through broadening the definition of capital to include the human capital (education and health), and emphasising the physical infrastructure within the physical capital (structures and business equipment).

Detailed evidences/arguments against all these three assumptions are included in the following section:

ENDOGENOUS (NEW) GROWTH THEORY

The Solow model of economic growth has proved inadequate to explain the actual rates of growth across countries and over time. Further, the model's theory of convergence, which suggests that the growth rate across countries would tend to equalize over time, has not been validated by facts. Beginning the 1980s, this has inspired new research, both theoretical and empirical, to look into its assumptions and to identify the additional or other determinants (called the fourth wheel, in addition to the Solow's three wheels, viz. labour, capital and technology) of output and growth. Recall that under the Solow model, the saving rate affects the growth rate only up to the **steady** state position, beyond which technology and population growth alone determines the growth rate in real GDP. Further, both technical progress (the crucial determinant of growth) and growth rate in population (which affects positively the growth rate in the total income and not in per capita income) are treated as exogenous variables in the model and, accordingly, the model is branded as an exogenous growth theory. Accordingly, the growth rate beyond the steady state becomes exogenous in any economy and the Solow model leaves little scope for the government to influence the growth rate. Such a scenario is incompatible with the significant roles policy makers have been making across the world in improving the growths of their economies. The pleasant experiences of China, the tiger economies of South East Asia (Singapore, Taiwan and South Korea), India and even Vietnam, Brazil, Indonesia and South Africa lately, among others, on the one hand; and the not so good experiences of the countries like those in Africa and part of Latin America, Europe and Russian Federation etc. on the other hand, points out that economic policies do matter in economic growth. To incorporate such factors, the alternative growth model has been advanced. The said model—which tries to explain technical progress, labour growth and the role of the government in promoting growth besides discovering the 'other' determinants—is termed as the **endogenous growth theory** or the **New Growth Theory**. The endogenous growth model is an extension of the exogenous growth model as it goes deeper in the question of the ultimate sources of growth, and provides a better explanation of growth over space and time. Though the alternative model of economic growth is not in a neat form as the Solow model (vide equation 16.6), it is free from the faulty assumptions of the latter model and it gives due recognition to 'other factors' of growth. Its salient tenets may be presented under the five heads as follows.

Technical Progress and Globalisation

The significance of technical progress in growth needs no exaggeration. It is embodied in the quality of labour and capital. Quality of labour, in turn, is governed by the knowledge, skill, ideas, information and entrepreneurial ability of the labour force, and it is influenced by factors such as education, training, dissemination, labour mobility, motivation and commitment to perform. Ideas like sowing seeds in straight lines and rotating crops in fields represent a great breakthrough in technology of farming, as **reservations against cancellation** (RACs) in railways in India. This is obvious from the facts regarding growth rates of the knowledge-based industries in relation to the traditional industries across various countries. These attributes are while costly to acquire, they, like the public goods, are non-rival in consumption. Robert Lucas (1988) has emphasised the role of this factor (**intellectual infrastructure**) in economic well-being, and combining this with the physical infrastructure, he has attempted to explain the jumps in immigrants' income when they move from the poor countries (like India) to the rich countries (like the US). Entrepreneurship, which is concerned with the organisation of a firm and risk taking, inherent in all businesses and growing over time, is of special significance. Schumpeter was perhaps the first economist to recognise the role of innovation/the entrepreneur in economic growth. The special contribution of **entrepreneurship** to growth is obvious from the many examples in the world. In this respect, it may suffice to just mention just a few names of the world famous entrepreneurs: Bill Gates, Steve Jobs, Warren Buffette, Marx Zuckerberg, Dhirubhai Ambani, Laxmi Nivas Mittal, Ratan Tata and Aditya Birla. Thus, countries/regions that have emphasised entrepreneurship, *ceteris paribus*, have grown faster than the others. The developed world stands way high up in relation to the developing world on this count. Within India, Gujarat, Maharashtra and Karnataka among others, provide ample proof of this in comparison to Rajasthan, Orissa, Bihar etc. Factor mobility and commitment to progress contributes to the quality of labour. Opportunities are unfortunately not uniformly distributed geographically and all people do not have the same attitude to work. Some people are more attached to the lands of their origin and to relatives than others. This obviously affects the economy's growth. Governments are making efforts to spread opportunities as uniformly as possible across their respective areas but this involves huge investments in infrastructure, which is prohibitive. Western people are relatively more mobile, have grown through greater individual responsibilities and under a more competitive spirit and, thus, are relatively more successful, even partly, through this factor. This could be due to the social factor, which includes caste, traditions, values, culture and institutions. This may also be influenced by the competitive spirit or the motivation to work and progress. Language plays a role in factor mobility and therefore in economic growth. English language is fairly popular in India and this gives us an extra strength over many other nations.

The invention and developments in the computer and its applications, and **internet** during the last two decades are credited to have brought in dramatic growth in the world economy, and its impact has varied significantly across countries. Such technological breakthroughs are compared with those in the **steam engine** in the late 18th century, railways in the 19th century, and **electrification**, automobiles and jet planes in the 20th century. These technical advances have expanded economic activities and made them more efficient. While these developments may have been available to all countries, the extent of their use/consumption depends on the skill of the work force and the available infrastructure—both physical and legal—in the country. Since all countries were never alike in the latter respects, technical progress has contributed to varying growth rates across countries, besides its contribution to the growth rate over time.

Globalisation by itself has contributed significantly to boost growth. Factories have and are moving to the low cost regions; firms are focusing on core activities and global market, and thereby taking the advantages of specialization, economies of scale and scope; world-wide mergers are taking place to achieve synergies and size, and to save on transaction costs; funds are raised globally to minimise the cost of capital and to supplement domestic saving; immigration rules are mended to facilitate smooth flow of workforce; the multinational firms are creating spillovers of technologies; and so on. Many of these factors have enabled the less developed countries, in particular, to enhance their growth rates. Thus, we have **coupling and decoupling theories**. Under the former, as countries get more and more integrated, the prosperity in one region brings prosperity to other region and vice versa. This, as seen in Chapter 7, comes through appropriate changes in trade and capital flows across countries under free trade and investment policy. The latter theory, viz.

decoupling, which is exactly opposite of the former, holds if the affected region is successful in enforcing stringent regulations to check those trade and capital flows. The experiences of the South East Asian financial crisis of 1997-98 and the recent great recession of 2007-09, do provide some evidences of the decoupling theory.

The endogenous model of growth explains the technical progress through economic incentives for research and development, training and education, and granting of patent rights to grant a temporary monopoly to the inventors of new products. The tax rebates are offered to firms engaging in research and development, and the basic research in educational institutions is funded, to some extent, through foundations supported by government funding. Special tax and other concessions are provided for knowledge-based industries to foster technical progress. Engineering, management and pharmaceutical studies are a part of technical education and investment and enrollments in these could be used to assess the degree of such progress. Increased capital itself would also lead to technical progress, for new investment fosters inventions and improvements in machines. Also, increase in the labour input would reduce waste and bottlenecks, and enhance the scope for learning and acquisition of new skills. In addition, it is said that **every child brings new hope for the future**. As mentioned above, there are evidences about the positive relationship between investment in information and communication technologies (ICT) and growth in total factor productivity (vide Calderon 2001).The data on such activities could be used to explain the technical progress, at least to some extent.

Capital Accumulation, Law of Diminishing Marginal Returns and Sectoral Allocation of Capital

Capital accumulation is regarded as an important factor of growth ever since Adam Smith. The validity of the law of diminishing marginal returns causing the irrelevance of the saving rate beyond the steady state has been challenged, and the significance of the sectoral allocation of capital in growth has been recognised by the endogenous model of growth. The endogenous growth theory does not accept the Solow model's key assumption of the law of diminishing marginal returns and thereby it treats saving/investment as a permanent source rather than merely a transitory source of growth. Paul Romer (1986) rejects the assumption of the law of diminishing marginal returns and his mentor Robert Lucas (1988) broadens the definition of capital to include 'human capital' (investment in education and health), besides physical capital (structures and business equipment and inventories). Even physical capital is distinguished by several categories, like the factories versus infrastructure (power, transportation and communication), small versus large factories, defence vs. civil, and public sector versus private sector investment and so on. While some of these physical capitals may be subject to the law of diminishing marginal returns, others, like the infrastructure, may not. Also, human capital or knowledge-based industries are not likely to be constrained by the said law. However, the international mobility of human capital is constrained by immigration policies, which are country specific. If the production function is not subject to the law of diminishing marginal returns, then the economy would never hit the steady state, and in that case the saving rate would always play a positive role in augmenting the national product and the rate of economic growth. To see the impossibility of the steady state position, consider the following production function, which is subject to constant marginal returns to capital:

$$\frac{Y}{L} = A\left(\frac{K}{L}\right) \quad \textbf{(16.17)}$$

Substitution of this into the steady state condition, viz., equation **(16.11)**, gives:

$$sA\left(\frac{K}{L}\right) = (d+n)\frac{K}{L}$$

$$\Rightarrow \quad sA = d + n$$

Since the last equation has only the parameters, this would rarely be true. If the said equation does not hold, the steady state does not exist. Further, even if the relationship holds, it would be independent of the value of the capital-labour ratio, and thereby fail to determine the said ratio at the steady state position. In the Solow model, equation **(16.11)** could determine the unique value of the capital-labour ratio because as the capital-labour increases, the per capita output increases, but at a decreasing rate. This tends to increase the left side of equation **(16.11)**, viz., $s\left(\frac{Y}{L}\right)$ at a slower rate than the increase in the right side of equation (16.11), viz. $(d+n)\frac{K}{L}$ which helps determine the unique value of the capital-labour ratio for the steady state. Thus, as the law of diminishing marginal returns does not hold or the steady state does not exist, the saving rate remains an important determinant of growth. Further, all capital is not subject to depreciation, for example, neither human capital nor natural capital depreciates. Recognition of this would reduce the average rate of depreciation for all capital (*d*) and thereby, further the attainment of the steady state position (vide equation **16.11**), accordingly retaining the role of saving rate in growth for a longer period than otherwise. Gupta (1989) found the saving rate a significant determinant of growth across countries. Cardarelli (2002) research has found that capital accumulation plays a larger role than technology in explaining the divergence in per capita income in Australia and New Zealand.

Even under the Solow model, the saving rate is a determinant of the growth rate in the per capita income until the economy reaches the steady state. Thus, Romer-Lucas are able to demonstrate the significance of the saving rate in the standard of living at all times through their rejection of the law of diminishing marginal returns to all capital input. This challenges the principal contention of the Solow model, viz., saving is just a temporary source of economic growth. Another implication of the constant returns to capital is that the marginal physical product of capital would be a constant and independent of the capital-labour ratio. For example, in the production function **(16.17)**, the MPP of capital = *A*, which is a constant. Under this situation, the real capital rental would be the same in the rich and poor countries, as they both would have uniform MPP of capital. This, in turn, provides a rationale for the seemingly two-way movement of capital among nations.

Capital is not equally productive across sectors. The Harrod–Domar and Solow models are one-sector models and, thus, are silent on the role of the sector-wise allocation of capital in growth. Nevertheless, the said models do suggest that the capital-output ratio affects the growth rate negatively. Further, it is known that the said ratio differs significantly across various sectors of an economy. For example, it is higher in industry rather than in agriculture, in capital goods industries than in consumption goods industries; and it is usually higher, the larger is the size of the firm and so on. In view of this, the average capital-output ratio in a country depends on the sector-wise and size-wise allocation of capital and, thus, the latter exert influence on the growth rate in the economy. Accordingly, the emphasis on agriculture versus industry and services affects the growth rate. Further, since agricultural performance heavily depends on nature (weather), countries that are more industrialised have achieved higher growth rates than the others. Examples of Japan, the United States, Germany and other industrialised countries vis-à-vis China, India, Indonesia and other less developed countries provide ample proof of this. It is argued that investment in birth control could yield higher return (and hence growth) than that in either industrial or agricultural activities, particularly in high population growth countries (e.g., India).

Public versus private sector is also relevant for the growth theory, as the former suffers from lack of incentives, indifferent attitude and lower productivity in relation to the private sector. It is because of this realisation that privatisation and disinvestment have been emphasised all over the world for the last over couple of decades. Within the industry, the growth rate is the least if investment is relatively more in defence related industries and the most if it is relatively more in non-defence industries. Infrastructure investment (transport, power and communication) is considered as the best from the long-term growth point of view, as it helps reduce production cost universally. Investment in residential property, in general, falls in between defence and non-defence sectors, with respect to the growth rate. Within the non-defence sector, the growth rate is more if more capital is invested in the knowledge-based industries than in traditional industries. Thus, the **Boston Consulting Group's** distinction of industries among the dog, cow, sunrise and star industries is relevant from the growth point of view. Due to the input-output relationship, growth is faster if all the related industries-agriculture-services are developed simultaneously, than otherwise. This is why **balanced growth** is recommended. However, globalisation has reduced the significance of this factor in growth. Although there is no consensus as to whether small size or the large size is conducive to the growth rate, economists do argue that the **industry size** has a bearing on the overall growth rate of the economy. While the small size may be beautiful from the social welfare point of view; large size, which brings economies of scale and economies of scope, could be beautiful from the growth point of view. Currently, **mergers and acquisitions** across countries are seen as the hot strategies for accelerating efficiency. Concentration on the core areas and outsourcing the side activities are yet other popular strategies adopted across the globe to augment factor productivity. All these factors affect the incremental capital-output ratio (ICOR) and, thereby, the growth rate.

Natural Resources are a part of capital. They contribute to output as do humans and human-made capital resources. However, the former, unlike the latter, do not grow over time, and are thus ignored in growth theories. Nevertheless, some natural resources, like mines and oil reservoirs, have continuously been discovered and exploited, and they have surely contributed to output growth. It is because of this factor that countries all over the world invest a lot of funds on such activities and enjoy the fruits of accelerated economic growth. Although there is now little scope for the physical land area to grow, history suggests otherwise. The data suggests that between 1820 and 1870, the land area of the United States of America grew at an annual rate of about 1.4 per cent and that surely had made a contribution to the growth rate during that period of the US economy. Also, the discovery of massive oil reserves in Norway during the 1970s and 1980s boosted its growth rate significantly. Nevertheless, natural resources are found only rarely and their discovery involves huge investment, therefore, they cannot be considered to help growth on a regular basis. We do have examples of countries like Japan, Switzerland, Singapore and Hong Kong, which are poor in natural resources and yet well developed; and countries like Canada, Norway and Russia, which are rich in such resources and yet not doing that well. Even the climate is considered a determinant of growth. Temperate climate favours growth while tropical climate harms it. Jefferson Sachs (1995) writes that, "Given the varied political, economic and social histories of regions around the world, it must be more than coincidence that all the tropics remained underdeveloped at the start of the 21st century. The United States and Europe lie outside the tropics, most of Central and South Africa, and South East Asia lie within".

Population/Work Force/Working Hours

The endogenous growth model measures the labour input by the labour force (working hours), in contrast to the Solow model, which makes no distinction between the population and labour input. What are relevant for economic growth are the labour input and not the population. While growth in population reduces the per capita income that in the labour force increases it. With a given population, the labour input can grow through an increase in the **work participation rate** as well as through increase in the average number of **working hours**. The work participation rate is affected by the change in the age composition of the population, child labour regulation, retirement age, minimum wage regulations, unemployment compensation system, social changes in the economy (such as women seeking outside jobs) etc. The hours of work are affected by the working hour rules, health of the work force, industrial relations etc. If one looks at the relevant historical data, he/she would find that neither the labour participation rate nor the working hours has remained invariant over time and space. In particular, the female participation rate has shown a significant increase in many countries over time and the improvement in health has contributed to increase in the retirement age. The hours of work differ significantly across occupations as well as countries. The private sector and the knowledge-based industries are credited with having longer work hours than traditional industries and the public sector, respectively. Similarly, the United States is believed to be having longer working hours than the most of European countries. Besides, hard and smart work always contributes more to the production. With the emphasis on globalisation, immigration has increased westward and thereby the actual work force has gone up faster than the number of workers.

Different countries are tapping this source of economic growth differently and it varies over time as well. The world average participation rate (labour force as a percentage of population 15 years or older) was at 79 per cent for male and 52 per cent for female in 2000, which went down to 77 per cent and 51 per cent in 2011, respectively. The rate varies across countries fairly significantly. The labour participation rate was relatively high in Brazil and China, and low in Germany, Japan and South Africa across both the genders. In India, it was higher for male but lower for female than the corresponding world average. In USA, UK, Russia and Australia, it was relatively low for male and high for female. Over time, the participation rate, in general, went up in Russia, Australia, Brazil and Germany, and went down in India, China, Japan, and USA, among others (vide World Development Indicators, 2013). Female work force participation rate, particularly in low and middle-income countries, is relatively low and it is this resource which must be tapped for enhancing the growth rate. It is argued that US workers work longer and harder than do Europeans and most others. Over time, the average work hours seems to have gone down. Estimates suggest that the average work year in the United States fell from 3100 to 1730 hours during the 20th century. It is thus the size of the work force and its productivity that would have accounted for the growth of output due to labour input.

There is yet another dimension here, viz. age composition of the population, which has bearing on the work force and the saving rate (vide Chapter 5), and hence on the growth. The larger is the share of the working age population and the lower is the share of the retirees in total population, the better are the growth prospects. This is known as the **demographic dividend** a country possess. The data on age composition of population indicates that India has a significant demographic dividend. . This is obvious as the proportion of its population in the age groups 0-14, 15-64 and 65 and above in 2012 stood at 29, 66 and 5 vis-à-vis the world population shares of 26, 66 and 8, respectively. The said proportions in USA and Japan stand at 20, 66 and 14; and 13, 63 and 24, respectively. India's advantage exists even in comparison to China, where the shares are 18, 73 and 9.

Economic Policy and Political System

The growth experiences of the OECD countries, tiger economies (Singapore, Hong Kong, Republic of Korea and Taiwan), baby tiger economies (Malaysia, Thailand and Indonesia), caged tiger economy (India), China, among others, and the empirical research [vide Barro (1997), Easterly (2001), Fischer (1993), Greenspan (2002), Hall (1999), Krugman (1994), Porter (1990), Sachs (1995), Sen (1999), Young (1996) etc.] have drawn our attention to the several other determinants (other than those identified by the Solow model) of the level of and the growth rate in per capita income. These include economic policy, political environment and aggregate demand. Economic policy is a rather broad area but the then Governor of Federal Reserve Bank, USA, Alan Greenspan (2002) has emphasised three aspects pertaining to growth, viz., **globalisation, institutional infrastructure and macroeconomic stability**. Experiences of highly open economies like Singapore, Hong Kong, Taiwan, Korea, Malaysia and Thailand have clearly demonstrated the fruits of globalisation. It is suggested that these countries have grown through export led growth and debt (external) led growth. Even China, and lately India, has attained high growth rates in the recent past through globalisation. The theory of international trade and investment suggests that the international movement of goods and capital are 'win-win' situation to all the participants. Countries concentrate on the production of those goods where they have comparative advantage, thereby bring benefits to all. Workers continue doing unpleasant jobs and sweating it out, for they have weak intellect and hard labour is best for them. The fact that practically all large countries have joined the World Trade Organisation (WTO), that seventeen countries have joined hands in having the common currency Euro in Europe, that several regional agencies (like the North American Frontier For Trade Agreement) embracing free trade within a region have emerged, and that increasingly more countries are moving towards a floating exchange rate system etc. clearly suggests globalisation is conducive to economic growth.

Institutional infrastructure includes property rights, rule of law, education and health system, healthy financial market, corruption free political system, fair and transparent economic system, stringent regulations against black money etc. Without the presence of such institutions, there would neither be motivation nor the ability to grow. If institutions are sound, people are confident that their contracts will be honoured, loans will be repaid, property will not be snatched, and the guilty will be punished and without much delay. Even the independence of the Central Bank of the country is hailed to help attain price stability and promote economic growth. This explains why the productivity of an Indian/Chinese/Pakistani/Sri Lankan multiplies when he/she moves from his home country to the United States, Canada, U.K., Singapore, Australia or such institutionally well-equipped countries.

Macroeconomic stability is concerned with sound fiscal, monetary and trade and exchange rate policies. Recall that these policies affect foreign investment and foreign trade, and thereby growth, unemployment and inflation. The erstwhile **financial repression** (regulated low interest rate, pre-emption of banks' funds through high cash reserve requirements and statutory liquidity ratios, etc.) in several countries had impinged on the roles of stabilisation policies, and thereby the stability and growth of those economies. Economic reforms have reduced, if not eliminated, such hurdles to growth. Further the policies are now more stable than before. If economic policies change frequently and abruptly, people lose confidence in government and the growth and other goal variables suffers. For a sustained growth, it is imperative that the government has a long-term vision with regard to fiscal and trade deficits (which have consequences on public debt-domestic and external), as well as reasonable targets for inflation and growth rates. To substantiate its significance, one just needs to review the experience of Latin American economies in last 25 years or so. These economies had suffered with high fiscal deficits, high public debts, inflation or/and unstable exchange rates during 1975 through 2000 and thus have had to be content with low growth rates. Also, several European countries (including PIIGS-Portugal, Italy, Ireland, Greece and Spain) have been currently facing similar difficulties since 2008. Recently, economists have found that the large debt to GDP ratio (over 90 per cent) retards economic growth (vide Reinhart and Rogoff 2010). When they checked these maladies through sound fiscal, monetary and exchange rate policies in the 1990s and onwards, they experienced remarkably improved economic performance. Similar is the story of Africa. Conducive political environment surely helps growth. Corruption and black money are other evils, which are causing serious damage across the globe. India is facing such maladies rather significantly for last about five years and to the extent that it disrupts rather frequently even the rule-making parliament. Political stability and peace brings good policies and thereby foster growth. Decisions become hard to arrive at, and a lot of the scarce money and human efforts gets spent in elections under unstable governments. Japan has almost lost the last two decades due at least partly to political instability. The USSR had difficulty in managing its communist system and it collapsed in 1989. Lately, Russia is progressing reasonably well. African countries are currently suffering from poor political environments and their economies are consequently in poor shape. Many Latin American countries have moved to a democratic system in last couple of decades, and they are more stable now than before. Sen (1999) has found that **most famines were caused not by crop failures but by faulty political systems** that prevented the market from functioning. He argues that minor agricultural disturbances become catastrophes if imports are not allowed, prices are not permitted to rise and farmers are forbidden from going for alternative crops. He cites the case of China, having had the largest record of famines in history in comparison to India, which has faced none since her independence in 1947. Greenspan cites the examples of Singapore, Hong Kong, Chile and Botswana as economies having high quality of governance that promote fast growth. Competition contributes to economic growth, and, both, economic policy and political environment are among the determinants of the extent of competition. Even Michael Porter (1990) recognises the significance of this factor in explaining the growth variations across nations. Thus, the governments have a significant role in economic growth through making and executing good rules, fostering technology and regulating the business, saving/investment rates, population, the type of capital, etc.

Case Study: India has suffered a significant decline in its growth rate in the last couple of years. Its growth rate hovered around 9 per cent during 2005-06 through 2010-11 (barring 2008-09 when it went down to 6.7, primarily due to the Great/global recession), which fell to 6.2 in 2011-12 and to below 5 per cent in 2013-14. Most people blame the government and its policies for this poor performance. Currently (March 2014), the country is on the eve of general elections, and the incumbent government is facing serious allegations for harming the growth, pointing wrong doings, such as (a) corruption (b) policy paralysis (c) trust deficit (d) risk deficit, etc. These problems have adversely affected foreign trade, foreign investments and have led to a significant depreciation of our exchange rate. The Rupee-dollar (USA) rate had hit the lowest rate at ₹68.83 per US dollar on

August 28, 2013, which has recovered since then standing at around ₹60.79/$ as on March 24, 2014. Even our saving and investment rates have fallen significantly during last 4-5 years. Between 2007-08 and 2011-12, the former fell from 36.8 per cent to 30.8 per cent and the latter from 38.1 per cent to 35.0 per cent.

Aggregate Demand

The classical as well as the new classical theory (natural rate hypothesis) suggests that the long run output is governed by the supply side alone. Further, it postulates that output equals the production capacity, which is determined by the quantity and productivity of the factors of production in the economy in the long run. This explains the role of capital accumulation, labour input and technology in growth. However, the theory ignores the role of demand for goods and services, which the Keynesians believe to be the **engine of growth,** at least in the short run, which the **natural rate hypothesis** also accepts. All productions are for sales and they are undertaken basically to sell only. Thus, if there is a paucity of demand (even due to price rigidity), the productive capacity would be left idle and, accordingly, growth would suffer. Also, if the demand exceeds the productive capacity (could be due to wage rigidity), the resources would be induced to expand (workers would be encouraged to work harder and for longer hours, capital assets would be operated more intensively and entrepreneurs would assume greater risks) and, thereby, accelerate growth. The growth process occurs out of the interaction of demand and supply. The fiscal and monetary policies, which exert influence on the aggregate demand, thus, have a role in economic growth. Similarly, net export is a component of aggregate demand and, thus, foreign trade has a role in growth. Investment plays a dual role, viz., it increases supply as it creates capacity and it increases demand as it is a component of the total expenditure. Further, investment is the most volatile component of demand and hence it is the major driver of growth. Consumption expenditure is the largest component of demand, but it is more stable than the other components and it is essentially driven by growth rather than driving it. In view of all this, aggregate demand is a determinant of growth. The larger the AD, *ceteris paribus*, the larger is the growth, and vice versa. Even geographical location is considered as a determinant of economic growth. While, temperate climate is conducive to growth, extreme ones (tropical) harm it.

The above provides a run down on the determinants of economic growth. The list is not exhaustive and there are some overlapping elements in these factors . Further, there is no mathematical model, like the Harrod–Domar or the Solow model, which would quantify their precise or even approximate contributions to growth. However, econometric studies have been performed and they do throw light on the individual contributions of several of the above factors on growth. Needless to say, these factors help explain the growth variations across countries and over time. Also, they defy the exogenous growth theory and also the theory of convergence. Since governments can influence most of these factors through appropriate regulating (agriculture, industry, labour, competition, international trade and capital flows, foreign exchange, immigration, etc.) and demand management (fiscal-monetary) policies, it enjoys the power to influence the economic growth rate. It is for this reason that the government is praised for high growth rate and blamed for stagnant and fluctuating growth rates.

Evidences on Sources of Growth

There are several empirical studies on growth rate across countries and over time. However, the present book is no place to go into many of them. Only two studies are reported here. Edward Dension (1985) studied the sources of economic growth in the United States of America during 1929-82. His findings suggest that during the period of his study, the annual growth rate stood at 2.9 per cent, and the contribution of the growth rates in the labour input and labour productivity (catch all for all non- labour determinants of growth) to it was 32 and 68 per cent, respectively. The distribution of the contribution of labour productivity growth, among its various sources, was found as follows:

Workers' education	14%
Capital formation	19%
Technical progress	28%
Economies of scale	9%
Other factors	–2%
(Resource allocation across industries, weather and work stoppages)	
All	68%

Thus, the labour productivity had turned out to be the most important source of economic growth and labour input took the second position. Further, the productivity of labour was enhanced the most through technical progress, second through capital formation and third by workers' education, and so on. Economies of scale denote the firm size variable and its role also turned out fairly important in promoting labour productivity. The contribution of the 'other factors' was found trivial. This is so because in the United States industry composition and industrial relations are not that important, and weather is fairly stable over years. If the study were replicated for developing countries, contribution of the 'other determinants' would not perhaps be found to be so minor.

Rudi Dornbusch (2001) has reported interesting results in growth for four countries. The same are reported below.

Table 16.2 Economic Growth and Labour Productivity Growth: 1990–98 (%)

Country	*Actual real GDP*	*Real GDP per employee*	*Real GDP per hour worked*
USA	3.0	1.7	1.5
Germany	1.4	2.1	2.5
France	1.4	1.3	1.8
UK	2.0	2.0	1.9

Source: Economic Times, December 14, 2001.

In the table above, the first column gives the growth rate in real GDP and the second and third columns give those due to labour productivity, measured in two different ways during the period 1990 through 1998 in select four countries. Thus, the difference in the rates in columns 1 and 2, and 1 and 3 give two alternative measures of the growth rate due to the labour input. The results suggest that the contribution of the labour productivity to economic growth has been overwhelming, no matter how the productivity is measured; it is over 100 per cent in Germany on both the measures and in France on the hourly basis. This is no wonder if one recalls the backward bending labour supply curve (vide section 9.3, Chapter 9) and note that all the four countries in the table are rich ones. It is no wonder that in rich countries particularly, labour productivity alone matters in growth.

Needless to say, these are simply a couple of examples. The relative significance of the various sources of economic growth varies from country to country, particularly from the developed to developing countries, as well as from one period to another. In general, the contribution of the growth in natural resources (land) is large during the early stages of development and almost insignificant at the later stages. Capital accumulation is a significant determinant, particularly in developing countries, and labour productivity remains the most reliable source of economic growth, everywhere, in the long run.

Limits to Economic Growth

Economic growth is highly desirable and every country must try hard to attain a high and sustainable growth rate such that it stays in the expansion phase of the business cycle as long as possible. Historical data suggest that the highest rate of growth that any country could achieve was 23.3 per cent in China in 1970. The said rate was preceded by 19.3 per cent in the previous year, and succeeded by 7.0 and 2.9 per cent in the following two years, respectively. Thus, the highest rate was not sustained even for a year. If we look at the sustainable rate; it stands at around 7 to 10 per cent in China and other fast developing countries including India, 4 to 5 per cent in the developed countries like United States, Canada, Japan, United Kingdom, France and Germany, and at 4-6 per cent in the world as a whole. The said growth rate is relatively low for the developed countries because the level of income happens to fall in the denominator of the growth rate formula. The pertinent question to probe is, is there a limit (upper) to growth rate? The answer is clearly in the affirmative and we need to look into the reasons for the same.

Recall that growth is determined by the growth in factor inputs and factor productivities. The former includes labour and capital—both natural (land) and human-made. The growth in labour input is restricted by that in population, age composition of population, health, years of education, childcare and household chores, trade-off between work and leisure (backward bending labour supply curve), immigration rules and such other factors. While some of these are natural constraints others are outcomes of conscious decisions and policies. Natural resources are limited, are mostly non-renewable and their exploitation is highly capital deepening. Human-made capital resources (investments in structures, capital equipment and business inventories) are constrained by domestic savings (which is constrained by income and consumption), foreign investments, and depreciation. This leaves factor productivity to foster growth. All the non-factor input determinants of growth affect the factor productivity and these are many as seen above under the endogenous growth theory section of this chapter. The important ones here include technology, institutional infrastructure, economic policy and demand. Technology/ideas flows only gradually and the other three, though are quite significant in the short-term, have minor long-term impacts. It is for all such factors that there is an upper limit to sustainable growth, which could be taken as the ones given by past experiences and indicated in the above paragraph. To the extent an economy has lagged behind these achievable rates, it has not realised its potentials. In view of this, while it is laudable that India has achieved a growth rate of over 6.7 per cent during 2003 through 2010 in a row and hit a growth rate of 9.6 per cent in 2006-07, the challenge she faces is to cross over this or at least sustain this over the next decade or longer. Similarly, China could be proud of having scored the two digit growth rates in several years during the last couple of decades; sustaining it during the next two decades and beyond is a challenge for her.

While **growth is** desirable, it is also **not a 'free lunch'**. It is true that growth alone can bring prosperity to everyone (Pareto optimal) but only if the **trickle-down** theory holds. Under the said theory, the benefits of growth percolate to the poorest of the poor, and so everyone enjoys the fruits of growth. While all economists may not subscribe to this view, the falling of the poverty level over time has provided a good proof of the said theory. However, recall from Chapter 2 that **growth is accompanied by negative effects (costs of growth) as well**. For example, it is associated with industrial hazards like air and water pollution, traffic congestion, violence, family tussles, mental stress, accidents, long working hours, deforestation, destruction of natural beauty/wildlife, over-exploitation of the non-renewable resources, etc. These factors do impose limits on efforts to maximise economic growth. Accordingly, economic development (or **inclusive growth**), which includes economic growth, education, freedom, health, entertainment, clean and conducive environment, gender, race and income equalities, law and order, justice and many more 'normal' goods, is often the over-riding objective, and this may impose a limit to economic growth. Many countries, India included, have designed and implemented many national, state and local level programmes to curb poverty and unemployment directly, and to eradicate illiteracy and hunger through food security and right to education bills. Legislations have been passed to stop child labour and racial/gender biases, to install safety and pollution controlling equipment, to stop cutting of trees, to preserve natural beauty and wildlife and regulations on several other undesirable outcomes of economic growth. Right to information bill has been passed and enforced and this is serving good cause for transparency which surely promotes growth. Non-renewable resources are conserved so as not to endanger sustainable growth. While some of these efforts may have harmed the economic prosperity but have surely boosted economic development.

Conclusion

The fundamental task of macroeconomics is to explain business cycles and to determine the sources of economic growth. Besides technology, the rate of saving is the single most important source of economic growth, at least until the economy hits the steady state. Saving alone provides funds for capital formation, which creates productive capacity for economic growth. The proper selection of investment projects, their execution and management is of immense significance in achieving high economic growth.

The **vicious circle of poverty** is often alleged as the significant hurdle in achieving economic prosperity by the less developed countries. According to this circle, a country is poor because it is poor. This is so because:

$$y^{\downarrow} \Rightarrow S^{\downarrow} \Rightarrow I^{\downarrow} \Rightarrow g^{\downarrow} \Rightarrow y^{\downarrow}$$

It says that the poor countries have low per capita income (y), which leads to low saving (S), which leaves little funds for investment (I), which results into low economic growth (g), which restricts the growth in per capita income (y), and this circle is repeated year after year.

The endogenous growth theory has thrown open a lot of avenues for the poor countries to grow out of this vicious circle. In particular, the supply side tax incentives for saving, which have been implemented vigorously throughout the world in the last 2-3 of decades, have recorded meaningful successes in boosting savings even in the less developed economies. Most countries today have schemes for contractual (compulsory and optional) savings, where in the households/workers enter into some contracts with employers/government/insurance or pension companies to save a certain amount on a regular basis, and where such savings attract tax breaks. Besides, inflation is under check lately and so financial savings are less subject to capital drain. Also, uncertainty about the future has increased and all these must tend to enhance saving. China, Malaysia, Indonesia and Thailand, among others, provide ample proof of this. Besides, national saving is not the only source of funds for investments. Foreign saving, net capital flows from abroad, is another source. If the return on investments is relatively attractive in the country and foreign exchange risks are not prohibitive, foreign savings could be tapped to augment domestic investments. China and the ASEAN (Association of the South East Asian Nations) nations have been fairly successful in this direction and India is making good progress in this direction. It is instructive to note here that while the domestic investment creates both employment and profit, the foreign investment merely generates employment. But foreign investment could additionally bring new technology, which may well trickle sustainable prosperity.

While investment funds are a prerequisite for growth, their appropriate utilisation is also of immense significance. The choices on the sector, specific industry and the entrepreneurship, among other factors, make a lot of difference. The creation of appropriate productive capacity is one thing and its utilisation is another. Idle capacity is doubly harmful. It blocks funds, which have significant opportunity costs, and contributes nothing to the actual production. It is rightly said that the **under-utilisation of resources (both human and non-human) is the worst enemy of economic growth**. One of the reasons often cited for the South East Asian financial/economic crisis of 1996-97 and even the subprime lending triggered great recession of 2007-09 happens to be the glut of productive capacity in certain sectors, like the real estate, banking and stock market. Thus, even large investments may not bring perceptible growth and small investments could well create sustainable growth slowly but steadily.

There are numerous other non-investment factors, detailed earlier, which exert influence on the speed of growth. To emphasise one such factor, note that growth does not mean growth in productive capacity alone. Increase in capacity must be accompanied with increase in demand for goods and services. If there is demand, productive capacity could expand through some means. It is the equilibrium between aggregate demand and aggregate supply that determines the output and the growth in it. Economic policies, with respect to regulations and stabilisation, enjoy significant impact on economic growth. Thus, the vicious circle could be won over and low-income countries need not take that as a binding constraint to economic growth.

The world is better placed today than ever before. We have international organisations like the World Bank, IMF, WTO, UNO, FAO, Asian Development Bank etc., which aid countries through finance and guidance. There are regional organisations like the European Economic Union, OECD, Paris Club, NAFTA, G-7, G-20 and so on, which work towards promoting regional and international growth. At the individual country level, there are all sorts of financial institutions and development organisations. We have the long history to teach the government and firms as to what could be the best for them. Above all, we have a relatively more useful macroeconomic theory and policy to guide us in all economic matters concerning growth. For all these reasons, among others, the future is bright and we ought to have higher growth rates in the future in relation to the past.

KEYWORDS

Sustainable growth; Arithmetic/Miracle of compounding; Rule of 72; Key facts of growth; Fundamental equation of growth; Solow residual; Harrod-Domar model; Solow model; Exogenous growth model; Endogenous growth model; New growth theory; Break even rate of investment; Steady state of the economy; Key determinant; Golden rule; Convergence theory; Capital flight; Factor homogeneity; Law of diminishing marginal returns; Public good; Decoupling theory; Fourth wheel; Entrepreneurship; Factor mobility; Research and development; Globalisation; Human capital; Physical-Institutional infrastructure; Knowledge based industries; Balanced growth; Industry size; Natural resources; Climate; Work participation rate; Working hours; Macroeconomic stability; Political environment; Aggregate demand; Engine of growth; Labour productivity; Limits to growth; Trickle-down theory; Costs of growth; Economic development; Inclusive growth; Vicious circle of poverty; Under-utilisation of resources.

REFERENCES

1. Barro Robert J, *Determinants of Economic Growth: A Cross Country Empirical Study*, (Cambridge, Massachusetts: MIT Press, 1997).
2. Calderon Cesar, 'Productivity in the OECD Countries: A Critical Appraisal of the Evidence, IMF Working Paper, (01/89, 2001).
3. Cardarelli Roberto, 'An Exploration into the Income Divergence between New Zealand and Australia, in New Zealand: Selected Issues', IMF Staff Country Report, (February, 2002).

4. Denison Edward E, *Trends in American Growth 1929-82*, (Washington D C: The Brookings Institution, 1985).
5. Domar Evsey D, 'Capital Expansion, Rate of Growth, and Employment', *Econometrica* 14, (April, 1946): 137-147.
6. Fischer Stanley, 'The Role of macroeconomic Factors in Growth', *Journal of Monetary Economics* 32, (December, 1993): 485-512.
7. Greenspan Alan, 'The Wealth of Nations Revisited', Mexico's Second International Conference on Macroeconomic Stability, Financial Markets and Economic Development, held on November 12,2002 at Banco de, Mexico.
8. Gupta G S, 'Growth Variations Across Developing Countries: How Much and Why'? *Indian Economic Journal* 36, (January-March, 1989): 49-64.
9. Hall Robert E., Charles Jones, 'Why Do Some Countries Produce so much More Output Per Worker than Others, *Quarterly Journal of Economics* 114, (February, 1999): 83-116.
10. Harrod Roy, 'An Essay in Dynamic Theory,' *Economic Journal* 49, (March, 1939): 14-33.
11. Krugman Paul, 'The Myth of Asia's Miracle,' *Foreign Affairs* 73, (November-December, 1994): 62-78.
12. Lucas Robert E, 'On the Mechanics of Economic Development,' *Journal of Monetary Economics* 22, (July, 1988): 3-42.
13. Government of India, *Eighth Five Year Plan, 1992-97*,Vol. 1, (New Delhi: Planning Commisson).
14. Porter Michael E, *The Competitiveness Advantages of Nations*, (London: Macmillan, 1990).
15. Reinhart, Carmen and Kenneth Rogoff, Growth in a Time of Debt, *American Economic Review,* 100,2 (January 2010), 573-8.
16. Romer Paul M, 'Increasing Returns and Long Run Growth', *Journal of Political Economy* 94, (October, 1986): 1002-37.
17. Sachs Jeffrey, Andrew Warner, 'Economic Reform and the Process of Global Integration', Brookings Papers on Economic Activity 1, (1995): 1-118.
18. Sen A K, Development as Freedom, (New York. Alfred A. Knopt, 1999).
19. Solow Robert M, 'A Contribution to the Theory of Economic Growth,' *Quarterly Journal of Economics* 70 (February, 1956): 65-94.
20. Solow Robert M, 'Perspectives on Growth Theory,' *Journal of Economic Perspectives* 8, (Winter, 1994): 45-54.
21. Young Alwyn, 'The Tyranny of Numbers: Confronting the Statistical Realities of the East Asian Growth Experience, *Quarterly Journal of Economics* 110, (August, 1996): 641-80.

Review Questions

1. The data on the growth rates in real GDP in each of the last three decades in selected countries are as follows:

Country	*Growth rate (annual)*		
	1980–90	*1990–2000*	*2000–12*
India	5.7	6.0	7.7
USA	3.5	3.6	1.6
UK	3.2	3.1	1.6
Japan	4.1	1.0	0.7
Singapore	6.7	7.2	5.9
Malaysia	5.3	7.0	4.9
Rep. of Korea	8.9	5.8	4.0
China	10.3	10.6	10.6
Sri Lanka	4.0	5.3	5.9
Australia	3.5	3.6	3.1
Russian Federation	1.9	-4.7	4.8
Germany	2.2	1.8	1.1
Brazil	2.7	2.7	3.7
World		2.8	2.6

Source: World Development Indicators, 2013

The year-to-year growth rates data for India and the United States for the period 1953 through 2012 are available in review question 1, Chapter 14, and data on several macroeconomic variables for all the countries above are available elsewhere in this text. Examine these data, and any other information that you can get from the library and other sources, and identify the sources of variations in the growth rates across countries and over time.

2. Analyse the virtues and pitfalls of economic growth. What, if any, is the ideal rate of growth?

3. Examine the relationship between economic growth and the growth of population. Would investment in birth control yield higher returns than that in either industrial or agricultural activities, particularly in countries with very high growth rates in population (e.g. India)? Why?

4. Neither under saving nor over saving is good for any economy. Discuss.

5. The country that would win the growth race in the future would be the one that would achieve excellence in technical progress. Do you agree? Why or why not?

6. Discuss the role of government in economic growth/development.

7. In long run, the "standard of living is governed by the capacity to produce". Comment.

8. Consider an economy which is subject to a Cobb-Douglas production function. Further, assume that the Solow model operates there with various parameters taking the following values:
Depreciation rate = 8%, Savings rate = 30%, Population growth rate = 2%, Share of capital in output = 35%, Initial capital-labour ratio = 3, and A (neutral technology parameter) = 1
Given the above, attempt the following questions:
(a) Write the production function for this economy.
(b) Determine the steady state level of capital stock per capita
(c) Determine the Golden Rule level of the saving rate
(d) Suggest an economic policy for achieving the Golden Rule outcomes for this economy

Chapter 17

State of Macroeconomics

Learning Objectives

After reading the chapter you should be able to:

1. Appreciate the contributions of macroeconomic theory and policy, which are evident in the measurement of macroeconomic variables, explanation of economic fluctuations and the policy prescriptions for taming business cycles, and in providing the theory for promoting sustainable and inclusive economic growth.
2. Comprehend that there is no free lunch and accordingly there are trade-offs in all significant economic decisions and depending on the priorities, decision-makers have to choose what to achieve at what cost. Believe that Economics is a useful social science to individuals as a worker, consumer and investor; to business to raise finance, execute production and sales; and to governments to formulate the fiscal, monetary, trade and foreign exchange rate policy, among several other such decisions.
3. Remember the economics' two fundamentals, supply and demand, which have become inevitable for everyone and everywhere.

Macroeconomics is concerned basically with three aspects:

- Measurement of national aggregates
- Fluctuations in national aggregates (business cycles) and the role of stabilisation policies in countering business cycles
- Growth in national aggregates

A thorough understanding of these three aspects would enable anyone to explain all macroeconomic events that have happened in the past and suggest an appropriate policy mix to handle such events.

Though there are many national aggregates, economics deals with economic variables only and macroeconomics with macroeconomic variables only. Macroeconomic variables are many and they are, for convenience, classified into (ultimate) target, indicator, intermediate and policy variables. The indicative and intermediate variables are useful primarily because it is through them that the macroeconomic policy exerts influence on the economy's goal variables. Their magnitudes per se are immaterial. Policy variables again are not of much concern in terms of their precise magnitudes, all that we wish is that they assume values such that the desired magnitudes of the ultimate target (or goal) variables are attained. It is thus the magnitudes of the target variables with which macro-economists are basically concerned. Among these, real national income, and resultant unemployment (if any) and price level or the rate of inflation, are of ultimate interest. In this concluding chapter, we look at where the present state of macroeconomics stands with regard to the measurement, stability and growth of these three variables, which are, real national income, unemployment and inflation.

Measurement of Economic Variables

Measurement of the size of an event precedes its understanding. Most countries in the world now have regular publications of data on national income and price indices, and these are compiled and published on regular basis for all countries by international organisations, like the UNO, World Bank, IMF and the WTO. Time series data on unemployment are, however, not available for all countries. For such defaulting countries, survey data on different bases (e.g., usual, weekly, daily) are occasionally published. The time lag, that is the gap between the actual period up to which data is available and the present period, varies across countries. In the developed countries, this lag is, in general, relatively small as compared to that in the developing countries. For example, in the United States income data becomes available in the next quarter, while in India the actual figures on income are available only after a couple of years. The time lag for the price index is relatively small and it varies across price indices. While the wholesale or producers' price index data are available fairly fast (within two weeks), the consumers' price indices take a month, and the GDP deflator data follows the GDP data schedule. The data on the monetary variables, foreign trade and investment are available with a relatively little time lag and they are quite reliable and easily accessible.

National income and inflation are well defined conceptually and all countries follow their standard definitions. However, while most countries measure the inflation rate by the changes in the consumers' price index (called the retail inflation); others use the wholesale price index (called the wholesale inflation) for this purpose. Measurement of unemployment across countries is unfortunately not so standardised and it suffers seriously from measurement error even in the developed countries. This is primarily because it is highly subjective and it is not easy to identify as to who is voluntary unemployed and who is not and what is the extent of underemployment, etc. In general, the data suffers from inaccuracies due to several factors, including the following:

(a) Non-market economy
(b) Black or parallel economy
(c) Measurement of services
(d) Arbitrariness in foreign exchange rates
(e) Changes in the quality of products
(f) Emergence of new products
(g) Unorganised sector
(h) Sampling errors
(i) Non-sampling (or compilation) errors
(j) Subjective errors

The relative size of these factors varies across countries and, hence, the data is not exactly comparable across nations. To give a classic example, in July 1991,

India devalued its currency by about 25 per cent, which reduced the country's per capita income in US dollars instantly by that percentage. No goods or services were destroyed, and yet, India was rendered poor in US dollar measurement by a mere stroke of a pen! The PPP income is, of course, not affected by devaluation/revaluation. It is argued that though the absolute magnitudes are not meaningfully comparable, the rates of changes in them are suitable for the purpose. This is so because the rate of change is unaffected so long as the inaccuracy proportion is a constant. Thus, if the share of the parallel economy remains constant over time, though the national income is underestimated, the rate of change in the national income, the growth rate, is correctly measured. Economics is a practical subject and, therefore, lots of empirical research is carried out in this discipline. If the data is inaccurate, we have 'the garbage in, garbage out'. To minimise the impact of this weakness, efforts have continuously been made to identify and correct as many sources of inaccuracy in data measurements as possible. The process is never ending. However, one can safely conclude that errors in variables' measurement are much lower today than they were ever before, and careful research could use them meaningfully to analyse economic events, and suggest policies to counter business cycles and to promote growth.

Needless to say, economic policies matter with regard to the measurement of macroeconomic variables. For example, the government can fund research in data collection methodologies and increase the budget for data collection. The latter would enable quality workers, larger sample sizes, and faster, more accurate processing and publication of data. Improvement in methodology, sample size, quality of work force and computerisation would improve the data quality and reduce the time lag. Thereby, government policy matters in the measurement of macroeconomic variables.

The contribution of macroeconomics with regard to the measurement of national aggregates needs no exaggeration. We are now able to measure our economic well-being and compare it with the past to see the improvements in the same (economic growth rate). Also, we can compare our standard of living with those of others both within the country and outside it (intra-country and inter-country comparisons). We have money, which has made the exchange so convenient worldwide. We have data on the goal and behaviour variables, which guide us in our decision-making. We have found merit in globalisation and are making use of this source to enhance happiness and prosperity. We are able to measure everything in common money and thus know how much each entity possess and owes. This list has no end as the fruits of developments in macroeconomics are enormous. The message is clear—the **bottom line for a country is**—attain as high a per capita income as possible (giving due recognition to the non-market and parallel economies and other imperfections in the measurement of national income and the quality of life), ensure proper health care for everyone, ensure no one goes to sleep hungry, secure clean and pollution free environment, and have high saving-investment rates to secure future consumption.

Business Cycles and Stabilisation Policies

Understanding an economic event precedes its management. There is almost a consensus that **business cycles** (ups and downs in the real income and unemployment over time) **are caused by, both, demand and supply shocks**, and that these could come through government initiatives/policies, natural factors, peoples'/business behavioural changes and new expectations (called **animal spirits**), innovations, etc. Further, these shocks take time to have full impact on the economy due to factors like the life cycle theory of consumption, acceleration theory of investment, long and variable lags of fiscal and monetary policies, etc. However, economists differ with regard to their relative roles. While the classicists emphasise on supply (real) shocks, the Keynesians stress on demand (monetary) shocks. The former believed in the wage-price flexibility (hence market clearing) without or with information barriers, the latter hypothesized the wage-price rigidity and other market imperfections. The role of expectations (animal spirits) and the **rational expectations theory** proposed by the new classicalists has been accepted even by the new Keynesians.

Supply shocks are caused by nature (discoveries/destructions of resources, weather and natural calamities like earthquake, floods, droughts, epidemics etc.), the workers (work-leisure preference and trade unions), firms (technology, cartel formations, mergers etc.), the government (taxation, subsidy, stipulations on pollution, safety regulations, immigration laws, trade and investment regulations, etc.) and by factors like **innovations**, wars and terrorism. The technology, supported by the inter-temporal substitution of labour, is emphasised as the single significant source of business cycles by the Real Business Cycle Theory Imperfect information or an 'information barrier' is considered the principal source of economic fluctuations in the Friedman-Lucas versions of the new-classical model. **Demand shocks** could emanate from the behaviour of the private sector (consumption and investment behaviour), government actions (money supply, interest rate, government expenditure, taxation and subsidies, exchange rate) and the behaviour of foreigners (net exports and capital flows).

The classicists believe in the relative **stability** of the private sector and argue that the instability of the government policies is the real source of the instability of the aggregate demand. In contrast, the Keynesians consider the private sector (particularly, investment spending and money demand) as the main source of instability from the demand side. The foreign sector is still relatively minor in countries like India and its behaviour is erratic only during crises, both abroad and home. However, growing **globalisation** and instability of the exchange rate are enhancing its significance. The role of **wage-price rigidities** is emphasised by all the Keynesians as the most prominent source of business cycles.

The Great Depression of 1929-33 is believed to have been caused by the leftward shift in the aggregate demand curve not countered by the liberal monetary and fiscal policies. What caused the shift in the AD curve, there is a difference of opinion. While, the **Keynesians** (also known as the non-monetarists) put the blame on the erosion of wealth due to bust of **stock market bubble of 1927-29** and the loss of business confidence, resulting into a fall in consumption and investment, and debt-deflation hypothesis, resulting into redistribution of income in favour of the rich causing a further fall in consumption spending, both leading to the leftward shift in the IS curve; the **monetarists** argue in terms of the loss of the depositors confidence in banks, leading to bank failures, rise in the currency ratio and a consequent fall in the money supply, triggering a leftward shift in the LM curve. Leftward shift in the IS or/and LM curves led to a leftward shift in the aggregate demand (AD) curve, causing a fall in real GDP and price. The stagflation of the 1970s occurred due to then activated role of the cartel by the organization of petroleum exporting countries (OPEC), leading to an **oil price hike** and corresponding increase in the cost of production across the board, resulting into a leftward shift in short run aggregate supply (SAS) curve, resulting in a fall in GDP and an increase in price/inflation. The adverse supply shocks dominated during 1973 through 1982 period. The prosperity of the 1980s and 1990s is explained through the emphasis on globalization (discovery of new markets for goods, services and capital, and liberal immigration), the **invention of internet**, leading to investments in computers, software and telecommunications equipment, and growth of the knowledge based industries. Entrepreneurs made huge profits in the information technology sector that led to yet another **stock market bubble** during 1996-2000. While the internet related innovations led to increased labour productivity, causing to a rightward shift in SAS curve, the stock price bubble led to a rightward shift in AD curve, which together triggered an increase in GDP and reduction in the rate of inflation. This period was so good to almost all economies and is thus termed as the **"Goldilocks" economy puzzle**, meaning neither too hot nor too cold. The slowdown of the early 21st century is explained by the bust of the IT boom. The recovery and prosperity during 2002-07 came through the **housing price bubble,** triggered by the long lasting low mortgage rate, tax incentives on housing loans, enhanced financial leverage on housing, securitization of mortgage debts, etc. The recent great recession (2007-09) was triggered by the long duration low interest rate regime, causing fall out of sub-prime lending and housing sector boom, bank failures, which busted leading to bank failures, securitization, and collapse of some merchant banks (Lehman Brothers) and sick business houses, resulting into twin shocks of both adverse supply and adverse demand. These experiences have exposed the ancient **myth that prices can only go up and can never fall**. The recent European crisis (**PIIGS**-Portugal, Italy, Ireland, Greece and Spain) was triggered by the low interest rate regime, excessive borrowings, bank failures, and so on.

Free markets need regulations. Stabilisation polices are recognised to play a significant role in moderating/countering business cycles. The inflation (and the **hyperinflation**), in the long run, is always associated with growth in the money supply, triggered by unsustainable fiscal deficits. Long run unemployment, called the **natural rate of unemployment**, is due to job separation and job finding issues, and mismatch troubles, both of which are part of labour market difficulties. Thus, in the long run, inflation and unemployment are unrelated issues. However, in the short run, there is a trade-off between the two, given by the **short run Phillips Curve**. The post late 1960's emergence of the permanent income hypothesis, lags in policy effects, the natural rate hypothesis, adaptive expectations and rational expectations theories changed the opinion against inflation and unemployment trade-off. Even the most anti-stabilization policy model of the classicists, which is, the Lucas "**policy irrelevance**" model recognizes the role of 'surprise' policies in effecting unemployment and inflation in the short run. Economists differ in the approach to these stabilization policies, that is, whether they should be conducted actively or passively and through the set rules or discretion. Nevertheless, there is a consensus that **at least one of the fiscal and monetary policies is always available to tame business cycles**. Yet another issue is that if there is any trade-off between inflation and unemployment, even in the short run, then the question is which one is more serious and which of the two fiscal or monetary policy should focus on which of the two goals. While there is no resolution on the relative importance of the two goals, it is now clear that **monetary policy's principal responsibility lies with controlling inflation/deflation while managing the growth rate is the mandate for the governments**. Also, with the spread of globalization, a new issue has emerged, i.e. in addition to aim at the potential level of output (= natural level of output), called the **internal equilibrium**, a country must also try to secure an **external equilibrium**, where the foreign exchange market is in equilibrium or the balance of payments is zero. Sometime the two goals conflict and to strike a balance, policy is needed. Of course, two goals require two policy instruments but which one is a debatable issue. For this, Robert Mundell has suggested an **assignment rule** under which the fiscal policy may be made responsible to secure internal equilibrium and the monetary policy to take care of the external equilibrium.

Moving to the actual applications of the policies, it is evident that the fiscal policy dominated to tame business cycles until around 1970, the monetary policy assumed that role during 1970 through 2001, and both policies are sharing this role thereafter. The return of **fiscal activism** is evident in the tax rebates announced in 2001 and 2003 in USA and several other countries, fiscal stimulus which was mounted simultaneously by the G-20 (a group of developed, emerging and large economies) constituted by then US president George Bush (Junior), to counter 2007-09 great recession, etc. Recall that fiscal policy is less effective under globalization, floating exchange rate system, binding governments' inter-temporal budget constraint, and high interest sensitiveness of investment;, while monetary policy is of little significance under fixed exchange rate system and low interest rate. Since world was less global until 1970 than later, it was on the fixed exchange rate system, and debt did not become a serious worry, the fiscal tool was practiced more than the monetary then. Post 1970, quite the opposite is happening, we have more open economies, most countries are on the floating exchange rate, and the governments' debt has become an over-riding constraint, under such a situation, the monetary policy has much sharper teeth than the fiscal policy. The **puzzle** of both policies being in use currently is explained through the role of regionalization, some countries (like China) which are on almost the fixed exchange rate have become more prominent in the world, some countries have moved to a common currency, governments having learnt to live with debts, fact that the fiscal bears a direct effect on the GDP as compared to the monetary policy, and so on.

Though business cycles have been tamed both with regard to their frequency and length of occurrence, and severity to a neat extent, they still persist. This is because these policies suffer from some inherent/outside limitations, which are as follows:

(a) Inaccurate estimates and forecasts of economic events

(b) Unstable policy multipliers/elasticities due to changing structure of the economy

(c) Uncertain private sector's expectations and reactions to policy

(d) Long and variable policy lags

(e) Incompatible priorities

(f) Political costs of policies

(g) Policy-related constraints

Due to measurement problems mentioned above and the obvious imperfections in forecasting techniques, policy makers do not have the exact figures on the current and future magnitudes of unemployment and inflation. It is obvious that if data is inaccurate, no policy can be fully effective. For example, if unemployment is estimated at 5 per cent, and the policy makers desire it at 4 per cent, they would design a policy to reduce the said variable by just 1 per cent. However, if the actual unemployment was 7 per cent (and not 5 per cent) the objective at 4 per cent would not be attained. Similarly, though a lot of empirical research has been going on, no one has the true values of the several policy multipliers, which give the response of target variables (unemployment, inflation, and GDP) to the changes in the policy variables. Thus, if the income elasticity of money demand was estimated at 1.5, and the inflation target was 4 per cent, then for the 8 per cent expected growth in national income, the money supply would be increased by 16 per cent (= $1.5 \times 8 + 4$). However, if the said elasticity differed from 1.5, the inflation rate would differ from 4 per cent even if the income actually went up exactly by 8 per cent. Thus, both undershooting and over-shooting a target could be possible. Since the structure of various economies is changing with time, the estimation problem exists and would sustain, though hopefully in a milder form. Similar problem will arise even if the Taylor Rule was applied to set the nominal interest rate when data on inflation rate or/and GDP gap were inaccurate. It is natural that people and business will respond to policies, which the policy makers cannot predict and incorporate.

Policies exert influence on the goal variables only after a **time lag**, which is long and variable, and hence the exact timings of the policies and economic events may not match, and could even be counter-effective. Under such a scenario, policy makers might use an easy policy (to avoid, say, the current deflationary threat) when in fact a dear policy was needed (when the policy became effective, the economy was experiencing inflation), and thus go wrong. As seen in Chapter 1, and elsewhere, the various **economic goals** are not always compatible. For example, inflation control competes with the control on unemployment in the short run. Policy makers differ in their recommendations partly because quite often different policies are alternative tools to handle a situation and partly because they attach different significance to different policy goals. There is a lot of **ideology** in macroeconomics. For example, recession could be countered either through an easy monetary or an easy fiscal policy; but since classicists are pro-monetarist, they would recommend the former while the Keynesians, being pro-fiscal, would recommend the latter. Also, while some lawmakers hate unemployment more than inflation (perhaps the Democrats in the United States), the others may hate inflation more than unemployment (perhaps the Republicans in the United States); and, if so, they could well differ in the matter of policy recommendations. Also, if the policy makers do not like either inflation or unemployment, they would refuse to act, and problems would continue. As if these issues are not enough against the effective/meaningful stabilisation policies, there are **political costs** associated with the right policy. Since most political leaders like to retain their powers, or consider safeguarding their chairs as good for the economy, they cannot afford to displease the majority of their voters. For example, subsidies of various kinds and reservations for the small sector and weaker and minority communities are now deemed socially harmful by the most, and an exit policy is the need of the hour, yet no significant changes in the existing policies have been forthcoming. Instead of seeking the maximum social welfare, policy makers may be looking for maximum political welfare. In addition, as detailed in Chapter 10, each policy has its own constraints and so may not be available at a particular juncture. Thus, all these constraints render the otherwise effective fiscal and monetary policies less effective with respect to cyclical unemployment and inflation. It is hard for economists to overcome these hurdles to make policies effective.

The emphasis on **globalisation** and the **floating exchange rate** system has undermined the role of the fiscal policy and enhanced that of the monetary policy in regulating business cycles. The traditional inter-dependence of these two policies, where the fiscal deficit was largely to be monetised, is being checked and the monetary policy is gaining increasing independence and significance over time. There is a dichotomy in the view that the monetary policy may be entrusted with the management of inflation and the fiscal policy with that of unemployment. The credit for the world having controlled inflation lately is being accorded to the central bank being made more autonomous and empowered to manage the same. However, expansionary fiscal policy has remained a rather popular policy, at least among the poor people, though it is still alleged that it benefits the present generation at the cost of future generations.

Unlike the 1960s when the **Phillips' curve** provided a menu to policy makers to counter all business cycles, today there is no formula/equation or even a reliable econometric model to guide us in mitigating such fluctuations. However, tools exist and policies matter and they have surely been used in the real world to check the amplitudes and duration of business cycles. Business cycles are partly due to nature and partly created by human factor/policies. Economists do make mistakes in diagnosing economic events due to data imperfections etc., and they, accordingly, recommend alternative medicines and doses. This is because, like in medical science, we **have alternatives and our faith in them varies**. Also, the faith is sometime derived from 'trials and errors', and **our priorities in achieving conflicting objectives are different**. Yet, the fact remains that **business cycles are less frequent, shorter lasting and less deep today than ever before, and the Great Depression and hyperinflation are history**. Further, expansions have been longer and recessions shorter during the post-war (World War II) rather than the pre-war period. Surely, macroeconomic developments share the credit with the skills of policy makers in this achievement. There are opinions that the monetary policy should concentrate on attaining price stability and the fiscal policy on securing as low an unemployment rate as feasible, which goes hand in hand with the highest sustainable growth rate. However, to date most Central Banks have the dual mandate of endeavouring to provide, both, stable price and high growth rate, besides ensuring healthy and orderly financial market. The other significant contributions of macroeconomics towards business cycles' theories include:

(a) There are voluntary and natural unemployment
(b) Hyperinflation is associated with high growth in money supply
(c) Information barriers exist
(d) Decision makers make rational expectations
(e) Wage-price rigidities are a fact of life

(f) There is a trade-off between inflation and unemployment rates in the short run, and not in the long run

(g) Stabilisation policies are not neutral to income, employment and other real magnitudes at least in the short run. In the long run, output always gravitate around its natural level.

In conclusion, business cycles are neither pure real nor pure monetary phenomenon, they are rather a mixed phenomenon. Thus, there is only the **eclectic (heterodox) theory of business cycle**. At times, either the supply or the demand shock might trigger a cycle, but over time there are evidences of both. Also, both the fiscal and monetary policies (and even the trade and exchange rate policies to some extent) are usually available to counter business cycles and the two policies are more complementary than competitive. Also, the failure of the demand management policies and the success of supply side policies during 1970s and of the opposite during the other times is a false dichotomy, as both are useful. In addition, the great recession of 2007-09 has taught the policy-makers the virtues of cooperation among all players (country group, G20) to act simultaneous in the well-deliberated direction to attack the common malady. While ending this part, a mention must be made that while fluctuations are generally considered as bad, they have some good side effects too. One, unless a person (country) faces bad time, she may not appreciate the plight of the vulnerable parts of the universe (countries). Two, by stabilizing, you eliminate not only the recessions but also the booms!

Economic Growth

Ultimately, it is the level of the real national income, or rather real per capital income (a measure of the standard of living) and the growth rate in it over a period of time that matters. There is a consensus among economists that the **standard of living in a country is governed largely by its productive capacity**, which depends positively on the factors of production, viz., labour, capital and technology The alternative growth strategies under the **endogenous model** (Chapter 16) do exert some influence on the economic growth rate, but there are differences of opinion on their precise roles. While the output tends to hit its natural level in the long run, its short-run level is influenced by the demand factors. Note that when we talk of growth, we are concerned to find what determines the natural level of output.

Education, knowledge, skills and ideas (not mutually separable), together referred to as the human capital or **intellectual infrastructure**, are universally recognised as the significant contributors to economic growth. **Physical infrastructure** (transport, electricity, water, etc.) is a complementary factor for technology to make an impact. Although technical know-how can be imported, infrastructure cannot and, thus, it does constraints growth. Investment in human capital and infrastructure are considered the 'secrets' of growth. Entrepreneurship is a proven virtue for economic growth. Invention of the computer and such other machines has contributed to factor productivity.

Saving (not hoarded) contributes to the physical capital and thereby promotes economic growth. Large chronic fiscal deficits retard national savings and thus harm economic growth. Foreign capital could supplement national saving, particularly in the low-income countries, but it must not lead to chronic current account deficits and unsustainable external debt. The law of diminishing marginal returns to capital has been challenged and accordingly the saving rate enjoys the status of being a permanent source of economic growth. Allocation of capital across various sectors and business sizes affects the capital-output ratio and, thereby, the growth rate.

Population growth, though leads to an increase in the quantity of labour and, thus, national income, harms the standard of living (per capita income). The law of diminishing marginal returns applies to labour and the population growth affects the quality of labour, i.e., human capital or technology. Increase in the labour participation rate (like the housewives opting for outside jobs), work ethics, labour mobility, commitment to progress and average hours of work are considered the desirable changes for promoting economic growth. Improvements in the security and legal system, property rights etc. do contribute to growth.

Economic policies favouring globalisation, institutional infrastructure (legal, property rights and regulating) and sound macroeconomic stability have proved their worth in effecting economic growth. Demand management policies are significant not only in taming business cycles but also in generating adequate demand so that potentials for output growth can be fully exploited. Output is determined by the interaction of aggregate supply and aggregate demand. Unless there is demand, production would not be forthcoming even if there is productive capacity. Thus, demand also plays a role in economic growth. Since investment is a component of expenditure, it affects demand, besides affecting the supply through enhancing the productive capacity. Since fiscal and monetary policies influence aggregate demand, and even aggregate supply (supply side economics), they play a role in economic growth. The regulating policies exert influence on the sectoral allocation of capital and labour and, hence, on aggregate supply and economic growth. A sound political system would create and foster good economic policies, thereby promoting growth. Black market and corruption have significant negative effects on growth. Thus, the government has a role in economic growth. Unfortunately, even geography, on which a country has no control, also effects growth. It is believed that temporal climate is adverse to growth.

The emergence of international and regional organisations like the World Bank, IMF, WTO, FAO, Asian Development Bank, European Union, North American Frontier for Trade Agreement, G-8, G20 and Paris Club have only facilitated growth. Needless to say, a part of the reported growth rates across countries has been merely due to improvements in data quality coming through reductions in the non-market economy and black economy, and data measurement and collection. Though **there is no precise mathematical model like the Harrod-Domar model to explain the growth variations across countries and time, the endogenous growth theory provides a good account of the same.**

There is an upper limit to the sustainable growth rate, which comes from the limits on labour and capital increases, slow changes in factor productivity and the **speed limit** set by the natural rate of unemployment and the hazards/costs of growth. It hovers around 8-10 per cent for the low-income countries, 6-7 per cent for the middle-income ones and 4-5 per cent for the rich nations. If a country exceeds this limit in a given year, it must be either because it had a poor previous year or a windfall through great monsoon, discovery of some big natural resources or a significant technological breakthrough etc. Unfortunately, such experiences are rare. Most of the time, every country's performance is below its potential. The reasons for the poor performance must be found in one or more of the following factors:

(a) Natural calamities, like earthquakes and epidemic

(b) Poor weather/rainfall/climate

(c) Human-made calamities, like wars, terrorism, riots, scams and industrial relation trouble

(d) Political instability, including policy paralysis, mid-term elections, coalition compulsion

(e) Economic instability, like high fiscal and/or trade deficit, serious recession, hyperinflation, etc.

The above events either destroy some of the production resources or render them less productive. While not much can be done to control the first two events, particularly in the short run, the last three factors are very much in our hands. If we can take care of these and learn from other countries experiences, growth would be no problem. It is in such instances that the tools of macroeconomics would come handy to aid growth.

CONCLUSION

Economics is designed to explain the economies' history, assist in designing suitable economic policies, and to predict the likely future economic scenario. Since the world economy is dynamic, economics cannot remain static. Thus, we have witnessed enormous developments, both in macroeconomic theory and practice, ever since its founder's (John Maynard Keynes) work in the general theory. The current state of knowledge has evolved over time and often triggered by unexpected events, (like Great Depression, fiat money, hyperinflation, oil price hike, stagflation, invention of internet, sub-mortgage crisis, falls of giant business, financial innovations, debt crisis, etc.) Needless to say, it is highly useful to understand the past, the present day world and foresee what is in store in future. However, as economics is an inexact social science, measurement is imprecise and the future is full of uncertainty, differences of opinion are inevitable. Nevertheless, the differences, are little in theory and more in policy, sustain largely in terms of the extent and not in kind, and are often due to differences in setting priorities. Further, as the difference between micro and macroeconomics is getting blurred over time, so is the difference among economists in macroeconomics. Briefly recollecting developments with regard to the significant/controversial issues, the following may be stated:

(a) There is a consensus that though GDP is still not free of measurement errors, real GDP is the best available measure of a country's overall economic well-being and performance.

(b) There is a consensus with regard to the ultimate objectives of economic policies, which are high and fast growing income, price stability, social justice and sovereignty (independence or current account sustainability).

(c) There is a near consensus that there is a trade-off between inflation and unemployment rates (or between inflation and economic growth) in the short run, but not in the long run.

(d) Economists differ with regard to the relative costs of unemployment and inflation, and accordingly, they attach varying priorities to these economic ills.
(e) There is a consensus that business cycles are caused by either or both demand and supply supplyshocks, which could be either favourable or adverse and which could be triggered through the private sectors' behaviours, policies, natural factors and/or innovations.
(f) There is a consensus that incentives matter and thereby the fiscal, monetary, trade and exchange rate, and incomes' policies are useful in taming business cycles and promoting growth.
(g) Economists differ with regard to the choice of a policy tool to tackle a particular economic ill.
(h) There is a consensus that productivity alone matters for the long run growth.
(i) Big government (Keynesian) at home, free trade and capital flows abroad (Smithian-Adam Smith) is the emerging new consensus for global economies.

Macroeconomics research has contributed immensely in all of its three areas, viz., measurement, stability and growth. The biggest contribution of macroeconomics in the 20th century is deemed to be in the field of the **measurement of economic variables**. Though the data is far from perfect, its coverage and accuracy levels have improved, time lag has reduced and accessibility has become remarkable. Efforts in this direction are still on and would never end, for the data is never perfect. It is said that there are three kinds of lies: lies, damn lies and data. The wealth of data and developments in macroeconomic theory greatly helps the people to understand economic events so far faced by the world and the events likely to occur in future. Given such understanding, households and business organisations are better prepared to plan and execute their consumption, saving, investment, production, export, import and balance sheet, etc. To understand the occurrence of business cycles, economists have advanced theories and tested them through the real-life data. Since no individual theory could account for all historical cycles of various characters, currently we have the **eclectic (heterodox) theory** for this purpose. Fiscal, monetary, trade and foreign exchange rate policies have been advanced and their relative roles in countering cycles have been well assessed. These developments help policy makers to formulate meaningful economic policies to stabilise the economy against impending business cycles. In the field of economic growth, it is now well known that growth can go on but it has to be achieved more through productivity enhancement than through increasing factor inputs. Roles of technology, globalisation, institutional infrastructure, macroeconomic stability and aggregate demand, among other factors, in productivity have been well established. It is because of the appreciation of these roles of economics that economists are currently playing a rather active role, both, in government and in the corporate world. It is heartening to note that even elections are currently fought through economic issues. The field is alive and responsive to economic events, and surely progress would continue in the future.

Economics was once labeled a '**dismal science**'. However, this must be judged through a recap of some interesting propositions put forth by this field of study:

- There is nothing like free lunch.
- Unemployment is bad as it results in 'GDP loss'; there are voluntary and natural unemployment.

- Every new child brings new hopes for the future but reduces the per capita income.
- Law of diminishing marginal returns operates; population growth was to outpace food supply which has not happened.
- Business cycles are facts of life; they are generally bad but have some good side effects.
- High inflation is bad; deflation is worse.
- Economic growth and price stability are desirable; to attain one you may have to sacrifice the other.
- Competition is good; it would destroy the capitalist world which still survives.
- Labour supply curve is backward bending.
- Workers take holidays during recessions; work longer during good times.
- Fruits of growth hardly percolate to the poorest of the poor.
- Demand and supply both play roles in output and price; productivity alone matters in the long run.
- Supply creates its own demand; demand creates its own supply.
- Fiscal, trade and current account deficits are not necessarily bad, though they ought to be sustainable.
- With the free movements in goods, services, capital, price, interest rate and exchange rate, there would be nothing legitimate to fear from inflation, fiscal, trade deficits/surpluses, positive/negative net foreign investment and debtor/creditor status.
- Two economists, three opinions; true only in policy prescriptions.
- There is a need for two-handed economist.
- Future is uncertain; accurate predictions are impossible.
- There is no government, even firm or bank, with no economist!

The above statements only prove that economics is interesting and useful rather than a dismal science. A through reading and understanding of this text would surely have convinced the readers of this fact.

KEYWORDS

Measurement; Bottom line;; Business cycles; Demand-Supply shocks; Animal spirit; Great Depression; Hyperinflation; Fiscal-Monetary policy; Eclectic/Heterodox theory of business cycles; Forecasts of economic events; Policy multipliers; Long and variable policy lags; Incompatible priorities; Political costs; Standard of living; Productive capacity; Mathematical model; Harrod-Domar model; Endogenous growth theory; Natural calamities; Human-made calamities; Climate, Significant/Controversial issues; Stability; Growth; Dismal science; No free lunch; Competition; Productivity; Fiscal-Trade-Current account deficit; Two-handed economist; Predictions, Demand, Supply.

Reference

1. Gupta G.S, "Economics, Economists and Economy: Facts, Fallacies and Feuds", Presidential Address, Gujarat Economic Association Conference (Bharuch, Gujarat, February 12-13, 2005).

Review Questions

1. Briefly contrast the four schools of thought, viz.,
   - Classical
   - Keynesian
   - New Classical
   - New Keynesian

   in terms of their contentions, with regard to the sources and cures of business cycles.
2. Identify the four most significant developments in macroeconomics and explain their roles both in the stability of the world economy (business cycles—causes and roles of stabilising policies in countering them) as well as its growth.
3. Given the present state of knowledge on the growth theory and growth experiences of the various countries (particularly, Japan, China, "Asian tigers" and Latin America), suggest some policy options to stimulate long-term growth prospects for the Indian economy.

Appendix

Comprehensive Case Studies

Macroeconomics deals with the macro economic variables, and their fluctuations and growth over time. For case studies, one could choose any one or more significant macroeconomic events that happened in the recent past in the world and analyse the same or/and select any one or more countries and analyse the movements over time in their macroeconomic indicators. Under this part of the text, we have included both types of topics for case studies. Thus, we have two case studies on significant macroeconomic events, namely

(a) The Great Recession 2007-09

(b) The Euro Area Crisis 2007-12

Also, there are country level cases on

(c) The Japan's Lost Two Decades and Continuing Struggle

(d) Commentary on the Economic Issues in Argentina

(e) Commentary on the Russia's Growing Clout

In addition, the Appendix includes the time series data on significant macroeconomic indicators for selected eight countries, for easy access to students/ readers, to comprehend and analyse those economies, problems and performances. The data must be supplemented with the data available in various chapters and from internet. An understanding of these through the fundamentals of macroeconomic theory and policy would enable the readers to appreciate the events, see what the policy-makers did to handle the problems, and what more or less could have been attempted to manage the situation in the best possible way. It is hoped that the Japan's detailed case would encourage students to study the other countries too similarly, using the data provided here, given elsewhere in this textbook and available on internet and other sources.

At this stage, it may be worthwhile to explain our choice of the eight countries and the list of macroeconomic indicators.

Select Countries, Macroeconomic Variables and Data

Select Countries Goldman Sachs has identified four countries that were expected to dominate the economic scene during the next decade and beyond. These are Brazil, Russia, India and China, jointly known as BRIC. A careful look at their sizes and recent past performances vis-à-vis those of the other large economies and the world would explain the choice (vide Table A-1):

Table A-1 Select Data for Select Countries

Country	*Measured GNP at Current Prices ($ billions)* 2011	*Population (millions)* 2011	*Land Area (thousand square km.)* 2011	*Growth Rate (%)* 2000-2011
Brazil	2108	197	8515	3.8
Russia	1522	143	17098 (1)	5.1
India	1766	1242 (2)	3287 (6)	7.8
China	6643 (2)	1344 (1)	9600 (4)	10.8
USA	15418 (1)	312 (3)	9832 (3)	1.6
Japan	5740 (3)	128	378	0.7
World	66354	6974	134269	2.7

Note: Numbers in parentheses give the rank in the world

A careful look at these demonstrates the role the BRIC countries are expected to play in the next decade and beyond. The USA and Japan's economies are important as they happen to be the number one and three, respectively in terms of their national incomes. Besides, each of these countries has experienced serious fluctuations in their crucial macroeconomic variables during the past two decades. For example, the 1990s was one of the best periods for the United States, as it invented the internet, attained a relatively good growth rate and it turned the fiscal deficit to fiscal surplus. However, the economy remained highly unstable during the first decade of the current millennium. During the decade it has faced two recessions in 2001 and 2007-09, and had a great period in between the two recessions. Lately, the country is recovering from the recession but is still struggling with low growth rate and twin deficits. As is dealt in detail below, the two decades of the 1990s and 2000s are considered as the lost decades for Japan. In the last decade or so, a number of countries have faced economic/financial crises, and studies on some of them would help understand the reasons behind such happenings and the policies adopted to cope and counter them. On this ground, Argentina and Thailand have been included for the purpose. Argentina, being among the most prosperous economies of Latin America, suffered a severe economic crisis in 2001-2002. The 1997-1998 financial crises began in Thailand and spread across Indonesia, Malaysia and South Korea. A group of countries in Europe, called the PIIGS (group of countries includes Portugal, Ireland, Italy, Greece and Spain) have faced serious financial difficulties during 2008-12, and two (viz. Greece and Spain), the most troubled of these five, are studied separately under the case, The Euro Area crisis.

Select Macroeconomic Variables and Data On each of the select countries and on some groups of them, the pertinent macroeconomic data are presented in Tables A-2 through A-9. The data include those on the three target variables, which every country is concerned with. These are growth rate, inflation rate and the rate of unemployment. Further, the tables include data on four macroeconomic prices, viz. interest rate, wage rate, exchange rate and share price, which have close bearings on the national goals. Also, included are data on two well-known imbalances, namely fiscal deficit and current account balance, each of which must be balanced over long run. Data on money supply, government expenditure, and foreign exchange reserves are included to assess the applications of stabilization policies. Lastly, the tables have data on nominal GDP and population to give a feel about the size of various countries. Incidentally, there are some blanks in these tables but they were inevitable due to data unavailability. In what follows, we present the various case studies in the order outlined above.

Table A-2 Argentina (Population in 2011: 40.8 million)

Year	*Growth rate (GDP)*	*Infln rate (CPI)*	*Unem rate**	*Interest rate (Lend)*	*Wage rate*	*Share Price*	*Forex rate**	*Forex Res.#*	*Curr. A/c bal*	*Broad Money Supply*	*Govt Con. exp*	*Fiscal deficit*	*GDP at current prices*
	%	%	%	%	Index No.	Index No.	Peso per $	$ bill.	$ bill.	Peso bill.	Peso bill.	Peso Bill.	Peso bill.
1990	–1.8	2315	9.2	NA	26.1	NA	0.49	4.6	4.6	7.9	NA	0.2	69
1991	10.5	172	6.3	NA	65.0	26.6	0.95	6.0	–0.6	19.1	NA	1.0	181
1995	–2.8	3.4	16.0	17.9	100.0	28.3	.9998	14.3	–5.1	52.0	34.4	1.4	258
1996	5.4	0.2	16.6	10.5	100.7	37.5	.9997	18.1	–6.8	61.8	34.0	5.2	272
2000	–0.8	4.2	14.7	11.1	NA	33.7	.9995	25.1	–9.0	90.5	39.2	6.8	284
2001	–4.4	–1.1	18.1	27.7	NA	24.5	.9995	14.5	–3.3	73.1	38.0	8.7	269
2002	–10.9	25.9	17.5	51.7	NA	26.8	3.063	10.5	8.7	83.9	38.2	3.5	313
2003	8.8	13.4	16.8	19.2	NA	49.0	2.901	14.2	8.0	116.8	43.0	0.4	376
2004	9.0	4.4	13.6	6.8	NA	74.0	2.923	18.9	3.3	147.5	49.8	9.4	448
2005	9.2	9.6	11.6	6.2	NA	100.0	2.904	27.2	5.3	177.2	63.4	NA	532
2006	8.5	10.9	10.2	8.6	NA	117.2	3.054	30.9	7.8	220.6	81.2	NA	654
2007	8.7	8.8	8.5	11.1	NA	144.5	3.096	44.7	7.4	267.8	105.0	NA	812
2008	7.0	8.6	7.9	19.5	NA	118.5	3.144	44.9	6.8	305.4	139.3	NA	1038
2009	0.7	6.3	8.7	15.7	NA	109.0	3.710	46.1	8.3	352.5	174.0	NA	1145
2010	9.2	10.8	7.8	10.6	NA	170.5	3.896	49.7	1.4	485.2	215.3	NA	1443
2011	8.9	9.5	7.5	14.1	NA	208.1	4.110	43.2	–1.6	605.1	279.0	NA	1842
2012	1.9	10.0	7.2	14.1	NA	167.0	4.537	39.9	0.5	796.4	359.6	NA	2164
Lat-est@	5.5	NA	6.4	NA	NA	NA	7.95	NA	–3.5	NA	NA	2.4 %	NA

Source: International Financial Statistics Yearbook, IMF, 2013; Notes: * Period averages, # End of period, – not available @ *Economist*, March 20, 2014

Table A-3 Brazil

(Population in 2011: 197 million)

Year	Growth rate (GDP)	Infln rate (CPI)	Unem rate*	Interst rate (Lend)	Wage rate	Share price	Forex rate*	Forex Res.#	Curr. A/c bal	Broad Money supply	Govt Con Exp	Fiscal deficit	GDP at current prices
	%	%	%	%	Index No.	Index No.	Reais per $	$ bill.	$ bill.	Reais bill.	Reai bill.	Reais bill.	Reais bill.
1990	–4.3	2948	3.7	NA	NA	NA	0.248	7.4	–3.8	NA	2	0.7	NA
1991	1.3	NA	NA	NA	NA	NA	1.419	8.0	–1.5	NA	11	0.3	NA
1995	4.2	65.9	6.1	NA	NA	14.0	0.918	49.7	–18.1	168	127	NA	646
1996	2.7	15.8	7.0	NA	NA	21.2	1.005	58.3	–23.2	188	144	NA	779
2000	4.4	7.0	9.2	56.8	NA	100.0	1.830	32.5	–24.2	274	210	NA	1101
2001	1.3	6.8	10.1	57.6	NA	51.0	2.350	35.6	23.2	322	258	NA	1302
2002	2.7	8.5	11.7	62.9	NA	41.7	2.920	37.2	–7.6	398	304	NA	1478
2003	1.2	14.7	12.3	67.1	NA	52.3	3.078	48.8	4.2	413	330	NA	1670
2004	5.7	6.6	11.5	54.9	NA	81.0	2.925	52.5	11.7	493	373	NA	1941
2005	3.2	6.9	9.8	55.4	NA	100	2.434	53.2	14.0	582	428	NA	2147
2006	4.0	4.2	10.0	50.8	NA	138.3	2.175	85.1	13.6	662	475	NA	2369
2007	6.1	3.6	9.3	43.7	NA	193.2	1.947	179.4	1.6	781	539	NA	2661
2008	5.2	5.7	7.9	47.3	NA	200.7	1.834	192.8	–28.2	1073	612	NA	3032
2009	–0.3	4.9	8.1	44.7	NA	191.6	1.999	231.9	–24.3	1165	687	NA	3239
2010	7.5	5.0	6.7	40.0	NA	244.2	1.759	280.6	–47.3	1362	797	NA	3770
2011	2.7	6.6	6.0	43.9	NA	223.3	1.673	343.4	–52.5	1617	857	NA	4143
2012	NA	5.4	5.5	36.6	NA	216.1	1.953	362.1	–54.2	1765	945	NA	4403
Lat-est@	1.9	5.7	4.8	13.2	NA	NA	2.33	NA	–81.6	NA	NA	4.0%	NA

Source: International Financial Statistics Yearbook, IMF, 2006. Notes: * Period averages, # End of period @ *Economist*, March 20, 2014

Table A-4 China (Population in 2011: 1344 million)

Year	*Growth rate (GDP)*	*Inflat rate (CPI)*	*Unem rate**	*Interst rate (Lend)*	*Wage rate*	*Share Price*	*Forex rate**	*Forex Res.#*	*Curr. A/c balan*	*Broad Money supply*	*Govt Con. Exp.*	*Fiscal deficit*	*GDP at current prices*
	%	%	%	%	Index No.	Index No.	Yuan per $	$ bill.	$ bill.	Yuan bill.	Yua bill.	Yuan bill.	Yuan bill.
1990	3.8	3.1	2.5	9.4	NA	NA	4.78	30	12.0	1468	225	15	1832
1991	9.2	3.5	2.3	8.6	NA	NA	5.32	44	13.3	1860	283	24	2128
1995	8.9	16.9	2.9	12.1	NA	NA	8.35	74	1.6	6074	699	91	5851
1996	9.8	8.3	3.0	10.1	NA	NA	8.31	105	7.2	7610	785	87	6833
2000	7.9	0.3	3.1	5.9	NA	NA	8.28	166	20.5	13596	1171	277	8934
2001	8.3	0.7	3.6	5.9	NA	169.9	8.28	212	17.4	15830	1750	438	10966
2002	9.1	–0.8	3.8	5.3	NA	136.6	8.28	286	35.4	18500	1876	310	12033
2003	10.0	1.2	4.2	5.3	NA	128.5	8.28	403	45.9	22122	2004	292	13582
2004	10.1	3.9	4.3	5.6	NA	128.4	8.28	610	68.7	25321	2233	NA	15988
2005	11.3	1.8	4.2	5.6	NA	100	8.19	819	132.4	29876	2640	204	18493
2006	12.7	1.5	4.2	6.1	NA	141.4	7.97	1066	231.8	34558	3053	161	21631
2007	14.2	4.8	4.1	7.5	NA	369.1	7.61	1528	353.2	40340	3590	156	26581
2008	9.6	5.9	4.1	5.3	NA	266.8	6.95	1946	420.6	47517	4175	NA	31405
2009	9.2	–0.7	4.3	5.3	NA	239.7	6.83	2399	243.3	60623	4569	NA	34090
2010	10.3	3.3	4.1	5.8	NA	247.9	6.77	2847	237.8	72585	5336	NA	40151
2011	9.4	5.4	4.1	6.6	NA	233.7	6.46	3181	136.1	85159	6193	NA	47156
2012	7.8	2.2	4.1	6.0	NA	194.3	6.31	3312	193.1	97415	NA	NA	51932
Latest@	7.7	2.0	4.1	4.19	NA	NA	6.20	NA	188.6	NA	NA	1.9%	NA

Source: International Financial Statistics Yearbook, IMF, 2006. Notes: * Period averages, # End of period, – not available @ *Economist*, March 20, 2014

Table A-5 India

(Population in 2011: 1242 million)

*Year ***	*Growth rate (GDP)*	*Inflat rate (CPI)*	*Unem rate**	*Interst rate (Lending)*	*Wage rate*	*Share Price*	*Forex rate**	*Forex Res.#*	*Curr. A/c balan*	*Broad Money Supply#*	*Govt Con. Exp.*	*Fiscal deficit*	*GDP at current prices*
	%	%	%	%	Index No.	Index No.	₹ per $	$ bill.	$ bill.	₹ bill.	₹ bill.	₹ bill.	₹ bill.
1990	5.9	9.0	NA	16.5	NA	15	17.5	1.5	–7.0	2430	660	435	5110
1991	/0.9	13.9	NA	17.9	NA	23	22.7	3.6	–4.3	2875	743	358	5890
1995	7.4	10.2	NA	15.5	NA	53	32.4	17	–5.6	5250	1288	599	10736
1996	7.8	9.0	NA	16.0	NA	53	35.4	20	–6.0	6233	1457	669	12436
2000	4.3	4.0	NA	12.3	NA	72	44.9	37	–3.2	10693	2644	1087	19302
2001	5.5	3.7	NA	12.1	NA	47	32.4	46	–4.6	13368	2912	1007	21678
2002	4.0	4.4	NA	11.9	NA	44	45.9	68	1.4	15609	3016	1162	23382
2003	8.1	3.8	NA	11.5	NA	52	67.7	99	7.1	17643	3248	958	26222
2004	7.0	3.8	NA	10.9	NA	75	41.3	127	6.9	20595	3545	1038	29715
2005	9.5	4.2	NA	10.8	NA	100	43.1	132	–10.3	23808	4016	1174	33905
2006	9.6	6.1	NA	11.2	NA	155	44.9	171	–9.3	30163	4435	963	39533
2007	9.3	6.4	NA	13.0	NA	216	47.2	267	–8.1	36988	5130	1281	45821
2008	6.7	8.4	NA	13.3	NA	208	48.6	247	–31.0	44440	6153	3217	53036
2009	8.6	10.9	NA	12.2	NA	194	46.6	265	–26.2	52454	7712	4257	61089
2010	9.3	12.0	NA	8.3	NA	252	45.3	275	–52.3	62253	8910	3792	72670
2011	6.2	8.9	NA	10.2	NA	246	44.1	271	–60.0	72222	10427	5245	83535
2012	5.0	9.3	NA	10.6	NA	240	46.0	271	NA	80273	11868	5098	94610
Latest@	4.7	8.1	9.9	8.78	NA	NA	61.0	NA	–49.2	NA	NA	4.9 %	NA

Source: International Financial Statistics Yearbook, IMF, 2013. Notes: * Period average; # end of period

** Year beginning April 1. – not available, @ *Economist*, March 20, 2014

Table A-6 Japan

(Population in 20011: 128 million)

Year	*Growth rate (GDP)*	*Inflat rate (CPI)*	*Unem rate**	*Interst rate (Lend)*	*Wage rate*	*Share Price*	*Forex rate**	*Forex Res.#*	*Curr. A/c balan*	*Broad Money supply*	*Govt Con. Exp.*	*Fiscal deficit*	*GDP at current prices*
	%	%	%	%	Index No.	Index No.	Yen per $	$ bill.	$ bill.	Yen trill.	Yen trill.	Yen trill.	Yen trill.
1990	5.3	3.1	2.1	7.0	100.9	170.7	145	79	44	495	59	6.8	442
1991	3.1	3.3	2.1	7.5	101.9	145,1	135	72	68	508	62	–7.8	469
1995	1.4	–0.1	3.2	3.5	99.8	108.5	94	172	111	549	75	NA	493
1996	2.2	0.1	3.4	2.7	101.6	126.8	109	207	66	561	77	NA	503
2000	2.8	–0.7	4.7	2.1	103.4	122.0	108	347	120	630	85	NA	501
2001	0.4	–0.8	5.0	2.0	101.1	94.1	122	395	88	647	90	NA	506
2002	0.3	–0.9	5.4	1.9	99.4	77.2	125	461	112	668	91	NA	499
2003	1.7	–0.2	5.3	1.8	99.4	72.3	116	663	136	682	91	NA	499
2004	2.4	0	4.7	1.8	99.3	88.1	108	834	172	689	92		504
2005	1.3	–0.3	4.4	1.7	100	100	110	834	166	701	92	4.1	504
2006	1.7	0.2	4.1	1.7	100.6	128.2	116	880	171	708	92	0.9	507
2007	2.2	0.1	3.8	1.9	100.6	131.1	118	953	212	720	93	2.4	513
2008	–1.1	1.4	4.0	1.9	99.8	93.5	103	1009	159	735	93	2.9	501
2009	–5.5	–1.3	5.1	1.7	97.1	68.4	94	1022	147	754	94	7.6	471
2010	4.7	–0.7	5.1	1.6	97.7	69.8	88	1061	204	775	95	6.7	482
2011	–0.5	–0.3	4.6	1.5	97.5	64.8	80	1258	119	797	96	8.3	471
2012	2.0	0	4.4	1.4	97.7	60.6	80	1227	61	817	98	NA	476
Latest@	2.6	1.4	3.7	0.61	NA	NA	102	NA	23	NA	NA	8.1%	NA

Source: International Financial Statistics Yearbook, IMF, 2006. Notes: * Period averages, # End of period, @ *Economist*, March 20, 2014

Table A-7 Russian Federation

(Population in 2011: 143 million)

Year	*Growth rate (GDP)*	*Inflat rate (CPI)*	*Unem rate**	*Interst rate (Lend)*	*Wage rate*	*Share Price*	*Forex rate**	*Forex Res.#*	*Curr. A/c balan*	*Broad Money supply*	*Govt Con. Exp.*	*Fiscal deficit*	*GDP at current prices*
	%	%	%	%	Index No.	Index No.	Ruble per $	$ bill.	$ bill.	Rubles bill.	Rubles bill.	Rubles bill.	Rubles bill.
1990	–3.0	NA	NA	NA	NA	NA	NA	NA	NA	NA	NA	NA	NA
1991	–5.1	NA	0.1	NA	NA	NA	NA	NA	NA	NA	NA	NA	NA
1995	–4.1	198.5	8.9	320.3	NA	NA	4.56	14.2	7.0	276	273	70	NA
1996	–3.6	47.6	9.9	146.8	NA	NA	5.12	11.3	10.8	357	391	148	NA
2000	10.0	20.8	10.6	24.4	NA	NA	28.13	24.3	46.8	1569	1102	–174	NA
2001	5.1	21.5	9.1	17.9	NA	26.5	29.17	32.5	33.9	2138	1470	–275	8984
2002	4.7	15.8	8.0	15.7	NA	42.2	31.35	44.1	29.1	2860	1911	–179	10780
2003	7.9	13.7	8.3	13.0	NA	59.4	30.69	73.2	35.4	3961	2331	–314	13282
2004	7.2	10.9	8.1	11.4	NA	80.1	28.81	120.8	58.6	5299	2890	–826	17123
2005	6.4	12.7	7.6	10.7	NA	100	28.28	175.9	84.4	7223	3646	–1623	21736
2006	8.2	9.7	7.2	10.4	NA	192.1	27.19	295.6	92.3	10127	4680	NA	26934
2007	8.5	9.0	6.1	10.0	NA	241.1	25.58	466.8	71.3	14236	5751	NA	32869
2008	5.2	14.1	6.2	12.2	NA	197.7	24.85	411.7	103.9	16277	7360	NA	41882
2009	–7.8	11.7	8.4	15.3	NA	142.4	31.74	416.6	50.4	19096	8067	NA	39502
2010	4.3	6.9	7.5	10.8	NA	198.4	30.37	443.6	67.5	23791	8671	NA	46727
2011	4.3	8.4	6.6	8.5	NA	222.5	29.38	453.9	97.2	28755	10041	NA	56424
2012	NA	5.1	5.5	9.1	NA	204.0	30.84	486.6	74.8	32226	11665	NA	63304
Latest@	1.2	6.2	5.6	9.19	NA	NA	35.9	NA	33.0	NA	NA	0.5%	NA

Source: International Financial Statistics Yearbook, IMF, 2006. Notes: * Period averages, # End of period, @ *Economist*, March 20, 2014

Table A-8 Thailand

(Population in 2011: 70 million)

Year	*Growth rate (GDP)*	*Inflat rate (CPI)*	*Unem rate**	*Interst rate (Lend)*	*Wage rate*	*Share Price*	*Forex rate**	*Forex Res.#*	*Curr. A/c balan*	*Broad Money supply*	*Govt Con. Exp.*	*Fiscal deficit*	*GDP at current prices*
	%	%	%	%	Index No.	Index No.	Baht per $	$ bill.	$ bill.	Baht bill.	Baht bill.	Baht bill.	Baht bill.
1990	1.2	6.0	2.2	14.4	NA	NA	25.6	13	–7.3	1529	205	–107	2183
1991	8.6	5.7	2.7	15.4	NA	NA	25.5	18	–7.6	1832	231	–100	2507
1995	9.6	5.8	1.1	13.3	NA	NA	24.9	35	–13.6	3557	414	–135	4186
1996	5.9	5.8	1.1	13.3	NA	NA	25.3	37	–14.7	3935	470	–43	4611
2000	4.7	1.6	2.4	7.8	NA	50	40.1	32	9.3	5638	558	108	4923
2001	2.2	1.6	3.3	7.3	NA	44	44.4	32	6.2	6562	581	123	5134
2002	5.3	0.7	2.4	6.9	NA	53	43.0	38	7.0	6647	604	77	5451
2003	7.0	1.8	2.2	5.9	NA	70	41.5	41	8.0	7062	635	–24	5929
2004	6.2	2.8	2.1	5.5	NA	96	40.2	49	6.9	7471	721	NA	6504
2005	4.5	4.5	1.9	5.8	NA	100	40.2	51	-7.6	7927	839	NA	7103
2006	5.6	4.6	1.6	7.4	NA	104	37.9	65	2.3	8573	926	NA	7850
2007	4.9	2.3	1.4	7.1	NA	111	34.5	85	15.7	9110	1039	NA	8530
2008	2.5	5.4	1.4	7.0	NA	100	33.3	109	2.2	9946	1128	NA	9076
2009	–2.3	-0.9	1.5	6.0	NA	84	34.3	135	21.9	10618	1214	NA	9042
2010	7.8	3.3	1.0	5.9	NA	123	31.7	168	9.9	11778	1310	NA	10105
2011	0.1	3.8	0.7	6.9	NA	149	30.5	167	5.9	13561	1400	NA	10539
2012	6.5	3.0	0.7	7.1	NA	174	31.1	173	2.8	14967	1544	NA	11375
Latest@	0.4	2.0	0.6	3.63	NA	NA	32.1	NA	–2.8	NA	NA	2.6%	NA

Source: *International Financial Statistics Yearbook*, IMF, 2006. Notes: * Period averages, # End of period, @ *Economist*, March 20, 2014

Table A-9 United States of America

(Population in 2011: 312 million)

Year	Growth rate (GDP)	Inflat rate (CPI)	Unem rate*	Interst rate (Lend)	Wage rate	Share Price	Forex rate*	Forex Res.#	Curr. A/c balan	Broad Money supply	Govt Con. Exp.	Fiscal deficit	GDP at current prices
	%	%	%	%	Index No.	Index No.	$ per Euro	$ bill.	$ bill.	US $ bill.	US $ bill.	US $ bill.	US $ bill.
1990	1.9	5.4	5.6	10.0	65.1	28.3	1.27	72.3	–79	3767	1018	236	5803
1991	–0.2	4.2	6.8	8.5	67.2	32.3	1.24	66.7	3.7	3890	1062	266	5986
1995	2.5	2.8	5.6	8.83	74.5	46.5	1.31	74.8	–114	4243	1137	146	7400
1996	3.8	2.9	5.4	8.27	76.9	57.4	1.27	64.0	–125	4502	1171	111	7817
2000	3.7	3.4	4.0	9.23	86.4	126.7	0.92	56.6	–415	6110	1417	–255	9817
2001	1.1	2.8	4.7	6.92	89.2	96.6	0.90	52.6	–389	7581	1524	–92	10286
2002	1.8	1.6	5.8	4.68	92.4	87.5	0.94	68.0	–472	7918	1640	231	10642
2003	2.5	2.3	6.0	4.12	95.1	85.3	1.13	74.9	–528	8267	1757	396	11142
2004	3.5	2.7	5.5	4.34	97.5	97.8	1.24	75.9	–665	8739	1860	400	11853
2005	3.1	3.4	5.1	6.19	100	100	1.25	54.1	–746	9448	1978	267	12623
2006	2.7	3.2	4.6	7.96	101.5	108.2	1.26	54.9	–801	10299	2093	138	13377
2007	1.9	2.9	4.6	8.05	104.3	124.9	1.37	59.5	–710	11505	2218	230	14029
2008	–0.3	3.8	5.8	5.09	107.2	106.7	1.47	66.6	–677	12444	2381	756	14292
2009	–3.1	-0.4	9.3	3.25	110.2	84.2	1.39	119.7	–382	13025	2460	1478	13974
2010	–2.4	1.6	9.6	3.25	112.4	101.1	1.33	121.4	–442	12667	2552	1467	14499
2011	1.8	3.2	9.0	3.25	114.4	113.5	1.39	136.9	–466	13497	2580	1403	15076
2012	2.2	2.1	8.1	3.25	115.3	122.9	1.29	139.1	–475	14149	2591	1238	15685
Latest@	2.5	1.1	6.7	2.77	NA	NA	NA		–379	NA	NA	2.9%	NA

Source: International Financial Statistics Yearbook, IMF, 2006. Notes: * Period averages, # End of period, @ *Economist*, March 20, 2014

Case A1: The Great Recession: 2007-09

The growing prosperity of the global economy which hit its recent peak in 2006, with a growth rate of 5.1 per cent, slowed a bit in 2007, fell significantly in 2008, turned negative in 2009, and has resumed its momentum thereafter. Since this happens to be the serious most recession post the Great Depression of 1929-33 and the first fall in the world's real GDP in over 40 years, the period 2007-09 has been described as the GREAT RECESSION, also termed as GLOBAL RECESSION. The most striking fall out of this recession happens to be the collapse of the Lehman Brothers, the fourth largest US investment bank, on September 15, 2008. The case first briefly analyses the relevant macroeconomic data on the meaningfully selected eight countries and the world, and then proceeds on the factors responsible for the crisis, the policy interventions implemented in the world around, and the lessons learnt to appreciate the business cycles and stabilization policy. Some questions are put at the end for students to analyse and learn.

Macroeconomic Data The relevant data of the relevant select eight countries and the world for four years are given in Table A-10. The selected relevant macroeconomic indicators consists of three ultimate goal variables (growth rate, inflation rate and unemployment rate), two monetary policy related magnitudes (interest rate and growth rate of money supply) and two fiscal policy related indicators (fiscal imbalance as per cent to GDP and public debt as per cent to GDP) and one the most significant determinant of economic growth (investment rate). The eight select countries include five (USA, UK, Germany, Japan and Russia) of the G-7 and 4 from the BRICS group (Brazil, Russia, India and China), Russia being the common in the two groups. Four years data is included so that one can compare the normal year data with the crisis year data. A careful look at the data indicate that the growth rate had suffered in all the select countries during 2008 and in all but Germany in 2009, and that the recovery has been slow particularly with regard to unemployment. Further, the data suggest that the effect of the recession on inflation was little as it continued to remain fairly stable even during the bad time. As expected, during the recession period, in general, the interest rate and investment rate fell, while the money supply, fiscal deficit as per cent of GDP and government debt as per cent of GDP increased.

Factors causing Great Recession The recession began in USA and soon spread to Europe and other parts of the globe. Accordingly, the reasons for recession must begin with issues in USA. Several hypotheses have been advanced. The important ones are as follows:

(a) Great Moderation during 1986-2006: The two decades preceding the Great Recession happened to be, in general, the period of prosperity and economic stability in most parts of the world, barring the mild recession in 2001 and the lost two decades of Japan. In particular, the trade-off between inflation and unemployment, which was observed in the 1960s and early 1980s, was not visible anymore and the Central Banks had gained the credibility for controlling inflation, and to the extent that economists started believing in "inflation is dead". This lead to complacency both among the public (households and firms) and the policy-makers and enhanced their appetite to assume risk.

(b) Sub-Prime Mortgages and the Collapse of the Real Estate Market: Net inflows of capital in USA from high saving countries like China and the desire to tame the recession of 2001, led the Federal Bank not only to reduce the interest rate to a very low level but also to leave it at that level for several years in a row. Further due to increased flow of capital from Asia, and the improved appetite for assuming high risk, banks became soft and loaned money for housing on meagre down payments to people whose credit worthiness was highly doubtful. This got further boost as housing price was booming, so much so that owning a house became a business even to people who could not afford one. The glut of housing led to the collapse of the real estate market in 2006, which was followed through default in mortgages, foreclosures and accumulation of non-performing assets by banks. Thus, low interest rate, high leverage on mortgage loans, housing glut and crash in real estate market led to sick banks. The latter caused reduction in financial services, including loans for business, investment suffered, production was cut and workers lost jobs.

(c) Financial Innovations (Securitization): To get out the crisis, experts came out with some new ideas like bundling toxic mortgages into some sort of a security and then raising funds through selling that security, called securitization. Thus, risky mortgages were passed out to big banks. The latter put a large number of such toxic mortgages into different bundles, as one does to have a diversified portfolio, having low risk. However, since the real estate market fell throughout the US, the prices of various mortgages were highly correlated, and the bundles did not prove really diversified portfolios. The pooled mortgages were used to back securities, called Collateralised Debt Obligations (CDOs). The CDOs were sliced into tranches by degree of exposure to default. The banks managed to get high credit ratings for the tranches from the credit rating agencies, like Standard & Poor and Moody's, and thus could sell them to investors, as interest rate continued to remain low. Thus, through securitisation, sub-mortgaged loans, promising income stream over a long period, were transferred into a lump sums today. Investment banks borrowed short term at low interest rate and invested in long dated CDOs. As the real estate market remained subdued, mortgaged backed CDOs value got eroded and investment banks had no choice but to declare significant losses. This is how the Lehman Brothers which collapsed and some others (like American Insurance Group) who could retain their solvency became the victim of securitization.

(d) Labour Market Distortions: The distortions in financial market led to loss of financial services which impacted the real economy. As asset (real estate and stocks) prices fell, people's wealth was reduced and so the aggregate demand fell. Production cut followed and good number of workers lost jobs and unemployment soared. However, workers did not compete; opted for social security, and thus wages did not fall and thereby the threat of deflation could be avoided.

(e) Economic Policy: The too easy monetary policy of keeping the interest rate low for several years in a row is considered to be equally responsible for the Great Recession. It is instructive to note that, in order to tame the 2001 recession, the US Federal Reserve Bank lowered its policy rate, viz. federal fund rate,

Table A-10 Macroeconomic Data

(per centages)

Country and Year	*Growth rate*	*Inflation rate (CPI)*	*Unemployment rate*	*Increase in Broad Money**	*Interest rate (lending)*	*Fiscal balance as % of GDP*	*Central Govt debt as % of GDP*	*Investment to GDP ratio*
USA								
2007	1.9	2.9	4.6	11.7	8.05	–2.2	45.1	19.6
2008	–0.3	3.8	5.8	8.2	5.09	–5.2	53.6	18.1
2009	–3.1	–0.4	9.3	4.7	3.25	–10.2	65.2	14.7
2010	2.4	1.6	9.6	–2.8	3.25	–10.0	74.1	15.5
Germany								
2007	3.4	2.3	8.7	11.4	5.96	–0.3	40.8	19.3
2008	0.8	2.6	7.5	7.4	5.97	–0.4	43.1	19.2
2009	5.1	0.3	7.8	–0.2	4.96	–2.2	47.6	16.4
2010	4.0	1.1	7.1	1.1	3.77	–3.2	55.6	17.4
Japan								
2007	2.2	0.1	3.8	0.6	1.88	–2.4	144.1	22.9
2008	–1.1	1.4	4.0	0.7	1.91	–2.9	153.1	23.0
2009	–5.5	–1.3	5.1	2.1	1.72	–7.6	166.8	19.7
2010	4.7	–0.7	5.1	2.0	1.60	–6.7	174.8	19.8
India								
2007	9.3	6.4	NA	22.3	13.02	–0.5	56.5	37.0
2008	6.7	8.4		20.5	13.31	–4.9	56.1	34.2
2009	8.6	10.9		18.0	12.19	–5.4	54.3	34.5
2010	9.3	12.0		17.8	8.33	–3.6	50.0	34.9

contd.

China								
2007	14.2	4.8	4.1	16.7	7.47	NA	NA	41.4
2008	9.6	5.9	4.1	17.8	5.31			44.0
2009	9.2	–0.7	4.3	28.4	5.31			48.2
2010	10.3	3.3	4.1	18.9	5.81			48.2
Brazil								
2007	6.1	2.,3	9.3	18.7	50.81	–1.9	57.4	18.3
2008	5.2	6.4	7.9	17.8	43.72	–1.2	56.6	20.7
2009	–0.3	–1.1	8.1	16.3	47.25	–3.5	60.0	17.8
2010	7.5	5.6	6.7	15.8	44.65	–1.7	52.2	20.2
Russia								
2007	8.5	9.0	6.1	40.6	10.03	6.2	7.2	21.2
2008	5.2	14.1	6.2	14.3	12.23	5.6	6.5	22.0
2009	–7.8	11.7	8.4	17.3	15.31	–4.2	8.7	21.6
2010	4.3	6.9	7.5	24.6	10.82	–1.9	9.1	21.4
U.K.								
2007	3.6	2.3	5.4	15.7	5.52	–2.7	46.4	18.3
2008	–1.0	3.6	5.7	17.8	4.63	–4.6	56.5	17.1
2009	–4.0	2.2	7.6	–0.1	0.63	–10.9	72.2	14.1
2010	1.8	3.3	7.9	4.0	0.50	–10.0	85.5	15.1
World								
2007	5.0	3.8	NA	NA	NA	NA	NA	NA
2008	2.3	5.8						
2009	–1.3	2.3						
2010	4.5	3.4						

Sources: (a) IMF: *International Financial Statistics*, 2013, (b) www.worldbank.org/indicator/all

- Data on increase in broad money is for Europe instead of Germany
- NA: Not available/applicable

from 6.6 per cent in May 2000 in 11 instalments to a low of 1.75 per cent in Dec 2001, followed by further reduction to 1.24 per cent in Nov 2002 and finally to 1.00 per cent in May 2003. Thereafter the rate was increased bit by bit to reach to 5.25 per cent by June 2006, and after which the reduction trend restarted and the federal fund rate came down to 0.25 per cent in Dec 2008. Since Jan 2009 the rate remained within the range 0–0.25 per cent. In addition, banking regulations were inadequate as the capital adequacy factor was altogether missing while banks were advancing mortgage based loans. Even the credit rating agencies failed to check the malady.

It is argued that the US government initiatives such as the 2008 tax rebate, President Bush's warning of a possible Great Depression around the Lehman Brothers bankruptcy, the Troubled Asset Relief Program (TARP), the American Recovery and Reinvestment Act, Cash for Clunkers and US Treasury mortgage modification programs aggravated early weakness in the economy and led to great recession. The public criticised ("too big to fall") the governments' for not bailing out the Lehman but did not quite appreciate when the bailout was extended to AIG (American International Group) and Bear Stearns, etc. and Fortis in Europe. It seems the governments' communications regarding the economic strength and policy increased public uncertainty, causing people to panic, spent less and save more for uncertain future, which aggravated the recession. Such a public reaction became strong as the symptoms of this recession appeared similar to those of the Great Depression. Like this one, the Great Depression was initiated by the busting of the asset (stocks) price, bank failures, wealth erosion, fall in aggregate demand, cuts in production, increase in unemployment, and so on. The only major difference was in terms of the fall in wage rate and deflation, which did not happen during the Great Recession.

(f) Globalisation: Over time, globalisation has increased and accordingly there is **contagious** (also called **coupling) effect**. Globalisation links all countries through trade, investment and even migration. This makes nations interdependent. Further, the USA happens to account for over 20 per cent of the world GDP and thus recession in USA quickly spread to the rest of the world. Europe was the immediate and most seriously affected region. This has given rise to the Euro Area (PIGGS) Crisis, which is described in another case in the Text. Even large and emerging nations, like China and India, have been adversely affected by the sub-mortgage crisis of USA as reflected in their falling growth rates, etc.

All the above factors, and possibly others, are jointly responsible for the Great Recession.

Policy Interventions to Counter Great Recession Though the US internal policy to cope with great recession has been criticised, its leadership role in coordinating with the rest of the world has received acclamation. The then US president, George Bush, Jr. constituted a group of 20 countries (called G-20), which includes the large, developed and emerging nations to study the crisis, debate and arrive at a coordinated approach to handle the situation as meticulously as possible. The first meeting of the G-20 was held in Washington, DC in Nov 2008, second in London in April 2009, third in Pittsburgh in September 2009, fourth in Singapore in 2012, and the last in Sydney in February 2014. Through these meetings and mutual trust, the group, instead of following the policy of "**beggar thy neighbour**", pledged to fight all forms of protectionism and to maintain trade and foreign investments. Also, they committed to maintain the supply of credit by providing more liquidity and recapitalising the banks, and to implement rapidly the stimulus plans. In addition, they decided to maintain low interest rate as long as necessary and to try to strengthen the International Monetary Fund. With such broad commitments, the G-20 launched simultaneously the biggest peacetime Keynesian stimulating fiscal and monetary policies, and communicating those well to all under the globe. It is estimated that a stimulus package worth an average of 2 per cent of GDP in 2009 and another package worth 1.6 per cent of GDP in 2010 was implemented by the G-20 (vide *The Economist*, Sept. 2009, Page 80) to neutralise the crisis.

The data in Table A-10 on interest rate and money supply growth rate reflect the monetary stimulus and those on fiscal imbalance and public debt as proportions to GDP those of fiscal stimulus undertaken by the select eight countries. These efforts have tried to avoid the earlier mistakes of inappropriate and poorly communicated policy, making the policy credible and effective. Accordingly, the real interest rates have been kept low, fiscal deficits have been allowed to widen; trades and exchange rates have been left essentially to the market forces, and stringent regulations on banks' capital requirements have been implemented. In addition, the international institutions, like the World Bank, IMF and WTO, have extended the required assistance to tame the Great Recession. It is these policies, which have distinguished this recession from the Great Depression of the 1930s, and salvaged the world from the second Great Depression.

Even good policies have adverse side effects. The stimulus in monetary policy brought down the short-term interest rate close to zero, which rendered the monetary policy ineffective. To overcome this **liquidity trap** handicap, the Japan's Central Bank, Federal Reserve Bank of USA, the Bank of Japan, the Bank of England and European Central Bank discovered and applied some unconventional tool of monetary policy. Under this, they implemented **Quantitative Easing** (QE) in several installments, wherein they purchased bonds (mortgage backed securities, long term government bonds and other private assets) sometimes in well announced lump sums and other times through prior announced every month and printed currency against those purchases. For example, in November 2008, the Federal Reserve Bank initiated the purchases of $600 billion in mortgage securities. When the economy showed signs of recovery, the purchases were halted for some time and resumed again when needed. The Fed set targets for such securities and purchased them in monthly installments. In the first round of QE, it purchased $30 billion worth of these assets every month. In the second round, $600 billion worth of such bonds were purchased during Nov 2010 through June 2011. On Sept. 13, 2012, the third round was launched under which Fed announced an open-ended purchase of $ 40 billion per month. Subsequently, on December 12, 2012, the Fed announced an increase in the amount of open-ended purchases from $40 to $85 per month. The tapering of QE was announced on June 19, 2013, and by the end of March 2014, the QE have come down to $65/month. According to the Fed announcement, the QE programme could be wrapped up by mid 2014. The Bank of England applied QE beginning in 2009 with purchases of around 165 billion pounds and continued with this tool each year since then taking the total purchases to 375 billion pounds by July 2012. The European Central Bank purchased corporate debt worth about 60 billion in May 2009. The Bank of Japan has been using this tool to stimulate its economy since 2001.

Through the QE measure, the Central Banks enhanced liquidity and lowered the interest rate to encourage banks to advance more credit for durable consumption spending and investments so as to boost aggregate demand and thereby to increase production, employment and economic growth. Also, a good part of the money so created moved out of the country to Europe and some emerging nations, including India, which benefitted and progressed. The recently launched easing of the QE is tending to reverse the capital flows in favour of USA and causing exchange rate instability in affected countries including India. Indian rupee depreciated to its lowest ever level of ₹68.83 per US dollar on August 28, 2013, which has since recovered to ₹59.89/$ by March 28, 2014. Incidentally note that though both the QE and monetisation leads to increase in money supply, the two are different. While QE is through prior announced targets, is on large scale and involves purchases of both the private sector and governments' assets (securities), the monetisation does not follow prior announcement, is on small scale and involves only government securities. In other words, while QE means creating money to stimulate the economy, monetisation means creating money to finance government deficits or pay off government debt. Further, the goal of QE is to increase the money supply rather than to decrease the interest rate, which cannot be decreased if it is already close to zero. Accordingly, QE is considered as a **last resort** in the hands of the Central Bank to stimulate the economy.

Recovery from Great Recession The coordinated policy interventions by the G-20 and the renewed confidence of the public and business did work and the recession was countered successfully and fairly quickly. The world moved from a negative growth rate of 1.3 per cent in 2009 to a positive growth rate of 4.5 per cent in 2010, 3.3 per cent in 2011 and 2.6 per cent in 2012. Thus, the global GDP fell just for a year in 2009, thanks particularly for the coordinated interventions by G-20. However, the decline in the unemployment rate came slow and it is still higher than the average of the past decade in many countries including USA. In addition, the recession has damaged several European economies so much that they are still in what is known as the Euro Area Financial Crisis or its ugly name, the PIIGS crisis. This is pursued further in another case study in this text.

To conclude, the low interest rate regime, the asset price bubble of 2002–06 and the excess leverage in sub-prime mortgages were the principal factors in causing the great recession, and the new tool of securitisation served to aggravate the crisis. The coordinated effort of the G-20 and the big timely stimulus packages by the group could ensure the earlier exit from it. It is believed that if such packages were absent, as they were during the Great Depression of 1929–33, the world would have perhaps faced a second Great Depression. Needless to say, the Keynesian theory and the latter developments in stabilisation policy, which did not exist during the early 1930s, are credited to have rescued us from the global recession going the worse.

Questions

1. Examine the data in the Table A-10 and explain why the period 2007–09 is considered as the Great Recession. Feel free to look for additional data in the Text or even on internet to justify your answer.
2. How Quantitative Easing (QE) is different from open market operations? Explain the process through which QE leads to increase in bank credit and money supply and decrease in long term interest rate.
3. While both quantitative easing and monetisation involves printing money, their effect on interest rate varies. Explain using the IS-LM model.
4. In the framework of the IS-LM-BP and AD-AS-BP models, examine the
   (a) Effect of each cause of the Great Recession on the GDP, price, interest rate and unemployment,
   (b) Verify if your answers to the above question are consistent with the cause–effect relationships in explaining the said recession.
5. Compare this Great Recession with the material on the Great Depression available elsewhere in the text and comment on the similarities and differences between the two, all in terms of the factors causing them, consequences on the economies and policy measures adopted to handle the crisis.
6. Two significant quotations on business cycles have come from the experts recently. These are
   (a) "Depression prevention has been solved" (Robert Lucas, Lecture at American Economic Association meeting in 2003)
   (b) "The Death of Inflation" (*Economist*, April 13, 2013)
   Do you agree with these statements? Why or why not?

Case A2: The Euro Area Crisis 2007–12

The single currency, Euro, was born on January 01, 1999 in Europe to serve as the common currency for a group of European countries. Initially, eleven European countries had joined this group and the new currency was valued at par with the US dollar, i.e. US $1=Euro 1. The eleven member nations were Austria, Belgium, Finland, France, Germany, Ireland, Italy, Luxemburg, Netherlands, Portugal and Spain. After two years, Greece joined the group in 2001. The currencies of the member nations remained in circulation until end 2001 and the Euro replaced all of them in early 2002. The European Central Bank was established to issue the Euro coins and notes as well as to conduct the monetary policy for the Euro Area. Subsequently, Slovenia joined in 2007, Cyprus and Malta in 2008, Slovakia in 2009, Estonia in 2011 and Latvia in 2014, taking the current member countries to 18. Under the Maastricht Treaty, the formation of the group had to meet certain conditions so that the group could be viable in the long run. The conditions are in terms of some common standards with respect to significant economic variables. These consist of

(a) Inflation rate should not exceed 1.5 the average inflation rate of the three member countries with the lowest inflation,
(b) Fiscal deficit as per cent to GDP should not have exceeded 3 per cent in the previous year,
(c) Government debt to GDP should not exceed 60 per cent,
(d) Long-term interest rate for 10 years bond should not exceed 2 per cent of the average that rate in three countries with the lowest inflation rate, and
(e) Should have been a member of the European ERM (Exchange Rate Management) for at least two consecutive years and should not have had devaluation in last two years.

Obviously, only the countries which could meet with the stipulations with respect to these five parameters could join the member. The idea behind the common currency was to serve like the United States of America and to promote trade, investment and migration within the group.

The Pros and Cons of the Common Currency By going for the common currency, the group has avoided the foreign exchange risk in the exchange of goods, services and capital within the group, and thereby has moved to promote trade and investments within the region. However, as there is no free lunch, each of the member country has had to surrender the monetary sovereignty and thus has lost the power of monetary policy to tame business cycles and promote growth and price stability, among other such objectives. Of the then 15 member European Monetary Union in 1999, the three countries, viz. UK, Denmark and Sweden, who were otherwise qualified to join the group, opted to remain outside the group, may be they did not wish to surrender their monetary sovereignty.

The Factors Causing the Crisis Multiple factors are responsible for the Euro zone crisis. The significant ones are explained below.

(a) The globalisation that intensified since the 1980s throughout the world has brought prosperity to the globe but one of its side effects has been in terms of the enhanced interdependence among countries as well. Accordingly, both the prosperity as well as recession in one part of the world gets transmitted to the rest of the world real fast through the much-improved communication and transport network, thanks particularly to the invention of the internet in the post mid 1990s. This movement has undermined the significance of the each nation's AD–AS (aggregate demand–aggregate supply) model in the nation's economic performance in favour of the GAD-GAS (global AD-global AS) model. While there have been many countries, like the South East Asian nations, China, etc. which have derived great benefits through globalisation; there are many nations that have suffered due to the contagion effect. While the international trade is also increasing over time, it is the capital flows across countries which has multiplied many times and led to serious consequences, both good as well as bad. The good effects are in terms of the net capital flows into developing nations, and thereby improving the factor productivity and global growth. The bad effects have been in terms of the financial crises, which it times lead to real crises, these flows are held responsible for. In the 1980s, the debt crisis plagued the Latin American and African countries; currently this crisis is causing serious problems in Europe and particularly in the Euro zone. This case highlights the suffering brought about by the globalisation.

(b) The case is on the Euro Area crisis which is yet to exit fully. The low interest rate regime and sub-mortgaged triggered asset price bubble bust erupted in USA in 2007, got spread through securitisation and capital flows across the whole world in a short time and turned into a Great Recession (GR) during 2007–09. To counter the GR, various policy measures were designed and implemented, the most significant of which happened to be the formation of the group of 20 nations (called G-20) and the consequent coordinated stimulus programme implemented simultaneously by all its members and many other countries. The members applied the fiscal tools by enhanced government spending and cuts in taxes, expansionary monetary policy through what has come to be known as the Quantitative Easing (QE) under which the Central Banks bought long-term government bonds, mortgages backed bonds and other private assets to steer low interest rate regime towards promoting credit expansion, consumption and investment, etc. Further, at the level of institutions the IMF's fund position was enhanced and the WTO warned against following the "beggar-thy-neighbour" policy of protection. These measures did achieve the desired results and the GR recession was practically over in less than two years by the end of 2009. While the recession may have exited, its baby may have been dumped in the Euro region in the name of the Euro Area Crisis. This happened because the low interest rate regime and the monetary stimulus through the quantitative Easing in the US and Japan and encouraged the European nations to borrow from those countries and invest in the home countries, which led to heavy debts in Europe. As the recession in the West started subsiding, capital tended to move back, putting pressure on the debt ridden Europe to service the debt.

The case first looks at the Euro Area's economic performance since its adoption of the common currency, focusing on the problems the group has faced particularly since the beginning of the Great Recession in 2007. In the next part, a detailed analysis is carried out for the two most affected countries in the group, viz. Greece and Spain. Towards the end, case presents some questions which the students/readers may like to attempt while analysing the case.

Euro Area's Relative Economic Performance The macroeconomic data on selected variables and for the selected groups and individual countries for 2001 through 2012 are provided in Table A-11. The individual countries list is kept small and the countries are chosen so that only advanced nations are compared and they come from different regions including the Euro area (Germany), non-Euro area Europe (UK) and the famous benchmark country (USA). This comparison should help us to evaluate, at least to certain extent, the pros and cons of the decision in favour of common currency. The data suggest that ever since the Euro Area fully adopted the common currency in 2002, the Euro Area's relative performance on the economic front has not been that good:

(a) The Euro zone's growth rate has always fallen below even the world's average growth rate, not to compare with that of the high performing countries. Further, in seven out of the 11 years (2002 to 2012), the growth rate in the Euro Area has been below even the average growth rate in all the so called advanced countries, of which the group happens to be a part. Furthermore, the story is exactly the same even if one compares the group's growth rate with that of the USA. One is thus led to believe that the group's efforts on this criterion have not been worthwhile.

(b) On the criterion of inflation (CPI), the group has achieved a stable inflation rate which has varied only marginally between 1.6 and 3.3 per cent during the 12 years, with an outlier of 0.3 per cent in 2009 – the year in which most countries experienced either very low inflation or some deflation. As a matter of fact, inflation was almost dead in most countries, and surely in advanced ones.

(c) In terms of unemployment, the data for the group of countries do not exist. Between the three individual countries whose data are included in the table, unemployment rate has been higher in Germany an all the normal years as compared to both USA and UK, and it has been at about the same rate in the latter two countries. However, the point to note here is that while the recession had little bearing on the unemployment rate in Germany,. it did cause the rate to increase significantly in both USA and UK.

(d) In terms of the nominal exchange rate (data not included here), Euro value in terms of the US dollar appreciated from 1.06255 Euros/$ in 2002 to Euro 0.77829/$ in 2012. However, in the real effective exchange rate (REER) index based on relative consumer prices' term (data not included in the Table), the common currency has remained fairly stable, as it has varied only little between 87.4 in 2002 to 91.3 in 2012.

(e) The recession has practically exited from the global economy by 2010. Even the advanced countries as a group, has more or less recovered from the recession by 2010. However, the Euro Area is still not out of soup, as its growth rate has turned negative even in 2012. Still worse are some countries within the Euro Area whose performance has even worsened during the post—the Great Recession. The latter group of countries has been given a notorious name, PIIGS, which is an acronym for Portugal, Ireland, Italy, Greece and Spain. Each of these five countries is experiencing a negative growth rate since 2008 for almost each year. In terms of inflation, they are subject to a low rate but

Table A-11 Economic Performance in Select (Groups of) Countries

(Percentages)

Country/ Variable	*2002*	*2003*	*2004*	*2005*	*2006*	*2007*	*2008*	*2009*	*2010*	*2011*	*2012*
Euro Area											
Growth rate	0.9	0.7	2.0	1.8	3.3	3.3	0.5	–3.8	1.9	1.7	–0.5
Inflation rate*	2.3	2.1	2.2	2.2	2.2	2.1	3.3	0.3	1.6	2.7	2.5
Unemployment	NA	NA	NA	NA	NA	NA	NA	NA	NA	NA	NA
World											
Growth rate	2.5	3.4	4.9	4.4	5.1	5.0	2.3	–1.3	4.5	3.3	2.6
Inflation rate*	3.5	3.6	3.6	3.7	3.6	3.8	5.8	2.3	3.4	4.5	3.7
Unemployment	NA	NA	NA	NA	NA	NA	NA	NA	NA	NA	NA
Adv. Eco.											
Growth rate	1.5	1.9	3.0	2.5	2.9	2.6	–0.1	–3.7	2.7	1.5	1.2
Inflation rate*	1.5	1.8	2.0	2.3	2.3	2.2	3.4	0.1	1.5	2.6	1.9
Unempl. Rate	NA	NA	NA	NA	NA	NA	NA	NA	NA	NA	NA
USA											
Growth rate	1.8	2.5	3.5	3.1	2.7	1.9	–0.3	–3.1	2.4	1.8	2.2
Inflation rate*	1.6	2.3	2.7	3.4	3.2	2.9	3.8	–0.4	1.6	3.2	2.1
Unempl. rate	5.8	6.0	5.5	5.1	4.6	4.6	5.8	9.3	9.5	9.0	8.1
U.K.											
Growth rate	2.4	3.8	2.9	2.8	2.6	3.6	–1.0	–4.0	1.8	1.0	0.3
Inflation rate*	1.3	1.4	1.3	2.0	2.3	2.3	3.6	2.2	3.3	4.5	2.8
Unempl. Rate	5.2	5.0	4.8	4.8	5.4	5.4	5.7	7.6	7.9	8.1	7.9
Germany											
Growth rate	NA	–0.4	0.7	0.8	3.9	3.	0.8	5.1	4.0	3.1	0.9
Inflation rate*	1.4	1.0	1.7	1.5	1.6	2.3	2.6	0.3	1.1	2.1	2.0
Unempl. rate	9.8	10.5	10.6	11.7	10.8	8.7	7.5	7.8	7.1	6.5	6.8

Source: IMF: International Financial Statistics, 2013

- CPI rate – NA: Not available/applicable

three of these (viz. Italy, Portugal and Spain) have occasionally landed into deflation.

The PIGGS Group and its Crisis The PIGGS group of countries consists of Portugal, Ireland, Italy, Greece and Spain. While the whole Euro area is adversely affected by the great recession, the PIIGs group has suffered the most and hence the name. To give some figure, within the Euro zone, the unemployment rate in 2012 happened to be the lowest at 4.5 per cent in Austria as compared to over 24 per cent both in Spain and Greece. Also, within the PIGGS group, the impact of the crisis has varied. For example, the Greece has the highest public debt to GDP per centage of over 100 each year during the post 2001 as compared to Ireland, Spain and Portugal who have never (or rarely) hit 100 per cent during the period. On the basis of economic growth, the poorest of the poor performance has been recorded by Greece and Spain amid PIIGS. While it would be interesting to study all of them, the Case takes the cases of Greece and Spain only for a detailed analysis.

Before we move into details, it may be recalled that since these countries are on the common currency, they have no exchange rate tool and no monetary policy, possess little role in trade and capital flows' regulations due to WTO (World Trade Organisation) membership, and thus are left with mere fiscal policy tool for countering business cycles. One should hasten to add that the European Central Bank could surely use its monetary tool for the whole of the Euro Zone. Further, macroeconomic theory and policy tells us that under full globalisation and floating exchange rate system, fiscal policy ceases to have any effect on the real magnitudes, including real GDP and unemployment. It appears that due to such developments, the national economic policies have relatively lost their function of stabilising their own economies.

Like the South East Asian Nations during 1990s, the PIIGS group has achieved economic progress through large-scale capital inflows in the past. As USA, UK, Japan and other nations resorted to QE, those countries money supply increased faster, interest rate fell somewhat, thence the capital outflows picked up from those nations to other countries including the Euro region. These outflows caused a depreciation of the currencies of countries from which the capital outflow occurred and appreciation of the currencies of the receiving countries (PIIGS and others). This worsened the trade balance of countries receiving the capital flows. Due to the global recession during 2007–09, these flows not only could not be sustained but also tended to reverse. The PIIGS group landed into high sovereign debts which had to be serviced. First casualty was Greece, followed by Ireland, Portugal, Spain and Italy. The foreign debt had not only to be repaid but also the interest on them, which is said to stand at an average rate of 7 per cent, had to be paid. These and such other developments led to financial crisis in PIIGS.

The macroeconomic data on the most relevant variables for the last about 10 years, covering the pre-great recession (GR), the GR period and the post-GR period on the select two of the five PIGGS group countries are given in Table A-12. The select indicators include the three ultimate goal variables (viz. growth rate, inflation rate and unemployment rate), two prices (viz. interest rate and share price), two imbalances (viz. fiscal deficit and current account deficit), two fiscal instruments (government consumption expenditure and tax revenue), one which happens to be

Table A-12 Macroeconomic Indicators of Greece and Spain

(Percentages)

Indicator	*2001*	*2005*	*2006*	*2007*	*2008*	*2009*	*2010*	*2011*	*2012*
Greece (Pop. 2012 = 11.3 mill.)	NA	NA	NA	NA	NA	NA	NA	NA	NA
Growth rate	4.2	3.3	5.5	3.5	–0.2	–3.1	–4.9	–7.1	–6.4
Infl. rate**	3.4	3.5	3.2	2.9	4.2	1.2	4.7	3.3	1.5
Unemp. rate	10.8	9.9	8.9	8.3	7.7	9.5	12.5	17.7	24.1
Int. rate@	8.59	8.47	7.89	7.70	8.65	8.59	9.79	10.16	8.19
Share Price*	89.3	100	126.4	154.6	104	68.8	52.4	36.3	22.6
Fiscal deficit % GDP	4.6	5.6	5.9	6.7	9.9	15.6	10.6	9.8	NA
Current A/c Deficit % GDP	NA	7.6	11.3	14.6	15.0	11.2	10.4	9.9	2.5
Govt. Consumption % GDP	18	18	17	18	18	21	18	17	18
Tax Revenue as % GDP	22.0	20.3	20.5	20.8	20.4	19.6	20.1	21.3	NA
Investment as % GDP	23.2	21.4	24.6	26.7	24.0	18.6	17.5	16.1	13.6
Govt. Debt as % GDP	127	125	129	126	121	137	129	107	161@@
Spain (Pop. 2012 = 46.2 mill.)									
Growth rate	3.7	3.6	4.1	3.5	0.9	–3.7	–0.3	0.4	–1.4
Infl. rate**	3.6	3.4	3.5	2.8	4.1	–0.3	1.8	3.2	2.4
Unemp. rate	13.1	9.2	8.5	8.3	11.3	18.0	20.1	21.0	25.1
Int. rate*	NA	7.97	8.73	9.89	11.02	10.72	7.36	5.96	6.96
Share Price @	80	100	126.1	153.6	118.5	98.9	98.8	92.6	71.7
Fiscal deficit % GDP	–0.2	–1.6	–2.3	–2.5	2.3	8.6	5.2	3.6	NA
Current A/c Deficit % GDP	NA	7.5	9.0	10.0	9.6	4.8	4.5	3.8	1.1
Govt. Consumption % GDP	17	18	18	18	19	21	21	21	20
Tax Revenue as % GDP	15.8	12.9	13.5	13.9	10.5	8.6	11.4	9.6	NA
Investment as % GDP	26.4	29.5	30.9	31.0	29.1	24.0	22.8	21.5	19.7
Govt. Debt as % GDP	55	39	34	30	34	47	49	56	85@@

Sources: (a) IMF: International Financial Statistics, 2013, (b) www.worldbank.org/indicator/all
** Consumer price index * Lending rate @ Index numbers @@ CIA World Fact book estim
NA: Not available/applicable

the most important determinant of growth (investment rate) and the last one which is a measure of the country's solvency level (public debt). A comparative study of these data reveals the following:

(a) Taking up the high level goals first, Greece is experiencing a negative growth rate since 2009 and Spain also since 2009 barring a small positive (0.4 per cent) rate in 2011. In terms of the size, Greece's position is worse than Spain. Inflation is no problem in either country rather deflation occurred in Spain in 2009. Unemployment has been a serious problem in both the countries as it has been around 20 per cent in Spain in all years since 2009 and in two digits hitting 24.1 per cent in 2012 in Greece.

(b) Coming to prices, interest rate have been relatively high in the two nations vis-a-vis other countries in Euro region. This is obviously so due to debt crisis and low credit ratings. Share price index has fallen drastically to about 23 per cent in 2012 in seven years in Greece and to about 72 per cent in Spain.

(c) Fiscal deficit, in general, widened during 2004 through 2009 and narrowed in later years. The current account has been in deficit all throughout in both the countries, though its trend has been mixed while witnessing narrowing the level by 2012.

(d) Looking at the fiscal measures, while the government consumption as per cent to GDP is about the same in two countries, hovering between 17 and 21 per cent, the tax to GDP per cent has been about twice in Greece (20 to 22 per cent) to that in Spain (9 to 16 per cent). The data do reflect some fiscal stimulus.

(e) The investment rate has fallen significantly in both the economies, which has surely damaged the economic growth. In terms of the debt burden, Greece's debt ratio stands at around double of that of Spain.

The economic position of both the nations has been bad, particularly since 2007 or 2008. All the five PIIGS group countries have crossed the 60 per cent and 3 per cent deadlines for debt and fiscal deficit ratios, respectively, requirements for being the Euro member. This explains as to why these two countries are in economic crisis.

What is the way out of this crisis? The group is surviving through the massive Euro zone assistance coming from the European Central Bank and Germany, the groups' largest and strongest economy, and the austerity measures implemented by their governments. The domestic governments have been supporting the private sector by reductions in taxes, faster disbursements of the rebates on VAT, export promotion schemes, etc. The rating agencies, S & P and Moody's have downgraded their external debts which are leading to cascading consequences. Huge losses of banks are being transferred to governments, worsening the public debt burden. Being a member of the Euro, these countries do not have the luxury of printing the money and infusing inflation. Austerity measures by the private sector through cutting consumption may only adversely affect demand instead of providing funds for investments and debt repayments. With the global crisis, the manufacturing industry began to decline in many countries especially in the PIIGS group of countries, worsening even their balance of payments. While the IMF and European Union have assisted, funds are a constraint even for them. The only solution looks like the one applied for the Latin American debt crisis in early 1980s of the two-fold attack. First, on domestic front, stick to fiscal discipline, reduce consumption and increase saving and investment, try to cut wages to improve the comparative advantage for boosting exports, etc. On the external front, reschedule the debts, get them reduced through generous forgiveness and discounts from the affordable creditors, plead with the creditors to accept the repayments in terms of domestic assets of the debtor nations, and continue seeking assistance and guidance from the multinational financial institutions like the European Central Bank, World Bank and IMF. In addition, efforts may be mounted to coordinate the fiscal policy within the Euro region to complement with the coordinated monetary policy under Euro. The PIIGS recession is serious and it is not easy to exit from it. It will take time but surely will be out, hopefully in foreseeable future!

Questions

1. Assess the pros and cons of the common currency, Euro.
2. Critically examine the monetary policy tool of quantitative Easing for stimulating a recession prone country, giving due considerations to "beggar-thy-neighbour" policy.
3. Could the PIIGS crisis have been avoided? How?
4. Use the macroeconomic tools of the IS–LM–BP and the AD-SAS-BP to explain the evolution of the PIIGS crisis.

CASE A3: THE JAPAN'S LOST TWO DECADES AND CONTINUING STRUGGLE

Japan has created history on several occasions. First, in the mid-19th century, the country embraced the West to become an industrialized nation after centuries of isolation. Second, damaged by the World War II, it, together with Germany, achieved high economic growth rate during the post-war years lasting through 1960s and a bit beyond. To cite some hard facts, in 1820, the GDP per capita (PPP at 1990 dollars) was $669 in Japan as compared to that in India at $533, in China at $600 and USA at $ 1,257. The figures changed to $1,926, $619, $439 and $ 9,561, respectively in 1950; and to $ 27,967, $2,897, $5,003 and $ 37,562, respectively in 2003. Thus, while Japan's PCI multiplied by 41.8 times that of India, China and USA multiplied by 5.4, 8.3 and 29.9 times, respectively during those 183 years. Such astonishing results happened in Japan due to the post-war experiencing of democratizing, intelligent and hard working work force, accompanied with high saving and investment rates, and technological developments. Japan has always encouraged private industry to flourish, is blessed with unmatched engineering capacity in high tech manufacturing, and has highly skilled and disciplined labour force. Since Japanese are relatively risk averse and have bequest motive, etc., they save more and spend less. Accordingly, the resulting growth came less from domestic demand and more through exports. In the beginning of 1970s, financial sector was liberalised and the interest rate was de-regulated, which created strong banking which in turn facilitated growth. Third, the decades of the 1990s and 2000s have been bad for Japan, falling saving and investment rates, and thence the growth rate (to not only low levels but in some years even to the negative figures); increasing unemployment rate, fiscal deficit and current account (of balance of payments) surplus; falling inflation rate (turning into deflation), falling interest rate, generally falling share and property prices, and first appreciating until 1995 then fluctuating both ways the foreign exchange rate; and political instability, among other factors taking adverse numbers. Accordingly, the 1990's and 2000's have been termed as the lost two decades for Japan. The downward trend has not yet been quite arrested and even the political stability is far from secured.

Currently (March 2014), the latest available data indicate that the country is facing the following problems, among others:

(a) Low growth rate
(b) Threat of deflation
(c) Relatively high unemployment–job shortage
(d) High fiscal deficit and perhaps the most heavily indebted nation in the world in terms of the public debt as percentage to GDP (estimated at 214% in 2012, as compared to 64 per cent in USA, 126% in Italy, 161% in Greece, and so on—vide CIA World Fact book, 2013)
(e) Falling saving and investment rates (each has fallen from around 33 to around 22 % of GDP)
(f) Ageing population and shrinking workforce, leading to rising health care cost (24 per cent of Japanese are in the age group of 65 and above, the birth rate in Japan is the lowest (8 per 1000) among the developed countries, and the growth rate in population is at zero)

(g) Swathes of the depopulated country side

(h) Political instability (the current Prime Minister is the 9th PM since 2001, and 16th since 1990)

Economic Scenario during the Post 1990 In the decades following the World War-II, Japan implemented stringent tariffs and policies to encourage the people to save a good part of their incomes. With more money in banks, loans and credit became easier to obtain, and so the investment soared. This lead to economic prosperity and the country performed remarkably well until around 1970. It attained an average growth rate of 9.5 per cent during 1955 through 1970. However, the tempo could not be sustained any more. The growth rate fell to an average of 3.8 per cent during 1971 to 1990 and to a low of 0.8 in the last two decades ending 2010. Japan's per capita income level had reached almost the level of the US toward the end of the 1980s. With this happening, Japan's era of high growth, which was based on the technological catching up, came to an end. The year-wise (with some gaps) detailed data available in Table A-6 would indicate the Japan's performance with respect to all important macroeconomic indicators during the last decades and they would leave one to conclude that the country is still not out of the trouble. In particular, during the decade of the 1990s, the average rate of growth was not only around 1 per cent, it was even negative in two of the ten-year period. Further, during the decade 2000-2009, the average growth rate achieved comes to even lower than 1 per cent, with negative rates again in 2 out of 10 years. Post 2009, the situation has improved somewhat, the country still faced recession in 2011. On the unemployment front, the position is no better. The said rate was at 2.1 per cent in 1990, which rose monotonously to hit 4.7 per cent in 1999 and to 5.4 per cent in 2002, fluctuating up and down, and eventually hitting 4.6 per cent in 2012. These rates happen to be the highest in the Japan's history since it began compiling the data in 1953.

The interesting phenomena is noticed when one compares the above trends with those in other macroeconomic magnitudes. For example, the inflation rate fell from 3.1 per cent in 1990 to –0.3 per cent in 1999, fluctuating a bit in future yet landing again at –0.3 per cent 2012. Of the 23 years period, the country has witnessed deflation in 10 years, inflation in 11 years and the zero rates in the remaining two years. Looking at the nominal interest rate, one observes a monotonically downward trend, as it fell from 7.0 per cent in 1990 to 2.2 per cent in 1999 and to 1.4 per cent in 2012. The fall may be due to the threat from deflation and easy monetary policy to tame recession. The nominal wage rate has remained stagnant with a marginal fall of around three per cent during the 23 years. The share price lost over 30 per cent of its value during the 1990s and again about 50 per cent since then until 2012. The Japanese currency swung significantly both ways during the period, first appreciating by over 50 per cent during 1990 through 1995, then depreciating until 1998, and later changing the course more frequently, and eventually indicating an overall appreciation of about 40 per cent during 1990–2012. The current (March 20, 2014) exchange rate marks over 20 per cent devaluation of yen over its 2012 average value. Japan's current account (of its balance of payments) has always been having positive balance, though it has fluctuated both ways during the 23 years period, its size has grown by about 40 per cent during the period. However, if one looks at the latest available data March 20, 2014), the current account deficit falls below its 1990 level. Last but not the least, the foreign exchange holdings of Japan has witnessed a positive trend almost uniformly (multiplying by a factor of 15 plus) throughout the period.

The rapid ageing of Japanese society is a widely known phenomenon. The total population has remained more or less static and the working age population had started falling around 1995. This has caused the fall in workforce, which in the absence of sufficient growth in factor productivity, has been responsible for poor economic performance. Thus, Japan has faced such an adverse supply shock as well.

Diagnosis of the Problem What could have caused this downward spiral? During the 1980s, the interest rate was relatively low and banks were eager to lend, which was based more on relationship and collateral than on expected cash flows. In consequence, people borrowed to invest in real estate and stocks, and even banks invested in such assets. This resulted into soaring prices of such assets in Japan. Japan's stock market index Nikkie rose from its level of about 13,000 in December 1985 to about 38,916 in December 1989. Even the real estate prices tripled during the 1980s. Recognizing that the bubble was unsustainable, the Bank of Japan sharply raised interest rate in late 1990 which caused the bursting of the bubble and the stock price crashed. The fall in land prices followed during the early 1990s. These eroded the wealth of households, which worsened the position of the borrowers who defaulted on their bank loans. In consequence, there happened a phenomenal rise in non-performing loans/assets of banks.. Thus, banks suffered, some even became insolvent, and financial crisis resulted. In consequence, there was credit crunch which affected adversely the investment and growth. The erosion of private wealth reduced the purchasing power, there by impinging on domestic demand, leading to accumulation of inventories, cuts in production and increase in unemployment.

There was a Plaza Accord (so known as it was agreed to in a meeting held at Hotel Plaza in New York) among the Finance Ministers of the G-5 countries (USA, UK, Japan, Germany and France) in September 1985 under which they agreed to encourage depreciation of the US dollar. Yen had depreciated from 210 per US dollar in 1978 to 239 in 1985, and through the Accord it appreciated to 138 a dollar in 1989. This affected adversely Japan's competitive advantage and accordingly exports fell. Japanese being relatively frugal (their consumption expenditure even in 2012 is around 61 per cent of GDP in comparison to that of 72 per cent of US), fall in exports led to fall in aggregate demand, causing recession. During the 1990s the interest rate in Japan declined drastically making loans cheap and saving unattractive. This led Japanese to move their savings abroad and foreigners to borrow from Japan. In consequence investment suffered, which hampered growth.

Japan experienced **political instability** during the 1990s and 2000s which still persists. The country has had 7 Prime Ministers in each of the two lost decades (1990–1999 and 2000–09). In 2001, Junichiro Koizumi of the Liberal Democratic Party (LDP) was elected to the position and completed his term of five years in 2006. He provided stability to the otherwise unstable government and carried out economic reforms. Several institutions, such as post office including the vast pool of post office savings, were privatized. Protections that large firms had enjoyed for long were removed and the innovations were encouraged. Banks were persuaded to write off non-performing loans within three years and some prudential norms for them were imposed. Such measures did help revive the economy and accordingly the early part of the 2000s was fairly healthy for Japan. Even many thought that the slump was gone by 2004. However, deflation continued and so did high unemployment rate. Koizumi was re-elected but he resigned and his successor Shinzo Abe survived just for a year when he resigned in mid-September 2007. The new Prime Minister, Mr. Yasuo Fukuda, from the same party as M/S Koizumi and Abe, was elected on September 23, 2007, who too lasted just for a year. The four more Prime Ministers had come after Mr. Fukuda, each lasting for about a year, and finally Mr. Shinzo Abe is back as the Prime Minister since December 26, 2012.

Economic Policies Though most Prime Ministers had rather short term during the 1990s, Japanese government did not sit silent on the happenings in the economy. The government initiated large spending programs to try to stimulate the economy. Japanese government spent over US dollar one trillion on public works projects during the 1990s. In consequence, Japan's fiscal deficit increased to 10 per cent of GDP in 1999 and remained high during next few years, taking the Japan's gross debt to GDP ratio from 58 per cent to 114 per cent in 2000, to 144 per cent in 2005, to 190 per cent in 2011 and to 214 per cent in 2012. The Keynesian model of stimulating the depressed economy through government expenditure did not work enough to cure the recession. The critics have argued that the Japanese government was slow in initiating the expansion and when spending was increased it was not adequate in relation to the size of the country. Further, since there was political instability, a sizeable part of the expenditure was considered as wasteful. In addition, following the Ricardo–Barro theory of equivalence, people started worrying about increased future tax liabilities and thereby economizing on their spending. This rendered fiscal policy less effective.

Bank of Japan did make efforts to use its monetary policy to stimulate the economy. The discount rate, the policy rate of the country, has been frequently and heavily used in Japan to manage the money and credit levels for long. However, its use became much more pronounced during the 1990s. The said rate stood at 6 per cent in 1990, was lowered to 4.50 per cent in 1991, 3.25 per cent in 1992, 1.75 per cent in 1993, 0.50 per cent in 1995, 0.15 per cent in 1999, and to 0.10 per cent in 2001. Since the discount rate is a signal rate, the other interest rates followed suit. For example, the lending rate fell from 7 per cent in 1990 to 2.2 per cent in1999 and to 1.4 per cent in 2012, which stands at 0.61 currently (March 20, 2014). However, the easy credit/money policy did not do enough good to revive the economy. The said policy was partly crowded by large-scale bank failures, causing loss of public confidence in banks and banks becoming more conscious. Remember that when people lose confidence in banks, they move from financial assets (bank deposits etc.) to currency and when banks try to avoid risk, they hold their assets more in cash than in loans. People go for liquidity when interest rate is too low (liquidity trap). Each of these moves lowers the money multiplier (ratio of money to the high-powered money) and thereby adversely affects the quantity of money in the economy. Incidentally note that macroeconomic theory suggests that when the interest rate is too low, the country could be in **liquidity trap** and if so the monetary policy is impotent with regard to its effect on income and unemployment. However, under such a situation, the fiscal policy is quite strong, provided it has a reasonable scale and is well focused! Further, could monetary policy influence price expectations and thereby soften recession? To fight deflation, particularly when the short-term interest rate is close to zero, Japan applied the Quantitative Easing (QE) tool of the monetary policy for the first time on March 19, 2001. Towards this end, the Bank of Japan purchased more government bonds than would be required to set interest rate to zero. In addition, the Bank even bought the private asset-backed securities and equities and extended the terms of its commercial papers purchasing operation. With QE, Bank of Japan flooded commercial banks with excess liquidity to promote private lending, investment and thereby economic growth. Paul Krugman has argued that Japan's lost two decades is an example of a liquidity trap. Some economists have called QE as "an expansion of the Central Bank's balance sheet" and accordingly the recession is also called as a "balance sheet recession".

The policy-makers have trade and exchange rate policy as well to counter the recession. Japan has consistently been having trade and even current account surplus. This means its exports have always exceeded its imports. Promoting exports further may not be desirable and, in fact, its surplus is significantly the outcome of deficits in USA, with which USA has been unhappy. Accordingly, instead of devaluing yen to encourage net exports, Japan had agreed for the Plaza Accord to let yen appreciate. Due to yen appreciation and low interest rate in Japan, firms were encouraged to invest less domestically and to shift production facilities and investments abroad. The off-shore assets are now providing income for the elderly in Japan, which, though a part of GNP, is not even counted in GDP on which the growth is currently measured.

Japan is currently busy coming out with the "biggest monetary stimulus in history", called the Quantitative and Qualitative Easing (QQE). Under this the liquidity flowing from Japan could help fill the gap that may be left as a result of the tapering of monetary stimulus in the US. The estimates are that Japanese banks, which have been snapping up regional lenders, could pump an extra \$60bn–\$140bn into South East Asian economies alone. India could expect to receive a good part of it.

Questions

1. Understand the dynamics of the Japanese economy.
2. What do the macroeconomic indicators on Japan tell? Understand the gravity of the problem and the relationship among the economic ills. Use the IS-LM-SAS framework and infer the shifts in them so as to get the results (in terms of changes in real income, unemployment, interest rate and price) consistent with the happenings in Japan during the period under analysis. In what ways the Japanese slump is similar to the Great Depression of 1929–33 and how the two differ?
3. Relate the factors causing the recession with the consequences on the economy as described in the Case.
4. Evaluate the limitations of the fiscal, monetary and trade policies, and suggest some ways out when an economy faces the situation like Japan's during the 1990s and 2000s, and even beyond. In particular, examine the validity of the **Ricardo–Barro equivalence theory**, the efficacy of the monetary policy under liquidity trap, and the usefulness of the trade policy in the presence of trade surplus.

CASE A4: COMMENTARY ON THE ECONOMIC ISSUES IN ARGENTINA

(a) Argentina is rich in natural resources (land area = 2780 thousand sq km–26th rank) and in human development (per capita income PPP= $15,347 in 2012 and HDI = 0.811 in 2012–45th rank). Thus, the country has good opportunities for investment. Its per capita PPP income at US $ 15,347 in 2012 puts it among the high-income countries.

(b) Argentina is one of the largest economies in South America and it, jointly with Brazil and Mexico, represents Latin America at the G-20.

(c) During most of the 20th century, the country has suffered from recurring economic crises, persistent fiscal and current account deficits, high inflation, mounting external debt and capital flight.

(d) Argentina has had low saving rate but good investment opportunities. The country borrowed extensively from abroad and experienced good growth until 1998, barring a couple of years. In 1999, after the three years boom, Argentina faced recession for four long years, ending in 2002. The economy was once again on fairly high growth path until 2009, when the global recession impacted the economy and the growth rate came down to 0.2 per cent. During 2010–2011, the country again hit a growth rate of about 9 per cent but again 2012 recorded a low growth rate of just 1.9 per cent; however the year 2013 has shown good improvement.

(e) High inflation has been a weakness of the Argentina's economy. It suffered hyperinflation during 1989 and 1990, the inflation rates being 3080 and 2315 per cent, respectively. The inflation is currently hovering around 9 per cent since 2005, though the country had experienced mild deflation during 1999–2001. The high inflation has been at least partly due to the continued expansionary fiscal and monetary policies.

(f) The country has suffered two-digit unemployment rates for the most part of the 1990s until 2006, since when the rate is down to around 7 per cent.

(g) Experienced a highly volatile exchange rate, fluctuating between 0.00676 in 1984 and 4.07633 in 1977, standing at about 0.49 in 1990, 1.00 in 2000 and 4.54 peso per US dollar in 2012. The country instituted the currency board system of exchange rate with fixed one to one rate between peso and US dollar in 1990. Exchange rate stabilized but the board broke down in and peso plummeted to 3.063 in 2002. The country is on the floating exchange rate since then. This helped the economy to rebound and grow well until it was hit by the Global recession in 2009.

(h) Argentina's fiscal deficits soared after 1995 and the country faced financial difficulties in serving its debt. The country was unable to pay even the interest on its debt and was forced to default. Interest rate went up and it had to seek loans from International Monetary Fund on stringent conditions. The country fell into a sovereign default again in 2001. It attempted debt restructuring but has not been able to negotiate with capital markets. Government nationalized the private retirement plans to get some resources. Its debt to GDP ratio stands at around 42 per cent in 2012.

(i) In 2001–02, political dissatisfaction reached high such that there were riots on the streets and the country had five different presidents within a span of a few months.

(j) Lately, the country's economic parameters are reasonably sound. The country shows tremendous potential for being a world-class economy but it seems to be having problems of poor governance and poor economic policies.

Question: Analyse how Argentina could come out of its economic crisis during 1999–2002 through support from the IMF in spite of the stringent conditions?

Case A5: Commentary on the Russia's Growing Clout

(a) Russia was disintegrated from Soviet Union in 1989, taking about half of the Union.

(b) The country has democracy but it has degenerated into managed democracy. The Centre dictates Russian internal politics and economics, though through democratic and market-based decisions.

(c) The country has the largest land area in the world, its GDP happens to be the 10th largest in the world, and the country is rich in natural resources, particularly fossil fuels, precious metals and timber. Its economy is largely based on exports of oil, gas and other natural resources. Its vast oil reserve makes Russia the resurgent superpower. However, its future hinges equally on the way it modernizes its economy.

(d) Soviet Union was the founder of economic planning. Five-year plans and annual plans were the chief mechanisms the Soviet government used to translate economic policies into programmes. The government's role was to ensure that the plans were fulfilled. Responsibility for production flowed from the top to bottom. One of the chief reformers of the late 1980s, Boris Yeltsin, oversaw the substantial dissolution of the nearly 60 years old central planning system in the early 1990s.

(e) In early 1990s, under the leadership of Boris Yeltsin, Russia had made great strides toward developing a market economy by implementing basic tenets such as market-determined prices, privatization of state owned enterprises and opening of the economy for foreign trade and investments. Price controls were lifted on about 90 per cent of consumer goods and 80 per cent of raw materials. Taxes were raised and fiscal deficit was reduced from about 20 per cent in 1991 to about 3 per cent in 1993, and turned into surplus in 2000 and onwards.

(f) The state run enterprises and individuals had built up large foreign currency deposits and the country's currency ruble had depreciated significantly during 1999 and onwards. These prompted the Russian Central Bank to follow a highly expansionary monetary policy in 2000 and onwards until 2008, where the annual growth rate in money supply ranged between 34 and 41 per cent. Subsequently, when inflation became high the Monetary growth was suddenly brought down to 14 per cent in 2008 and has remained around that level until not.

(g) The country suffered multi-year recession until 1998, performed well during 1999 through 2008, went into recession in late 2008 and early 2009 under the impact of the Global Recession of 2007–09, and is back to a reasonable growth rate.

(h) Unemployment rate was low during the first half of the 1990s but it remained in two digits during the second half of that decade. Subsequently, it has been brought down gradually and currently it stands at a reasonable rate of around five per cent.

(i) The country has suffered hyperinflation; the inflation rate remained in three digits until 1995, in two digits during 1995 through 2005, and continues to remain above the world average level even now.

(j) Interest rate has been relatively high in Russia all through. The share market has been yielding consistently good returns. The foreign exchange rate in terms of the US dollar depreciated rather significantly in 1999, then fluctuated marginally both ways, but has followed a general depreciation trend all through.

(k) An important symptom of Russian macroeconomic instability has been severe fluctuations in the exchange rate of its currency in relation to the US dollar, particularly during 1992 through 2000. Nevertheless, in order to stabilize the currency, Russia launched on full convertibility of ruble on current account to boost its foreign trade in goods and services.

(l) The country has been building on foreign exchange reserves and has always enjoyed a positive balance on its current account of the balance of payments. The country's public debt has been rather low and it stood at 12.2 per cent of its GDP in 2012.

(m) Corruption in Russia is a well-known old story. Even with economic prosperity, corruption shows no sign of a retreat.

(n) Russia is increasingly in news these days for its highflying economy and its controversial politics. A billionaire entrepreneur declared recently "anything is possible in Russia right now".

Question: Evaluate the Yeltsin period's macroeconomic reforms and the clout that Russia enjoys currently in the global economy.

Glossary

Acceleration principle—relates investment directly and proportionately to the change in output, current or lagged.

Accommodating policy—a policy to offset a shock; like an expansionary monetary and/or fiscal policy to counter an adverse supply shock so as to protect the GDP from falling, or an expansionary monetary policy to accompany an increase in government expenditure so as prevent increase in interest rate.

Active policy—a policy that is in response to the current state of the economy; also known as discretionary policy.

Adaptive expectations theory—a theory under which expectations about the future values of a variable are formed entirely on the basis of that variable's historical/past data.

Aggregate demand curve—a curve that gives the quantity of all goods and services (which means real GDP) that households, firms, governments and foreigners plan or desire to buy at each price. Also, it is the locus of various combinations of (real) income (or output) and (general) price at which both the product and the money market are simultaneously in equilibrium.

Aggregate supply curve—a curve that gives the quantity of all goods and services (=real GDP) that all firms wish to produce (and sell) at each price. Also, it is the locus of various combinations of (real) income (or output) and (general) price at which the factor market is in equilibrium.

Animal spirits—peoples' expectations about the state of the economy which exerts influence on investment and thence on output and employment.

Arbitrage—act of buying in market where the item is cheap and selling simultaneously in the market where it is costly, thus making profit without any investment.

Assignment (or Mundell's) rule—it suggests that fiscal policy should be responsible for economic growth and monetary policy for price stability.

Asymmetric information—a situation under which one group of the people have better information than the other, like workers are usually poorly informed than the firms about the market trends. Milton Friedman has advanced the Fooling of Workers' theory to explain the upward sloping short run aggregate supply (SAS) curve.

Augmented Phillips curve—Phillips curve that includes expected inflation, in addition to the rate of unemployment, as a determinant of the inflation rate.

Automatic (or built-in) stabilisers—changes in tax revenues and transfer payments which happen independent of any new policy initiative such that they move counter-cyclical, like tax revenues fall (transfer payments increase) during recessions and rise (transfer payments fall) during prosperity which tend to dampen cyclical fluctuations.

Autonomous expenditure (variable)—expenditures (variables) which are fixed and cannot be explained by the model.

Autonomous expenditure multiplier—gives the number of times by which the GDP in rupees increases when the government expenditure or any other autonomous expenditure is increased by one rupee. It is also known as the Keynesian multiplier.

Balanced budget multiplier—gives the number of times by which the GDP increases in rupees when each of the government expenditure and tax revenues is increased by one rupee.

Balance of payments deficit (surplus)—sum of the deficits (surplus) in current account and capital account of the balance of payments; or the net capital outflow (inflow) from the country.

Bank rate—is the interest rate at which the Central Bank of the country (RBI) advances loans to its member banks.

Barro–Ricardo equivalence theorem—proposition that government expenditures financed through borrowing or tax increases are equivalent in their effects on the economy, as the forward looking people fully understand that government debt means future taxes.

Beggar-thy-neighbour policy—is a policy which increases domestic output at the cost of the output of other nations; like the restrictive trade policy or currency devaluation when the economy is on the fixed exchange rate.

Black money/parallel/underground economy—exists when production or income is hidden either to evade taxes or because it is illegal; like not or under reporting of production/incomes, bribes, drugs, dangerous weapons, etc.

BP curve—locus of various combinations of income and interest rate (or exchange rate or price) at which the foreign exchange market (or balance of payments) is in equilibrium.

Business cycles—fluctuations in real GDP over time.

Capitalism—economic system in which most property is privately owned and major economic decisions (what, how and for whom to produce) are based on the market (demand–supply) with little intervention from the governments.

Cash reserve ratio (CRR)—it is a monetary policy tool which requires every member bank to maintain a certain percentage of their demand and time liabilities as reserves with the Central bank of the country (RBI).

Classical dichotomy—segmentable model in which real variables are determined in one part and the nominal variables in the other part of a macroeconomic model, implying no relationship between the two sets of variables. This means neutrality of money.

Classical model (old)—a long run macroeconomic model advanced by the pre-Keynesian economists which assumes wage-price flexibility and perfect information.

Classical model (new)—a long run macroeconomic model advanced by the new classical economists which assumes wage-price flexibility but imperfect information.

Command economy—an economic system in which most property is publicly owned and under which all key economic functions (like what, how and for whom to produce) are decided by the central planning authority.

Convergence theory—states that the low per capita income countries grow at a faster rate than the high per capita income countries and thus all countries tend to converge to the same rate of growth in per capita income under the conditional convergence, and to the same per capita income under the absolute convergence in the long-run.

Crawling peg—an exchange rate policy under which the exchange rate is devalued (re-valued) roughly equal to the inflation rate differential between the country (major trade partner) and its major trade partners (country).

Crowding out—decrease in investment (or net export) that results when government expenditure increase causing interest rate to move up (or currency to appreciate).

Currency board—a monetary system under which the currency is issued against full (or near full) backing of assets denominated in a key foreign currency, like the US dollar.

Current account convertibility—prevails in the country when its currency is convertible into any foreign currency for carrying out any legal transactions on the current account of the balance of payments.

Cyclical unemployment—deviation of actual unemployment from the natural rate of unemployment; also, it equals the sum of structural, frictional, seasonal, and wait unemployment.

Dead weight loss—a loss to the society that occurs due to some market intervention by the governments, like taxes, price or quantity controls, entry restrictions, etc.

Deflationary gap—measures the shortfall in the (gap between the required and actual) autonomous expenditure (like government expenditure) to attain the full employment output level.

Deflation–debt hypothesis—proposition that deflation causes transfers of resources from debtors to creditors and thereby reduces average propensity to consume and thence aggregate demand, which could lead to recession.

Depression—a situation when the rate of decline in GDP is large, lasts for multi years and spread across many economies, or a period of recession which is deep, lasting long, and well spread globally.

Dollarisation—occurs when a country adopts/legalise a foreign currency as its own currency and thereby loses the seigniorage revenue.

Economic growth rate—rate of increase in real GDP per year measured in percentage.

Economics—a discipline which deals with the allocation of scarce resources among their alternative uses.

Exchange rate, nominal—official price of one currency in terms of some other currency.

Exchange rate–real—price of a basket of goods and services in one country in terms of the same basket of goods and services in some other currency.

Extinguishing policy—a policy to counter inflationary pressure; like a restrictive monetary, fiscal and/or trade policy to offset an adverse supply shock so as prevent increase in price.

Fiat money—money declared by a fiat (decree or governments order) and whose intrinsic value may be very small compared to its face value.

Fiscal (or budget) deficit—positive gap between governments' total expenditure and its non-debt receipts in a given year.

Fisher's effect—stands for the one-for-one effect of expected inflation on the nominal interest rate.

Fooling of the workers' model—the short run aggregate supply model which is based on the Milton Friedman's theory of asymmetric information wherein the workers do not possess the correct information on the general price level, though they do on the prices of the goods and services they buy which happen to move at different rates and in different directions.

Frictional unemployment—unemployment in between graduation and actual placement, and in between jobs caused by job quitting or retrenchment; also known as the turnover unemployment.

Gross domestic product (GDP)—quantity (or value) of all goods and services that is produced in the country by all agents of production (residents and non-residents) in a given period. Also, it equals the total expenditure on all domestically produced goods and services. Further, it equals all incomes that the factors of production receive towards all the domestic production.

GDP at factor cost—GDP valued at the factors cost.

GDP at market prices—GDP valued at the market prices, which includes the factors cost and indirect taxes net of indirect subsidies.

GDP deflator—ratio of nominal GDP and real GDP; also it is a measure of the prices of all goods and services produced in the economy in the year relative to the base year.

GDP measured—GDP valued at the official (actual) exchange rate.

GDP Nominal—GDP valued at the current prices.

GDP PPP—GDP valued at the PPP exchange rate.

GDP real—GDP valued at the base year (or constant) prices.

Golden rule—gives the saving rate that maximises the per capita consumption at the steady state in the Solow model of economic growth.

Great recession—recession spread globally.

Gross national product (GNP)—quantity (or value at the base year price for real GNP and value at the current prices for nominal GNP) of all goods and services that is produced by the residents (households, firms and governments) anywhere in the world.

High-power money (or reserve money, monetary base, government money)—the money which has power to create more money. It consists of currency and bank reserves, hold in vaults as well as with the Central Bank of the country.

Hyperinflation—situation when inflation rate is very high, like 1,000 percent or more per year.

Hysteresis theory—suggests that the natural rate of unemployment is influenced by the actual historical unemployment rates.

Imputed value—estimated price of a good which is not marketed, like the rent of an owner occupied house or the price of the services rendered by the President of the country.

Indexation—a system by which all the monetary transactions are automatically and exactly adjusted for inflation/deflation.

Inflation (deflation)—rate of increase (decrease) in percentage in the general (macro) price over the previous year/per year; like the retail inflation in India in April 2014 was recently declared at 8.6 percent, which means the consumer price index (all India) in India increased by 8.6 per cent between April 2013 and April 2014.

Inflation tax—revenue that the issuers of money (RBI) get from the holders of money (households, firms and banks) caused entirely by the inflation.

Information barriers (or imperfect information) model—a model of the short run aggregate supply wherein neither the workers nor the firms have the correct information on the general price level though they know the prices of the goods they trade in.

Inside lag—time between a shock to the economy and the policy action taken to respond to it.

International trade (exchange rate) effect—measures the effect of price on aggregate demand through change in the real exchange rate, net export and so on.

International trilemma (or impossible trinity)—an issue which all open economies have to resolve by choosing any two of the three systems, viz. integration (no restrictions on international movements of goods, services and capital), regulation (of the exchange rate) and sovereignty (independence on the money supply).

IS curve—locus of various combinations of income and interest rate (or exchange rate) at which the product market is in equilibrium.

J-curve—measures the effect of devaluation on the trade deficit over time.

Keynesian model (old)—a short run macroeconomic model advanced by John Maynard Keynes and his followers which assumes wage-price rigidity without rationalising the same.

Keynesian model (new)—a short run macroeconomic model advanced by new Keynesian economists which retains the Keynesian assumption of wage-price rigidity but offers economic rationale for it.

Keynes (interest rate) effect—measures the effects of price on aggregate demand through change in real money supply, interest rate and investment.

Kuznets' curve—describes the inverted U-shaped relationship between the income inequality and the per capita income.

Laffer's curve—describes the inverted U-shaped relationship between the tax revenue and the tax rate.

Large open economy—an open economy which can regulate its domestic interest rate and even influence the world interest rate.

Laspeyres price index—price measure based on a fixed (base year) basket of goods.

Leading indicators—intermediate economic variables which fluctuate ahead of the goal (target) variables and thus signal the direction of the forthcoming business cycles.

Life cycle theory—a theory of consumption under which people decide their consumption spending on the basis of their expected average life-time (working to retirement years) income, and they save and borrow to smooth consumption in the face of income fluctuations.

Liquidity—it is the ease with which an asset can be converted at its market price into money. Money is thus perfectly liquid.

Liquidity trap—situation under which the interest rate is so low that the demand for money is infinitely elastic and the LM curve is horizontal at that interest rate.

LM curve—locus of various combinations of income and interest rate at which the money market is in equilibrium.

Long run—a period when prices and wages are flexible, information is perfect and expectations match with actual.

Long-run aggregate supply (LAS) curve (line)—curve (vertical line) which describes that the supply of all goods and services is fixed at the potential (or natural rate) level of GDP irrespective of the (general) price level in the long run. Also, it is the locus of various combinations of output and price at which the factor market is in equilibrium in the long run.

Lucas critique—points out that the macroeconomic models based on the adaptive expectations theory are flawed as they ignore the effects of the current policies on the people's expectations, which have significant effects both on aggregate demand and aggregate supply.

Macroeconomics—a branch of economics which deals with the behaviour of the economy as a whole in terms of variables like GDP, unemployment, inflation, money supply, interest rate, fiscal deficit, current account deficit, exchange rate, exports, imports, etc.

Marginal Standing Facility—it is the facility extended by the RBI under which the member banks while faced with cash crunch can borrow for over–night from the RBI up to 2 percent of their demand and time liabilities at the interest rate equal to repo rate plus one percent.

Microeconomics—a branch of economics which deals with the behaviour of the individual households, firms, and markets for individual products in terms of the variables like consumption, production and price of wheat, milk, potatoes, cars, houses, air fare, hair cut, college fee for MBA, hotel tariff, pizza hut pizza, electricity tariff, etc.

Misery index—measure of peoples' unhappiness, defined as the sum of the rates of inflation and unemployment.

Monetarism—a belief that changes in the money supply are the primary cause of business cycles.

Money illusion—arises when people base their decisions on the basis of the nominal values of variables, like you spend more on consumption when your salary goes up by 10 percent even when the inflation rate was 10 percent.

National income—is same as the net national product at factor cost, which equals the GDP at market prices minus depreciation, minus net indirect taxes, plus net factor income from abroad.

Natural rate hypothesis—a theory which states that the demand management policies (fiscal–monetary) exerts influence on output and employment only in the short run and these variables return to their natural levels in the long run as predicated by the classical model.

Natural rate of output—the output level associated with the natural rate of unemployment.

Natural rate of unemployment (called as NAIRU)–(non accelerating inflation rate of unemployment)—rate of unemployment which prevails in any economy in the long run, and around which unemployment fluctuates in the short run.

Neutral policy—a policy to do nothing in the face of a shock.

Okun's law—states a negative relationship between the rate of economic growth and the change in the rate of unemployment. Alternatively, it describes a negative relationship between the deviations of output from its natural level and the deviations of the unemployment rate from its natural level.

Open market operations (OMO)—it is a monetary policy tool under which the Central Bank of the country (RBI) conducts purchases and sales of government bonds in the open market.

Outside lag—time between the policy action on a shock to the economy and its effect on the economy.

Paasche price index—price measure based on a changing (over time) basket of goods.

Passive policy—a policy which is ruled based rather than the need based.

Permanent income hypothesis—a theory of consumption under which consumption spending is decided on the basis of the permanent income (like the annuity of the life time income); and saving and borrowing are used to smooth consumption in the face of fluctuations in the transitory income.

Pigou (real balance) effect—measures the effect of price on aggregate demand through change in real wealth, consumption, investment and so on.

Primary deficit—positive gap between the fiscal deficit and interest on public debt in a given year.

PPP exchange rate—exchange rate given by the relative price of goods and services in the concerned two countries.

Pump priming—a policy under which the increased government expenditure is financed fully through increase in money supply so that the output is increased while the interest rate is left unaffected.

Purchasing power parity—rule of one price by which the nominal exchange rate indicates the differences in price levels in the concerned two countries.

Quantitative (or credit) easing—a relatively new monetary policy instrument under which the Central Bank of the country creates money (currency) through buying government and private assets backed securities (like mortgage backed securities).

Quantity theory of money—classical theory of money demand describing the direct and proportional relationship between the nominal demand for money and the nominal income, or the quantity of money and the price level.

Random walk hypothesis—a theory that changes in the variable under question over time are unpredictable or random.

Rational expectations hypothesis—a theory under which expectations on a variable are formed optimally using all the relevant past, current and likely future scenarios on all the relevant policy and non policy variables.

Real business cycle—business cycle theory that economic fluctuations are caused primarily by shocks in real (supply) factors, like technology, labour and leisure trade-off, rather than shocks in monetary factors.

Recession—situation when the real GDP has fallen in last two consecutive quarters or more.

Repo rate—it is the interest rate at which the Central Bank of the country (RBI) advances loans to its member banks against government securities for over–night under the Liquidity Adjustment Facilities.

Retail inflation—is based on the consumers price index—combined (or all India).

Reverse Repo rate—it is the interest rate at which the member banks can park their surplus funds with the Central Bank of the country (RBI) for overnight under the Liquidity Adjustments Facilities.

Sacrifice ratio—is a measure of the loss of real GDP in percentage caused by a one percent reduction in inflation rate. Also, it describes a positive relationship between growth and inflation.

Say's law—supply creates its own demand .

Seigniorage—profit that the issuers of currency (RBI and governments) make under their monopoly power to print currency.

Short run (or medium term)—a period when some prices and wages are fixed and others are variable, there are information barriers, or workers and firms are subject to misperceptions.

Short run aggregate supply (SAS) curve—curve which describes the positive relationship between the supply of all goods and services and the (general) price in the short run (or the medium term). Also, it is the locus of various combinations of output and price at which the factor market is in equilibrium in the short-run.

Solow growth model—indicates that the growth rate in per capita income depends positively on the saving rate (though only up to the steady state) and technology, and negatively on the growth rate in population. It is also called as the exogenous growth theory.

Solow residual—a change in economic growth rate that cannot be accounted for by changes in factor inputs; or a measure of the contribution of total factor productivity to economic growth;.

Square root formula (or Baumol–Tobin model)—rationalises the transactions demand for money as a positive function of income and negative function of interest rate.

Stagflation (or slumpflation)—situation when unemployment and inflation occur simultaneously.

Staggered wage—price contracts occur when firms set their wage–price contracts at different times.

Statutory Liquidity Requirements (SLR)—it is a government regulation under which all commercial banks are required to hold a certain percentage of their demand and time liabilities in the form of government and other notified bonds.

Steady–state equilibrium—situation where real per capita income and other real per capita variables are constant.

Sterilisation—policy action under which the Central Bank of the country (like RBI) buys foreign currency when there is net capital inflow and simultaneously sells government bonds through the open market operations, and sells foreign currency when there is net capital outflow and simultaneously buys government bonds through the open market operations so as to nullify their effects on the money supply.

Structural deficit—fiscal deficit that would occur with current fiscal policy when the economy was at full employment.

Structural unemployment—unemployment that is due to mismatch of skills and job requirements, and mismatch of locations of vacancies and availability of unemployed persons.

Supply side economics—theory which operates through the management of aggregate supply, which includes incentives to work, save, invest and risk-taking.

Taylor's rule—prescribes a formula for the monetary authority to set the nominal interest rate (like the federal fund rate or repo rate) such that it varies positively with the inflation rate and negatively with the output gap, ensuring that the real interest rate is constant at 2 percent.

Tobin's Q—is the ratio of the market capitalisation to the replacement cost of a company's capital assets.

Transfer payments (public)—refers to the payments that the governments make to the individuals by way of social security, pensions, unemployment compensation, accidental deaths, etc which have nothing in exchange (no quid pro quo).

Trickle-down theory—suggests that the benefits of economic growth percolate through the bottom of the pyramid.

Unemployment rate—proportion (percentage) of unemployed persons in total workforce, where workforce is the sum of the unemployed persons and employed persons; note workforce plus persons not in workforce (= children + retirees + students + in beds due to long sickness, etc.) equals population.

Velocity of money—the number of times an average rupee is used to transact in goods and services during a year.

Very short run—a period when all prices are fixed.

Very short run aggregate supply curve (line)—curve (horizontal line) which describes that at the fixed price, the supply of all goods and services is infinitely price elastic up to the potential (full employment) level of output and it remains at its potential level even at all prices above the fixed price in the very short run. Also, it is the locus of various combinations of output and price at which the factor market is in equilibrium in the very short run.

Wage-price rigidity—Keynesian model of wage–price rigidity for short-run aggregate supply (SAS) where wage–price adjustments are slow and demand and supply may not equal always.

Wage-price spiral—process through which price changes cause wage changes, which cause further price changes and the process moves on.

Wholesale inflation—based on the wholesale price index.

Yield curve (or term structure of interest rate)—describes a relationship between the nominal interest rate and the duration (maturity) of the borrowing/lending (bond).

Answers to Numerical Questions

Chapter 2

Q2. (a) GNP at market price = 39,000
GDI = 11,700
PIP = 28,275
PS = 11,700
FD = –975

Q3. GNP_M = 6,046
GDP_M = 6,039
N.I = 4,888
S = 852
Rental Income = 43

Q4. GDP_M = 710, National income = 610

Chapter 3

Q3. (a) $\dot{P} = 3.9\%$
(b) $\dot{P} = 2.08\%$
(c) $\dot{P} = 2.38\%$

Q6. $u = 11.11\%$

Chapter 4

Q1. M_3 = 3,200
H = 900
FD = 485
PD = 160
CAD = 110
BOPD = 20

Q4. Arithmetic averaging:
$NEER_1$ = 9.40625
$NEER_2$ = 9.796875
Depreciation rate = 4.1%
$REER_2$ = 9.9507
Index of $REER_2$ = 1.2710

REER devalued by 27.1%
Geometric averaging:
$NEER_1 = 2.8202$
$NEER_2 = 3.3764$
Depreciation rate = 19.72%
$REER_2$ Index = 1.2641
REER devalued by 26.41%

Chapter 5

Q2. (a) Autonomous $C = 50$
(b) APC = 0.823 and MPC = 0.734
(c) $S = -50 + 0.25\,Y + 8.5\dfrac{Y}{Y_{MP}} + 0.50\,i$

Chapter 8

Q8. (a) $M_3 = 87{,}955$ and Reserve money = 15,589
(b) Money multiplier = 5.64
(c) Money multiplier = 5.53

Chapter 9

Q9. (a) $\dfrac{\partial^2\theta}{\partial L^2} = -0.075\,L^{-1.5}K^{0.7}$, which is negative and hence the law of diminishing returns holds.

(b) $\dfrac{\partial^2\theta}{\partial L\partial K} = 0.105\,L^{-1.5}\,K^{-0.3}$, which is positive and hence MPP_L goes up as K increases. This implies that the labour productivity is higher in countries having more capital intensive production (like USA) than in countries having less capital intensive production (like India).

(c) $L = [0.71\,(P_K/P_L)(3.33\text{ Q})^{1.43}]^{0.58}$

And $K = [15.55\,(P_L/P_K)(Q^2)]^{0.416}$

These demand functions do indicate that the demand for an input varies inversely with its own price and directly with the price of the other input. At the given values of prices of labour, capital and output, the results are as follows:

$L = 11.69$, $K = 1{,}084$, $Q = 136.66$, $TR = 232.32$, $TC = 279.5$ and Profit = –47.18

(d) No, technology is contained in constant 0.3.

Q10. Inflation rate = 5.8 %

Chapter 11

Q4. (a) $Y = 2400$, $i = 10\%$
(b) $Y = 2533$, $i = 13.33\%$

Q.10. (a) Tax rate = 16.59% and Growth rate in private investment = 9.78%
(b) ICOR = 1.4068

Chapter 12

Q5. (a) IS: $Y = 2500 - 3750\ i$
(b) LM: $Y = 1125 + 10{,}000\ i$
(c) $i = 0.10$, $Y = 2125$, C = 1400, $I = 200$, $NX = -205$ and BD = 105
(d) If G goes up by 110; $Y = 2325$, $i = 0.12$ and BD = 65
If M goes up by 100, $Y = 2398$, $i = 0.0273$ and BD = 50.4
(e) $Y = 2650$

Chapter 13

Q13. (a) Base values of G and M: $Y = 2{,}225$; $P = 1.0$ and $i = 0.0833$
(i) G up by 100: $Y = 2{,}407$; $P = 4.64$ and $i = 0.48$
(ii) M up by 100: $Y = 2{,}229$; $P = 1.09$ and $i = 0.0683$
(iii) G up by 100 and M up by 100: $Y = 2{,}410$; $P = 4.70$ and $i = 0.4670$
(b) Base values of G and M: $Y = 2{,}223.5$; $P = 0.97$ and $E = 28.2$
(c) Base values of G and M: $Y = 2{,}225$; $P = 1.0$ and $M = 772.4$

Chapter 14

Q2. (a) AD equation: $Y = 41.7 + 583.3/P$
(b) $Y = 100$, $P = 10$ and $i = 5$
(c) $Y = 120$, $P = 7.45$ and $i = 1$
(d) Short-run Philips curve equation:

$$\dot{P} = 0.6\left[\frac{Y}{Y_n} - 1\right] + \dot{P}^e$$

Short-run inflation rate = –5%

Chapter 15

Q13. (a) GDP Loss = 2 $(u - u_n)$ (GDP)
USA: \$ 1286.2 billion
Japan: \$ 47.7 billions
(b) Misery Index = $u + p$
USA: 10.2%
Japan: 4.1%
(c) Inflation tax revenue = p(RM/P)
USA: \$56.28
Japan: - \$5.205
For other countries, calculate using the formula given above.

Chapter 16

Q8. (a) $Y/L = (K/L)^{0.35}$
(b) $K/L = 5.42$
(c) $s = 35\ \%$
(d) To achieve the Golden Rule outcomes for the economy, government should aim to raise the saving rate, which could be done through its own control of the fiscal deficit and through providing incentives on private saving- like tax rebate.

Index